MindTap

QUICK START GUIDE

1. To get started, navigate to www.cengagebrain.com and select "Register a Product."

A new screen will appear prompting you to add a Course Key. A Course Key is a code given to you by your instructor — this is the first of two codes you will need to access MindTap. Every student in your course section should have the same Course Key.

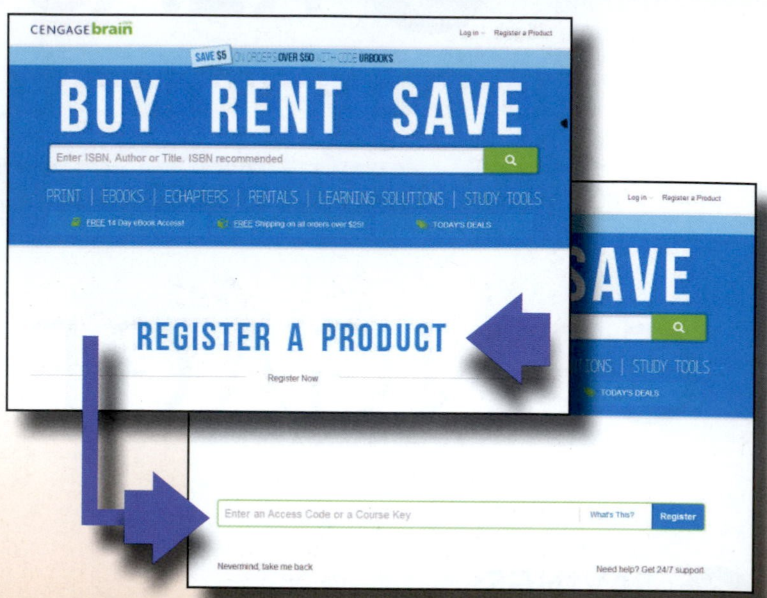

2. Enter the Course Key and click "Register."

If you are accessing MindTap through your school's Learning Management System, such as BlackBoard or Desire2Learn, you may be redirected to use your Course Key/Access Code there. Follow the prompts you are given and feel free to contact support if you need assistance.

3. Confirm your course information above and proceed to the log in portion below.

If you have a CengageBrain username and password, enter it under "Returning Students" and click "Login." If this is your first time, register under "New Students" and click "Create a New Account."

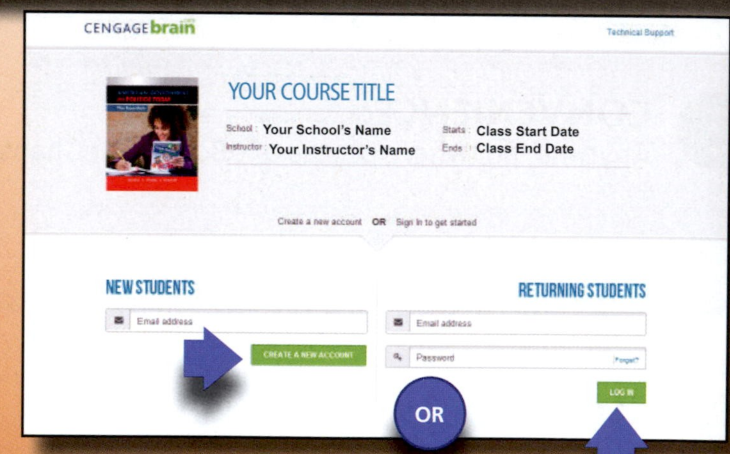

4. Now that you are logged in, you can access the course for free by selecting "Start Free Trial" for 20 days or enter in your Access Code.

Your Access Code is unique to you and acts as payment for MindTap. You may have received it with your book or purchased separately in the bookstore or at www.cengagebrain.com. Enter it and click "Register."

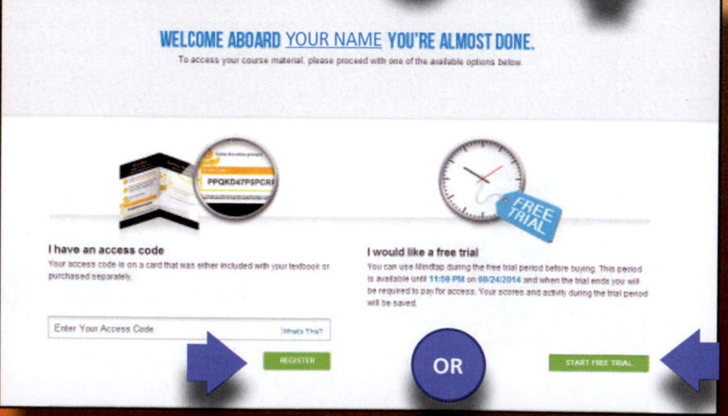

NEED HELP?

For CengageBrain Support: Login to **Support.Cengage.com.** Call **866-994-2427** or access our **24/7 Student Chat!**
Or access the **First Day of School PowerPoint Presentation** found at **www.cengagebrain.com.**

The Brief

AMERICAN PAGEANT

120°W
110°W
100°W
90°W
49°N
WASHINGTON
1889
Columbia R.
OREGON COUNTRY
(By Agreement
with Britain, 1846)
OREGON
1859
IDAHO
1890
42°N
40°N
MONTANA
1889
Missouri R.
NORTH DAKOTA
1889
SOUTH DAKOTA
1889
WYOMING
1890
NEBRASKA
1867
LOUISIANA
PURCHASE
(From France, 1803)
Great
Salt
Lake
NEVADA
1864
UTAH
1896
MEXICAN CESSION
(1848)
PACIFIC
OCEAN
CALIFORNIA
1850
Colorado R.
COLORADO
1876
KANSAS
1861
ARIZONA
1912
OKLAHOMA
1907
NEW MEXICO
1912
30°N
GADSDEN PURCHASE
(From Mexico, 1853)
TEXAS
(Independent Republic,
Annexed 1845)
Rio Grande
TEXAS
1845
Nueces R.
PACIFIC OCEAN
HAWAI'I
1959
HAWAI'I
(Annexed 1898)
20°N
0 50 100 Km.
0 50 100 Mi.
160°W
155°W
RUSSIA
70°N
ALASKA
1959
CANADA
60°N
ALASKA PURCHASE
(From Russia, 1867)
MEXICO
170°E
50°N
PACIFIC OCEAN
0 200 400 Km.
0 250 400 Mi.
180°
170°W
160°W
150°W
140°W

CANADA
Lake Superior
St. Lawrence R.
Lake Michigan
Lake Huron
Lake Ontario
Lake Erie
MAINE 1820
VT. 1791
N.H.
MASS.
CONN.
R.I.
NEW YORK
WISCONSIN 1848
INNESOTA 1858
MICHIGAN 1837
IOWA 1846
PENNSYLVANIA
NEW JERSEY
MASON-DIXON LINE
1790
DELAWARE
MARYLAND
OHIO 1803
INDIANA 1816
ILLINOIS 1818
MISSOURI 1821
WEST VIRGINIA 1863
KENTUCKY 1792
VIRGINIA
THE ORIGINAL THIRTEEN COLONIES
2010
THE ORIGINAL UNITED STATES (By Treaty with Britain, 1783)
36°30'N MISSOURI COMPROMISE LINE
NORTH CAROLINA
TENNESSEE 1796
ARKANSAS 1836
Mississippi R.
SOUTH CAROLINA
GEORGIA
MISSISSIPPI 1817
ALABAMA 1819
LOUISIANA 1812
(Seized from Spain, 1810, 1813)
FLORIDA (By Treaty with Spain, 1819)
FLORIDA 1845
ATLANTIC OCEAN
N
Territorial Growth of the United States
1820 Date of states admission to the Union
Geographic center of population by decade
0 150 300 Km.
0 150 300 Mi.
Gulf of Mexico
BAHAMAS
CUBA
DOMINICAN REPUBLIC
HAITI
PUERTO RICO (Acquired from Spain, 1898)
VIRGIN IS. (Acquired from Denmark, 1916–1917)
PUERTO RICO
VIRGIN ISLANDS
19°N
18°N
68°W
67°W
66°W
65°W
0 25 50 Km.
0 25 50 Mi.
90°W
80°W
70°W
60°W

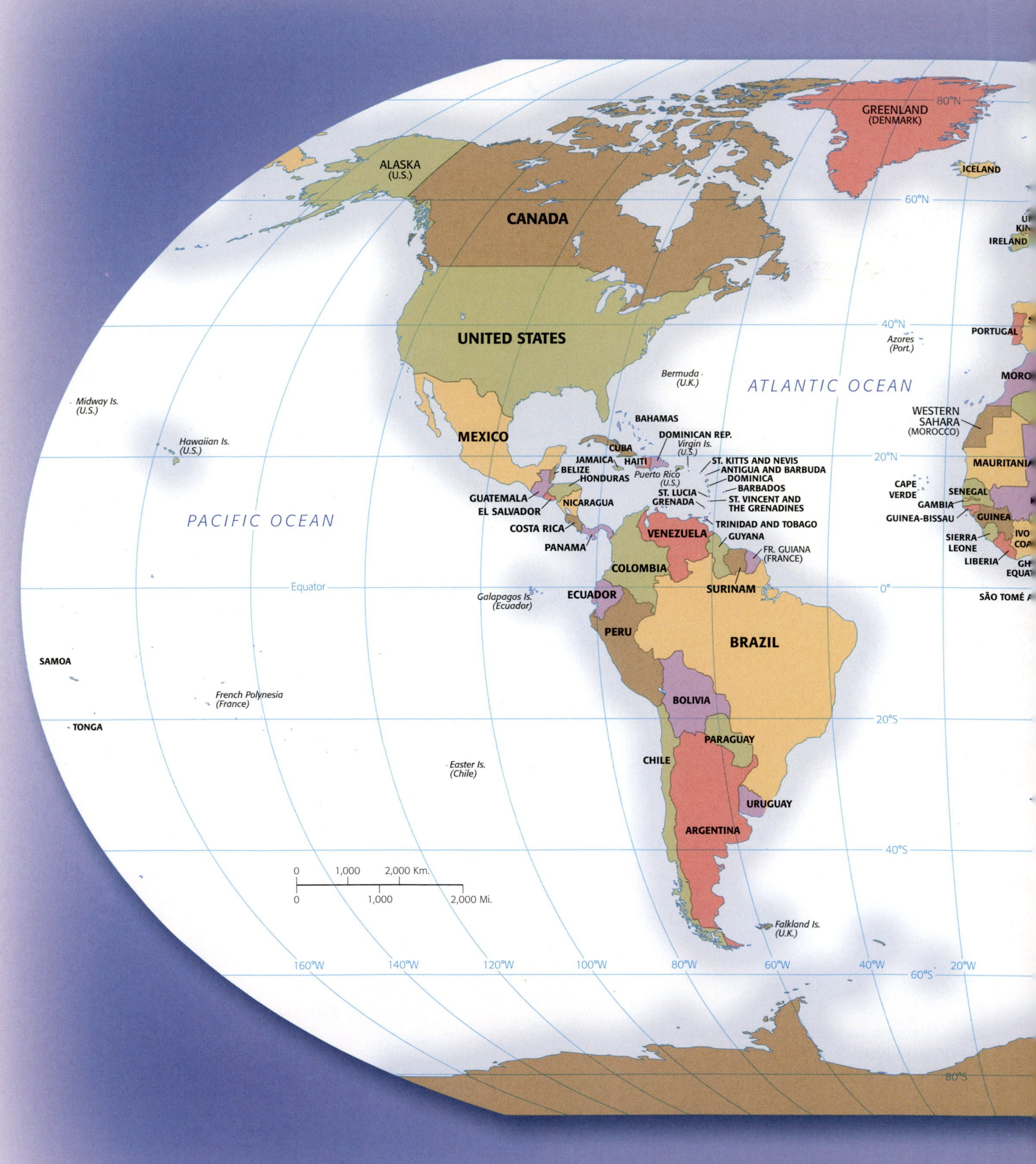

GREENLAND
(DENMARK)
ICELAND
ALASKA
(U.S.)
CANADA
IRELAND
UNITED STATES
PORTUGAL
Azores
(Port.)
Bermuda
(U.K.)
ATLANTIC OCEAN
Midway Is.
(U.S.)
WESTERN
SAHARA
(MOROCCO)
BAHAMAS
Hawaiian Is.
(U.S.)
MEXICO
DOMINICAN REP.
Virgin Is.
(U.S.)
CUBA
JAMAICA
HAITI
ST. KITTS AND NEVIS
ANTIGUA AND BARBUDA
DOMINICA
BARBADOS
ST. LUCIA
ST. VINCENT AND
THE GRENADINES
GRENADA
TRINIDAD AND TOBAGO
BELIZE
HONDURAS
Puerto Rico
(U.S.)
MAURITANIA
CAPE
VERDE
SENEGAL
GAMBIA
GUINEA-BISSAU
GUINEA
SIERRA
LEONE
LIBERIA
GUATEMALA
EL SALVADOR
NICARAGUA
COSTA RICA
PANAMA
PACIFIC OCEAN
VENEZUELA
GUYANA
FR. GUIANA
(FRANCE)
COLOMBIA
SURINAM
Galapagos Is.
(Ecuador)
ECUADOR
PERU
BRAZIL
SÃO TOMÉ
SAMOA
French Polynesia
(France)
TONGA
BOLIVIA
PARAGUAY
CHILE
Easter Is.
(Chile)
URUGUAY
ARGENTINA
0 1,000 2,000 Km.
0 1,000 2,000 Mi.
Falkland Is.
(U.K.)
80°N
60°N
40°N
20°N
Equator
0°
20°S
40°S
60°S
80°S
160°W
140°W
120°W
100°W
80°W
60°W
40°W
20°W

RUSSIA
KAZAKHSTAN
MONGOLIA
UZBEKISTAN
KYRGYZSTAN
TAJIKISTAN
TURKMENISTAN
N. KOREA
S. KOREA
JAPAN
PACIFIC OCEAN
PEOPLE'S REPUBLIC OF CHINA
AFGHANISTAN
PAKISTAN
BHUTAN
NEPAL
BANGLADESH
INDIA
MYANMAR (BURMA)
LAOS
TAIWAN
VIETNAM
THAILAND
CAMBODIA (KAMPUCHEA)
PHILIPPINES
SRI LANKA
BRUNEI DARUSSALAM
MALAYSIA
SINGAPORE
MALDIVES
INDIAN OCEAN
INDONESIA
TIMOR LESTE
PAPUA NEW GUINEA
PALAU
Mariana Islands (U.S.)
Guam (U.S.)
Wake I. (U.S.)
MARSHALL ISLANDS
FEDERATED STATES OF MICRONESIA
KIRIBATI
NAURU
SOLOMON IS.
TUVALU
VANUATU
FIJI
New Caledonia (France)
AUSTRALIA
NEW ZEALAND
NORWAY
SWEDEN
FINLAND
ESTONIA
LATVIA
LITHUANIA
BELARUS
DEN.
GERMANY
POLAND
CZ.
SLK.
UKRAINE
MOLDOVA
AUS.
HUNG.
SLN.
CR.
ROMANIA
ITALY
B. H.
SE.
K.
BULGARIA
MO.
MAC.
ALBANIA
GREECE
GEORGIA
TURKEY
ARMENIA
AZERBAIJAN
CYPRUS
MALTA
TUNISIA
LEBANON
ISRAEL
SYRIA
IRAQ
IRAN
JORDAN
KUWAIT
BAHRAIN
QATAR
SAUDI ARABIA
UNITED ARAB EMIRATES
OMAN
YEMEN
LIBYA
EGYPT
NIGER
CHAD
SUDAN
ERITREA
DJIBOUTI
ETHIOPIA
SOMALIA
BENIN
NIGERIA
CENTRAL AFRICAN REP.
SOUTH SUDAN
CAMEROON
UGANDA
KENYA
GABON
RWANDA
DEM. REP. OF CONGO
BURUNDI
CONGO
TANZANIA
SEYCHELLES
COMOROS
ANGOLA
ZAMBIA
MALAWI
MADAGASCAR
NAMIBIA
ZIMBABWE
MAURITIUS
BOTSWANA
MOZAMBIQUE
SWAZILAND
SOUTH AFRICA
LESOTHO
20°E
40°E
60°E
80°E
100°E
120°E
140°E
160°E
ABBREVIATIONS
AUS. AUSTRIA
BEL. BELGIUM
B. H. BOSNIA AND HERZEGOVINA
CR. CROATIA
CZ. CZECH REPUBLIC
DEN. DENMARK
HUNG. HUNGARY
K. KOSOVO
LUX. LUXEMBOURG
MAC. MACEDONIA
MO. MONTENEGRO
NETH. NETHERLANDS
SE. SERBIA
SLK. SLOVAKIA
SLN. SLOVENIA
SWITZ. SWITZERLAND

The Brief

AMERICAN PAGEANT

A HISTORY OF THE REPUBLIC

VOLUME II: SINCE 1865

NINTH EDITION

David M. Kennedy

Stanford University

Lizabeth Cohen

Harvard University

Mel Piehl

Valparaiso University

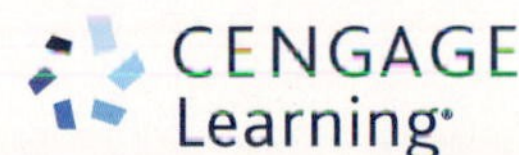

Australia • Brazil • Mexico • Singapore • United Kingdom • United States

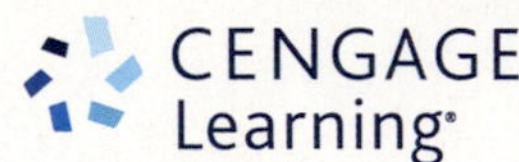

***The Brief American Pageant: A History of the Republic Volume II: Since 1865* Ninth Edition**
David M. Kennedy / Lizabeth Cohen / Mel Piehl

Product Director: Paul R. Banks

Product Manager: Clint Attebery

Senior Content Developer: Margaret McAndrew Beasley

Content Developer: Kate MacLean

Product Assistant: Andrew Newton

Marketing Development Manager: Kyle Zimmerman

Senior Content Project Manager: Carol Newman

Senior Art Director: Cate Rickard Barr

Manufacturing Planner: Fola Orekoya

IP Analyst: Alexandra Ricciardo

Production Service and Compositor: Cenveo® Publisher Services

Text Designer: Lisa Devenish, Devenish Design

Cover Designer: Diana Graham

Cover Image: American calendar art of sailor raising the American flag aboard ship, 1917. The Everett Collection.

Library of Congress Control Number: 2015946508

Student Edition:
ISBN: 978-1-285-19331-1

Loose-leaf Edition:
ISBN: 978-1-305-86528-0

Cengage Learning
20 Channel Center Street
Boston, MA 02210
USA

Printed in the United States of America
Print Number: 01 Print Year: 2015

BRIEF CONTENTS

CONTENTS

Part Five

STRUGGLING FOR JUSTICE AT HOME AND ABROAD

1901–1945

Part Six

MAKING MODERN AMERICA

1945 To The Present

MAPS

CHARTS AND TABLES

PREFACE

This new edition of *The Brief American Pageant*, a concise version of *The American Pageant*, sixteenth edition, includes significant innovations. As always, this Brief Edition presents the core content of *The American Pageant* in an efficient and engaging fashion. It preserves the central distinguishing features of *The American Pageant*—its strong narrative and consistent focus on the great themes of American history: liberty, democracy, the struggle for justice in a modern industrial economy, and America's place in the world.

A new feature of this edition is Contending Voices, which presents paired quotes from the past to encourage critical thinking about controversial issues. The Thinking Globally features highlight the global context of key moments in American history. More highlighted quotes throughout the text help students hear the language of real people who experienced historical events.

In addition, the Examining the Evidence features enable students to deepen their understanding of the historical craft by conveying how historians develop interpretations of the past through research in many different kinds of primary sources. Here students learn to probe a wide range of historical documents and artifacts: correspondence between Abigail and John Adams in 1776, and what it reveals about women's place in the American Revolution; the Gettysburg Address and the light it sheds not only on President Lincoln's brilliant oratory but also on his vision of the American nation; a letter from a black freedman to his former master in 1865 that illuminates his family's experience in slavery as well as their hopes for a new life; the manuscript census of 1900 and what it teaches us about immigrant households on the Lower East Side of New York at the dawn of the twentieth century; and a new kind of architectural structure—the shopping mall—and how it changed both consumers' behavior and politicians' campaign tactics after World War II.

The text incorporates these features while preserving the liveliness and readability that have long been *The American Pageant's* hallmark. We are often told that the *Pageant* is the sole American history text that has a distinctive personality—defined by clarity, concreteness, a consistent chronological narrative, strong emphasis on major themes, avoidance of clutter, access to a variety of interpretive perspectives, and a colorful writing style leavened, as appropriate, with wit. That personality, we strongly believe, is what has made *The Brief American Pageant* both appealing and useful to countless students for several decades.

The Brief American Pageant's goal is not to teach the art of prophecy but the much subtler and more difficult arts of seeing things in context, of understanding the roots and direction and pace of change, and of distinguishing what is truly new under the sun from what is not. The study of history, it has been rightly said, does not make one smart for the next time, but wise forever. We hope that *The Brief American Pageant* will help to develop this art of critical thinking in its readers, and that those who use the book will take from it both a fresh appreciation of what has gone before and a seasoned perspective on what is to come.

New to the Ninth Edition

Like *The American Pageant*, *The Brief American Pageant* provides students with a firm foundation in American history. *The Brief American Pageant* has also followed the lead of its parent text in terms of revisions for this most recent edition. For this edition we have consolidated and combined two chapters (eighth edition Chapters 29 and 30) into a single chapter (ninth edition Chapter 29; now titled Wilsonian Progressivism in Peace and War), resulting in renumbering of subsequent chapters for a total of 41 chapters in the ninth edition. Other changes include the following:

- **Part Six on the post-1945 era** has been substantially revised, reorganized, and updated to impart greater thematic coherence on the most recent past. Reflecting an emerging scholarly consensus, our new framework roughly divides the period into two eras, which can be summarized as follows: a midcentury era defined by sustained economic growth, broadly shared prosperity, and the international context of Cold War confrontation with the Soviet Union, followed by a new historical phase, originating in the pivotal decade of the 1970s, that has seen more fitful growth alongside both decreasing economic equality and increasing social inclusiveness, as well as a struggle to define America's international role after the collapse of the Soviet Union in 1991.

- **Contending Voices** features, all new to the ninth edition, offer paired quotes from original historical sources, accompanied by questions prompting students to assess conflicting perspectives on often hotly debated subjects. This feature is designed to nurture students' historical thinking skills by exposing them to the contested nature of history as well as historical interpretation.

- The **marginal glossary** has been substantively revised for the ninth edition to focus on the key terms—events, movements, organizations, laws, and so on—that are essential to the student's ability to understand larger historical developments. In contrast to previous editions, the glossary no longer includes general vocabulary definitions, which can be easily accessed in online or print dictionaries.

- A **strong global context** once again deepens the *Pageant's* treatment of American history. Within each chapter, both text and graphics help students compare American developments to developments around the world. Boxed quotes bring more international voices to the events chronicled in the narrative. In addition, the expanded "Thinking Globally" essays present a different context for the American experience within world history.
- The text includes **updated coverage throughout** with updated scholarship and new documentary photos, political cartoons, graphs, and tables.

Notes on Content Revisions

Chapter 1: New images and revised treatment of the Indian civilizations of Mexico, South America, and North America; new Contending Voices: "Europeans and Indians" (Juan Ginés de Sepulveda, Bartolomé de Las Casas)

Chapter 2: Enhanced treatment of changing early Indian cultures and of the links between the West Indies and North American slavery; new Contending Voices: "Old World Dreams and New World Realities" (Richard Hakluyt, George Percy)

Chapter 3: New Contending Voices: "Anne Hutchinson Accused and Defended" (John Winthrop, Anne Hutchinson)

Chapter 4: New Contending Voices: "Berkeley Versus Bacon" (Nathaniel Bacon, William Berkeley)

Chapter 5: Substantially revised treatment of lives of enslaved African Americans; new Contending Voices: "Race and Slavery" (Samuel Sewall, Virginia slave code of 1705)

Chapter 6: New map of French and Indian War; new Contending Voices: "The Proclamation of 1763" (Royal Proclamation of 1763, George Washington)

Chapter 7: New Contending Voices: "Reconciliation or Independence?" (John Dickinson, Thomas Paine)

Chapter 8: Expanded discussion of international context of the American Revolution; new Contending Voices: "Two Revolutions: French and American" (Friedrich von Gentz, John Quincy Adams)

Chapter 9: New material on the debate over the Constitution; a revised and expanded discussion of the impact of *both* the Revolution and the Constitution on ideas of equality, religious freedom, and civic virtue; new Contending Voices: "Debating the New Constitution" (Jonathan Smith, Patrick Henry)

Chapter 10: Focused discussion of Hamiltonian Federalists vs. Jeffersonian Republicans; new Contending Voices: "Human Nature and the Nature of Government" (Alexander Hamilton, Thomas Jefferson)

Chapter 11: New boxed quotes and information on Marshall and the federal judiciary; new Contending Voices: "The Divisive Embargo" (Federalist pamphlet, W. B. Giles)

Chapter 12: New Contending Voices: "Sizing Up the Monroe Doctrine" (Klemens von Metternich, Colombian newspaper)

Chapter 13: New attention to spreading American democracy in global context; new Thinking Globally feature: "Alexis de Tocqueville on Democracy in America and Europe"; revised Varying Viewpoints essay on Jacksonian Democracy; new Contending Voices: "Taking the Measure of Andrew Jackson" (Maryland supporter, Thomas Jefferson)

Chapter 14: Revised treatment of anti-immigrant sentiment; new Contending Voices: "Immigration, Pro and Con" (Know-Nothing party platform, Orestes Brownson)

Chapter 15: Revised Examining the Evidence feature on "Dress as Reform"; revised material on later fate of the Oneida Community; revised Varying Viewpoints essay on "Reform: Who? What? How? and Why?"; new Contending Voices: "The Role of Women" (differing newspaper commentaries on Seneca Falls)

Chapter 16: Expanded coverage of international context of antislavery, including religiously motivated abolitionism; revised Varying Viewpoints essay on the true nature of slavery; new Contending Voices: "Perspectives on Race and Slavery" (William A. Smith, American Anti-Slavery Society)

Chapter 17: New Contending Voices: "Warring over the Mexican War" (*New York Evening Post*, Henry Clay)

Chapter 18: New Contending Voices: "The Compromise of 1850" (John C. Calhoun, Daniel Webster)

Chapter 19: New material on John Brown and Harper's Ferry; new Contending Voices: "Judging John Brown" (Harriet Tubman, Abraham Lincoln); revised Varying Viewpoints essay includes attention to international context of southern secession

Chapter 20: New Contending Voices: "War Aims: Emancipation or Union?" (Horace Greeley, Abraham Lincoln)

Chapter 21: Revised Thinking Globally feature: "The Era of Nationalism" compares Lincoln's American nationalism with that of contemporaries in Germany and Italy; new Contending Voices: "The Controversy over Emancipation" (*Cincinnati Enquirer*, Abraham Lincoln)

Chapter 22: New material on radical Reconstruction, including blacks' roles in the Reconstruction regime; new

Contending Voices: "Radical Republicans and Southern Democrats" (Thaddeus Stevens, James Lawrence Orr)

Chapter 23: New Contending Voices: "The Spoils System" (George Washington Plunkitt, Theodore Roosevelt); revised Varying Viewpoints essay on "The Populists: Radicals or Reactionaries?"

Chapter 24: New material on subsidies for railroad-building, and their advantages and disadvantages for the public; new Contending Voices: "Class and the Gilded Age" (Populist platform, William Graham Sumner); revised Varying Viewpoints essay on "Industrialization: Boon or Blight?"

Chapter 25: This chapter now includes revised discussion of religious conservatism as well as social reform, and expanded treatment of women as urban social reformers. Also revised and expanded are the discussions of moral controversies, women and family life in the cities, and the revived but altered suffrage movement. The new discussion of literature and the arts is now organized around the distinct but related cultural movements of realism, naturalism, and regionalism—all of which reflected in different ways the emerging national urban civilization. New Contending Voices: "The New Immigration" (Henry Cabot Lodge, Grover Cleveland)

Chapter 26: More quotes from both the Plains Indians and the soldiers who fought against them; new Contending Voices: "The Ghost Dance and the Wounded Knee Massacre" (James McLaughlin, Black Elk)

Chapter 27: New material on the debate over imperialism and race; new Contending Voices: "Debating Imperialism" (Albert Beveridge, George Hoar); revised Varying Viewpoints essay on "Why Did America Become a World Power?"

Chapter 28: New material on Roosevelt's conservation policies, including debates over "mixed use" versus "preservation"; expanded treatment of Roosevelt's break with Taft, and the Roosevelt ("New Nationalism") versus Wilson ("New Freedom") versus Taft (Republican Old Guard) ideological campaign of 1912; new Contending Voices: "Debating the Muckrakers" (Theodore Roosevelt, Ida Tarbell); revised Varying Viewpoints essay highlights female and international role in Progressive reform, with differing American and European emphases.

Chapter 29: Completely revised and reorganized treatment of "Wilsonian Progressivism at Home and Abroad" highlights the links between Wilson's domestic reform program and his eventual leadership of the idealistic American crusade in World War I; new Contending Voices: "Battle of the Ballot" (Carrie Chapman Catt, Mrs. Barclay Hazard)

NOTE: Due to the consolidation of two chapters (eighth edition Chapters 29 and 30) into a single chapter (ninth edition Chapter 29), subsequent chapters have been renumbered for a total of 41 chapters in the ninth edition.

Chapter 30: Substantially revised treatment of American literature and culture in the 1920s, with emphasis on the intersection of American developments with the wider international movement of modernism in the arts; new Contending Voices: "All that Jazz" (Henry van Dyke, Duke Ellington)

Chapter 31: Expanded coverage of American isolationism, including economic isolation; new Contending Voices: "Depression and Protection" (Willis Hawley, economists' petition)

Chapter 32: Revised discussion of the Social Security Act and the Fair Labor Standards Act points out their initial exclusion of several categories of workers, for example, farm laborers and domestic workers; new Contending Voices: "The New Deal at High Tide" (Franklin Roosevelt, Herbert Hoover); revised Varying Viewpoints essay describes various radical critiques of the New Deal, as well as historians of the constraints school who stress the limits on FDR's ability to change American society.

Chapter 33: Substantially revised section on the Atlantic Charter as an attempt to revive liberal hopes for a new democratic world order; fresh emphasis on the isolationist-internationalist debate; new Contending Voices: "To Intervene or Not to Intervene" (Sterling Morton, Franklin Roosevelt)

Chapter 34: New Thinking Globally feature: "America and the World in Depression and War: A Study in Contrasts"; increased attention to the impact of race during the war; new Contending Voices: "War and the Color Line" (Franklin Roosevelt, African American soldier)

Chapter 35: Revised and reorganized treatment of the origins of the Cold War, as well as expanded discussion of the long economic boom in the decades after World War II and its impact on American politics and society; new Contending Voices: "Debating the Cold War" (George Kennan, Henry Wallace)

Chapter 36: The chapter presents a fresh treatment of the Eisenhower and Kennedy administrations under the new title "American Zenith," emphasizing the pervasive affluence and confidence of the immediate postwar era; includes a new treatment of the beat writers as critics of a conformist society; new Contending Voices: "The 'Kitchen Debate'" (Richard Nixon, Nikita Khrushchev)

Chapter 37: New Thinking Globally feature, "The Global 1960s," locates American cultural upheavals of the time in relation to similar youth-led upheavals around the globe; new Contending Voices: "Differing Visions of Black Freedom" (Martin Luther King, Jr., Malcolm X)

Chapter 38: The revised and compressed chapter treats the 1970s in the context of "Challenges to the Postwar

Order," highlighting the economic troubles, international conflicts, and increasing loss of faith in American government and other institutions in the wake of Vietnam and Watergate; new Contending Voices: "The Political Mobilization of Business" (Lewis Powell, Douglas Fraser)

Chapter 39: Revised Varying Viewpoints essay on "Where Did Modern Conservatism Come From?"; new Contending Voices: "Who Ended the Cold War?" (Margaret Thatcher, Mikhail Gorbachev)

Chapter 40: Extensively revised treatment of the 1990s and the Clinton administration as an attempt to adjust to a post-Cold War world as well as growing conflict over the role of government; fresh discussions of cultural pluralism, the postmodern mind, and the increasing fragmentation of American culture into narrow niches; new Contending Voices: "Welfare Reform Divides the Democrats" (Joseph Lieberman, Marian Wright Edelman)

Chapter 41: Almost entirely new chapter on America in the post-9/11 era, includes discussion of the global war on terror in Iraq and Afghanistan, and the growing political polarization and gridlock between the two parties, especially after the elections of George W. Bush and Barack Obama; new Contending Voices: "Populist Politics in a Polarized Age" (Tea Party activist, Occupy Wall Street activist)

Pedagogical Features

The special pedagogical features of *The Brief American Pageant* are many and varied, and may be used in different ways by students and instructors.

- **"What if . . . ?"** questions at the end of each part-opening essay prompt students to consider how history might have changed if certain events turned out differently, reinforcing the contingent nature of history. This element is unique to the Brief Edition.
- **Chapter Outlines** begin each chapter to provide a roadmap for the student. This element is unique to the Brief Edition.
- **Focus Questions** come at the beginning of each chapter, pointing to the key issues and ideas in the account that follows, and guiding the student's reading and understanding. This element is unique to the Brief Edition.
- **Chronologies** have been updated to include even more political occurrences and historical events.
- **Marginal Glossary** highlights and defines in a concise, accessible way the key terms—events, movements, organizations, laws, and so on—that are essential to the student's ability to understand larger historical developments. In contrast to previous editions, the glossary no longer includes general vocabulary definitions.
- **Key Terms** are listed at the end of the chapter, with page numbers included, for ease of reference.
- **People to Know** are listed at the end of each chapter, providing students with a useful study tool as they learn about some of the most important individuals in American history.
- **Examining the Evidence** features enable students to deepen their understanding of the historical craft by conveying how historians develop interpretations of the past through research in many different kinds of primary sources.
- **Contending Voices** features offer students two different perspectives on a single event or issue, and include a question to help develop critical thinking skills.
- **Chapter Summaries** provide a handy review that highlights the chapter's main points. This element is unique to the Brief Edition.

Teaching and Learning Aids

Instructor Resources

MindTap™ for *The Brief American Pageant*, 9e is a personalized, online digital learning platform providing students with an immersive learning experience that builds critical thinking skills. Through a carefully designed chapter-based learning path, MindTap allows students to easily identify the chapter's learning objectives, improve writing skills by completing unit-level essay assignments, read short, manageable sections from the e-book, and test their content knowledge with a chapter test that employs Aplia™ questions (see Chapter Test description below).

- *Setting the Scene:* Each chapter within MindTap begins with a brief video that introduces the chapter's major themes in a compelling, visual way that encourages students to think critically about the subject matter.
- *Review Activities:* Each chapter within MindTap includes reading comprehension assignments designed to cover the content of each major heading within the chapter.
- *Chapter Test*: Each chapter within MindTap ends with a summative chapter test. It covers each chapter's learning objectives and is built using Aplia critical thinking questions. All chapter tests include at least one map-based activity. Aplia provides automatically graded critical thinking assignments with detailed, immediate explanations on every question. Students can also choose to see another set of related questions if they did not earn all available points in their first attempt and want more practice.
- *Reflection Activity:* Every chapter ends with an assignable, gradable reflection activity, intended as a brief writing assignment through which students can apply a

theme or idea they've just studied. Reflection activities are based upon primary source features within the book.

- *Unit Activities:* Chapters in MindTap are organized into multi-chapter units. Each unit includes a brief set of higher-level activities for instructors to assign, designed to assess students on their writing and critical thinking skills, and their ability to engage larger themes, concepts, and material across multiple chapters.

- *Classroom Activities*: MindTap includes a brief list of class activity ideas for instructors. These are designed to increase student collaboration, engagement, and understanding of selected topics or themes. These activities, including class debate scenarios and primary source discussion guides, can enrich an online or in-class experience for both instructors and students.

MindTap also includes a variety of other tools that support history teaching and learning:

- The Instructor Resource Center provides additional 4,000+ primary source documents that professors can search within and add to any chapter in MindTap.

- Questia allows professors to search a database of thousands of peer-reviewed journals, newspapers, magazines, and full-length books—all assets can be added to any relevant chapter in MindTap.

- Kaltura allows instructors to create and insert inline video and audio into the MindTap platform.

- ReadSpeaker reads the text out loud to students in a voice they can customize.

- Note taking and highlighting are organized in a central location that can be synced with EverNote on any mobile device accessible to students.

- ConnectYard allows instructors to create digital "yards" and communicate with students based upon their preferred social media sites—without "friending" students.

MindTap for *The Brief American Pageant* goes well beyond an eBook and a homework solution. It is truly a *personal learning experience* that allows instructors to synchronize the reading with engaging assignments. To learn more, ask your Cengage Learning sales representative to demo it for you—or go to www.Cengage.com/MindTap.

Instructor Companion Website

This website is an additional resource for class preparation, presentation, and testing for instructors. Accessible through Cengage.com/login with your faculty account, you will find an Instructor's Manual, PowerPoint presentations (descriptions below), and testbank files (please see Cognero description).

- *Instructor's Manual:* For each chapter, this manual contains: focus questions, chapter themes, a chapter summary, suggested lecture topics, and discussion questions.

- *PowerPoint® Lecture Tools:* These presentations are ready-to-use, visual outlines of each chapter. They are easily customized for your lectures. There are presentations of only lecture or only images, as well as combined lecture and image presentations. Also available is a per-chapter JPEG library of images and maps.

- *Cengage Learning Testing, powered by Cognero®:* A test bank that contains multiple-choice and essay questions for each chapter. Cognero® is a flexible, online system that allows you to author, edit, and manage test bank content. Create multiple test versions instantly and deliver through your LMS with no special installs or downloads required. The following test bank format types are available for download from the Instructor Companion Site: Blackboard, Angel, Moodle, Canvas, and Desire2Learn. You can import these files directly into your LMS to edit, manage questions, and create tests.

Cengagebrain.com

Save your students time and money. Direct them to www.cengagebrain.com for choice in formats and savings and a better chance to succeed in your class. Cengagebrain.com, Cengage Learning's online store, is a single destination for more than 10,000 new textbooks, eTextbooks, eChapters, study tools, and audio supplements. Students have the freedom to purchase a-la-carte exactly what they need when they need it. Students can save 50 percent on the electronic textbook and can pay as little as $1.99 for an individual eChapter.

Custom Options

Nobody knows your students like you, so why not give them a text that is tailored to their needs? Cengage Learning offers custom solutions for your course—whether it's modifying *The Brief American Pageant* to match your syllabus or combining multiple sources to create something truly unique. You can pick and choose chapters and include your own material, to create a text that fits the way you teach. Ensure that your students get the most out of their textbook dollar by giving them exactly what they need. Contact your Cengage Learning representative to explore custom solutions for your course.

Reader Program

Cengage Learning publishes a number of readers, some containing exclusively primary sources, others a combination of primary and secondary sources, and some designed to guide students through the process of historical inquiry. Visit Cengage.com/history for a complete list of readers.

Student Resources

MindTap™ for *The Brief American Pageant, 9e* incorporates a set of resources designed to help students develop historical thinking skills, and identify the relevance of those skills beyond the history classroom. These resources include interactive tutorials for map skills, essay writing, and critical thinking, as well as other opportunities to read and write about history. With MindTap, students can access the entire e-book, plus many more valuable study tools.

***Writing for College History, 1e* [ISBN: 9780618306039]** Prepared by Robert M. Frakes, Clarion University. This brief handbook for survey courses in American history, Western civilization/European history, and world civilization guides students through the various types of writing assignments they encounter in a history class. Providing examples of student writing and candid assessments of student work, this text focuses on the rules and conventions of writing for the college history course.

***The History Handbook, 2e* [ISBN: 9780495906766]** Prepared by Carol Berkin of Baruch College, City University of New York and Betty Anderson of Boston University. This book teaches students both basic and history-specific study skills such as how to read primary sources, research historical topics, and correctly cite sources. Substantially less expensive than comparable skill-building texts, *The History Handbook* also offers tips for Internet research and evaluating online sources.

***Doing History: Research and Writing in the Digital Age, 2e* [ISBN: 9781133587880]** Prepared by Michael J. Galgano, J. Chris Arndt, and Raymond M. Hyser of James Madison University. Whether you're starting down the path as a history major, or simply looking for a straightforward and systematic guide to writing a successful paper, you'll find this text to be an indispensable handbook to historical research. This text's "soup to nuts" approach to researching and writing about history addresses every step of the process, from locating your sources and gathering information, to writing clearly and making proper use of various citation styles to avoid plagiarism. You'll also learn how to make the most of every tool available to you—especially the technology that helps you conduct the process efficiently and effectively.

***The Modern Researcher, 6e* [ISBN: 9780495318705]** Prepared by Jacques Barzun and Henry F. Graff of Columbia University. This classic introduction to the techniques of research and the art of expression is used widely in history courses, but is also appropriate for writing and research methods courses in other departments. Barzun and Graff thoroughly cover every aspect of research, from the selection of a topic through the gathering, analysis, writing, revision, and publication of findings, presenting the process not as a set of rules but through actual cases that put the subtleties of research in a useful context. Part One covers the principles and methods of research; Part Two covers writing, speaking, and getting one's work published.

***Rand McNally Historical Atlas of the World, 2e* [ISBN: 9780618841912]** This valuable resource features more than 70 maps that portray the rich panoply of the world's history from preliterate times to the present. They show how cultures and civilization were linked and how they interacted. The maps make it clear that history is not static. Rather, it is about change and movement across time. The maps show change by presenting the dynamics of expansion, cooperation, and conflict. This atlas includes maps that display the world from the beginning of civilization; the political development of all major areas of the world; expanded coverage of Africa, Latin America, and the Middle East; the current Islamic World; and the world population change in 1900 and 2000.

Acknowledgments

Many people contributed to *The Brief American Pageant.* Foremost among them are the countless students and teachers who have written unsolicited letters of comment or inquiry. We also offer thanks to the following colleagues for their particular contributions to improving the text:

Sheryl Ballard-Smith, Houston Community College
William Barnhart, Caldwell University
Edward Bond, Alabama A&M University
Thomas Born, Blinn College
Shearer Bowman, University of Kentucky
Steven Boyd, University of Texas at San Antonio
Tracy Campbell, University of Kentucky
Coreen Derifield, East Central College
Thomas Devine, California State University, Northridge
Mike Downs, Tarrant County College, Southeast Campus
Vance Kincade, Arcadia University
Jennifer Lawrence, Tarrant County College
Nancy Maurer, University of Central Florida
Bob McConaughy, Austin Community College, Rio Grande Campus
Lindsey McNellis, University of Central Florida
Manuel Medrano, University of Texas at Brownsville
Russell Mitchell, Tarrant County College, Southeast Campus
Jaime Olivares, Houston Community College
Kathleen Riley, Ohio Dominican University
John Sacher, University of Central Florida
Manfred Silva, El Paso Community College
Sandra Slater, College of Charleston
Bianka Stumpf, Central Carolina Community College
Gary Topping, Salt Lake Community College
Amanda Wallace-Wittnebel, University of Texas at San Antonio
Chad Wooley, Tarrant County College

D.M.K.
L.C.
M.P.

Sail, sail thy best, ship of Democracy,

Of value is thy freight, 'tis not the Present only,

The Past is also stored in thee,

Thou holdest not the venture of thyself alone, not of the Western continent alone,

Earth's résumé entire floats on thy keel, O ship, is steadied by thy spars,

With thee Time voyages in trust, the antecedent nations sink or swim with thee,

With all their ancient struggles, martyrs, heroes, epics, wars, thou bear'st the other continents,

Theirs, theirs as much as thine, the destination-port triumphant . . .

Walt Whitman
Thou Mother with Thy Equal Brood, 1872

The Brief AMERICAN PAGEANT

Chapter 22

The Ordeal of Reconstruction

1865–1877

With malice toward none, with charity for all, with firmness in the right as God gives us to see the right, let us strive on to finish the work we are in, to bind up the nation's wounds, to care for him who shall have borne the battle and for his widow and orphan, to do all which may achieve and cherish a just and lasting peace among ourselves and with all nations.

ABRAHAM LINCOLN, SECOND INAUGURAL ADDRESS, MARCH 4, 1865

Chapter Outline

- The Defeated South
- The Freed Slaves
- President Andrew Johnson's Reconstruction Policies
- Moderate and Radical Republicans
- Congressional Reconstruction Policies
- Military Reconstruction, 1867–1877
- Freed People Enter Politics
- "Black Reconstruction" and the Ku Klux Klan
- The Impeachment of Andrew Johnson
- The Legacy of Reconstruction
- *Examining the Evidence: Letter from a Freedman to His Old Master, 1865*
- *Varying Viewpoints: How Radical Was Reconstruction?*

The battle was done, the buglers silent. Bone-weary and bloodied, the American people, North and South, now faced the staggering challenges of peace. Four questions loomed large. How would the South, physically devastated by war and socially revolutionized by emancipation, be rebuilt? How would the liberated blacks fare as free men and women? How would the Southern states be reintegrated into the Union? And who would direct the process of Reconstruction—the Southern states themselves, the president, or Congress?

FOCUS QUESTIONS

1. What were the major problems facing the South and the nation after the Civil War?
2. How did African Americans and whites, Southerners and Northerners, each respond to the end of slavery and approach race relations under new conditions of freedom?
3. How did Andrew Johnson's political incompetence and missteps enable the Radical Republicans to gain control of Reconstruction policy?
4. What were the actual effects of congressional Reconstruction in the South, and how did militant white opposition and growing northern apathy eventually bring an end to Reconstruction in the Compromise of 1877?
5. What were the primary successes and failures of Reconstruction, and what legacy did it leave for later generations of Americans?

CHRONOLOGY

1863	▪ Lincoln announces "10 percent" Reconstruction plan
1864	▪ Lincoln vetoes Wade-Davis Bill
1865	▪ Lincoln assassinated ▪ Johnson issues Reconstruction proclamation ▪ Congress refuses to seat Southern congressmen ▪ Freedmen's Bureau established ▪ Southern states pass Black Codes
1866	▪ Congress passes Civil Rights Bill over Johnson's veto ▪ Congress passes Fourteenth Amendment ▪ Johnson-backed candidates lose congressional election ▪ *Ex parte Milligan* case ▪ Ku Klux Klan founded
1867	▪ Reconstruction Act ▪ Tenure of Office Act ▪ United States purchases Alaska from Russia
1868	▪ Johnson impeached and acquitted ▪ Johnson pardons Confederate leaders
1870	▪ Fifteenth Amendment ratified
1870–1871	▪ Force Acts
1872	▪ Freedmen's Bureau ended
1877	▪ Reconstruction ends

The Problems of Peace

Other questions also clamored for answers. What should be done with the captured Confederate ringleaders? All Confederate officials were subject to charges of treason, and during the war a popular Northern song had been "Hang Jeff Davis to a Sour Apple Tree." Davis was clapped into prison for two years, but no treason trials were ever held. President Andrew Johnson pardoned all "rebel" leaders as a sort of Christmas present in 1868. Congress removed their civil disabilities thirty years later.

Dismal indeed was the picture presented by the war-wracked South when the rattle of musketry faded. Not only had an age perished, but a civilization had collapsed, in both its economic and its social structure. The moonlight-and-magnolia Old South, largely imaginary in any case, had forever gone with the wind.

Handsome cities of yesteryear, such as Charleston and Richmond, were rubble-strewn and weed-choked. An Atlantan returned to his once-fair hometown and remarked, "Hell has laid her egg, and right here it hatched." Economic life had creaked to a halt. Banks and businesses had locked their doors, ruined by runaway inflation. Factories were smokeless, silent, dismantled. The transportation system had broken down completely. Efforts to untwist the rails corkscrewed by Sherman's soldiers proved bumpily unsatisfactory.

Agriculture—the economic lifeblood of the South—was almost hopelessly crippled. Once-white-carpeted cotton fields yielded a lush harvest of nothing but green weeds. The slave-labor system had collapsed, seed was scarce, and livestock had been driven off by plundering Yankees. Pathetic instances were reported of men hitching themselves to plows, while women and children gripped the handles.

The princely planter aristocrats were humbled by the war—at least temporarily. Reduced to proud poverty, they faced charred and gutted mansions, lost investments, and almost worthless land. Their investment of more than $2 billion in slaves, their primary form of wealth, had evaporated with emancipation.

Beaten but unbent, many high-spirited white Southerners remained dangerously defiant. They cursed the "damn yankees" and spoke of "your government" in Washington instead of "our government." Conscious of no crime, these former Confederates continued to believe that their view of secession was correct and that the "lost cause" was still a just war. One popular anti-Union song ran,

I'm glad I fought agin her, I only wish we'd won,
And I ain't axed any pardon for anything I've done.

Such attitudes boded ill for the prospects of painlessly binding up the Republic's wounds.

Freedmen Define Freedom

Confusion abounded in the still-smoldering South about the precise meaning of "freedom" for blacks. Emancipation took effect haltingly and unevenly in different parts of the conquered Confederacy. As Union armies marched in and out of various localities, many blacks found themselves emancipated and re-enslaved. A North Carolina slave estimated that he had celebrated freedom about twelve times. In some regions planters stubbornly protested that slavery was legal until state legislatures or the Supreme Court might act. For many slaves the shackles of bondage were not struck off in a single mighty blow; long-suffering blacks often had to pry off their chains link by link.

The variety of responses to emancipation, by whites as well as blacks, illustrated the sometimes startling complexity of the master–slave relationship. Loyalty to the plantation master prompted some slaves to resist the liberating Union armies, while other slaves' pent-up bitterness burst violently forth on the day of liberation. In one instance, a group of Virginia slaves laid twenty lashes on the back of their former master—a painful dose of his own favorite medicine.

Prodded by the bayonets of Yankee armies of occupation, all masters were eventually forced to recognize their slaves' permanent freedom. The once-commanding planter would assemble his former human chattels in front of the porch of the "big house" and announce their liberty. Though some blacks initially responded to news of their emancipation with suspicion and uncertainty, they soon celebrated their newfound freedom. Many took new names in place of the ones given by their masters and demanded that whites formally address them as "Mr." or "Mrs."

Tens of thousands of emancipated blacks took to the roads, some to test their freedom, others to search for long-lost spouses, parents, and children. Emancipation thus strengthened the black family, and many newly freed men and women formalized "slave marriages" for personal and pragmatic reasons, including the desire to make their children legal heirs.

Whole communities sometimes moved together in search of opportunity. From 1878 to 1880, some twenty-five thousand blacks from Louisiana, Texas, and Mississippi surged in a mass exodus to Kansas.

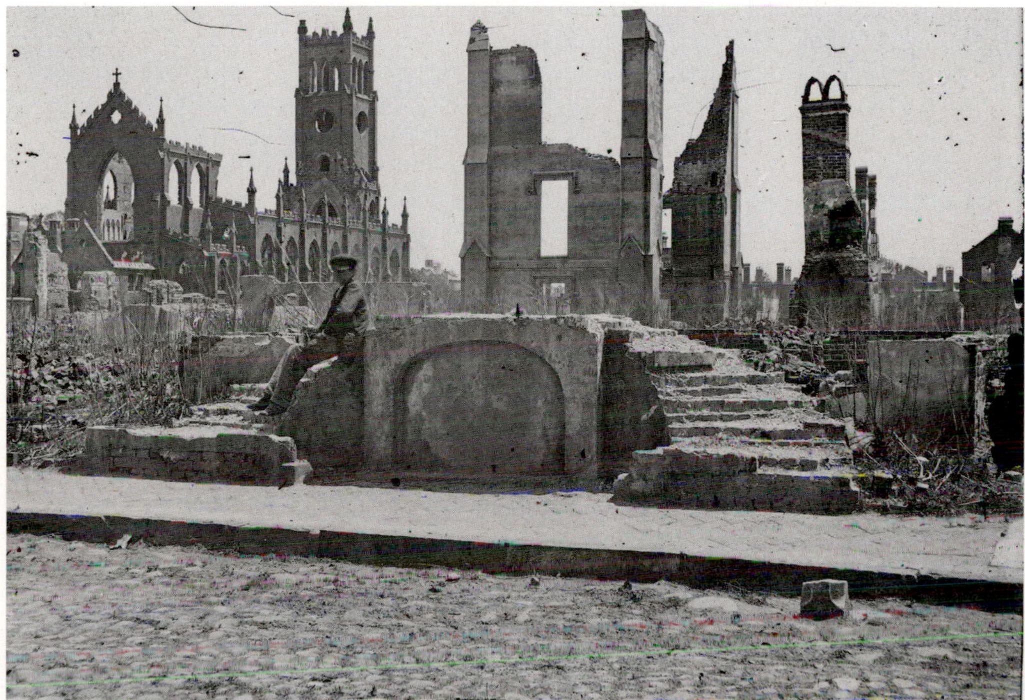

Library of Congres

Charleston, South Carolina, in Ruins, April 1865 Rebel troops evacuating Charleston blew up military supplies to deny them to General William Tecumseh Sherman's forces. The explosions ignited fires that all but destroyed the city.

Houston H. Holloway, age twenty at the time of his emancipation, recalled his feelings upon hearing of his freedom:

"I felt like a bird out of a cage. Amen. Amen. Amen. I could hardly ask to feel any better than I did that day. . . . The week passed off in a blaze of glory."

The reunion of long-lost relatives also inspired joy; one Union officer wrote home:

"Men are taking their wives and children, families which had been for a long time broken up are united and oh! such happiness. I am glad I am here."

The church became the focus of black community life in the years following emancipation. As slaves, blacks had worshiped alongside whites, but now they formed their own churches pastored by their own ministers. Black churches grew robustly. The 150,000-member black Baptist Church of 1850 reached 500,000 by 1870, while the African Methodist Episcopal Church quadrupled in size from 100,000 to 400,000 in the first decade after emancipation. These churches formed the bedrock of black community life, and they soon gave rise to other benevolent, fraternal, and mutual aid societies. All these organizations helped blacks protect their newly won freedom.

Emancipation also meant education for many blacks. Learning to read and write had been a privilege generally denied to them under slavery. Freedmen wasted no time establishing societies for self-improvement, which undertook to raise funds to purchase land, build schoolhouses, and hire teachers. With qualified black teachers in short supply, they accepted the aid of Northern white women sent by the American Missionary Association. They also turned to the federal government for help. The freed blacks were going to need all the friends—and power—they could muster in Washington.

The Freedmen's Bureau

Abolitionists had long preached that slavery was a degrading institution. Now the emancipators were faced with the brutal reality that the former slaves were overwhelmingly unskilled, unlettered, without property or money, and with scant knowledge of how to survive as free people. To cope with this problem throughout the conquered South, Congress created the **Freedmen's Bureau** on March 3, 1865.

Freedmen's Bureau (1865–1872) *Created to aid newly emancipated slaves by providing food, clothing, medical care, education, and legal support. Its achievements were uneven and depended largely on the quality of local administrators.*

On paper at least, the bureau was intended to be a kind of primitive welfare agency. It was to provide food, clothing, and education both to freedmen and to white refugees. The bureau was also authorized to distribute up to forty acres of abandoned or confiscated land to black settlers. Headed by General Oliver O. Howard, who later founded and served as president of Howard University in Washington, D.C., the bureau achieved its greatest successes in education. It taught an estimated 200,000 blacks how to read. Many former slaves had a passion for learning, partly because they wanted to close the gap between themselves and the whites and partly because they longed to read the Word of God.

But in other areas the bureau's accomplishments were meager—or even mischievous. Although the bureau was authorized to settle former slaves on forty-acre tracts, little confiscated Confederate land actually passed into black hands. Instead local administrators often collaborated with planters in expelling blacks from towns and cajoling them into signing labor contracts to work for their former masters. Still, the white South resented the bureau as a meddlesome federal interloper that threatened to upset white racial dominance. President Andrew Johnson, who shared the white supremacist views of most white Southerners, repeatedly tried to kill it, and the bureau expired in 1872.

Women from the North enthusiastically embraced the opportunity to go south and teach in Freedmen's Bureau schools for emancipated blacks. One volunteer explained her motives:

"I thought I must do something, not having money at my command, what could I do but give myself to the work. . . . I would go to them, and give them my life if necessary."

Johnson: The Tailor President

Few presidents have ever been faced with a more perplexing sea of troubles than that confronting Andrew Johnson. What manner of man was this dark-eyed, black-haired Tennessean, now chief executive by virtue of the bullet that killed Lincoln?

Educating Young Freedmen and Women, 1870s Freed slaves in the South regarded schooling as the key to improving their children's lives and the fulfillment of a long-sought right that had been denied blacks in slavery. These well-dressed school children are lined up outside their rural, one-room schoolhouse alongside their teachers, both black and white.

No citizen, not even Lincoln, has ever reached the White House from humbler beginnings. Born to impoverished parents in North Carolina and orphaned early, Johnson never attended school but was apprenticed to a tailor at age ten. Ambitious to get ahead, he taught himself to read, and later his wife taught him to write and do simple arithmetic. Like many another self-made man, he was inclined to overpraise his maker.

Johnson early became active in politics in Tennessee, where he had moved when seventeen years old. He shone as an impassioned champion of the poor whites against the planter aristocrats, and as a two-fisted stump speaker before angry and heckling crowds. Elected to Congress, he attracted much favorable attention in the North when he refused to secede with his own state. After Tennessee was partially liberated by Union armies, he was appointed war governor of the state.

Political exigency next thrust Johnson into the vice presidency. Lincoln's Union party in 1864 needed to attract support from the War Democrats and other pro-Southern elements, and Johnson, a Democrat, seemed to be the ideal man.

"Old Andy" Johnson was no doubt a man of parts—unpolished parts. He was intelligent, able, forceful, and steadfastly devoted to duty and to the Constitution. Yet the man who had raised himself from the tailor's bench to the president's chair was a misfit. A Southerner who did not understand the North, a Tennessean who had earned the distrust of the South, a Democrat who had never been accepted by the Republicans, a president who had not been elected to the office, he was not at home in a Republican White House. Hotheaded, contentious, and stubborn, Johnson was the wrong man in the wrong place at the wrong time. A Reconstruction policy devised by the angels might well have failed in his tactless hands.

Examining the Evidence

Letter From a Freedman to His Old Master, 1865

What was it like to experience the transition from slavery to freedom? Four million southern blacks faced this exhilarating and formidable prospect with the end of the war. For historians, recovering the African American perspective on emancipation is challenging. Unlike their white masters, freed blacks left few written records. But one former slave captured in a letter to his "Old Master" (whose surname he bore) the heroic determination of many blacks to build new independent and dignified lives for themselves and their families.

During the war Jourdon Anderson escaped slavery in Tennessee with his wife and two daughters. After relocating to the relative safety of Ohio, he received a communication from his former owner asking him to return. In his bold reply, reportedly "dictated by the old servant" himself, Anderson expressed his family's new expectations for life as free people and an uneasiness about his former master's intentions. He made reference to his "comfortable home," his daughters' schooling, the church that he and his wife were free to attend regularly, and the peace of mind that came with knowing that "my girls [would not be] brought to shame by the violence and wickedness of their young masters." To test the white man's sincerity, Anderson and his wife asked for the astronomical figure of $11,680 in back wages from decades as slaves. He closed by reiterating that "the great desire of my life is to give my children an education and have them form virtuous habits." This rare letter demonstrates that many black correspondents may have been illiterate, but they were hardly inarticulate. And they asserted themselves as parents, workers, and citizens not only from the distance of a former free state such as Ohio but also deep within the former slave states of the South.

1. Was the tone of Anderson's letter (and postscript) serious, sarcastic, or tongue-in-cheek? What specific phrases support your answer?
2. How did the eventual accomplishments of Reconstruction correspond with the initial expectations of people like Anderson and his former owner?
3. What does this letter reveal about the complicated relationships between freedmen and their former masters? Is the relationship a "personal" one, or was it entirely dominated by Jourdon Anderson's having been held by Colonel P. H. Anderson as "property"?

Letter from a Freedman to his Old Master.

The following is a genuine document. It was *dictated* by the old servant, and contains his ideas and forms of expression. [Cincinnati Commercial.

DAYTON, Ohio, August 7, 1865.

To my Old Master, Col. P. H. ANDERSON, *Big Spring, Tennessee.*

SIR: I got your letter and was glad to find that you had not forgotten Jordan, and that you wanted me to come back and live with you again, promising to do better for me than anybody else can. I have often felt uneasy about you. I thought the Yankees would have hung you long before this for harboring Rebs. they found at your house. I suppose they never heard about your going to Col. Martin's to kill the Union soldier that was left by his company in their stable. Although you shot at me twice before I left you, I did not want to hear of your being hurt, and am glad you are still living. It would do me good to go back to the dear old home again and see Miss Mary and Miss Martha and Allen, Esther, Green and Lee. Give my love to them all, and tell them I hope we will meet in the better world, if not in this. I would have gone back to see you all when I was working in the Nashville Hospital, but one of the neighbors told me Henry intended to shoot me if he ever got a chance.

I want to know particularly what the good chance is you propose to give me. I am doing tolerably well here; I get $25 a month, with victuals and clothing; have a comfortable home for Mandy (the folks here call her Mrs. Anderson), and the children, Milly Jane and Grundy, go to school and are learning well; the teacher says Grundy has a head for a preacher. They go to Sunday-School, and Mandy and me attend church regularly. We are kindly treated; sometimes we over-

As to my freedom, which you say I can have, there is nothing to be gained on that score, as I got my free-papers in 1864 from the Provost-Marshal-General of the Department at Nashville. Mandy says she would be afraid to go back without some proof that you are sincerely disposed to treat us justly and kindly—and we have concluded to test your sincerity by asking you to send us our wages for the time we served you. This will make us forget and forgive old sores, and rely on your justice and friendship in the future. I served you faithfully for thirty-two years, and Mandy twenty years, at $25 a month for me, and $2 a week for Mandy. Our earnings would amount to $11,680. Add to this the interest for the time our wages has been kept back and deduct what you paid for our clothing and three doctor's visits to me, and pulling a tooth for Mandy, and the balance will show what we are in justice entitled to. Please send the money by Adams Express, in care of V. Winters, esq., Dayton, Ohio. If you fail to pay us for faithful labors in the past we can have little faith in your promises in the future.

P. S.—Say howdy to George Carter, and thank him for taking the pistol from you when you were shooting at me.

New York Tribune Tuesday, August 22, 1865

Presidential Reconstruction

Even before the shooting war had ended, the political war over Reconstruction had begun. Abraham Lincoln believed that the Southern states had never legally withdrawn from the Union. Their formal restoration to the Union would therefore be relatively simple. Accordingly, Lincoln in 1863 proclaimed his **"10 percent" Reconstruction plan**. It decreed that a state could be reintegrated into the Union when 10 percent of its voters in the presidential election of 1860 had taken an oath of allegiance to the United States and pledged to abide by emancipation. The next step would be formal erection of a state government. Lincoln would then recognize the purified regime.

"10 percent" Reconstruction plan (1863) *Introduced by President Lincoln, it proposed that a state be readmitted to the Union once 10 percent of its voters had pledged loyalty to the United States and promised to honor emancipation.*

Lincoln's proclamation provoked a sharp reaction in Congress, where Republicans feared the restoration of the planter aristocracy to power and the possible re-enslavement of blacks. Republicans therefore rammed through Congress in 1864 the **Wade-Davis Bill**. The bill required that 50 percent of a state's voters take the oath of allegiance and demanded stronger safeguards for emancipation than Lincoln's as the price of readmission. Republicans were outraged when Lincoln "pocket-vetoed" this bill by refusing to sign it after Congress had adjourned.

Wade-Davis Bill *Passed by Congressional Republicans in response to Abraham Lincoln's "10 percent plan," but never signed or enacted by Lincoln, it would have required that 50 percent of a state's voters pledge allegiance to the Union, and intended to set stronger safeguards for emancipation. Reflected divisions between Congress and the President, and between radical and moderate Republicans, over the treatment of the defeated South.*

The controversy surrounding the Wade-Davis Bill had revealed deep differences between the president and Congress. Unlike Lincoln, many in Congress insisted that the seceders had indeed left the Union—had "committed suicide" as republican states—and had therefore forfeited all their rights. They could be readmitted only as "conquered provinces" on such conditions as Congress should decree.

The episode further revealed differences among two emerging Republican factions, moderates and radicals. The majority moderate group tended to agree with Lincoln that the seceded states should be restored to the Union as simply and swiftly as reasonable—though on Congress's terms, not the president's. The minority radical group believed that before the South could be restored, its social structure should be uprooted, the haughty planters punished, and the newly emancipated blacks protected by federal power.

After President Lincoln's assassination in April 1865, some radicals hoped that spiteful Andy Johnson, who shared their hatred for the planter aristocracy, would also share their desire to reconstruct the South with a rod of iron. But Johnson soon disillusioned them. He quickly recognized several of Lincoln's 10 percent governments, and on May 29, 1865, he issued his own Reconstruction proclamation. It disfranchised certain leading Confederates and called for special state conventions, which were required to repeal secession, repudiate all Confederate debts, and ratify the slave-freeing Thirteenth Amendment.

Johnson, savoring his dominance over the high-toned aristocrats who now begged his favor, granted pardons in abundance. Bolstered by the political resurrection of the planter elite, the recently rebellious states moved rapidly in the second half of 1865 to organize governments. But as the pattern of the new governments became clear, Republicans of all stripes grew furious.

The Baleful Black Codes

Among the first acts of the new Southern regimes sanctioned by Johnson was the passage of the iron-toothed **Black Codes**. These laws were designed to regulate the affairs of the emancipated blacks, much as the slave statutes had done in pre-Civil War days. The Black Codes aimed, first of all, to ensure a stable and subservient labor force. Dire penalties were therefore imposed by the codes on blacks who "jumped" their labor contracts, which usually committed them to work for the same employer for one year, and generally at pittance wages.

Black Codes (1865–1866) *Laws passed throughout the South to restrict the rights of emancipated blacks, particularly with respect to negotiating labor contracts. Increased Northerners' criticisms of President Andrew Johnson's lenient Reconstruction policies.*

The codes also sought to restore as nearly as possible the pre-emancipation system of race relations. Freedom was legally recognized, as were some other privileges, such as the right to marry. But all the codes forbade a black to serve on a jury or vote, and some codes even barred blacks from renting or leasing land.

These oppressive laws mocked the ideal of freedom, so recently purchased by buckets of blood. The Black Codes imposed terrible burdens on the unfettered blacks, struggling against mistreatment and poverty to make their way as free people. Thousands of impoverished former slaves slipped into virtual peonage as sharecropper farmers, as did many landless whites.

Contending Voices

Radical Republicans and Southern Democrats

Representative Thaddeus Stevens (1792–1868), a leading radical Republican, argued in September 1865 for a sweeping plan of compulsory land redistribution and political reform to smash the Southern plantation system:

"The whole fabric of southern society *must* be changed, and never can it be done if this opportunity is lost. . . . If the South is ever to be made a safe republic let her lands be cultivated by the toil of the owners or the free labor of intelligent citizens."

Two months later, the new governor of South Carolina, James Lawrence Orr (1822–1873), voiced elite Southerners' insistence that emancipated slaves must be kept tied to the South's prewar economic system, even if now by contract rather than bondage:

"[Emancipated slaves] must be restrained from theft, idleness, vagrancy and crime, and taught the absolute necessity of strictly complying with their contracts for labor. . . . The labor of every negro in the State is needed, if not to till the soil, in some other useful employment—for the culture of cotton and rice; and, in menial occupations, it is very doubtful whether any laborers in this country or in Europe can supply his place."

Why were these competing visions of the political future of the post–Civil War South so linked to labor and land policies?

The Black Codes made an ugly impression in the North. If the former slaves were being re-enslaved, people asked one another, had not the Boys in Blue spilled their blood in vain? Had the North really won the war?

Congressional Reconstruction

These questions grew more insistent when the congressional delegations from the newly reconstituted Southern states presented themselves in the Capitol in December 1865. To the shock and disgust of the Republicans, many former Confederate leaders were on hand to claim their seats.

The appearance of these ex-rebels was a natural but costly blunder. Voters of the South, seeking able representatives, had turned instinctively to their experienced statesmen. But most of the Southern leaders were tainted by active association with the "lost cause." Among them were four former Confederate generals, five colonels, and various members of the Richmond cabinet and Congress. Worst of all, there was the shrimpy but brainy Alexander Stephens, ex-vice president of the Confederacy, still under indictment for treason.

The presence of these "whitewashed rebels" infuriated the Republicans in Congress. The war had been fought to restore the Union, but not on these kinds of terms. Most Republicans balked at giving up the political advantage they had enjoyed while the South had been "out" from 1861 to 1865. They had passed much legislation that favored the North, such as the Morrill Act, the **Pacific Railroad Act**, and the Homestead Act. On the first day of the congressional session, December 4, 1865, they banged shut the door in the face of the newly elected Southern delegations.

Looking to the future, the Republicans were alarmed to realize that a restored South would be stronger than ever in national politics. Before the war a black slave had counted as three-fifths of a person in apportioning congressional representation. But now, owing to full counting of free blacks, the eleven rebel states were entitled to twelve more votes in Congress and twelve more presidential electoral votes than they had previously enjoyed. Again, angry voices in the North raised the cry, "Who won the war?"

Republicans had good reason to fear that ultimately they might be elbowed aside. Southerners might join hands with Democrats in the North and win control of Congress or maybe even the White House. If that happened, they could perpetuate the Black Codes, virtually re-enslaving the blacks. They could dismantle the economic program of the Republican party and possibly even repudiate the national debt. President Johnson thus deeply disturbed the congressional Republicans when he announced on December 6, 1865, that the recently rebellious states had satisfied his conditions and that in his view the Union was now restored.

Pacific Railroad Act (1862) *Helped fund the construction of the Union Pacific transcontinental railroad with the use of land grants and government bonds.*

Johnson Clashes with Congress

A clash between president and Congress was now inevitable. It exploded into the open in February 1866, when the president vetoed a bill (later repassed) extending the life of the controversial Freedmen's Bureau.

Aroused, the Republicans swiftly struck back. In March 1866 they passed the **Civil Rights Bill**, which conferred on blacks the privileges of American citizenship and struck at the Black Codes. President Johnson resolutely vetoed this forward-looking measure, but in April congressmen steamrollered it over his veto—something they repeatedly did henceforth. The hapless president, dubbed "Andy Veto," had his presidential wings clipped short, as Congress increasingly assumed the dominant role in running the government.

Civil Rights Bill (1866) *Passed over Andrew Johnson's veto, the bill aimed to counteract the Black Codes by conferring citizenship on African Americans and making it a crime to deprive blacks of their rights to sue, testify in court, or hold property.*

The Republicans now undertook to rivet the principles of the Civil Rights Bill into the Constitution as the **Fourteenth Amendment**, so that no future Congress could repeal the law. The proposed amendment, as approved by Congress and sent to the states in June 1866 and ratified in 1868, was sweeping. The amendment (1) conferred civil rights, including citizenship but excluding the franchise, on the freedmen; (2) reduced proportionately the representation of a state in Congress and in the Electoral College if it denied blacks the ballot; (3) disqualified from federal and state office former Confederates who as federal officeholders had once sworn to "support the Constitution of the United States"; and (4) guaranteed the federal debt, while repudiating all Confederate debts. (See the text of the Fourteenth Amendment in the Appendix.)

Fourteenth Amendment (ratified 1868) *Constitutional amendment that extended civil rights to freedmen and prohibited states from taking away such rights without due process.*

The radical faction was disappointed that the Fourteenth Amendment did not grant the right to vote, but all Republicans agreed that no state should be welcomed back into the Union fold without first ratifying the Fourteenth Amendment. Yet President Johnson advised the Southern states to reject it, and all of the "sinful eleven," except Tennessee, defiantly spurned the amendment.

Swinging 'Round the Circle with Johnson

As 1866 lengthened, the battle grew between Congress and the president. Now the issue was whether Reconstruction was to be carried on with or without the Fourteenth Amendment. The Republicans would settle for nothing less; indeed, they soon insisted on even more.

The crucial congressional elections of 1866—more crucial than some presidential elections—were fast approaching. Johnson was naturally eager to escape from the clutch of Congress by securing a majority favorable to his soft-on-the-South policy. Invited to dedicate a Chicago monument to Stephen A. Douglas, he undertook to speak at various cities en route in support of his views.

Johnson's famous "swing 'round the circle," beginning in the late summer of 1866, was a seriocomedy of errors. The president delivered a series of "give 'em hell" speeches, in which he accused the radicals in Congress of having planned large-scale antiblack riots and murder in the South. As he spoke, hecklers hurled insults at him. Reverting to his stump-speaking days in Tennessee, he shouted back angry retorts, amid cries of "You be damned!" and "Don't get mad, Andy!" The dignity of his high office sank to a new low.

As a vote-getter, Johnson was highly successful—for the opposition. His inept speechmaking heightened the cry to "Stand by Congress" against the "Tailor of the Potomac." When the ballots were counted, the Republicans had rolled up more than a two-thirds majority in both houses of Congress.

Republican Reconstruction

The Republicans now had a veto-proof Congress and virtually unlimited control of Reconstruction policy. But moderates and radicals still disagreed over the best course to pursue in the South.

The radicals were led in the Senate by the courtly and principled idealist Massachusetts Senator Charles Sumner, who tirelessly labored not only for black freedom but for racial equality. In the House the most powerful radical was crusty and vindictive Pennsylvania Congressman Thaddeus Stevens. An unswerving friend of blacks, he insisted that after his death he be buried in a black cemetery. Still opposed to rapid restoration of the Southern states, the radicals led by Sumner and Stevens wanted to keep them out

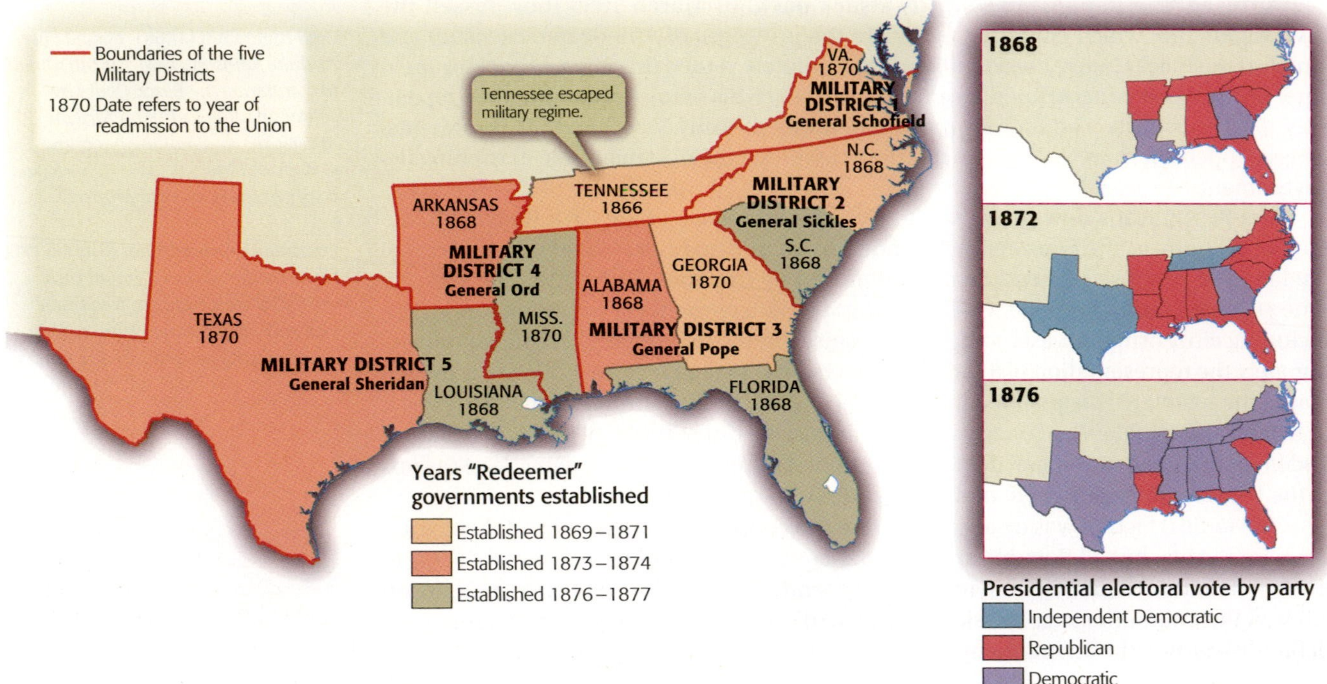

Map 22.1 Military Reconstruction, 1867 (five districts and commanding generals) For many white Southerners, military Reconstruction amounted to turning the knife in the wound of defeat. An often-repeated story of later years had a Southerner remark, "I was sixteen years old before I discovered that damnyankee was two words."

as long as possible and apply federal power to bring about a drastic social and economic transformation in the South.

But moderate Republicans, invoking the principles of states' rights and self-government, preferred policies that restrained the states from abridging citizens' rights, rather than policies that directly involved the federal government in individual lives. The actual policies adopted by Congress showed the influence of both these schools of thought, though the moderates, as the majority faction, had the upper hand. And one thing both groups had come to agree on by 1867 was the necessity to enfranchise black voters, even if it took federal troops to do it.

Reconstruction Act (1867) *Passed by the newly elected Republican Congress, it divided the South into five military districts, disenfranchised former confederates, and required that Southern states both ratify the Fourteenth Amendment and write state constitutions guaranteeing freedmen the franchise before gaining readmission to the Union.*

Against a backdrop of vicious and bloody race riots that had erupted in several Southern cities, Congress passed the **Reconstruction Act** on March 2, 1867 (see Map 22.1). This drastic legislation divided the South into five military districts, each commanded by a Union general and policed by blue-clad soldiers, about twenty thousand all told.

Congress additionally laid down stringent requirements for the readmission of the seceded states. The wayward states were required to ratify the Fourteenth Amendment, giving the former slaves their rights as citizens, and to guarantee in their state constitutions full suffrage for their former adult male slaves. Yet the act, reflecting moderate sentiment, stopped short of giving the freedmen land or education at federal expense. The overriding purpose of the moderates was to create an electorate in Southern states that would vote those states back into the Union on acceptable terms and thus free the federal government from direct responsibility for the protection of black rights. As later events would demonstrate, this approach proved woefully inadequate to the cause of justice for the blacks.

Fifteenth Amendment (ratified 1870) *Prohibited states from denying citizens the franchise on account of race. It disappointed feminists who wanted the Amendment to include guarantees for women's suffrage.*

The radical Republicans still worried that once the unrepentant states were readmitted, they would amend their constitutions to withdraw the ballot from the blacks. They therefore sought the ironclad safeguard of incorporating black suffrage in the federal Constitution. This goal was finally achieved by the **Fifteenth Amendment**, passed by Congress in 1869 and ratified by the required number of states in 1870. (See the Appendix.)

Military Reconstruction of the South not only usurped certain functions of the president as commander in chief but set up a martial regime of dubious legality. The Supreme Court had already ruled, in the case ***Ex parte Milligan*** (1866), that military tribunals could not try civilians, even during wartime, in areas where the civil courts were open. Peacetime military rule seemed starkly contrary to the spirit of the Constitution, but the circumstances were extraordinary and for the time being the Supreme Court avoided offending the Republican Congress.

The prominent suffragist and abolitionist Susan B. Anthony (1820–1906) was outraged over the proposed exclusion of women from the Fourteenth Amendment. In a conversation with her former male allies Wendell Phillips and Theodore Tilton, she reportedly held out her arm and declared:

"Look at this, all of you. And hear me swear that I will cut off this right arm of mine before I will ever work for or demand the ballot for the negro and not the woman."

Prodded into line by federal bayonets, the Southern states got on with the task of constitution making. By 1870 all of them had reorganized their governments and had been accorded full rights. The hated "bluebellies" (federal troops) remained until the new regimes—usually called "radical" regimes—appeared to be firmly entrenched. Yet when the U.S. Army finally left a state, its government swiftly passed into the hands of white "Redeemer" regimes, which were inevitably Democratic. Finally, in 1877, the last federal muskets were removed from state politics, and the "solid" Democratic South congealed.

Ex parte Milligan **(1866)** *Civil War Era case in which the Supreme Court ruled that military tribunals could not be used to try civilians if civil courts were open.*

The passage of the three Reconstruction-era Amendments—the Thirteenth, Fourteenth, and Fifteenth—delighted former abolitionists but deeply disappointed advocates of women's rights. Women had played a prominent part in the prewar abolitionist movement, and in the eyes of many women the struggle for black freedom and the crusade for women's rights were one and the same. Now, feminist leaders reeled with shock when the Fourteenth Amendment, which defined equal national citizenship, for the first time inserted the word *male* into the Constitution in referring to a citizen's right to vote. When the Fifteenth Amendment proposed to prohibit denial of the vote on the basis of "race, color, or previous condition of servitude," women's rights leaders Susan B. Anthony and Elizabeth Cady Stanton wanted the word *sex* added to the list. They lost this battle, too. Fifty years would pass before the Constitution granted women the right to vote.

The Realities of Radical Reconstruction in the South

Blacks now had freedom, of a sort. By 1867 Republican hesitation over black voting had given way to a hard determination to enfranchise the former slaves wholesale and immediately, while thousands of white Southerners were being denied the right to vote. By glaring contrast, most of the Northern states, before ratification of the Fifteenth Amendment in 1870, withheld the ballot from their tiny black minorities. White Southerners naturally concluded that the Republicans were hypocritical in insisting that blacks in the South be allowed to vote.

Having gained their right to suffrage, Southern black men seized the initiative and began to organize politically. Their primary vehicle became the Union League, originally a pro-Union organization based in the North. Assisted by Northern blacks, freedmen turned the League into a network of political clubs that educated members in their civic duties and campaigned for Republican candidates. The League's mission soon expanded to include building black churches and schools, representing black grievances before local employers and governments, and recruiting militias to protect black communities from white retaliation.

Though African American women did not obtain the right to vote, they too assumed new political roles. Black women faithfully attended the parades and rallies common in black communities during the early years of Reconstruction and helped assemble mass meetings in the newly constructed black churches. They even showed up at the constitutional conventions held throughout the South in 1867, monitoring the proceedings and participating in informal votes outside the convention halls.

The Granger Collection, New York

Freedmen Voting, Richmond, Virginia, 1871 The exercise of democratic rights by former slaves constituted a political and social revolution in the South and was bitterly resented by many whites.

But black men elected as delegates to the state constitutional conventions held the greater political authority. They formed the backbone of the black political community. At the conventions, they sat down with whites to hammer out new state constitutions, which most importantly provided for universal male suffrage.

scalawags *Derogatory term for pro-Union Southerners whom Southern Democrats accused of plundering the resources of the South in collusion with Republican governments after the Civil War.*

carpetbaggers *Pejorative used by Southern whites to describe Northern businessmen and politicians who came to the South after the Civil War to work on Reconstruction projects or invest in Southern infrastructure.*

The sight of former slaves holding office deeply offended their onetime masters, who lashed out with fury at the freedmen's white allies, labeling them **scalawags** and **carpetbaggers**. The so-called scalawags were Southerners, often former Unionists and Whigs, whom former Confederates wildly accused of plundering the treasuries of the Southern radical governments. The carpetbaggers were supposedly sleazy Northerners who had packed all their worldly goods into a carpetbag suitcase at war's end and had come South to seek personal power and profit. In fact, most were former Union soldiers and Northern businessmen and professionals who wanted to play a role in modernizing the "New South."

How well or badly did the radical regimes rule? White southerners regularly portrayed the "Black Reconstruction" governments as run by ignorant and corrupt former slaves. Black voters did make up a majority of the electorate in five states, but only in South Carolina did blacks predominate in the lower house of the legislature. Black political participation expanded exponentially during Reconstruction. Many of the newly elected black legislators were literate and able; more than a few came from the ranks of the prewar free blacks who had acquired considerable education. Though no blacks were elected governors of their states, more than a dozen black congressmen and two black United States senators, Hiram Revels and Blanche K. Bruce, both of Mississippi, served in Washington, D.C.

In some radical regimes, there was truth to the charges of graft and corruption. This was especially true in South Carolina and Louisiana, where conscienceless promoters and other pocket-padders used politically inexperienced blacks as cat's-paws. The worst "black-and-white" legislatures purchased as "legislative supplies" such "stationery" as hams, perfumes, suspenders, bonnets, corsets, champagne, and a coffin. Yet this sort of corruption was no more outrageous than the scams and felonies being perpetrated in the North at the same time, especially in Boss Tweed's New York.

The radical legislatures also passed much desirable legislation. For the first time in Southern history, steps were taken toward establishing adequate public schools. Tax systems were streamlined; public works were launched; and property rights were guaranteed to women. Many of these welcome reforms were retained by the all-white "Redeemer" governments that later returned to power.

Ku Klux Klan *An extremist, paramilitary, right-wing secret society founded in the mid-nineteenth century and revived during the 1920s. It was anti-foreign, anti-black, anti-Jewish, anti-pacifist, anti-communist, anti-internationalist, anti-evolutionist, and anti-bootlegger, but pro-Anglo-Saxon and pro-Protestant. Its members, cloaked in sheets to conceal their identities, terrorized freedmen and sympathetic whites throughout the South after the Civil War. By the 1890s, Klan-style violence and Democratic legislation succeeded in virtually disenfranchising all Southern blacks.*

The Ku Klux Klan

Deeply embittered, some Southern whites resorted to savage measures against "radical" rule. Many whites resented the success and ability of black legislators as much as they resented alleged "corruption." A number of secret organizations mushroomed forth, the most notorious of which was the "Invisible Empire of the South," or **Ku Klux Klan**, founded in Tennessee in 1866. Hooded nightriders, their horses' hoofs muffled, would hammer on blacks' cabin doors or use other tactics to frighten them. Those stubborn

Dallas Historical Society, Texas, USA/The Bridgeman Art Library

Klansmen in Costume Members of the Ku Klux Klan like these two garbed men utilized terrorist violence on behalf of a political agenda: the disenfranchisement of African Americans and their Republican allies and the reinstatement of white supremacist rule by "Redeemer" governments.

souls who persisted in their "upstart" ways were flogged, mutilated, or even murdered. In one Louisiana parish in 1868, whites in two days killed or wounded two hundred victims; a pile of twenty-five bodies was found half-buried in the woods. By such atrocious terror tactics were blacks "kept in their place"—that is, down.

Force Acts (1870–1871) *Passed by Congress following a wave of Ku Klux Klan violence, the acts banned clan membership, prohibited the use of intimidation to prevent blacks from voting, and gave the U.S. military the authority to enforce the acts.*

Congress, outraged by this night-riding lawlessness, passed the harsh **Force Acts** of 1870 and 1871. Federal troops were able to stamp out much of the "lash law," but by this time the Invisible Empire had already done its work of intimidation. The Klan remained a refuge for numerous scoundrels and cutthroats who hid under its sheets, often continuing to operate under the guise of "dancing societies," "missionary clubs," and "rifle clubs."

White resistance undermined attempts to empower blacks politically. The white South for many decades openly flouted the Fourteenth and Fifteenth Amendments. Wholesale disfranchisement of the blacks, starting conspicuously about 1890, was achieved by intimidation, fraud, and trickery. Among various underhanded schemes were the literacy tests, unfairly administered by whites to the advantage of illiterate whites. In the eyes of white Southerners, the goal of white supremacy fully justified these dishonorable devices.

Impeachment and Acquittal for Johnson

Radicals meanwhile had been sharpening their hatchets for President Johnson. Not content with curbing his authority, they decided to remove him altogether by constitutional processes (for impeachment, see Art. I, Sec. II, para. 5, Art. I, Sec. II, paras. 6, 7, Art. II, Sec. IV, in the Appendix).

Tenure of Office Act (1867) *Required the President to seek approval from the Senate before removing appointees. When Andrew Johnson removed his secretary of war in violation of the act, he was impeached by the House but remained in office when the Senate fell one vote short of removing him.*

As an initial step, Congress in 1867 passed the **Tenure of Office Act**—as usual over Johnson's veto. Contrary to precedent, the new law required the president to secure the consent of the Senate before he could remove his cabinet members, including the secretary of war, Edwin M. Stanton, a holdover from the Lincoln administration. Although outwardly loyal to Johnson, Stanton was secretly serving as a spy and informer for the radicals.

The remarkable ex-slave Frederick Douglass (1817?–1895) wrote in 1882:

"Though slavery was abolished, the wrongs of my people were not ended. Though they were not slaves, they were not yet quite free. No man can be truly free whose liberty is dependent upon the thought, feeling, and action of others, and who has himself no means in his own hands for guarding, protecting, defending, and maintaining that liberty. Yet the Negro after his emancipation was precisely in this state of destitution. . . . He was free from the individual master, but the slave of society. He had neither money, property, nor friends. He was free from the old plantation, but he had nothing but the dusty road under his feet. He was free from the old quarter that once gave him shelter, but a slave to the rains of summer and the frosts of winter. He was, in a word, literally turned loose, naked, hungry, and destitute, to the open sky."

Johnson provided the radicals with a pretext to begin impeachment proceedings when he abruptly dismissed Stanton early in 1868. The House of Representatives immediately voted 126 to 47 to impeach Andrew Johnson for "high crimes and misdemeanors," as required by the Constitution, charging him with various violations of the Tenure of Office Act. Two additional articles related to Johnson's verbal assaults on the Congress, involving "disgrace, ridicule, hatred, contempt, and reproach."

With evident zeal the radical-led Senate now sat as a court to try Johnson on the dubious impeachment charges. The House conducted the prosecution. The trial aroused intense public interest and, with only one thousand tickets printed, proved to be the biggest show of 1868. Johnson kept his dignity and maintained a discreet silence. His battery of attorneys argued that the president had fired Stanton merely to put a test case before the Supreme Court. The House prosecutors, including oily-tongued Benjamin F. Butler and embittered Thaddeus Stevens, had a harder time building a compelling case for impeachment.

On May 16, 1868, the day for voting in the Senate, the tension was electric, and heavy breathing could be heard in the galleries. By a margin of only one vote, the radicals failed to muster the two-thirds majority for Johnson's removal. Seven resistant Republican senators, courageously putting country above party, voted "not guilty."

Diehard radicals were infuriated. "The Country is going to the Devil!" cried the crippled Stevens as he was carried from the hall. But the nation, though violently aroused, accepted the verdict with a good temper that did credit to its political maturity.

The nation thus narrowly avoided a bad precedent that would have gravely weakened one of the three branches of the federal government. Johnson was clearly guilty of bad speeches, bad judgment, and bad temper, but not of "high crimes and misdemeanors." From the standpoint of the radicals, his greatest crime had been to stand inflexibly in their path.

The Purchase of Alaska

Johnson's administration, though largely reduced to a figurehead, achieved its most enduring success in the field of foreign relations. The Russians by 1867 were in a mood to sell the vast and chilly expanse of land now known as Alaska. The region had been ruthlessly "furred out" and was a growing economic liability to them. The Russians were therefore eager to unload their "frozen asset" on the Americans. They preferred the United States to any other purchaser primarily because they wanted to strengthen the American Republic as a barrier against their ancient enemy, Britain.

In 1867 Secretary of State William Seward, an ardent expansionist, signed a treaty with Russia that transferred Alaska to the United States for the bargain price of $7.2 million. But Seward's enthusiasm for these frigid wastes was not shared by his ignorant or uninformed countrymen, who jeered at "**Seward's Folly**," "Seward's Icebox," and "Walrussia."

Seward's Folly (1867) *Popular term for Secretary of State William Seward's purchase of Alaska from Russia. The derisive term reflected the anti-expansionist sentiments of most Americans immediately after the Civil War.*

Then why did Congress and the American public sanction the purchase? For one thing Russia, alone among the great powers, had been conspicuously friendly to the North during the recent Civil War. Americans did not feel that they could offend their good friend the tsar by hurling his walrus-covered icebergs back into his face. Besides, the territory was rumored to be still teeming with furs, fish, and gold, and it might yet "pan out" profitably—as it later did with natural resources that included vast deposits of oil and gas.

The Heritage of Reconstruction

Many white Southerners regarded Reconstruction as a more grievous wound than the war itself. It left a festering scar that would take generations to heal. They resented the upending of their social and racial systems, the political empowerment of blacks, and the insult of federal intervention in their local affairs. Yet given the explosiveness of the issues that had caused the war and the bitterness of the fighting, the wonder is that Reconstruction was not far harsher than it was. Northern policymakers groped for the right policies, influenced as much by Southern responses to defeat and emancipation as by any specific plans of their own.

The Republicans acted from a mixture of idealism and political expediency. They wanted both to protect the freed slaves and to promote the fortunes of the Republican party. In the end their efforts backfired badly. Reconstruction conferred only fleeting benefits on the blacks, and it virtually extinguished the Republican party in the South for nearly one hundred years.

Moderate Republicans never fully appreciated the extensive effort necessary to make the freed slaves completely independent citizens, nor the lengths to which Southern whites would go to preserve their system of racial dominance. Had Thaddeus Stevens's radical program of drastic economic reforms and heftier protection of political rights been enacted, things might well have been different. But deep-seated racism, ingrained American resistance to tampering with property rights, and rigid loyalty to the principle of local self-government, combined with spreading indifference in the North to the plight of blacks, formed too formidable an obstacle. Despite good intentions by Republicans, the Old South was in many ways more resurrected than reconstructed, which spelled continuing woe for generations of Southern blacks.

Varying Viewpoints

How Radical Was Reconstruction?

Few topics have triggered as much intellectual warfare as the "dark and bloody ground" of Reconstruction. The period provoked questions—sectional, racial, and constitutional—about which people felt deeply and remain deeply divided even today. Scholarly argument goes back conspicuously to a Columbia University historian, William A. Dunning, who wrote about Reconstruction as a kind of national disgrace, foisted on a prostrate region by vindictive and self-seeking radical Republican politicians.

In the 1920s, widespread suspicion that the Civil War itself had been a tragic and unnecessary blunder shifted attention to Northern politicians. Scholars such as Howard Beale argued that the radical Republicans had masked a ruthless desire to exploit Southern resources and expand Republican power in the South behind a false "front" of concern for the freed slaves.

Although ignored by his contemporaries, the scholar and founder of the National Association for the Advancement of Colored People W. E. B. Du Bois wrote a sympathetic history of Reconstruction in 1935 that became the basis of historians' interpretations ever since. Following World War II, Kenneth Stampp and others, influenced by the modern civil rights movement, built on Du Bois's argument and claimed that Reconstruction had been a noble though ultimately failed attempt to extend American principles of equity and justice. By the early 1970s, this view had become orthodoxy, and it generally holds sway today. Yet some scholars, such as Michael Benedict and Leon Litwack, disillusioned with the inability to achieve full racial justice in the 1960s and 1970s, claimed to discover that Reconstruction was never really very radical and argued that the Freedmen's Bureau and other agencies had merely allowed white planters to maintain local political and economic control.

More recently, Eric Foner has powerfully reasserted the argument that Reconstruction was a truly radical and noble attempt to establish an interracial democracy. Drawing on the work of Du Bois, Foner has emphasized that Reconstruction allowed blacks to form political organizations and churches and to establish some measure of economic independence. In South Africa, the Caribbean, and other areas once marked by slavery, these opportunities were much harder to come by. Many of the benefits of Reconstruction were erased by white Southerners during the Gilded Age, but in the twentieth century, constitutional principles and organizations developed during Reconstruction provided the foundation for the modern civil rights movement—which some have called the Second Reconstruction.

Steven Hahn's *A Nation Under Our Feet: Black Political Struggles in the Rural South from Slavery to the Great Migration* (2003) is the latest contribution to the literature on Reconstruction. Hahn emphasizes the assertiveness and ingenuity of African Americans in creating new political opportunities for themselves after emancipation.

CHAPTER SUMMARY ★ ★ ★ ★ ★ ★ ★ ★ ★ ★ ★ ★ ★ ★

With the Civil War over, the nation faced the difficult problems of rebuilding the South, assisting the freed slaves, reintegrating the Southern states into the Union, and deciding who would direct the Reconstruction process.

The South was economically devastated and socially revolutionized by emancipation. As slave owners reluctantly confronted the end of slave labor, blacks took their first steps in freedom. Black churches and freedmen's schools helped the former slaves begin to shape their own destinies.

The new President Andrew Johnson was politically inept and personally contentious. His attempt to implement a moderate plan of Reconstruction, along the lines originally suggested by Lincoln, fell victim to Southern whites' severe treatment of blacks and his own political blunders.

Republicans imposed harsh military Reconstruction on the South after their gains in the 1866 congressional elections. The Southern states reentered the Union with new radical governments, which rested partly on the newly enfranchised blacks, but also had support from some sectors of Southern society. These governments were sometimes corrupt, but they also implemented important reforms, especially in education. For a time, acting from a mixture of idealism and political expediency, Republicans tried seriously to build a new Republican party in the South to guarantee black rights. But the divisions between moderate and radical Republicans meant that Reconstruction's aims were often limited and confused, despite successful passage of the important Fourteenth and Fifteenth Amendments guaranteeing black civil and voting rights.

Embittered whites hated the radical governments and mobilized reactionary terrorist organizations such as the Ku Klux Klan to restore white supremacy. The radical Republican House of Representatives impeached Johnson, but the Senate failed narrowly to convict him. In the end, the inadequate Reconstruction policy, which never really addressed the deep economic and social legacy of slavery and the Civil War, failed disastrously and created as much or more bitterness than the war itself.

KEY TERMS

- Freedmen's Bureau (350)
- "10 percent" Reconstruction plan (353)
- Wade-Davis Bill (353)
- Black Codes (353)
- Pacific Railroad Act (354)
- Civil Rights Bill (355)
- Fourteenth Amendment (355)
- Reconstruction Act (356)
- Fifteenth Amendment (356)
- *Ex parte Milligan* (357)
- scalawags (358)
- carpetbaggers (358)
- Ku Klux Klan (359)
- Force Acts (360)
- Tenure of Office Act (360)
- Seward's Folly (361)

PEOPLE TO KNOW

- General Oliver O. Howard
- Andrew Johnson
- Thaddeus Stevens
- Hiram Revels
- Edwin M. Stanton
- William Seward

Part 4

FORGING AN INDUSTRIAL SOCIETY

1865–1909

A nation of farmers fought the Civil War in the 1860s. By the time the Spanish-American War broke out in 1898, America was an industrial nation. For generations Americans had plunged into the wilderness and plowed their fields. Now they settled in cities and toiled in factories. Between the Civil War and the century's end, economic and technological change came so swiftly and massively that it seemed to many Americans that a whole new civilization had emerged.

In some ways it had. The sheer scale of the new industrial civilization was dazzling. Transcontinental railroads knit the country together from sea to sea. New industries such as oil and steel grew to staggering sizes—and made mega-millionaires out of entrepreneurs such as oilman John D. Rockefeller and steelmaker Andrew Carnegie.

Drawn by the allure of industrial employment, Americans moved to the city. In 1860 only about 20 percent of the population were city dwellers. By 1900 that proportion had doubled, as rural Americans and European immigrants alike flocked to mill town and metropolis in search of steady jobs.

These sweeping changes challenged the spirit of individualism that Americans had celebrated since the seventeenth century. Even on the western frontier, that historic bastion of rugged loners, the hand of government was increasingly felt, as large armies were dispatched to subdue the Plains Indians and federal authority was invoked to regulate the use of natural resources. The rise of powerful monopolies called into question the government's traditional hands-off policy toward business, and a growing band of reformers increasingly clamored for government regulation of private enterprise. The mushrooming cities, with their needs for transport systems, schools, hospitals, sanitation, and fire and police protection, required bigger governments and budgets than an earlier generation could have imagined. As never before, Americans struggled to adapt old ideals of private autonomy to the new realities of industrial civilization.

With economic change came social and political turmoil. Labor violence brought bloodshed to places such as Chicago and Homestead, Pennsylvania. Small farmers, squeezed by debt and foreign competition, rallied behind the People's, or "Populist," party, a radical movement of the 1880s and 1890s that attacked the power of Wall Street, big business, and the banks. Anti-immigrant sentiment swelled. Bitter disputes over tariffs and monetary policy deeply divided the country, setting debtors against lenders, farmers against manufacturers, the West and South against the Northeast. And in this unfamiliar era of big money and expanding government, corruption flourished, from town hall to Congress, fueling loud cries for political reform.

The bloodiest conflict of all pitted Plains Indians against the relentless push of westward expansion. As railroads drove their iron arrows through the heart of the West, the Indians

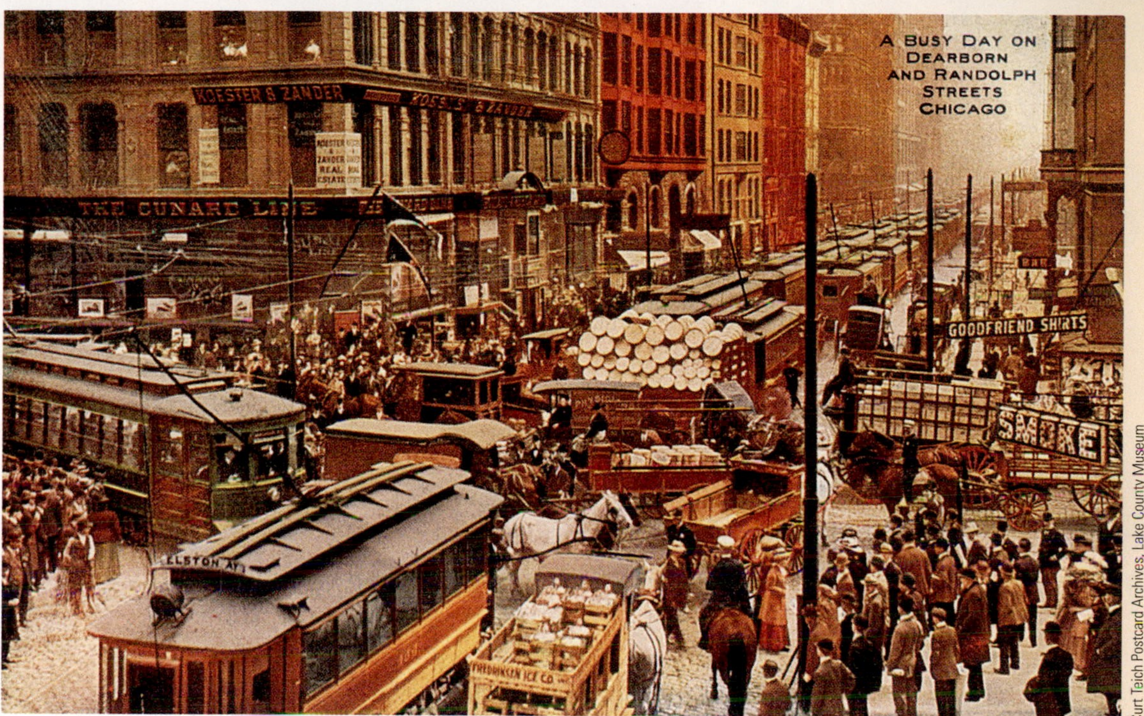

Curt Teich Postcard Archives, Lake County Museum

Dearborn Street, Chicago Loop, Around 1900 "America is energetic, but Chicago is in a fever," marveled a visiting Englishman about turn-of-the-century Chicago. Street scenes like this were common in America's booming new cities, especially in the "Lord of the Midwest."

lost their land and life-sustaining buffalo herds. By the 1890s, after three decades of fierce fighting with the U.S. Army, the Indians who had once roamed across the vast rolling prairies were struggling to preserve their shattered cultures within the confinement of reservations.

The South remained the one region largely untouched by the Industrial Revolution sweeping the rest of America. For the most part, the South's rural way of life and its peculiar system of race relations were largely unperturbed by the changes happening elsewhere. The post-emancipation era inflicted new forms of racial injustice on African Americans, the vast majority of whom continued to live in the Old South. State legislatures systematically deprived black Americans of their political rights, including the right to vote. Segregation of schools, housing, and all kinds of public facilities made a mockery of African Americans' Reconstruction-era hopes for equality before the law.

The new wealth and power of industrial America nurtured a growing sense of national self-confidence. Literature flowered, and a golden age of philanthropy dawned. The reform spirit spread. So did a restless appetite for overseas expansion. In a brief war against Spain in 1898, the United States, born in a revolutionary war of independence and long the champion of colonial peoples yearning to breathe free, seized control of the Philippines and itself became an imperial power. Uncle Sam's venture into empire touched off a bitter national debate about America's role in the world and ushered in a long period of argument over the responsibilities, at home and abroad, of a modern industrial state.

What if . . . ?

- **What if industrial workers and small farmers in the post–Reconstruction era had joined in a political movement strong enough to challenge the "Captains of Industry" for control of the American economy?**
- **How would the course of American economic, social, and political development, and the character of America's foreign policy, have been different?**

Chapter

23

Political Paralysis in the Gilded Age

1869–1896

Grant . . . had no right to exist. He should have been extinct for ages. . . . That, two thousand years after Alexander the Great and Julius Caesar, a man like Grant should be called—and should actually and truly be—the highest product of the most advanced evolution, made evolution ludicrous. . . . The progress of evolution, from President Washington to President Grant, was alone evidence enough to upset Darwin. . . . Grant . . . should have lived in a cave and worn skins.

HENRY ADAMS, THE EDUCATION OF HENRY ADAMS, 1907

Chapter Outline

- Ulysses S. Grant, Soldier-President
- Corruption and Reform in the Post–Civil War Era
- The Depression of the 1870s
- Political Parties and Partisans
- The Compromise of 1877 and the End of Reconstruction
- Class Conflict and Ethnic Clashes
- Civil Service Reform
- Grover Cleveland and the Tariff
- President Harrison and the "Billion-Dollar" Congress
- Populists
- Cleveland and the Depression of the 1890s
- *Makers of America: The Chinese*
- *Varying Viewpoints: The Populists: Radicals or Reactionaries?*

The population of the post–Civil War Republic continued to vault upward by vigorous leaps, despite the awful bloodletting in both Union and Confederate ranks. Census takers reported over 39 million people in 1870, a gain of 26.6 percent over the preceding decade, as the immigrant tide surged again. The United States was now the third-largest nation in the Western world, ranking behind Russia and France.

But the civic health of the United States did not keep pace with its physical growth. The Civil War and its aftermath spawned waste, extravagance, speculation, and graft. Disillusionment ran deep among idealistic Americans in the postwar era. They had spilled their blood for the Union, emancipation, and Abraham Lincoln, who had promised "a new birth of freedom." Instead, they got a bitter dose of corruption and political stalemate—beginning with Ulysses S. Grant, a great soldier but an utterly inept politician.

FOCUS QUESTIONS

1. Why was the Gilded Age a period of political patronage, corruption, and stalemate between the two major parties? Given these negative factors, why did political participation achieve such high levels?
2. How did the disputed Hayes–Tilden election of 1877 lead to the Compromise of 1877 and the end of Reconstruction?
3. What did the end of Reconstruction mean for blacks, and how did the South's racial segregation and sharecropping system trap both poor whites and blacks in poverty?
4. What caused the rise of industrial and agricultural conflict in the 1880s–1890s? Why were both Republicans and Democrats unable to address this discontent?
5. How did the severe depression of the 1890s stir growing social protest and class conflict and fuel the rise of the radical Populist party?

CHRONOLOGY

1868	▪ Grant defeats Seymour for the presidency
1869	▪ Fisk and Gould corner gold market
1871	▪ Tweed scandal in New York
1872	▪ Crédit Mobilier scandal exposed ▪ Liberal Republicans break with Grant ▪ Grant defeats Greeley for presidency
1873	▪ Panic of 1873
1875	▪ Whiskey Ring scandal ▪ Civil Rights Act of 1875 ▪ Resumption Act
1876	▪ Hayes-Tilden election standoff and crisis
1877	▪ Compromise of 1877 ▪ Reconstruction ends ▪ Railroad strikes paralyze nation
1880	▪ Garfield defeats Hancock for presidency
1881	▪ Garfield assassinated; Arthur assumes presidency
1882	▪ Chinese Exclusion Act
1883	▪ *Civil Rights Cases* ▪ Pendleton Act sets up Civil Service Commission
1884	▪ Cleveland defeats Blaine for presidency
1888	▪ Harrison defeats Cleveland for presidency
1890	▪ "Billion-Dollar" Congress ▪ McKinley Tariff Act ▪ Sherman Silver Purchase Act (repealed 1893)
1892	▪ Homestead steel strike ▪ Coeur d'Alene (Idaho) silver miners' strike ▪ People's party candidate James B. Weaver wins twenty-two electoral votes ▪ Cleveland defeats Harrison and Weaver to regain presidency
1893	▪ Depression of 1893 begins ▪ Republicans regain House of Representatives
1895	▪ J. P. Morgan's banking syndicate loans $65 million in gold to federal government
1896	▪ *Plessy v. Ferguson* legitimizes "separate but equal" doctrine

The "Bloody Shirt" Elects Grant

Wrangling between Congress and Andrew Johnson had soured the people on professional politicians, and the notion still prevailed that a good general would make a good president. Stubbly bearded General Grant was by far the most popular northern hero to emerge from the war. Grateful citizens of Philadelphia, Washington, and New York showered him with gifts of houses and cash, which the general, silently puffing on his cigar, unapologetically accepted.

Grant was a hapless greenhorn in the political arena. His one presidential vote had been cast for the Democratic ticket in 1856. A better judge of horseflesh than of humans, his cultural background was breathtakingly narrow. He once reportedly remarked that Venice, Italy, would be a fine city if only it were drained.

The Republicans, freed from the Union party coalition of war days, enthusiastically nominated Grant for the presidency in 1868. The party's platform sounded a clarion call for continued Reconstruction of the South under the glinting steel of federal bayonets. Yet Grant, always a man of few words, coined a popular campaign slogan when he declared, "Let us have peace."

Expectant Democrats, meeting in their own nominating convention, denounced military Reconstruction but could agree on little else. Wealthy eastern delegates demanded a platform promising that federal war bonds be redeemed in gold, while the poorer midwesterners backed the "Ohio Idea" calling for redemption in greenbacks. Debt-burdened agrarian Democrats thus hoped to keep more money in circulation and to keep interest rates lower. This dispute introduced a bitter contest over monetary policy that continued to convulse the Republic until the century's end.

Midwestern delegates got the platform but not the candidate. The nominee, former New York governor Horatio Seymour, scuttled the Democrats' faint hope for success by repudiating the Ohio Idea. Republicans whipped up enthusiasm for Grant by energetically **"waving the bloody shirt"**—that is, reviving gory memories of the Civil War—which became for the first time a prominent feature of a presidential campaign.* "Vote as You Shot" was a powerful Republican slogan aimed at Union army veterans.

"waving the bloody shirt" *The use of Civil War imagery by political candidates and parties to draw votes to their side of the ticket.*

Grant won, with 214 electoral votes to 80 for Seymour. But despite his great popularity, the former general scored a majority of only 300,000 in the popular vote (3,013,421 to 2,706,829). Most white voters apparently supported Seymour, and the ballots of three still-unreconstructed southern states (Mississippi, Texas, and Virginia) were not counted at all. An estimated 500,000 former slaves gave Grant his margin of victory. To remain in power, the Republican party somehow had to continue to control the South—and to keep the ballot in the hands of the grateful freedmen. Republicans could not take future victories "for Granted."

The Era of Good Stealings

A few skunks can pollute a large area. Although the great majority of businesspeople and government officials continued to conduct their affairs with decency and honor, the whole postwar atmosphere stunk of corruption. The Man in the Moon, it was said, had to hold his nose when passing over America. Freewheeling railroad promoters sometimes left gullible bond buyers with only "two streaks of rust and a right of way." Unethical stock-market manipulators were a cinder in the public eye. Too many judges and legislators put their power up for hire. Cynics defined an honest politician as one who, when bought, would stay bought.

Notorious in the financial world were two millionaire partners, "Jubilee Jim" Fisk and Jay Gould. The corpulent and unscrupulous Fisk provided the "brass," while the undersized and cunning Gould provided the brains. The crafty pair concocted a plot in 1869 to corner the gold market. Their slippery game would work only if the federal Treasury refrained from selling gold. The conspirators worked on President Grant directly, and also through Grant's brother-in-law, who received $25,000 for his complicity. For weeks, Fisk and Gould madly bid the price of gold skyward, so that they could later profit from its heightened value. But on "Black Friday" (September 24, 1869), the bubble burst when the Treasury, contrary to Grant's supposed assurances, was compelled to release gold. The price of gold plunged, and numerous honest businesspeople were driven to the wall. A congressional probe concluded that Grant had done nothing crooked, though he had acted stupidly and indiscreetly.

Tweed Ring *A symbol of Gilded Age corruption, "Boss" Tweed and his deputies ran the New York City Democratic party in the 1860s and swindled $200 million from the city through bribery, graft, and vote-buying. Boss Tweed was eventually jailed for his crimes and died behind bars.*

The infamous **Tweed Ring** in New York City vividly displayed the ethics (or lack of ethics) typical of the age. Burly "Boss" Tweed—240 pounds of rascality—employed bribery, graft, and fraudulent elections to milk the metropolis of as much as $200 million. Honest citizens were cowed into silence. Protesters found their tax assessments raised.

Tweed's luck finally ran out. The *New York Times* secured damning evidence in 1871 and courageously published it, though offered $5 million not to do so. Gifted cartoonist Thomas Nast pilloried Tweed mercilessly, after spurning a heavy bribe to desist. New York attorney Samuel J. Tilden headed the prosecution, gaining fame that later paved the path to his presidential nomination. Unbailed and unwept, Tweed died behind bars.

More serious than Boss Tweed's peccadilloes were the misdeeds of the federal government. President Grant's cabinet was a rodent's nest of grafters and incompetents. Favor seekers haunted the White House, plying Grant himself with cigars, wine, and horses. Several dozen of Grant's in-laws attached themselves to the public payroll.

Crédit Mobilier scandal (1872) *A construction company was formed by owners of the Union Pacific Railroad for the purpose of receiving government contracts to build the railroad at highly inflated prices—and profits. In 1872 a scandal erupted when journalists discovered that the Crédit Mobilier Company had bribed congressmen and even the vice president to allow the ruse to continue.*

The easygoing Grant was first tarred by the **Crédit Mobilier scandal**, which erupted in 1872. Union Pacific Railway insiders had formed the Crédit Mobilier construction

*The expression is said to have derived from a speech by Representative Benjamin F. Butler of Massachusetts, who allegedly waved before the House the bloodstained nightshirt of a Klan-flogged carpetbagger.

company and then cleverly hired themselves at inflated prices to build the railroad line, earning dividends as high as 348 percent. Fearing that Congress might blow the whistle, the company furtively distributed shares of its valuable stock to key congressmen. A newspaper exposé and congressional investigation of the scandal led to the formal censure of two congressmen and the revelation that the vice president of the United States had also accepted payments from Crédit Mobilier.

The breath of scandal in Washington also reeked of alcohol. In 1874–1875 a sprawling Whiskey Ring robbed the Treasury of millions in excise-tax revenues. When President Grant's own private secretary turned up among the culprits, the president volunteered a written statement to a jury that helped exonerate the thief. Further rottenness in the Grant administration came to light in 1876, forcing Secretary of War William Belknap to resign after pocketing bribes from suppliers to the Indian reservations. Grant, ever loyal to his crooked cronies, accepted Belknap's resignation "with great regret."

Bettmann/CORBIS

Can the Law Reach Him? 1872 Cartoonist Thomas Nast attacked "Boss" Tweed in a series of cartoons like this one that appeared in *Harper's Weekly* in 1872. Here Nast depicts the corrupt Tweed as a powerful giant, towering over a puny law force.

The Liberal Republican Revolt of 1872

By 1872 a powerful wave of disgust with Grantism was beginning to build up throughout the nation, even before some of the worst scandals had been exposed. Reform-minded citizens banded together in the Liberal Republican party. Voicing the slogan "Turn the Rascals Out," they urged purification of the Washington administration as well as an end to military Reconstruction.

The Liberal Republicans muffed their chance when their Cincinnati nominating convention astounded the country by nominating the brilliant but erratic Horace Greeley for the presidency. Although Greeley was a fearless editor of the *New York Tribune*, he was dogmatic, emotional, petulant, and notoriously unsound in his political judgments.

More astonishing still was the action of the office-hungry Democrats, who foolishly proceeded to endorse Greeley's candidacy. In swallowing Greeley the Democrats "ate crow" in large gulps, for the eccentric editor had long blasted them as traitors, slave drivers, saloon keepers, horse thieves, and idiots. Yet Greeley pleased the Democrats, North and South, when he pleaded for clasping hands across "the bloody chasm." The Republicans dutifully renominated Grant. The voters were thus presented with a choice between two candidates who had made their careers in fields other than politics and who were both eminently unqualified, by temperament and lifelong training, for high political office.

In the mud-spattered campaign that followed, regular Republicans denounced Greeley as an atheist, a free-lover, and a vegetarian, while Democrats derided Grant as a drunken swindler. But the regular Republicans, chanting "Grant us another term," pulled the president through. The count in the electoral column was 286 to 66, in the popular column 3,596,745 to 2,843,446.

Liberal Republican agitation frightened the regular Republicans into cleaning their own house before they were thrown out of it. The Republican Congress in 1872 passed a general amnesty act, removing political disabilities from all but some five hundred former Confederate leaders. Congress also moved to reduce high Civil War tariffs and to fumigate the Grant administration with mild civil-service reform. Like many American third parties, the Liberal Republicans left some enduring footprints, even in defeat.

Depression and Demands for Inflation

panic of 1873 *A worldwide depression that began in the United States when one of the nation's largest banks abruptly declared bankruptcy, leading to the collapse of thousands of banks and businesses. The crisis intensified debtors' calls for inflationary measures such as the printing of more paper money and the unlimited coinage of silver. Conflicts over monetary policy greatly influenced politics in the last quarter of the nineteenth century.*

Grant's woes deepened in the paralyzing economic **panic of 1873**. Bursting with startling rapidity, the crash was one of those periodic plummets that roller-coastered the economy in this age of unbridled capitalist expansion. Overreaching promoters had laid more railroad track, sunk more mines, erected more factories, and sowed more grain fields than existing markets could bear. Bankers, in turn, had made too many imprudent loans to finance those enterprises. When profits failed to materialize, loans went unpaid, and the whole credit-based house of cards fluttered down. The United States did not suffer alone. Nations worldwide underwent a similar economic collapse in 1873.

Boom times became gloom times as more than fifteen thousand American businesses went bankrupt. In New York City, an army of unemployed riotously battled police. Black Americans were hard hit. The Freedman's Savings and Trust Company had made unsecured loans to several companies that went under. Black depositers, who had entrusted over $7 million to the bank, lost their savings, and black economic development and black confidence in savings institutions went down with the bank.

Hard times inflicted the worst punishment on debtors, who intensified their clamor for inflationary policies. Proponents of inflation breathed new life into the issue of greenbacks. During the war $450 million of the "folding money" had been issued, but it had depreciated under a cloud of popular mistrust and dubious legality.* By 1868 the Treasury had already withdrawn $100 million of the "battle-born currency" from circulation, and "hard-money" people everywhere looked forward to its complete disappearance. But now afflicted agrarian and debtor groups—"cheap-money" supporters—pressed for a reissuance of the greenbacks. With a crude but essentially accurate grasp of monetary theory, they reasoned that more money meant cheaper money and, hence, rising prices and easier-to-pay debts. Creditors, of course, reasoning from the same premises, advocated precisely the opposite policy.

The "hard-money" advocates took a notable step in 1874 when they persuaded Grant to veto a bill to print more paper money. They scored another victory in the Resumption Act of 1875, which pledged the government to the further withdrawal of greenbacks from circulation and to the redemption of all paper currency in gold at face value, beginning in 1879.

Down but not out, debtors now looked for relief to another precious metal, silver. The "sacred white metal," they claimed, had received a raw deal. In the early 1870s, the Treasury stubbornly and unrealistically maintained that an ounce of silver was worth only one-sixteenth as much as an ounce of gold. Silver miners thus stopped selling their shiny product to the federal mints, and Congress dropped the coinage of silver dollars in 1873. Fate then played a sly joke when new silver discoveries later in the 1870s shot production up and forced silver prices down. Westerners from silver-mining states now joined with debtors in assailing the "Crime of '73," demanding a return to the "Dollar of Our Daddies." Like the demand for more greenbacks, the demand for the coinage of more silver was nothing more nor less than another scheme to promote inflation.

Hard-money Republicans resisted this scheme and counted on Grant to hold the line against it. He did not disappoint them. The Treasury began to accumulate gold stocks against the appointed day for resumption of metallic-money payments. Coupled with the reduction of greenbacks, this policy was called "contraction." It had a noticeable deflationary effect—the amount of money per capita in circulation actually decreased between 1870 and 1880, from $19.42 to $19.37. Contraction probably worsened the impact of the depression. But the new policy did restore the government's credit rating, and it brought the embattled greenbacks up to their full face value. When Redemption Day came in 1879, few greenback holders bothered to exchange the lighter and more convenient bills for gold.

Republican hard-money policy had a political backlash. It helped elect a Democratic House of Representatives in 1874, and in 1878 it spawned the Greenback Labor party, which polled over a million votes and elected fourteen members of Congress. The contest over monetary policy was far from over.

---

*The Supreme Court in 1870 declared the Civil War Legal Tender Act unconstitutional. With the concurrence of the Senate, Grant thereupon added to the bench two justices who could be counted on to help reverse that decision, which happened in 1871. This is how the Court grew to its current size of nine justices.

Pallid Politics in the Gilded Age

The political seesaw was delicately balanced throughout most of the **Gilded Age** (a sarcastic name given to the three-decade-long post–Civil War era by Mark Twain in 1873). Even a slight nudge could tip the teeter-totter to the advantage of the opposition party. Every presidential election was a squeaker, and the majority party in the House of Representatives switched six times in the eleven sessions between 1869 and 1891. Wobbling in such shaky equilibrium, politicians tiptoed timidly, producing a political record that was often trivial and petty.

Gilded Age *A term originally coined by Mark Twain, given to the period 1865–1896, indicating both the fabulous wealth and the widespread corruption of the era.*

Few significant economic issues separated the major parties. Democrats and Republicans saw very nearly eye-to-eye on questions such as the tariff and civil-service reform, and majorities in both parties substantially agreed even on the much-debated currency question. Yet despite their rough agreement on these national matters, the two parties were ferociously competitive with each other. They were tightly and efficiently organized, and they commanded fierce loyalty from their members. Voter turnouts reached heights unmatched before or since. Nearly 80 percent of eligible voters cast their ballots in presidential elections in the three decades after the Civil War. On election days, droves of the party faithful tramped behind marching bands to the polling places, and "ticket splitting," or failing to vote the straight party line, was as rare as a silver dollar.

How can this apparent paradox of political consensus and partisan fervor be explained? The answer lies in the sharp ethnic and cultural differences in the membership of the two parties—in distinctions of style and tone, and especially of religious sentiment. Republican voters tended to adhere to those creeds that traced their lineage to Puritanism. They stressed strict codes of personal morality and believed that government should play a role in regulating both the economic and the moral affairs of society. Democrats, among whom immigrant Lutherans and Roman Catholics figured heavily, were more likely to adhere to faiths that took a less stern view of human weakness. Their religions professed toleration of differences in an imperfect world, and they spurned government efforts to impose a single moral standard on the entire society. These differences in temperament and religious values often produced raucous political contests at the local level, where issues such as prohibition and education loomed large.

Democrats had a solid electoral base in the South and in the northern industrial cities, teeming with immigrants and controlled by well-oiled political machines. Republican strength lay largely in the Midwest and the rural and small-town Northeast. Grateful freedmen in the South continued to vote Republican in significant numbers. Another important bloc of Republican ballots came from the members of the Grand Army of the Republic (GAR)—a politically potent organization of several hundred thousand Union veterans of the Civil War.

The lifeblood of both parties was **patronage**—disbursing jobs by the bucketful in return for votes, kickbacks, and party service. Boisterous infighting over patronage beset the Republican party in the 1870s and 1880s. A "Stalwart" faction, led by the handsome and imperious Senator Roscoe ("Lord Roscoe") Conkling of New York, unblushingly embraced the time-honored system of swapping jobs for votes. Opposed to the Conklingites were the so-called Half-Breeds, who flirted coyly with civil-service reform, but whose real quarrel with the Stalwarts was over who should grasp the ladle that dished out the spoils. The champion of the Half-Breeds was James G. Blaine, a radiantly personable congressman from Maine with a fine physical presence, a thrilling speaking voice, and an elastic conscience. But despite all the color of their personalities, Conkling and Blaine succeeded only in stalemating each other and deadlocking their party.

patronage *A system, prevalent during the Gilded Age, in which political parties granted jobs and favors to party regulars who delivered votes on election day. Patronage was both an essential wellspring of support for both parties and a source of conflict within the Republican party.*

The Hayes-Tilden Standoff, 1876

Hangers-on around Grant, like fleas urging their ailing dog to live, begged the "Old Man" to try for a third term in 1876. The general, blind to his own ineptitudes, showed a disquieting willingness. But the House, by a lopsided bipartisan vote of 233 to 18, spiked the third-term boom. It passed a resolution that sternly reminded the country—and Grant—of the antidictator implications of the two-term tradition.

The Political Legacy of the Civil War Union veterans of the Civil War supported Republican candidate Rutherford B. Hayes in 1876. The Grand Army of the Republic (GAR), the Union veterans' organization, voted heavily for the GOP (Grand Old Party) in the post–Civil War years. (Left: The Granger Collection, NYC; Right: Collection of Janice L. and David J. Frent)

With Grant out of the running and with the Conklingites and Blaineites neutralizing each other, the Republicans turned to a compromise candidate, Rutherford B. Hayes, who was obscure enough to be dubbed "the Great Unknown." His foremost qualification was having served as three-term governor of the potent "swing" state of Ohio, which was so crucial to the cliffhanging electoral contests of the day that it regularly produced presidential candidates.

Pitted against the humdrum Hayes was the Democratic nominee, Samuel J. Tilden, who had risen to fame as the man who bagged Boss Tweed in New York. Campaigning against Republican scandal, Tilden racked up 184 electoral votes of the needed 185, with 20 votes in four states doubtful because of irregular returns (see Map 23.1). Oregon eventually fell completely to Hayes, but surely Tilden could pick up at least one of the other three, especially in view of the fact that he had polled 247,448 more popular votes than Hayes, 4,284,020 to 4,036,572.

Both parties scurried to send "visiting statesmen" to the three still-contested southern states of Louisiana, South Carolina, and Florida. These states had all submitted two sets of returns, one Democratic and one Republican. As the weeks drifted by, the paralysis tightened, generating a dramatic constitutional crisis. The Constitution merely specifies that the electoral returns from the states shall be sent to Congress, and in the presence of the House and Senate they shall be opened by the president of the Senate (see the Twelfth Amendment in the Appendix). But who should count them? On this point the Constitution was silent. If counted by the president of the Senate (a Republican), the Republican returns would be selected. If counted by the Speaker of the House (a Democrat), the Democratic returns would be chosen. How could the impasse be resolved?

The Compromise of 1877 and the End of Reconstruction

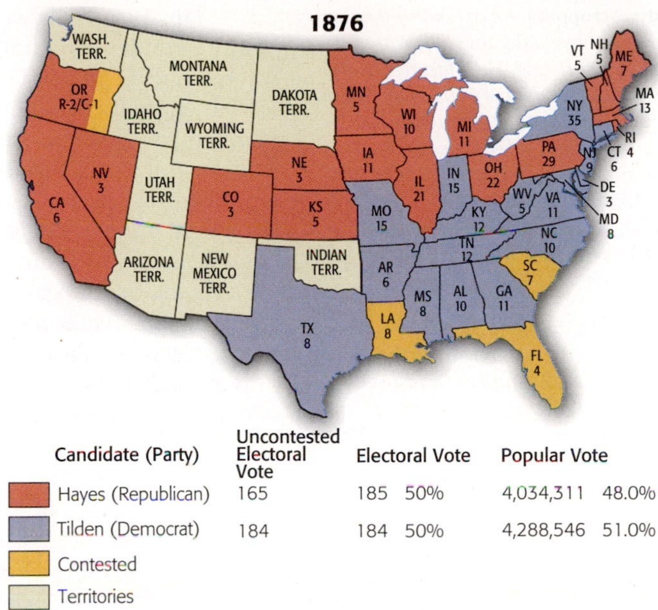

Map 23.1 Hayes-Tilden Disputed Election of 1876 (with electoral vote by state) Nineteen of the twenty disputed votes composed the total electoral count of Louisiana, South Carolina, and Florida. The twentieth was one of Oregon's three votes, cast by an elector who turned out to be ineligible because he was a federal officeholder (a postmaster), contrary to the Constitution (see Art. II, Sec. I, para. 2).

Clash or compromise was the stark choice. The danger loomed that there would be no president on inauguration day, March 4, 1877. "Tilden or Blood!" cried Democratic hotheads, and some of their "Minute Men" began to drill with arms. But behind the scenes, frantically laboring statesmen gradually hammered out an agreement in the Henry Clay tradition—the **Compromise of 1877**.

The election deadlock itself was to be broken by the Electoral Count Act, which passed Congress early in 1877. It set up an electoral commission consisting of fifteen men selected from the Senate, the House, and the Supreme Court.

In February 1877, about a month before Inauguration Day, the Senate and House met together in an electric atmosphere to settle the dispute. The roll of the states was tolled off alphabetically. When Florida was reached—the first of the three southern states with two sets of returns—the disputed documents were referred to the electoral commission, which sat in a nearby chamber. After prolonged discussion the members agreed, by the partisan vote of eight Republicans to seven Democrats, to accept the Republican returns. Outraged Democrats in Congress, smelling defeat, undertook to launch a filibuster "until hell froze over."

Renewed deadlock was avoided by the rest of the complex Compromise of 1877, already partially concluded behind closed doors. The Democrats reluctantly agreed that Hayes might take office in return for his withdrawing intrusive federal troops from the two states in which they remained, Louisiana and South Carolina. Among various concessions, the Republicans assured the Democrats a place at the presidential patronage trough and support for a bill subsidizing the Texas and Pacific Railroad's construction of a southern transcontinental line. Not all of these promises were kept in later years, including the Texas and Pacific subsidy. But the deal held together long enough to break the dangerous electoral standoff.

Compromise of 1877 *The agreement that finally resolved the 1876 election and officially ended Reconstruction. In exchange for the Republican candidate, Rutherford B. Hayes, winning the presidency, Hayes agreed to withdraw the last of the federal troops from the former Confederate states. This deal effectively completed the southern return to white-only, Democratic-dominated electoral politics.*

The compromise bought peace at a price. Partisan violence was averted by sacrificing the civil rights of southern blacks. With the Hayes-Tilden deal, the Republican party quietly abandoned its commitment to racial equality. That commitment had been weakening in any case. Many Republicans had begun to question the worthiness of Reconstruction and became less willing to send dollars and enlisted sons to bolster southern state governments.

The **Civil Rights Act of 1875** was in a sense the last feeble gasp of the congressional radical Republicans. The act supposedly guaranteed equal accommodations in public places and prohibited racial discrimination in jury selection, but the law was born toothless and stayed that way for nearly a century. The Supreme Court pronounced much of the act unconstitutional in the *Civil Rights Cases* (1883), declaring that the Fourteenth Amendment prohibited only *government* violations of civil rights, not the denial of civil rights by *individuals*. When President Hayes withdrew the blue-clad federal troops that were propping up Reconstruction governments, the bayonet-backed Republican regimes collapsed.

Civil Rights Act of 1875 *The last piece of federal civil rights legislation until the 1950s, the law promised blacks equal access to public accommodations and banned racism in jury selection, but it provided no means of enforcement and was therefore ineffective. In 1883, the Supreme Court declared most of the act unconstitutional.*

The Birth of Jim Crow in the Post–Reconstruction South

Reconstruction was officially ended. Relying shamelessly on fraud and intimidation, white Democrats ("Redeemers") reassumed political power in the South and ruthlessly suppressed the now-friendless blacks. Blacks who tried to assert their rights faced unemployment, eviction, and physical harm.

sharecropping *An agricultural system that emerged after the Civil War in which black and white farmers rented land and residences from a plantation owner in exchange for giving him a certain "share" of each year's crop. Sharecropping was the dominant form of southern agriculture after the Civil War, and landowners manipulated this system to keep tenants in perpetual debt and unable to leave their plantations.*

Jim Crow *System of racial segregation in the American South from the end of Reconstruction until the mid-twentieth century. Based on the concept of "separate but equal" facilities for blacks and whites, the Jim Crow system sought to prevent racial mixing in public, including restaurants, movie theaters, and public transportation. An informal system, it was generally perpetuated by custom, violence, and intimidation.*

***Plessy v. Ferguson* (1896)** *A Supreme Court case that upheld the constitutionality of segregation laws, saying that as long as blacks were provided with "separate but equal" facilities, these laws did not violate the Fourteenth Amendment. This decision provided legal justification for the Jim Crow system until the 1950s.*

Many blacks (as well as poor whites) were forced into **sharecropping** and tenant farming under conditions scarcely better than slavery. Through the "crop-lien" system, storekeepers extended credit to small farmers for food and supplies and in return took a lien on their customers' harvests. Shrewd merchants manipulated the system so that farmers remained perpetually in debt to them. For generations to come, southern blacks were condemned to eke out a harsh and threadbare living.

With white southerners back in the political saddle, daily discrimination against blacks grew increasingly oppressive. What had started as the informal separation of blacks and whites in the immediate postwar years developed by the 1890s into systematic state-level codes of segregation known as **Jim Crow** laws. Southern states also enacted literacy requirements, voter-registration laws, and poll taxes—and tolerated violent intimidation of black voters—to ensure full-scale disfranchisement of the South's freedmen. The Supreme Court validated the South's segregationist social order in the case of ***Plessy* v. *Ferguson*** (1896). It ruled that "separate but equal" facilities were constitutional under the "equal protection" clause of the Fourteenth Amendment.

But in reality the quality of African American life was grotesquely unequal to that of whites. Segregated in inferior schools and separated from whites in virtually all public facilities, blacks were assaulted daily by reminders of their second-class citizenship. To ensure the stability of this political and economic "new order," southern whites dealt harshly with any black who dared to violate the South's racial code of conduct. A record number of blacks were lynched during the 1890s, most often for the "crime" of asserting themselves as equals. It would take a second Reconstruction, nearly a century later, to redress the racist imbalance of southern society.

Class Conflicts and Ethnic Clashes

The year 1877 marked more than the end of Reconstruction. As the curtains officially closed on regional warfare, they opened on scenes of class struggle. The explosive atmosphere was largely a by-product of the long years of depression and deflation following the panic of 1873. Railroad workers faced particularly hard times, while they watched the railroads continue to rake in huge profits. When the presidents of the nation's four largest railroads collectively decided in 1877 to cut employees' wages by 10 percent, the workers struck back. President Hayes's decision to call in federal troops to quell the unrest brought the striking laborers an outpouring of working-class support. Work stoppages spread like wildfire in cities from Baltimore to St. Louis. When the battling between workers and soldiers ended after several weeks, over one hundred people were dead.

The failure of the great railroad strike exposed the weakness of the labor movement in the face of massive government intervention on the side of the railroads. The federal courts, the United States Army, state militias, and local police all lent their muscle to keeping the engines of big business operating at full throttle, and the workers be damned. Meanwhile, racial and ethnic fissures among workers fractured labor unity. Divisions were particularly acute between the Irish and the Chinese in California (see "Makers of America: The Chinese," p. 375). By 1880 the Golden State counted seventy-five thousand Asian newcomers, about 9 percent of its entire population.

Mostly poor, uneducated, single males from K'uang-t'ung (Guangdong) province in southern China, they had originally come to dig in the gold fields and lay the tracks of the transcontinental railroads across the West. When those jobs ended, the Chinese who remained had to turn to the most menial jobs, often as cooks, laundrymen, or domestic servants. Without women or families, they were deprived of the children who in other immigrant communities eased their parents' assimilation through their exposure to the English language and American customs in school.

In San Francisco, Irish-born demagogue Denis Kearney incited his followers, many of them recently arrived European immigrants, to violent abuse of the hapless Chinese. Taking to the streets, gangs of Kearneyites terrorized the Chinese by shearing off their precious pigtails. Some victims were murdered outright.

The Chinese

Between 1800 and 1925, at least 3 million Chinese left their homeland to labor around the globe. The once great Chinese Empire was disintegrating while its population was exploding, creating severe land shortages and opening up the unstable country to European imperial powers bent on unlocking the riches of a nation closed to outsiders for centuries. Chinese men, faced with economic hardship and political turmoil in their homeland and lured by labor shortages as far afield as Southeast Asia, Australia, and the Americas, migrated by the tens of thousands to work the plantations and dig the mines that fueled a burgeoning global economy. By 1900, more than 300,000 Chinese had entered the United States to contribute their muscle to building the West, wrenching minerals from stubborn rock, and helping to lay the transcontinental railroads that stitched together the American nation.

Chinese emigrants, mostly poor laborers, had set off for destinations as diverse as Vietnam, Cuba, and Peru since the sixteenth century. But until the 1848 discovery of gold in California, there were fewer than 50 Chinese living in the United States. By 1852, at least twenty-five thousand Chinese had arrived in California, which they dubbed the "golden mountain." At that decade's end, Chinese workers made up nearly a quarter of the state's manual laborers, even though they were only a tenth of the population. Employers nationwide viewed the Chinese as cheap labor, recruiting them to cut sugar cane in the South and break strikes in New England shoe factories.

Although Chinese immigrants included a few merchants and artisans, most were unskilled country folk. In some cases families pooled their money to send out a son, but most travelers, desperately poor, obtained their passage through Chinese middlemen, who advanced them ship fare in return for the emigrants' promise to work off their debts after they landed.

The Chinese America of the late-nineteenth-century West was overwhelmingly a bachelor society. Women of good repute rarely made the passage. Of the very few Chinese women who did venture to California at this time, most became prostitutes. Many of them had been deceived by the false promise of honest jobs.

Although a stream of workers returned to China, many Chinese stayed. "Chinatowns" sprang up wherever economic opportunities presented themselves. Chinese in these settlements spoke their own language, enjoyed the fellowship of their own compatriots, and sought safety from prejudice and violence. Many immigrant clubs and associations were American adaptations of Chinese traditions of loyalty to clan. The poorest and most alienated immigrants also established *tongs*—literally, "meeting halls"—secret societies that acquired a sinister reputation among non-Chinese.

Mounting anti-Chinese agitation demanded political action against the immigrants, and in 1882 the Chinese Exclusion Act barred nearly all Chinese from the United States for six decades. Many of the bachelors died or returned home. Slowly, however, those men and the few women who remained raised families and reared a new generation of Chinese Americans. They were joined by thousands more immigrants who made the journey illegally or took advantage of the few exceptions permissible under the Exclusion Act. But this second generation still suffered from discrimination, eking out their living in jobs despised by Caucasian laborers or taking daunting risks in small entrepreneurial ventures. Yet many hard-working Chinese did manage to open their own restaurants, laundries, and other small businesses. Such enterprises formed a solid economic foundation for their small community and remain a source of livelihood for many Chinese Americans even today.

University of California at Berkeley, Bancroft Library

Chinese Butcher Shop, San Francisco, California, c. 1890

Chinese Exclusion Act (1882) *Federal legislation that prohibited most further Chinese immigration to the United States. This was the first major legal restriction on immigration in U.S. history.*

Congress slammed the door on Chinese immigrant laborers when it passed the **Chinese Exclusion Act** in 1882, prohibiting nearly all further immigration from China. The door stayed shut until 1943. Some exclusionists even tried to strip native-born Chinese Americans of their citizenship, but the Supreme Court ruled in *U.S. v. Wong Kim Ark* in 1898 that the Fourteenth Amendment guaranteed citizenship to all persons born in the United States. This doctrine of "birthright citizenship" provided important protections to Chinese Americans as well as to other immigrant communities.

Garfield and Arthur

As the presidential campaign of 1880 approached, "Rutherfraud" Hayes was a man without a party, repudiated by the Republican Old Guard. Seeking a new standard-bearer, the Republicans finally settled on dark-horse candidate Congressman James A. Garfield from the electorally powerful state of Ohio. His vice-presidential running mate was a notorious Stalwart henchman, Chester A. Arthur of New York.

Energetically waving the bloody shirt, Garfield barely squeaked out a victory over the Democratic candidate, Civil War hero Winfield Scott Hancock. Garfield polled only 39,213 more votes than Hancock—4,453,295 to 4,414,082—but his margin in the electoral column was a comfortable 214 to 155.

The new president was an energetic and able man, but he was immediately ensnared in political conflict between his secretary of state, James G. Blaine, and Blaine's Stalwart nemesis, Senator Roscoe Conkling. Then, as the Republican factions dueled, tragedy struck. A disappointed and mentally deranged office seeker, Charles J. Guiteau, shot President Garfield in the back in a Washington railroad station. Garfield died eleven weeks later, on September 19, 1881, and Chester Arthur assumed the presidency.

Garfield's death did have one positive outcome: it shocked politicians into reforming the shameful spoils system. The unlikely instrument of reform was Chester Arthur. Arthur's record of cronyism and fondness for fine wines and elegant clothing (including eighty pairs of trousers) suggested that he was little more than a foppish dandy. But as the new president, Arthur surprised his critics by prosecuting several fraud cases and giving his former Stalwart pals the cold shoulder.

Pendleton Act (1883) *Congressional legislation that established the Civil Service Commission, which granted federal government jobs on the basis of examinations instead of political patronage, thus reining in the spoils system.*

Disgust with Garfield's murder also gave the Republican party itself a previously undetected taste for reform. The medicine finally applied to the long-suffering federal government was the **Pendleton Act** of 1883—the so-called Magna Carta of civil-service reform. It made compulsory campaign contributions from federal employees illegal, and it established the Civil Service Commission to make appointments to federal jobs on the basis of competitive examinations rather than party pull.

Although at first covering only about 10 percent of federal jobs, civil service reform did rein in the most blatant political abuses. Yet like many well-intentioned reforms, it bred unintended problems of its own. With the "plum" federal posts now beyond their reach, politicians were forced to look elsewhere for money, the "mother's milk of politics." Increasingly, they turned to the bulging coffers of the big corporations. A new breed of boss emerged—less skilled at mobilizing small armies of immigrants and other voters on election day, but more adept at milking dollars from manufacturers and lobbyists.

The Blaine-Cleveland Mudslingers of 1884

President Arthur's surprising display of integrity offended too many powerful Republicans, and his ungrateful party refused to nominate him in 1884. Instead they turned to James G. Blaine, whose persistence in pursuit of the presidential nomination finally paid off. The dashing Maine politician, blessed with almost every asset except a reputation for honesty, was the clear choice of the Republican convention in Chicago, though reformers gagged at his candidacy.

Blaine's enemies publicized the Republican nominee's fishy-smelling "Mulligan letters," written by Blaine to a Boston businessman. These damning documents linked Blaine to a corrupt deal involving federal favors to a southern railroad, and one of them ended with the furtive warning "Burn this letter." Some reformers, unable to swallow Blaine, bolted to the Democrats. They were sneeringly dubbed Mugwumps, a word of Indian derivation meaning "sanctimonious" or "holier than thou."

Victory-starved Democrats turned enthusiastically to a noted reformer, Grover Cleveland. A burly bachelor with a soup-straining mustache and a taste for chewing tobacco, Cleveland was a solid but not brilliant lawyer of forty-seven. He had rocketed from the Buffalo mayor's office to the governorship of New York and the presidential nomination in three short years. Known as "Grover the Good," he enjoyed a well-deserved reputation for probity in office.

But Cleveland's admirers soon got a shock. Resolute Republicans, digging for dirt in the past of bachelor Cleveland, unearthed the fact that he had been involved in an amorous affair with a Buffalo widow. Cleveland had provided financial support for her illegitimate son, now eight years old. Demoralized Democratic elders hurried to Cleveland and urged him to lie like a gentleman, but their ruggedly honest candidate insisted, "Tell the truth."

The campaign of 1884 sank to perhaps the lowest level in American experience, as the two parties grunted and shoved for the hog trough of office. Few fundamental differences separated them. Even the bloody shirt had faded to pale pink.* Personalities, not principles, claimed the headlines. Crowds of Democrats surged through city streets, chanting—to the rhythm of left, left, left, right, left—"Burn, burn, burn this letter!" Republicans taunted in return, "Ma, ma, where's my pa?" Defiant Democrats shouted back, "Gone to the White House, ha, ha, ha!"

The contest hinged on the state of New York, where Blaine blundered badly in the closing days of the campaign. A witless Republican clergyman damned the Democrats in a speech as the party of "Rum, Romanism, and Rebellion"—insulting with one swift stroke the culture, the faith, and the patriotism of New York's numerous Irish Americans. Blaine was present at the time but lacked the presence of mind to repudiate the statement immediately. The pungent phrase, shortened to "RRR," stung and stuck. Blaine's silence seemed to give assent, and the wavering Irishmen who then deserted his camp helped to account for Cleveland's paper-thin plurality of about a thousand votes in New York State, enough to give him the presidency. Cleveland swept the solid South and squeaked into office with 219 to 182 electoral votes and 4,879,507 to 4,850,293 popular votes.

*Neither candidate had served in the Civil War. Cleveland had hired a substitute to go in his stead while he supported his widowed mother and two sisters. Blaine was the only candidate nominated by the Republicans from Grant through McKinley (1868–1900) who had not been a Civil War officer.

Contending Voices

The Spoils System

In a famous series of newspaper interviews in 1905, George Washington Plunkitt (1842–1924), a political "boss" in the same Tammany Hall Democratic political "machine" that had spawned William Marcy ("Boss") Tweed, candidly described his ethical and political principles, which included a distinction between "honest graft and dishonest graft." Here he condemns civil-service reform while defending the efficacy of the patronage system.

"This civil service law is the biggest fraud of the age. It is the curse of the nation. There can't be no real patriotism while it lasts. How are you goin' to interest our young men in their country if you have no offices to give them when they work for their party? . . . First, this great and glorious country was built up by political parties; second, parties can't hold together if their workers don't get the offices when they win; third, if the parties go to pieces, the government they built up must go to pieces, too; fourth, then there'll be h– to pay."

Future U.S. president Theodore Roosevelt (1858–1919), by contrast, served as a civil-service commissioner and charged the patronage system with "tending to degrade American politics."

"The men who are in office only for what they can make out of it are thoroughly unwholesome citizens, and their activity in politics is simply noxious. . . . Decent private citizens must inevitably be driven out of politics if it is suffered to become a mere selfish scramble for plunder, where victory rests with the most greedy, the most cunning, the most brazen. The whole patronage system is inimical to American institutions; it forms one of the gravest problems with which democratic and republican government has to grapple."

Who benefited and who lost out in the process of reforming the civil service and curbing political patronage?

Library of Congress Images

"I Want My Pa!" Malicious anti-Cleveland cartoon.

"Old Grover" Takes Over

Bull-necked Cleveland in 1885 was the first Democrat to take the oath of presidential office since Buchanan, twenty-eight years earlier. Huge question marks hung over his portly frame (5 feet 11 inches, 250 pounds). Could the "party of disunion" be trusted to govern the Union? Would desperate Democrats, ravenously hungry after twenty-four years of exile, trample the frail sprouts of civil-service reform in a stampede to the patronage trough? Could Cleveland restore a measure of respect and power to the maligned and enfeebled presidency?

Cleveland was a man of principles, most of them safely orthodox by the standards of the day. A staunch apostle of the hands-off creed of laissez-faire, the new president summed up his political philosophy in 1887 when he vetoed a bill to provide seeds for drought-ravaged Texas farmers. "Though the people support the government," he declared, "the government should not support the people." As tactless as a mirror and as direct as a bulldozer, Cleveland was outspoken, unbending, and profanely hot-tempered.

At the outset Cleveland narrowed the North–South chasm by naming to the cabinet two former Confederates. As for the civil service, Cleveland was whipsawed between the demands of the Democratic faithful for jobs and the demands of the Mugwumps, who had helped elect him, for reform. Believing in the merit system, Cleveland at first favored the cause of the reformers, but he eventually caved in to the carpings of Democratic bosses and fired almost two-thirds of the 120,000 federal employees, including 40,000 incumbent (Republican) postmasters, to make room for "deserving Democrats."

Military pensions gave Cleveland some of his most painful political headaches. The politically powerful Grand Army of the Republic (GAR) routinely lobbied hundreds of often questionable private pension bills through a compliant Congress. As a non-veteran, Cleveland was in an awkward position to fight the pension grabbers, but he conscientiously read each bill and ended up vetoing several hundred of them.

Cleveland also risked his political neck by prodding the hornet's nest of the tariff issue. Jacked up to new high levels during the Civil War, the tariff duties were producing enormous revenues while comfortably sheltering American industry. By 1881 the Treasury was running an annual surplus amounting to an embarrassing $145 million. Congress could reduce the surplus either by squandering it on pensions or other "pork-barrel" bills or by lowering the tariff—something big industrialists vehemently opposed.

With his characteristic bluntness, Cleveland tossed an appeal for lower tariffs like a bombshell into the lap of Congress in late 1887. The response was electric. Democrats were deeply frustrated by the obstinacy of their chief. Republicans rejoiced at his apparent recklessness, bellowing loudly that lower tariffs would mean higher taxes, lower wages, and increased unemployment. The old warrior Blaine gloated, "There's one more president for us in [tariff] protection." For the first time in years, a real issue divided the two parties as the 1888 presidential election loomed.

Dismayed Democrats, seeing no alternative, dejectedly renominated Cleveland at their St. Louis convention, while eager Republicans turned to Benjamin Harrison of Indiana, the grandson of former president William Henry ("Tippecanoe") Harrison. The tariff was the prime issue, and the two parties flooded the country with some 10 million pamphlets on the subject. Republicans raised an unprecedented $3 million war chest, largely by "frying the fat" out of nervous industrialists. The money was widely used to line up corrupt "voting cattle," known as "repeaters" or "floaters," especially in crucial swing states like Indiana.

On election day, Harrison nosed out Cleveland, 233 to 168 electoral votes. A change of about 7,000 ballots in New York would have reversed the outcome. Cleveland actually polled more popular votes, 5,537,857 to 5,447,129, but he nevertheless became the first sitting president to be voted out of his chair since Martin Van Buren in 1840.

Republicans Return under Harrison

After a four-year famine, the Republicans under Harrison licked their lips hungrily for federal offices to lavish upon the party faithful. But in the House of Representatives they had only three votes more than the necessary quorum of 163 members, and the Democrats were preparing to obstruct all House business by refusing to answer roll calls, demanding roll calls to determine the presence of a quorum, and other similar delaying tactics.

Into this tense cockpit stepped the new Republican Speaker of the House, Thomas B. Reed of Maine. A tall, hulking figure, Reed was a master debater who spoke with a harsh nasal drawl and wielded a verbal harpoon of sarcasm. To one congressman who quoted Henry Clay's saying that he would "rather be right than be president," Reed caustically retorted that he "would never be either." Opponents cringed at the crack of his quip.

"Czar" Reed soon bent the intimidated House to his imperious will. Employing clever parliamentary tactics to the full, Reed utterly dominated the "Billion-Dollar" Congress—the first in history to appropriate that sum. Congress showered pensions on Civil War veterans and increased government purchases of silver. To keep the revenues flowing in—and to protect Republican industrialists from foreign competition—the Billion-Dollar Congress also passed the McKinley Tariff Act of 1890, boosting rates to their highest peacetime level ever (an average of 48.4 percent on dutiable goods).

Sponsored in the House of Representatives by rising Republican star William McKinley of Ohio, the new tariff act brought fresh woes to farmers. Debt-burdened farmers had no choice but to buy high-priced manufactured goods from protected American industrialists, but they were compelled to sell their own agricultural products into highly competitive, unprotected world markets. Mounting discontent against Bill McKinley and his McKinley Bill caused many rural voters to rise in wrath. In the congressional elections of 1890, Republicans lost their precarious majority and were reduced to just 88 seats, compared with 235 Democrats. Ominously for conservatives, the new Congress also included nine members of the Farmers' Alliance, a militant organization of southern and western farmers.

The Drumbeat of Discontent

Politics was no longer "as usual" in 1892, when the newly formed People's party, or "Populists," burst upon the scene. Rooted in the Farmers' Alliances in the great agricultural belts of the West and South, the Populists met in Omaha and adopted a scorching platform that denounced the "prolific womb of governmental injustice." They demanded inflation through free and unlimited coinage of silver at the ratio of sixteen ounces of silver to one ounce of gold. They further called for a graduated income tax; government ownership of the railroads, telephone, and telegraph; the direct election of U.S. senators; a one-term limit on the presidency; the adoption of the initiative and referendum to allow citizens to shape legislation more directly; a shorter workday; and immigration restrictions. As their presidential candidate the Populists uproariously nominated the eloquent old Greenbacker, General James B. Weaver.

An epidemic of nationwide strikes in the summer of 1892 raised the prospect that the Populists could weld together a coalition of aggrieved workers and indebted farmers in a revolutionary joint assault on the capitalist order. At Andrew Carnegie's Homestead steel plant near Pittsburgh, company officials called in three hundred armed Pinkerton

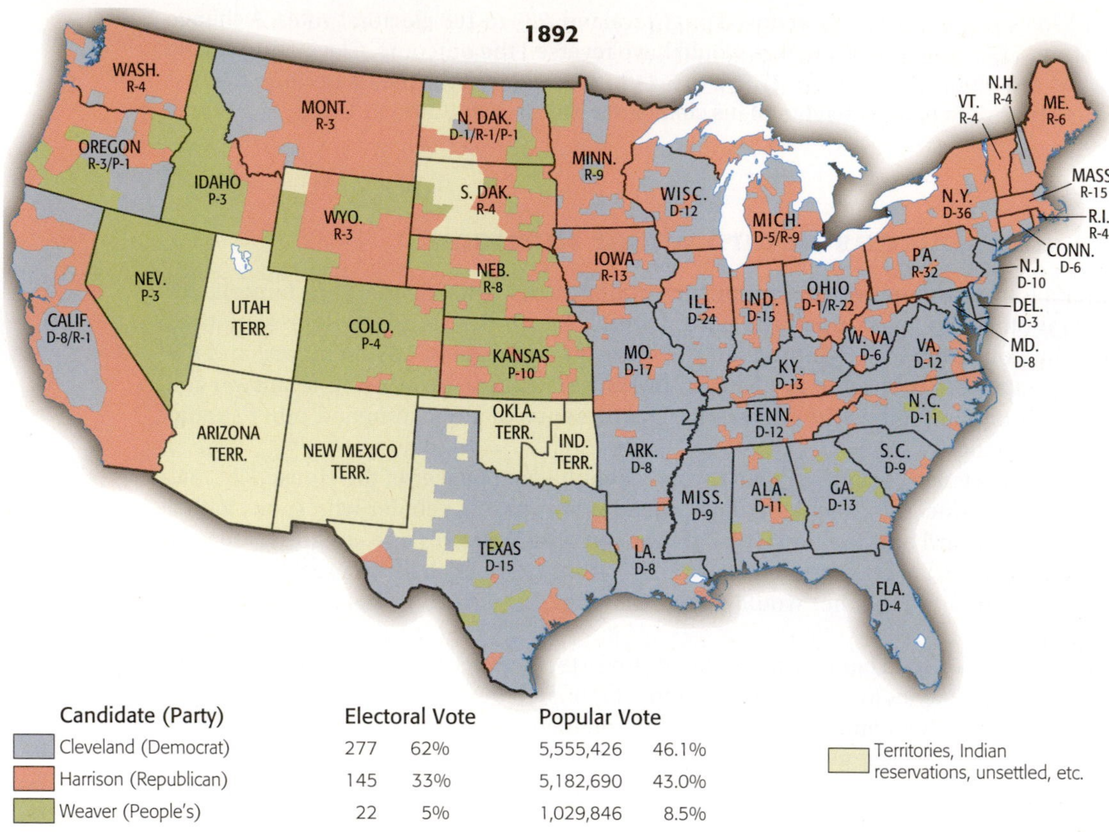

Map 23.2 Presidential Election of 1892 (showing vote by county) Note the concentration of Populist strength in the semiarid farming regions of the western half of the country.

Homestead Strike (1892) *A strike at a Carnegie steel plant in Homestead, Pennsylvania, that ended in an armed battle between the strikers and three hundred armed Pinkerton detectives hired by Carnegie, and federal troops, which killed ten people and wounded more than sixty. The strike was part of a nationwide wave of labor unrest in the summer of 1892 that helped the Populists gain some support from industrial workers.*

detectives in July to crush the obstinate **Homestead Strike** by steelworkers angry over pay cuts. Defiant strikers, armed with rifles and dynamite, forced their assailants to surrender after a vicious battle that left ten people dead and some sixty wounded. Troops were eventually summoned, and both the strike and the union were broken. That same month, federal troops bloodily smashed a strike among silver miners in Idaho's Coeur d'Alene district.

The Populists made a remarkable showing in the 1892 presidential election (see Map 23.2). Singing "Good-bye, Party Bosses," they rolled up 1,029,846 popular votes and 22 electoral votes for General Weaver. They thus became one of the few third parties in U.S. history to break into the electoral column. But they fell far short of an electoral majority. Industrial laborers, especially in the urban East, did not rally to the Populist banner in appreciable numbers. Populist electoral votes came from only six midwestern and western states, four of which (Kansas, Colorado, Idaho, and Nevada) fell completely into the Populist basket.

A popular protest song of the 1890s among western farmers was titled "The Hayseed." One stanza ran,

I once was a tool of oppression,
And as green as a sucker could be,
And monopolies banded together
To beat a poor hayseed like me.

The South, although a hotbed of agrarian agitation, proved especially unwilling to throw in its lot with the new party. Race was the reason. The more than 1 million southern black farmers, organized in the Colored Farmers' National Alliance, shared a host of complaints with poor white farmers, and for a time their common economic goals promised to overcome their racial differences. Recognizing the crucial edge that black votes could give them in the South, Populist leaders such as Georgia's Tom

The Populists: Radicals or Reactionaries?

Taking their cue from contemporary satirical commentaries such as Mark Twain and Charles Dudley Warner's *The Gilded Age* (1873), the first historians who wrote about the post–Civil War era judged it harshly. They condemned its politicians as petty and corrupt, lamented the emergence of a new plutocratic class, and railed against the arrogance of corporate power. Such a view is conspicuous in Charles and Mary Beard's *The Rise of American Civilization* (4 vols., 1927–1942), perhaps the most influential American history text ever written.

The Beards were leaders of the so-called progressive school of historical writing that flourished in the early years of the twentieth century. Progressive historians were chillingly antibusiness and warmly pro-labor, pro-farmer, and pro-reform. They identified Populism as virtually the only organized opposition to the social, economic, and political order that took shape in the last decades of the nineteenth century. The Populists thus became heroes to historians such as John D. Hicks, whose work *The Populist Revolt* (1931) is the classic portrayal of the Populists as embattled farmers hurling defiance at Wall Street and the robber barons in defense of their simple, honest way of life. Bowed but unbroken by the defeat of their great champion, William Jennings Bryan, in the presidential election of 1896, the Populists, Hicks claimed, left a reformist legacy that flourished again in the progressive era and the New Deal.

Hicks's point of view was the dominant one until the 1950s, when it was sharply criticized by Richard Hofstadter in *The Age of Reform* (1955). The city-born-and-bred Hofstadter argued that the Populists were best understood not as picturesque protesters, but as "harassed little country businessmen" bristling with provincial prejudices not just against Wall Street, but also irrationally against urbanism, immigrants, the East, and modernity itself. Hofstadter thus exposed a "dark side" of Populism that contained elements of backwoods anti-intellectualism, paranoia, and even anti-Semitism.

In the 1960s several scholars, inspired by the work of C. Vann Woodward, as well as by sympathy with the protest movements of that turbulent decade, began to rehabilitate the Populists as authentic reformers with genuine grievances. Especially notable in this vein was Lawrence Goodwyn's *Democratic Promise: The Populist Movement in America* (1976), which portrayed Populism as the last gasp of popular political revolt against urban industrialism and finance capitalism, a democratic "moment" in American history that expired with the Populists' absorption into the Democratic party.

Two subsequent works, Edward L. Ayers's *Promise of the New South* (1992) and Robert C. McMath's *American Populism* (1993), synthesized many of the older perspectives and presented a balanced view of the Populists as radical in many ways but also limited by their nostalgia for a lost agrarian past. In the last decade Charles Postel's *The Populist Vision* (2007) made the strongest argument yet for the movement's forward-looking elements, while Eric Rauchway's *Blessed Among Nations* (2006) argued that Populism was a reaction to America's increased reliance on foreign investment. Although Hofstadter had made a similar point about resentment of foreign economic control, the impact of the international economy on domestic politics is again a direction for research.

CHAPTER SUMMARY ★ ★ ★ ★ ★ ★ ★ ★ ★ ★ ★ ★ ★

After the soaring ideals and tremendous sacrifices of the Civil War, the post–Civil War era was generally one of political disillusionment and even cynicism. Politicians from the White House to the courthouse were deeply enmeshed in corruption and scandal, while the actual economic, ethnic, and racial problems afflicting industrializing America festered beneath the surface without being seriously addressed.

The popular war hero Grant was a poor politician and his administration was rife with corruption. Despite occasional futile reform efforts by both high-minded "Mugwumps" and third-party agrarians, politics in the Gilded Age was monopolized by the two patronage-fattened parties, which competed vigorously for spoils while essentially agreeing on most national policies. Cultural and religious differences, different ethnic and regional bases, and deeply felt local issues fueled intense party competition and unprecedented voter participation. Periodic complaints by political reformers and "soft-money" farmers' advocates failed to make much of a dent on politics or the *laissez-faire* business economics of the time.

The deadlocked and bitterly contested 1876 election led to the crass Compromise of 1877, which put an end to Reconstruction at the price of abandoning southern blacks. An oppressive economic system that combined tenant farming and sharecropping with racial segregation and oppression was thereafter fastened on the South, enforced by sometimes lethal violence. Racial prejudice against Chinese immigrants was also linked with labor unrest in the 1870s and 1880s.

Garfield's assassination by a disappointed office seeker spurred the beginnings of civil-service reform but made politics more dependent on big business. Cleveland, the first Democratic president since the Civil War, proposed a lower tariff, creating the first real issue in national politics for some time. But the weakness of conventional politics was exposed by a major economic depression that began in 1893. This crisis, the worst of the nineteenth century, deepened the growing outcry from suffering farmers and workers against a government and economic system that seemed biased toward big business and the wealthy.

KEY TERMS

"waving the bloody shirt" (368)
Tweed Ring (368)
Crédit Mobilier scandal (368)
panic of 1873 (370)
Gilded Age (371)
patronage (371)
Compromise of 1877 (373)
Civil Rights Act of 1875 (373)
sharecropping (374)
Jim Crow (374)
Plessy v. *Ferguson* (374)
Chinese Exclusion Act (376)
Pendleton Act (376)
Homestead Strike (380)
grandfather clause (381)

PEOPLE TO KNOW

Jay Gould
Horace Greeley
Rutherford B. Hayes
James A. Garfield
Chester Arthur
Grover Cleveland
Thomas B. Reed
Tom Watson
William Jennings Bryan
J. P. Morgan

MindTap is a fully online, highly personalized learning experience built upon Cengage Learning content. MindTap combines student learning tools—readings, multimedia, activities, and assessments—into a singular Learning Path that guides students through the course.

Chapter 24

Industry Comes of Age

1865–1900

The wealthy class is becoming more wealthy, but the poorer class is becoming more dependent. The gulf between the employed and the employer is growing wider; social contrasts are becoming sharper; as liveried carriages appear, so do barefooted children.

HENRY GEORGE, 1879

Chapter Outline

- The Railroad Boom
- Speculators and Financiers
- Early Efforts at Government Regulation
- Lords of Industry
- Industry in the South
- Workers and Unions
- *Examining the Evidence: The Photography of Lewis W. Hine*
- *Varying Viewpoints: Industrialization: Boon or Blight?*

As the nineteenth century drew toward a close, observers were asking, "Why are the best men not in politics?" One answer was that they were being lured away from public life by the lusty attractions of the booming private economy. As America's Industrial Revolution slipped into high gear, talented men ached for profits, not the presidency. They dreamed of controlling corporations, not Congress. What the nation lost in civic leadership, it gained in an astounding surge of economic growth. As late as 1870, agriculture was the nation's biggest business. By 1900 its share of the economy was half that. Until the end of the Civil War the United States imported more merchandise than it exported. By 1900 it annually delivered more than $600 million worth of manufactured goods into the world's marketplace. Americans did not achieve this economic transformation all by themselves. Foreign investment, labor, trade, and technology made it possible. Although in many ways still a political dwarf, the United States was about to stand up before the world as an industrial colossus—and the lives of millions of working Americans would be transformed in the process.

FOCUS QUESTIONS

1. How did the transcontinental railroad network promote the post–Civil War transformation of American industry?
2. How did the American economy come to be dominated by monopolistic corporations in industries such as steel and oil, and what was the public and governmental response to these huge combinations?
3. Why was the South generally excluded from industrial development, and what were the economic, social, and racial problems that the region faced as a result?
4. How did industrialization alter American society, particularly the role of the working class and of women?
5. Why did late-nineteenth-century American labor unions generally fail to mobilize American workers?

CHRONOLOGY

1862	▪ Congress authorizes transcontinental railroad
1866	▪ National Labor Union organized ▪ First working transatlantic telegraph cable
1869	▪ Transcontinental railroad joined near Ogden, Utah ▪ Knights of Labor organized ▪ Suez Canal completed
1870	▪ Standard Oil Company organized
1876	▪ Bell invents telephone
1879	▪ Edison invents electric light
1886	▪ Haymarket Square bombing ▪ *Wabash* case ▪ American Federation of Labor formed
1887	▪ Interstate Commerce Act
1890	▪ Sherman Anti-Trust Act
1901	▪ United States Steel Corporation formed

The Iron Colt Becomes an Iron Horse

The government-business entanglements that increasingly shaped politics after the Civil War also undergirded the industrial development of the nation. The unparalleled outburst of railroad construction was a crucial case. When Lincoln was shot in 1865, there were only 35,000 miles of steam railways in the United States, mostly east of the Mississippi. By 1900 the figure had spurted up to 192,556 miles, or more than that for all Europe combined, and much of the new track ran west of the Mississippi.

Transcontinental railroad building was so costly and risky as to require government subsidies, as it had in many other industrializing nations. Everywhere, the construction of railway systems promised greater national unity and economic growth. Congress began to advance liberal loans to two favored cross-continent companies in 1862 and added enormous donations of acreage paralleling the tracks. All told, Washington rewarded the railroads with 155,504,994 acres, and the western states contributed 49 million more—a total area larger than Texas (see Map 24.1).

In later years much criticism was leveled at the "giveaway" of so valuable a birthright to greedy corporations. But the government did receive beneficial returns, including preferential rates for postal service and military traffic. Critics also overlooked the fact that western land had very little value until the railroads made it accessible for settlers and merchants. Little wonder that communities fought one another for the privilege of playing host to the railroads, often offering monetary or other attractions to entice the rail lines to their town.

Deadlock in the 1850s over the location of the proposed transcontinental railroad was broken when the South seceded, leaving the field to the North. In 1862, the year after the guns first spoke at Fort Sumter, Congress made provision for starting the long-awaited line. One weighty argument for action was the urgency of bolstering the Union, already disrupted, by binding the Pacific Coast more securely to the rest of the Republic.

The Union Pacific Railroad—note the word *Union*—was thus commissioned by Congress to thrust westward from Omaha, Nebraska. The laying of rails began in earnest after the Civil War ended in 1865, and with juicy loans and land grants available, the "groundhog" promoters made all possible haste.

Sweaty construction gangs, which included many Irish "Paddies" (Patricks), worked at a frantic pace. On one record-breaking day, a sledge-and-shovel army of some five thousand men laid ten miles of track. A favorite song was:

Then drill, my Paddies, drill;
Drill, my heroes, drill;
Drill all day,
No sugar in your tay [tea]
Workin' on the U.P. Railway.

When hostile Indians attacked, the laborers would drop their picks and seize their rifles. At rail's end, workers tried to find relaxation and conviviality in tented towns known as "hells on wheels," often teeming with as many as ten thousand men and a sprinkling of painted prostitutes and performers.

Rail laying at the California end was undertaken by the Central Pacific Railroad. This line pushed boldly eastward from boomtown Sacramento, over and through the towering, snow-clogged Sierra Nevada. Four farseeing men—the so-called Big Four—were the chief financial backers of the enterprise. The quartet included the heavyset, enterprising ex-governor Leland Stanford of California, who had useful political connections, and the burly, energetic Collis P. Huntington, an adept lobbyist.

The Central Pacific, which was granted the same princely subsidies as the Union Pacific, had the same incentive to haste. Some ten thousand Chinese laborers sweated from dawn to dusk under their basket hats. Hundreds lost their lives in premature explosions and other mishaps. The towering Sierra Nevada presented a formidable barrier; and the nerves of the Big Four were strained when their workers could chip only a few inches a day through solid rock, while the Union Pacific was sledgehammering westward across the plains.

A "wedding of the rails" was finally consummated near Ogden, Utah, in 1869, as the two locomotives gently kissed cowcatchers. The colorful ceremony included the breaking of champagne bottles and the driving of a last ceremonial (golden) spike, with ex-governor Leland Stanford clumsily wielding a silver maul.* In all, the Union Pacific built 1,086 miles, the Central Pacific 689 miles.

---

*The spike was promptly removed and is now exhibited at the Stanford University Museum.

Map 24.1 Federal Land Grants to Railroads The heavy red lines indicate areas within which the railroads might be given specific parcels of land. As shown in the inset, land was reserved in belts of various widths on either side of a railroad's right of way. Until the railroad selected the individual mile-square sections it chose to possess, *all* such sections within the belt were withdrawn from eligibility for settlement. The "time zones" were introduced in 1883 (see p. 389), and their boundaries have since been adjusted.

Underwood Archives/Getty Images

The Union Pacific and the Central Pacific Link at Promontory Point, Utah, May 10, 1869 Railroad financiers, dignitaries, spectators, and Chinese (Central Pacific) and Irish (Union Pacific) work gangs witnessed the historic joining that created the nation's first transcontinental railroad. After the two locomotives chugged within a few feet of each other, Central Pacific chief and former California governor Leland Stanford tapped a golden spike into a prepared hole on the last tie with a silver-plated maul. The golden spike was whisked away to be preserved for posterity at the Stanford University Museum, but the iron one that replaced it was hardly ordinary. It was wired to a Union Pacific telegraph line, while a copper plate on the maul was connected to a Central Pacific wire. When they touched, they closed a telegraphic circuit that sent the news to cities all over the country.

In 1892 James Baird Weaver (1833–1912), nominee of the Populists, wrote regarding the railroad magnates:

"In their delirium of greed the managers of our transportation systems disregard both private right and the public welfare. Today they will combine and bankrupt their weak rivals, and by the expenditure of a trifling sum possess themselves of properties which cost the outlay of millions. Tomorrow they will capitalize their booty for five times the cost, issue their bonds, and proceed to levy tariffs upon the people to pay dividends upon the fraud."

With the westward trail now blazed, four other transcontinental lines were completed before the century's end. None of them secured monetary loans from the federal government, as had the Union Pacific and the Central Pacific. But all of them except the Great Northern received generous grants of land.

The Northern Pacific Railroad, stretching from Lake Superior to Puget Sound, reached its terminus in 1883. The Atchison, Topeka, and Santa Fe, stretching through the southwestern deserts to California, was completed in 1884. The Southern Pacific ribboned from New Orleans to San Francisco and was consolidated in the same year.

The last of the five nineteenth-century transcontinental railroads, the Great Northern, ran north of the Northern Pacific from Duluth to Seattle. Its creator was James J. Hill, a far-visioned Canadian American who organized his railroad so soundly that it rode through later financial storms with flying colors.

Yet the romance of the rails was not without its sordid side. Pioneer builders were often guilty of gross overoptimism, laying down rails that went "from nowhere to nothing" in order to get the lavish federal land bounties. When prosperity failed to smile, railroad companies went into bankruptcy, carrying down with them the savings of trusting investors. Many of the large railroads in the post–Civil War decades passed through seemingly endless bankruptcies, mergers, or reorganizations.

Revolution by Railways

The metallic fingers of the railroads intimately touched countless phases of American life. For the first time, a sprawling nation became physically bound together with ribs of iron and steel. The railroads emerged as the nation's biggest business, employing more people than any other industry and gobbling up nearly 20 percent of investment dollars, from foreign and domestic investors alike.

More than any other single factor, the railroad network spurred the amazing economic growth of the post–Civil War years. By stitching North America together from ocean to ocean, the puffing locomotives opened up the West with its wealth of resources. Trains hauled raw materials to factories and sped them back as finished goods for sale across the continent, making the United States the largest integrated national market in the world. The forging of the rails themselves provided the largest single source of orders for the adolescent steel industry.

The screeching iron horse especially stimulated mining and agriculture, particularly in the West. The railroads took farmers out to their land, carried the fruits of their toil to market, and brought them their manufactured necessities. Clusters of farm settlements paralleled the railroads, just as earlier they had followed the rivers.

Railways were a boon for cities and played a leading role in the great cityward movement of the last decades of the century. The iron monsters could carry food to enormous concentrations of people and at the same time ensure them a livelihood by providing both raw materials and markets.

Railroad companies also stimulated the mighty stream of immigration. Seeking settlers to whom their land grants might be sold at a profit, they advertised seductively in Europe and sometimes offered to transplant the newcomers free to their farms.

The land also felt the impact of the railroad—especially the broad, ecologically fragile midsection of the continent. Settlers following the railroads plowed up the tallgrass prairies of Iowa, Illinois, Kansas, and Nebraska and planted well-drained, rectangular cornfields. On the shortgrass prairies of the high plains in the Dakotas and Montana, range-fed cattle rapidly displaced the buffalo, which were hunted to near- extinction. The white pine forests of Michigan, Wisconsin, and Minnesota disappeared into lumber that was rushed by rail to prairie farmers who used it to build houses and fences.

Time itself was bent to the railroads' needs. Until the 1880s every town in the United States had its own "local" time, dictated by the sun's position. When it was noon in Chicago, it was 11:50 A.M. in St. Louis and 12:18 P.M. in Detroit. For railroad operators worried about keeping schedules and avoiding wrecks, this patchwork of local times was a nightmare. Thus, on November 18, 1883, the major rail lines decreed that the continent would henceforth be divided into four "time zones." Most communities quickly adopted railroad "standard" time.

Finally, the railroad, more than any other single factor, was the maker of millionaires. A raw new aristocracy, consisting of "lords of the rail" such as eastern railroad magnate Cornelius Vanderbilt and "palace car" inventor George Pullman, replaced the old southern "lords of the lash." The multiwebbed lines became the playthings of Wall Street, and colossal wealth was amassed by stock speculators and corporate railroad manipulators.

Wrongdoing in Railroading

Corruption lurks nearby when fabulous fortunes can materialize overnight. The fleecings administered by the railroad construction companies, such as the Crédit Mobilier, were but the first of the bunco games that the railroad promoters learned to play. Methods soon became more refined, as fast-fingered financiers executed multimillion-dollar maneuvers beneath the noses of a bedazzled public. Jay Gould was the most adept of these ringmasters of rapacity. For nearly thirty years he boomed and busted the stocks of the Erie, the Kansas Pacific, the Union Pacific, and the Texas and Pacific in an incredible circus of speculative skullduggery.

One of the favorite devices of the moguls of manipulation was "stock watering." The term originally referred to the practice of making cattle thirsty by feeding them salt, and then having them bloat themselves with water before they were weighed in for sale. Using a variation of this technique, railroad stock promoters grossly inflated their claims about a given line's assets and profitability and sold stocks and bonds far in excess of the railroad's actual value. "Promoters' profits" were often the tail that wagged the iron horse itself. Railroad managers were forced to charge extortionate rates and wage ruthless competitive battles in order to pay off the exaggerated financial obligations with which they were saddled.

The public interest was frequently trampled underfoot as the railroad titans waged their brutal wars. Crusty old Cornelius Vanderbilt, when told that the law stood in his way, reportedly exclaimed: "Law! What do I care about the law? Hain't I got the power?" His son, William H. Vanderbilt, when asked in 1883 about public discontent with the discontinuance of a fast mail train, reportedly snorted, "The public be damned!"

While abusing the public, the railroaders blandly bought and sold people in public life. They bribed judges and legislatures, elected their own agents to high office, and showered free passes on journalists and politicians in exchange for favorable treatment.

Railroad kings were, for a time, virtual industrial monarchs. As manipulators of a huge natural monopoly, they exercised more direct control over the lives of more people than did the president of the United States. They increasingly shunned the crude bloodletting of cutthroat competition and began to cooperate with one another to rule the railroad dominion. Sorely pressed to show at least some returns on their bloated investments, they entered into defensive alliances to protect precious profits.

The earliest form of combination was the "pool"—an agreement to divide the business in a given area and share the profits. Other rail barons granted secret rebates or kickbacks to powerful shippers in return for steady and assured traffic. Often they slashed their rates on competing lines, but they more than made up the difference on noncompeting ones, where they might actually charge more for a short haul than for a long one. As a result, small farmers usually paid the highest rates, while large customers got the best deals.

Government Bridles the Iron Horse

It was neither healthy nor politically acceptable that so many people should be at the mercy of so few. Impoverished farmers, especially in the Midwest, began to wonder whether the nation had not escaped from the slavery power only to fall into the hands of the money power, as represented by the railroad plutocracy.

But the American people, usually quick to respond to political injustice, were slow to combat economic injustice. Dedicated to free enterprise and to the principle that competition is the soul of trade, they remembered that Jefferson's ideals were hostile to governmental interference with business. Above all, there shimmered the "American dream": the hope that in a catch-as-catch-can economic system, anyone might become a millionaire.

The depression of the 1870s finally goaded the farmers into protesting against being "railroaded" into bankruptcy. Under pressure from organized agrarian groups such as the Grange (see p. 441), many midwestern legislatures tried to regulate the railroad monopoly. The scattered state efforts screeched to a halt in 1886. The Supreme Court, in the case of ***Wabash, St. Louis & Pacific Railroad Company* v. *Illinois***, decreed that individual states had no power to regulate *inter*state commerce. If the mechanical monster were to be corralled, the federal government would have to do the job.

Wabash, St. Louis & Pacific Railroad Company v. Illinois (1886) *A Supreme Court decision that prohibited states from regulating the railroads because the Constitution grants Congress the power to regulate interstate commerce. As a result, reformers turned their attention to the federal government, which now held sole power to regulate the railroad industry.*

Interstate Commerce Act (1887) *Congressional legislation that established the Interstate Commerce Commission, compelled railroads to publish standard rates, and prohibited rebates and pools. Railroads quickly became adept at using the act to achieve their own ends, but it gave the government an important means to regulate big business.*

Congress ignored President Cleveland's grumbling indifference to the problem and passed the **Interstate Commerce Act** in 1887, which prohibited rebates and pools and required the railroads to publish their rates openly. The act also forbade unfair discrimination against shippers and outlawed charging more for a short haul than for a long one over the same line. Most importantly, the Interstate Commerce Act set up the Interstate Commerce Commission (ICC) to administer and enforce the new legislation.

Despite acclaim, the Interstate Commerce Act emphatically did not represent a popular victory over corporate wealth. One of the leading corporation lawyers of the day, Richard Olney, shrewdly noted that the new commission "can be made of great use to the railroads. It satisfies the popular clamor for a government supervision of railroads, at the same time that such supervision is almost entirely nominal. . . . The part of wisdom is not to destroy the Commission, but to utilize it."

What the new legislation did do was provide an orderly forum where competing business interests could resolve their conflicts in peaceable ways. The country could now avoid ruinous rate wars among the railroads and deflect angry "confiscatory" attacks on the lines by pitchfork-prodded state legislatures. The Interstate Commerce Act tended to stabilize, not revolutionize, the existing business system.

Yet the act still ranks as a red-letter law. It was the first large-scale attempt by Washington to regulate business in the interest of society at large. The act foreshadowed the doom of freewheeling, buccaneering business practices and served full notice that there was a public interest in private enterprise that the government was bound to protect.

Miracles of Mechanization

Postwar industrial expansion, partly a result of the railroad network, rapidly began to assume mammoth proportions. When Lincoln was elected in 1860, the Republic ranked only fourth among the manufacturing nations of the world. By 1894 it had bounded into first place. Why the sudden upsurge?

Liquid capital, previously scarce, was now becoming abundant. The word *millionaire* had not been coined until the 1840s, and in 1861 only a handful of individuals were eligible for this class. But the Civil War, partly through profiteering, created immense fortunes, and these accumulations could now be combined with borrowings from foreign capitalists. Investors from abroad loaned more money to the United States in the postwar period than any country had previously received. Unlike in other countries, in America they mostly put the money into private hands, not public coffers. Investors primarily from Britain, but from France, Germany, the Netherlands, and Switzerland as well, sometimes owned all or part of an American business. Other times they simply lent their money to the thousands of European companies set up to manage investment in U.S. industry. Either way, Europeans were usually content to let Americans run the business.

Innovations in transportation fueled growth, too, by bringing the nation's amazingly abundant natural resources—particularly coal, oil, and iron—to the factory door. A shipping system through the Great Lakes carried the rich iron deposits of the Mesabi range of Minnesota to Chicago and Cleveland for refining. This priceless bonanza, where mountains of red-rusted ore could be scooped up by steam shovels, ultimately became a cornerstone of a vast steel empire. Copper, bauxite, and zinc made similar journeys from mine to manufacture.

The sheer size of the American market encouraged innovators to invent mass-production methods. With cheap transportation crisscrossing the nation and an ever larger population able and eager to consume, anyone who could make an appealing new product available for a good price in large quantities—and figure out how to market it—thrived. Industrialists continued to refine the pre–Civil War "American system" of using specialized machinery to make interchangeable parts, culminating in 1913 with Henry Ford's fully developed, moving, assembly line for his Model T (see "The American System" in Chapter 12, p. 178 and "Putting America on Rubber Tires" in Chapter 30, pp. 526–527).

The captains of industry had a major incentive to invent machines: they made it possible to replace expensive, skilled craft labor with unskilled workers, now cheap and plentiful as a result of massive immigration. Steel, the keystone industry, built its strength largely on the sweat of low-priced immigrant labor from eastern and southern Europe, working in two 12-hour shifts, seven days a week.

Just as industry served as a hothouse of invention, brilliant ideas gave rise to whole new lines of business. Between 1860 and 1890, some 440,000 patents were issued. Business operations were facilitated by such machines as the cash register, the stock ticker, and the typewriter ("literary piano"), while the refrigerator car, the electric dynamo, and the electric railway speeded urbanization. One of the most ingenious inventions was the telephone, introduced by Alexander Graham Bell in 1876. America was suddenly turned into a nation of "telephoniacs," as a gigantic communications network was built on Bell's invention. The social impact of the telephone further expanded when it lured "number please" women away from the stove to the switchboard.

The most versatile inventor of all was Thomas Alva Edison (1847–1931), who as a boy had been considered so dull witted that he was taken out of school. Edison was a gifted tinkerer and a tireless worker, not a pure scientist. "Genius," he said, "is 1 percent inspiration and 99 percent perspiration." Wondrous devices poured out of his "invention factory" in New Jersey—the phonograph, the mimeograph, the dictaphone, and the moving picture. He is probably best known for his perfection in 1879 of the electric lightbulb, which turned night into day and transformed ancient human habits as well. People had previously slept an average of nine hours a night; now they slept just a bit more than seven.

The Trust Titan Emerges

vertical integration *The practice perfected by Andrew Carnegie of controlling every step of the industrial production process in order to increase efficiency and limit competition.*

horizontal integration *The practice perfected by John D. Rockefeller of dominating a particular phase of the production process in order to monopolize a market, often by forming trusts and alliances with competitors.*

trust *A mechanism by which one company grants control over its operations, through ownership of its stock, to another company. The Standard Oil Company became known for this practice in the 1870s as it eliminated its competition by taking control of smaller oil companies.*

Standard Oil Company (1870–1911) *John D. Rockefeller's company, formed in 1870, which came to symbolize the trusts and monopolies of the Gilded Age. By 1877 Standard Oil controlled 95 percent of the oil refineries in the United States. It was also one of the first multinational corporations and at times distributed more than half of its kerosene production outside the United States. By the turn of the century it had become a target for trust-busting reformers, and in 1911 the Supreme Court ordered it to break up into several dozen smaller companies.*

interlocking directorates *The practice of having executives or directors from one company serve on the board of directors of another company. J. P. Morgan introduced this practice to eliminate banking competition in the 1890s.*

Despite pious protests to the contrary, competition was the bugbear of most business leaders of the day. Tycoons like Andrew Carnegie, the steel king; John D. Rockefeller, the oil baron; and J. Pierpont Morgan, the bankers' banker, exercised their genius in devising ways to circumvent competition. Carnegie pioneered the "**vertical integration**" of production by directly controlling every phase of his steel-making operation from mining to marketing. His miners dug the ore from Minnesota's Mesabi range; Carnegie ships floated it across the Great Lakes; Carnegie railroads delivered it to blast furnaces at Pittsburgh. When the molten metal finally poured from the glowing crucibles into the waiting ingot molds, no other hands but those in Carnegie's employ had touched the product.

Rockefeller pursued the less economically justifiable technique of "**horizontal integration**," which simply meant allying with competitors to monopolize a given market. He perfected a device for controlling bothersome rivals—the **trust**. Stockholders in various smaller oil companies assigned their stock to the board of directors of Rockefeller's **Standard Oil Company**, formed in 1870, which then consolidated and concerted the operations of the previously competing enterprises. "Let us prey" was said to be Rockefeller's unwritten motto. Ruthlessly wielding vast power, Standard Oil soon cornered virtually the entire world petroleum market. Weaker competitors, left out of the trust agreement, were forced to the wall. Rockefeller's stunning success inspired many imitators, and the word *trust* came to be generally used to describe any large-scale business combination.

The imperial Morgan devised still other schemes for eliminating "wasteful" competition. The depression of the 1890s drove into his welcoming arms many bleeding businesspeople, wounded by cutthroat competition. His prescribed remedy was to consolidate rival enterprises and to ensure future harmony by placing officers of his own banking syndicate on their various boards of directors. These came to be known as **interlocking directorates**.

The Supremacy of Steel

"Steel is king!" might well have been the exultant war cry of the new industrialized generation. The mighty metal ultimately held together the new civilization, from skyscrapers to coal scuttles, while providing it with food, shelter, and transportation. Steel making, notably rails for railroads, typified the dominance of heavy industry, which concentrated on making "capital goods," as distinct from the production of "consumer goods" such as clothes and shoes.

Now taken for granted, steel was a scarce commodity in the wood-and-brick America of Abraham Lincoln. Steel was expensive and was used largely for special products like cutlery. Yet within an amazing twenty years after 1870, the United States outdistanced all foreign competitors and was pouring out more than one-third of the world's supply of steel. By 1900 the Americans were producing as much as Britain and Germany combined.

What wrought the transformation? Chiefly, the invention in the 1850s of a method of making cheap steel—the Bessemer process. William Kelly, a Kentucky manufacturer of iron kettles, had earlier discovered that cold air blown on red-hot iron caused the metal to become white-hot by igniting the carbon and thus eliminating impurities. But Kelly was unable to win acceptance for the product. Only after Bessemer, a British inventor, joined forces with Kelly did the Bessemer-Kelly process make possible the new steel civilization.

Kingpin among steelmasters was Andrew Carnegie, an undersized, charming Scotsman. As a towheaded lad of thirteen, he was brought to America by his impoverished parents in 1848 and got a job as a bobbin boy at $1.20 a week. Mounting the ladder of success so fast that he was said to have scorched the rungs, he forged ahead by working hard, doing extra chores, cheerfully assuming responsibility, and smoothly cultivating influential people.

After accumulating some capital, Carnegie entered the steel business in the Pittsburgh area. By 1900 he was producing one-fourth of the nation's Bessemer steel, and the partners in these pre-income tax days were dividing profits of $40 million a year as their take-home pay, with the "Napoleon of the Smokestacks" himself receiving a cool $25 million.

Into the picture now stepped the financial giant of the age, J. Pierpont Morgan. "Jupiter" Morgan had made a legendary reputation for himself and his Wall Street banking house by financing the reorganization of railroads, insurance companies, and banks. An impressive figure of a man, with massive shoulders, shaggy brows, piercing eyes, and a bulbous, acne-cursed red nose, he had established an enviable reputation for integrity. Morgan did not believe that "money power" was dangerous, except when in dangerous hands—and he did not regard his own hands as dangerous.

The force of circumstances brought Morgan and Carnegie into collision. By 1900 the canny little Scotsman, weary of turning steel into gold, was eager to sell his holdings. Morgan had meanwhile plunged heavily into the manufacture of steel pipe tubing. Carnegie, cleverly threatening to invade the same business, was ready to ruin his rival if he did not receive his price. The steelmaster's agents haggled with the imperious Morgan for eight agonizing hours, and the financier finally agreed to buy out Carnegie for over $400 million. Fearing that he would die "disgraced" with so much wealth, Carnegie dedicated the remaining years of his life to giving it away for public libraries, pensions for professors, and other such philanthropic purposes—in all disposing of about $350 million.

Morgan moved rapidly to expand his new industrial empire. He took the Carnegie holdings, added others, "watered" the stock liberally, and in 1901 launched the enlarged United States Steel Corporation. Capitalized at $1.4 billion, it was America's first billion-dollar corporation—a larger sum than the total estimated wealth of the nation in 1800. The Industrial Revolution had come into its own.

Rockefeller Grows an American Beauty Rose

Another new industry was born almost overnight when in 1859 the first oil well—"Drake's Folly" in Pennsylvania—poured out its liquid "black gold." Kerosene, derived from petroleum, was the first major product of the infant oil industry. Replacing whale oil as the fuel for America's lamps, kerosene became the country's fourth most valuable export by the 1870s.

But what technology gives, technology takes away. By 1885 Thomas Edison's new electric lightbulbs had rendered kerosene largely obsolete. Oil might thus have remained a modest, even a shrinking, industry but for yet another turn of the technological tide—the invention of the automobile. By 1900 the gasoline-burning internal combustion engine had clearly bested its rivals, steam and electricity, and the oil business got a new, long-lasting, and hugely profitable lease on life.

John D. Rockefeller—lanky, shrewd, ambitious, abstemious (he neither drank, smoked, nor swore)—came to dominate the oil industry. Born to a family of precarious income, he became a successful businessman at age nineteen. One upward stride led to another, and in 1870 he organized the Standard Oil Company of Ohio, nucleus of the great trust formed in 1882.

In the jungle world of big business, a kind of primitive savagery prevailed. Rockefeller—"Reckafellow," as Carnegie had once called him—showed little mercy to his competitors. His son later explained that the giant American Beauty rose could be produced "only by sacrificing the early buds that grew up around it." His father pinched off the small buds with complete ruthlessness. By 1877 Rockefeller controlled 95 percent of all the oil refineries in the country. Employing spies and extorting secret rebates from the railroads, he even forced the lines to pay him rebates on the freight bills of his competitors!

Rockefeller thought he was simply obeying a law of nature. "The time was ripe" for aggressive consolidation, he later reflected. "The day of combination is here to stay. Individualism has gone, never to return." On the other side of the ledger, Rockefeller's oil monopoly did turn out a superior product at a relatively cheap price achieved through its large-scale methods of production and distribution. This, in truth, was the tale of the other trusts as well. The efficient use of expensive machinery called for bigness, and consolidation proved more profitable than ruinous price wars.

Other trusts blossomed along with the American Beauty of oil. These included the sugar trust, the tobacco trust, the leather trust, and the harvester trust, which amalgamated some two hundred competitors. The meat industry arose on the backs of bawling western herds, and meat kings such as Gustavus F. Swift and Philip Armour took their places among the new royalty. Wealth was coming to dominate the commonwealth.

These untrustworthy trusts, and the "pirates" who captained them, were disturbingly new. They eclipsed an older American aristocracy of modestly successful merchants and professionals. An arrogant class of "new rich" was now elbowing aside the patrician families in the mad scramble for power and prestige. Not surprisingly, the ranks of the antitrust crusaders were frequently spearheaded by the "best men"—genteel old-family do-gooders who were not radicals but conservative defenders of their own vanishing influence.

Robber Barons Cyrus Field, Jay Gould, Cornelius Vanderbilt, and Russell Sage Kept Afloat on the Broken Backs of America's Workingmen, 1883

The Gospel of Wealth

Monarchs of yore invoked the divine right of kings, and America's industrial plutocrats took a somewhat similar stance. Some candidly credited heavenly help and justified their social position with what came to be known as the "Gospel of Wealth." "Godliness is in league with riches," preached the Episcopal bishop of Massachusetts, and hardfisted John D. Rockefeller piously declared that "the good Lord gave me my money."

But most defenders of wide-open capitalism relied more heavily on the survival-of-the-fittest theories of English philosopher Herbert Spencer and Yale Professor William Graham Sumner. Later mislabeled **Social Darwinists**, these theorists argued that individuals won their stations in life by competing on the basis of their natural talents. The wealthy and powerful had simply demonstrated greater abilities than the poor. Spencer and Sumner owed less to English evolutionary naturalist Charles Darwin, who stressed the adaptation of organisms, than to British laissez-faire economists David Ricardo and Thomas Malthus. In fact, Spencer, not Darwin, coined the phrase "survival of the fittest." "The millionaires are a product of natural selection," Sumner declared. In 1883 he asked, "What do social classes owe each other?" then answered his own question: nothing. Some Social Darwinists later applied this theory to explain why some nations were more powerful than others or had the right to dominate "lesser peoples," often defined by race.

Social Darwinists *Believers in the idea, popular in the late nineteenth century, that people gained wealth by "survival of the fittest." Therefore, the wealthy had simply won a natural competition and owed nothing to the poor, and indeed service to the poor would interfere with this organic process. Some Social Darwinists also applied this theory to whole nations and races, explaining that powerful peoples were naturally endowed with gifts that allowed them to gain superiority over others. This theory provided one of the popular justifications for U.S. imperial ventures like the Spanish-American War.*

Self-justification by the wealthy inevitably involved contempt for the poor. Many of the rich, especially the newly rich, had pulled themselves up by their own bootstraps; hence, they concluded that those who stayed poor must be lazy and lacking in enterprise. The Reverend Russell Conwell of Philadelphia became rich by delivering his lecture "Acres of Diamonds" thousands of times. In it he charged, "There is not a poor person in the United States who was not made poor by his own shortcomings." Such attitudes were a formidable roadblock to social reform.

Plutocracy, like the earlier slavocracy, took its stand firmly on the Constitution. The clause that gave Congress sole jurisdiction over interstate commerce was a godsend to the monopolists; their high-priced lawyers used it time and again to thwart controls by the state legislatures. Giant trusts likewise sought refuge behind the Fourteenth Amendment, which had been originally designed to protect the rights of the ex-slaves as persons. The courts ingeniously interpreted a corporation to be a legal "person" and decreed that, as such, it could not be deprived of its property by a state without "due process of law" (see Art. XIV, para. 1 in the Appendix).

Contending Voices

Class and the Gilded Age

Industrial millionaires were condemned in the Populist platform of 1892:

"The fruits of the toil of millions are boldly stolen to build up colossal fortunes for a few . . . and the possessors of these, in turn despise the Republic and endanger liberty. From the same prolific womb of governmental injustice we breed the two great classes—tramps and millionaires."

But Yale professor William Graham Sumner (1840–1910), in his 1893 book What Social Classes Owe to Each Other, *defended millionaires:*

"In no sense whatever does a man who accumulates a fortune by legitimate industry exploit his employees, or make his capital 'out of' anybody else. The wealth which he wins would not be but for him. . . . If we should set a limit to the accumulation of wealth, we should say to our most valuable producers, 'We do not want you to do us the services which you best understand how to perform, beyond a certain point.' It would be like killing off our generals in war."

In what ways did the opening of new class fissures in the Gilded Age challenge traditional American ideals of social opportunity?

Government Tackles the Trust Evil

At long last the masses of the people began to mobilize against monopoly. They first tried to control the trusts through state legislation, as they had earlier attempted to curb the railroads. Failing here, as before, they were forced

Sherman Anti-Trust Act (1890) *A law that forbade trusts or combinations in business, this was landmark legislation because it was one of the first congressional attempts to regulate big business for the public good. At first the law was mostly used to restrain trade unions, as the courts tended to side with companies in legal cases. In 1914 the act was revised so it could more effectively be used against monopolistic corporations.*

to appeal to Congress. After prolonged pulling and hauling, the **Sherman Anti-Trust Act** of 1890 was finally signed into law.

The Sherman Act flatly forbade combinations in restraint of trade, without making any distinction between "good" trusts and "bad" trusts. Bigness, not badness, was the sin. The law proved ineffective, largely because it had only baby teeth or no teeth at all, and because it contained legal loopholes through which clever corporation lawyers could wriggle. But the act was unexpectedly effective in one respect. Contrary to its original intent, the Sherman Act was used to curb labor unions or labor combinations that were deemed to be restraining trade.

Early prosecutions of the trusts by the Justice Department under the Sherman Act of 1890, as it turned out, were neither vigorous nor successful. Not until 1914 were the paper jaws of the Sherman Act fitted with reasonably sharp teeth. Until then, there was some question as to whether the government would control the trusts or the trusts the government.

But the iron grip of monopolistic corporations was being threatened. A revolutionary new principle had been written into the law books by the Sherman Anti-Trust Act of 1890, as well as by the Interstate Commerce Act of 1887. Private greed should henceforth be subordinated to public need.

The South in the Age of Industry

The industrial tidal wave that washed over the North after the Civil War caused only feeble ripples in the backwater of the South. The plantation system had degenerated into a pattern of absentee landownership. White and black sharecroppers now tilled the soil for a share of the crop, or they became tenants, in bondage to landlords who controlled needed credit and supplies.

Southern agriculture received a boost in the 1880s, when machine-made cigarettes replaced the roll-your-own variety and tobacco consumption shot up. James Buchanan Duke took full advantage of the new technology to mass produce the dainty "coffin nails." In 1890, in what was becoming a familiar pattern, he absorbed his main competitors into the American Tobacco Company. The cigarette czar later showed such generosity to Trinity College, near his birthplace in Durham, North Carolina, that the trustees gratefully changed its name to Duke University.

Industrialists tried to coax the agricultural South out of the fields and into the factories, but with only modest success. The region remained overwhelmingly rural. Prominent among the boosters of a "new South" was silver-tongued Henry W. Grady, editor of the *Atlanta Constitution*. He tirelessly exhorted the ex-Confederates to become "Georgia Yankees" and outplay the North at the commercial and industrial game.

Yet formidable obstacles lay in the path of southern industrialization. One was the paper barrier of regional rate-setting systems imposed by the northern-dominated railroad interests. Railroads gave preferential rates to manufactured goods moving southward from the North, but in the opposite direction they discriminated in favor of southern raw materials. The net effect was to keep the South in a kind of servitude to the Northeast—as a supplier of raw materials to the manufacturing metropolis, unable to develop a substantial industrial base of its own.

A bitter example of this economic discrimination against the South was the "Pittsburgh plus" pricing system in the steel industry. Rich deposits of coal and iron ore near Birmingham, Alabama, worked by low-wage southern labor, should have given steel manufacturers there a competitive edge, especially in southern markets. But the steel lords of Pittsburgh brought pressure to bear on the compliant railroads. As a result, Birmingham steel, no matter where it was delivered, was charged a fictional fee, as if it had been shipped from Pittsburgh. This stunting of the South's natural economic advantages throttled the growth of the Birmingham steel industry.

In manufacturing cotton textiles, the South fared considerably better. Southerners had long resented shipping their fiber to New England, and now their cry was, "Bring the mills to the cotton." Beginning about 1880, northern capital began to erect cotton mills in the South, largely in response to tax benefits and the prospect of cheap and nonunionized labor.

The textile mills proved a mixed blessing to the economically blighted South. They slowly wove an industrial thread into the fabric of southern life, but at a considerable human cost. Cheap labor was the South's major attraction for potential investors, and keeping labor cheap became almost a religion among southern industrialists. The mills took root in the chronically depressed Piedmont region of southern Appalachia. Blacks were excluded from the mills, so rural southern whites, often derided as "hillbillies" or "lintheads," worked from dawn to dusk amid the whirring spindles. Paid at half the rate of their northern counterparts, most were perpetually in debt to the company store. But despite their depressed working conditions and poor pay, many southerners saw employment in the mills as a salvation. With many mills anxious to tap the cheap labor of women and children, mill work often offered destitute farm-fugitive families their only chance to remain together.

Henry W. Grady (1851–1889), editor of the Atlanta Constitution, *urged the new South to industrialize. In a Boston speech in 1889, he described the burial in Georgia of a Confederate veteran:*

"The South didn't furnish a thing on earth for that funeral but the corpse and the hole in the ground. . . . They buried him in a New York coat and a Boston pair of shoes and a pair of breeches from Chicago and a shirt from Cincinnati, leaving him nothing to carry into the next world with him to remind him of the country in which he lived, and for which he fought for four years, but the chill of blood in his veins and the marrow in his bones."

The Impact of the New Industrial Revolution on America

Economic miracles wrought during the decades after the Civil War enormously increased the wealth of the Republic. The standard of living rose sharply, and well-fed American workers enjoyed more physical comforts than their counterparts in any other industrial nation. Urban centers mushroomed as the insatiable factories demanded more American labor and as immigrants swarmed like honeybees to the new jobs (see "Makers of America: The Poles," p. 523).

Early Jeffersonian ideals were withering before the smudgy blasts from the smokestacks. As agriculture declined in relation to manufacturing, America could no longer aspire to be a nation of small freehold farms. Jefferson's concepts of free enterprise, with neither help nor hindrance by Washington, were being thrown out the factory window.

Older ways of life also wilted in the heat of the factory furnaces. The very concept of time was revolutionized. Rural American migrants and peasant European immigrants, used to living by the languid clock of nature, now had to regiment their lives by the factory whistle. The seemingly arbitrary discipline of industrial labor did not come easily and sometimes had to be forcibly taught by corporate managers.

Probably no single group was more profoundly affected by the new industrial age than women. Propelled into industry by recent inventions, chiefly the typewriter and the telephone switchboard, millions of stenographers and "hello girls" discovered new economic and social opportunities. The "Gibson Girl," a magazine image of an independent and athletic "new woman" created in the 1890s by the artist Charles Dana Gibson, became the romantic ideal of the age. For middle-class women, careers often meant delayed marriages and smaller families. Most women workers, however, toiled neither for independence nor for glamour but out of economic necessity. They faced the same long hours and dangerous working conditions as did their mates and brothers, and they earned less because wages for "women's jobs" were usually set below men's.

The clattering machine age likewise accentuated class division. "Industrial buccaneers" flaunted bloated fortunes, and their rags-to-riches spouses displayed glittering diamonds. Such extravagances evoked bitter criticism. Some of it was envious, but much of the criticism rose from the small and increasingly vocal group of socialists and other radicals, many of whom were recent European immigrants. The existence of an oligarchy of money was amply demonstrated by the fact that in 1900 about one-tenth of the people owned nine-tenths of the nation's wealth.

A nation of farmers and independent producers was becoming a nation of wage earners. In 1860 half of all workers were self-employed; by the century's end, two of every three working Americans depended on wages. Real wages were rising, but with dependence on wages came vulnerability to the swings of the economy and the whims of the employer. Illness or unemployment could mean catastrophe for an entire family. Nothing more sharply defined the growing difference between working-class and middle-class conditions of life than the precariousness of the laborer's lot.

Finally, strong pressures for foreign trade developed as the tireless industrial machine threatened to saturate the domestic market. Aided by developments such as the laying of a transatlantic telegraph in 1866 and the opening of the Suez Canal in 1869, international trade became ever faster, cheaper, and easier. American products and companies like Standard Oil radiated out all over the world. The flag follows trade, and empire tends to follow the flag—a harsh lesson that America was soon to learn.

In Unions There Is Strength

The sweat of the laborer lubricated the vast new industrial machine. Yet wage workers did not share proportionately with their employers the benefits of the age of big business.

The worker, suggestive of the Roman galley slave, was becoming a lever puller in a giant mechanism. Individual originality and creativity were being stifled, and less value than ever before was being placed on manual skills. Before the Civil War, the worker might have toiled in a small plant whose owner hailed the employee in the morning by first name and inquired after the family's health. But now the factory hand was employed by a corporation—depersonalized, bodiless, soulless, and often conscienceless. Employers could take advantage of the vast new railroad network and bring in unemployed workers from the four corners of the country and beyond to beat down high wage levels. During the 1880s and 1890s, several hundred thousand unskilled immigrant workers poured into the country from Europe, creating a labor market more favorable to the boss than the worker.

Individual workers were powerless to battle single handedly against giant industry. The corporation could dispense with the individual worker much more easily than the worker could dispense with the corporation. Employers could retain high-priced lawyers, buy up the local press, import strikebreakers ("scabs"), and employ thugs to beat up labor organizers. In 1886 Jay Gould reputedly boasted, "I can hire one-half of the working class to kill the other half."

Corporations had still other weapons in their arsenals. They could call upon conservative federal judges to issue injunctions against strikers, and if defiance continued, the corporations could then request state or federal authorities to send in troops. Employers could lock the doors of their plants—a procedure called the "lockout"—and starve rebellious workers into submission. They could compel them to sign "ironclad oaths" or "yellow dog contracts," both solemn agreements not to join a labor union. They could put the names of labor agitators on a "black list" and circulate it among fellow employers. A corporation might even own the "company town," where high-priced grocery stores and "easy" credit often sank workers into perpetual debt—a status that strongly resembled serfdom.

The middle-class public, annoyed by recurrent strikes, grew deaf to the outcry of the worker. Carnegie and Rockefeller had battled their way to the top, and the view was common that the laborer could do likewise. Somehow the strike seemed like a foreign importation—socialistic and hence unpatriotic. Big business might combine into trusts to raise prices, but the worker must not combine into unions to raise wages. Unemployment seemed to be an act of God, who somehow would take care of the laborer.

Labor Limps Along

Labor unions, which had been few and disorganized in 1861, were given a strong boost by the Civil War, when manpower shortages put a premium on labor. By 1872, there were several hundred thousand organized workers and thirty-two national unions, representing such crafts as the bricklayers, typesetters, and shoemakers.

Examining the Evidence

The Photography of Lewis W. Hine

The pell-mell onrush of industrialization after the Civil War spawned countless human abuses, few more objectionable than the employment of children, often in hazardous jobs. For decades, reformers tried to arouse public outrage against child labor, and they made significant headway at last with the help of photography—especially the photographs of Lewis W. Hine (1874–1940). A native of Wisconsin, Hine in 1908 became the staff photographer for the National Child Labor Committee, an organization committed to ending child labor. This 1909 photo of young "doffers," whose job it was to remove fully wound bobbins from textile spinning machines, is typical of Hine's work. He shows the boys climbing dangerously on the whirling mechanism, and his own caption for the photo names the mill—"Bibb Mill No. 1, Macon, Georgia"—but not the boys, as if to underline the impersonal, dehumanizing nature of their work and the specific responsibilities of their employer. His other subjects included child workers on Colorado beet farms, in Pennsylvania coal mines, and Gulf Coast fish canneries, and in the glass, tobacco, and garment trades. Hine's images contributed heavily to the eventual success of the campaign to end child labor in the New Deal era. Hine is also celebrated as one of the fathers of documentary photography.

Library of Congress Prints and Photographs Division [LC-USZ6-1222]

1. Why might Hine's graphic images have succeeded in stirring public opinion more powerfully than factual and statistical demonstrations of the evil of child labor?
2. Given Hine's own reform objectives, can his photographs—or any so-called documentary images—be taken at face value as literal, accurate information about the past?
3. Which details in Lewis Hine's photo especially emphasize the exploitation and dangers experienced by child laborers?

The **National Labor Union**, organized in 1866, represented a giant bootstride by workers. One of the earliest national-scale unions to organize in the Americas or Europe, it aimed to unify workers across locales and trades to challenge their ever more powerful bosses. The union lasted six years and attracted the impressive total of some 600,000 members, including the skilled, unskilled, and farmers, though it excluded the Chinese and made only nominal efforts to include women and blacks. Black workers organized their own Colored National Labor Union, but persistent white racism prevented the two national unions from working together. The National Labor Union agitated for the arbitration of industrial disputes and the eight-hour workday, winning the latter for government workers. But the devastating depression of the 1870s dealt it a knockout blow. Wage reductions in 1877 touched off such disruptive strikes on the railroads that nothing short of federal troops could restore order.

A new organization—the **Knights of Labor**—seized the torch dropped by the defunct National Labor Union. Officially known as the Noble and Holy Order of the Knights of Labor, the organization began inauspiciously in 1869 as a secret society, with a private ritual, passwords, and a special handshake. Secrecy, which continued until 1881, was intended to forestall possible reprisals by employers.

National Labor Union (1866–1872) *This first national labor organization in U.S. history gained 600,000 members from many parts of the work force, although it limited the participation of Chinese, women, and blacks. The organization devoted much of its energy to fighting for an eight-hour workday before it dissolved in 1872.*

Knights of Labor *The second national labor organization, organized in 1869 as a secret society and opened for public membership in 1881. The Knights were known for their efforts to organize all workers, regardless of skill level, gender, or race. After the mid-1880s their membership declined for a variety of reasons, including the Knights' participation in violent strikes and discord between skilled and unskilled members.*

The Knights of Labor, like the National Labor Union, sought to include all workers in "one big union." Their slogan was "An injury to one is the concern of all." A welcome mat was rolled out for the skilled and unskilled, for men and women, for whites and blacks, some ninety thousand of whom joined. The Knights barred only liquor dealers, professional gamblers, lawyers, bankers, and stockbrokers.

Setting up broad goals, the embattled Knights campaigned for economic and social reform, including producers' cooperatives and codes for safety and health. The ordinary workday was then ten hours or more, and the Knights waged a determined campaign for the eight-hour stint.

Under the eloquent but often erratic leadership of Terence V. Powderly, an Irish American of nimble wit and fluent tongue, the Knights won a number of strikes for the eight-hour day. When the Knights staged a successful strike against Jay Gould's Wabash Railroad in 1885, membership mushroomed to about three-quarters of a million workers.

Unhorsing the Knights of Labor

Despite their outward success, the Knights were riding for a fall. They became involved in a number of May Day strikes in 1886, about half of which failed. A focal point was Chicago, home to about eighty thousand Knights. The city was also honeycombed with a few hundred anarchists, many of them foreign-born, who were advocating a violent overthrow of the American government.

Haymarket Square (1886) *A May 4th rally that turned violent when someone threw a bomb into the middle of the meeting, killing several people. Eight anarchists were arrested for conspiracy contributing to the disorder, although evidence linking them to the bombing was thin. Four were executed, one committed suicide, and three were pardoned in 1893.*

Tensions rapidly built up to the bloody **Haymarket Square** episode. Labor disorders had broken out, and on May 4, 1886, the Chicago police advanced on a meeting called to protest alleged brutalities by the authorities. Suddenly a dynamite bomb was thrown that killed or injured several dozen people, including police.

Hysteria swept the Windy City. Eight anarchists were rounded up. Although nobody proved that they had anything to do directly with the bomb, a judge and jury held that since they had preached incendiary doctrines, they could be charged with conspiracy. Five were sentenced to death: one of these men committed suicide, and four were executed. The other three anarchists were given stiff prison terms. They were eventually pardoned in 1892 by Illinois governor John P. Altgeld, a German-born Democrat of strong liberal tendencies.

The Haymarket Square bomb helped blow the props from under the Knights of Labor. They were associated in the public mind, though mistakenly, with the anarchists. The eight-hour movement suffered correspondingly, and subsequent strikes by the Knights met with scant success. By the 1890s the Knights had melted away to only 100,000 members, and these gradually fused with other protest groups of that decade.

The AF of L to the Fore

American Federation of Labor *A national federation of trade unions that included only skilled workers, founded in 1886. Led by Samuel Gompers for nearly four decades, the AFL sought to negotiate with employers for a better kind of capitalism that rewarded workers fairly with better wages, hours, and conditions. The AFL's membership was almost entirely white and male until the middle of the twentieth century.*

The elitist **American Federation of Labor**, born in 1886, was largely the brainchild of squat, square-jawed Samuel Gompers. This colorful Jewish cigar maker, born in a London tenement and removed from school at age ten, was brought to America when thirteen. Taking his turn at reading informative literature to fellow cigar makers in New York, he was pressed into overtime service because of his strong voice. Rising spectacularly in the labor ranks, he was elected president of the American Federation of Labor every year except one from 1886 to 1924.

Gompers adopted a down-to-earth approach, soft-pedaling attempts to engineer sweeping social reform. A bitter foe of socialism, he shunned politics for economic strategies and goals. Gompers had no quarrel with capitalism, but he demanded a fairer share for labor. All he wanted, he said, was "more." Promoting what he called "pure and simple" unionism, he sought better wages, hours, and working conditions.

German Historical Museum/akg-images

***The Strike*, by Robert Koehler, 1886** Scenes like this were becoming more typical of American life in the late nineteenth century as industrialism advanced spectacularly and sometimes ruthlessly. Here Koehler (1850–1917) shows an entire community of men, women, and children—many of them apparently immigrant newcomers—challenging the power of the "boss." The scene is tense but orderly, though violence seems to be imminent as one striker reaches for a rock.

The AF of L thus established itself on solid but narrow foundations. Although attempting to speak for all workers, it fell far short of being representative of them. Composed of skilled craftsmen, such as the carpenters and bricklayers, it was willing to let unskilled laborers, including women and especially blacks, fend for themselves. The AF of L weathered the panic of 1893 reasonably well, and by 1900 it could boast a membership of 500,000.

Labor disorders continued, peppering the years from 1881 to 1900 with an alarming total of over 23,000 strikes. These disturbances involved 6,610,000 workers, with a total loss to both employers and employees of $450 million. The strikers lost about half their strikes and won or compromised the remainder. Perhaps the gravest weakness of organized labor was that it still embraced only a small minority of all working people—about 3 percent in 1900.

But attitudes toward labor had begun to change perceptibly by 1900. The public was beginning to concede the right of workers to organize, to bargain collectively, and to strike. As a sign of the times, Labor Day was made a legal holiday by act of Congress in 1894. A few enlightened industrialists had come to perceive the wisdom of avoiding costly economic warfare by bargaining with the unions and signing agreements. But the vast majority of employers continued to fight organized labor, which achieved its grudging gains only after recurrent strikes and frequent reverses. If the age of big business had dawned, the age of big labor was still some distance over the horizon.

Varying Viewpoints

Industrialization: Boon or Blight?

The capitalists who forged an industrial America in the late nineteenth century were once called captains of industry—a respectful title that bespoke awe for their wondrous material accomplishments. But these economic innovators have never been universally admired. During the Great Depression of the 1930s, when the entire industrial order they had created seemed to have collapsed utterly, it was fashionable to speak of them as robber barons—a term implying scorn for their high-handed methods. This sneer often issued from the lips and pens of leftist critics such as Matthew Josephson, who sympathized with the working classes allegedly brutalized by the factory system.

Criticism has also come from writers nostalgic for the preindustrial past. These critics believe that industrialization stripped away the traditions, values, and pride of native farmers and immigrant craftspeople. Conceding that economic development elevated the material standard of living for working Americans, this interpretation contends that the Industrial Revolution diminished their spiritual "quality of life." Accordingly, historians such as Herbert Gutman and David Montgomery portray labor's struggle for control of the workplace as the central drama of industrial expansion.

Nevertheless, even these historians concede that class-based protest has never been as powerful a force in the United States as in certain European countries. Many historians believe that this is so because greater social mobility in America dampened class tensions.

In the 1960s, historians led by Stephan Thernstrom began to test this long-standing belief. Looking at such factors as occupation, wealth, and geographic mobility, they tried to gauge the nature and extent of social mobility in the United States. Most of these historians concluded that, although relatively few Americans made rags-to-riches leaps, large numbers experienced small improvements in their economic and social status. Few sons of laborers became corporate tycoons, but many more became line bosses and white-collar clerks.

Such studies have subsequently been criticized by historians who point out the difficulties involved in defining social status. For instance, some white-collar clerical workers received lower wages than manual laborers did. Were they higher or lower on the social scale? Furthermore, James Henretta has pointed out that different groups defined success differently: whereas Jewish immigrants often struggled to give their sons professional educations, the Irish put more emphasis on acquiring land, and Italians on building small family-run businesses.

Meanwhile, leftist historians such as Michael Katz have argued that the degree of social mobility in America has been overrated. These historians argue that industrial capitalism created two classes: a working class that sold its labor and a business class that controlled resources and bought labor. Although most Americans took small steps upward, they generally remained within the class in which they began. Thus, these historians argue, the inequality of a capitalistic class system persisted in America's seemingly fluid society.

CHAPTER SUMMARY ★ ★ ★ ★ ★ ★ ★ ★ ★ ★ ★ ★ ★ ★

Aided by government land grant subsidies and loans, the first transcontinental rail line was completed in 1869, soon followed by others. This rail network opened vast new markets and prompted industrial growth. The power and corruption of the railroads led to public demands for regulation. State regulation was declared unconstitutional, but in 1887 the federal government took a small step with the Interstate Commerce Act.

New technology and types of business organization, sometimes employing harsh competitive practices, led to the growth of huge corporate trusts. Andrew Carnegie and John D. Rockefeller led the way in the steel and oil industries. Initially, the oil industry supplied kerosene for lamps; it eventually expanded by providing gasoline to fuel automobiles. Cheap steel transformed industries from construction to rail building, and the powerful railroads dominated the economy and reshaped American society. Many sectors of the economy came to be dominated by monopolistic trusts that used "interlocking directorates" and other pressure tactics to control competitors. Business-oriented ideologies such as the religious "gospel of wealth" and naturalistic "Social Darwinism" celebrated the wealthy as "fittest" to survive and denigrated poverty as a sign of moral and natural failure.

While industrialization did raise the general economy and standard of living, its benefits were very unevenly distributed. The South remained in underdeveloped "Third World" dependence, despite "New South" proclamations, while the industrial working class struggled at the bottom of the growing class divisions of American society. Increasingly transformed from independent producers and farmers to dependent wage earners, America's workers became vulnerable to illness, industrial accidents, and unemployment.

Workers' attempts at labor organization were generally ineffective, hindered by corporate and governmental opposition and their own backward-looking ideologies. The National Labor Union enjoyed brief success but then collapsed, and the Knights of Labor also disappeared after the Haymarket bombing. Gompers's AF of L successfully organized skilled craft laborers but ignored most industrial workers, women, and blacks. Middle class public attitudes toward organized labor slowly became more positive after 1900, but business retained the upper hand and only a small minority of workers were unionized.

KEY TERMS

Wabash, St. Louis & Pacific Railroad Company v. *Illinois* (390)
Interstate Commerce Act (390)
vertical integration (392)
horizontal integration (392)
trust (392)
Standard Oil Company (392)
interlocking directorates (392)
Social Darwinists (395)
Sherman Anti-Trust Act (396)
National Labor Union (399)
Knights of Labor (399)
Haymarket Square (400)
American Federation of Labor (400)

PEOPLE TO KNOW

Cornelius Vanderbilt
Alexander Graham Bell
Thomas Alva Edison
Andrew Carnegie
John D. Rockfeller
Samuel Gompers

Chapter 25

America Moves to the City

1865–1900

What shall we do with our great cities? What will our great cities do with us . . . ? [T]he question . . . does not concern the city alone. The whole country is affected . . . by the condition of its great cities.

LYMAN ABBOT, 1891

Chapter Outline

- The Rise of the City
- Skyscrapers, Tenements, and Suburbs
- The "New Immigrants"
- New Jobs for Women
- Nativists and Immigration Restriction
- Churches in the City
- Black Leaders: Booker T. Washington and W. E. B. Du Bois
- Literary Achievements
- The "New Woman" and the New Morality
- Art and Entertainment in Urban America
- *Makers of America: The Italians*
- *Examining the Evidence: Manuscript Census Data, 1900*

Born in the country, America moved to the city in the decades following the Civil War. By the year 1900 the United States' upsurging population nearly doubled from the 40 million people enumerated in the census of 1870. Yet, in the very same period, the population of American cities *tripled.* This cityward drift affected not only the United States but the entire industrializing world. European peasants, pushed off the land in part by competition from cheap American foodstuffs, were pulled into cities—in both Europe and America—by the new lure of industrial jobs. A revolution in American agriculture thus fed the industrial and urban revolutions in Europe, as well as in the United States.

FOCUS QUESTIONS

1. What features characterized the new industrial city, and what was its impact on American society?
2. Why did the massive "New Immigration" from southern and eastern Europe stir opposition from many native-born Americans, and how did political machines, social reformers, and churches adapt to the new urban and immigrant era?
3. What were the major challenges facing American religious life in the late nineteenth century? How did the growth of Catholicism, Judaism, and other "immigrant" faiths as well as "new" religions alter the character of an historically Protestant America?
4. What were the major changes in American educational and cultural life in the late nineteenth century, and how did the intellectual and literary turn toward "realism" and "pragmatism" reflect the new conditions of an urban and scientific civilization?
5. Why were there such fierce debates over morality in the late nineteenth century, especially over issues concerning sex, women, and the family?

CHRONOLOGY

1859	▪ Charles Darwin publishes *On the Origin of Species*
1862	▪ Morrill Act provides public land for higher education
1863	▪ World's first subway system opens in London
1866	▪ American Society for the Prevention of Cruelty to Animals (ASPCA) created
1869	▪ Wyoming Territory grants women the right to vote
1871	▪ *Woodhull and Claflin's Weekly* published
1872	▪ Metaphysical Club meets in Cambridge, Massachusetts
1873	▪ Comstock Law
1874	▪ Woman's Christian Temperance Union (WCTU) organized ▪ Chautauqua education movement launched ▪ Impressionist artists debut in Paris
1876	▪ Johns Hopkins University graduate school established
1879	▪ Henry George publishes *Progress and Poverty* ▪ Dumbbell tenement introduced ▪ Mary Baker Eddy establishes Christian Science ▪ Salvation Army begins work in America
1881	▪ Booker T. Washington becomes head of Tuskegee Institute ▪ American Red Cross founded ▪ Henry James publishes *The Portrait of a Lady* ▪ Barnum and Bailey first join to stage "Greatest Show on Earth"
1882	▪ First immigration-restriction laws passed
1883	▪ Brooklyn Bridge completed ▪ Metropolitan Opera House built in New York
1884	▪ Mark Twain publishes *The Adventures of Huckleberry Finn*
1885	▪ Chicago's Home Insurance Building built, the world's first skyscraper ▪ Linotype invented
1886	▪ Statue of Liberty erected in New York harbor
1887	▪ American Protective Association (APA) formed
	▪ Hatch Act supplements Morrill Act
1888	▪ Edward Bellamy publishes *Looking Backward* ▪ American all-star baseball team tours world
1889	▪ Jane Addams founds Hull House in Chicago
1890	▪ National American Woman Suffrage Association (NAWSA) formed
1891	▪ Basketball invented
1893	▪ Lillian Wald opens Henry Street Settlement in New York ▪ Anti-Saloon League formed ▪ World's Columbian Exposition held in Chicago ▪ New Zealand grants women right to vote
1895	▪ Stephen Crane publishes *The Red Badge of Courage*
1897	▪ Library of Congress opens ▪ Robert Gould Shaw Memorial erected on Boston Common
1898	▪ Charlotte Perkins Gilman publishes *Women and Economics*
1899	▪ Kate Chopin publishes *The Awakening*
1900	▪ Theodore Dreiser publishes *Sister Carrie*
1907	▪ Henry Adams privately publishes *The Education of Henry Adams*
1909	▪ National Association for the Advancement of Colored People (NAACP) founded

The Urban Frontier

The growth of American metropolises was spectacular. In 1860 no city in the United States could boast a million inhabitants; by 1890 New York, Chicago, and Philadelphia had spurted past the million mark. By 1900 New York, with some 3.5 million people, was the second largest city in the world, outranked only by London. Throughout the world,

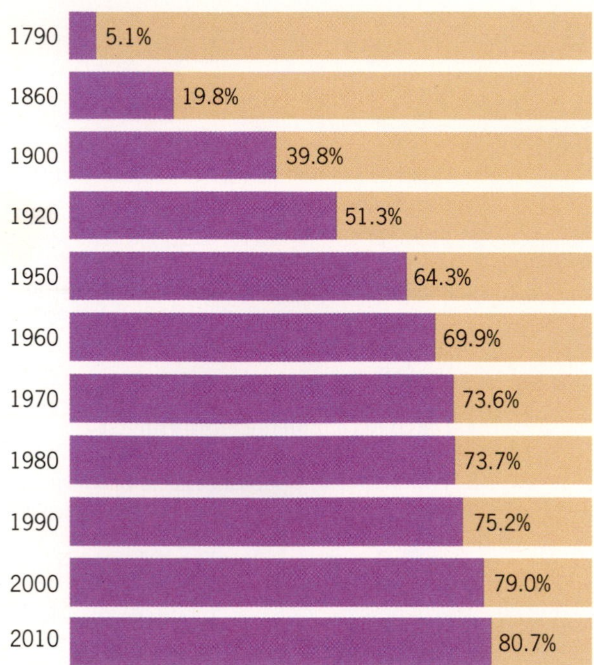

Figure 25.1 The Shift to the American City This chart shows the percentage of total population living in locales with a population of twenty-five hundred or more. Note the slowing of the cityward trend from 1970 on. (Sources: *Historical Statistics of the United States;* U.S. Census Bureau.)

cities were exploding; not only London, but also Paris, Berlin, Tokyo, Moscow, Mexico City, Calcutta, and Shanghai all doubled or tripled in size between 1850 and 1900. The population of Buenos Aires multiplied by more than ten.

American cities grew both up and out. The cloud-brushing skyscrapers allowed more people and workplaces to be packed onto a parcel of land. Appearing first as a ten-story building in Chicago in 1885, the skyscraper was made usable by the perfecting of the electric elevator. An opinionated Chicago architect, Louis Sullivan (1856–1924), contributed formidably to the further development of the skyscraper with his famous principle that "form follows function."

Cities also spread out, turning many Americans into commuters who traveled daily by mass-transit electric trolleys and later subways between their urban job in the central city and their suburban home. The compact and communal "walking city" gave way to the immense and impersonal megalopolis, carved into distinctly different districts for business, industry, and residential neighborhoods—which in turn were segregated by race, ethnicity, and social class.

Rural life could not compete with the siren song of the city (see Figure 25.1). Industrial jobs, above all, drew people off farms in America, as well as abroad, and into factory centers. But the urban lifestyle also held powerful attractions. The predawn milking of cows had little appeal when compared with the late-night glitter of city lights, particularly alluring to young adults yearning for independence. Electricity, indoor plumbing, and telephones all made life in the big city more enticing. Engineering marvels such as the skyscraper and New York's awesome Brooklyn Bridge, a harp-like suspension span dedicated in 1883, further added to the seductive glamour of the gleaming cities.

Cavernous department stores such as Macy's in New York and Marshall Field's in Chicago attracted urban middle-class shoppers and provided urban working-class jobs, many of them for women. The bustling emporiums also heralded a dawning era of consumerism and accentuated widening class divisions. When Carrie Meeber, novelist Theodore Dreiser's fictional heroine in *Sister Carrie* (1900), escapes from rural boredom to Chicago, it is the spectacle of the city's dazzling department stores that awakens her fateful yearning for a richer, more elegant way of life.

The move to the city also introduced Americans to new ways of living. Household products sold in bulk at the local store, without wrapping, gave way to city goods that came in throwaway bottles, boxes, bags, and cans. Cheap ready-to-wear clothing and swiftly changing fashions pushed old suits and dresses out of the closet. And the mountains of waste that city-dwellers generated created a new urban-age issue and testified to a cultural shift away from the virtues of thrift to the convenience of consumerism.

The jagged skyline of America's perpendicular civilization could not fully conceal the canker sores of feverish growth. Criminals flourished like lice in the teeming asphalt jungles. Impure water, uncollected garbage, unwashed bodies, and droppings from draft animals enveloped many cities in a satanic stench.

The cities were monuments of contradiction. They represented "humanity compressed," remarked one observer, "the best and the worst combined, in a strangely composite community." They harbored merchant princes and miserable paupers, stately banks and sooty factories, green-grassed suburbs and treeless ghettos. The glaring contrasts that assaulted the eye in New York reminded one visitor of "a lady in ball costume, with diamonds in her ears, and her toes out at the boots."

Worst of all were the human pigsties known as slums. They seemed to grow ever more crowded, more filthy, and more rat infested, especially after the perfection in 1879 of the "dumbbell" tenement. So named because of the outline of its floor plan, the dumbbell was usually seven or eight stories high, with shallow, sunless, and ill-smelling air shafts providing minimal ventilation. Several families were sardined onto each floor of the barracks-like structures, and they shared a malodorous toilet in the hall. "Flophouses" abounded where the poor and unemployed might sleep for a few cents on verminous

[LC-USZC4-1584]/Library of Congress Prints and Photographs Division Washington, D.C. 20540 USA

Mulberry Street on New York City's Lower East Side, c. 1900 Population densities in early-twentieth-century American cities were among the highest in the world. Mulberry Street, shown in this photo, was at the heart of New York's "Little Italy" neighborhood.

mattresses. Small wonder that slum dwellers strove mightily to escape their wretched surroundings—as many of them did. But the slums remained, foul places inhabited by successive waves of newcomers.

Cities were dangerous for everyone. In 1871 two-thirds of downtown Chicago burned in a raging fire that left 90,000 people homeless and destroyed more than 15,000 buildings. Closely packed wooden structures fed the insatiable flames, prompting Chicago and other wary cities to require stone and iron buildings downtown. The wealthiest began to leave the risky city behind and head for semirural suburbs. These leafy "bedroom communities" eventually ringed the brick-and-concrete cities with a greenbelt of affluence.

★ The New Immigration

The powerful pull of the American urban magnet was felt even in faraway Europe. A seemingly endless stream of immigrants continued to pour in from the old "mother continent." In each of the three decades from the 1850s through the 1870s, more than 2 million migrants had stepped onto America's shores. By the 1880s the stream had swelled to a rushing torrent, as more than 5 million migrants cascaded into the country.

Until the 1880s most immigrants had come from the British Isles and western Europe, chiefly Germany and Ireland. Also significant were the more than 300,000 Chinese. Many of these earlier immigrants had faced virulent nativism, especially the Irish and Chinese. In fact, the latter were legally excluded in 1882 (see pp. 374–376). But by the last decades of the century, the "old" European immigrants had adjusted well to American life by building supportive ethnic organizations and melding into established farm communities or urban craft unions. Although many still lived, worked, and worshipped among their own, they were largely accepted as "American" by the native-born.

But in the 1880s the character of the immigrant stream changed drastically. The so-called **New Immigrants**—Italians, Croats, Slovaks, Greeks, Poles, Jews, and others—came from southern and eastern Europe. Many of them worshiped in Roman Catholic

New Immigrants *Immigrants from southern and eastern Europe who formed a recognizable wave of immigration from the 1880s until 1924, in contrast to the immigrants from western Europe who had come before them. These new immigrants congregated in ethnic urban neighborhoods, where they worried many native-born Americans, some of whom responded with nativist anti-immigrant campaigns and others of whom introduced urban reforms to help the immigrants assimilate.*

or Eastern Orthodox churches or in Jewish synagogues. They came from countries with little history of democratic government and where opportunities for advancement were few. These new peoples totaled only 19 percent of newcomers in the 1880s; but by the first decade of the twentieth century, they constituted an astonishing 66 percent of the total inflow. They clustered in cities like New York and Chicago, where the "Little Italys" and "Little Polands" soon claimed more inhabitants than the largest cities of the same nationality in the Old World (See "Makers of America: The Italians").

Why were these bright-shawled and quaint-jacketed strangers hammering on the gates? In part they left their native countries because Europe seemed to have no room for them. Rapid population growth, American food imports, and European industrialization shook the peasantry loose from its ancient habitats and customary occupations, creating a vast, footloose army of the unemployed. Europeans by the millions drained out of the countryside and into European cities. Most stayed there, but some kept moving and left Europe altogether. About 60 million Europeans abandoned the Old Continent in the nineteenth and early twentieth centuries. More than half of them moved to the United States, while their compatriots spread out across the globe to South America, Canada, Africa, and Australia. Masses of people were already in motion in Europe before they felt the tug of the American magnet. This European diaspora, dominated by immigration to the United States, was, in many ways, simply a by-product of the urbanization of Europe.

"America fever" proved highly contagious in Europe. The United States was often painted as a land of fabulous opportunity in the "America letters" sent by friends and relatives already transplanted. The land of the free was also blessed with freedom from military conscription and institutionalized religious persecution. Beginning in the 1880s, savage persecution of minorities in Europe, especially of Jews in Russia, drove tens of thousands of battered refugees to American shores. Virtually unique among the New Immigrants, Jews had experienced city life in Europe, and many of them brought their urban skills of tailoring and shopkeeping to America's seaboard Atlantic cities, especially New York. Destitute and devout, eastern European Jews were frequently given a frosty reception not only by old-stock Americans but also by those German Jews who had arrived decades earlier and prospered in the United States, some of them as garment manufacturers who now employed their coreligionists as cheap labor.

The new immigrants struggled heroically to preserve their traditional cultures. Catholics expanded their parochial school system, and Jews established Hebrew schools. Foreign-language newspapers abounded. Yiddish theaters, kosher food stores, Polish parishes, Greek restaurants, and Italian social clubs all attested to the desire to keep old ways alive. Yet time took its toll on these efforts to preserve Old World customs. The children of the immigrants grew up speaking English, and often rejected the Old Country manners of their mothers and fathers in their desire to plunge headlong into the mainstream of American life.

Mary Antin (1881–1949), who came to America from Russian Poland in 1894 when thirteen years of age, later wrote in The Promised Land *(1912):*

"So at last I was going to America! Really, really going, at last! The boundaries burst. The arch of heaven soared. A million suns shone out for every star. The winds rushed in from outer space, roaring in my ears, 'America! America!'"

Reactions to the New Immigration

America's government system, nurtured in wide-open spaces, was ill suited to the cement forests of the great cities. Beyond minimal checking to weed out criminals and the insane, the federal government did virtually nothing to ease the assimilation of immigrants into American society. State governments, usually dominated by rural representatives, did even less. City governments, overwhelmed by the sheer scale of rampant urban growth, proved woefully inadequate to the task. By default, the business of ministering to the immigrants' needs fell to the unofficial "governments" of the urban political machines, led by "bosses" such as New York's notorious Boss Tweed.

The Italians

Who were the "New Immigrants," these southern and eastern Europeans who flocked to the United States between 1880 and 1920? Prominent and typical among them were Italians, some 4 million of whom sailed to the United States during the four decades of the New Immigration.

They came from the southern provinces of their native land, the heel and toe of the Italian boot. These areas had lagged behind the prosperous, industrial region of northern Italy. Unification of the nation of Italy had raised hopes of similar progress in the downtrodden south, but it was slow in coming. Southern Italian peasants tilled their fields without fertilizer or machinery, using hand plows and rickety hoes that had been passed down for generations.

From such demeaned conditions, southern Italians set out for the New World. Almost all of them were young men who intended to spend only a few months in America, stuff their pockets with earnings, and return home. At least half of Italian immigrants did indeed repatriate—as did comparable numbers of the other New Immigrants, with the conspicuous exception of the Jews, who had fled their native lands to escape religious persecution. Almost all Italian immigrants sailed through New York harbor, sighting the Statue of Liberty as they debarked from crowded ships. Many soon moved on to other large cities, but so many remained that, in the early years of the twentieth century, more Italians resided in New York than in Florence, Venice, and Genoa combined.

Although most Italian immigrants huddled in the cities, they did not abandon their rural upbringings entirely. Much to their neighbors' consternation, they often kept chickens and raised vegetables in small garden plots nestled between decaying tenement houses.

Those who bade a permanent farewell to Italy clustered in tightly knit communities that boasted opera clubs, Italian-language newspapers, and courts for playing bocci—a version of lawn bowling imported from the Old Country. Pizza emerged from the hot wood-burning ovens of these Little Italys, its aroma and flavor wafting into the hearts and stomachs of all Americans.

Italians typically earned their daily bread as industrial laborers—most famously as longshoremen and construction workers. They owed their prominence in the building trades to the "padrone system." The *padrone*, or labor boss, met immigrants upon arrival and secured jobs for them in New York, Chicago, the West, or wherever there was an immediate demand for industrial labor.

Lacking education, the Italians, as a group, remained in blue-collar jobs longer than some of their fellow New Immigrants. Many Italians, valuing vocation over schooling, sent their children off to work as early in their young lives as possible. Before World War I, less than 1 percent of Italian children enrolled in high school. Over the next fifty years, Italian Americans and their offspring gradually prospered, moving out of the cities into the more affluent suburbs. Many served heroically in World War II and availed themselves of the GI Bill to finance the college educations and professional training their immigrant forebears had lacked.

An Italian Immigrant Family Arriving at Ellis Island, ca. 1905

Taking care of the immigrants was big business, indeed. Trading jobs and services for votes, a powerful boss might claim the loyalty of thousands of followers. In return for their support at the polls, the boss provided jobs on the city's payroll, found housing for new arrivals, tided over the needy with gifts of food and clothing, patched up minor scrapes with the law, and helped get schools, parks, and hospitals built in immigrant neighborhoods. Reformers gagged at this cynical exploitation of the immigrant vote, but the political boss gave valuable assistance that was forthcoming from no other source.

The nation's social conscience gradually awakened to the plight of the cities and their immigrant masses. Prominent in this awakening were several Protestant clergymen such as Walter Rauschenbusch of New York City and Washington Gladden of Columbus, Ohio, who both sought to apply the lessons of Christianity to the slums and factories. Preaching the "social gospel," they insisted that churches tackle the burning social issues of the day. The Sermon on the Mount, they declared, was the science of society, and some social gospelers predicted that socialism was the logical outcome of Christianity. These "Christian socialists" did much to prick callous consciences and prepare the path for the later progressive reform movement.

One middle-class woman who was deeply dedicated to uplifting the urban masses was Jane Addams (1860–1935). Born into a prosperous Illinois family, Addams was one of the first generation of college-educated women and sought suitable outlets for her large talents. Inspired by a visit to England, in 1889 she established Hull House in Chicago as the most prominent American settlement house. Soft-spoken but tenacious, Addams became a kind of urban American saint in the eyes of many admirers. The philosopher William James told her, "You utter instinctively the truth we others vainly seek." She was a broad-gauge reformer who courageously condemned war as well as poverty, and she eventually won the Nobel Peace Prize in 1911. But her pacifism also earned her the enmity of some Americans, including the Daughters of the American Revolution, who expelled her from membership in their august organization.

Located in a poor immigrant neighborhood of Greeks, Italians, Russians, and Germans, Hull House offered instruction in English, counseling to help newcomers cope with American big-city life, child-care services for working mothers, and cultural activities for neighborhood residents. Following Jane Addams's lead, women founded **settlement houses** in other cities as well—notably Lillian Wald's Henry Street Settlement in New York, which opened its doors in 1893.

settlement houses *Mostly run by middle-class native-born women, settlement houses in immigrant neighborhoods provided housing, food, education, child care, cultural activities, and social connections for new arrivals to the United States. Many women, both native-born and immigrant, developed lifelong passions for social activism in the settlement houses. Jane Addams's Hull House in Chicago and Lillian Wald's Henry Street Settlement in New York City were two of the most prominent.*

The settlement houses became centers of women's activism and of social reform on behalf of women, children, blacks, and consumers. The women of Hull House, for example, successfully lobbied in 1893 for an Illinois anti-sweatshop law that protected women workers and prohibited child labor. They were led by Florence Kelley, a guerrilla warrior in the urban jungle who battled for decades on behalf of the underprivileged at both Hull House and the Henry Street Settlement. Armed with the insights of socialism and endowed with the voice of an actress, Kelley was a lifelong battler for the welfare of women, children, blacks, and consumers. She served for three decades as general secretary of the National Consumers League.

The pioneering work of Addams, Wald, and Kelley helped blaze the trail that many women—and some men—later followed into careers in urban reform and the new profession of social work. For these female reformers, and for many other women, the city offered a new kind of frontier opportunity.

Narrowing the Welcome Mat

Antiforeignism, or "nativism," earlier touched off by the Irish and German arrivals in the 1840s and 1850s, bared its ugly face in the 1880s with fresh ferocity. The New Immigrants had come for much the same reasons as the Old—to escape the poverty and squalor of Europe and to seek new opportunities in America. But "nativists" viewed the eastern and southern Europeans as culturally and religiously exotic hordes and often gave them a rude reception. The newest newcomers aroused widespread alarm. Their high birthrate, common among people with a low standard of living, raised worries that the original Anglo-Saxon stock would soon be outbred and outvoted. Still more horrifying was the

Examining the Evidence

Manuscript Census Data, 1900

Article I of the Constitution requires that a census of the American people be taken every ten years, in order to provide a reliable basis for congressional apportionment. Early censuses gathered little more than basic population numbers, but over the years the census takers have collected information on other matters as well, including occupational categories, educational levels, and citizenship status, yielding copious raw data for historical analysis. The census of 1890 was the first to use punch cards and electric tabulating machines, which greatly expanded the range of data that could be assembled and correlated—though the basic information was still hand recorded by individual canvassers who went door to door to question household members and fill out the census forms. Those handwritten forms, as much as the aggregate numbers printed in the final census tally, can furnish invaluable insights to the historian. Despite its apparent bureaucratic formality, the form shown here richly details the lives of the residents of a tenement house on New York's Lower East Side in 1900. See in particular the entries for the Goldberg family.

1. In what ways does this document reflect the great demographic changes that swept late-nineteenth-century America?
2. What light does the document shed on the character of immigrant "ghettos"?
3. What is the most common occupation of those listed? What is second? What might you conclude about the economic status of these residents of Manhattan?

TWELFTH CENSUS OF THE UNITED STATES.

SCHEDULE No. 1.—POPULATION.

State: New York
County: New York
Supervisor's District No. 1
Enumeration District No. 180
Sheet No. 2
Township or other division of county: Boro. Manhattan
Name of incorporated city, town, or village, within the above-named division: New York
Ward of city: 4
Enumerated by me on the 2d day of June, 1900, Harman Wechsler, Enumerator.

National Archives

prospect that it would be "mongrelized" by a mixture of "inferior" southern European blood and that the fairer Anglo-Saxon types would disappear. One New England writer cried out in anguish:

> *O Liberty, white Goddess! is it well*
> *To leave the gates unguarded?*

Native-born Americans voiced additional fears. They blamed the immigrants for the degradation of urban government. Some trade unionists assailed the alien arrivals for their willingness to work for "starvation" wages, which seemed to the immigrants like princely sums, and for importing in their intellectual baggage such seemingly dangerous doctrines as socialism, communism, and anarchism. Many business leaders who had welcomed the flood of cheap manual labor began to fear that they had embraced a Frankenstein's monster.

Antiforeign organizations, reminiscent of the "Know-Nothings" of antebellum days, were now revived in a different guise. Notorious among them was the American Protective Association (APA), which was created in 1887 and soon claimed a million members. In pursuing its nativist goals, the APA urged voting against Roman Catholic candidates for office and sponsored the publication of lustful fantasies about runaway nuns.

Organized labor was quick to throw its growing weight behind the move to choke off the rising tide of foreigners. Frequently used as strikebreakers, the wage-depressing immigrants were hard to unionize because of the language barrier. Labor leaders argued, not illogically, that if American industry was entitled to protection from foreign goods, American workers were entitled to protection from foreign laborers.

Congress finally nailed up partial bars against the inpouring immigrants. The first restrictive law, in 1882, banged the gate shut in the faces of paupers, criminals, and convicts, all of whom had to be returned at the expense of the greedy or careless shipper. Congress further responded to pained outcries from organized labor when in 1885 it prohibited the importation of foreign workers under contract—usually for substandard wages.

In later years, other federal laws lengthened the list of undesirables to include the insane, polygamists, prostitutes, alcoholics, anarchists, and people carrying contagious diseases. A proposed literacy test, long a favorite of nativists because it favored the Old Immigrants over the New, met vigorous opposition. The test was not enacted until 1917,

Picture Research Consultants & Archives

Looking Backward Older immigrants, trying to keep their own humble arrival in America "in the shadows," sought to close the bridge that had carried them and their ancestors across the Atlantic.

after three presidents had vetoed it on the grounds that literacy was more a measure of opportunity than of intelligence.

In 1886, four years after the first immigration restrictions were passed, the Statue of Liberty arose in New York harbor, a gift from the people of France. On its base were inscribed the words of Emma Lazarus:

Give me your tired, your poor,
Your huddled masses yearning to breathe free,
The wretched refuse of your teeming shore.

To many nativists, those noble words described only too accurately the "scum" washed up by the New Immigrant tides. Yet the uprooted immigrants, unlike "natives" lucky enough to have had parents who caught an earlier ship, became American citizens the hard way. These new immigrants stepped off the boat ready to put their shoulders to the nation's industrial wheels. The Republic owes much to these latecomers—for their brawn, their brains, their courage, and the yeasty diversity they brought to American society.

Contending Voices

The New Immigration

Writing in 1891 in support of a literacy test for immigrants, Massachusetts Republican Henry Cabot Lodge (1850–1924) emphasized a distinction between the recent stream of immigrants from southern and eastern Europe and earlier arrivals from Great Britain and Germany:

"Thus it is proved, first, that immigration to this country is increasing, and, second, that it is making its greatest relative increase from races most alien to the body of the American people and from the lowest and most illiterate classes among those races."

Six years later, Democratic president Grover Cleveland (1837–1908) disputed the merits of just such a distinction:

"It is said . . . that the quality of recent immigration is undesirable. The time is quite within recent memory when the same thing was said of immigrants who, with their descendants, are now numbered among our best citizens."

What political factors might account for the contrasting positions taken by these two public officials?

Churches Confront the Urban Challenge

The swelling size and changing character of the urban population posed sharp challenges to American churches, which, like other national institutions, had grown up in the country. Protestant churches in particular suffered heavily from the shift to the city, where many of their traditional doctrines and pastoral approaches seemed irrelevant.

As they lost their bearings in the new urban world, some churches were tending to become merely sacred diversions or amusements. Reflecting the wealth of their prosperous parishioners, many of the old-line churches were distressingly slow to raise their voices against social and economic vices. John D. Rockefeller was a pillar of the Baptist Church; J. Pierpont Morgan, of the Episcopal Church. Trinity Episcopal Church in New York City actually owned some of the city's worst slum property. Cynics remarked that the Episcopal Church had become "the Republican party at prayer." The mounting emphasis was on materialism; too many devotees worshiped at the altar of avarice. Money was the accepted measure of achievement, and the new gospel of wealth proclaimed that God caused the righteous to prosper.

Into this spreading moral vacuum stepped a new generation of **liberal Protestants**. With roots in earlier revolts against orthodox Calvinism, liberal ideas came into the mainstream of American Protestantism between 1875 and 1925, leading to frequent and bitter controversies with fundamentalists. Entrenched in the leadership and seminaries of the dominant denominations, liberal Protestants adapted religious ideas to modern culture, attempting to reconcile Christianity with new scientific and economic doctrines. They rejected biblical literalism, urging Christians to view biblical stories as models for Christian behavior rather than as dogma. They stressed the ethical teachings of the Bible and allied themselves with the reform-oriented "social gospel" movement. Friendly to urban revivalists such as Dwight Moody, a former shoe salesman who captivated audiences with his message of forgiveness, optimistic liberal Protestants focused on earthly salvation and personal growth. They helped many Protestant Americans reconcile their religious faith with modern, cosmopolitan ways of thinking.

liberal Protestants *Members of a branch of Protestantism that flourished from 1875 to 1925 and encouraged followers to use the Bible as a moral compass rather than to believe that the Bible represented scientific or historical truth. Many liberal Protestants became active in the "social gospel" and other reform movements of the era.*

Simultaneously, the Roman Catholic and Jewish faiths were gaining enormous strength from the New Immigration. By 1900 Roman Catholics had become the largest single denomination, numbering nearly 9 million communicants. Cardinal James Gibbons (1834–1921) of Baltimore, an urban Catholic leader devoted to American unity, was immensely popular with Roman Catholics and Protestants alike. Acquainted with every president from Andrew Johnson to Warren Harding, he employed his liberal sympathies to assist the American labor movement.

By 1890 the variety-loving Americans could choose from 150 religious denominations, two of them brand new. One was the band-playing Salvation Army, whose soldiers without swords invaded America from England in 1879 and established a beachhead on the street corners. Appealing frankly to the down-and-outers, the boldly named Salvation Army did much practical good, especially with free soup.

The other important new faith was the Church of Christ, Scientist (Christian Science), founded by Mary Baker Eddy in 1879 after she had suffered much ill health. Preaching that the true practice of Christianity heals sickness, she set forth her views in a book entitled *Science and Health with Key to the Scriptures* (1875), which sold an amazing 400,000 copies before her death. A fertile field for converts was found in America's hurried, nerve-wracked, and urbanized civilization. By the time Eddy died in 1910, she had founded an influential church that embraced several hundred thousand devoted worshipers.

Urbanites also participated in a new kind of religious-affiliated organization, the Young Men's and Women's Christian Associations. The YMCA and the YWCA, established before the Civil War, grew by leaps and bounds. Combining physical education with social service and religious instruction, the "Y's" appeared in virtually every major American city by the end of the nineteenth century.

Chicago History Museum

Morning Service at Moody's Church, 1908 Thousands of Chicagoans found the gospel and a helping hand at evangelist Dwight Lyman Moody's church. Although Moody himself died in 1899, his successors continued to attract throngs of worshipers to his church, which could hold up to ten thousand people.

The old-time religion received many blows from modern trends, including a boom sale of books on comparative religion and on historical criticism as applied to the Bible. Most unsettling of all were the writings of the English naturalist Charles Darwin. In the lucid prose of *On the Origin of Species* (1859), Darwin set forth the sensational theory that higher forms of life had slowly evolved from lower forms, through a process of random biological mutation and adaptation.

Darwin's idea of "natural selection" broke new ground. Nature, in his view, blindly selected organisms for survival or death based on random, inheritable variations that they happened to possess. Some traits conferred advantages in the struggle for life and hence better odds of passing them on to offspring. By providing a material explanation for the evolutionary process, Darwin's theory explicitly rejected the "dogma of special creation," which ascribed the design of each fixed species to divine agency.

Darwin's radical ideas evoked the wrath of scientists and laymen alike. Many zoologists, like Harvard's Louis Agassiz, held fast to the old doctrine of "special creation." By 1875, however, the majority of scientists in America and elsewhere had embraced the theory of organic evolution, though not all endorsed natural selection as its agent.

Clergymen and theologians responded to Darwin's theory in several ways. By 1875, after most natural scientists had embraced evolution, the religious community split into two camps. A conservative minority condemned what they thought was the "bestial hypothesis" of Darwinism. Their rejection of scientific consensus spawned a muscular view of biblical authority that eventually gave rise to fundamentalism in the twentieth century.

Most religious thinkers parted company with conservatives, refusing to accept the Bible as either history or science, and sought ways to reconcile Darwinism with Christianity. They heralded the revolutionary theory as a newer and grander revelation of the Almighty. As one commentator observed:

Some call it Evolution,
Others call it God.

While the liberal efforts at compromise did succeed in keeping many Americans in the pews, these compromises also tended to relegate religious teaching to matters of personal faith, private conduct, and family life. As science began to explain more of the external world, commentators on nature and society increasingly refrained from adding religious perspectives to the discussion.

The Lust for Learning

Public education continued its upward climb. The ideal of tax-supported elementary schools was still gathering strength. Beginning about 1870, more and more states were making at least a grade-school education compulsory, and this gain, incidentally, helped check the frightening abuses of child labor.

Spectacular indeed was the spread of the high schools, especially by the 1880s and 1890s. By 1900 some six thousand high schools were educating teenage boys and girls. In addition, the states provided free textbooks in increasing numbers during the last two decades of the century.

Teacher-training schools, then called "normal schools," also experienced a striking expansion after the Civil War. In 1860 only twelve normal schools were operating; in 1910, there were more than three hundred. Kindergartens, earlier borrowed from Germany, began to gain strong support. The New Immigration in the 1880s and 1890s brought vast new strength to the private Catholic parochial schools, which were fast becoming a major pillar of the nation's educational structure. In the realm of adult education, the Chautauqua movement, launched in upstate New York in 1874, sponsored public lectures and home study courses that reached hundreds of thousands of participants.

Crowded cities, despite their cancers, generally provided better educational facilities than the old one-room, one-teacher red schoolhouse. The success of the public schools is confirmed by the falling of the illiteracy rate from 20 percent in 1870 to 10.7 percent in 1900. Americans were developing a profound faith, often misplaced, in formal education as the sovereign remedy for their ills.

W. E. B. Du Bois (1868–1963) In 1961, at the end of a long lifetime of struggle for racial justice in the United States, Du Bois renounced his American citizenship at the age of ninety-three and took up residence in the newly independent African state of Ghana.

Booker T. Washington and Education for Black People

War-torn and impoverished, the South lagged far behind other regions in public education, and African Americans suffered most severely. A staggering 44 percent of nonwhites were still illiterate in 1900. Some help came from northern philanthropists, but the foremost champion of black education was an ex-slave, Booker T. Washington, who had slept under a board sidewalk to save pennies for his schooling. Called in 1881 to head the black normal and industrial school at Tuskegee, Alabama, he began with forty students in a tumbledown shanty. Undaunted, he taught black students useful trades so that they could gain self-respect and economic security. But Washington stopped short of advocating *social* equality with whites, acquiescing in segregation in return for the right to develop economic and educational resources of the black community.

Washington's commitment to training young blacks in agriculture and the trades guided the curriculum at the **Tuskegee Institute** and made it an ideal place for slave-born George Washington Carver to teach and research. After Carver joined the faculty in 1896, he became an internationally famous agricultural chemist who boosted the Southern economy by discovering hundreds of new uses for the lowly peanut (shampoo, axle grease), sweet potato (vinegar), and soybean (paints).

Other black leaders, notably Dr. W. E. B. Du Bois, assailed Booker T. Washington for an approach that would condemn their race to manual labor and perpetual inferiority. Born in Massachusetts, Du Bois was a mixture of African, French, Dutch, and Indian blood ("Thank God, no Anglo-Saxon," he would add). After a determined struggle, he earned a Ph.D. at Harvard, the first of his race to achieve that goal. Du Bois demanded complete equality for blacks, social as well as economic, and helped to found the National Association for the Advancement of Colored People (NAACP) in 1909. Rejecting Washington's gradualism and separatism, he argued that the "talented tenth" of the black community should be given full and immediate access to the mainstream of American life. An exceptionally skilled historian, sociologist, and poet, Du Bois died as a self-exile in Africa in 1963, at the age of ninety-five.

Tuskegee Institute *A normal and industrial school led by Booker T. Washington in Tuskegee, Alabama. It focused on training young black students in agriculture and the trades to help them achieve economic independence. Washington justified segregated, vocational training as a necessary first step on the road to racial equality, although critics accused him of being too "accommodationist."*

W. E. B. Du Bois (1868–1963) wrote in his 1903 classic, The Souls of Black Folk:

"It is a peculiar sensation, this double consciousness, this sense of always looking at one's self through the eyes of others, of measuring one's self through the eyes of others. . . . One ever feels his two-ness—an American, a Negro; two souls, two thoughts, two unreconciled strivings; two warring ideals in one dark body, whose dogged strength alone keeps it from being torn asunder."

The Hallowed Halls of Ivy

Colleges and universities also shot up like lusty young saplings in the decades after the Civil War (see Table 25.1). Even women and African Americans were finding new opportunities for higher education. The educational battle for women, only partially won before the war, turned into a rout of the masculine diehards. Women's colleges such as Vassar were gaining ground, and universities open to both genders were blossoming, notably in the Midwest. By 1900 every third college graduate was a woman. By the turn of the century the black academies planted during Reconstruction had blossomed into a crop of southern black colleges. Howard University in Washington, D.C., Hampton Institute in Virginia, Atlanta University, and numerous others nurtured higher education for blacks until the civil rights movement of the 1960s made widespread attendance at white institutions possible.

Table 25.1 Educational Levels, 1870–2011

Year	Number Graduating from High School	Number Graduating from College	Median Number of School Years Completed*	High School Graduates as a Percentage of 17-Year-Old Population
1870	16,000	9,371		2.0%
1880	23,634	12,896		2.5%
1890	43,731	15,539		3.5%
1900	94,883	27,410		6.4%
1910	156,429	37,199	8.1	8.8%
1920	311,266	48,622	8.2†	16.8%
1930	666,904	122,484	8.4†	29.0%
1940	1,221,475	186,500	8.6	50.8%
1950	1,199,700	432,058	9.3	59.0%
1960	1,858,023	392,440	10.5	69.5%
1970	2,888,639	792,316	12.2	76.9%
1980	3,042,214	929,417	12.5	71.4%
1990	2,574,162	1,051,344	12.7	73.4%
2000	2,832,844	1,237,875	NA	69.8%
2010	3,434,672	1,650,014	NA	79.7%
2011	3,402,920††	1,715,913	NA	77.9%††

*People twenty-five years and over.
†1910–1930 based on retrogressions of 1940 data; 1940 was the first year measured.
††Projected figure.

Sources: *Digest of Education Statistics*, 2012, a publication of the National Center for Education Statistics; *Statistical Abstract of the United States*, relevant years; Folger and Nam, Education of the American Population, a 1960 Census Monograph.

The truly phenomenal growth of higher education owed much to the Morrill Act of 1862. This enlightened law provided a generous grant of public lands to the states for support of public higher education. The Hatch Act of 1887 extended the Morrill Act by providing federal funds for the establishment of state agricultural experiment stations. Together these two pieces of legislation spawned over a hundred **land-grant colleges** that evolved into state universities, including such institutions as the University of California (1868), Ohio State University (1870), and Texas A&M (1876).

land-grant colleges *Colleges and universities created from allocations of public land through the Morrill Act of 1862 and the Hatch Act of 1887. These grants helped fuel the boom in higher education in the late nineteenth century, and many of today's public universities derive from them.*

Private philanthropy richly supplemented government grants to higher education. Many of the new industrial millionaires, developing tender social consciences, donated immense fortunes to educational enterprises. In the twenty years from 1878 to 1898 these money barons gave away about $150 million. Among the noteworthy new private universities were Cornell (1865) and Leland Stanford Junior (1891), the latter founded in memory of the deceased fifteen-year-old only child of a builder of the Central Pacific Railroad. The University of Chicago, opened in 1892, speedily forged into a front-rank position, owing largely to the lubricant of John D. Rockefeller's oil millions.

Towering among the new professionalized institutions of higher learning was Johns Hopkins University, opened in 1876, which developed the nation's first high-grade graduate school. Several generations of American scholars, repelled by snobbish English cousins and attracted by painstaking Continental methods, had attended German universities. Reputable scholars no longer had to go abroad for a gilt-edged graduate degree; Dr. Woodrow Wilson, among others, received his Ph.D. from Johns Hopkins.

Homegrown influences shaped the modern American university as much as German models. Antebellum colleges had stressed the "unity of truth," or the idea that knowledge and morality existed in a single system united by theology and moral philosophy. After the Darwinian challenge made religion and science seem less compatible, university reformers struggled to preserve the unity of moral and intellectual purpose. When that effort failed, university educators abandoned moral instruction and divorced "facts" from "values."

Other pressures also helped doom the traditional curriculum. Industrialization and science brought insistent demands for "practical" courses, and specialization, not synthesis, became the primary goal of a university education. The turn toward electives and pre-professional training received a powerful boost in the 1870s when Dr. Charles W. Eliot became president of Harvard College. As a sign of the secularizing times, Eliot changed Harvard's motto from *Christo et Ecclesiae* (For Christ and Church) to *Veritas* (Truth).

One of America's most brilliant intellectuals, the slight and sickly William James (1842–1910) served for thirty-five years on the Harvard faculty. Through his numerous writings he made a deep mark on many fields. His *Principles of Psychology* (1890) helped to establish the modern discipline of psychology. In *The Will to Believe* (1897) and *Varieties of Religious Experience* (1902), James explored the philosophy and psychology of religion. In his most famous work, *Pragmatism* (1907), he declared that America's greatest contribution to the history of philosophy was the concept of **pragmatism**—that truth of an idea was to be tested, above all, by its practical consequences.

pragmatism *A distinctive American philosophy that emerged in the late nineteenth century around the theory that the true value of an idea lay in its ability to solve problems. The pragmatists thus embraced the provisional, uncertain nature of experimental knowledge. Among the most well-known purveyors of pragmatism were John Dewey, Oliver Wendell Holmes, Jr., and William James.*

The Appeal of the Press

Books continued to be a major source of edification and enjoyment for both juveniles and adults. Public libraries—the poor person's university—made encouraging progress in the late nineteenth century, especially in Boston and New York. The magnificent Library of Congress building, which opened its doors in 1897, provided thirteen acres of floor space in the largest and costliest edifice of its kind in the world. A new era was inaugurated by the generous gifts of Andrew Carnegie, who contributed $60 million for the construction of public libraries all across the United States and around the world. By 1900 there were about nine thousand free public libraries in America.

Roaring newspaper presses, spurred by the invention of the Linotype in 1885, more than kept pace with the demands of a word-hungry public. But the heavy investment in machinery and plant was accompanied by a growing fear of offending advertisers and subscribers. Bare-knuckle editorials were, to an increasing degree, being supplanted by feature articles and noncontroversial syndicated material. The day of slashing, journalistic giants such as Horace Greeley was passing.

Sensationalism, at the same time, was capturing the public taste. The semiliterate immigrants, combined with strap-hanging urban commuters, created a profitable market for news that was simply and punchily written. Sex, scandal, and other human-interest stories burst into the headlines, as a vulgarization of the press accompanied the growth of circulation. Critics complained in vain about these "presstitutes."

Two new journalistic tycoons emerged. Joseph Pulitzer, Hungarian born and near blind, was a leader in the techniques of sensationalism in his ownership of the *St. Louis Post-Dispatch* and the *New York World*. His use of colored comics featuring the "Yellow Kid" gave the name **yellow journalism** to his lurid sheets. A close and ruthless competitor was youthful William Randolph Hearst, who had been expelled from Harvard College for a crude prank. Able to draw on his California father's mining millions, Hearst built up a powerful chain of newspapers, beginning with the *San Francisco Examiner* in 1887. Unfortunately, Pulitzer and Hearst both prostituted the press in their struggle for increased circulation; they "stooped, snooped, and scooped to conquer." Their flair for scandal and sensation was happily somewhat offset by the strengthening of the news-gathering Associated Press, which had been founded in the 1840s.

yellow journalism *A scandal-mongering practice of journalism that emerged in New York during the Gilded Age out of the circulation battles between Joseph Pulitzer's* New York World *and William Randolph Hearst's* New York Journal. *The expression has remained a pejorative term referring to sensationalist journalism practiced with unethical, unprofessional standards.*

Apostles of Reform

Magazines partly satisfied the public appetite for good reading, notably old standbys such as *Harper's*, the *Atlantic Monthly*, and *Scribner's Monthly* and new western entrants such as the California-based *Overland Monthly*. Possibly the most influential journal was the liberal and highly intellectual *Nation*, whose modest circulation of ten thousand consisted largely of professors, preachers, and publicists. Launched in 1865 by the Irish-born critic Edwin L. Godkin, the *Nation* crusaded for civil-service reform, honesty in government, and a moderate tariff. Godkin believed that by reaching the most influential readers his ideas might spread to tens of millions.

Another journalist-author, Henry George, was an original thinker who left an enduring mark. Poor in formal schooling, he was rich in idealism and in the milk of human kindness. After seeing poverty at its worst in India and land-grabbing at its greediest in California, George penned his classic treatise *Progress and Poverty* (1879), which undertook to solve "the great enigma of our times"—"the association of progress with poverty." According to George, property owners unjustifiably profited from the pressure of growing population on a fixed supply of land. A single 100 percent tax on those windfall profits would eliminate unfair inequalities and stimulate economic growth.

George's controversial single-tax ideas so horrified the propertied classes that his manuscript was rejected by numerous publishers. Finally published in 1879, the book ultimately sold some 3 million copies. George also lectured widely in America, where he influenced thinking about the maldistribution of wealth, and in Britain, where he left an indelible mark on Fabian socialism. George's proposals resounded for decades, and his concern for the gap between rich and poor inspired numerous later American reformers. Edward Bellamy, a quiet Massachusetts Yankee, was another journalist-reformer of remarkable power. In 1888 he published a socialistic novel, *Looking Backward*, in which the hero, falling into a hypnotic sleep, awakens in the year 2000. The hero "looks backward" and finds that the social and economic injustices of 1887 have melted away under an idyllic government, which has nationalized big business to serve the public interest. To a nation already alarmed by the trust evil, the book had a magnetic appeal and sold over a million copies. Scores of Bellamy Clubs sprang up to discuss this mild utopian socialism, and they heavily influenced American reform movements near the end of the century.

The New Morality

Like other radical reformers, Victoria Woodhull shook the pillars of conventional morality when she publicly proclaimed her belief in free love in 1871. Woodhull was a beautiful and eloquent divorcée, sometime stockbroker, and tireless feminist propagandist. Together with her sister Tennessee Claflin she published a far-out periodical, *Woodhull and Claflin's Weekly*. The sisters again shocked "respectable" society in 1872 when their journal struck a blow for the new morality by charging that Henry Ward Beecher, the most famous preacher of his day, had for years been carrying on an adulterous affair.

Pure-minded Americans sternly resisted these affronts to their moral principles. Their foremost champion was a portly crusader, Anthony Comstock, who made lifelong war on the "immoral." Armed after 1873 with a federal statute—the notorious Comstock Law—this self-appointed defender of sexual purity boasted that he had confiscated no fewer than 202,679 "obscene pictures and photos"; 4,185 "boxes of pills, powders, etc., used by abortionists"; and 26 "obscene pictures, framed on walls of saloons."

The antics of the Woodhull sisters and Anthony Comstock exposed to daylight the battle going on in late-nineteenth-century America over sexual attitudes and the place of women. Switchboards and typewriters in the booming cities became increasingly the tools of women's independence. Young workingwomen headed to dance halls and nightclubs when the day was done, enjoying a new sense of freedom in the cities. This "new morality" began to be reflected in soaring divorce rates, the spreading practice of birth control, and increasingly frank discussion of sexual topics. By 1913, said one popular magazine, the chimes had struck "sex o'clock in America."

Families and Women in the City

The new urban environment was hard on families. Paradoxically, the crowded cities were emotionally isolating places. Urban families had to go it alone, separated from clan, kin, and village. Many families cracked under the strain of providing the virtually exclusive

In 1906 progressive reformer Jane Addams (1860–1935) argued that granting women the vote would improve the social and political condition of American cities:

"City housekeeping has failed partly because women, the traditional housekeepers, have not been consulted as to its multiform activities. The men have been carelessly indifferent to much of the civic housekeeping, as they have been indifferent to the details of the household. . . . City government demands the help of minds accustomed to detail and a variety of work, to a sense of obligation to the health and welfare of young children, and to a responsibility for the cleanliness and comfort of other people."

arena for intimate companionship and emotional satisfaction. The late-nineteenth-century urban era launched the "divorce revolution" that transformed the United States' social landscape in the twentieth century.

Urban life also dictated changes in work habits and even in family size. Not only fathers but mothers and even children as young as ten years old often worked, and usually in widely scattered locations. In the city more children meant more mouths to feed, more crowding in sardine-tin tenements, and more human baggage to carry in the uphill struggle for social mobility. Not surprisingly, birthrates were still dropping, and family size continued to shrink as the nineteenth century lengthened. Marriages were being delayed, and more couples learned the techniques of birth control.

Women were growing more independent in the urban environment, and in 1898 they heard the voice of a major feminist prophet, Charlotte Perkins Gilman. In that year the freethinking and original-minded Gilman published *Women and Economics*. In this classic of feminist literature, Gilman called on women to abandon their dependent status and contribute to the larger life of the community through productive involvement in the economy. Rejecting all claims that biology gave women a fundamentally different character from men, she argued that "our highly specialized motherhood is not so advantageous as believed." She advocated centralized nurseries and cooperative kitchens to facilitate women's participation in the work force—anticipating by more than half a century the day-care centers and convenience-food services of a later day.

Gilman's call for female participation in wage labor reflected epochal changes already under way, but strict codes still prescribed which women might work and what jobs they might hold. Because employment of wives and mothers was considered taboo, the vast majority of working women were single. Race, ethnicity, and class also shaped job opportunities. White-collar jobs like social worker, telephone operator, and department-store clerk were largely reserved for native-born women, while immigrant women clustered in particular industries, as Jewish women did in the garment trade. Black women had few opportunities beyond domestic service.

Beyond addressing the world of work, fiery feminists also continued to insist on the ballot. They had been demanding the vote since before the Civil War, but many high-minded female reformers had temporarily shelved the cause of women to battle for the rights of blacks. In 1890 militant suffragists formed the **National American Woman Suffrage Association (NAWSA)**. Its founders included aging pioneers like Elizabeth Cady Stanton, who had helped organize the first women's rights convention in 1848, and her long-time comrade Susan B. Anthony, the radical Quaker who had courted jail by trying to cast a ballot in the 1872 presidential election.

National American Woman Suffrage Association (NAWSA) *An organization founded in 1890 to demand the vote for women. NAWSA argued that women should be allowed to vote because their responsibilities in the home and family made them indispensable in the public decision-making process. During World War I, NAWSA supported the war effort and lauded women's role in the Allied victory, which helped to finally achieve nationwide woman suffrage in the Nineteenth Amendment (1920).*

By 1900 a new generation of women had taken command of the suffrage battle. Their most effective leader was Carrie Chapman Catt, a pragmatic and businesslike reformer of relentless dedication. Significantly, under Catt the suffragists de-emphasized the argument that women deserved the vote as a matter of right, because they were in all respects the equals of men. Instead Catt stressed the desirability of giving women the vote if they were to continue to discharge their traditional duties as homemakers and mothers. Women thus had a special public responsibility for such things as children's education, public health, and safety, the argument ran.

By thus linking the ballot to a traditional definition of women's role, suffragists registered encouraging gains as the new century opened, despite continuing showers of rotten eggs and the jeers of male critics. Women were increasingly permitted to vote in local elections. Wyoming Territory—later called "the Equality State"—granted the first unrestricted suffrage to women in 1869. This important breach in the dike once made, many states followed Wyoming's example. Paralleling these triumphs, most of the states by 1890 had passed laws to permit wives to own or control their property after marriage.

The reborn suffrage movement and other women's organizations largely excluded black women from their ranks. Fearful that an integrated campaign would handicap its efforts to get the vote, the National American Woman Suffrage Association limited membership to whites. Black women, however, created their own associations. Journalist and teacher Ida B. Wells inspired black women to mount a nationwide antilynching crusade. She also helped launch the black women's club movement, which culminated in the establishment of the National Association of Colored Women in 1896.

Women also took a lead in the growing crusade against alcohol and the saloon. In 1874 the **Woman's Christian Temperance Union (WCTU)** was organized with the white ribbon as its symbol of purity. The saintly Frances E. Willard—also a champion of planned parenthood—was its leading spirit. Less saintly was the mentally deranged "Kansas Cyclone," Carrie A. Nation, who smashed saloon bottles and bars with her hatchet. Female prohibitionists, singing "The Lips That Touch Liquor Must Never Touch Mine," began sweeping new states into the "dry column"—setting the stage for the great, but temporary, triumph of 1919 when the national prohibition amendment (Eighteenth) was attached to the Constitution.

Woman's Christian Temperance Union (WCTU) *Founded in Ohio in the 1870s to combat the evils of excessive alcohol consumption, the WCTU went on to embrace a broad reform agenda, including campaigns to abolish prostitution and gain the right to vote for women.*

Postwar Fiction, Lowbrow and High

Not all social activity proved so serious. Post–Civil War Americans devoured millions of "dime novels," usually depicting the wild West. Paint-bedaubed Indians and quick-triggered gunmen such as "Deadwood Dick" shot off vast quantities of gunpowder, and virtue invariably triumphed. These lurid "paperbacks" were frowned on by parents, but goggle-eyed youths read them in haylofts or in schools behind the broad covers of geography books. The king of dime novelists was Harlan F. Halsey, who made a fortune by dashing off about 650 novels, often one in a day.

General Lewis Wallace—lawyer, soldier, and author—was a colorful figure. Having fought with distinction in the Civil War, he sought to combat the prevailing wave of Darwinian skepticism with his novel *Ben Hur: A Tale of the Christ* (1880). A phenomenal success, the book sold an estimated 2 million copies in many languages, including Arabic and Chinese, and later appeared on stage and screen. It was the *Uncle Tom's Cabin* of the anti-Darwinists, who found in it support for the Holy Scriptures.

An even more popular writer was Horatio ("Holy Horatio") Alger, a Puritan-reared New Englander, who in 1866 forsook the pulpit for the pen. He wrote more than a hundred volumes of juvenile fiction that sold over 17 million copies. His stock formula depicted a poor boy, who through a combination of virtue, honesty, hard work, and bravery, achieved success, wealth, and honor—a kind of survival of the purest, especially nonsmokers, nondrinkers, nonswearers, and nonliars.

Literature and the arts were not immune to the era's sweeping changes. Confronted by new cities and industries, American writers and artists forsook the romantic sentimentality of an earlier age and generated three interrelated currents in the arts: **realism**, **naturalism**, and **regionalism**. All three movements responded to the Gilded Age's urban, industrial transformation.

Realism quickly came to dominate post–Civil War American literature. Foregoing romantic pageantry, American authors increasingly found their subjects in the coarse human comedy and material drama of the world around them. William Dean Howells (1837–1920), the celebrated "father of American realism," emerged as the era's preeminent advocate of unsentimental literature. A printer's son from Ohio with limited formal education, he wrote his way into high literary circles of the East and in 1871 became editor of the prestigious Boston-based *Atlantic Monthly*. In his thirty-six novels, Howells wrote about ordinary people and about controversial social themes such as divorce and labor conflict. His most famous novel, *The Rise of Silas Lapham* (1885), describes the trials of a newly rich paint manufacturer caught up in the caste system of Brahmin Boston.

Two recipients of Howells's patronage and friendship—Mark Twain and Henry James—carried literary realism to new heights. With only meager schooling in frontier

realism *Mid-nineteenth-century movement in European and American literature and the arts that sought to depict contemporary life and society as it actually was, in all its unvarnished detail. Adherents eschewed the idealism and nostalgia of the earlier romantic sensibility.*

naturalism *An offshoot of mainstream realism, this late-nineteenth-century literary movement purported to apply detached scientific objectivity to the study of human characters shaped by degenerate heredity and extreme or sordid social environments.*

regionalism *A recurring artistic movement that, in the context of the late nineteenth century, aspired to capture the peculiarities, or "local color," of America's various regions in the face of modernization and national standardization.*

Culture Club/Getty Images

Mark Twain (1835–1910) Born Samuel Langhorne Clemens, he was not only America's most popular author but also a renowned platform lecturer. This photograph was taken in Dublin, New Hampshire, in August 1906 by Albert Bigelow Paine, Mark Twain's biographer.

Missouri, mustachioed Mark Twain (1835–1910) typified a new breed of American authors in revolt against the elegant refinements of the old New England school of writing. Christened Samuel Langhorne Clemens, he had served for a time as a Mississippi river boat pilot. After a stint in the Confederate militia, he journeyed westward to Nevada and California, a trip he described with a mixture of truth and tall tales in *Roughing It* (1872). One year later Twain teamed up with Charles Dudley Warner in 1873 to write *The Gilded Age*, an acid satire on post–Civil War politicians and speculators that gave a name to an era. Many other books flowed from Twain's busy pen. *The Adventures of Tom Sawyer* (1876) preceded *The Adventures of Huckleberry Finn* (1884), an American masterpiece that defied Twain's own definition of a classic as "a book which people praise and don't read." His later years were soured by bankruptcy growing out of unwise investments, and he was forced to take to the lecture platform and amuse what he called "the damned human race." Journalist, humorist, satirist, and foe of social injustice, Twain made his most enduring contribution in capturing frontier realism and humor in the authentic American dialect.

Twain's homegrown vernacular met its match in Henry James's elegant prose. Brother of Harvard philosopher William James, Henry James (1843–1916) was a New Yorker who took as his dominant literary theme the confrontation of innocent Americans with subtle Europeans. James penned a remarkable number of brilliant novels, including *The Portrait of a Lady* (1881) and *The Wings of the Dove* (1902). *The Bostonians* (1886) was one of the first novels about the rising feminist movement. James frequently made women his central characters, exploring their inner reactions to complex situations with a deftness that marked him as a master of "psychological realism." Long resident in England, he became a British subject shortly before his death.

Like her friend James, Edith Wharton (1862-1937) took a magnifying glass to the inner psychological turmoil and moral shortcomings of post–Civil War high society. Born into money, Wharton lived in the blue-blooded social circles of New York and Paris. After an unhappy marriage, she increasingly turned to writing. Her novels, including *The House of Mirth* (1905) and *The Age of Innocence* (1920) exposed the futile struggles and interior costs of striving characters stuck on the social ladder.

While realist authors often treated middle- and upper-class characters in everyday settings, naturalistic novelists placed lower-class or marginal characters in extreme or sordid environments, including the urban jungle. Stephen Crane (1871–1900), the fourteenth son of a Methodist minister, exemplified this naturalistic urge in his writing. His *Maggie: A Girl of the Streets* (1893), a brutal tale about a poor prostitute driven to suicide, proved too grim to find a publisher, so Crane had to have it printed privately. He rose quickly to prominence with *The Red Badge of Courage* (1895), the stirring story of a bloodied young Civil War recruit under the extreme stress of fire. Crane himself had never seen a battle and wrote entirely from the printed Civil War records. Sharing the misfortune of his many characters, he died of tuberculosis in 1900, when only twenty-nine.

Candid, naturalistic portrayals of contemporary life and social problems were the literary order of the day by the turn of the century. Jack London (1876–1916) turned from popular nature books such as *The Call of the Wild* (1903) to depicting a possible fascistic revolution in *The Iron Heel* (1907). Frank Norris (1870–1902), like London a Californian, wrote *The Octopus* (1901), an earthy saga of the stranglehold of the railroad and corrupt politicians on California wheat ranchers.

Conspicuous among the naturalistic novelists rising in the literary firmament was Theodore Dreiser (1871–1945), a homely, gangling writer from Indiana. He burst on the literary scene in 1900 with *Sister Carrie*, a graphic narrative of a poor working girl in Chicago and New York. She becomes one man's mistress, then elopes with another, and finally strikes out on her own to make a career on the stage. The fictional Carrie's disregard for prevailing moral standards so offended Dreiser's publisher that the book was soon withdrawn from circulation, though it later reemerged as an acclaimed American classic.

Sharing a common documentary impulse with realist and naturalistic fiction, regionalism as a movement sought to chronicle the peculiarities of local ways of life before the coming wave of industrial standardization. Regionalist writers accentuated the differences among still-distant American locales, while at the same time partially demystifying regional differences among national audiences bent on postwar reunification.

Twain, London, and Bret Harte, among other western writers, simultaneously popularized and debunked the lusty legends of the Old West. A foppishly dressed New Yorker, Harte (1836-1902) struck it rich in California with his stories of the gold rush, especially "The Luck of Roaring Camp" (1868) and "The Outcasts of Poker Flat" (1869).

Interest in local-color writing about the South also revived in the aftermath of Reconstruction. Two black writers, Paul Laurence Dunbar (1872–1906) and Charles W. Chesnutt (1858–1932), brought their distinctive voices to late-nineteenth-century literature. In Dunbar's acclaimed book of poetry, *Lyrics of Lowly Life* (1896), he used black dialect and folklore to capture the spontaneity and richness of southern black culture. Chesnutt did the same through his short stories, collected in *The Conjure Women* (1899).

Pioneering women also contributed to the post-Civil War southern literary scene. The daring Louisiana feminist author Kate Chopin (1851-1904) wrote candidly about adultery, suicide, and women's ambitions in *The Awakening* (1899). Largely ignored after her death, Chopin was rediscovered by later readers who saw in her work the feminist yearnings that stirred beneath the surface of the Gilded Age.

Some important authors defied categorization. The gifted Henry Adams (1838–1918)—son of Charles Francis Adams, grandson of John Quincy Adams, and great-grandson of John Adams—turned unrivaled family connections into a prolific career as a historian, novelist, and critic. In his nine-volume *History of the United States During the Administrations of Jefferson and Madison* (1889–1891), Adams defended his patrician heritage from posthumous attack. In *Mont-Saint Michel and Chartres* (1905), Adams celebrated the bygone beauty and unity of the High Middle Ages. He channeled his own failure to come to grips with the chaotic modern age into his autobiographical work, *The Education of Henry Adams* (1907).

Artistic Triumphs

Realism and regionalism (more so than naturalism) also energized the American art world, much as they did the literary sphere. Philadelphia's native son Thomas Eakins (1836-1920) created a veritable artistic catalogue of his hometown's social, scientific, and sporting life at the end of the nineteenth century. Boston-born Winslow Homer (1836–1910), who as a youth had secretly drawn sketches in school, was perhaps the greatest painter of the group. Earthily American and largely resistant to foreign influences, Homer revealed rugged realism and boldness of conception. His canvases of the sea and of fisherfolk were masterly, and probably no American artist has excelled him in portraying the awesome power of the ocean.

Following in the footsteps of the expatriate writers Henry James and Edith Wharton, prominent American painters working in the realist style made their living abroad. James Whistler (1834–1903) did much of his work, including the celebrated portrait of his mother, in England. This eccentric and quarrelsome Massachusetts Yankee had earlier been dropped from West Point after failing chemistry. "Had silicon been a gas," he later jested, "I would have been a major general." Another gifted portrait painter, likewise self-exiled in Britain, was John Singer Sargent (1856–1925), whose depictions of the British nobility and American nouveau riche were highly prized. Mary Cassatt, an American exile in Paris, painted sensitive portrayals of women and children that earned her a place in the pantheon of the French Impressionist painters.

The most gifted sculptor yet produced by America was Augustus Saint-Gaudens (1848–1907). Born in Ireland of an Irish mother and a French father, he became an adopted American. Among his most moving works is the Robert Gould Shaw memorial, erected in Boston in 1897. It depicts Colonel Shaw, a young white "Boston Brahmin" officer, leading his black troops into battle in the Civil War.

Music, too, was gaining popularity. America of the 1880s and 1890s was assembling high-quality symphony orchestras, notably in Boston, Philadelphia, and Chicago. The famed Metropolitan Opera House of New York was erected in 1883. In its fabled "Diamond Horseshoe" the newly rich, often under the pretense of enjoying the imported singers, would flaunt their jewels, gowns, and furs. While symphonies and operas were devoted to bringing European music to elite American audiences, new strains of homegrown American music were sprouting in the South, another outgrowth of the regionalist trend. Black folk traditions such as spirituals and "ragged music" were evolving into the blues, ragtime, and jazz that would transform American popular music in the twentieth century.

A marvelous invention was the reproduction of music by mechanical means. The phonograph, though a squeakily imperfect instrument when invented by the deaf Edison, had by 1900 reached over 150,000 homes. Americans were rapidly being dosed with "canned music," as the "sitting room" piano increasingly gathered dust.

City Beautiful movement *A turn-of-the-century movement among progressive architects and city planners, who aimed to promote order, harmony, and virtue while beautifying the nation's new urban spaces with grand boulevards, welcoming parks, and monumental public buildings.*

Wrenching changes to the nation's cities inspired a new generation of architects and planners to reshape American urban space with the **City Beautiful movement**. Its proponents wanted the new American city not just to look beautiful but to convey a confident sense of harmony, order, and monumentality. To achieve these effects they copied European styles of beaux-arts classicism and planning ideas from the master builder of Paris, Baron Georges-Eugène Haussmann. Aiming to assert America's prominence among the greatest urban cultures of the Western world, architects constructed grandiose urban landmarks such as New York's Grand Central Terminal (1913). City planners such as Daniel Burnham redesigned Chicago and Washington, D.C., in the belief they could make them perfect, progressive cities, inspiring civic virtue in their inhabitants. To this end, they joined contemporary landscape architects and park builders like Frederick Law Olmsted, who sought to foster virtue and egalitarian values with his designs for New York's Central Park (1873) as well as the campus of Stanford University (1891).

World's Columbian Exposition (1893) *Americans saw this world's fair, held in Chicago, as their opportunity to claim a place among the world's most "civilized" societies, by which they meant the countries of western Europe. The fair honored art, architecture, and science, and its promoters built a mini-city in which to host the fair that reflected all the ideals of city planning popular at the time. For many, this was the high point of the City Beautiful movement.*

Burnham's first major project, which came to symbolize the City Beautiful movement, was his design for the great **World's Columbian Exposition**. Held in Chicago in 1893, the exposition, with Burnham's imposing landscape of pavilions and fountains, honored the four-hundredth anniversary of Columbus's first voyage. This so-called dream of loveliness was visited by 27 million people. It did much to raise American artistic standards and promote city planning, although many fair goers proved more interested in the contortions of a hootchy-kootchy dancer named "Little Egypt."

The Business of Amusement

Fun and frolic were not neglected by the workaday American. People sought their pleasures fiercely, as they had overrun their continent and built their cities fiercely. And now they had more time to play. Varied diversions beckoned. The legitimate stage still flourished, as appreciative audiences responded to the lure of the footlights. Vaudeville, with its coarse jokes and graceful acrobats, continued to be immensely popular during the 1880s and 1890s, as were minstrel shows in the South, now performed by black singers and dancers rather than by whites wearing blackface.

The circus—high tented and multiringed—finally emerged full-blown. Phineas T. Barnum, the master showman who had early discovered that "the public likes to be humbugged," joined hands with James A. Bailey in 1881 to stage the "Greatest Show on Earth."

Colorful "Wild West" shows, first performed in 1883, were even more distinctively American. Headed by the knightly, goateed, and free-drinking William F. ("Buffalo Bill") Cody, the troupe included war-whooping Indians, live buffalo, and deadeye sharpshooters such as the girlish Annie Oakley. Rifle in hand, she could at thirty paces perforate a tossed-up card half a dozen times before it fluttered to the ground.

Baseball, already widely played before the Civil War, was clearly emerging as the national pastime, if not a national mania. A league of professional players was formed in the 1870s, and in 1888 an all-star baseball team toured the world, using the pyramids as a backstop while in Egypt. Basketball was invented in 1891 by James Naismith, a YMCA instructor in Springfield, Massachusetts. Designed as an active, indoor sport that could be played during the winter months, basketball spread rapidly and enjoyed enormous popularity in the next century.

The trend toward spectator sports was exemplified by football, a rugged game that at first used the dangerous flying-wedge formation. The Yale–Princeton game of 1893 drew fifty thousand cheering fans, while foreigners jeered that the nation was getting "sports on the brain."

Even pugilism, with its long background of bare-knuckle brutality, gained a new gloved respectability in 1892. Agile "Gentleman Jim" Corbett wrested the world championship from the aging and alcoholic John L. Sullivan, the "Boston Strong Boy."

The land of the skyscraper was plainly becoming more standardized, owing largely to the new industrialization. Despite their distinct ethnic and racial neighborhoods, Americans increasingly shared a common culture—playing, reading, shopping, and talking alike. As the century drew to a close, the explosion of cities paradoxically made Americans more diverse and more similar at the same time.

Buffalo Bill Historical Center/The Art Archive at Art Resource, NY

Buffalo Bill's Wild West Show, ca. 1907 By the late 1800s, the "Wild West" was already passing into the realm of myth—and popular entertainment. Famed frontiersman William F. ("Buffalo Bill") Cody (1846–1917) made his fortune showing off his tame cowboys and Indians to enthusiastic urban audiences in Europe as well as the United States. Buffalo Bill's "Wild West"—an extravaganza featuring skilled horsemen from around the globe, including Turks, South American gauchos, Arabs, and Cossacks—was even more motley than the real one.

CHAPTER SUMMARY ★★★★★★★★★★★★★

The United States moved from the country to the city in the post–Civil War decades. Mushrooming urban development was attractive and exciting for many who migrated from farms and small towns, but urban development also created severe social problems, including overcrowding, slums, and a sharp divide between rich and poor.

After the 1880s the cities were also flooded with the "New Immigrants" from southern and eastern Europe. With their culturally different customs and non-Protestant religions, the newcomers often met with nativist hostility and discrimination. Congress began to throw up barriers to immigration, including a complete ban on the Chinese.

Religion had to adjust to social, cultural, and intellectual changes. The immigrant faiths of Roman Catholicism and Judaism gained considerable strength, while conflicts over evolution and biblical interpretation divided American Protestantism into fundamentalist and modernist wings.

American education expanded rapidly, especially at the secondary and collegiate levels; major new research universities were founded, both by state governments and by wealthy industrialists. Women's opportunities for education advanced in both separate institutions and coeducation. Black leaders Washington and Du Bois divided over the question of manual education versus development of an elite "talented tenth."

Significant conflicts over moral values, especially relating to sexuality and the role of women, began to appear. The new urban environment provided expanded opportunities for women but also created difficulties for the family. Families grew more isolated from society, the divorce rate rose, and average family size shrank.

American literature and the arts reflected the social and moral issues of the new urban, industrial age. The major literary and artistic movements of realism, naturalism, and regionalism reflected the new energy and sophistication of American culture, which gained national acclaim and increasing international respect. Leisure-time amusements and sports became enormously popular but also more standardized, in keeping with the new industrial nation.

KEY TERMS

New Immigrants (407)
settlement houses (410)
liberal Protestants (413)
Tuskegee Institute (416)
land-grant colleges (417)
pragmatism (418)
yellow journalism (418)
National American Woman Suffrage Association (NAWSA) (420)
Woman's Christian Temperance Union (WCTU) (421)
realism (421)
naturalism (421)
regionalism (421)
City Beautiful movement (424)
World's Columbian Exposition (424)

PEOPLE TO KNOW

Jane Addams
Charles Darwin
Booker T. Washington
W. E. B. Du Bois
Joseph Pulitzer
William Randolph Hearst
Carrie Chapman Catt
Mark Twain
Henry James
Winslow Homer
Augustus Saint-Gaudens

Chapter 26

The Great West and the Agricultural Revolution

1865–1896

• • •

Up to our own day American history has been in a large degree the history of the colonization of the Great West. The existence of an area of free land, its continuous recession, and the advance of American settlement westward, explain American development.

FREDERICK JACKSON TURNER, 1893

The White Man, who possesses this whole vast country from sea to sea, . . . cannot know the cramp we feel in this little spot, with the undying remembrance of the fact . . . that every foot of what you proudly call America, not very long ago belonged to the red man.

WASHAKIE (SHOSHONE INDIAN), 1878

Chapter Outline

- The Conquest of the Indians
- The Mining and Cattle Frontiers
- The Industrialization of Agriculture
- Farmers Protest
- Challenge from the People's Party
- Panic and Depression
- Bryan versus McKinley, 1896
- *Makers of America: The Plains Indians*
- *Examining the Evidence: Robert Louis Stevenson's Transcontinental Journey, 1879*
- *Thinking Globally: The Great Frontier*
- *Varying Viewpoints: Was the West Really "Won"?*

When the Civil War crashed to a close, the frontier line was still wavering westward. A long fringe of settlement, bulging outward here and there, ran roughly north through central Texas and on to the Canadian border. Between this jagged line and the settled areas on the Pacific slope, there were virtually no white people. The few exceptions were the islands of Mormons in Utah, occasional trading posts and gold camps, and several scattered Mexican settlements throughout the Southwest.

Sprawling in expanse, the Great West was a rough square that measured about a thousand miles on each side. Embracing mountains, plateaus, deserts, and plains, it was the habitat of the Indian, the buffalo, the wild horse, and the coyote. Twenty-five years later—that is, by 1890—the entire domain had been carved into states and the four territories of Utah, Arizona, New Mexico, and "Indian Territory," or Oklahoma. Pioneers flung themselves greedily on this enormous prize, as if to ravish it. Probably never before in human experience had so huge an area been transformed so rapidly.

FOCUS QUESTIONS

1. Why did the western Indians clash with the expanding United States? What were the causes and consequences of their defeat?
2. What were the principal stages of frontier settlement in the West, and how did each affect the region's development?

CHRONOLOGY

c. 1700–1800	▪ New Indian peoples move onto Great Plains
1858	▪ Pikes Peak gold rush
1859	▪ Nevada Comstock lode discovered
1862	▪ Homestead Act
1864	▪ Sand Creek massacre ▪ Nevada admitted to Union
1867	▪ National Grange organized
1876	▪ Battle of the Little Bighorn ▪ Colorado admitted to Union
1877	▪ Nez Percé War
1881	▪ Helen Hunt Jackson publishes *A Century of Dishonor*
1884	▪ Federal government outlaws Indian Sun Dance
1885	▪ Canadian Pacific Railway, first transcontinental rail line, completed across Canada
1885–1890	▪ Local chapters of Farmers' Alliances formed
1887	▪ Dawes Severalty Act
1889	▪ Oklahoma opened to U.S. citizen settlement
1889–1890	▪ North Dakota, South Dakota, Montana, Washington, Idaho, and Wyoming admitted to Union
1890	▪ Census Bureau declares frontier line ended ▪ Emergence of People's party (Populists) ▪ Battle of Wounded Knee
1891	▪ Construction of Trans-Siberian Railroad begins
1892	▪ Populist party candidate James B. Weaver polls more than 1 million votes in presidential election
1893	▪ Frederick Jackson Turner publishes "The Significance of the Frontier in American History"
1894	▪ "Coxey's Army" marches on Washington ▪ Pullman strike
1896	▪ McKinley defeats Bryan for presidency ▪ Utah admitted to Union
1897	▪ Dingley Tariff Act
1900	▪ Gold Standard Act
1907	▪ Oklahoma admitted to Union
1924	▪ Indians granted U.S. citizenship
1934	▪ Indian Reorganization Act

3. What was the significance of the closing of the frontier in 1890 for American history? Why did the West remain a distinctive American region even as it left its frontier past behind?
4. How did the agricultural revolution transform Great Plains farming? What were the consequences for farmers?
5. What were the causes of western and southern farmers' protests? How were their grievances expressed in the Populist Party?

The Clash of Cultures on the Plains

Native Americans numbered about 360,000 in 1860, many of them scattered across the vast grasslands of the trans-Missouri West. But to their misfortune, the Indians stood in the path of the advancing white pioneers. An inevitable clash loomed between an acquisitive, industrializing nation and the Indians' lifeways, highly evolved over centuries to adapt to the demanding environment of the sparsely watered western plains.

Migration and conflict—and sometimes dramatic cultural change—were no strangers to the arid West, even before the whites began to arrive. The Comanches had driven the Apaches off the central plains into the upper Rio Grande valley in the eighteenth century. Harried by the Mandans and Chippewas, the Cheyenne had abandoned their villages along the upper reaches of the Mississippi and Missouri Rivers in the century before the Civil War. The Sioux, displaced from the Great Lakes woodlands in the late eighteenth century, emerged onto the plains to prey upon the Crows, Kiowas, and Pawnees. Mounted on Spanish-introduced horses, peoples like the Cheyenne and the Sioux transformed themselves into wide-ranging nomadic traders and deadly efficient buffalo hunters.

When white soldiers and settlers edged onto the plains just before the Civil War, they accelerated a fateful cycle that exacerbated already fierce enmities among the Indians and ultimately undermined the foundations of Native American culture. White intruders unwittingly spread cholera, typhoid, and smallpox among the native peoples of the plains, with devastating results. Equally harmful, whites put further pressure on the shrinking bison population by hunting and by grazing their own livestock on the prairie grasses. As the once-mammoth buffalo herds dwindled, warfare intensified among the Plains tribes for ever-scarcer hunting grounds.

The federal government tried to sign treaties with various "chiefs" at Fort Laramie in 1851. The treaties marked the beginning of the **reservation system** in the West. But the white treaty makers misunderstood both Indian government and Indian society. "Tribes" and "chiefs" were often fictions of the white imagination, which could not grasp the fact that many Native Americans, living in scattered bands, recognized only the authority of their immediate families or perhaps a band elder. And the nomadic culture of the Plains Indians was utterly alien to the concept of living out one's life in the confinement of a defined territory.

reservation system *The system that allotted land with designated boundaries to Native American tribes in the West, beginning in the 1850s and ending with the Dawes Severalty Act of 1887. Within these reservations, most land was used communally, rather than owned individually. The U.S. government encouraged and sometimes violently coerced Native Americans to stay on the reservations at all times.*

In the 1860s the federal government tried to herd the Plains Indians into confines such as the "Great Sioux Reservation" in the Dakotas and the Indian Territory of present-day

Buffalo Bill Historical Center/The Art Archive at Art Resource, NY

The Buffalo Hunt, by Frederic Remington, 1890 A New Yorker who first went west at the age of nineteen as a cowboy and ranch cook, Remington (1861–1909) became the foremost artist of the vanishing way of life of the old Far West. Once a common sight on the high plains, the kind of buffalo kill that Remington records here was a great rarity by the time he painted this scene in 1890. The once-vast herds of bison had long since been reduced to a pitiful few by the white man's rifles and the increasingly concentrated use of the land by ever more constricted Indians.

One disheartened Indian complained to the white Sioux Commission created by Congress:

"Tell your people that since the Great Father promised that we should never be removed we have been moved five times. . . . I think you had better put the Indians on wheels and you can run them about wherever you wish."

Oklahoma, where dozens of southern Plains tribes were forced to move. Promises from Washington that they would be left alone and provided with food, clothing, and other supplies were often violated by corrupt federal agents who regularly cheated the Indians.

For more than a decade after the Civil War, fierce warfare between Indians and the U.S. Army raged in various parts of the West (see Map 26.1). Army troops met formidable adversaries in the Plains Indians, whose superb horsemanship gave them baffling mobility. Fully one-fifth of all U.S. Army personnel on the frontier were African American—dubbed "Buffalo Soldiers" by the Indians.

Receding Native Population

The Indian wars in the West were often savage clashes. Aggressive whites sometimes shot peaceful Indians on sight. At Sand Creek, Colorado, in 1864, Colonel J. M. Chivington's militia massacred in cold blood some four hundred Indians who apparently thought they had been promised immunity. Women were shot praying for mercy, children had their brains dashed out, and braves were tortured, scalped, and unspeakably mutilated.

Cruelty begot cruelty. In 1866 a Sioux war party ambushed Captain William Fetterman's command of eighty-one soldiers and civilians in Wyoming's Bighorn Mountains, killing every man and mutilating the corpses. As the cycle of ferocious warfare intensified, the federal government in 1868 abandoned its attempt to construct the Bozeman Trail through Montana. The sprawling "Great Sioux Reservation" was guaranteed to the Sioux tribes.

But in 1874 a new round of warfare with the Plains Indians began when Colonel George Armstrong Custer, a famed Civil War officer, led a "scientific" expedition into the Black Hills of South Dakota and announced that he had discovered gold there. Hordes of greedy gold-seekers soon swarmed into the Sioux lands. The aggrieved Sioux, aided by the Cheyenne and Arapaho, took to the warpath, inspirited by the influential and wily Sitting Bull.

Colonel Custer's Seventh Cavalry set out to suppress the Indians and force them onto the reservation. Attacking what turned out to be a superior force of some 2,500 well-armed warriors along the Little Bighorn River in present-day Montana, the "White Chief with Yellow Hair" and about 250 officers and men were completely wiped out in 1876 when two supporting columns failed to come to their rescue.* But in a series of battles across the northern plains in the ensuing months, the U.S. Army relentlessly hunted down the Indians who had destroyed Custer's troops.

The Nez Percé Indians of northeastern Oregon were goaded into a daring fight in 1877, when U.S. authorities tried to herd them onto a reservation. Chief Joseph finally surrendered his band after a tortuous, seventeen-hundred-mile, three-month trek across the Continental Divide toward Canada. There Chief Joseph hoped to rendezvous with Sitting Bull, who had taken refuge north of the border after the **Battle of the Little Bighorn**. Betrayed into believing that they would be returned to their ancestral lands in Idaho, the Nez Percés instead were sent to a dusty reservation in Kansas, where 40 percent of them perished from disease. The survivors eventually returned to Idaho.

Fierce Apache tribes of Arizona and New Mexico were the most difficult to subdue. Led by Geronimo, whose eyes blazed with hatred of the whites, they were pursued into Mexico by federal troops. Scattered remnants of the warriors were finally persuaded to surrender after the Apache women had been exiled to Florida.

Battle of the Little Bighorn (1876)
A particularly violent example of the warfare between whites and Native Americans in the late nineteenth century, also known as "Custer's Last Stand." In two days, June 25 and 26, 1876, the combined forces of 2,500 Sioux, Cheyenne, and Arapaho Indians defeated and killed more than 250 U.S. soldiers, including Colonel George Custer. The battle came as the U.S. government tried to compel Native Americans to remain on the reservations and Native Americans tried to defend territory from white gold-seekers. This Indian advantage did not last long, however, as the union of these Indian fighters proved tenuous and the U.S. Army soon exacted retribution.

*When whites annihilated Indians, the engagement (in white history books) was usually a "battle"; when Indians slaughtered whites, it was a "massacre." "Strategy," when practiced by Indians, was "treachery."

This relentless fire-and-sword policy of the whites at last shattered the spirit of the Indians. The vanquished Native Americans were finally ghettoized on reservations, where they were compelled to eke out an existence as wards of the government.

The "taming" of the Indians was engineered by a number of factors. Of cardinal importance was the federal government's willingness to back its land claims with military force. Almost as critical was the railroad, which shot an iron arrow through the heart of the West. The Indians were also ravaged by the white people's diseases, to which they showed little resistance, and by their firewater, which they could resist even less.

Above all, the virtual extermination of the buffalo doomed the Plains Indians' nomadic way of life. When the white Americans ventured onto the Great Plains after the Civil War, some 15 million buffalo, or American bison, still blackened the prairies. In 1868 a Kansas Pacific locomotive

Civil War veteran and long-time Indian fighter General Philip Sheridan (1831–1888) reflected on the wars against the Indians:

"We took away their country and their means of support, broke up their mode of living, their habits of life, introduced disease and decay among them, and it was for this and against this they made war. Could anyone expect less?"

What alternative paths might U.S.-Indian relations have followed during the era of America's intensive westward expansion?

Map 26.1 Indian Wars, 1860–1890 Surrendering in 1877, Chief Joseph of the Nez Percés declared: "Our chiefs are killed. . . . The old men are all dead. . . . The little children are freezing to death. . . . I want to have time to look for my children. . . . Hear me, my chiefs. My heart is sick and sad. From where the sun now stands I will fight no more forever."

Contending Voices

The Ghost Dance and the Wounded Knee Massacre

James McLaughlin (1842–1923), a U.S. Indian Service agent involved in events precipitating the bloody 1890 confrontation at Wounded Knee, depicted the Sioux's "Ghost Dance" as a dangerous practice hindering their assimilation and progress:

"The [Ghost Dance] doctrine was artfully framed to appeal to the cupidity of the Indian and to inflame him against the whites, carrying with it promise of return to the free life, with plenty of buffalo and no prospect of work. . . . A more pernicious system of religion could not have been offered to a people who stood on the threshold of civilization, and who hungered for a realization of dreams that would free them from present poverty, probable hunger, and the prospect of toil."

Oglala Sioux chief Black Elk (1863–1950), meanwhile, recounted the horrifying aftermath of the massacre instigated by that very civilizing impulse:

"[A]fter the soldiers marched away from their dirty work, a heavy snow began to fall. . . . The snow drifted deep in the crooked gulch, and it was one long grave of butchered women and children and babies, who had never done any harm and were only trying to run away."

had to wait eight hours for a herd to amble across the tracks. These huge, shaggy, lumbering beasts were the staff of life for the Native Americans (see "Makers of America: The Plains Indians," p. 433). Their flesh provided food; their dried dung provided fuel ("buffalo chips"); their hides provided clothing, lariats, and harnesses.

With the building of the railroad, the massacre of the herds began in deadly earnest. The creatures were slain for their hides, for a few choice cuts of meat, or for sheer amusement. The telescope-eyed crack shot William "Buffalo Bill" Cody killed over four thousand buffalo in eighteen months while employed by the Kansas Pacific. "Sportsmen" on lurching railroad trains would lean out the windows and blaze away at the animals to satisfy their lust for slaughter or excitement. Such wholesale butchery left fewer than a thousand buffalo alive by 1885, and the once-numerous beasts were in danger of complete extinction. The whole story is a shocking example of the greed and waste that accompanied the conquest of a continent.

The End of the Trail

By the 1880s, the national conscience began to stir uneasily over the plight of the Indians. Helen Hunt Jackson, a Massachusetts writer of children's literature, pricked the moral sense of Americans in 1881 when she published *A Century of Dishonor*. The book chronicled the sorry record of governmental ruthlessness and chicanery in dealing with the Indians. Her later novel *Ramona* (1884), a story of injustice to the California Indians, sold some 600,000 copies and further inspired sympathy for the Indians.

Debate seesawed. Humanitarians wanted to treat the Indians kindly and persuade them thereby to "walk the white man's road." Yet hard-liners insisted on the current policy of forced containment and brutal punishment. Neither side showed much respect for Native American culture. Christian reformers, who often administered educational facilities on the reservations, sometimes withheld food to force the Indians to give up their tribal religion and assimilate to white society. In 1884 these zealous white souls joined with military men in successfully persuading the federal government to outlaw the sacred Sun Dance. When the "Ghost Dance" religious movement later spread to the Dakota Sioux, the army bloodily stamped it out in 1890 at the so-called **Battle of Wounded Knee**. In the fighting thus provoked, an estimated two hundred Indian men, women, and children were killed, as well as twenty-nine invading soldiers.

Battle of Wounded Knee (1890) *A battle between the U.S. Army and the Dakota Sioux, in which two hundred Native Americans and twenty-nine U.S. soldiers died. Tensions erupted violently over two major issues: the Sioux practice of the "Ghost Dance," which the U.S. government had outlawed, and the dispute over whether Sioux reservation land would be broken up because of the Dawes Act.*

The misbegotten offspring of the movement to reform Indian policy was the **Dawes Severalty Act** of 1887. Reflecting the forced-civilization views of the reformers, the act dissolved many tribes as legal entities, wiped out tribal ownership of land, and set up individual Indian family heads with 160 free acres. If the Indians behaved themselves like "good white settlers," they would get full title to their holdings, as well as citizenship, in twenty-five years. The probationary period was later extended, but full citizenship was granted to all Indians in 1924.

Dawes Severalty Act (1887) *An act that broke up Indian reservations and distributed land to individual households. Leftover land was sold for money to fund U.S. government efforts to "civilize" Native Americans.*

The federal efforts at forced assimilation included boarding schools for Indian children, beginning in 1879 with the Carlisle Indian School in Pennsylvania. "Kill the Indian and save the man" was the motto for these schools, where Native American children, separated from their tribes, were taught English and inculcated with white values and customs.

The Plains Indians

The last of the native peoples of North America to bow before the military might of the whites, the Indians of the northern Great Plains long defended their lands and their ways of life against the American cavalry. After the end of the Indian wars, toward the close of the nineteenth century, the Plains tribes struggled on, jealously guarding their communities against white encroachment, preserving much of their ancestral culture to this day.

Before Europeans first appeared in North America in the sixteenth century, the vast plain from northern Texas to Saskatchewan was home to some thirty different tribes. There was no typical Plains Indian; each tribe spoke a distinct language, practiced its own religion, and formed its own government.

Indians had first trod the arid plains to pursue sprawling herds of antelope, elk, and especially buffalo, but they were not exclusively hunters. The women were expert farmers, coaxing lush gardens of pumpkins, squash, corn, and beans from the dry but fertile soil. Still, the shaggy pelt and heavy flesh of the buffalo constituted the staff of life on the plains. Hunted by men, the great bison were butchered by women, who used every part of the beast. They fashioned horns into spoons, turned sinews into strong bowstrings, and wove buffalo hair into ropes. Meat not immediately eaten was pounded into pemmican—thin strips of smoked or sun-dried buffalo flesh mixed with berries.

The nomadic Plains Indians had long dispersed in small bands during the winter, gathering together in the summer for larger-scale religious ceremonies, socializing, and communal buffalo hunts. Then in the sixteenth century, the mounted Spanish *conquistadores* ventured into the New World, and their steeds quickly spread over the plains. The horse revolutionized Indian societies, turning the Plains tribes into efficient hunting machines that promised to banish hunger from the prairies. But the plains pony also ignited a furious competition for grazing land and for ever more horses, so wars became increasingly bitter and frequent.

The European invasion soon eclipsed the short-lived era of the horse. After many battles the Plains Indians found themselves crammed together on tiny reservations, clinging with tired but determined fingers to their traditions. Although much of Plains Indian culture persists to this day, the Indians' free-ranging way of life passed into memory. As Black Elk, an Oglala Sioux, put it, "Once we were happy in our own country and we were seldom hungry, for then the two-legged and the four-legged lived together like relatives, and there was plenty for them and for us. But then the Wasichus [white people] came, and they made little islands for us . . . and always these islands are becoming smaller, for around them surges the gnawing flood of Wasichus."

A Comanche Village, by George Catlin, 1834

The Indian spokesman Plenty Coups said in 1909:

"I see no longer the curling smoke rising from our lodge poles. I hear no longer the songs of the women as they prepare the meal. The antelope have gone; the buffalo wallows are empty. Only the wail of the coyote is heard. The white man's medicine is stronger than ours. . . . We are like birds with a broken wing."

The government also sent "field matrons" to the reservations to teach Native American women the art of sewing and to preach the virtues of chastity and hygiene.

The Dawes Act struck directly at tribal organization and tried to make rugged individualists out of the Indians. This legislation ignored the inherent reliance of traditional Indian culture on tribally held land. The forced-assimilation doctrine of the Dawes Act remained the cornerstone of the government's official Indian policy until the Indian Reorganization Act ("the Indian New Deal") of 1934 partially reversed the individualistic approach and belatedly tried to restore the tribal basis of Indian life (see p. 561).

Under these new federal policies, defective though they were, the Indian population started to mount slowly. The total number had been reduced by 1887 to about 243,000—the result of bullets, bottles, and bacteria—but the census of 2010 counted about 5.3 million Native Americans and Alaska Natives, urban and rural.

Mining: From Dishpan to Ore Breaker

The conquest of the Indians and the coming of the railroad were life-giving boons to the mining frontier. The golden gravel of California continued to yield "pay dirt," and in 1858 an electrifying discovery of gold convulsed Colorado. Avid "fifty-niners" rushed west with "Pike's Peak or Bust" inscribed on the canvas of their covered wagons. But there were more miners than minerals, and many gold-grubbers creaked wearily back with the added inscription, "Busted, by Gosh." But some bearded fortune seekers stayed on in Colorado to mine silver or extract nonmetallic wealth from the earth in the form of golden grain.

"Fifty-niners" also poured feverishly into Nevada in 1859, after the fabulous Comstock lode had been uncovered. A fantastic amount of gold and silver, worth more than $340 million, was mined by the "Kings of the Comstock" from 1860 to 1890. The scantily populated state of Nevada was prematurely railroaded into the Union in 1864, partly to provide three electoral votes for President Lincoln.

Smaller "lucky strikes" drew frantic gold and silver seekers into Montana, Idaho, and other western states. Boomtowns, known as "Helldorados," sprouted like magic. Every third cabin was a saloon, where sweat-stained miners drank adulterated liquor ("rotgut") in the company of accommodating women. Lynch law and vigilante justice, as in early California, preserved a crude semblance of order. And when the "diggings" petered out, the gold seekers decamped, leaving behind picturesque "ghost towns," such as Virginia City, Nevada. Begun with a boom, these towns ended with a whimper.

Once the loose surface gold was gobbled up, ore-breaking machinery was imported to smash the gold-bearing quartz. This operation was so expensive that it could ordinarily be undertaken only by corporations pooling the wealth of stockholders. Gradually the age of big business came to the **mining industry**. Dusty, bewhiskered miners, dishpans in hand, were replaced by impersonal corporations with their costly machinery and trained engineers.

mining industry *After gold and silver strikes in Colorado, Nevada, and other western territories in the second half of the nineteenth century, fortune-seekers by the thousands rushed to the West to dig. These metals were essential to U.S. industrial growth and were also sold into world markets. After surface metals were removed, people sought ways to extract ore from under the ground, leading to the development of heavy mining machinery. This, in turn, led to the consolidation of the mining industry, because only big companies could afford to buy and build the necessary machines.*

Yet the mining frontier had played a vital role in conquering the continent. Magnet-like, it attracted population and wealth while advertising the wonders of the Wild West. Women as well as men found opportunity, running boardinghouses or working as prostitutes. They won a kind of equality on the rough frontier that earned them the vote in Wyoming (1869), Utah (1870), Colorado (1893), and Idaho (1896) long before their sisters in the East could cast a ballot. The amassing of precious metals helped finance the Civil War, facilitated the building of railroads, and intensified the already bitter conflict between whites and Indians. The outpouring of silver and gold enabled the Treasury to resume specie payments in 1879 and injected the silver issue into American politics. Finally, the mining frontier added to American folklore and literature, as the writings of Bret Harte and Mark Twain so colorfully attest.

Beef Bonanzas and the Long Drive

Dressed to Kill Cowboys came in all varieties and sizes in the wild and woolly frontier West—and in all kinds of garb as well.

When the Civil War ended, the grassy plains of Texas supported several million tough, longhorn cattle. These scrawny beasts were killed primarily for their hides. There was no way to get their meat profitably to market.

The problem of marketing was neatly solved when the transcontinental railroads thrust their iron fingers into the West. Cattle could now be shipped alive to the stockyards, and "beef barons" such as the Swifts and Armours turned the highly industrialized meatpacking business into a main pillar of the economy. Drawing on the gigantic stockyards at Kansas City and Chicago, the meatpackers could ship their fresh products to the East Coast in the newly perfected refrigerator cars.

A spectacular feeder of the new slaughterhouses was the "Long Drive." Texas cowboys—black, white, and Mexican—drove herds numbering from one thousand to ten thousand head slowly over the unfenced and unpeopled plains until they reached a railroad terminal. The bawling beasts grazed en route on the free government grass. Favorite terminal points were fly-specked "cow towns" such as Dodge City and Abilene (Kansas), Ogallala (Nebraska), and Cheyenne (Wyoming). From 1866 to 1888, bellowing herds totaling over 4 million steers were driven northward from the beef bowl of Texas.

What the Lord giveth, the Lord also can taketh away. The railroad made the Long Drive; and the railroad unmade the Long Drive, primarily because the locomotives ran both ways. The same rails that bore the cattle from the open range to the kitchen range brought out the sheepherder and the homesteader. Both of these intruders, sometimes amid flying bullets, built barbed-wire fences that were too numerous to be cut down by the cowboys. Furthermore, the terrible winter of 1886–1887, with blinding blizzards and temperatures reaching 68 degrees below zero, left thousands of dazed cattle starving and freezing. The only escape for the stockman was to make cattle raising a big business and avoid the perils of overproduction. Breeders learned to fence their ranches, lay in winter feed, import blooded bulls, and produce fewer and meatier animals. They also learned to organize. The Wyoming Stock-Growers, Association, especially in the 1880s, virtually controlled the territory and its legislature.

This was the heyday of the cowboy. The equipment of the lone cowhand—from "shooting irons" and ten-gallon hat to chaps and spurs—served a useful, not an ornamental, function. A "genuwine" gun-toting cowpuncher, riding where men were men and smelled like horses, could justifiably boast of his toughness.

These bowlegged Knights of the Saddle, with colorful trappings and cattle-lulling songs, became part of American folklore. Many of them, perhaps five thousand, were blacks, who especially enjoyed the new-found freedom of the open range.

The Farmers' Frontier

Miners and cattlemen created the romantic legend of the West, but it was the sober sodbuster who wrote the final chapter of frontier history. A fresh day dawned for western farmers with the **Homestead Act** of 1862. The new law allowed a settler to acquire as much as 160 acres of land (a quarter-section) by living on it for five years, improving it, and paying a nominal fee of about $30.

Homestead Act (1862) *A federal law that sold settlers 160 acres of land for about $30 if they lived on it for five years and improved it by, for instance, building a house on it. The act helped make land accessible to hundreds of thousands of westward-moving settlers, but many people also found disappointment when their land was infertile or they saw speculators grabbing up the best land.*

The Homestead Act marked a drastic departure from previous policy. Before the act, public land had been sold primarily for revenue; now it was to be given away to encourage a rapid filling of empty spaces and to provide a stimulus to the family farm—"the backbone of democracy." During the forty years after its passage, about half a million families took advantage of the Homestead Act to carve out new homes in the vast open stretches. Yet five times that many families *purchased* their land from the railroads, land companies, or the states.

Nebraska State Historical Society

Nebraska Homesteaders in Front of Their Sod House, 1887 These two brothers and their families had escaped to Canada from the slave South during the Civil War. Returning to the United States in the 1880s, they took advantage of the Homestead Act to stake out farms in Custer County, Nebraska.

The Homestead Act often turned out to be a cruel hoax. The standard 160 acres, quite adequate in the well-watered Mississippi basin, frequently proved pitifully inadequate on the rain-scarce Great Plains. Thousands of homesteaders, perhaps two out of three, were forced to give up the one-sided struggle against drought.

Naked fraud was spawned by the Homestead Act and similar laws. Perhaps ten times more of the public domain wound up in the clutches of land-grabbing promoters than in the hands of bona fide farmers. Unscrupulous corporations would use "dummy" homesteaders—often their employees or immigrants bribed with cash or beer—to grab the best properties, containing timber, minerals, and oil. Settlers would later swear that they had "improved" the property by erecting a "twelve-by-fourteen" dwelling, which turned out to measure twelve by fourteen *inches*.

The railways also played a major role in developing the agricultural West, largely through the profitable marketing of crops. Some railroad companies induced Americans and European immigrants to buy the cheap land earlier granted to the railroads by the government. The Northern Pacific Railroad at one time had nearly a thousand paid agents in Europe distributing roseate leaflets in various languages.

Agriculture expanded once the myth of the Great American Desert was shattered. Pioneer explorers had assumed that the soil must be sterile, simply because it was not heavily watered and did not support immense forests. But once the prairie sod was broken with heavy iron plows pulled by four yokes of oxen, the earth proved astonishingly fruitful.

Lured by higher wheat prices resulting from crop failures elsewhere in the world, settlers in the 1870s rashly pushed still farther west, onto the poor, marginal lands beyond the

In making the arduous journey across the western prairies, many women settlers discovered new confidence in their abilities. Early on in her trek, Mary Richardson Walker (1811–1897) confided in her diary that:

"my circumstances are rather trying. So much danger attends me on every hand. A long journey before me, going I know not whither, without mother or sister to attend me, can I expect to survive it all?"

Only a month later, she recorded that:

"in the afternoon we rode thirty-five miles without stopping. Pretty well tired out, all of us. Stood it pretty well myself."

100th meridian. Geologist John Wesley Powell, explorer of the Colorado River's Grand Canyon, warned in 1874 that beyond the 100th meridian so little rain fell that agriculture was impossible without massive irrigation. Ignoring Powell's advice, farmers heedlessly chewed up the crusty earth in western Kansas, eastern Colorado, and Montana. They quickly went broke as a six-year drought in the 1880s further desiccated the already dusty region. In the wake of the devastating drought, some pioneers tried the new "dry farming" technique of frequent shallow cultivation. But over time "dry farming" created a finely pulverized surface soil that contributed to the "Dust Bowl" several decades later (see pp. 560–561).

Other adaptations to the western environment were more successful. Tough strains of wheat, resistant to cold and drought, were imported from Russia and blossomed into billowing yellow carpets. Barbed wire, perfected by Joseph F. Glidden in 1874, solved the problem of how to build fences on the treeless prairies. Eventually, federally financed irrigation projects on a colossal scale caused the Great American Desert to bloom. In the long run, hydraulic engineers had more to do with shaping the modern West than all the trappers, miners, cavalrymen, and cowboys ever did.

The Great West experienced a fantastic surge in migration from the 1870s to the 1890s. A parade of new western states proudly joined the Union. Boomtown Colorado, offspring of the Pikes Peak gold rush, was greeted in 1876 as the "Centennial State." In 1889–1890 a Republican Congress, eagerly seeking more Republican electoral and congressional votes, admitted in a wholesale lot six new states: North Dakota, South Dakota, Montana, Washington, Idaho, and Wyoming. The Mormon church—belatedly, in many Americans' eyes—banned polygamy in 1890, but not until 1896 was Utah deemed worthy of admission. Only Oklahoma, New Mexico, and Arizona remained to be lifted into statehood from contiguous territory on the mainland of North America.

In a last gaudy fling, the federal government made available to settlers vast stretches of fertile plains formerly occupied by the Indians in Oklahoma ("the Beautiful Land"). Scores of overeager and well-armed "sooners," illegally jumping the gun, entered Oklahoma Territory before the opening date. They had to be evicted repeatedly by federal troops. On April 22, 1889, all was in readiness for the legal opening, and some fifty thousand "boomers" were poised expectantly on the boundary line. At high noon the bugle shrilled, and a horde of "eighty-niners" poured in on lathered horses or careening vehicles. That night a lonely spot on the prairie had mushroomed into the tent city of Guthrie, with over ten thousand people. By the end of the year Oklahoma boasted 60,000 inhabitants, and Congress made it a territory. In 1907 it became the "Sooner State."

The Fading Frontier

In 1890—a watershed date—the superintendent of the census announced that for the first time in America's experience a frontier line was no longer discernible. All the unsettled areas were now broken into by isolated bodies of American settlement. The "closing" of the frontier inspired one of the most influential essays ever written about American history—Frederick Jackson Turner's "The Significance of the Frontier in American History," in 1893.

As the nineteenth century neared its sunset, the westward-tramping American people were disturbed to find that their fabled free land was going or had gone. The secretary of war had prophesied in 1827 that five hundred years would be needed to fill the West. But as the nation finally recognized that its land was not inexhaustible, seeds were planted to preserve the vanishing resource. The government set aside lands for national parks—first Yellowstone in 1872, followed by Yosemite and Sequoia in 1890.

The frontier was more than a place: It was also a state of mind and a symbol of opportunity. Its passing ended a romantic phase of the nation's internal development and created new economic and psychological problems. Traditionally footloose, Americans have been notorious for their mobility. The nation's farmers, unlike the peasants of Europe, seldom remained rooted to their soil.

Much has been said about the frontier as a "safety valve." The theory is that when hard times came, the unemployed who cluttered the city pavements merely moved west, took up farming, and prospered. In truth, relatively few eastern city dwellers migrated to the frontier during depressions. Most of them did not know how to farm; few of them

Examining the Evidence

Robert Louis Stevenson's Transcontinental Journey, 1879

The celebrated Scottish writer Robert Louis Stevenson, author of such enduring classics as *Treasure Island, Kidnapped*, and *The Strange Case of Dr. Jekyll and Mr. Hyde*, journeyed from Scotland to California in 1879 to rendezvous with his American fiancée, Frances Osbourne. Between New York and San Francisco, Stevenson traveled on the transcontinental railroad line completed just ten years earlier, and he dutifully recorded his impressions of America, the West in particular, as he made his way toward California. Stevenson's account of his trip provides an unusually gifted writer's vivid portrait of the trans-Mississippi West at the close of the era of the Indian wars. Like all travelogues, Stevenson's colorful tale may reveal as much about the traveler as it does about the things he saw. Yet historians frequently make use of such documents to reconstruct the original appearance and texture of places that were once the exotic destinations of adventurous travelers, before they were transformed by the onrush of modernity.

1. In the passages reproduced here, inspired by the view as Stevenson's train passed through Nebraska and Wyoming, what features of the landscape does the author find most remarkable?
2. What does Stevenson's extended comparison of traveling across the plains to being "at sea" convey about cultured European views of the American West in the late nineteenth century? Why do the buffalo and the cabins he sees not disrupt his perception of the West's "emptiness"?
3. What is Stevenson's view of the Indians, as well of those who built the railroad (including Chinese laborers)?

THE PLAINS OF NEBRASKA

. . . We were at sea—there is no other adequate expression—on the plains of Nebraska. . . . It was a world almost without a feature; an empty sky, an empty earth; front and back, the line of railway stretched from horizon to horizon, like a cue across a billiard-board; on either hand, the green plain ran till it touched the skirts of heaven. . . . [G]razing beasts were seen upon the prairie at all degrees of distance and diminution; and now and again we might perceive a few dots beside the railroad which grew more and more distinct as we drew nearer till they turned into wooden cabins, and then dwindled and dwindled in our wake until they melted into their surroundings, and we were once more alone upon the billiard-board. The train toiled over this infinity like a snail; and being the one thing moving, it was wonderful what huge proportions it began to assume in our regard. . . .

[That] evening we left Laramie [Wyoming]. . . . And yet when day came, it was to shine upon the same broken and unsightly quarter of the world. Mile upon mile, and not a tree, a bird, or a river. Only down the long, sterile cañons, the train shot hooting and awoke the resting echo. That train was the one piece of life in all the deadly land; it was the one actor, the one spectacle fit to be observed in this paralysis of man and nature. And when I think how the railroad has been pushed through this unwatered wilderness and haunt of savage tribes, and now will bear an emigrant for some £12 from the Atlantic to the Golden Gates; how at each stage of the construction, roaring, impromptu cities, full of gold and lust and death, sprang up and then died away again, and are now but wayside stations in the desert; how in these uncouth places pig-tailed Chinese pirates worked side by side with border ruffians and broken men from Europe, talking together in a mixed dialect, mostly oaths, gambling, drinking, quarrelling and murdering like wolves; how the plumed hereditary lord of all America heard, in this last fastness, the scream of the 'bad medicine waggon' charioting his foes; and then when I go on to remember that all this epical turmoil was conducted by gentlemen in frock coats, and with a view to nothing more extraordinary than a fortune and a subsequent visit to Paris, it seems to me, I own, as if this railway were the one typical achievement of the age in which we live, as if it brought together into one plot all the ends of the world and all the degrees of social rank, and offered to some great writer the busiest, the most extended, and the most varied subject for an enduring literary work. . . .

Source: *Across the Plains* by Robert Louis Stevenson (New York: Charles Scribner's Sons, 1897).

could raise enough money to transport themselves west and then pay for livestock and expensive machinery.

But the safety-valve theory does have some validity. Free acreage did lure to the West a host of immigrant farmers who otherwise might have remained in the eastern cities to clog the job markets and crowd the slums. And the very *possibility* of westward migration may have induced urban employers to maintain wage rates high enough to discourage workers from leaving.

But the real safety valve by the late nineteenth century was in western cities like Denver and San Francisco, where failed farmers, busted miners, and displaced easterners found ways to seek their fortunes. Indeed, after about 1880 the area from the Rocky Mountains to the Pacific Coast was the most urbanized region in America, measured by the percentage of people living in cities.

U.S. history cannot be properly understood unless it is viewed in light of the westward-moving experience. As Frederick Jackson Turner wrote, "American history has been in a large degree the history of the colonization of the Great West." The story of settling and taming the trans-Mississippi West in the late nineteenth century was but the last chapter in the saga of the colonizing of various American "wests" since Columbus's day.

And yet the trans-Mississippi West formed a distinct chapter in that saga and retains even to this day much of its uniqueness. There the Native American peoples waged their last struggle against colonization, and there most Native Americans live today. There "Anglo" culture collided most directly with Hispanic culture, and the Southwest remains the most Hispanicized region in America. There America faced across the Pacific to Asia, and there most Asian Americans dwell today. There the scale and severity of the environment posed their largest challenges to human ambitions, and there the environment continues to mold social and political life, and the American imagination, as in no other part of the nation.

The westward-moving pioneers and the country they confronted have assumed mythic proportions in the American mind. For better or worse, those pioneers planted the seeds of American civilization in the immense western wilderness. The life we live, they dreamed of; the life they lived, we can only dream.

The Farm Becomes a Factory

The situation of American farmers, once jacks-and-jills-of-all-trades, was rapidly changing. They had raised their own food, fashioned their own clothing, and bartered for other necessities with neighbors. Now high prices persuaded farmers to concentrate on growing single "cash" crops, such as wheat or corn, and use their profits to buy foodstuffs at the general store and manufactured goods in town or by mail order. The Chicago firm of Aaron Montgomery Ward sent out its first catalogue—a single sheet—in 1872. Farmers were becoming a part of the world economy, as their crops journeyed by rail and ship to distant parts of the globe.

Large-scale farmers were now both specialists and businesspeople. As cogs in the vast industrial machine, they were intimately tied to banking, railroading, and manufacturing. They had to buy expensive machinery to plant and to harvest their crops. The speed of harvesting wheat was immensely increased in the 1870s by the invention of the twine binder and then in the 1880s by the "combine"—the combined reaper-thresher, which was drawn by twenty to forty horses and both reaped and bagged the grain.

This amazing **mechanization of agriculture** in the postwar years was almost as striking as the mechanization of industry. Those who remained on the farms achieved miracles of production, making America the world's breadbasket and butcher shop. The farm was attaining the status of a factory—an outdoor grain factory. The enormous bonanza wheat farms of the Minnesota-North Dakota area foreshadowed the gigantic agribusinesses of the next century. By 1890 at least a half-dozen of them were larger than fifteen thousand acres.

mechanization of agriculture *The development of engine-driven machines, like the combine, which helped to dramatically increase the productivity of land in the 1870s and 1880s. This process contributed to the consolidation of agricultural business that drove many family farms out of existence.*

Agriculture was a big business from the outset in California's phenomenally productive (and phenomenally irrigated) Central Valley. California farms, carved out of giant Spanish Mexican land grants and the railroads' huge holdings, were from the outset more than three times larger than the national average. With the advent of the railroad refrigerator car in the 1880s, California fruits and vegetable crops, raised on sprawling tracts by ill-paid migrant Mexican and Chinese farmhands, sold at a handsome profit in the rich urban markets of the East.

Deflation Dooms the Debtor

Once the farmers became chained to a one-crop economy—wheat or corn—they were in the same leaky boat with the southern cotton growers. The grain farmers were no longer the masters of their own destinies. They were engaged in one of the most fiercely competitive of businesses, for the price of their product was determined in a world market by the world output. If the wheat fields of Argentina, Russia, and other foreign countries flourished, the price of the farmers' grain would fall and American sodbusters would face ruin, as they did in the 1880s and 1890s.

Low prices and a deflated currency were the chief worries of the frustrated farmer in all regions. If a family had borrowed $1,000 in 1855, when wheat was worth about a dollar a bushel, they expected to pay back the equivalent of one thousand bushels, plus interest, when the mortgage fell due. But if they let their debt run to 1890, when wheat had fallen to about fifty cents a bushel, they would have to pay back the price of two thousand bushels for the $1,000 they had borrowed, plus interest. This unexpected burden struck them as unjust, though their steely-eyed creditors often branded the complaining farmers as slippery and dishonest rascals.

The deflationary pinch on the debtor flowed partly from the static money supply. There were simply not enough dollars to go around, and as a result prices were forced down. In 1870 the currency in circulation for each person was $19.42; in 1890 it was only $22.67. Yet during these twenty years, business and industrial activity, increasing manyfold, had intensified the scramble for available currency.

The forgotten farmers were caught on a treadmill. Despite unremitting toil, they operated year after year at a loss. In a vicious circle, their farm machinery increased their output of grain, lowered the price, and drove them even deeper into debt. Mortgages engulfed homesteads at an alarming rate; by 1890 Nebraska alone reported more than 100,000 farms blanketed with mortgages. The repeated crash of the sheriff-auctioneer's hammer kept announcing to the world that another sturdy American farmer had become landless in a landed nation.

Ruinous rates of interest, running from 8 to 40 percent, were charged on mortgages, largely by agents of eastern loan companies. The windburned sons and daughters of the sod, who felt that they deserved praise for developing the country, cried out in despair against the loan sharks and the Wall Street octopus.

Farm tenancy rather than farm ownership was spreading like stinkweed. The trend was especially marked in the sharecropping South, where cotton prices also sank dismayingly. By 1880 one-fourth of all American farms were operated by tenants. The United States was ready to feed the world, but under the new industrial feudalism the farmers were about to sink into a status suggesting Old World serfdom.

Unhappy Farmers

Even Mother Nature ceased smiling as her powerful forces conspired against agriculture. Mile-wide clouds of grasshoppers, leaving "nothing but the mortgage," periodically ravaged prairie farms. The terrible cotton boll weevil was also wreaking havoc in the South by the early 1890s.

The good earth was going sour. Floods washed the topsoil off millions of once-lush southern acres. A long succession of droughts seared the trans-Mississippi West, beginning in the summer of 1887. Whole towns were abandoned. "Going home to the wife's folks" and "in God we trusted, in Kansas we busted" were typical laments of many impoverished farmers as they fled their weather-beaten shacks and sunbaked sod houses.

To add to their miseries, the soil-tillers were gouged by their government—local, state, and national. Their land was overassessed, and they paid painful local taxes, whereas wealthy easterners could conceal their stocks and bonds in safe-deposit boxes. High protective tariffs in these years poured profits into the pockets of manufacturers. Farmers, on the other hand, had no choice but to sell their low-priced products in a fiercely competitive, unprotected world market, while buying high-priced manufactured goods in a protected home market.

The farmers were also "farmed" by the corporations. Trusts raised prices on farmers' machinery and supplies to extortionate levels, while operators pushed storage rates to the ceiling at grain warehouses and elevators. The railroad octopus often pushed freight rates so high that the farmers sometimes lost less if they burned their corn for fuel than if they shipped it.

Farmers still made up nearly one-half of the population in 1890, but they were hopelessly disorganized. The manufacturers and the railroad barons knew how to combine to promote their own interests, and so, increasingly, did industrial workers. But the farmers were by nature independent and individualistic—dead set against consolidation or regimentation. They never did organize successfully to restrict production until forced to do so by the federal government nearly half a century later, in Franklin Roosevelt's New Deal days. What they did manage to organize was a monumental political uprising.

The Farmers Take Their Stand

Agrarian unrest had flared forth earlier, in the Greenback movement shortly after the Civil War. Prices sagged in 1868, and a host of farmers unsuccessfully sought relief from low prices and high indebtedness by demanding an inflation of the currency with paper money.

The National Grange of the Patrons of Husbandry—better known as the Grange—was organized in 1867. Its leading spirit was Oliver H. Kelley, a shrewd and energetic Minnesota farmer then working as a clerk in Washington. Kelley's first objective was to

The Granger Collection, New York

The Farmers' Grievances This poster from 1875 expresses one of the agrarian radicals' fundamental premises: that all other walks of life were dependent—or even parasitic—on the indispensable work of farmers. In his famous "Cross of Gold" speech in 1896, Populist presidential candidate William Jennings Bryan put it this way: "Burn down your cities and leave our farms, and your cities will spring up again as if by magic; but destroy our farms and the grass will grow in the streets of every city in the country."

Thinking Globally

The Great Frontier

The American pioneers who surged westward in the nineteenth century were part of a great global land grab that changed lives and landscapes on several continents. From the Australian outback to the Canadian prairies, from the Argentine pampas to the Russian steppes and the African savannas, millions of mostly white settlers poured into vast new territories and claimed them as their own.

Everywhere, the settlers encountered indigenous peoples who had lived on those lands since time immemorial. With their superiority in weaponry, transportation, and political organization, everywhere the newcomers prevailed. By the century's close, they had displaced or destroyed countless native peoples and extended their dominion over parts of the planet once considered too remote or rugged to be habitable.

The American frontier soon became the stuff of legend, and even the subject of a scholarly explanation of American uniqueness—Frederick Jackson Turner's fabled "frontier thesis," which hailed the grit and gumption of the pioneers and commended them as the agents of civilization and democracy. Yet far from being unique, those westering Americans had much in common with settlers in sister societies abroad. Argentina had its cowboys (gauchos), and Australia had its colorful backcountry outlaws, such as Ned Kelly, whose exploits rivaled those of Billy the Kid. The Russians and South Africans had their own versions of "Manifest Destiny," and like the Americans they often cloaked them in the language of racial superiority.

The world's various frontiers also reflected the particularities of geography and history. Australians soon conceded that much of their continent—the world's driest—was too arid for traditional farming. Most of the Outback proved suitable only for enormous "sheep stations," sometimes measuring tens of thousands of acres. Consequently, small-farm homesteading of the American and Canadian type never took root, nor did cities of any consequence emerge in the parched Australian interior.

Canada's westward movement came later than that in the United States and proceeded more peaceably. Only after the Ottawa government promised in 1871 to build a transcontinental railroad connecting eastern Canada to its western provinces did settlement being in earnest. And unlike in America, where restless pioneers typically struck out on their own and made much mischief among themselves and with the Indians they encountered, in Canada, settlers were generally preceded by government authorities—usually the red-jacketed North-West Mounted Police, or "Mounties"—who established at least a semblance of order before large numbers of pioneers appeared on the scene. As a result, Canada's frontier was markedly less violent than America's. Canada, then and now a more law-abiding society than the United States, never had a "Wild West" like that of its southern neighbor.

In Argentina and Russia, inherited patterns of landholding and politics shaped their nineteenth-century frontiers. When Argentina's General Julio Roca vanquished the native Araucanians in 1879, he flung open the horizonless pampas to white settlement. But he also retained the venerable custom, handed down from Spanish colonial times, of apportioning the land in gigantic *estancias* (ranches) to a few favored fellow soldiers and friends. These lordly landowners then employed wage workers, mostly Italian immigrants, who turned the fertile Argentine interior into a beef bowl and breadbasket to the world. The immigrants themselves, however, had little hope of ever possessing land of their own.

Russia's frontier lay to the east and long felt the heavy hand of the tsar. For centuries autocratic rulers had strong-armed landowning nobles to move their serfs onto the "virgin lands" beyond the settled edge of European Russia. By the nineteenth century, imperial Russia had pushed its frontier onto the rolling steppes of central Asia, home to Tartars, Kalmyks, Kazahks, and myriad other indigenous peoples. Only military conquest and a strengthened state bureaucracy made possible European settlement in those regions. Between 1867 and 1897, more than a million of the tsar's subjects left for the hinterland. As elsewhere, the railroad proved essential to the growth of the tsarist empire, especially after the government began construction of the Trans-Siberian line in 1891.

enhance the lives of isolated farmers through social, educational, and fraternal activities. The Grange spread like an old-time prairie fire and by 1875 claimed some 800,000 members, chiefly in the Midwest and South.

The Grangers gradually raised their goals from individual self-improvement to improvement of the farmers' collective plight. In a determined effort to escape the clutches of the trusts, they established cooperatively owned stores, grain elevators, and warehouses, and even made a failed attempt to manufacture harvesting machinery.

Embattled Grangers also went into politics, enjoying their most gratifying success in the grain-growing regions of the upper Mississippi Valley. There, through state legislation,

Royal Canadian Mounted Police/Picture Research Consultants & Archives

North-West Mounted Police, c. 1890 Empowered by an act of Parliament in 1873 to establish Canadian authority and order in the Northwest Territories, this force made frontier settlement somewhat more peaceful in Canada than in the United States. In 1920 the North-West Mounted Police absorbed the Dominion Police and became the famed Royal Canadian Mounted Police, or "Mounties."

The Dutch-descended Afrikaners, or Boers, in southern Africa found their frontier to the north, and unlike their American counterparts, they made scant claim to be spreading democracy. Rather, they sought to escape British rule in the Cape Colony—in particular, to escape from the threat of racial equality for blacks after Britain abolished slavery in the 1830s. The Afrikaners' "Great Trek" took them into the land of the Zulus, who ferociously resisted the oncoming Boers but eventually, like indigenous peoples everywhere, were forced to submit to white rule.

In the Americas, Australia, Asia, and Africa, the great frontier of the nineteenth century was the companion of conquest. The frontier brought opportunity to some and oppression to others. In many places it nurtured democracy; elsewhere it invigorated autocracy. And everywhere it expanded the domains of European civilization—for better or worse.

they strove to regulate railway rates and the storage fees charged by railroads and grain elevator operators. Many of the state courts, notably in Illinois, were disposed to recognize the principle of public control of private business for the general welfare. A number of the so-called Granger Laws, however, were bitterly fought through the high courts by the well-paid lawyers of the "interests." Following judicial reverses, most severely at the hands of the Supreme Court in the *Wabash* decision of 1886 (see p. 390), the Grangers' influence faded.

Farmers' grievances likewise found a vent in the Greenback Labor party, which combined the inflationary appeal of the earlier Greenbackers with a program for improving the lot of labor. In 1878, the high-water mark of the movement, the Greenback Laborites polled over a million votes and elected fourteen members of Congress. In the presidential election of 1880 the Greenbackers ran General James B. Weaver, an old Granger who spoke to perhaps half a million citizens but polled only 3 percent of the popular vote.

Prelude to Populism

A striking manifestation of rural discontent came through the Farmers' Alliance, founded in Texas in the late 1870s (see p. 379). Farmers came together in the Alliance to socialize, but more importantly they hoped to break the strangling grip of the railroads and manufacturers through cooperative buying and selling. Local chapters spread throughout the South and the Great Plains during the 1880s, until by 1890 members numbered more than a million hard-bitten souls.

Unfortunately, the Alliance weakened itself by ignoring the plight of landless tenant farmers, sharecroppers, and farmworkers. Even more debilitating was the Alliance's exclusion of blacks, who counted for nearly half the agricultural population of the South. In the 1880s a separate Colored Farmers' National Alliance emerged to attract black farmers, and by 1890 membership numbered more than 250,000. The long history of racial division in the South, however, made it difficult for white and black farmers to work together in the same organization.

Populists *Officially known as the People's Party, the Populists represented Westerners and Southerners who believed that U.S. economic policy inappropriately favored Eastern businessmen instead of the nation's farmers. Their proposals included nationalization of the railroads, a graduated income tax, and, most significantly, the unlimited coinage of silver.*

Out of the Farmers' Alliances a new political party emerged in the early 1890s—the People's Party. Better known as the **Populists**, these frustrated farmers attacked Wall Street and the "money trust." They called for nationalizing the railroads, telephones, and telegraph; instituting a graduated income tax; and building government-owned warehouses where they could store their grain until market prices rose. They also wanted the free and unlimited coinage of silver—yet another of the debtors' demands for inflation that echoed continuously throughout the Gilded Age.

Numerous fiery prophets leapt forward to trumpet the Populist cause. The free coinage of silver struck many Populists as a cure-all, especially after William Hope Harvey produced an enormously popular pamphlet called *Coin's Financial School* (1894). Illustrated by clever woodcuts, the booklet showed how "Coin" Harvey overwhelmed the bankers and professors of economics with his brilliant arguments on behalf of free silver. Another notorious spellbinder was red-haired Ignatius Donnelly of Minnesota, three times elected to Congress. The queen of the Populist "calamity howlers" was Mary Elizabeth ("Mary Yellin") Lease, a tall, athletic woman known as the "Kansas Pythoness." She reportedly demanded that Kansans should raise "less corn and more hell." The *New York Evening Post* snarled, "We don't want any more states until we can civilize Kansas." To many easterners, complaint, not corn, was rural America's staple crop.

Yet the Populists, despite their oddities, were not to be laughed away. They were leading a deadly earnest and impassioned campaign to relieve the farmers' many miseries. Smiles faded from Republican and Democratic faces alike as countless thousands of Populists began to sing "Good-bye, My Party, Good-bye."

In 1892 the Populists had jolted the traditional parties by winning several congressional seats and polling more than 1 million votes for their presidential candidate, James B. Weaver. Racial divisions continued to hobble the Populists in the South, but in the West their ranks were swelling. Could the People's Party now reach beyond its regional bases in agrarian America, join hands with urban workers, and mount a successful attack on the northeastern citadels of power?

Coxey's Army and the Pullman Strike

The panic of 1893 and the severe ensuing depression strengthened the Populists' argument that farmers and laborers alike were being victimized by an oppressive economic and political system. Ragged armies of the unemployed began marching to protest their plight. In the growing hordes of displaced industrial toilers, the Populists saw potential political allies.

The most famous marcher was "General" Jacob S. Coxey, a wealthy Ohio quarry owner who set out for Washington in 1894 with a small band of supporters. His platform included a demand that the government relieve unemployment by an inflationary $500 million federal public works program. Coxey himself rode in a carriage with his wife and infant son, appropriately named Legal Tender Coxey, while his tiny "army" tramped along behind, singing:

We're coming, Grover Cleveland,
500,000 strong.
We're marching on to Washington
to right the nation's wrong.

After the Pullman strike collapsed, Eugene Debs (1855–1926) said:

"No strike has ever been lost."

In 1897 he declared:

"The issue is Socialism versus Capitalism. I am for Socialism because I am for humanity."

The "Commonweal Army" of Coxeyites finally straggled into the nation's capital, but the "invasion" took on the aspects of a comic opera when "General" Coxey and his "lieutenants" were arrested for walking on the grass.

Elsewhere, violent flare-ups accompanied labor protests, notably in Chicago. Most dramatic was the crippling **Pullman strike** of 1894. Eugene V. Debs, a charismatic labor leader, had helped organize the American Railway Union of about 150,000 members. The Pullman Palace Car Company, which maintained a model town near Chicago for its employees, was hit hard by the depression and cut wages by about one-third, while holding the line on rent for company houses. The workers finally struck—in some places overturning Pullman cars—and paralyzed railway traffic from Chicago to the Pacific Coast.

Pullman strike (1894) *A strike by railroad workers upset by drastic wage cuts. The strike was led by socialist Eugene Debs but not supported by the American Federation of Labor. Eventually President Grover Cleveland intervened, and federal troops forced an end to the strike. The strike highlighted both divisions within labor and the government's new willingness to use armed force to combat work stoppages.*

The turmoil in Chicago was serious but not completely out of hand. At least this was the judgment of Governor John Peter Altgeld of Illinois, a friend of the downtrodden, who had pardoned the Haymarket Square anarchists the year before (see p. 400). But U.S. attorney general Richard Olney, an archconservative and an ex-railroad attorney, urged the dispatch of federal troops on the legal grounds that the strikers were interfering with the U.S. mail. President Cleveland supported Olney with the ringing declaration, "If it takes the entire army and navy to deliver a postal card in Chicago, that card will be delivered."

To the delight of conservatives, federal troops, bayonets fixed, crushed the Pullman strike. Debs was sentenced to six months' imprisonment for contempt of court because he had defied a federal court injunction to cease striking. Ironically, the lean labor agitator spent much of his enforced leisure reading radical literature, which led to his later leadership of the socialist movement in America.

Embittered cries of "government by injunction" now burst from organized labor. This was the first time that such a legal weapon had been used conspicuously by Washington to break a strike, and it was all the more distasteful because defiant workers who were held in contempt could be imprisoned without jury trial. Signs multiplied that employers were striving to smash labor unions by court action. Nonlabor elements of the country, including the Populists and other debtors, were likewise incensed. They saw in the brutal Pullman episode further proof of an unholy alliance between business and the courts.

Golden McKinley and Silver Bryan

The smoldering grievances of the long-suffering farmers and depression-plagued laborers gave ominous significance to the election of 1896. Conservatives of all stripes feared an impending upheaval, while down-and-out husbandmen and discontented workers cast about desperately for political salvation. Increasingly, monetary policy—whether to maintain the gold standard or inflate the currency by monetizing silver—loomed as the issue on which the election would turn.

The leading candidate for the Republican presidential nomination in 1896 was former congressman William McKinley of Ohio, sponsor of the ill-starred tariff bill of 1890 (see p. 379). He had been a Civil War officer; he hailed from the electorally potent state of Ohio; and he could point to long years of honorable service in Congress.

As a presidential candidate, McKinley was largely the creature of a fellow Ohioan, Marcus Alonzo Hanna, who had made his fortune in the iron business and now coveted

The Sacrilegious Candidate A hostile cartoonist makes sport of Bryan's flamboyant Cross of Gold speech in 1896.

the role of president maker. As a wholehearted Hamiltonian, Hanna believed that a prime function of government was to aid business. Hanna also believed that in some measure prosperity "trickled down" to the laborer, whose dinner pail would be full when business flourished. Critics assailed this idea as equivalent to feeding the horses in order to feed the sparrows.

The hardheaded Hanna, although something of a novice in politics, organized his preconvention campaign for McKinley with consummate skill and a liberal outpouring of his own money. The convention steamroller, well lubricated with Hanna's dollars, nominated McKinley on the first ballot at St. Louis in June 1896. The Republican platform condemned Democratic incapacity in hard times and declared for the gold standard.

Dissension riddled the Democratic camp. Cleveland no longer led his party. The depression had driven the last nail into his political coffin. Dubbed "the Stuffed Prophet," he was undeniably the most unpopular man in the country. Labor-debtor groups remembered too vividly his intervention in the Pullman strike, the backstairs Morgan bond deal, and especially his stubborn hard-money policies. Ultraconservative in finance, Cleveland now looked more like a Republican than a Democrat on the money issue.

Rudderless, the Democratic convention met in Chicago in July 1896, with the silverites lusting for victory. Shouting insults at the absent Cleveland, the delegates refused to endorse their own administration. They had the enthusiasm and the numbers; all they lacked was a leader.

A new Moses suddenly appeared in the person of William Jennings Bryan of Nebraska. Then only thirty-six years of age and known as "the Boy Orator of the Platte,"* Bryan stepped confidently onto the platform before fifteen thousand people. His masterful presence was set off by a peninsular jaw and raven-black hair. He radiated honesty, sincerity, and energy.

The convention-hall setting was made to order for a magnificent oratorical effort. A hush fell over the delegates as Bryan stood before them. With an organ-like voice that rolled into the outer corners of the huge hall, he delivered a fervent plea for silver. Rising to supreme heights of eloquence, he thundered, "We will answer their demands for a gold standard by saying to them: 'You shall not press down upon the brow of labor this crown of thorns, you shall not crucify mankind upon a cross of gold!'"

The Cross of Gold speech was a sensation. Swept off its feet in a tumultuous scene, the Democratic convention nominated Bryan the next day. The platform demanded inflation through the unlimited coinage of silver at the ratio of 16 ounces of silver to 1 of gold, though the market ratio was about thirty-two to one. This meant that the silver in a dollar would be worth about fifty cents.

Democratic "Gold Bugs," unable to swallow Bryan, bolted their party over the silver issue. A conservative senator from New York, when asked if he was a Democrat still, reportedly replied, "Yes, I am a Democrat still—very still." The Democratic minority, including Cleveland, charged that the Populist silverites had stolen both the name and the clothes of their party. Many of them, including Cleveland, not too secretly hoped for a McKinley victory.

The Populists now faced a dilemma because the Democratic majority had appropriated their main plank—"16 to 1," that "heaven-born ratio." The bulk of the Populists, fearing a hard-money McKinley victory, endorsed "fusion" with the Democrats and Bryan for president, sacrificing their identity in the mix. Singing "The Jolly Silver Dollar of the Dads," they became in effect the "Demo-Pop" or "Popocratic" party, though a handful of the original Populists refused to support Bryan and went down with their colors nailed to the mast.

*One contemporary sneered that Bryan, like the Platte River, was "six inches deep and six miles wide at the mouth."

Class Conflict: Plowholders Versus Bondholders

Mark Hanna smugly assumed that he could make the tariff the focus of the campaign. But Bryan, a dynamo of energy, forced the free-trade issue into a back seat when he took to the stump in behalf of free silver. Sweeping through 27 states and traveling 18,000 miles, Bryan made nearly 600 speeches—36 in one day—and even invaded the East, "the enemy's country." Vachel Lindsay caught the spirit of his oratorical orgy:

Prairie avenger, mountain lion,
Bryan, Bryan, Bryan, Bryan,
Gigantic troubadour, speaking like a siege gun,
*Smashing Plymouth rock with his boulders from the West.**

Free silver became almost as much a religious as a financial issue. Hordes of fanatical free-silverites, singing "No Crown of Thorns, No Cross of Gold," hailed Bryan as the messiah to lead them out of the wilderness of debt.

Bryan created panic among eastern conservatives with his threat of converting their holdings overnight into fifty-cent dollars. "In God we trust, with Bryan we bust," the Republicans sneered, while one clergyman cried, "That platform was made in Hell." Widespread fear of Bryan and the "silver lunacy" enabled "Dollar Mark" Hanna, now chairman of the Republican National Committee, to shine as a money raiser. He "shook down" the trusts and plutocrats and piled up an enormous "slush fund" for a "campaign of education"—or of propaganda, depending on one's point of view. Republicans appealed to the "belly vote" with their prize slogan, "McKinley and the full dinner pail." The McKinleyites amassed the most formidable political campaign chest thus far in American history—about $16 million, as contrasted with about $1 million for the poorer Democrats (roughly "16 to 1"). With some justification, the Bryanites accused Hanna of "buying" the election and of floating McKinley into the White House on a tidal wave of mud and money.

Bryan's cyclonic campaign began to lose steam as the weeks passed. Fear was probably Hanna's strongest ally, as it was Bryan's worst enemy. Some Republican businesspeople threatened wage reductions or told their workers not to come to work on Wednesday morning if Bryan won. Such were some of the "dirty tricks" of the "Stop Bryan, Save America" crusade.

Hanna's campaign methods paid off. On election day McKinley triumphed decisively. The vote was 271 to 176 in the Electoral College, and 7,102,246 to 6,492,559 in the popular vote. Driven by fear and excitement, an unprecedented outpouring of voters flocked to the polls. McKinley ran strongly in the populous East, where he carried every county of New England, and in the upper Mississippi Valley. Bryan's states, concentrated in the debt-burdened South and the trans-Mississippi West, involved more acreage than McKinley's but less population (see Map 26.2).

The free-silver election of 1896 was perhaps the most significant political turning point since Lincoln's victories in 1860 and 1864. Despite Bryan's strength in the South and West, the results vividly demonstrated his lack of appeal to the unmortgaged farmer and especially to the eastern urban laborer. Many wage earners in the East, threatened as they were by free silver, voted for their jobs and full dinner pails. Living precariously on a fixed wage, the factory workers had no reason to favor inflation, which was the heart of the Bryanites' program.

The Bryan-McKinley battle heralded the advent of a new era in American politics. The outcome represented a resounding victory for big business, the big cities, middle-class values, and financial conservatism. Bryan's defeat marked the last serious effort to win the White House with mostly agrarian votes. The future of presidential politics lay not on the farms, with their dwindling populations, but in the mushrooming cities, with their growing hordes of freshly arriving immigrants.

The Grand Old Party's smashing victory of 1896 also heralded a Republican grip on the White House for sixteen consecutive years—indeed, for all but eight of the next

---

*Reprinted with permission of Macmillan Publishing Company, Inc., from *Collected Poems*, by Vachel Lindsay. Copyright 1920 by Macmillan Publishing Company, Inc., renewed 1948 by Elizabeth C. Lindsay.

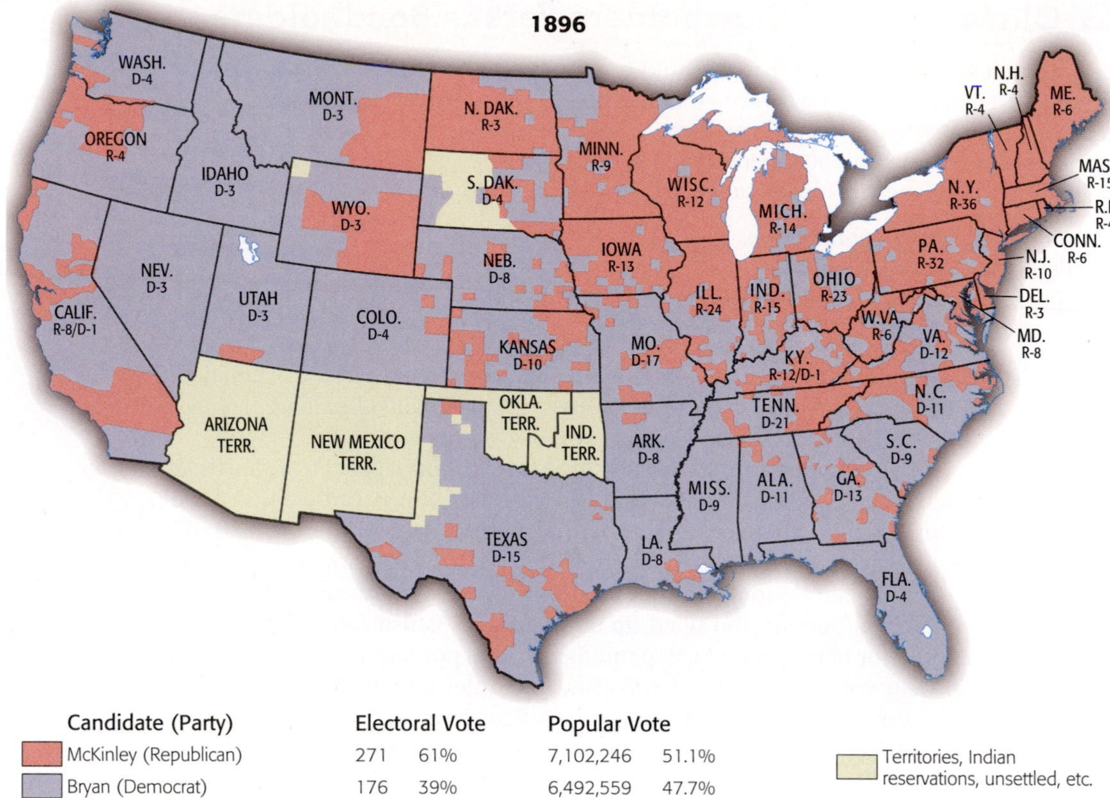

Map 26.2 Presidential Election of 1896 (with electoral vote by state) This election tolled the death knell of the Gilded Age political party system, with its razor-close elections, strong party loyalties, and high voter turnouts. Bryans' sweep of the southern states and strong showing in the West gave him only 176 electoral votes to McKinley's 271 from the more populous North and East. For years after 1896, Republicans predominated, and citizens showed declining interest in either joining parties or voting.

thirty-six years. McKinley's election thus imparted a new character to the American political system. The long reign of Republican political dominance that it ushered in was accompanied by diminishing voter participation in elections, the weakening of party organizations, and the fading away of issues such as the money question and civil-service reform, which came to be replaced by concern for industrial regulation and the welfare of labor. Scholars have dubbed this new political era the period of the **fourth party system**, signaling a break with the previous "third party system," in place since 1860, of remarkably high voter turnouts and close contests between Democrats and Republicans.

fourth party system *A term scholars have used to describe national politics from 1896 to 1932, when Republicans had a tight grip on the White House and issues such as industrial regulation and labor concerns became paramount, replacing older concerns such as civil-service reform and monetary policy.*

Republican Stand-pattism Enthroned

An eminently "safe" McKinley took the inaugural oath in 1897. Though a man of considerable ability, he was an ear-to-the-ground politician who seldom got far out of line with majority opinion. His cautious, conservative nature caused him to shy away from the flaming banner of reform. Business was given a free rein, and the trusts, which had trusted him in 1896, were allowed to develop more mighty muscles without serious restraints.

Almost as soon as McKinley took office, the tariff issue, which had played second fiddle to silver in the "Battle of '96," quickly forced itself to the fore. In due course the Dingley Tariff Bill was jammed through the House in 1897 under the pounding gavel of the rethroned "Czar" Reed. The proposed new rates were high, but not high enough to satisfy the paunchy lobbyists, who once again descended upon the Senate. Over 850 amendments were tacked onto the overburdened bill. The resulting piece of patchwork finally established the average rates at 46.5 percent, substantially higher than the Democratic Wilson-Gorman Act of 1894 and in some categories even higher than the McKinley Act of 1890.

With the return of prosperity under McKinley in 1897, the money issue that overshadowed politics since the Civil War gradually faded away. The **Gold Standard Act** of 1900, passed over last-ditch silverite opposition, provided that paper currency was to be freely redeemed in gold. Electrifying discoveries of new gold deposits in Canada's fabled Klondike, as well as in Alaska, South Africa, and Australia, brought huge new quantities of gold onto world markets. Moderate inflation thus took care of the currency needs of an explosively expanding nation, as its circulatory system greatly improved. The tide of "silver heresy" rapidly receded, and the "Popocratic" fish were left gasping high and dry on a golden-sanded beach.

Gold Standard Act (1900) *An act that guaranteed that paper currency would be redeemed freely in gold, putting an end to the already dying "free-silver" campaign.*

Varying Viewpoints

Was the West Really "Won"?

For more than half a century, the Turner thesis dominated historical writing about the West. In his famous essay of 1893, "The Significance of the Frontier in American History," historian Frederick Jackson Turner argued that not only the West but the national character had been uniquely shaped by the westward movement. The struggle to overcome the hazards of the western wilderness had transformed *Europeans* into tough, inventive, and self-reliant *Americans*.

Turner's thesis raised a question that Americans found especially intriguing in 1893, just three years after the census superintendent had declared the frontier closed forever. What new forces, Turner asked, would shape a distinctive American national character now that the testing ground of the frontier had been plowed and tamed? Turner's hypothesis that the American character was forged in the western wilderness is surely among the most provocative statements ever made about the nation's formative influences. But as the frontier era recedes ever further into the past, scholars are less persuaded that Turner's thesis adequately explains the national character.

Modern historians like David J. Weber challenge Turner's assumptions by suggesting that the line of the frontier did not define the quavering edge of "civilization," but instead marked the boundary between diverse and equally legitimate cultures. The frontier should therefore be understood not as the place where "civilization" triumphed over "savagery," but as the principal site of interaction between those cultures.

Several so-called New Western historians take this argument still further. Scholars such as Patricia Nelson Limerick, Richard White, and Donald Worster suggest that the cultural and ecological damage inflicted by advancing "civilization" must be reckoned with in any final accounting of what these pioneers accomplished. These same scholars insist that the West did not lose its regional identity after 1890. The West, they argue, is still a unique part of the national mosaic, a region whose history, culture, and identity remain every bit as distinctive as those of New England or the Old South.

But where Turner saw the frontier as the principal shaper of the region's character, the New Western historians emphasize the effects of ethnic and racial confrontation, topography, climate, and the roles of government and big business as the factors that have made the modern West. The pioneer "conquests" of Native Americans and Hispanics were less than complete, they contend, and the West therefore remains, uniquely among American regions, an unsettled arena of commingling and competition among these groups. Moreover, in these accounts the West's distinctively challenging climate and geography yielded to human habitation not through the efforts of heroic individual pioneers, but only through massive corporate—and especially federal government—investments in projects like the transcontinental railroads and irrigation systems. Such developments still give western life its special character today.

CHAPTER SUMMARY ★★★★★★★★★★★★★

At the close of the Civil War, the Great Plains and Mountain West were still controlled by Indians who hunted buffalo on horseback and fiercely resisted white encroachment on their land and way of life. But the whites' railroads, mining, and livestock activities gradually broke up the Indians' land, while disease and the destruction of the buffalo reduced their numbers and ended their way of life. After a series of sharp military clashes, the federal government eventually forced the Indians onto largely barren reservations.

Attempting to coerce Indians into adopting white ways, the government passed the Dawes Act, which eliminated tribal ownership of land, while often insensitive "humanitarians" created a network of Indian boarding schools that further assaulted traditional culture.

The mining and cattle frontiers created colorful chapters in western history. Farmers carried out the final phase of settlement, lured by free homesteads, railroads, and irrigation. The census declared the end of the frontier in 1890, concluding a formative phase of American history. The frontier was less of a "safety valve" for American class conflict than many believed, but it may have had some impact on keeping American wage rates relatively high. The newest western frontier was actually in western cities, which helped make the West the most urbanized (by percentage) region of the United States by the 1890s.

Beginning in the 1870s, farmers began pushing onto the treeless prairies beyond the 100th meridian, using techniques of dry farming that gradually contributed to soil erosion. Irrigation projects, later financed by the federal government, allowed specialized farming in some areas of the arid West, including California. The "closing" of the frontier in 1890 signified the end of traditional westward expansion, but the Great West remained a unique social and environmental region.

As the farmers opened vast new lands, agriculture was becoming a mechanized business dependent on specialized production and international markets. Once declining prices and other woes doomed the farmers to permanent debt and dependency, they began to protest their lot, first through the Grange and then through the Farmers' Alliances, the prelude to the People's (Populist) Party. The Populists made spectacular gains in the West and the South, but racial divisions undermined southern Populism.

The major depression of the 1890s accelerated farmer protest and labor unrest and strikes, leading to a growing class conflict. In 1896 pro-silver hero William Jennings Bryan captured the Democratic Party's nomination, and with Populist support as well led a fervent campaign against the "goldbug" Republicans and their candidate William McKinley. McKinley's success in winning urban workers away from Bryan proved a turning point in American politics, signaling the triumph of the city, the middle class, and a new party system. The return of prosperity in McKinley's first term ended the late-nineteenth-century preoccupation with monetary issues and made Republicans the dominant party for two generations.

KEY TERMS

reservation system (429)
Battle of the Little Bighorn (430)
Battle of Wounded Knee (432)
Dawes Severalty Act (432)
mining industry (434)
Homestead Act (435)
mechanization of agriculture (439)
Populists (444)
Pullman strike (445)
fourth party system (448)
Gold Standard Act (449)

PEOPLE TO KNOW

Frederick Jackson Turner
Jacob S. Coxey
William McKinley
Marcus Alonzo Hanna

Chapter 27

Empire and Expansion

1890–1909

• • •

We assert that no nation can long endure half republic and half empire, and we warn the American people that imperialism abroad will lead quickly and inevitably to despotism at home.

DEMOCRATIC NATIONAL PLATFORM, 1900

Chapter Outline

In the years immediately following the Civil War, Americans remained astonishingly indifferent to the outside world. Enmeshed in struggles over Reconstruction and absorbed in efforts to heal the wounds of civil war, build an industrial economy, make their cities habitable, and settle the sprawling West, most citizens took little interest in international affairs. But the sunset decades of the nineteenth century witnessed a momentous shift in U.S. foreign policy. America's new diplomacy reflected the far-reaching changes that were reshaping agriculture, industry, and the social structure. American statesmen also responded to the intensifying scramble of other nations for international advantage in the dawning "age of empire." By the beginning of the twentieth century, America had acquired its own empire, an astonishing departure from its venerable anticolonial traditions. The world now had to reckon with a new great power, potentially powerful but with diplomatic ambitions and principles that remained to be defined.

FOCUS QUESTIONS

1. Why did the United States abandon its historic isolationism and turn outward to develop imperial great power ambitions at the end of the nineteenth century?
2. What were the causes of the Spanish-American War, and how did the war lead to the acquisition of an American empire in the Philippines, Guam, and Puerto Rico?
3. Why was there such a vigorous national debate over imperialism, and how did the Filipino rebellion against U.S. rule contribute to doubts about America's overseas role?
4. How did the United States become increasingly involved in China and the rest of East Asia, and what were the Open Door policy toward China and Theodore Roosevelt's diplomacy with Japan intended to achieve?
5. How did Theodore Roosevelt vigorously assert American power in Panama and elsewhere in Latin America, and why did the "Roosevelt Corollary" to the Monroe Doctrine stir controversy?

CHRONOLOGY

1820	▪ New England missionaries arrive in Hawaii
1889	▪ Samoa crisis with Germany ▪ Pan-American Conference
1890	▪ Mahan publishes *The Influence of Sea Power upon History*
1891	▪ New Orleans crisis with Italy
1892	▪ Valparaiso crisis with Chile
1893	▪ White planter revolt in Hawaii ▪ Cleveland refuses Hawaii annexation
1895	▪ Cubans revolt against Spain
1895–1896	▪ Venezuelan boundary crisis with Britain
1898	▪ *Maine* explosion in Havana harbor ▪ Spanish-American War ▪ Teller Amendment ▪ Dewey's victory at Manila Bay ▪ Hawaii annexed
1899	▪ Senate ratifies treaty acquiring Philippines ▪ Aguinaldo launches rebellion against United States in the Philippines ▪ First American Open Door note
1900	▪ Hawaii receives full territorial status ▪ Foraker Act for Puerto Rico ▪ Boxer Rebellion and U.S. military expedition to China ▪ Second Open Door note ▪ McKinley defeats Bryan for presidency
1901	▪ Supreme Court *Insular Cases* ▪ Platt Amendment ▪ McKinley assassinated; Roosevelt becomes president ▪ Filipino rebellion suppressed ▪ Hay-Pauncefote Treaty with Britain gives United States exclusive right to build Panama Canal
1902	▪ U.S. troops leave Cuba ▪ Colombian senate rejects U.S. proposal for canal across Panama
1903	▪ Panamanian revolution against Colombia ▪ Hay-Bunau-Varilla Treaty gives United States control of Canal Zone in newly independent Panama
1904	▪ Roosevelt Corollary to the Monroe Doctrine
1904–1914	▪ Construction of the Panama Canal
1905	▪ United States takes over Dominican Republic customs service ▪ Roosevelt mediates Russo-Japanese peace treaty
1906	▪ San Francisco Japanese education crisis ▪ Roosevelt arranges Algeciras conference
1906–1909	▪ U.S. Marines occupy Cuba
1907	▪ Great White Fleet makes world voyage
1907–1908	▪ "Gentlemen's Agreement" with Japan
1908	▪ Root-Takahira agreement
1917	▪ Puerto Ricans granted U.S. citizenship

Imperialist Stirrings

Many developments fed the nation's ambition for overseas expansion. Both farmers and factory owners began to look beyond American shores as agricultural and industrial production boomed. Many Americans believed that the United States had to expand or explode. Their country was bursting with a new sense of power generated by the robust growth in population, wealth, and productive capacity—and it was trembling from the hammer blows of labor violence and agrarian unrest. Overseas markets might provide a safety valve to relieve those pressures.

Other forces whetted the popular appetite for overseas involvement. The lurid "yellow press" of Joseph Pulitzer and William Randolph Hearst described foreign exploits as manly adventures, the kind of dashing derring-do that was the stuff of young boys' dreams. Pious missionaries, inspired by books such as the Reverend Josiah Strong's *Our Country: Its Possible Future and Its Present Crisis*, looked overseas for new souls to harvest. Strong trumpeted the superiority of Anglo-Saxon civilization and summoned Americans to spread their religion and their values to "backward" peoples. At the same time, aggressive Americans such as Theodore Roosevelt and Congressman (later Senator) Henry Cabot Lodge were interpreting Darwinism to mean that the earth belonged to the strong and the fit—that is, to Uncle Sam. This view was strengthened as latecomers to the colonial scramble began to scoop up leavings from the banquet table of earlier diners in Africa, China, and elsewhere. If America was to survive in the competition of modern nation-states, perhaps it, too, would have to become an imperial power.

The development of a new steel navy also focused attention overseas. Captain Alfred Thayer Mahan's book of 1890, *The Influence of Sea Power upon History, 1660–1783*, argued that control of the sea was the key to world dominance. Mahan helped stimulate the naval race among the great powers that gained momentum around the turn of the century. Red-blooded Americans joined in the demands for a mightier navy and for an American-built isthmian canal between the Atlantic and the Pacific.

The undiplomatic note to Britain by Secretary of State Richard Olney (1835–1917) read:

"Today the United States is practically sovereign on this continent, and its fiat is law upon the subjects to which it confines its interposition. . . . Its infinite resources combined with its isolated position render it master of the situation and practically invulnerable as against any or all other powers."

America's new international assertiveness manifested itself in a number of diplomatic crises or near-wars in the late 1880s and early 1890s. The American and German navies nearly came to blows in 1889 over the faraway Samoan Islands in the South Pacific, which were formally divided between the two nations in 1899. (German Samoa eventually became an independent republic; American Samoa remains an American territory.) The lynching of eleven Italians in New Orleans in 1891 brought America and Italy to the brink of war, until the United States agreed to pay compensation. In the ugliest affair, American demands on Chile after the deaths of two American sailors in the port of Valparaiso in 1892 made hostilities between the two countries seem inevitable. The threat of attack by Chile's modern navy spread alarm on the Pacific Coast, until the Chileans finally agreed to pay an indemnity. The willingness of Americans to risk war over such distant and minor disputes demonstrated the aggressive new national mood.

America's new belligerence combined with old-time anti-British feeling to create a serious crisis between the United States and Britain in 1895–1896. The jungle boundary between British Guiana and Venezuela had long been in dispute, but the discovery of gold in the contested area brought the conflict between Britain and Venezuela to a head. President Cleveland and his pugnacious secretary of state, Richard Olney, stepped into the affair with a combative note to Britain invoking the Monroe Doctrine and declaring that the United States was now calling the tune in the Western Hemisphere. Unimpressed British officials shrugged off Olney's salvo as just another twist of the lion's tail and replied that the affair was none of Uncle Sam's business. President Cleveland—"mad clear through," as he put it—sent a bristling special message to Congress that called for a U.S. commission to determine where the line ought to go and threatened war if the British would not accept the boundary it set.

The entire country, irrespective of political party, was swept off its feet in an outburst of hysteria. War seemed inevitable. Fortunately, sober second thoughts prevailed on both sides of the Atlantic. A rising challenge from Kaiser Wilhelm's Germany and a looming war with the Dutch-descended Boers in South Africa left Britain in no mood for war with America. London backed off and consented to arbitration.

The chastened British, their eyes fully opened to the European peril, now cultivated Yankee friendship and inaugurated an era of "patting the Eagle's head," which replaced a century or so of America's "twisting the lion's tail." Sometimes called the **Great Rapprochement**—or reconciliation—between the United States and Britain, the new Anglo-American cordiality became a cornerstone of both nations' foreign policies as the twentieth century opened.

Great Rapprochement *After decades of occasionally "twisting the lion's tail," American diplomats began to cultivate close, cordial relations with Great Britain at the end of the nineteenth century—a relationship that would intensify further during World War I.*

Spurning the Hawaiian Pear

Enchanted Hawaii had early attracted the attention of Americans. In the morning years of the nineteenth century, the breeze-brushed islands were a way station and provisioning point for Yankee shippers, sailors, and whalers. In 1820 the first New England missionaries arrived, preaching the twin blessings of Protestant Christianity and protective calico. Soon American sugar production flourished on the Hawaiian Islands, and the U.S. government assumed a greater interest. The State Department, beginning in the 1840s, sternly warned other powers to keep their hands off the islands. America's grip was further tightened in 1887 by a treaty with the native government guaranteeing priceless naval-base rights at spacious Pearl Harbor.

But trouble was brewing in the insular paradise. Old World pathogens had scythed the indigenous Hawaiian population to one-sixth of its size at the time of first European contact, leading the American sugar lords to import large numbers of Asian laborers. By century's end Chinese and Japanese immigrants outnumbered both whites and native Hawaiians, prompting fears that Tokyo might intervene on behalf of its often-abused nationals. Then sugar markets went sour in 1890 when the **McKinley Tariff** Act raised barriers against the Hawaiian product. White American planters' mounting efforts to secure annexation by the United States were blocked by Queen Liliuokalani, who insisted that native Hawaiians should control the islands. Though only a tiny minority, the white planters staged a successful coup early in 1893. They were openly assisted by American troops, who landed under the unauthorized orders of the expansionist American minister to Honolulu. "The Hawaiian pear is now fully ripe," he wrote exultantly to his superiors in Washington, "and this is the golden hour for the United States to pluck it."

McKinley Tariff (1890) *Shepherded through Congress by President William McKinley, this tariff raised duties on Hawaiian sugar and set off renewed efforts to secure the annexation of Hawaii to the United States.*

A treaty of annexation was rushed to Washington, but before it could be railroaded through the Senate, Republican president Harrison's term expired and Democratic president Cleveland came in. Suspecting that his powerful nation had gravely wronged the deposed Queen Liliuokalani and her people, "Old Grover" abruptly withdrew the treaty. A subsequent investigation determined that a majority of Hawaiian natives opposed annexation. Although Queen Liliuokalani could not be reinstated, the sugarcoated move for annexation had to be temporarily abandoned. The Hawaiian pear continued to ripen until 1898, when the United States acquired its overseas empire (see Map 27.1).

War with Spain over Cuba

Cuba's masses, frightfully misgoverned, again rose against their Spanish oppressors in 1895. The roots of their revolt were partly economic. Sugar production—the backbone of the island's prosperity—was crippled when the American tariff of 1894 restored high duties on the toothsome product.

The desperate ***insurrectos*** sought to drive out their Spanish overlords by adopting a scorched-earth policy, torching cane fields and sugar mills and dynamiting passenger trains. American sympathies went out to the Cuban underdogs. Sentiment aside, American business had about $50 million of investment in Cuba and conducted annual trade of about $100 million.

insurrectos *Cuban insurgents who sought freedom from colonial Spanish rule. Their destructive tactics threatened American economic interests in Cuban plantations and railroads.*

Fuel was added to the Cuban conflagration in 1896 with the coming to power of the Spanish General ("Butcher") Weyler. He undertook to crush the rebellion by herding many civilians into barbed-wire reconcentration camps, where they could not give assistance to the armed *insurrectos*. Lacking proper sanitation, these enclosures turned into deadly pestholes where the victims died miserably.

Atrocities in Cuba were red meat for the sensational new "yellow journalism." William Randolph Hearst and Joseph Pulitzer engaged in a titanic duel for circulation, each attempting to outdo the other with screeching headlines and hair-raising "scoops." Where atrocity stories did not exist, they were invented. Hearst sent the gifted artist Frederic Remington to Cuba to draw sketches, allegedly with the pointed admonition, "You furnish the pictures and I'll furnish the war." Among other outrages, Remington depicted Spanish customs officials brutally disrobing and searching an American woman. Most readers of Hearst's *Journal*, their indignation soaring, had no way of knowing that such tasks were performed by female attendants.

Maine **(1898)** *American battleship dispatched to keep a "friendly" watch over Cuba in early 1898. It mysteriously blew up in Havana harbor on February 15, 1898, with a loss of 260 sailors. Later evidence confirmed that the explosion was accidental, resulting from combustion in one of the ship's internal coal bunkers. But many Americans, eager for war, insisted that it was the fault of a Spanish submarine mine.*

Then early in 1898 Washington sent the battleship ***Maine*** to Cuba, ostensibly for a "friendly visit" but actually to protect and evacuate Americans if a dangerous flare-up

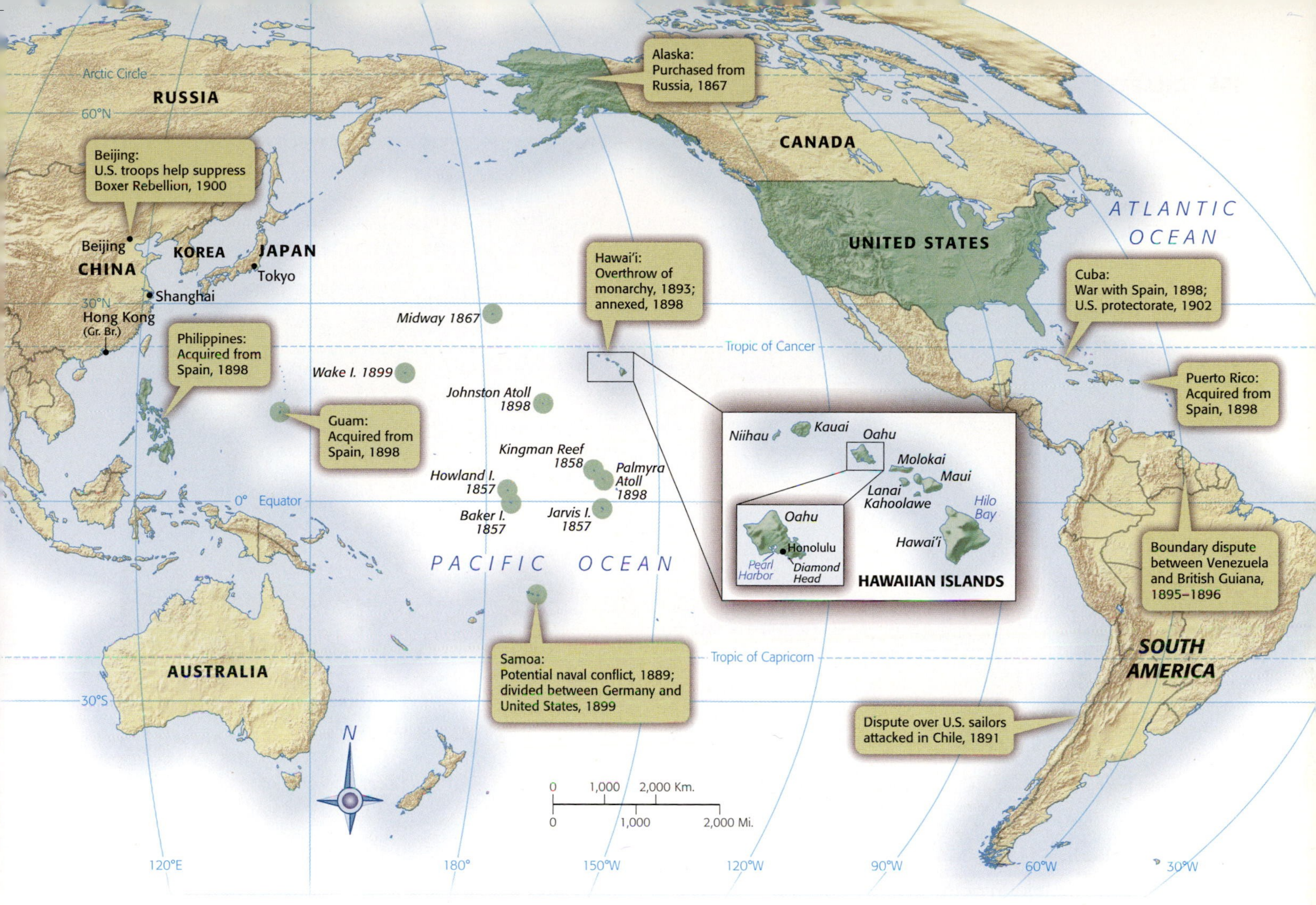

Map 27.1 United States Expansion, 1857–1917 With the annexation of the Philippines, Hawaii, and Puerto Rico in 1898, the United States became an imperial power.

should occur. Tragedy struck on February 15, 1898, when the *Maine* mysteriously blew up in Havana harbor, with a loss of 260 sailors.

Two investigations of the iron coffin ensued, one by U.S. naval officers and the other by Spanish officials. The Spaniards concluded that the explosion had been internal and presumably accidental; the Americans argued that the blast had been caused by a submarine mine. Not until 1976 did U.S. Navy Admiral H. G. Rickover confirm the original Spanish finding with overwhelming evidence that the initial explosion had resulted from spontaneous combustion in one of the coal bunkers adjacent to a powder magazine.

But Americans in 1898, now mad for war, blindly embraced the less likely explanation. Lashed to fury by the yellow press, they leapt to the inaccurate conclusion that the Spanish government had been guilty of intolerable treachery. The battle cry of the hour became:

> *Remember the Maine!*
> *To hell with Spain!*

Nothing would do but to hurl the "dirty" Spanish flag from the hemisphere.

The national war fever burned ever higher, even though American diplomats had already gained Madrid's agreement to Washington's two basic demands: an end to reconcentration and an armistice with the Cuban rebels. The cautious McKinley found himself in a jam. He did not want hostilities, but neither did he want continuing Spanish control nor a fully independent Cuba. More impetuous souls denounced the president as "Wobbly Willy" McKinley. Fight-hungry Theodore Roosevelt reportedly snarled

The Explosion of the *Maine*, February 15, 1898 Encouraged and amplified by the "yellow press," the outcry over the tragedy of the *Maine* helped drive the country into an impulsive war against Spain.

that the "white-livered" occupant of the White House did not have "the backbone of a chocolate éclair."

McKinley, recognizing the inevitable, eventually yielded and gave the people what they wanted. But public pressure did not fully explain McKinley's course. He did not trust Spanish promises, and he worried that Democrats would win the upcoming presidential election of 1900 if he remained indecisive. On April 11, 1898, McKinley sent his war message to Congress, urging armed intervention to free the oppressed Cubans. The legislators responded uproariously with what was essentially a declaration of war. In a burst of self-righteousness, they likewise adopted the hand-tying **Teller Amendment**. This proviso proclaimed to the world that when the United States had overthrown Spanish misrule, it would give the Cubans their freedom—a declaration that caused imperialistic Europeans to smile skeptically.

Teller Amendment (1898) *A proviso to President William McKinley's war plans that proclaimed to the world that when the United States had overthrown Spanish misrule, it would give Cuba its freedom. The amendment testified to the ostensibly "anti-imperialist" designs of the initial war plans.*

Dewey's May Day Victory at Manila

The American people plunged into the war lightheartedly, like schoolchildren off to a picnic. Bands blared incessantly "There'll Be a Hot Time in the Old Town Tonight" and "Hail, Hail, the Gang's All Here," thus leading some foreigners to believe that those were the national anthems.

The war got off to a giddy start for American forces. Even before the declaration of war, on February 25, 1898, while Navy Secretary John D. Long was away from the office, his hot-blooded assistant secretary Theodore Roosevelt took matters into his own hands. Roosevelt cabled Commodore George Dewey, commanding the American Asian squadron, to descend upon Spain's Philippines in the event of war.

Dewey carried out his orders magnificently on May 1, 1898. Sailing boldly with his six warships at night into the fortified harbor of Manila, he trained his guns the next morning on the Spanish fleet. The entire collection of antiquated and overmatched vessels was quickly destroyed.

Taciturn George Dewey became a national hero overnight. An amateur poet blossomed forth with this:

Oh, dewy was the morning
Upon the first of May,
And Dewey was the Admiral
Down in Manila Bay.
And dewy were the Spaniards' eyes,
Them orbs of black and blue;
And dew we feel discouraged?
I dew not think we dew!

Yet Dewey was in a perilous position. He had destroyed the enemy fleet, but he could not storm the forts of Manila with his sailors. His nerves frayed, he was forced to wait in the sweltering bay while troop reinforcements were slowly assembled in America. The appearance of German warships in Manila harbor added to the tension.

Long-awaited American troops, finally arriving in force, captured Manila on August 13, 1898, in collaboration with Filipino insurgents commanded by their well-educated, part-Chinese leader, Emilio Aguinaldo. Dewey, to his later regret, had brought this shrewd and magnetic revolutionary from exile in Asia so that he might weaken Spanish resistance.

These thrilling events in the Philippines had meanwhile focused attention on Hawaii. An impression spread that America needed the archipelago as a coaling and provisioning way station in order to send supplies and reinforcements to Dewey. A joint resolution of annexation was rushed through Congress and approved by McKinley on July 7, 1898. Hawaii received full territorial status in 1900.

The Confused Invasion of Cuba

Shortly after the outbreak of war, the Spanish government ordered a fleet of warships to Cuba. But the decrepit Spanish "armada" was soon forced into bottle-shaped Santiago harbor, where it was blockaded by the much more powerful American fleet. Sound strategy seemed to dictate that an American army be sent in from the rear to drive out the Spanish ships. Leading the ill-equipped American invading force was the grossly overweight General William R. Shafter, a would-be warrior so blubbery that he had to be carried about on a door.

The **Rough Riders**, a part of the invading army, now charged onto the stage of history. This colorful regiment of volunteers, short on discipline but long on dash, consisted largely of western cowboys and other hardy characters, with a sprinkling of ex-polo players and ex-convicts. Commanded by Colonel Leonard Wood, the group was organized principally by the glory-chasing Theodore Roosevelt, who had resigned from the Navy Department to serve as lieutenant colonel.

Rough Riders (1898) *Organized by Theodore Roosevelt, this was a colorful, motley regiment of Cuban war volunteers consisting of western cowboys, ex-convicts, and effete Ivy Leaguers. Roosevelt emphasized his experience with the regiment in subsequent campaigns for governor of New York and vice president under William McKinley.*

About the middle of June a bewildered American army of seventeen thousand men finally embarked from Tampa, Florida, amid scenes of indescribable confusion. Shafter's landing near Santiago, Cuba, met little opposition. Brisk fighting broke out on July 1 at El Caney and Kettle Hill, up which Colonel Roosevelt and his Rough Riders charged, with strong support from two crack black regiments. They suffered heavy casualties, but the colorful colonel, having the time of his life, shot a Spaniard with his revolver and rejoiced to see his victim double up like a jackrabbit. He later wrote a book on his exploits, which the famed satirist Finley Peter Dunne's character "Mr. Dooley" remarked ought to have been entitled *Alone in Cubia* [*sic*].

The American army, fast closing in on Santiago, spelled doom for the Spanish fleet. On July 3 the Spanish ships steamed out of the harbor and into the teeth of the waiting American warships. "Don't cheer, men," Captain Philip of the *Texas* admonished his seamen. "The poor devils are dying." Shortly thereafter Santiago surrendered.

Contending Voices

Debating Imperialism

The contest over American imperialism took place on the Senate floor as well as around the globe. In 1900 Senator Albert J. Beveridge (1862–1927), Republican from Indiana, returned from an investigative trip to the Philippines to defend its annexation:

"The Philippines are ours forever. . . . And just beyond the Philippines are China's illimitable markets. We will not retreat from either. We will not abandon our opportunity in the Orient. We will not renounce our part in the mission of our race: trustee, under God, of the civilization of the world."

Two years later Senator George F. Hoar (1826–1904), Republican from Massachusetts, broke with his party to denounce American annexation of the Philippines and other territories:

"You cannot maintain despotism in Asia and a republic in America. If you try to deprive even a savage or a barbarian of his just rights you can never do it without becoming a savage or a barbarian yourself."

Was the alleged conflict between American power and American democratic ideals a fundamentally new problem at the turn of the twentieth century, or a new variation on a recurring tension in the country's history?

Hasty preparations were then made for a descent on Puerto Rico before the war should end. There the American army met even less resistance. By this time Spain was ready for an armistice, which was signed on August 12, 1898.

If the Spaniards had held out a few months longer in Cuba, the American army might have melted away. Malaria, typhoid fever, dysentery, and yellow fever incapacitated numerous soldiers and sailors. Others suffered from fetid canned meat known as "embalmed beef." All told, nearly four hundred men lost their lives to bullets; over five thousand succumbed to bacteria and other causes.

America's Course (Curse?) of Empire

Late in 1898 Spanish and American negotiators met in Paris. War-racked Cuba, as expected, was freed from its Spanish overlords. The Americans had little difficulty in securing the remote Pacific island of Guam, which they had captured early in the conflict from astonished Spaniards who had not even known that a war was on. Spain also ceded Puerto Rico to the United States. Ironically, the last remnant of Spain's vast New World empire thus became the first territory ever annexed to the United States without the express promise of eventual statehood. In the decades to come, American investment in the island and Puerto Rican immigration to the United States would make this acquisition one of the weightier consequences of this somewhat carefree war (see "Makers of America: The Puerto Ricans," pp. 460–461).

Knottiest of all was the problem of the Philippines, a veritable apple of discord. These lush islands not only embraced an area larger than the British Isles but also contained an ethnically diverse population of some 7 million souls. McKinley was confronted with a devil's dilemma. He did not feel that America could honorably give the islands back to Spanish misrule, especially after it had fought a war to free Cuba. And America would be turning its back on its responsibilities, he believed, if it simply pulled up anchor and sailed away.

McKinley viewed all the choices open to him as trouble-fraught. The Filipinos, if left to govern themselves, might fall into anarchy. One of the major powers, possibly aggressive Germany or Japan, might then seize them and suck the United States into a major war. Seemingly the least of the evils was to acquire all the Philippines and then perhaps give the Filipinos their freedom later.

President McKinley, ever sensitive to public opinion, kept a carefully attuned ear to the ground. The rumble that he heard seemed to call for taking possession of the entire group of islands. Zealous Protestant missionaries were eager to win Filipino converts from Catholicism. (The Philippines had been substantially Christianized by Spanish Catholics before the founding of Jamestown in 1607.) Wall Street had generally opposed the war; but awakened by the booming of Dewey's guns, it was clamoring for profits in the Philippines.

A tormented McKinley later claimed that he went down on his knees seeking divine guidance and heard an inner voice telling him to take all the Philippines and Christianize and civilize them. Accordingly, he decided for outright annexation of the islands. Because Manila had been captured *after* the armistice was signed, the Americans agreed to pay Spain $20 million for the Philippine Islands—the last great Spanish haul from the New World.

The signing of the pact of Paris touched off one of the most impassioned foreign-policy debates in American history. Except for glacial Alaska, coral-reefed Hawaii, and a handful of Pacific atolls, the Republic had hitherto absorbed only contiguous territory on the North American continent. All previous acquisitions had been thinly peopled and eligible for ultimate statehood. But in the Philippines the nation had on its hands a distant tropical area, thickly populated by Asians of a different culture, tongue, and government institutions.

President William McKinley (1843–1901) later described his decision to annex the Philippines:

"When next I realized that the Philippines had dropped into our laps, I confess I did not know what to do with them. . . . I went down on my knees and prayed Almighty God for light and guidance. . . . And one night late it came to me this way. . . . That there was nothing left for us to do but to take them all, and to educate the Filipinos, and uplift and civilize and Christianize them and by God's grace do the very best we could by them, as our fellow men, for whom Christ also died. And then I went to bed and went to sleep, and slept soundly."

Opponents of annexation argued that such a step would dishonor and ultimately destroy American's venerable commitments to self-determination and anticolonialism. "Goddamn the United States for its vile conduct in the Philippine Isles!" burst out the usually mild-mannered Professor William James. The Harvard philosopher could not believe that the United States could "puke up its ancient soul in five minutes without a wink of squeamishness." The **Anti-Imperialist League** sprang into being to fight the McKinley administration's expansionist moves. The organization counted among its members some of the most prominent people in the United States, including the presidents of Stanford and Harvard Universities and the novelist Mark Twain. The anti-imperialist blanket even stretched over such strange bedfellows as the labor leader Samuel Gompers and the steel titan Andrew Carnegie.

Anti-Imperialist League (1898–1921) *A diverse group formed to protest American colonial oversight in the Philippines. It included university presidents, industrialists, clergymen, and labor leaders. Strongest in the Northeast, the Anti-Imperialist League was the largest lobbying organization on a U.S. foreign-policy issue up to that time. It declined in strength after the United States signed the Treaty of Paris (which approved the annexation of the Philippines), and especially after hostilities broke out between Filipino nationalists and American forces.*

Anti-imperialists raised many objections. The Filipinos thirsted for freedom; to annex them would violate the "consent of the governed" philosophy of the Declaration of Independence and the Constitution. Despotism abroad might well beget despotism at home. Imperialism was costly and unlikely ever to turn a profit. Finally, annexation would propel the United States into the political and military cauldron of East Asia.

Yet the expansionists or imperialists could sing a seductive song. They appealed to patriotism, invoked America's "civilizing mission," and played up possible trade profits. Manila, they claimed, might become another Hong Kong. Rudyard Kipling, the British poet laureate of imperialism, urged America down the slippery path with a quotable poem:

> *Take up the White Man's burden—*
> *Ye dare not stoop to less—*
> *Nor call too loud on Freedom*
> *To cloak your weariness.*

In short, the wealthy Americans must help to uplift (and exploit) the underprivileged, underfed, and underclad of the world.

Over heated protests, the Senate approved the treaty with Spain with just one vote to spare on February 6, 1898. America was now officially an empire.

Perplexities in Puerto Rico and Cuba

From the outset, the status of Puerto Rico was anomalous—neither a state nor a territory, and with little prospect of eventual independence. The **Foraker Act** of 1900 accorded the Puerto Ricans a limited degree of popular government, and in 1917 Congress granted Puerto Ricans U.S. citizenship but withheld full self-rule. Although the American regime worked wondrous improvements in education, sanitation, and transportation, many of the inhabitants still aspired to independence. Great numbers of Puerto Ricans ultimately moved to New York City, where they added to the complexity of the melting pot.

Foraker Act (1900) *Sponsored by Senator Joseph B. Foraker, a Republican from Ohio, this accorded Puerto Ricans a limited degree of popular government. The first comprehensive congressional effort to provide for governance of territories acquired after the Spanish-American War, it served as a model for a similar act adopted for the Philippines in 1902.*

The annexation of Puerto Rico (and the Philippines) posed a thorny legal problem: Did the Constitution follow the flag? Did American laws, including tariff laws and the Bill of Rights, apply with full force to the newly acquired possessions? "Who are we?" a group

Makers of America

The Puerto Ricans

At dawn on July 26, 1898, the U.S. warship *Gloucester* steamed into Puerto Rico's Guanica harbor, fired at the Spanish blockhouse, and landed some thirty-three hundred troops. Within days, the Americans had taken possession of the Caribbean island a thousand miles southeast of Florida. In so doing they set in motion changes on the island that ultimately brought a new wave of immigrants to U.S. shores.

Puerto Rico had been a Spanish possession since Christopher Columbus claimed it in 1493. The Spaniards enslaved many of the island's forty thousand Taino Indians and set them to work on farms and in mines. Many Tainos died of exhaustion and disease, and in 1511 the Indians rebelled. The Spaniards crushed the uprising, killed thousands of Indians, and began importing African slaves—thus establishing the basis for Puerto Rico's multiracial society.

The first Puerto Rican immigrants to the United States arrived as political exiles in the nineteenth century. From their haven in America, they agitated for the island's independence from Spain. The Puerto Rican political émigrés in the United States returned home after the Americans conquered the island in 1898. But they were soon replaced by poor islanders looking for work. When Congress granted Puerto Ricans U.S. citizenship in 1917, thereby eliminating immigration hurdles, many islanders hurried north to find jobs. Over the ensuing decades, Puerto Ricans went to work in Arizona cotton fields, New Jersey soup factories, and Utah mines. The majority, however, clustered in New York City and found work in the city's cigar factories, shipyards, and garment industry. Migration slowed somewhat after the 1920s as the Great Depression shrank the job market on the mainland and as World War II made travel hazardous.

When World War II ended in 1945, the sudden advent of cheap air travel sparked an emigration explosion. As late as the 1930s, the tab for a boat trip to the mainland exceeded the average Puerto Rican's yearly earnings. But with an airplane surplus after World War II, the six-hour flight from Puerto Rico to New York cost under fifty dollars. The Puerto Rican population on the mainland quadrupled between 1940 and 1950 and tripled again by 1960. In 1970, 1.5 million Puerto Ricans lived in the United States, one-third of the island's total population.

United States citizenship and affordable air travel made it easy for Puerto Ricans to return home. Thus to a far greater degree than most immigrant groups, Puerto Ricans kept one foot in the United States and the other on their native island. By some estimates, 2 million people a year journeyed to and from the island during the postwar period. This transience worked to keep Puerto Ricans' educational attainment and English proficiency far below the national average. At the same time, the immigrants encountered a deep-seated racism in America unlike anything on their multiracial island. Throughout the postwar years, Puerto Ricans remained one of the poorest groups in the United States. Still, Puerto Ricans have fared better economically in the United States than on the island, where, in 1970, 60 percent of all inhabitants lived below the poverty line. In recent years Puerto Ricans have attained more schooling, and many have attended college. Invigorated by the civil rights movement of the 1960s, Puerto Ricans also became more politically active, electing growing numbers of congressmen and state and city officials.

Insular Cases (1901–1904) *Beginning in 1901, a badly divided Supreme Court decreed in these cases that the Constitution did not follow the flag. In other words, Puerto Ricans and Filipinos would not necessarily enjoy all American rights.*

Platt Amendment (1901) *Following its military occupation, the United States successfully pressured the Cuban government to write this amendment into its constitution. It limited Cuba's treaty-making abilities, controlled its debt, and stipulated that the United States could intervene militarily to restore order when it saw fit.*

of Puerto Rican petitioners asked Congress in 1900. "Are we citizens or are we subjects?" Beginning in 1901 with the ***Insular Cases***, a badly divided Supreme Court decreed, in effect, that the flag did outrun the Constitution, and that the outdistanced document did not necessarily extend with full force to the new windfall. Puerto Ricans (and Filipinos) might be subject to American rule, but they did not enjoy all American rights.

Cuba, scorched and chaotic, presented another challenge. However, an American military government under General Leonard Wood of Rough Rider fame wrought miracles in governance, finance, education, agriculture, and public health. Wood and Colonel William C. Gorgas also launched a frontal attack on yellow fever. Spectacular experiments performed by Dr. Walter Reed and others on American soldiers, who volunteered as human guinea pigs, proved that the stegomyia mosquito was the lethal carrier. Cleaning up breeding places for mosquitoes wiped out yellow fever in Havana.

The United States, honoring its self-denying Teller Amendment of 1898, withdrew from Cuba in 1902. Old World imperialists could scarcely believe their eyes. But the Washington government feared that if Cuba were left on its own a grasping power like Germany might secure dangerous lodgment near America's soft underbelly. The Cubans were therefore forced to write into their own constitution of 1901 the so-called **Platt Amendment**.

bpk, Berlin/Art Resource, NY

The First Puerto Ricans The Spanish conquistadores treated the native Taino Indian peoples in Puerto Rico with extreme cruelty, and the Indians were virtually extinct by the mid-1500s.

The Platt Amendment placed restrictions on Cubans' political and financial autonomy and permitted the United States to intervene with troops to restore order when it saw fit. The Cubans also promised to sell or lease coaling or naval stations to their powerful "benefactor." The Cubans loathed the amendment, which served McKinley's ultimate purpose of bringing Cuba under American control. ("Plattism" survives as a colloquial term of derision even in modern-day Cuba.) The United States finally abrogated the amendment in 1934, although Uncle Sam still occupies one remaining base, Guantanamo, under an agreement that can be revoked only by the consent of both parties (see p. 572).

New Horizons in Two Hemispheres

In essence, the Spanish-American War was a kind of colossal coming-out party. Dewey's thundering guns merely advertised the fact that the nation was already a world power. The war itself was short (113 days), spectacular, low in casualties, and theatrically successful—despite the bungling. Secretary of State John Hay called it a "splendid

The New Jingoism An enthusiastic Uncle Sam cheers the U.S. Navy in the "splendid little war" of 1898. Many Americans, however, were less than enthused about America's new imperial adventure.

little war." American prestige rose sharply, and the European great powers grudgingly accorded the Republic more respect.

An exhilarating new martial spirit thrilled America, buoyed along by the newly popular military marching-band music of John Philip Sousa. Most Americans did not start the war with consciously imperialistic motives, but after falling through the cellar door of imperialism in a drunken fit of idealism, they wound up with imperialistic and colonial fruits in their grasp. Captain Mahan's big-navyism seemed vindicated, and popular support grew for more and better battleships. A masterly organizer, Secretary of War Elihu Root, established a general staff and founded the War College in Washington.

One of the most beneficial results of the conflict was the further closing of the "bloody chasm" between North and South. Thousands of patriotic southerners had flocked to the Stars and Stripes, and gray-bearded General Joseph ("Fighting Joe") Wheeler—a Confederate cavalry hero—was given a command in Cuba. He allegedly cried, in the heat of battle, "To hell with the Yankees! Dammit, I mean the Spaniards!"

Even so, the newly imperial nation was not yet prepared to pay the full bill for its new status. By taking on the Philippine Islands, the United States became a full-fledged East Asian power. But the distant islands eventually became a "heel of Achilles"—a kind of indefensible hostage given to Japan, as events proved in World War II. Here and elsewhere, the Americans had shortsightedly assumed burdensome commitments that they proved unwilling to defend with appropriate naval and military outlays.

"Little Brown Brothers" in the Philippines

The liberty-loving Filipinos assumed that they, like the Cubans, would be granted their freedom after the Spanish-American War. They were tragically deceived. Washington excluded them from the peace negotiations with Spain and made clear its intention to stay in the Philippines indefinitely. Bitterness toward the occupying American troops erupted into open insurrection on February 4, 1899, under Emilio Aguinaldo. Having plunged into war with Spain to free Cuba, the United States was now forced to deploy some 126,000 troops ten thousand miles away to rivet shackles onto a people who asked for nothing but freedom—in the American tradition.

The poorly equipped Filipino rebels soon melted into the jungle to wage vicious guerrilla warfare. Just months earlier, American soldiers had believed they were rescuing innocent Philippine victims of Spanish tyranny. Now they were fighting the Filipinos, whom they came to see as dangerous enemies of the United States. This shift contributed to a mounting "race war" in which both sides perpetrated sordid atrocities. Uncle Sam's soldiers adopted the "water cure"—forcing water down victims' throats until they yielded information or died. American-built reconcentration camps rivaled those of "Butcher" Weyler in Cuba. Having begun the Spanish war with noble ideals, America now dirtied its hands. One New York newspaper published a reply to Rudyard Kipling's famous poem:

We've taken up the white man's burden
Of ebony and brown;
Now will you kindly tell us, Rudyard,
How we may put it down?

The Americans broke the back of the Filipino insurgency in 1901 when they captured Aguinaldo. But sporadic fighting dragged on for many dreary months, eventually claiming the lives of 4,234 Americans and as many as 200,000 Filipinos.

Future president William H. Taft, an able and amiable Ohioan who weighed some 350 pounds, became civil governor of the Philippines in 1901. Forming a strong attachment to the Filipinos, he called them his "little brown brothers." But McKinley's "benevolent assimilation" of the Philippines proceeded with painful slowness. Millions of American dollars did lead to better roads, improved public sanitation, and an unusually good school system. But all this vast expenditure was ill received. The Filipinos hated compulsory Americanization and pined for liberty. They finally got their freedom on the Fourth of July, 1946. In the meantime, thousands of Filipinos emigrated to the United States (see "Makers of America: The Filipinos," p. 464).

Hinging the Open Door in China

Ominous events had meanwhile been brewing in enfeebled China. After its defeat by Japan in 1894–1895, the imperialistic European powers, notably Russia and Germany, moved in. Like vultures descending upon a wounded animal, they began to tear away valuable leaseholds and economic spheres of influence from the Manchu government.

A growing group of Americans viewed the vivisection of China with alarm. Churches were worried about their missionary strongholds. Merchants feared that Europeans would monopolize Chinese markets. An alarmed American public demanded that Washington do something. Secretary of State John Hay, a witty poet-novelist-diplomat, finally decided upon a dramatic move.

In the summer of 1899, Hay dispatched to all the great powers a communication soon known as the **Open Door note**. He urged them to announce that in their leaseholds or spheres of influence they would respect certain Chinese rights and the ideal of fair competition. Tellingly, Hay had not bothered to consult the Chinese themselves.

Open Door note (1899–1900) *A set of diplomatic letters in which Secretary of State John Hay urged the great powers to respect Chinese rights and free and open competition within their spheres of influence. The notes established the "Open Door policy," which sought to ensure access to the Chinese market for the United States, despite the fact that it did not have a formal sphere of influence in China.*

American Missionary Grace Roberts Teaching in China, 1903 A long history of American missionary involvement in China nurtured a sentimental affection for that country among Americans that persisted well into the twentieth century.

The Filipinos

At the beginning of the twentieth century, the United States, its imperial muscles just flexed in the war with Spain, found itself in possession of the Philippines. Uncertain of how to manage this empire, which seethed resentfully against its new masters, the United States promised to build democracy in the Philippines and to ready the islanders for home rule. Almost immediately after annexation, the American governor of the archipelago sent a corps of Filipino students to the United States, hoping to forge future leaders steeped in American ways who would someday govern an independent Philippines.

Most Filipino immigrants to the United States in these years, however, came not to study but to toil. With Chinese immigration banned, Hawaii and the Pacific Coast states turned to the Philippines for cheap agricultural labor. Beginning in 1906, the Hawaiian Sugar Planters Association aggressively recruited Filipino workers. By the 1920s thousands of young Filipino men had reached the Hawaiian Islands and been assigned to sugar plantations or pineapple fields.

Those Filipinos venturing as far as the American mainland found work less arduous but also less certain than did their countrymen on Hawaiian plantations. Many mainlanders worked seasonally—in winter as domestic servants, busboys, or bellhops; in summer journeying to the fields to harvest lettuce, strawberries, sugar beets, and potatoes. Eventually Filipinos, along with Mexican immigrants, came to make up the largest share of California's agricultural work force.

A mobile society, Filipino Americans also were overwhelmingly male; there was only one Filipino woman for every fourteen Filipino men in California in 1930. Thus, the issue of intermarriage became acutely sensitive. California and many other states prohibited the marriage of Asians and Caucasians in demeaning laws that remained on the books until 1948. Undeterred by such overt discrimination and the vigilante violence sometimes directed at them, especially in Washington and California, Filipinos challenged restrictive state laws and the hooligans who found in them an excuse for mayhem. But Filipinos, who did not become eligible for American citizenship until 1946, long lacked political leverage.

After World War II, Filipino immigration accelerated. Between 1950 and 1970, the number of Filipinos in the United States nearly doubled, with women and men stepping aboard the new transpacific airliners in roughly equal numbers. Many of these recent arrivals were solidly middle class and sought in America a better life for their children. Today, the Philippines sends more immigrants to American shores than does any other Asian nation.

Library of Congress Prints and Photographs Division

Filipino Laborers at Work on a Hawaiian Pineapple Plantation, Between 1910 and 1925

The phrase *Open Door* quickly caught the American public's fancy. But Hay's proposal caused much squirming in the leading world capitals, though all the great powers except Russia eventually agreed to it.

Open Door or not, patriotic Chinese did not care to be used as a doormat by the Europeans. In 1900 a superpatriotic group, known as the "Boxers" for their training in martial arts, broke loose with the cry, "Kill Foreign Devils." In what became known as the **Boxer Rebellion**, they murdered more than two hundred foreigners and thousands of Chinese Christians and besieged the foreign diplomatic community in the capital, Beijing (Peking).

Boxer Rebellion (1900) *An uprising in China directed against foreign influence. It was suppressed by an international force of some eighteen thousand soldiers, including several thousand Americans. The Boxer Rebellion paved the way for the revolution of 1911, which led to the establishment of the Republic of China in 1912.*

A multinational rescue force of some eighteen thousand soldiers, including several thousand Americans, arrived in the nick of time to quell the rebellion and prop the Open Door open. The victorious allied invaders acted angrily and vindictively. They assessed prostrate China an excessive indemnity of $333 million, of which America's share was to be $24.5 million. When Washington discovered that this sum was much more than enough to pay damages and expenses, it remitted about $18 million to be used for the education of a selected group of Chinese students in the United States—a not-so-subtle initiative to further the westernization of Asia.

Secretary Hay let fly another paper broadside in 1900, announcing that henceforth the Open Door would embrace the territorial integrity of China. Those principles helped spare China from possible partition in those troubled years and were formally incorporated into the Nine-Power Treaty of 1922, only to be callously violated by Japan's takeover of Manchuria a decade later (see pp. 537–538).

Imperialism or Bryanism in 1900?

President McKinley's renomination by the Republicans in 1900 was a foregone conclusion. He had won a war, acquired rich though burdensome colonial territories for the United States, safeguarded the gold standard, and brought the promised prosperity of the full dinner pail. An irresistible vice-presidential boom had developed for "Teddy" Roosevelt (TR), the cowboy-hero of the Cuban campaign. Capitalizing on his war-born popularity, he had been elected governor of New York, where the local political bosses had found him headstrong and difficult to manage. They therefore devised a scheme to kick the colorful colonel upstairs into the vice presidency.

This plot to railroad Roosevelt worked beautifully. Gesticulating wildly, Roosevelt sported a cowboy hat that made him stand out like a white crow at the Republican convention. To cries of "We Want Teddy!" he was handily nominated. A wary Mark Hanna reportedly moaned that there would now be only one heartbeat between "that damned cowboy" and the presidency of the United States.

William Jennings Bryan was the odds-on choice of the Democrats, meeting at Kansas City. Their platform proclaimed that the paramount issue was Republican overseas imperialism.

McKinley, the soul of dignity, once again campaigned safely from his front porch. Bryan again took to the stump in a cyclonic campaign. Lincoln, he charged, had abolished slavery for 3.5 million Africans; McKinley had reestablished it for 7 million Filipinos. Roosevelt out-Bryaned Bryan, touring the country with revolver-shooting cowboys. Flashing his monumental teeth and pounding his fist into his palm, Roosevelt denounced all the dastards who would haul down Old Glory.

McKinley handily triumphed by a much wider margin than in 1896: 7,218,491 to 6,356,734 popular votes, and 292 to 155 electoral votes. But victory for the Republicans was not a mandate for imperialism. If there was any mandate at all, it was for the two *Ps*: prosperity and protectionism. Meanwhile, the New York bosses gleefully looked forward to watching the nettlesome Roosevelt "take the veil" as vice president.

TR: Brandisher of the Big Stick

Kindly William McKinley had scarcely served another six months when, in September 1901, he was murdered by a deranged anarchist in Buffalo, New York. Roosevelt rode a buckboard out of his campsite in the Adirondack Mountains to take the oath of office, becoming, at age forty-two, the youngest president thus far in American history.

Born into a wealthy and distinguished New York family, Roosevelt, a red-blooded blue blood, had fiercely built up his spindly, asthmatic body by a stern and self-imposed routine of exercise. He graduated from Harvard with Phi Beta Kappa honors and published, at the age of twenty-four, the first of some thirty volumes of muscular prose. He worked as a ranch owner and cowboy in the Dakotas before pursuing his political career full time. Barrel-chested, bespectacled, with mulelike molars, squinty eyes, droopy mustache, and piercing voice, he was ever the delight of cartoonists.

The Rough Rider's high-voltage energy was electrifying. Believing that it was better to wear out than to rust out, he would shake the hands of some six thousand people at one stretch or ride long miles on horseback. Incurably boyish and bellicose, Roosevelt ceaselessly preached the virile virtues and denounced pacifist "flubdubs" and "mollycoddles." An ardent champion of military and naval preparedness, he adopted as his pet proverb, "Speak softly and carry a big stick, [and] you will go far."

His outsized ego caused it to be said of him that he wanted to be the bride at every wedding and the corpse at every funeral. He loved people and mingled with those of all ranks, from Catholic cardinals to professional prizefighters. "TR" commanded an idolatrous personal following. After visiting him, a journalist wrote, "You go home and wring the personality out of your clothes."

Above all, TR believed that the president should lead boldly. He had no real respect for the delicate checks and balances among the three branches of government. The president, he felt, may take any action in the general interest that is not specifically forbidden by the laws or the Constitution.

Building the Panama Canal

Roosevelt soon applied his bullish energy to foreign affairs. The Spanish-American War had reinvigorated interest in the long-talked-about canal across the Central American isthmus. An isthmian canal would plainly augment the strength of the navy by increasing its mobility. Such a waterway would also make easier the defense of such recent acquisitions as Puerto Rico, Hawaii, and the Philippines (see Map 27.2).

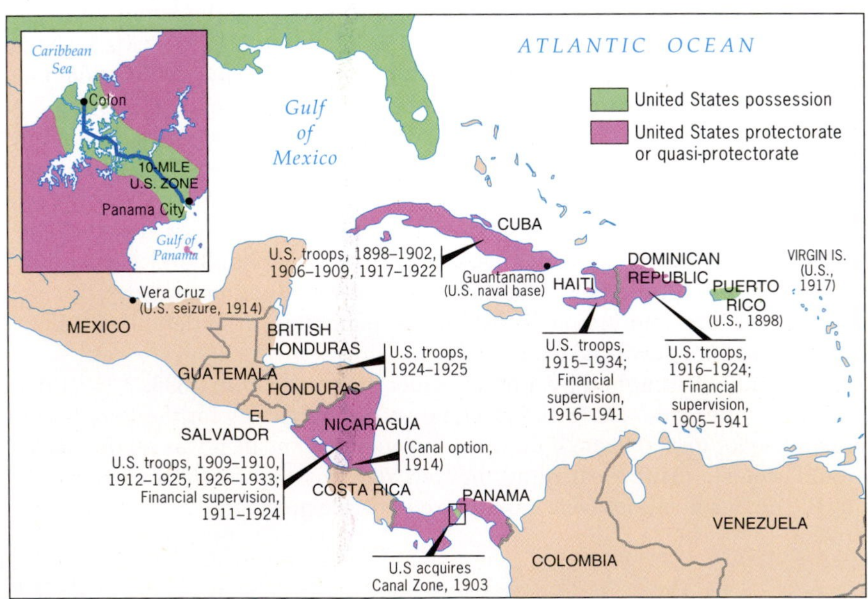

Map 27.2 Big Stick in the Caribbean In 1901 Roosevelt declared: "If a man continually blusters . . . a big stick will not save him from trouble; and neither will speaking softly avail, if back of the softness there does not lie strength, power. . . . If the boaster is not prepared to back up his words his position becomes absolutely contemptible."

Initial obstacles in the path of the canal builders were legal rather than geographical. By the terms of the ancient Clayton-Bulwer Treaty, concluded with Britain in 1850, the United States could not secure exclusive control over an isthmian route. But by 1901 America's British cousins were willing to yield ground. Confronted with an unfriendly Europe and bogged down in the South African Boer War, they consented to the **Hay-Pauncefote Treaty** in 1901. It not only gave the United States a free hand to build the canal but conceded the right to fortify it as well.

Hay-Pauncefote Treaty (1901) *A treaty signed between the United States and Great Britain giving Americans a free hand to build a canal in Central America. The treaty nullified the Clayton-Bulwer Treaty of 1850, which prohibited Britain or the United States from acquiring territory in Central America.*

But where exactly should the canal be dug? Many American experts favored a route across Nicaragua, but agents of an old French canal company were eager to salvage something from their costly failure in S-shaped Panama. Represented by a young, energetic, and unscrupulous engineer, Philippe Bunau-Varilla, the New Panama Canal Company suddenly dropped the price of its holdings from $109 million to the fire sale price of $40 million.

Congress in June 1902 finally decided on the Panama route. The scene now shifted to Colombia, of which Panama was a restive part. The Colombian senate rejected an American offer of $10 million and annual payment of $250,000 for a six-mile-wide zone across Panama. Roosevelt railed against "those dagos" who were frustrating his ambitions. Meanwhile, impatient Panamanians were ripe for a revolt. Scheming Bunau-Varilla was no less disturbed by the prospect of losing the company's $40 million if the Americans should turn to the Nicaraguan route. Working hand in glove with the Panama revolutionists, Bunau-Varilla helped incite a rebellion on November 3, 1903. United States naval forces prevented Colombian troops from crossing the isthmus to quell the uprising.

Roosevelt moved rapidly to make steamy Panama a virtual outpost of the United States. Just three days after the insurrection, he hastily extended the right hand of recognition. Fifteen days later, Bunau-Varilla, who was now the Panamanian minister despite his French citizenship, signed the Hay–Bunau-Varilla Treaty in Washington. The price of the canal strip was left the same, but the zone was widened from six to ten miles. The French company gladly pocketed its $40 million from the U.S. Treasury.

Theodore Roosevelt and His Big Stick in the Caribbean, 1904 Roosevelt's policies seemed to be turning the Caribbean into a Yankee pond.

Roosevelt, it seems clear, did not actively plot to tear Panama from the side of Colombia. But the conspirators knew of his angrily expressed views, and they counted on his using the big stick to hold Colombia at bay. The Rough Rider became so indiscreetly involved in the Panama affair as to create the impression that he had been a secret party to the intrigue, and the so-called rape of Panama marked an ugly downward lurch in U.S. relations with Latin America.

Canal construction began in 1904, in the face of daunting difficulties ranging from labor troubles to landslides and lethal tropical diseases. Colonel William C. Gorgas, the quiet and determined exterminator of yellow fever in Havana, ultimately made the Canal Zone "as safe as a health resort." At a cost of some $400 million, an autocratic West Point engineer, Colonel George Washington Goethals, ultimately brought the project to completion in 1914, just as World War I was breaking out.

★ TR's Perversion of Monroe's Doctrine

Latin American debt defaults prompted further Rooseveltian involvement in affairs south of the border. Nations such as Venezuela and the Dominican Republic were chronically in arrears in their payments to European creditors.

Roosevelt feared that if the Germans or British got their foot in the door as bill collectors, they might remain in Latin America, in flagrant violation of the Monroe Doctrine. He therefore declared a brazen policy of "preventive intervention," better known as the **Roosevelt Corollary** to the Monroe Doctrine. He announced that in the event of future financial malfeasance by the Latin American nations, the United States itself would intervene, take over the customshouses, pay off the debts, and keep the troublesome Europeans on the other side of the Atlantic. In short, no outsiders could push around the Latin American nations except Uncle Sam, Policeman of the Caribbean. This new brandishing of the big stick in the Caribbean became effective in 1905 when the United States took over the Dominican Republic's tariff collections. The big stick was vigorously wielded again in 1906 when revolutionary disorders in Cuba led to the sending of the U.S. Marines, who policed the country until they were temporarily withdrawn in 1909. In Latin American eyes this episode was but another example of the creeping power of the Colossus of the North.

Roosevelt Corollary (1904) *A brazen policy of "preventive intervention" advocated by Theodore Roosevelt in his Annual Message to Congress in 1904. Adding ballast to the Monroe Doctrine, his corollary stipulated that the United States would retain a right to intervene in the domestic affairs of Latin American nations in order to restore military and financial order.*

TR's rewriting of the Monroe Doctrine probably did more than any other single step to promote the "Bad Neighbor" policy begun in these years. As time wore on, the new corollary was used to justify wholesale interventions and repeated landings of the Marines, all of which helped turn the Caribbean into a "Yankee lake." To Latin Americans it seemed as though the revised Monroe Doctrine, far from providing a shield, was a cloak behind which the United States sought to strangle them.

★ Roosevelt on the World Stage

Booted and spurred, Roosevelt charged into international affairs far beyond Latin America. The outbreak of war between Russia and Japan in 1904 gave him a chance to perform as a global statesman. The Russians' threatened seizure of China's Manchuria would be a pistol pointed at Japan's strategic heart. The Japanese responded in 1904 with a devastating surprise pounce on the Russian fleet. They proceeded to administer a humiliating series of beatings to the inept Russians—the first serious military setback to a major European power since the sixteenth century. But as the war dragged on, Japan began to run short of men and yen. Tokyo officials therefore approached Roosevelt in the deepest secrecy and asked him to help sponsor peace negotiations.

Roosevelt was happy to oblige, as he wanted to avoid a complete Russian collapse so that the tsar's empire could remain a counterweight to Japan's growing power. At Portsmouth, New Hampshire, in 1905, TR guided the warring parties to a settlement that satisfied neither side. Japan was forced to drop its demands for a cash indemnity and Russian evacuation of Sakhalin Island, though it did gain effective control over Korea, which it formally annexed in 1910.

For achieving this agreement, as well as for helping arrange an international conference at Algeciras, Spain, in 1906 to mediate North African disputes, TR received the Nobel Peace Prize in 1906. But the price of his diplomatic glory was high for U.S. foreign relations. Two historic friendships withered on the windswept plains of Manchuria. America's relations with Russia, once friendly, soured as the Russians implausibly accused Roosevelt of robbing them of military victory. Japan, once America's protégé, felt robbed of its due compensation. Both newly powerful, Japan and America now became rivals in Asia, as fear and jealousy between them grew.

Japanese Laborers in California

America's Pacific Coast soon felt the effects of the Russo-Japanese War. The conflict's dislocations and tax burdens sent a new wave of Japanese immigrants into the spacious valleys of California. Although Japanese residents never amounted to more than 3 percent of the state's population, white Californians ranted about a new "yellow peril" and feared being drowned in an Asian sea.

A showdown on the influx came in 1906 when San Francisco's school board, coping with the aftermath of a frightful earthquake and fire, ordered the segregation of Chinese, Japanese, and Korean students in a special school to free more space for whites. Instantly the incident boiled into an international crisis. The people of Japan, understandably sensitive on questions of race, regarded this discrimination as an insult to them and their beloved children. On both sides of the Pacific, irresponsible war talk sizzled in the yellow press—the real "yellow peril." Roosevelt, the often-bellicose Rough Rider, was in this case

Japanese Workers Building a Road in California, c. 1910

Thinking Globally

The Age of Empire

The closing years of the nineteenth century witnessed an unprecedented explosion of imperialism, roughly defined as the forcible imposition of one country's rule on the unwilling inhabitants of another. Between 1870 and the outbreak of World War I in 1914, a handful of European states extended their sway over nearly one-quarter of the earth's surface. Other countries followed suit, notably Japan and eventually the United States.

All the imperial powers had in common a heritage of nationalism and a high degree of industrialization. They commanded the elaborate administrative apparatus of large unified states, along with quantities of wealth, technology, and murderous firepower utterly beyond the capacity of the so-called backward peoples they sought to dominate. As a result, imperialism was, from the start, a lopsided game. As one English wit mordantly noted in 1898:

Whatever happens, we have got
The Maxim gun, and they have not.

Yet ultimately, even with their enormously disproportionate advantages, the imperial states were unable to sustain the age of imperialism for much more than a century.

In many ways, modern imperialism resembled eighteenth-century mercantilism, as economically advanced states backed away from the free-trade doctrines that had energized the early stages of the Industrial Revolution and sought instead to create what one British imperialist called "a great self-sustaining and self-protecting empire." The new imperialism also differed from older colonialism in that the imperial powers sought not merely to exploit but also to transform, modernize, and "westernize" the "backward" societies under their control.

Imperialists often justified their dominion over less-developed societies with high-toned slogans. The British professed to be nobly shouldering "the white man's burden." The French piously invoked their *mission civilisatrice* (civilizing mission). The Germans touted the benefits of spreading their vaunted *Kultur* (culture). The Americans prated about the superiority of the Anglo-Saxons, as the Japanese did about their own "Yamato" race.

These protestations may have been sincere, but other motives more powerfully propelled the imperial enterprise. Prominent among them was the quest for new markets, as maturing industrial economies appeared to be exhausting the possibilities for economic growth at home. The need for reliable sources of products such as cotton, sugar, copper, coffee, and tea also figured conspicuously. An even more compelling incentive was the need to protect the huge investments of capital that built the railroads, highways, bridges, ports, mills, foundries, mines, smelters, and telegraphs of the developing world. By the eve of World War I, fully one-quarter of Britain's accumulated wealth was invested overseas.

But perhaps the most important factor driving the imperialist venture was simply the competitive nature of the international system itself. In an unstable, unpredictable world inhabited by ambitious and wary powers, no state thought it could afford to cede an advantage, however ill defined, to any real or imagined rival. Indeed, quite independently of their hard economic value, colonies came to be considered the necessary symbols of great-power status. This perverse logic proved to be a powerful dynamite: Once the imperial race began, it was difficult to stop. As Cecil Rhodes, the fabled British colonizer in southern Africa, once said, "I would annex the planets, if I could." So when Belgium's King Leopold took an interest in Africa's Congo basin in the 1870s, he touched off a mad imperial scramble that eventually involved Belgium, Britain, Germany, France, Italy, and Portugal. Less than two decades later, with the exceptions of Ethiopia and Liberia, the entire continent, much of it unexplored and of dubious economic value, lay under European domination.

In Asia, Germany annexed part of New Guinea in 1884. France completed its annexation of Indochina (present-day Vietnam, Laos, and Cambodia) that same year. Britain acquired Burma (now Myanmar) in 1885 and parts of Borneo and the Malay Peninsula soon after. Japan closed its grip on Okinawa in 1872, Formosa (Taiwan) in 1895, and Korea

unhappy that California might stir up a war. He therefore invited the entire San Francisco Board of Education to the White House.

TR finally broke the deadlock, but not until he had brandished his big stick and bared his big teeth. The Californians were induced to repeal the offensive school order and to accept what came to be known as the "Gentlemen's Agreement." By this secret understanding, worked out during 1907–1908, Tokyo agreed to stop the flow of laborers to the American mainland by withholding passports.

Worried that his intercession might be interpreted in Tokyo as prompted by fear, Roosevelt hit upon a dramatic scheme to impress the Japanese with the heft of his big stick. He daringly decided to send the entire U.S. battleship fleet on a highly visible voyage around the world.

A Young Ho Chi Minh Ho Chi Minh (1890–1969) attended the Congress of the Socialist Party in Tours, France, where the French Communist party was created in late December 1920.

in 1910. All those powers, in addition to Russia, also had designs on China. In the Open Door notes of 1899 and 1900 (see p. 463), the United States tried to temper the imperialists' appetites for Chinese territory and concessions, while at the same time America was becoming an imperial power itself with the takeover of the Philippines and Puerto Rico.

The imperialists brought not only their might and their majesty, their capital and their Maxim guns. They also brought their ideas, including concepts of nationalism, self-determination, and democracy. In 1919 a young Vietnamese nationalist named Nguyen Sinh Cung unsuccessfully petitioned the post–World War I peacemakers at Versailles for his country's right to self-determination. A little more than half a century later, under the name Ho Chi Minh, he secured Vietnam's independence by prevailing in a war first against the French and then against the Americans. By that time the United States had long since voluntarily relinquished the Philippines (in 1946, though Puerto Rico remains an American possession), and virtually all of Africa and Asia had been decolonized. With the handover of Hong Kong (1997) and Macao (1999) to the People's Republic of China, the age of empire effectively ended.

Late in 1907, sixteen sparkling-white smoke-belching battleships started from Virginia waters. Their commander pointedly declared that he was ready for "a feast, a frolic, or a fight." The Great White Fleet received tumultuous welcomes in Latin America, Hawaii, New Zealand, and Australia. The high point of the trip was an overwhelming reception in Japan, as tens of thousands of kimonoed schoolchildren turned out to wave tiny American flags and sing "The Star Spangled Banner."

In the warm diplomatic atmosphere created by the visit of the fleet, the United States signed the **Root-Takahira agreement** with Japan in 1908. The agreement pledged both powers to respect each other's territorial possessions in the Pacific and to uphold the Open Door in China. For the moment, at least, the two rising rival powers had found a means to maintain the peace.

Root-Takahira agreement (1908) *Agreement by which the United States and Japan agreed to respect each other's territorial possessions in the Pacific and to uphold the Open Door in China. The agreement was credited with easing tensions between the two nations, but it also resulted in a weakened American influence over further Japanese hegemony in China.*

Varying Viewpoints

Why Did America Become a World Power?

American imperialism has long been an embarrassing topic for students of American history, who remember the Republic's own revolutionary origins and anticolonial tradition. Perhaps for that reason, many historians have tried to explain the dramatic overseas expansionism of the 1890s as some kind of aberration—a sudden, singular, and short-lived departure from time-honored American principles and practices. Various explanations have been offered to account for this spasmodic lapse. Scholars such as Julius Pratt pointed to the irresponsible behavior of the yellow press. Richard Hofstadter ascribed America's imperial fling to the "psychic crisis of the 1890s," a crisis brought on, he argued, by the strains of the decade's economic depression and the Populist upheaval. Howard K. Beale emphasized the contagious scramble for imperial possessions by the European powers, as well as Japan, in these years.

In Beale's argument, the United States—and Theodore Roosevelt in particular—succumbed to a kind of international peer pressure: if other countries were expanding their international roles and even establishing colonies around the globe, could the United States safely refrain from doing the same? More recent scholars like Paul Kramer stress the degree to which American imperialists turned to European precedents for guidance and inspiration. Thus U.S. colonial officials in the Philippines and Puerto Rico studied and selectively adapted elements of British imperial policy.

Perhaps the most controversial interpretation of American imperialism has come from a so-called New Left school of writers, inspired by William Appleman Williams (and before him by V. I. Lenin's 1916 book *Imperialism: The Highest Stage of Capitalism*). Historians such as Williams and Walter LaFeber argue that the explanation for political and military expansion abroad is to be found in economic expansion at home. Increasing industrial output, so the argument goes, required ever more raw materials and, especially, overseas markets. That "revisionist" interpretation, in turn, has been sharply criticized by scholars who point out that foreign trade accounted for only a tiny share of American output and that the diplomacy of this period was far too complex to be reduced to "economic need."

Most recently, historians have highlighted the importance of race and gender in the march toward empire. Roosevelt and other imperialists perceived their world in gendered terms. Many feared American society had lost touch with manly virtues and grown soft and "feminine" since the closing of the frontier. Imperialists also saw the nations of the world in a strict racial hierarchy, with "primitive" blacks and Indians at the bottom and "civilized" Anglo-Saxons at the top. In this world view the conquest of "inferior" peoples seemed a natural tonic to restore the nation's masculine virility. Scholars who emphasize these explanations of imperialism are less likely to see the expansionism of the 1890s as an aberration in American history. Instead, they argue, these overseas adventures were part of a long tradition of race-fueled militarism, from the nation's earliest Indian wars to Cold War engagements in Korea and Vietnam.

CHAPTER SUMMARY ★ ★ ★ ★ ★ ★ ★ ★ ★ ★ ★ ★ ★ ★

The previously isolated United States dramatically turned its attention overseas in the 1890s, leading to a sudden burst of imperialism. Among the stimuli for the new imperialism were the desire for new economic markets, the sensationalistic "yellow press," Protestant missionary fervor, "Social Darwinist" ideology, great-power rivalry, and naval competition.

American intervention in the Venezuelan boundary dispute of 1895–1896 demonstrated an aggressive new assertion of the Monroe Doctrine and led to an American-British rapprochement after a severe war scare. Longtime American involvement in Hawaii climaxed in 1893 with a revolution against native rule by white American planters. The new government sought annexation by the United States, but President Cleveland blocked the effort.

The "splendid little" Spanish-American War began in 1898 over American outrage about Spanish oppression of Cuba. American support for the Cuban rebellion was whipped into intense popular fervor by the "yellow press." After the mysterious *Maine* explosion in February 1898, this public passion pushed a reluctant President McKinley into war, even though Spain was ready to concede on the major issues.

An astounding first development of the war was Admiral Dewey's naval victory in May 1898 in the rich Spanish islands of the Philippines in the Pacific. American troops, assisted by Filipino rebels, captured the Philippine city of Manila in another dramatic victory. Despite military confusion and many deaths from disease, American forces also easily and quickly overwhelmed the Spanish in Cuba and Puerto Rico.

McKinley's decision to take the Philippines precipitated a long and bitter national debate in Congress and the country over the wisdom and justice of American imperialism. The narrow pro-imperialist victory in the Senate made the Philippines, Guam, and Puerto Rico American colonial possessions. Despite continuing doubts about the wisdom of imperialism, the United States had asserted itself as a new international power, including in East Asia.

America's decision to take the Philippines stirred violent resistance from the Filipinos, who had expected independence. The brutal war to defeat the Filipino rebels was longer and costlier than the Spanish-American conflict.

Economic interests, missionary efforts, and European imperialistic intrusion led to growing American involvement in China and East Asia. Hay's Open Door policy helped prevent the European great powers from dismembering and colonizing China. The United States joined the international expedition to suppress the Boxer Rebellion.

McKinley readily defeated Bryan's anti-imperialist campaign in 1900 to win reelection. Assuming the presidency after McKinley's death, Theodore Roosevelt brought a new energy and assertiveness to American foreign policy. When his plans to build a canal in Panama were frustrated by the Colombian Senate, he supported a Panamanian revolt that enabled the strategically important canal to be built. He also revised the Monroe Doctrine by adding a "Roosevelt Corollary" that declared an American right to intervene in Latin America, stirring considerable resentment south of the U.S. border.

Roosevelt successfully negotiated an end to the Russo-Japanese War but angered both parties in the process. The United States and Japan were now competitors in the Pacific. Japanese immigration and Pacific Coast fears of a "yellow peril" added to tensions, but Roosevelt's diplomacy enabled the two countries to maintain a fragile peace.

KEY TERMS

- Great Rapprochement (453)
- McKinley Tariff (454)
- *insurrectos* (454)
- *Maine* (454)
- Teller Amendment (456)
- Rough Riders (457)
- Anti-Imperialist League (459)
- Foraker Act (459)
- *Insular Cases* (460)
- Platt Amendment (460)
- Open Door note (463)
- Boxer Rebellion (465)
- Hay-Pauncefote Treaty (467)
- Roosevelt Corollary (468)
- Root-Takahira agreement (471)

PEOPLE TO KNOW

- Josiah Strong
- Alfred Thayer Mahan
- Richard Olney
- Liliuokalani
- "Butcher" Weyler
- George Dewey
- Emilio Aguinaldo
- William H. Taft
- John Hay
- Theodore "Teddy" Roosevelt

MindTap is a fully online, highly personalized learning experience built upon Cengage Learning content. MindTap combines student learning tools—readings, multimedia, activities, and assessments—into a singular Learning Path that guides students through the course.

Part 5

STRUGGLING FOR JUSTICE AT HOME AND ABROAD

1901–1945

The new century brought astonishing changes to the United States. Victory in the Spanish-American War made it clear that the United States was a world power. Industrialization ushered in giant corporations, sprawling factories, sweatshop labor, and the ubiquitous automobile. A huge wave of immigration was altering the face of the nation, especially the cities, where a majority of Americans lived by 1920. With bigger cities came bigger fears—of crime, vice, poverty, and disease.

Changes of such magnitude raised vexing questions. What role should the United States play in the world? How could the enormous power of industry be controlled? How would the millions of new immigrants make their way in America? What should the country do about poverty, disease, and the continuing plague of racial inequality? All these issues turned on a fundamental point: should government remain narrowly limited in its powers, or did the times require a more potent government that would actively shape society and secure American interests abroad?

The progressive movement represented the first attempt to answer those questions. Reform-minded men and women from all walks of life and from both major parties shared in the progressive crusade for greater government activism. Buoyed by this outlook, Presidents Theodore Roosevelt, William Howard Taft, and Woodrow Wilson enlarged the capacity of government to fight graft, "bust" business trusts, regulate corporations, and promote fair labor practices, child welfare, conservation, and consumer protection. Progressive reformers, convinced that women would bring greater morality to politics, bolstered the decades-long struggle for female suffrage. Women finally secured the vote in 1920 with the ratification of the Nineteenth Amendment.

The progressive-era presidents also challenged America's tradition of isolationism in foreign policy. They felt the country had a moral obligation to spread democracy and an economic opportunity to reap profits in foreign markets. Roosevelt and Taft launched diplomatic initiatives in the Caribbean, Central America, and East Asia. Wilson aspired to "make the world safe for democracy" by rallying support for American intervention in the First World War.

The progressive spirit waned, however, as the United States retreated during the 1920s into what President Harding called "normalcy." Isolationist sentiment revived with a vengeance. Blessed with a booming economy, Americans turned their gaze inward to baseball heroes, radio, jazz, movies, and the first mass-produced American automobile, the Model T Ford. Presidents Harding, Coolidge, and Hoover backed off from the economic regulatory zeal of their predecessors.

"Normalcy" also had a brutal side. Thousands of suspected radicals were jailed or deported in the red scare of 1919 and 1920. Anti-immigrant passions flared until immigration quotas in 1924 squeezed the flow of newcomers to a trickle. Race riots scorched several northern cities in the

Bettmann/CORBIS

Marching for Suffrage Prominent New York socialite Mrs. Herbert Carpenter, bearing an American flag, marches in a parade for women's suffrage on Manhattan's Fifth Avenue, 1912.

summer of 1919, a sign of how embittered race relations had become in the wake of the migration of southern blacks to wartime jobs in northern industry. A reborn Ku Klux Klan staged a comeback, not just in the South but in the North and West as well.

"Normalcy" itself soon proved short lived, a casualty of the stock-market crash of 1929 and the Great Depression that followed. As Americans watched banks fail, businesses collapse, and millions of people lose their jobs, they asked with renewed urgency what role the government should play in rescuing the nation. President Franklin D. Roosevelt's answer was the "New Deal"—an ambitious array of relief programs, public works, and economic regulations that failed to cure the depression but furnished an impressive legacy of social reforms.

Most Americans came to accept an expanded federal governmental role at home under FDR's leadership in the 1930s, but they still clung stubbornly to isolationism. The United States did little in the 1930s to check the rising military aggression of Japan and Germany. By the early 1940s, events forced Americans to reconsider. Once Hitler's Germany had seized control of most of Europe, Roosevelt, who had long opposed the isolationists, found ways to aid a beleaguered Britain. When Japan attacked the American naval base at Pearl Harbor, Hawaii, in December 1941, isolationists at last fell silent. Roosevelt led a stunned but determined nation into the Second World War, and victory in 1945 positioned the United States to assume a commanding position in the post-war world order.

The Great Depression and the Second World War brought to a head a half-century of debate over the role of government and the place of the United States in the world. In the name of a struggle for justice, FDR established a new era of government activism at home and internationalism abroad. The New Deal's legacy set the terms of debate in American political life for the rest of the century.

What if . . .?

- **What if the Great Depression had never occurred, or had been swiftly overcome, in America and abroad?**
- **Would there then have been a New Deal—or a Second World War?**

Chapter 28

Progressivism and the Republican Roosevelt

1901–1912

When I say I believe in a square deal I do not mean . . . to give every man the best hand. If the cards do not come to any man, or if they do come, and he has not got the power to play them, that is his affair. All I mean is that there shall be no crookedness in the dealing.

THEODORE ROOSEVELT, 1905

Chapter Outline

- The Origins of Progressivism
- Progressive Political Reforms
- Progressive Women at the Forefront
- Roosevelt, Labor, and the Trusts
- Consumer Protection and Conservation
- The Roosevelt Legacy
- The Troubled Presidency of William Howard Taft
- Roosevelt's Progressive Revolt
- Roosevelt's New Nationalism vs. Wilson's New Freedom, 1912
- *Examining the Evidence:* Muller *v.* Oregon, *1908*
- *Makers of America: The Environmentalists*

Nearly 76 million Americans greeted the new century in 1900. Almost one in seven of them was foreign born. In the fourteen years of peace that remained before the Great War of 1914 engulfed the globe, 13 million more migrants would carry their bundles down the gangplanks to the land of promise.

Hardly had the twentieth century dawned on the ethnically and racially mixed American people than they were convulsed by a reform movement, the likes of which the nation had not seen since the 1840s. The new crusaders, who called themselves "progressives," waged war on many evils, notably monopoly, corruption, inefficiency, and social injustice. The progressive army was large, diverse, and widely deployed, but it had a single battle cry: "Strengthen the State." The "real heart of the movement," explained one progressive reformer, was to "use government as an agency of human welfare."

FOCUS QUESTIONS

1. What were the origins and central principles of the progressive movement?
2. What were the primary achievements of progressivism at the local, state, and national levels, and why were female reformers so important to its success?
3. How did President Theodore Roosevelt apply progressive principles to the American economy, and why were consumer protection and conservation such important progressive causes for Roosevelt?
4. How did William Howard Taft's policies split the Republican party and inspire Theodore Roosevelt's progressive revolt?
5. What made the election of 1912 a contest of ideologies as well as of candidates Roosevelt, Taft, and Wilson? Why did Wilson win the election?

CHRONOLOGY

1892	▪ Sierra Club founded
1899	▪ National Consumers League founded
1901	▪ Commission system established in Galveston, Texas ▪ Progressive Robert La Follette elected governor of Wisconsin ▪ Socialist Party of America formed
1902	▪ Lincoln Steffens and Ida Tarbell publish muckraking exposés ▪ Anthracite coal strike ▪ Newlands Act
1903	▪ Department of Commerce and Labor established ▪ Elkins Act ▪ Women's Trade Union League founded
1904	▪ *Northern Securities* case ▪ Roosevelt wins election to a first full term as president
1905	▪ *Lochner* v. *New York*
1906	▪ Hepburn Act ▪ Upton Sinclair publishes *The Jungle* ▪ Meat Inspection Act ▪ Pure Food and Drug Act
1907	▪ "Roosevelt panic"
1908	▪ *Muller* v. *Oregon* ▪ Taft defeats Bryan for presidency
1909	▪ Payne-Aldrich Tariff
1910	▪ Ballinger-Pinchot affair ▪ Washington State grants woman suffrage
1911	▪ Triangle Shirtwaist Company fire ▪ Standard Oil antitrust case ▪ U.S. Steel Corporation antitrust suit ▪ California grants woman suffrage
1912	▪ Taft wins Republican nomination over Roosevelt ▪ Wilson defeats Taft and Roosevelt for presidency ▪ Arizona, Kansas, and Oregon grant woman suffrage ▪ Children's Bureau established in Department of Labor
1913	▪ Seventeenth Amendment passed (direct election of U.S. senators) ▪ Federal Reserve Act ▪ San Francisco decides to build Hetch Hetchy Reservoir
1920	▪ Women's Bureau established in Department of Labor

Progressive Roots

The groundswell of the new reformist wave went far back—to the Greenback Labor party of the 1870s and the Populists of the 1890s, to the mounting unrest throughout the land as grasping industrialists concentrated more and more power in fewer and fewer hands. An outworn philosophy of hands-off individualism seemed increasingly out of place in the modern machine age. Progressive theorists were insisting that society could no longer afford the luxury of a limitless "let-alone" (laissez-faire) policy and a feeble Jeffersonian government. The people, through government, must substitute mastery for drift.

Well before 1900, perceptive politicians and writers had begun to pinpoint targets for the progressive attack. William Jennings Bryan, John Peter Altgeld, and the Populists loudly branded the "bloated trusts" with the stigma of corruption and wrongdoing. In 1894 Henry Demarest Lloyd charged headlong into the Standard Oil Company with his book entitled *Wealth Against Commonwealth*. Eccentric economist Thorstein Veblen assailed the new rich with his prickly pen in *The Theory of the Leisure Class* (1899), a savage attack on "predatory wealth" and "conspicuous consumption."

Other pen-wielding knights likewise entered the fray. The keen-eyed Danish immigrant Jacob A. Riis, a reporter for the *New York Sun*, shocked middle-class Americans in 1890 with *How the Other Half Lives*. His account was a damning indictment of the dirt, disease, vice, and misery of those rat-gnawed human rookeries known as the New York

Museum of the City of New York. The Art Archive at Art Resource, NY

Room in a Tenement Flat, 1910 Tenement life on the Lower East Side of New York City was exposed by the camera of Jacob Riis, who compiled a large photographic archive of turn-of-the-century urban life. Many families counted themselves lucky to share a single room, no matter how squalid.

slums. Novelist Theodore Dreiser used his blunt prose to batter promoters and profiteers in *The Financier* (1912) and *The Titan* (1914).

Socialists, many of whom were European immigrants inspired by the strong movements for state socialism in the Old World, began to register appreciable strength at the ballot box. High-minded messengers of the **social gospel** drew on their religious beliefs to demand better housing and living conditions for the urban poor. University-based economists urged new reforms modeled on European examples, importing policy ideas from Berlin to Baltimore. Feminists in multiplying numbers added social justice to suffrage on their list of needed reforms. With urban pioneers such as Jane Addams in Chicago and Lillian Wald in New York city blazing the way, women entered the fight to improve the lots of families living and working in the festering cities.

social gospel *A reform movement led by Protestant ministers who used religious doctrine to demand better housing and living conditions for the urban poor. Popular at the turn of the twentieth century, it was closely linked to the settlement-house movement, which brought middle-class, Anglo-American service volunteers into contact with immigrants and working people.*

Raking Muck with the Muckrakers

Beginning about 1902 the exposing of evil became a flourishing industry among American publishers. A group of aggressive popular magazines surged to the front, notably *McClure's*, *Cosmopolitan*, *Collier's*, and *Everybody's*. Waging fierce circulation wars, these magazines dug deep for the dirt that the public loved to hate. Enterprising editors financed extensive research and encouraged pugnacious writing by their bright young reporters, whom President Roosevelt branded as **muckrakers** in 1906.

muckrakers *Bright young reporters at the turn of the twentieth century who won this unfavorable moniker from Theodore Roosevelt but boosted the circulations of their magazines by writing exposés of widespread corruption in American society. Their subjects included business manipulation of government, white slavers, child labor, and the illegal deeds of the trusts. These reports helped spur the passage of reform legislation.*

Despite presidential scolding, these muckrakers boomed circulation, and some of their most scandalous exposures were published as best-selling books. In 1902 a brilliant New York reporter, Lincoln Steffens, launched a series of articles in *McClure's* titled "The Shame of the Cities." He fearlessly unmasked the corrupt alliance between big business and municipal government. Steffens was followed in the same magazine by Ida M. Tarbell, a pioneering woman journalist who published a devastating factual exposé of the Standard Oil Company. (Her father had been ruined by the oil interests.)

Plucky muckrakers fearlessly tilted their pen-lances at varied targets. They assailed the malpractices of life insurance companies and tariff lobbies. They roasted the beef trust, the "money trust," the railroad barons, and the corrupt amassing of American fortunes. David G. Phillips shocked an already startled nation by his series in *Cosmopolitan* titled "The Treason of the Senate" (1906). He boldly charged that seventy-five of the ninety senators did not represent the people at all but the railroads and trusts.

Some of the most effective fire of the muckrakers was directed at social evils. The ugly list included the immoral "white slave" traffic in women, the rickety slums, and the appalling number of industrial accidents. The sorry subjugation of America's 9 million blacks—of whom 90 percent still lived in the South and one-third were illiterate—was spotlighted in Ray Stannard Baker's *Following the Color Line* (1908). The abuses of child labor were brought luridly to light by John Spargo's *The Bitter Cry of the Children* (1906).

Vendors of potent patent medicines (often heavily spiked with alcohol) likewise came in for bitter criticism. These conscienceless vultures sold incredible quantities of adulterated or habit-forming drugs. Muckraking attacks in *Collier's* were substantiated by Dr. Harvey W. Wiley, chief chemist of the Department of Agriculture, who even performed experiments on himself.

Full of sound and fury, the muckrakers signified much about the nature of the progressive reform movement. They were long on lamentation but stopped short of revolutionary remedies. To right social wrongs they counted on publicity and an aroused public conscience, not drastic political change. They sought not to overthrow capitalism but to cleanse it. The cure for the ills of American democracy, they earnestly believed, was more democracy.

Contending Voices

Debating the Muckrakers

In his muckraker speech (1906), Theodore Roosevelt (1858–1919) chastised the new investigative journalists for being excessively negative and sensational:

"Now, it is very necessary that we should not flinch from seeing what is vile and debasing. There is filth on the floor and it must be scraped up with the muck-rake; and there are times and places where this service is the most needed of all the services that can be performed. But the man who never does anything else, who never thinks or speaks or writes, save of his feats with the muck-rake, speedily becomes, not a help to society, not an incitement to good, but one of the most potent forces for evil."

Years later, leading muckraker Ida Tarbell (1857–1944) offered her own take on Roosevelt's consternation:

"I felt at the time that Mr. Roosevelt had a good deal of the usual conviction of the powerful man in public life that correction should be left to him, a little resentment that a profession outside his own should be stealing his thunder."

Were the muckrakers ultimately a help or a hindrance to reform?

Political Progressivism

The question, "Who were the progressives?" evokes contradictory answers. Progressive reformers included militarists such as Theodore Roosevelt, who thrilled to the strenuous life, as well as pacifists such as Jane Addams, whose loftiest goals included the abolition of war. Female settlement workers hoping to "Americanize" recent immigrants mobilized alongside labor unionists and enlightened businessmen to strengthen the helping hand of government. In diverse ways, and sometimes with divergent aims, the progressives sought to modernize American institutions to achieve two chief goals: to use the state to curb monopoly power and to improve the common person's conditions of life and labor. Progressives emerged in both major parties, in all regions, and at all levels of government. The truth is that progressivism was less a monolithic minority movement and more a broadly dispersed majority mood.

One of the first objectives of progressives was to regain the power that had slipped from the hands of the people into those of the "interests." These ardent reformers pushed for direct primary elections so as to undercut power-hungry party bosses. They favored the **initiative** so that voters could directly propose legislation themselves, thus bypassing the boss-bought state legislatures. Progressives also agitated for the **referendum**, which would give the people the right to reject laws pushed through compliant legislatures by free-spending agents of big business. The **recall** would enable the voters to remove faithless elected officials who had been bribed

initiative *A progressive reform measure allowing voters to petition to have a law placed on the general ballot. Like the referendum and recall, it brought democracy directly "to the people" and helped foster a shift toward interest group politics and away from old political "machines."*

referendum *A progressive reform procedure allowing voters to place a bill on the ballot for final approval, even after being passed by the legislature.*

recall *A progressive ballot procedure allowing voters to remove elected officials from office.*

The suffrage campaign of the early twentieth century benefited from a new generation of women who considered themselves "feminists." At a mass meeting in New York in 1914, Marie Jenny Howe (1870–1934), a minister by training as well as a prominent early feminist, proclaimed:

"We intend simply to be ourselves, not just our little female selves, but our whole big human selves."

by bosses or lobbyists. The secret **Australian ballot** was likewise introduced in the states to counteract boss rule.

Direct election of U.S. senators became a favorite goal of progressives, especially after muckrakers had exposed the scandalous intimacy between greedy corporations and Congress. By 1900 the Senate had so many rich men that it was often sneered at as the "Millionaires' Club." Direct election was finally achieved by the Seventeenth Amendment to the Constitution, approved in 1913 (see the Appendix). But the expected improvement in caliber was slow in coming.

Woman suffrage, the goal of female reformers for many decades, likewise received powerful new support from the progressives early in the 1900s. The political reformers believed that women's votes would elevate the political tone, and the foes of the saloon felt that they could count on the support of enfranchised females. Many of the states, especially the more liberal ones in the West like Washington, California, and Oregon, gradually extended the vote to women. But by 1910 nationwide female suffrage was still a decade away.

Australian ballot *A system that allows voters privacy in marking their ballot choices. Developed in Australia in the 1850s, it was introduced to the United States during the progressive era to help counteract boss rule.*

Progressivism in the Cities and States

Progressives scored some of their most impressive gains in the cities. Frustrated by the inefficiency and corruption of machine-oiled city government, many localities followed the pioneering example of Galveston, Texas. In 1901 it had appointed expert-staffed commissions to manage urban affairs. Other communities adopted the city manager system, also designed to take politics out of municipal administration. Some of these "reforms" obviously valued efficiency more highly than democracy, as control of civic affairs was further removed from the people's hands.

Urban reformers likewise attacked "slumlords," juvenile delinquency, and wide-open prostitution (vice-at-a-price), which flourished in red-light districts unchallenged by bribed police. Public-spirited Americans looked to British and German cities for lessons on how to clean up their water supplies, light their streets, and run their trolley cars. The vogue of public ownership of utilities swept the nation as local governments tried to halt the corrupt sale of franchises.

Progressivism naturally bubbled up to the state level, notably in Wisconsin, which became a yeasty laboratory of reform. Pompadoured Governor Robert M. ("Fighting Bob") La Follette emerged as the most militant of the progressive Republican leaders. Elected governor in 1901, he waged a desperate fight with entrenched monopolies to win control of Wisconsin from crooked lumber and railroad interests and return it to the people. He also perfected a scheme for regulating public utilities while laboring in close association with experts on the faculty of the University of Wisconsin at Madison.

Other states marched steadily toward the progressive camp, as they undertook to regulate railroads and trusts, chiefly through public utilities commissions. Oregon was not far behind Wisconsin, and California made giant boot strides under the stocky Hiram W. Johnson. Elected Republican governor in 1910, this dynamic prosecutor of grafters helped break the dominant grip of the Southern Pacific Railroad on California politics and then, like La Follette, set up a political machine of his own.

Progressive Women

Women proved themselves an indispensable part of the progressive army. A crucial focus for women's activism was the settlement house movement (see p. 410). At a time when women could neither vote nor hold political office, settlement houses offered a side door to public life. They exposed middle-class women to the numerous problems plaguing

American cities and gave them the skill and confidence to tackle those evils. The women's club movement also turned from literary self-improvement to engagement with social issues and current events. "Dante has been dead for several centuries," observed the president of the General Federation of Women's Clubs in 1904. "I think it is time that we dropped the study of his *Inferno* and turned our attention to our own."

Nineteenth-century notions of "separate spheres" dictated that a woman's place was in the home, so most female progressives defended their new activities as an extension—not a rejection—of the traditional roles of wife and mother. Thus they were often drawn to moral and "maternal" issues such as keeping children out of sweltering sweatshops or ensuring that only safe food products found their way to the family table. Female activists agitated through organizations such as the National Consumers League (1899) and the Women's Trade Union League (1903) and through two new federal agencies, the Children's Bureau (1912) and the Women's Bureau (1920), both in the Department of Labor.

Campaigns for factory reform and temperance particularly attracted women foot soldiers. Unsafe and unsanitary sweatshops—factories where workers toiled long hours for low wages—were a public scandal in many cities. Florence Kelley, a former resident of Jane Addams's Hull House, became the state of Illinois's first chief factory inspector and one of the leading advocates for improved factory conditions. In 1899 Kelley took control of the newly founded National Consumers League, which mobilized female consumers to pressure for laws safeguarding women and children in the workplace. In the landmark case ***Muller* v. *Oregon*** (1908), crusading attorney Louis D. Brandeis persuaded the Supreme Court to accept the constitutionality of laws protecting women workers by presenting evidence of the harmful effects of factory labor on women's bodies. Although this argument calling for special protection for women seemed discriminatory by later standards and closed many "male" jobs to women, progressives at the time hailed Brandeis's achievement as a triumph. The American welfare state that emerged from female activism focused more on protecting women and children than on granting benefits to everyone, as was the case in much of western Europe, with its stronger labor overtones.

***Muller* v. *Oregon* (1908)** *A landmark Supreme Court case in which crusading attorney (and future Supreme Court justice) Louis D. Brandeis persuaded the Supreme Court to accept the constitutionality of limiting the hours of women workers. Coming on the heels of* Lochner v. New York*, it established a different standard for male and female workers.*

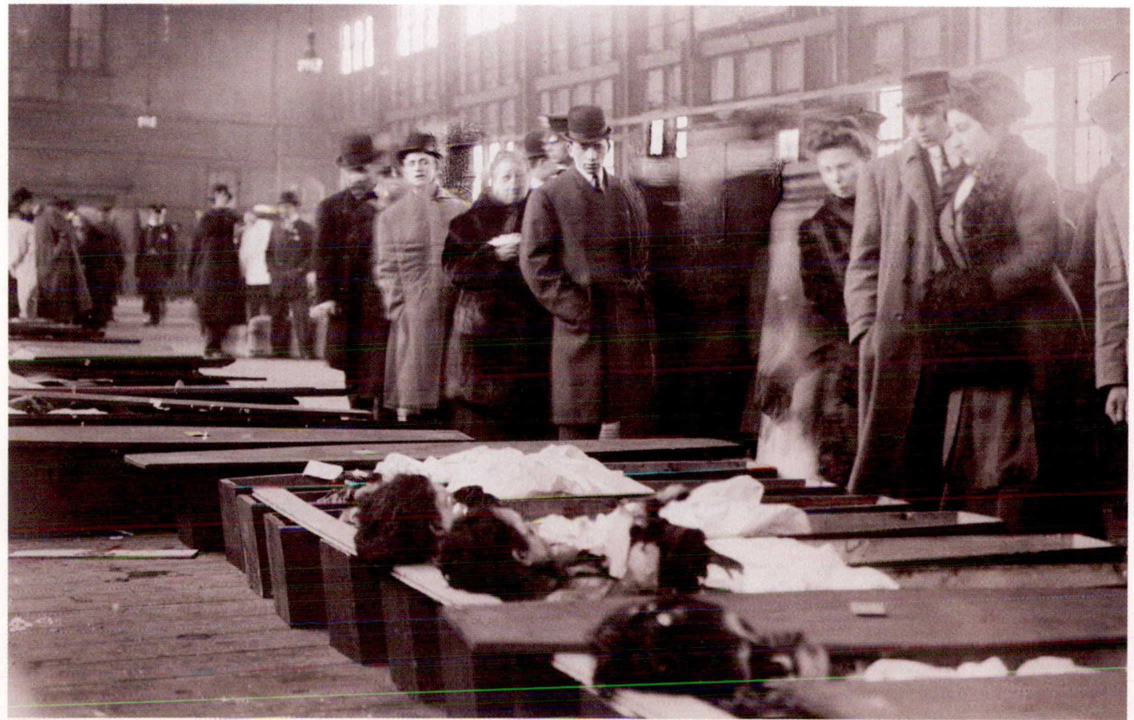

Bettmann/Corbis

The Wages of Negligence Family members arrive at the morgue to identify the bodies of victims of the Triangle Shirtwaist Company fire in 1911. Outrage over this calamity galvanized a generation of reformers to fight for better workplace safety rules.

***Lochner* v. *New York* (1905)** *A setback for labor reformers, this Supreme Court decision invalidated a state law establishing a ten-hour day for bakers. It held that the "right to free contract" was implicit in the due process clause of the Fourteenth Amendment.*

Crusaders for these humane measures did not always have smooth sailing. One dismaying setback came in 1905, when the Supreme Court in ***Lochner* v. *New York*** invalidated a New York law establishing a ten-hour day for bakers. Yet the reformist progressive wave finally washed up into the judiciary, and in 1917 the Court upheld a ten-hour law for factory workers.

Laws regulating factories were worthless if not enforced, a truth horribly demonstrated by a lethal fire in 1911 at the Triangle Shirtwaist Company in New York City. Locked doors and other flagrant violations of the fire code turned the factory into a death trap, incinerating one hundred forty-six workers, most of them young immigrant women. Lashed by the public outcry, including a massive strike of women in the needle trades, the New York legislature passed much stronger laws regulating the hours and conditions of sweatshop toil. By 1917 thirty states had put workers' compensation laws on their books, providing insurance to workers injured in industrial accidents. Gradually, the concept of the employer's responsibility to society was replacing the old dog-eat-dog philosophy of unregulated free enterprise.

Corner saloons naturally attracted the ire and fire of progressives, especially because the sale of alcohol was often intimately connected with prostitution and voter corruption. By 1900 cities such as New York and San Francisco had one saloon for about every two hundred people. Antiliquor campaigners received powerful support from several militant organizations, notably the Woman's Christian Temperance Union (WCTU). Founder Frances E. Willard, who would fall on her knees in prayer on saloon floors, mobilized nearly 1 million women to "make the world homelike" and built the WCTU into the largest organization of women in the world. She found a vigorous ally in the Anti-Saloon League, which was aggressive, well organized, and well financed.

Caught up in the crusade, some states and counties passed "dry" laws to control, restrict, or abolish alcohol. The big cities were generally "wet," for they had a large immigrant vote accustomed in the Old Country to the free flow of wine and beer. When World War I erupted in 1914, nearly one-half of the population lived in "dry" territory. Demon Rum was groggy and about to be floored—temporarily—by the Eighteenth Amendment in 1919.

TR's Square Deal for Labor

Theodore Roosevelt, although something of an imperialistic busybody abroad, was touched by the progressive wave at home. Like other reformers, he feared that the "public interest" was being submerged in the drifting seas of indifference. Everybody's interest was nobody's interest. Roosevelt decided to make it his. His sportsman's instincts spurred him into demanding a "square deal" for capital, labor, and the public at large. Broadly speaking, his program embraced three C's: control of the corporations, consumer protection, and conservation of natural resources.

The Square Deal for labor received its acid test in 1902, when a crippling strike broke out in the anthracite coal mines of Pennsylvania. Some 140,000 sooty workers, many of them illiterate immigrants, had long been frightfully exploited and accident-plagued. They demanded, among other improvements, a 20 percent increase in pay and a reduction of the working day from ten to nine hours.

Unsympathetic mine owners, confident that a chilled public would react against the miners, refused to arbitrate or even negotiate. One of their spokesmen, multimillionaire George F. Baer, wrote that workers would be cared for "not by the labor agitators, but by the Christian men to whom God in his infinite wisdom has given the control of the property interests of this country."

As coal supplies dwindled, factories and schools were forced to shut down, and even hospitals felt the icy grip of winter. Profoundly annoyed by the "extraordinary stupidity and bad temper" of the "wooden-headed" mine owners, Roosevelt threatened to seize the mines and operate them with federal troops. Faced with this first-time-ever threat to use federal bayonets against capital, rather than labor, the owners grudgingly consented to arbitration. A compromise decision ultimately gave the miners a 10 percent pay boost and a working day of nine hours. But their union was not officially recognized as a bargaining agent.

Keenly aware of the mounting antagonisms between capital and labor, Roosevelt urged Congress to create the new Department of Commerce and Labor. This goal was achieved in 1903. (Ten years later the agency was split in two.) An important arm of the new cabinet agency was the Bureau of Corporations, which was authorized to probe businesses engaged in interstate commerce. The bureau was highly useful in helping to break the stranglehold of monopoly and in clearing the road for the era of "trustbusting."

TR Corrals the Corporations

The sprawling railroad octopus sorely needed restraint. The Interstate Commerce Commission, created in 1887 as a feeble sop to the public, had proved woefully inadequate. Railroad barons could simply appeal the commission's decisions on rates to the federal courts—a process that might take ten years.

Spurred by the former-cowboy president, Congress passed effective railroad legislation, beginning with the **Elkins Act** of 1903. This curb was aimed primarily at the rebate evil. Heavy fines could now be imposed both on the railroads that gave rebates and on the shippers that accepted them.

Elkins Act (1903) *Law passed by Congress to impose penalties on railroads that offered rebates and customers who accepted them. The law strengthened the Interstate Commerce Act of 1887. The Hepburn Act of 1906 added free passes to the list of railroad no-no's.*

Still more effective was the Hepburn Act of 1906. Free passes, with their hint of bribery, were severely restricted. The once-infantile Interstate Commerce Commission was expanded, and its reach was extended to include express companies, sleeping-car companies, and pipelines. For the first time, the commission was given real molars when it was authorized to nullify existing shipping rates and stipulate maximum rates.

Railroads also provided Roosevelt with an opportunity to brandish his antitrust bludgeon. *Trusts* had come to be a fighting word in the progressive era. TR was determined to respond to the public outcry against the trusts by curbing but not eliminating them. He believed that there were "good" trusts with public consciences and "bad" trusts greedy for power, and that the goal was not to throw out the baby with the bathwater.

Roosevelt as a trustbuster first burst into the headlines in 1902 with an attack on the Northern Securities Company, a railroad holding company organized by financial titan J. P. Morgan and empire builder James J. Hill. These Napoleonic moguls of money sought to achieve a virtual monopoly of the railroads in the Northwest. Roosevelt was therefore challenging the most regal potentates of the industrial aristocracy.

The railway promoters appealed to the Supreme Court, which in 1904 upheld Roosevelt's antitrust suit and ordered the Northern Securities Company to be dissolved. The *Northern Securities* decision jolted Wall Street and angered big business but greatly enhanced Roosevelt's reputation as a trust smasher. Roosevelt's big stick crashed down on other giant monopolies, as he initiated over forty legal proceedings against the beef, sugar, fertilizer, harvester, and other monopolies.

Much mythology has inflated Roosevelt's reputation as a trustbuster. The Rough Rider understood the political popularity of monopoly smashing, but he did not consider it sound economic policy. Combination and integration, he felt, were the hallmarks of the age, and to try to stem the tide of economic progress by political means he considered the rankest folly. Bigness was not necessarily badness, so why punish success? Roosevelt's real purpose in assaulting the Goliaths of industry was to prove conclusively that the government, not private business, ruled the country. He believed in regulating, not fragmenting, the big business combines. The threat of dissolution, he felt, might make the sultans of the smokestacks more amenable to federal regulation—and it did.

In truth, Roosevelt never swung his trust-crushing stick with maximum force. His successor, William Howard Taft, actually "busted" more trusts than TR did. In one celebrated instance in 1907, Roosevelt even gave his personal blessing to J.P. Morgan's plan to have the U.S. Steel Corporation absorb the Tennessee Coal and Iron Company without fear of antitrust reprisals. When Taft then launched a suit against United States Steel in 1911, the political reaction from TR was explosive (see p. 490).

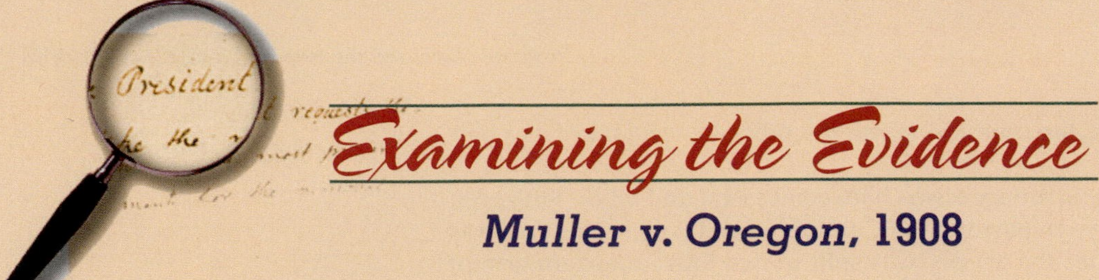

Examining the Evidence

Muller v. Oregon, 1908

Court records provide notably fruitful sources for historians. They not only tell often-colorful stories about the lives of ordinary men and women caught up in the legal system; they also by their very nature testify to the norms and values that lawyers employ to make their cases and that judges invoke to explain their decisions. The case of *Muller* v. *Oregon* (see p. 481) is especially instructive on both counts. The official Supreme Court records tell how on September 4, 1905, Joe Haselbock, a supervisor in Curt Muller's Grand Laundry in Portland, Oregon, asked an employee, Mrs. E. Gotcher, to remain after hours to do an extra load of laundry. That request violated Oregon's law prohibiting women from working more than ten hours per day. Mrs. Gotcher later complained to the authorities, and Muller was fined $10. Muller refused to pay and took his case all the way to the U.S. Supreme Court. In its landmark decision (below), the Court upheld the constitutionality of the Oregon statute, and Muller at last had to cough up his fine.

1. On what grounds did the Court justify its ruling?
2. What does Justice David J. Brewer's argument on behalf of the Court's decision suggest about the cultural identity and social role of women in early-twentieth-century American society?
3. Was Brewer's ruling really a "progressive" one? Why might progressives in the early twentieth century have regarded *Muller* as a great step forward, while Americans of the early twenty-first century might not?

(208 U.S. 412)
CURT MULLER, Plff. in Err.,
v.
STATE OF OREGON.

. . . That woman's physical structure and the performance of material functions place her at a disadvantage in the struggle for subsistence is obvious. This is especially true when the burdens of motherhood are upon her. . . . and as healthy mothers are essential to vigorous offspring, the physical well-being of woman becomes an object of public interest and care in order to preserve the strength and vigor of the race.

Still again, history discloses the fact that woman has always been dependent upon man. He established his control at the outset by superior physical strength, and this control in various forms, with diminishing intensity, has continued to the present. . . . It is still true that in the struggle for subsistence she is not an equal competitor with her brother. . . . Differentiated by these matters from the other sex, she is properly placed in a class by herself, and legislation designed for her protection may be sustained, even when like legislation is not necessary for men, and could not be sustained. It is impossible to close one's eyes to the fact that she still looks to her brother and depends upon him. . . . The two sexes differ in structure of body, in the functions to be performed by each, in the amount of physical strength, in the capacity for long continued labor, particularly when done standing, the influence of vigorous health upon the future well-being of the race, the self-reliance which enables one to assert full rights, and in the capacity to maintain the struggle for subsistence. This difference justifies a difference in legislation, and upholds that which is designed to compensate for some of the burdens which rest upon her.

We have not referred in this discussion to the denial of the elective franchise in the state of Oregon, for while that may disclose a lack of political equality in all things with her brother, that is not of itself decisive. The reason runs deeper, and rests in the inherent difference between the two sexes, and in the different functions in life which they perform. . . .

Caring for the Consumer

Roosevelt backed a noteworthy measure in 1906 that benefited both corporations and consumers. Big meatpackers were being shut out of certain European markets because some American meat had been found to be tainted. Foreign governments were threatening to ban all American meat imports.

At the same time, American consumers hungered for safer products. Their appetite for reform was whetted by Upton Sinclair's sensational novel *The Jungle*, published in 1906. Sinclair, a dedicated Socialist, intended his revolting tract to focus attention on the plight of the workers in the big meat-canning factories, but instead he appalled the public with his description of disgustingly unsanitary food products. (As he put it, he aimed for the nation's heart but hit its stomach.) The book described in noxious detail the filth, disease, and putrefaction in Chicago's damp, ill-ventilated slaughterhouses. A cynical jingle of the time ran:

Mary had a little lamb,
And when she saw it sicken,
She shipped it off to Packingtown,
And now it's labeled chicken.

Backed by a nauseated public, Roosevelt induced Congress to pass the **Meat Inspection Act** of 1906. The act decreed that the preparation of meat shipped over state lines would be subject to federal inspection from corral to can. The largest packers eventually accepted the act as an opportunity to drive their smaller, fly-by-night competitors out of business. At the same time, they could receive the government's seal of approval on their exports. As a companion to the Meat Inspection Act, the **Pure Food and Drug Act** of 1906 was designed to prevent the adulteration and mislabeling of foods and pharmaceuticals.

Meat Inspection Act (1906) *A law passed by Congress to subject meat shipped over state lines to federal inspection. The publication of Upton Sinclair's novel* The Jungle *earlier that year so disgusted American consumers with its description of conditions in slaughterhouses and meatpacking plants that it mobilized public support for government action.*

Pure Food and Drug Act (1906) *A law passed by Congress to inspect and regulate the labeling of all foods and pharmaceuticals intended for human consumption. This legislation, and additional provisions passed in 1911 to strengthen it, aimed particularly at the patent medicine industry. The more comprehensive Food, Drug, and Cosmetic Act of 1938 largely replaced this legislation.*

Earth Control

Wasteful Americans, assuming that their natural resources were inexhaustible, had looted and polluted their incomparable domain with unparalleled speed and greed. Western ranchers and timber men were especially eager to accelerate the destructive process, for they panted to build up the country, and the environmental consequences be hanged. But even before the end of the nineteenth century, far-visioned leaders saw that such a squandering of the nation's birthright would have to be halted or America would sink from resource richness to despoiled dearth.

A first serious step toward conservation was the Forest Reserve Act of 1891, authorizing the president to set aside public forest land as national forests and other reserves. Under this statute some 46 million acres of magnificent trees were rescued from the lumberman's saw in the 1890s and preserved for posterity.

A new day in the history of conservation dawned with Roosevelt (see "Makers of America: The Environmentalists," p. 486). Huntsman, naturalist, rancher, lover of the great outdoors, he was appalled by the pillaging of timber and mineral resources. Other dedicated conservationists, notably Gifford Pinchot, head of the federal Division of Forestry, had broken important ground before him. But Roosevelt seized the banner of leadership and charged into the fray with all the weight of his prestige, his energy, his firsthand knowledge, and his slashing invective.

Congress responded to the whip of the Rough Rider by passing the Newlands Act of 1902, which authorized Washington to use funds from the sale of public lands in the sun-baked western states for irrigation projects. Settlers repaid the cost of reclamation from their now-productive soil, and the money was put into a revolving fund to finance more

In his annual message to Congress in 1907, Roosevelt declared prophetically:

"We are prone to speak of the resources of this country as inexhaustible; this is not so. The mineral wealth of the country, the coal, iron, oil, gas, and the like, does not reproduce itself, and therefore is certain to be exhausted ultimately; and wastefulness in dealing with it today means that our descendants will feel the exhaustion a generation or two before they otherwise would."

The Environmentalists

Humans have long been awed by nature, but they have also yearned to be its masters. The earliest European colonists saw North America as a "howling wilderness" and toiled mightily with ax and plow to tame it. By the mid-nineteenth century, Americans commanded powerful new technologies that promised unbridled dominion over the natural world. Only then did voices begin to be heard in defense of the wounded earth—the first faint stirrings of what would come to be called "environmentalism."

In a pattern that would often be repeated, nature's earliest defenders tended to be well-off townsfolk and city dwellers such as Henry David Thoreau and Ralph Waldo Emerson. The Americans most likely to appreciate the value of pristine wilderness, it seemed, were those who had ceased to struggle against it. For the loggers, miners, and farmers who continued to sweat their living out of nature's grudging embrace, concern for environmental niceties often seemed like the sanctimonious piety of a privileged elite.

By the dawn of the twentieth century, many genteel, urban Americans had come to romanticize their pioneer forebears. Preservationists such as John Muir waxed lyrical about the mystic allure of unspoiled nature. Seizing the popular mood, Theodore Roosevelt deliberately constructed an image of himself as a manly outdoorsman, and as president he greatly expanded the system of national forests.

But Roosevelt was also a pioneer of another sort—as a prominent promoter of the progressive-era "conservation" movement, composed of a loose coalition of scientists, bureaucrats, and businesspeople dependent on stable access to America's rich endowment of natural resources. Progressive conservationists believed that nature must be neither uncritically reverenced nor wastefully exploited, but must instead be efficiently utilized. Thus the same TR who admired the wonders of Yosemite Valley in the company of John Muir also promoted the "rational use" philosophy that justified the systematic harvesting of millions of trees and the drowning of vast river valleys behind massive dams. This attitude toward nature triumphed in the New Deal era of the 1930s, when the federal government initiated colossal projects that undertook nothing less than reengineering the face of the continent—including the Tennessee Valley Authority, the Soil Conservation Service, and the Shelterbelt tree planting on the Great Plains.

The rise of ecological science in the post–World War II era fundamentally changed the debate about the relation of nature to civilization. Ecologists charged that the apparent "rationality" of the earlier conservationists dangerously neglected the stunningly complex interrelationships that linked together seemingly unrelated organisms—and to the perils of tampering even slightly with the delicate biological fabrics that nature had taken millennia to weave. Rachel Carson helped to popularize this new outlook in her sensational 1962 exposé, *Silent Spring*, about the far-reaching effects of pesticides on birds, plants, and animals—including humans.

The advent of ecological studies coincided with a revival of preservationist sentiment, especially in the suburbs, where Americans increasingly dwelled. Membership in environmental organizations such as the Sierra Club and the Audubon Society soared, as a generation infatuated with nature demanded a clean and green world. The first celebration of Earth Day on April 22, 1970 marked the maturation of modern-day environmentalism, which wedded scientific analysis with respect for nature's majesty. That same year saw the creation of the federal Environmental Protection Agency (EPA), soon to be followed by the Endangered Species Act and other legislation designed to regulate the relationship between humans and nature.

At the outset of the twenty-first century, developments like global warming served dramatic notice that planet Earth was an ecological system that did not recognize national boundaries. Yet while Americans took pride in the efforts they had made to clean up their own turf, who were they, having long since consumed their timberlands and tamed their free-flowing waters, to tell the Brazilians that they should not cut down their Amazon forest or the Chinese that they should not dam their rivers? For the peoples of the developing world, struggling to match America's standard of living, environmentalists often seemed like spoiled spoilers, preaching the same privileged pieties that had infuriated generations of working Americans.

Pinchots in the Great Outdoors Gifford Pinchot, the father of the modern Forest Service, poses with his family of fellow nature-lovers. His wife Cornelia was a driven feminist, political activist, and, as a passionate gardener, a proponent in her own right of people's "rational use" of the natural world.

such enterprises. Thanks to this epochal legislation, dozens of dams were thrown across virtually every major western river in the ensuing decades.

Roosevelt pined to preserve the nation's shrinking forests. By 1900 only about a quarter of the once-vast virgin timberlands remained standing. Lumbermen had already logged off most of the first-growth timber from Maine to Michigan, and the sharp thud of their axes was beginning to split the silence in the great fir forests of the Pacific slope. Roosevelt proceeded to set aside in federal reserves some 125 million acres, or almost three times the acreage thus saved from the saw by his three predecessors. He similarly earmarked millions of acres of coal deposits, as well as water resources useful for irrigation and power.

Conservation may have been Roosevelt's most enduring tangible achievement. He was buoyed in this effort by an upwelling national mood of concern about the disappearance of the frontier. An increasingly citified people worried that too much civilization might not be good for the national soul. City dwellers snapped up Jack London's *Call of the Wild* (1903) and other books about nature, and urban youngsters made the outdoor-oriented Boy Scouts of America the country's largest youth organization. Middle-class clubwomen raised money for nature preserves and organized the Massachusetts—and later National—Audubon Society to save wild native birds by banning the use of plumes to ornament fashionable ladies' hats. The Sierra Club, founded in 1892, dedicated itself to preserving the wildness of the western landscape.

The Yosemite Museum, Yosemite National Park

High Point for Conservation Roosevelt and famed naturalist-conservationist John Muir visit Glacier Point, on the rim of Yosemite Valley, California. In the distance is Yosemite Falls; a few feet behind Roosevelt is a sheer drop of 3,254 feet.

The preservationists lost a major battle in 1913 when the federal government allowed the city of San Francisco to build a dam for its municipal water supply in the spectacular, high-walled **Hetch Hetchy Valley** in Yosemite National Park. The Hetch Hetchy controversy laid bare a deep division among conservationists that persists to the present day. To the preservationists of the Sierra Club, including famed naturalist John Muir, Hetch Hetchy was a "temple" of nature that should be held inviolable by the civilizing hand of humanity. But other conservationists, including President Roosevelt and his chief forester, Gifford Pinchot, wanted to *use* the nation's natural endowment intelligently rather than lock it away as wilderness. With a policy of "multiple-use resource management," they sought to combine recreation, sustained-yield logging, watershed protection, and summer stock grazing on the same expanse of federal land.

Hetch Hetchy Valley *The federal government allowed the city of San Francisco to build a dam here in 1913. This was a blow to preservationists, who wished to protect the Yosemite National Park, where the dam was located.*

At first many westerners resisted the federal management of natural resources, but they soon learned how to take advantage of new agencies like the Forest Service and especially the Bureau of Reclamation. The largest ranches and timber companies in particular figured out how to work hand in glove with federal conservation programs devoted to the rational, large-scale, and long-term use of natural resources. The one-man-and-a-mule logger or the one-man-and-a-dog sheepherder had little clout in the new resources bureaucracy. Single-person enterprises were shouldered aside, in the interest of efficiency, by the combined bulk of big business and big government.

The Rough Rider Thunders Out

Roosevelt was handily elected president in 1904 and entered his new term buoyed by his enormous personal popularity. Yet the conservative Republican bosses grew increasingly restive as Roosevelt in his second term called ever more loudly for regulating corporations, taxing incomes, and protecting workers. Roosevelt, meanwhile, had

Baby, Kiss Papa Good-bye Theodore Roosevelt leaves his baby, "My Policies," in the hands of his chosen successor, William Howard Taft. Friction between Taft and Roosevelt would soon erupt, however, prompting Roosevelt to return to politics and challenge Taft for the presidency.

partly defanged himself after his election in 1904 by announcing that under no circumstances would he be a candidate for a third term.

Roosevelt suffered a sharp setback in 1907, when a short but punishing panic descended on Wall Street. The financial flurry featured frightened "runs" on banks, suicides, and criminal indictments against speculators. The financial world hastened to blame Roosevelt for the storm. It cried that this "quack" had unsettled industry with his boat-rocking tactics and branded the current distress the "Roosevelt panic." The hot-tempered president angrily lashed back at his critics when he accused "certain malefactors of great wealth" of having deliberately engineered the crisis to force the government to relax its assaults on trusts.

Still warmly popular in 1908, Roosevelt could easily have won a second presidential nomination and almost certainly the election. But he felt bound by his impulsive postelection promise after his victory in 1904. The departing president thus naturally sought a successor who would carry out "my policies." The man of his choice was amiable and ample-girthed William Howard Taft, his secretary of war and a mild progressive.

As the heir apparent, Taft had often been called upon in Roosevelt's absence to "sit on the lid"—all 350 pounds of him. At the Republican convention of 1908 in Chicago, Roosevelt used his control of the party machinery—the "steamroller"—to push through Taft's nomination on the first ballot. Three weeks later, in mile-high Denver in the heart of silver country, the Democrats again nominated twice-beaten William Jennings Bryan.

The dull campaign of 1908 featured the rotund Taft and the now-balding "Boy Orator" both trying to don the progressive Roosevelt mantle. The solid Judge Taft read cut-and-dried speeches, while Bryan griped that Roosevelt had stolen his policies from the Bryanite camp. A majority of voters chose stability with Roosevelt-endorsed Taft, who polled 321 electoral votes to 162 for Bryan. The victor's popular count was 7,675,320 to 6,412,294. The election's only surprise came from the Socialists, who amassed 420,793 votes for Eugene V. Debs, the hero of the Pullman strike of 1894 (see pp. 444–445).

Roosevelt, ever in the limelight, left soon after the election for a lion hunt in Africa. His numerous enemies clinked glasses while toasting "Health to the lions," and a few irreverently prayed that some big cat would "do its duty." But TR survived, still bursting with energy at the age of fifty-one in 1909.

Roosevelt was branded by his adversaries as a wild-eyed radical, but his reputation as an eater of errant industrialists now seems inflated. He fought many a sham battle, and the number of laws that he inspired was certainly not in proportion to the amount of noise he emitted. He was often under attack from the reigning business lords, but the more enlightened of them knew that they had a friend in the White House. Roosevelt should be remembered first and foremost as the cowboy who started to tame the bucking bronco of adolescent capitalism, thus ensuring it a long adult life.

TR's enthusiasm and perpetual youthfulness, like an overgrown Boy Scout's, appealed to the young of all ages. "You must always remember," a British diplomat cautioned his colleagues, "that the president is about six." He served as a political lightning rod to protect capitalists against popular indignation—and against socialism, which Roosevelt regarded as "ominous." He strenuously sought the middle road between unbridled individualism and paternalistic collectivism. His conservation crusade, which tried to mediate between the romantic wilderness-preservationists and the rapacious resource-predators, was probably his most typical and his most lasting achievement.

Several other contributions of Roosevelt lasted beyond his presidency. First, he greatly enlarged the power and prestige of the presidential office—and masterfully developed the technique of using the big stick of publicity as a political bludgeon. Second, he helped shape the progressive movement and beyond it the liberal reform campaigns later in the century. His Square Deal, in a sense, was the grandfather of the New Deal later launched by his fifth cousin, Franklin D. Roosevelt. Finally, to a greater degree than any of his predecessors, TR opened the eyes of Americans to the fact that they shared the world with other nations. As a great power, they had fallen heir to great responsibilities—and had been seized by great ambitions—from which there was no escaping.

Taft: A Round Peg in a Square Hole

William Howard Taft, with his ruddy complexion and upturned mustache, at first inspired widespread confidence. "Everybody loves a fat man," the saying goes, and the jovial Taft, with "mirthquakes" of laughter bubbling up from his abundant abdomen, was personally popular. He had graduated second in his class at Yale and established an admirable reputation as a lawyer and judge, though he was widely regarded as hostile to labor unions. He had served as a trusted administrator and troubleshooter under Roosevelt—in the Philippines, at home, and in Cuba.

But "good old Will" suffered from lethal political handicaps. Roosevelt had led the conflicting elements of the Republican party by the sheer force of his personality. Taft, in contrast, had none of the arts of a dashing political leader and none of Roosevelt's zest for the fray. Recoiling from the clamor of controversy, he generally adopted an attitude of passivity toward Congress. He was a poor judge of public opinion, and his candor made him a chronic victim of "foot-in-mouth" disease.

"Peaceful Bill" was no doubt a mild progressive, but at heart he was more wedded to the status quo than to change. Significantly, his cabinet did not contain a single representative of the party's "insurgent" wing, which was on fire for reform of current abuses, especially the tariff.

The Dollar Goes Abroad as a Diplomat

Though ordinarily lethargic, Taft bestirred himself to use the lever of American investments to boost American political interests abroad. Washington warmly encouraged Wall Street bankers to sluice their surplus dollars into foreign areas of strategic concern to the United States. New York bankers would thus strengthen American defenses and foreign policies while bringing further prosperity to their homeland—and to themselves. The almighty dollar thereby supplanted the big stick.

China's Manchuria was the object of Taft's most spectacular effort to practice **dollar diplomacy**. Newly ambitious Japan and imperialistic Russia, recent foes, controlled the railroads of this strategic province. President Taft saw in the Manchurian railway monopoly a possible slamming of the Open Door in the faces of U.S. merchants. But Secretary of State Philander Knox's attempt in 1909 to persuade U.S. investors to buy the Manchurian railroads and then turn them over to China ran into blunt Japanese and Russian opposition. Taft was showered with ridicule.

dollar diplomacy *Name applied by President Taft's critics to the policy of supporting U.S. investments and political interests abroad. First applied to the financing of railways in China after 1909, the policy then spread to Haiti, Honduras, and Nicaragua. President Woodrow Wilson disavowed the practice, but his administration undertook comparable acts of intervention in support of U.S. business interests, especially in Latin America.*

Another dangerous new trouble spot was the revolution-riddled Caribbean—now virtually a Yankee lake. Hoping to head off trouble, Washington urged Wall Street bankers to pump dollars into the financial vacuums in Honduras and Haiti. Again necessity was the mother of armed Caribbean intervention. Sporadic disorders in palm-fronded Cuba, Honduras, and the Dominican Republic brought American forces to these countries to restore order and protect American investments. A revolutionary upheaval in Nicaragua, partly fomented by American interests, resulted in the landing of twenty-five hundred Marines in 1912. The Marines remained in Nicaragua for thirteen years (see Map 29.1 on p. 499).

Taft the Trustbuster

Taft managed to gain some fame as a smasher of monopolies. The ironic truth is that the colorless Taft brought ninety suits against the trusts during his four years in office, compared with some forty-four for Roosevelt in seven and a half years.

The most sensational judicial actions during the Taft regime came in 1911. In that year the Supreme Court ordered dissolution of the mighty Standard Oil Company, which was judged to be a combination in restraint of trade in violation of the Sherman Anti-Trust Act of 1890. At the same time the Court handed down its famous "rule of reason." This doctrine held that only those combinations that "unreasonably" restrained trade were illegal. This fine-point proviso ripped a huge hole in the government's antitrust net.

Even more explosively, in 1911 Taft decided to press an antitrust suit against the U.S. Steel Corporation. This initiative infuriated Roosevelt, who had personally been involved in one of the mergers that prompted the suit. Once Roosevelt's protégé, President Taft was increasingly taking on the role of his antagonist. The stage was being set for a bruising confrontation.

Taft Splits the Republican Party

Lowering the barriers of the formidable protective tariff—the "Mother of Trusts"—was high on the agenda of the progressive members of the Republican party, and they at first thought they had a friend and ally in Taft. When the president called Congress into special session in March 1909, the House passed a moderately reductive bill. But senatorial reactionaries, led by Senator Nelson Aldrich of Rhode Island, tacked on hundreds of upward tariff revisions. Only such items as hides, sea moss, and canary seed were left on the duty-free list.

Payne-Aldrich Bill (1909) *While intended to lower tariff rates, this bill was eventually revised beyond all recognition, retaining high rates on most imports. President Taft angered the progressive wing of his party when he declared it "the best bill that the Republican party ever passed."*

Taft nevertheless signed the **Payne-Aldrich Bill**, thus betraying his campaign promises and outraging the progressive wing of his party, heavily drawn from the Midwest. Taft rubbed salt in the wound by proclaiming it "the best bill that the Republican party ever passed."

Taft revealed a further knack for shooting himself in the foot in his handling of conservation. The portly president was a dedicated conservationist, and his contributions—like the establishment of the Bureau of Mines to control mineral resources—actually equaled or surpassed those of Roosevelt. But his praiseworthy accomplishments were largely erased in the public mind by the noisy Ballinger-Pinchot quarrel that erupted in 1910.

When Secretary of the Interior Richard Ballinger opened public lands in Wyoming, Montana, and Alaska to corporate development, he was sharply criticized by Gifford Pinchot, chief of the Agriculture Department's Division of Forestry and a stalwart Rooseveltian. When Taft dismissed Pinchot on the narrow grounds of insubordination, a storm of protest arose from conservationists and from Roosevelt's friends, who were legion. The whole unsavory episode further widened the growing rift between the president and the former president, onetime bosom political partners.

New Nationalism (1912) *State-interventionist reform program devised by journalist Herbert Croly and advocated by Theodore Roosevelt during his Bull Moose presidential campaign. Roosevelt did not object to continued consolidation of trusts and labor unions. Rather, he sought to create stronger regulatory agencies to ensure that they operated to serve the public interest, not just private gain.*

The reformist wing of the Republican party was now up in arms, while Taft was being pushed increasingly into the embrace of the stand-pat Old Guard. By the spring of 1910, the Grand Old Party was split wide open, owing largely to the clumsiness of Taft. A suspicious Roosevelt returned triumphantly to New York in June 1910 and shortly thereafter stirred up a tempest. In a flaming speech at Osawatamie, Kansas, he proclaimed a doctrine—popularly known as the **New Nationalism**—that urged the national government to increase its power to remedy economic and social abuses.

Weakened by these internal divisions, the Republicans lost badly in the congressional elections of 1910. The Democrats emerged from their landslide victory with 228 seats to only 161 for the once-dominant Republicans. In a further symptom of the reforming temper of the times, a Socialist representative, Austrian-born Victor L. Berger, was elected from Milwaukee. The Republicans, by virtue of holdovers, retained the Senate, 51 to 41, but the insurgents in their midst were numerous enough to make that hold precarious.

The Granger Collection, NYC

Ex-President Theodore Roosevelt Watches President Taft Struggle with the Demands of Government, 1910

The Taft-Roosevelt Rupture

The sputtering uprising in Republican ranks had now blossomed into a full-fledged revolt. Early in 1911 the National Progressive Republican League was formed, with the fiery, white-maned Senator Robert La Follette of Wisconsin its leading candidate for the Republican presidential nomination. The assumption was that Roosevelt, an anti–third-termer, would not permit himself to be "drafted."

But the restless Rough Rider began to change his views about third terms as he saw Taft, hand in glove with the hated Old Guard, discard "my policies." In February 1912 Roosevelt formally wrote to seven state governors that he was willing to accept the Republican nomination. His reasoning was that the third-term tradition applied to three *consecutive elective* terms. Exuberantly he cried, "My hat is in the ring!" and "The fight is on and I am stripped to the buff!"

Roosevelt forthwith seized the Progressive banner, while La Follette, who had served as a convenient pathbreaker, was protestingly elbowed aside. Girded for battle, the Rough Rider came clattering into the presidential primaries then being held in many states. He shouted through half-clenched teeth that the president had fallen under the thumb of the reactionary bosses and that although Taft "means well, he means well feebly." The once-genial Taft, now in a fighting mood, retorted by branding Roosevelt supporters "emotionalists and neurotics."

A Taft-Roosevelt explosion was near in June 1912, when the Republican convention met in Chicago. The Rooseveltites, who were about 100 delegates short of winning the nomination, challenged the right of some 250 Taft delegates to be seated. Most of these contests were arbitrarily settled in favor of Taft, whose supporters held the throttle of the convention steamroller. The Roosevelt adherents, crying "fraud" and "naked theft," in the end refused to vote, and Taft won the Republican nomination. But Roosevelt, the supposedly good sportsman, refused to quit the game. Having tasted for the first time the bitter cup of defeat, he was now on fire to lead a third-party crusade.

The "Bull Moose" Campaign of 1912

Office-hungry Democrats, the "outs" since 1897, were jubilant over the disruptive Republican brawl in Chicago. If they could come up with an outstanding reformist leader, they had an excellent chance to win the White House. Such a leader appeared in New Jersey Governor Woodrow Wilson, once a mild conservative but now a militant progressive. Beginning professional life as a brilliant academic scholar of government, Wilson had risen in 1902 to the presidency of Princeton University, where he had achieved sweeping educational reforms.

Wilson entered politics in 1910 when New Jersey bosses nominated him for governor, expecting the novice to serve as a respectable "front" man who could be led around by the nose. But Wilson instead ran a passionate reform campaign in which he assailed the "predatory" trusts and promised to return state government to the people. As governor, Wilson drove through a sheaf of forward-looking measures that made reactionary New Jersey one of the more liberal states—and its zealous chief executive a leading contender for the presidency.

When the Democrats met in Baltimore in 1912, Wilson was nominated on the forty-sixth ballot, aided by William Jennings Bryan's switch to his side. The Democrats gave Wilson a strong progressive platform to run on, dubbed the **New Freedom** program.

New Freedom (1912) *Platform of reforms advocated by Woodrow Wilson in his first presidential campaign, including stronger antitrust legislation to protect small business enterprises from monopolies, banking reform, and tariff reductions. Wilson's strategy involved taking action to increase opportunities for capitalist competition rather than increasing government regulation of large trusts.*

Surging events had meanwhile been thrusting Roosevelt to the fore as a candidate for the presidency on a third-party Progressive ticket. The fighting ex-cowboy, angered by his recent rebuff, was eager to lead the charge. A pro-Roosevelt Progressive convention assembled in Chicago in August 1912. Dramatically symbolizing the rising political status of women, as well as Progressive support for the cause of social justice, settlement-house pioneer Jane Addams placed Roosevelt's name in nomination for the presidency. Thunderous applause erupted when Roosevelt fervently cried, "We stand at Armageddon, and we battle for the Lord!" A religious revival atmosphere suffused the convention, as the hoarse delegates sang "Onward Christian Soldiers" and the "Battle Hymn of the Republic." William Allen White, the caustic Kansas journalist, later wrote, "Roosevelt bit me and I went mad."

Picture Research Consultants & Archives

The Finishing Touch, 1912 Despite the excitement generated by Roosevelt's Progressive Party challenge in 1912, the GOP split that year helped to hand victory to the Democrats. This election-eve cartoon depicts Woodrow Wilson, attired in academic garb, preparing to slay Roosevelt the charging bull moose. The latter had already been injured by a slew of controversies, including allegations of improper campaign contributions during a previous election. Wilson's campaign manager and future treasury secretary, William McAdoo, holds the cape.

Fired-up Progressives entered the campaign with righteousness and enthusiasm. Roosevelt boasted that he felt "as strong as a bull moose," so the bull moose took its place with the donkey and the elephant in the American political zoo. As one poet whimsically put it:

I want to be a Bull Moose,
And with the Bull Moose stand
With antlers on my forehead
And a Big Stick in my hand.

The overshadowing question of the 1912 campaign was which of two varieties of progressivism would prevail—Roosevelt's New Nationalism or Wilson's New Freedom. Both men favored a more active government role in economic and social affairs, but they disagreed sharply over specific strategies. Roosevelt preached the theories spun out by the progressive thinker Herbert Croly in his book *The Promise of American Life* (1910). Croly and TR both favored continued consolidation of trusts and labor unions, paralleled by the growth of powerful regulatory agencies in Washington. Roosevelt and his "bull moosers" also campaigned for woman suffrage and a broad program of social welfare, including minimum-wage laws and publicly supported health care. Clearly, the bull moose Progressives looked forward to the kind of activist welfare state that Franklin Roosevelt's New Deal would one day make a reality.

Wilson's New Freedom, by contrast, favored small enterprise, entrepreneurship, and the free functioning of unregulated and unmonopolized markets. The Democrats shunned social- welfare proposals and pinned their economic faith on competition—on the "man on the make," as Wilson put it. The New Freedom Program called for banking reform and tariff reductions. But the keynote of Wilson's program was not regulation but fragmentation of the big industrial combines, chiefly by means of vigorous enforcement of the antitrust laws. The election of 1912 thus offered the voters a choice not merely of policies but of political and economic philosophies—a rarity in United States history.

Former professor Wilson won handily, with 435 electoral votes and 6,296,547 popular votes. The "third-party" candidate, Roosevelt, finished second, with 88 electoral votes and 4,118,571 popular votes. Taft won only 8 electoral votes and 3,486,720 popular votes. To the progressive tally must be added some support for the Socialist candidate, persistent Eugene V. Debs, who rolled up 900,672 votes, 6 percent of the total cast, or more than twice as many as he had netted four years earlier. Starry-eyed Socialists dreamed of being in the White House within eight years.

Taft went on to a fruitful old age. He taught law for eight pleasant years at Yale University and in 1921 became chief justice of the Supreme Court—a job for which he was far more happily suited than the presidency.

CHAPTER SUMMARY ★ ★ ★ ★ ★ ★ ★ ★ ★ ★ ★ ★ ★

The progressive movement of the early twentieth century became the greatest American reform crusade since abolitionism. Inaugurated by Populists, socialists, social gospelers, female reformers, and muckraking journalists, progressivism became a widely popular effort to strengthen government's power to correct the many social and economic problems associated with industrialization and urbanization.

Progressivism began at the city and state level, where it initially focused on "good government" political reforms to corral corrupt bosses. It then turned to correcting a host of social and economic evils that seemed to require national action by the federal government. Women played an especially critical role in galvanizing progressive social concern. Seeing involvement in such issues as reforming child labor, poor tenement housing, and consumer causes as a natural extension of their traditional roles as wives and mothers, female activists brought significant changes in both law and public attitudes in these areas.

At the national level, Roosevelt's Square Deal vigorously deployed the federal government to promote the public interest and mediate conflicts between labor interests on the one hand and the corporate trusts on the other. Rooseveltian progressivism also inspired attention to consumer and environmental concerns. Conservation became an important public crusade under Roosevelt, although sharp disagreements divided wilderness "preservationists" from moderate conservationists such as Roosevelt who favored the "multiple use" of nature.

Roosevelt personally selected his longtime subordinate Taft as his political successor, expecting him to carry out "my policies." But Taft proved to be a poor politician who fell under the thumb of the conservative Republican Old Guard and rapidly lost public support. The progressives' hostility to Taft split the Republican party, and when Roosevelt failed to win the nomination he launched a fiery third-party crusade in the 1912 election under the banner of his new Progressive party. Delighted at the Republican split, Democrats nominated New Jersey Governor Woodrow Wilson, a strong reformer. Roosevelt and Wilson offered competing progressive visions in the campaign. Roosevelt's New Nationalism stressed regulation and social welfare, while Wilson's New Freedom promoted economic fairness and competition. Wilson won the fiercely contested election, with Roosevelt second, Taft third, and Socialist Eugene Debs fourth.

KEY TERMS

social gospel (478)
muckrakers (478)
initiative (479)
referendum (479)
recall (479)
Australian ballot (480)
Muller v. *Oregon* (481)
Lochner v. *New York* (482)
Elkins Act (483)
Meat Inspection Act (485)
Pure Food and Drug Act (485)
Hetch Hetchy Valley (487)
dollar diplomacy (489)
Payne-Aldrich Bill (490)
New Nationalism (490)
New Freedom (492)

PEOPLE TO KNOW

Ida Tarbell
Henry Demarest Lloyd
Thorstein Veblen
Jacob A. Riis
Robert M. ("Fighting Bob") La Follette
Hiram W. Johnson
Florence Kelley
Frances E. Willard
Gifford Pinchot
John Muir

Chapter 29

Wilsonian Progressivism in Peace and War

1913–1920

American enterprise is not free; the man with only a little capital is finding it harder and harder to get into the field, more and more impossible to compete with the big fellow. Why? Because the laws of this country do not prevent the strong from crushing the weak.

Woodrow Wilson, The New Freedom, 1913

Chapter Outline

- Wilsonian Progressivism: Reforming the Tariff, the Banks, and the Trusts
- Wilson's Diplomacy in Mexico and Latin America
- War in Europe and American Neutrality
- The Reelection of Wilson, 1916
- German Submarines Push America into War, 1917
- Wilsonian Idealism and the Fourteen Points
- Wartime Propaganda and the Stifling of Dissent
- Workers, Blacks, and Women on the Home Front
- The American Doughboys
- The American Forces Fight in France
- Wilsonian Peacemaking in Paris
- The Senate Rejects the Versailles Treaty
- *Examining the Evidence: "Mademoiselle from Armentières"*
- *Varying Viewpoints: Woodrow Wilson: Realist or Idealist?*

Woodrow Wilson's two tumultuous presidential terms saw the apex of progressive achievements, as well as entanglement in a global war that helped snuff out the reform fires at home. That outcome was ironic because America entered the conflict buoyed by the same crusading idealism and confidence that had driven domestic progressivism.

FOCUS QUESTIONS

1. How did Wilsonian progressivism overcome the "triple wall of privilege"?
2. What were the central features of Wilson's moralistic foreign policy? How did he apply those principles to Latin America and then to Europe in World War I?
3. What was America's response to the outbreak of World War I? Why did Wilson's attempt to maintain neutrality turn into a critical stance toward Germany?
4. Why did America enter World War I?
5. Why did Woodrow Wilson proclaim America's entry into the war as an ideological crusade for universal democracy and freedom, rather than simply an attempt to curb German military power?
6. How did America mobilize for war, and what was the war's impact on labor, women, and African Americans?
7. Why was Wilson forced to compromise his idealistic Fourteen Points plan for peace at the Versailles Conference? Why was the battle over ratifying the Treaty of Versailles so bitter, and why was the Treaty defeated?

CHRONOLOGY

1913	▪ Underwood Tariff Act ▪ Sixteenth Amendment (income tax) ▪ Federal Reserve Act ▪ Huerta takes power in Mexico
1914	▪ Clayton Anti-Trust Act ▪ Federal Trade Commission established ▪ U.S. seizes port of Veracruz, Mexico ▪ World War I begins in Europe
1915	▪ La Follette Seamen's Act ▪ *Lusitania* torpedoed and sunk by German U-boat ▪ Germany declares submarine war area around British Isles
1916	▪ *Sussex* ultimatum and pledge ▪ U.S. exports to European belligerents skyrocket ▪ Workingmen's Compensation Act ▪ Federal Farm Loan Act ▪ Adamson Act ▪ Pancho Villa raids New Mexico ▪ Brandeis appointed to Supreme Court ▪ Jones Act ▪ Wilson defeats Hughes for presidency
1917	▪ Germany resumes unrestricted submarine warfare ▪ Zimmermann note ▪ Railroads placed under federal control ▪ United States enters World War I ▪ Espionage Act of 1917 ▪ Wilson calls for "peace without victory" ▪ Bolshevik Revolution
1918	▪ Wilson proposes Fourteen Points ▪ Sedition Act of 1918 ▪ Battle of Château-Thierry ▪ Second Battle of the Marne ▪ Meuse-Argonne offensive
1918–1919	▪ Armistice ends World War I ▪ Worldwide influenza pandemic
1919	▪ Paris Peace Conference and Treaty of Versailles ▪ Wilson's pro-League tour and collapse ▪ Eighteenth Amendment (prohibition of alcohol) passed ▪ First Senate defeat of Versailles Treaty
1920	▪ Final Senate defeat of Versailles Treaty after reconsideration ▪ Nineteenth Amendment (woman suffrage) passed ▪ Harding defeats Cox for presidency

Wilson: The Idealist in Politics

(Thomas) Woodrow Wilson, the second Democratic president since 1861, looked like the ascetic intellectual he was, with his clean-cut features, pinch-nose eyeglasses, and trim figure. Born in Virginia shortly before the Civil War and reared in Georgia and the Carolinas, the professor-politician was the first man from one of the seceded southern states to reach the White House since Zachary Taylor, sixty-four years earlier. Wilson's admiration for the Confederacy's attempt to win independence partly inspired his ideal of self-determination for people in other countries. Steeped in the traditions of Jeffersonian democracy, he shared Jefferson's faith in the masses—if they were properly informed.

Son of a Presbyterian minister, Wilson was reared in an atmosphere of fervent piety, and he deftly used the presidential pulpit to preach his inspirational political sermons. Convinced that Congress could not function properly unless the president got out in front and provided leadership, Wilson repeatedly relied on his eloquence to appeal over the heads of legislators to the sovereign people.

Splendid though Wilson's intellectual equipment was, he suffered from serious defects of personality. Incapable of acting the showman, like "Teddy" Roosevelt, Wilson lacked the common touch and knew it. Roosevelt "appeals to [the voters'] imagination; I do not," Wilson reflected. "I am a vague, conjectural personality, more made up of opinions and academic prepossessions than of human traits and red corpuscles."

Wilson Attacks the "Triple Wall of Privilege"

Few presidents have arrived at the White House with a clearer program than Wilson's or one destined to be so completely achieved. The new president called for an all-out assault on what he called the "triple wall of privilege": the tariff, the banks, and the trusts.

He tackled the tariff first. In a precedent-shattering move, he appeared in person before a joint session of Congress in 1913 and presented his appeal with stunning eloquence and effectiveness. Moved by Wilson's aggressive leadership, the House swiftly passed the **Underwood Tariff** Bill, which provided for a substantial reduction of rates. The bill was also a landmark in tax legislation. Under authority granted by the recently ratified Sixteenth Amendment, Congress enacted a graduated income tax, beginning with a modest levy on incomes over $3,000 (then considerably higher than the average family's income). By 1917 revenue from the income tax shot ahead of receipts from the tariff, a gap that has since vastly widened.

Underwood Tariff (1913) *This tariff provided for a substantial reduction of rates and enacted an unprecedented, graduated federal income tax. By 1917, revenue from the income tax surpassed receipts from the tariff, a gap that has since been vastly widened.*

A second bastion of the "triple wall of privilege" was the antiquated and inadequate banking and currency system, long since outgrown by the Republic's lusty economic expansion. The most serious shortcoming of the country's financial structure, still creaking along under the Civil War National Banking Act, was the inelasticity of the currency. Banking reserves were heavily concentrated in New York and a handful of other large cities and could not be mobilized in times of financial stress into areas that were badly pinched.

A House committee chaired by Congressman Arsene Pujo had already stirred public concern about the concentration of financial power by tracing the tentacles of the "money monster" into the hidden vaults of American banking and business. President Wilson's confidant, progressive-minded Massachusetts attorney Louis D. Brandeis, further fanned the flames of reform with his incendiary though scholarly book *Other People's Money and How the Bankers Use It* (1914).

In June 1913, in a second dramatic personal appearance before Congress, the president issued a ringing call for a decentralized bank in government hands, as opposed to Republican demands for a huge private bank. Again appealing to the sovereign people, Wilson scored another triumph. In 1913 he signed the **Federal Reserve Act**, the most important piece of economic legislation between the Civil War and the New Deal.

Federal Reserve Act (1913) *An act establishing twelve regional Federal Reserve Banks and a Federal Reserve Board, appointed by the president, to regulate banking and create stability on a national scale in the volatile banking sector. The law carried the nation through the financial crises of the First World War of 1914–1918.*

The new Federal Reserve Board, appointed by the president, oversaw a nationwide system of twelve regional reserve banks. These regional banks were owned by member financial institutions, but the final authority of the Federal Reserve Board guaranteed public control. The board was also empowered to issue paper money—"Federal Reserve Notes"—backed by commercial paper, such as the promissory notes of businesspeople. Thus the amount of money in circulation could be swiftly increased as needed for the legitimate requirements of business.

Without pausing for breath, Wilson pushed toward the last remaining rampart in the "triple wall of privilege"—the trusts. His third personal appearance before Congress in 1914 led to passage of the **Federal Trade Commission Act** of 1914. The new law empowered a presidentially appointed commission to turn a searchlight on industries engaged in interstate commerce, such as the meatpackers. The commissioners were expected to crush monopoly at the source by rooting out unfair trade practices, including unlawful competition, false advertising, mislabeling, adulteration, and bribery.

Federal Trade Commission Act (1914) *A banner accomplishment of Woodrow Wilson's administration, this law empowered a standing, presidentially appointed commission to investigate illegal business practices in interstate commerce like unlawful competition, false advertising, and mislabeling of goods.*

The knot of monopoly was further cut by the **Clayton Anti-Trust Act** of 1914. This act lengthened the Sherman Act's list of objectionable business practices to include price discrimination and interlocking directorates (whereby the same individuals served as directors of supposedly competing firms), an end often achieved through **holding companies**.

Clayton Anti-Trust Act (1914) *Law extending the anti-trust protections of the Sherman Anti-Trust Act and exempting labor unions and agricultural organizations from antimonopoly constraints. The act conferred long-overdue benefits on labor.*

holding companies *Companies that own part or all of other companies' stock in order to extend monopoly control. Often, a holding company does not produce goods or services of its own but only exists to control other companies. The Clayton Anti-Trust Act of 1914 sought to clamp down on these companies when they obstructed competition.*

The Clayton Act also conferred long-overdue benefits on workers by exempting labor and agricultural organizations from antitrust prosecution under the Sherman Act, while explicitly legalizing strikes and peaceful picketing. Union leader Samuel Gompers hailed the act as the Magna Carta of labor because it legally lifted human labor out of the category of "a commodity or article of commerce." But the rejoicing was premature, as conservative judges in later years continued to clip the wings of the union movement.

The Granger Collection, NYC

Reading the Death Warrant This cartoon appeared in a New York newspaper soon after Woodrow Wilson called for dramatic reform of the banking system before both houses of Congress. With the "money trust" of bankers and businessmen cowed, Wilson was able to win popular and congressional support for the Federal Reserve Act of 1913.

Wilson at the Peak

Having treated the nation to a dazzling demonstration of vigorous presidential leadership, Wilson pressed ahead with further reforms. The Federal Farm Loan Act of 1916 made credit available to farmers at low rates of interest—as long demanded by the Populists. The La Follette Seamen's Act of 1915 required decent treatment and a living wage for often-mistreated sailors on American merchant ships.

Wilson further helped workers with the **Workingmen's Compensation Act** of 1916, granting assistance to federal civil-service employees during periods of disability. In the same year the president endorsed an act restricting child labor on products flowing into interstate commerce, though the stand-pat Supreme Court soon invalidated the law. The **Adamson Act** of 1916 established an eight-hour day for all railroad employees on trains in interstate commerce, with extra pay for overtime.

Wilson earned the enmity of businesspeople and bigots but endeared himself to progressives when in 1916 he nominated for the Supreme Court the prominent reformer Louis D. Brandeis—the first Jew to be called to the high bench. Yet Wilson's progressivism had its limits, and it clearly stopped short of better treatment for blacks. The southern-bred Wilson actually presided over accelerated segregation in the federal bureaucracy. When a delegation of black leaders personally protested to him, the schoolmasterish president virtually froze them out of his office.

Workingmen's Compensation Act (1916) *Passed under Woodrow Wilson, this law granted assistance to federal civil-service employees during periods of disability. It was a precursor to labor-friendly legislation passed during the New Deal.*

Adamson Act (1916) *This law established an eight-hour day for all employees on trains involved in interstate commerce, with extra pay for overtime. The first federal law regulating the hours of workers in private companies, it was upheld by the Supreme Court in* Wilson v. New *(1917).*

Jones Act (1916) *Law according territorial status to the Philippines and promising independence as soon as a "stable government" could be established. The United States did not grant the Philippines independence until July 4, 1946.*

New Directions in Foreign Policy

In one important area, Wilson chose not to answer the trumpet call of the bull moosers. In contrast to Roosevelt and even Taft, Wilson recoiled from an aggressive foreign policy. Hating imperialism, he was repelled by TR's big stickism. Suspicious of Wall Street, he detested the so-called dollar diplomacy of Taft.

In office only a week, Wilson declared war on dollar diplomacy. He proclaimed that the government would no longer support American investors in Latin America and China. Shivering from this Wilsonian bucket of cold water, American bankers pulled out of the Taft-engineered six-nation loan to China the next day. Wilson's anti-imperialism also produced the **Jones Act** of 1916, which granted territorial status to the Philippines and promised independence as soon as a "stable government" could be established. Wilson's racial prejudices, however, made it difficult for him to anticipate anything other than a long political tutelage for the Filipinos. Indeed, not until July 4, 1946—thirty years later—did the United States accept Philippine independence.

Events in the Caribbean soon forced Wilson to eat some of his anti-imperialist words. In response to disorders in Haiti in 1914–1915, the president reluctantly dispatched marines to protect American lives and property. In 1916 he stole a page from the Roosevelt Corollary to the Monroe Doctrine as the United States took over supervision of Haiti's finances and police. In the same year, Wilson sent the leathernecked marines to quell riots in the Dominican Republic, which then came under the shadow of the American eagle's wings for the next eight years. In 1917 Wilson purchased from Denmark the Virgin Islands in the West Indies. Increasingly, the Caribbean Sea, with its vital approaches to the now-navigable Panama Canal, was taking on the earmarks of a Yankee preserve (see Map 29.1).

Moralistic Diplomacy in Mexico

Rifle bullets whining across the southern border served as a constant reminder that all was not quiet in Mexico. For decades Mexico had been sorely exploited by foreign investors in oil, railroads, and mines. By 1913 American capitalists had sunk about a billion dollars into the underdeveloped but generously endowed country.

But if Mexico was rich, the Mexicans were poor. Fed up with their miserable lot, the Mexicans at last revolted. Their revolution took an ugly turn in early 1913, when a conscienceless clique (with the support of President Taft's ambassador to Mexico) murdered the popular new revolutionary president and installed General Victoriano Huerta, a Huichol Indian, in the president's chair. All this chaos accelerated a massive migration of Mexicans to the United States. More than a million Spanish-speaking newcomers tramped across the southern border in the first three decades of the twentieth century. Settling mostly in Texas, New Mexico, Arizona, and California, they helped to create a unique borderland culture that blended Mexican and American folkways.

The revolutionary bloodshed also menaced American lives and property in Mexico. Cries for intervention burst from the lips of American jingoes such as publisher William Randolph Hearst, who owned a Mexican ranch larger than Rhode Island. Yet once again, President Wilson refused to practice the same old dollar diplomacy of his predecessors, deeming it "perilous" to determine foreign policy "in the terms of material interest."

Wilson strove as best he could to steer a moral course in Mexico. He sent his aggressive ambassador packing, imposed an arms embargo, and refused to recognize officially the murderous government of "that brute" Huerta, even though most foreign powers

Map 29.1 The United States in the Caribbean, 1898–1941 This map explains why many Latin Americans accused the United States of turning the Caribbean Sea into a "Yankee lake." The map also suggests that Uncle Sam was much less "isolationist" in his own backyard than he was in faraway Europe or Asia.

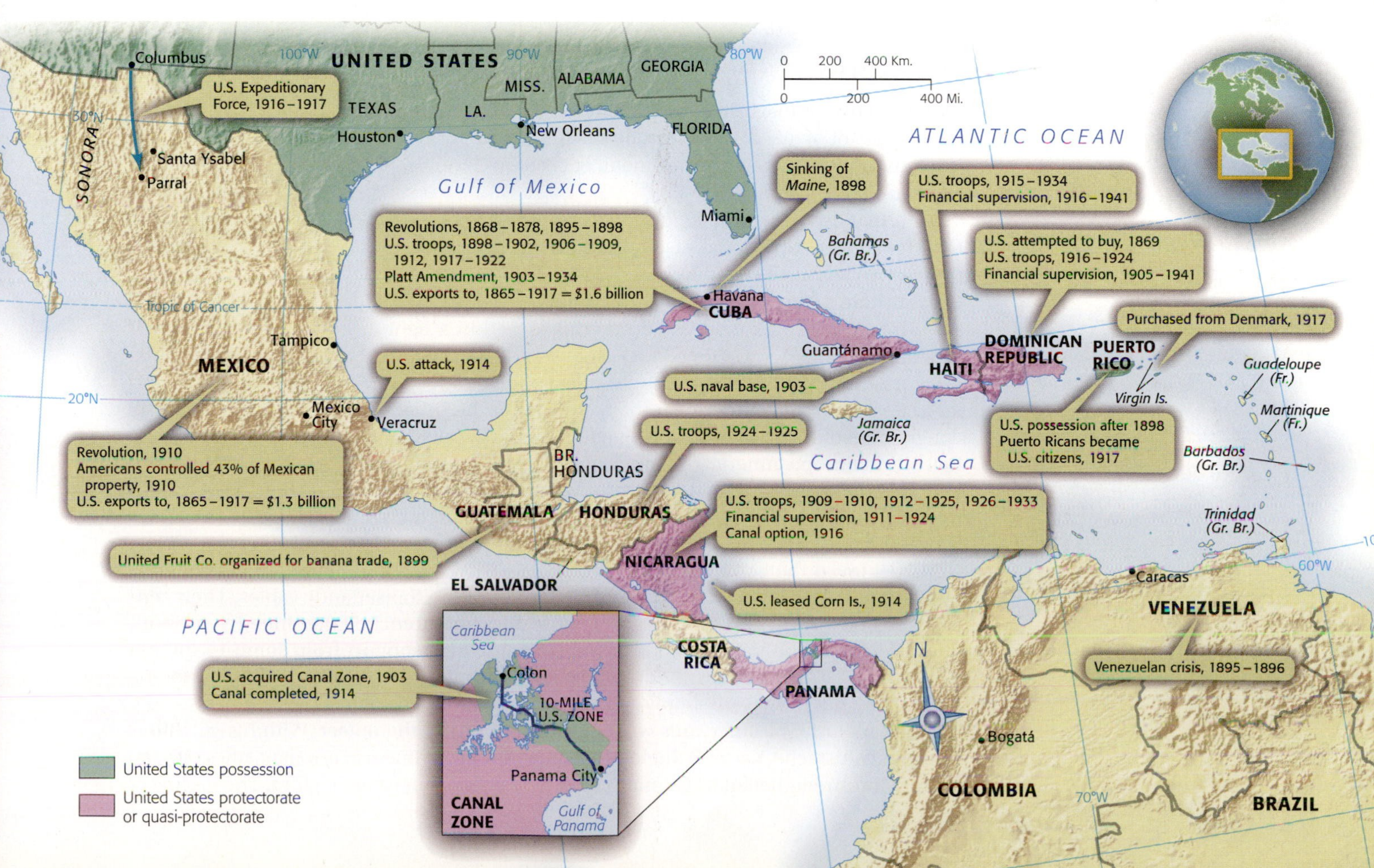

acknowledged Huerta's bloody-handed regime. "I am going to teach the South American republics to elect good men," the former professor declared. He put his munitions where his mouth was in 1914, when he allowed American arms to flow to Huerta's principal rivals, white-bearded Venustiano Carranza and the firebrand Francisco ("Pancho") Villa.

The Mexican volcano erupted at the Atlantic seaport of Tampico in April 1914, when a small party of American sailors was arrested. The Mexicans promptly released the captives and apologized, but they refused the affronted American admiral's demand for a twenty-one gun salute. Wilson ordered the navy to seize the Mexican port of Veracruz to thwart the arrival of a German steamer carrying Huerta-bound guns and ammunition.

Just as a full-dress shooting conflict seemed inevitable, Wilson was rescued by an offer of mediation from the ABC powers—Argentina, Brazil, and Chile. Huerta collapsed in July 1914 under pressure from within and without. He was succeeded by his archrival Carranza, who hotly resented Wilson's military meddling. The whole sorry **Tampico Incident** did not augur well for the future of United States–Mexican relations.

Tampico Incident (1914) *An arrest of American sailors by the Mexican government that spurred Woodrow Wilson to dispatch the American navy to seize the port of Veracruz in April 1914. Although war was avoided, tensions grew between the United States and Mexico.*

"Pancho" Villa, a combination of bandit and Robin Hood, had meanwhile emerged as the chief rival of President Carranza, whom Wilson now reluctantly supported. Challenging Carranza's authority while also punishing the gringos, Villa's men ruthlessly killed sixteen American mining engineers in northern Mexico in January 1916. A month later Villa and his followers, hoping to provoke a war between Wilson and Carranza, blazed across the border into Columbus, New Mexico, and murdered another nineteen Americans.

General John J. ("Black Jack," so called from his earlier service as an officer with the crack black Tenth Cavalry) Pershing, a ramrod-erect veteran of the Cuban and Philippine campaigns, was ordered to break up the bandit band. His hastily organized force of several thousand mounted troops penetrated deep into rugged Mexico with surprising speed. They clashed with Carranza's forces and mauled the Villistas but failed to capture Villa himself. As the threat of war with Germany loomed larger, the invading army was withdrawn in January 1917.

Thunder Across the Sea

Europe's powder magazine, long smoldering, blew up in the summer of 1914, when the flaming pistol of a Serb patriot killed the heir to the throne of Austria-Hungary in Sarajevo. An outraged Vienna government, backed by Germany, forthwith presented a stern ultimatum to Serbia.

An explosive chain reaction followed. Russia's mobilization in support of Serbia threatened Germany in the east, even as the tsar's ally, France, confronted Germany in the west. In alarm, the Germans struck suddenly at France through unoffending Belgium. Great Britain in turn was sucked into the conflagration on the side of France.

Almost overnight most of Europe was locked in a fight to the death. On one side were arrayed the **Central Powers**: Germany and Austria-Hungary, and later Turkey and Bulgaria. On the other side were the **Allies**, principally France, Britain, and Russia, and later Japan and Italy. Americans thanked God for the ocean moats and self-righteously congratulated themselves on having had ancestors wise enough to have abandoned the hell pits of Europe. Americans felt strong, snug, smug, and secure—but not for long.

Central Powers *Germany and Austria-Hungary, later joined by Turkey and Bulgaria, made up this alliance against the Allies in World War I.*

Allies *Great Britain, Russia, and France, later joined by Italy, Japan, and the United States, formed this alliance against the Central Powers in World War I.*

President Wilson issued the routine neutrality proclamation and called on Americans to be neutral in thought as well as deed. But such scrupulous evenhandedness proved difficult. Both sides wooed the United States, the great neutral in the West. The British enjoyed the boon of close cultural, linguistic, and economic ties with America and had the added advantage of controlling most of the transatlantic cables. Their censors sheared away war stories harmful to the Allies and drenched the United States with tales of German bestiality. Germany in turn looked for support from some 11 million Americans of German descent. Some recent immigrants did express noisy support for the Fatherland, but most were simply grateful to be so distant from the fray.

U-boats *German submarines, named for the German Unterseeboot, or "undersea boat," proved deadly for Allied ships in the war zone. U-boat attacks played an important role in drawing the United States into the First World War.*

The majority of Americans were anti-German from the outset. With his villainous upturned mustache, Kaiser Wilhelm II seemed the embodiment of arrogant autocracy, an impression strengthened by Germany's ruthless strike at neutral Belgium. The discovery in 1915 of German plans for industrial sabotage of American factories and ports further inflamed opinion against the kaiser and Germany. Still, most Americans earnestly hoped to stay out of the horrible war.

The Fatherland, *the chief German-American propaganda newspaper in the United States, cried:*

"We [Americans] prattle about humanity while we manufacture poisoned shrapnel and picric acid for profit. Ten thousand German widows, ten thousand orphans, ten thousand graves bear the legend 'Made in America.'"

America Earns Blood Money

When Europe burst into flames in 1914, the United States was bogged down in a worrisome business recession. But British and French war orders soon pulled American industry out of the morass of hard times and onto a peak of war-born prosperity. Part of this boom was financed by American bankers, notably the Wall Street firm of J.P. Morgan and Company, which eventually advanced to the Allies the enormous sum of $2.3 billion during the period of American neutrality.

American trade with Germany could legally have rivaled that of the Allies. But the British threw a noose-tight blockade around the German North Sea ports and began forcing American merchant vessels into their own ports. As a result trade between Germany and the United States virtually ceased.

Hard-pressed Germany did not tamely consent to being starved out. In retaliation for the British blockade, in February 1915 Berlin announced a submarine war area around the British Isles. The submarine was a weapon so new that existing international law could not be made to fit it. The old rule that a warship must stop and board merchant ships could hardly apply to submarines, which could easily be rammed or sunk if they surfaced.

The cigar-shaped marauders posed a dire threat to the United States—so long as Wilson insisted on maintaining America's neutral rights. Berlin officials declared that they would try not to sink *neutral* shipping, but they warned that mistakes would probably occur. Wilson now determined on a policy of calculated risk. He would continue to claim profitable neutral trading rights while hoping that no high-seas incident would force his hand to grasp the sword of war. The German submarines (known as **U-boats**, from the German *Unterseeboot*, or "undersea boat") meanwhile began their deadly work. In the first months of 1915, they sank about ninety ships in the war zone. Then the submarine issue became acute when the British passenger liner ***Lusitania*** was torpedoed and sank off the coast of Ireland on May 7, 1915, with the loss of 1,198 lives, including 128 Americans.

Lusitania *British passenger liner that sank after it was torpedoed by Germany on May 7, 1915. It ended the lives of 1,198 people, including 128 Americans, and pushed the United States closer to war.*

The *Lusitania* was carrying forty-two hundred cases of small-arms ammunition, a fact the Germans used to justify the sinking. But Americans were swept by a wave of shock and anger at this act of "mass murder" and "piracy." The eastern United States, closer to the war, seethed with talk of fighting, but the rest of the country showed a strong distaste for hostilities. The peace-loving Wilson had no stomach for leading a disunited nation into war and relied instead on a series of increasingly strong notes to take the German warlords sharply to task. "There is such a thing," he said, "as a man being too proud to fight." Wilson's policies incensed the war-thirsty Theodore Roosevelt, who assailed what he saw as the "weasel words" and spinelessness of the peace-loving professor in the White House.

Yet Wilson, sticking to his verbal guns, made some diplomatic progress. After another British liner, the *Arabic*, was sunk in August 1915, with the loss of two American lives, Berlin reluctantly agreed not to sink unarmed and unresisting passenger ships *without warning*. This pledge appeared to be violated in March 1916, when the Germans torpedoed a French passenger steamer, the *Sussex*. The infuriated Wilson informed the Germans that unless they renounced the inhuman practice of sinking merchant ships without warning he would break diplomatic relations—an almost certain prelude to war.

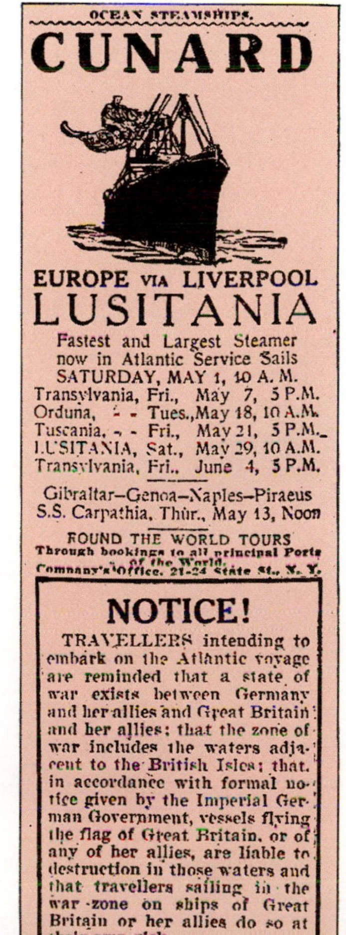

Advertisement from the *New York Herald*, May 1, 1915 Six days later the *Lusitania* was sunk. Notice the German warning.

Germany reluctantly knuckled under to President Wilson's *Sussex* ultimatum, agreeing not to sink passenger ships and merchant vessels without giving warning. But the Germans attached a long string to their *Sussex* pledge: the United States would have to persuade the Allies to modify what Berlin regarded as their illegal blockade. This, obviously, was something that Washington could not do. Wilson promptly accepted the

German pledge, without accepting the "string." He thus won a temporary but precarious diplomatic victory—precarious because Germany could pull the string whenever it chose, and the president might suddenly find himself tugged over the cliff of war.

Wilson Wins Reelection in 1916

Against this ominous backdrop, the presidential campaign of 1916 gathered speed. Both the bull moose Progressives and the Republicans met in Chicago. The Progressives uproariously renominated Theodore Roosevelt, but the Rough Rider, who loathed Wilson and all his works, had no stomach for splitting the Republicans again and ensuring the reelection of his hated rival. In refusing to run, he sounded the death knell of the Progressive party.

The Republicans drafted Supreme Court Justice Charles Evans Hughes, the cold, intellectual former governor of New York. The Republican platform condemned the Democratic tariff, assaults on the trusts, and Wilson's wishy-washiness in dealing with Mexico and Germany.

For his part, Wilson knew that his election in 1912 had owed largely to the Taft-Roosevelt split in the GOP. He had used his first term to identify himself as the candidate of progressivism and woo bull moose voters into the Democratic fold. Nominated by acclamation at the Democratic convention in St. Louis, Wilson now built his 1916 campaign on the slogan "He Kept Us Out of War."

On election day, Hughes swept the East and looked like a surefire winner. Wilson went to bed that night prepared to accept defeat, while New York newspapers displayed huge portraits of "The President-Elect—Charles Evans Hughes." But the rest of the country turned the tide. Midwesterners and westerners, attracted by Wilson's progressive reforms and antiwar policies, flocked to the polls for the president. The final result, in doubt for several days, hinged on California, which Wilson carried by some 3,800 votes out of about a million cast.

Wilson barely squeaked through, with a final vote of 277 to 254 in the Electoral College and 9,127,695 to 8,533,507 in the popular column (see Map 29.2). The pro-labor Wilson received strong support from the working class and from renegade bull moosers, whom Republicans failed to lure back into their camp. Wilson had not specifically promised to keep the country out of war, but probably enough voters relied on such implicit assurances to ensure his victory. Their hopeful expectations were soon rudely shattered.

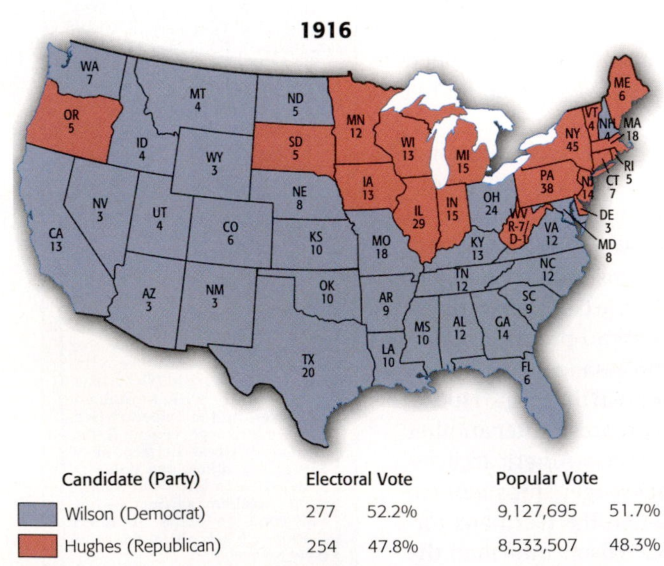

Map 29.2 Presidential Election of 1916 (with electoral vote by state) Wilson was so worried about being a lame-duck president in a time of great international tensions that he drew up a plan whereby Hughes, if victorious, would be appointed secretary of state, Wilson and the vice president would resign, and Hughes would thus succeed immediately to the presidency.

War by Act of Germany

Destiny dealt cruelly with Woodrow Wilson. The lover of peace, as fate would have it, was forced to lead a hesitant and peace-loving nation into war. As the last days of 1916 slipped through the hourglass, the president made one final, futile attempt to mediate between the embattled belligerents. On January 22, 1917, he delivered one of his most moving addresses, restating America's conviction that only a negotiated "peace without victory" would prove durable.

Germany's warlords responded with a blow of the mailed fist. On January 31, 1917, they announced to an astonished world that they intended to wage *unrestricted* submarine warfare, sinking *all* ships, including America's, in the war zone.

Why this rash act? War with America was the last thing Germany wanted. But after three ghastly years in the trenches, Germany's leaders decided that making distinctions between combatants and noncombatants was a luxury they could no longer afford. Thus they jerked on the string they had attached to their *Sussex* pledge in 1916, desperately hoping to bring Britain to its knees before the United States entered the war.

Wilson, his bluff called, broke diplomatic relations with Germany but refused to move closer to war unless the Germans undertook "overt" acts against American lives. To defend American interests short of war, the president asked Congress for authority to arm American merchant ships. When a band of midwestern senators launched a filibuster to block the measure, Wilson denounced them as a "little group of willful men" who were rendering a great nation "helpless and contemptible." But their obstructionism was a powerful reminder of the continuing strength of American isolationism.

Meanwhile, the sensational **Zimmermann note** was intercepted and published on March 1, 1917, infuriating Americans, especially westerners. German foreign secretary Arthur Zimmermann had secretly proposed a German-Mexican alliance, tempting anti-Yankee Mexico with veiled promises of recovering Texas, New Mexico, and Arizona.

Zimmermann note (1917) *Secret proposal by German foreign secretary Arthur Zimmerman for a German-Mexican alliance against the United States. When the note was intercepted and published in March 1917, it caused an uproar that made some Americans more willing to enter the war.*

On the heels of this provocation came the long-dreaded "overt" acts in the Atlantic, where German U-boats sank four unarmed American merchant vessels in the first two weeks of March. As one Philadelphia newspaper observed, "The difference between war and what we have now is that now we aren't fighting back." Simultaneously came the rousing news that a revolution in Russia had toppled the cruel regime of the tsars. America could now fight foursquare for democracy on the side of the Allies without the black sheep of Russian despotism in the Allied fold.

Subdued and solemn, Wilson at last stood before a hushed joint session of Congress on the evening of April 2, 1917, and asked for a declaration of war. He had lost his gamble that America could pursue the profits of neutral trade without being sucked into the ghastly maelstrom. A myth developed in later years that America was dragged unwittingly into war by munitions makers and Wall Street bankers, desperate to protect their profits and loans. Yet the weapons merchants and financiers were already thriving, unhampered by wartime government restrictions and heavy taxation. The simple truth is that British harassment of American commerce had been galling but endurable; Germany had resorted to the mass killing of civilians. President Wilson had drawn a clear, if risky, line against the depredations of the submarine. The German high command, in a last desperate throw of the dice, chose to cross it. In a figurative sense, America's war declaration of April 6, 1917, bore the unambiguous trademark "Made in Germany."

Wilsonian Idealism Enthroned

"It is a fearful thing to lead this great peaceful people into war," Wilson said in his war message. It proved fearful indeed. How could the president arouse the American people to shoulder this unprecedented burden? For more than a century, they had prided themselves on their isolation from the periodic outbursts of militarized violence that afflicted the Old World. Ominously, no fewer than six senators and fifty representatives (including the first congresswoman, Jeannette Rankin of Montana) had voted against the war resolution. Wilson could whip up no enthusiasm, especially in the landlocked Midwest, by calling on the nation to fight to make the world safe from the submarine.

To galvanize the country, Wilson would have to proclaim more glorified aims. Radiating the spiritual fervor of his Presbyterian ancestors, he declared the supremely ambitious goal of a crusade "to make the world safe for democracy." Brandishing the sword of righteousness, Wilson virtually hypnotized the nation with his lofty ideals. He contrasted the selfish war aims of the other belligerents, Allied and enemy alike, with America's shining altruism. America, he preached, did not fight for the sake of riches or territorial conquest. The Republic sought only to shape an international order in which democracy could flourish without fear of power-crazed autocrats and militarists.

In Wilsonian idealism the personality of the president and the necessities of history were perfectly matched. The high-minded Wilson genuinely believed in the principles he so eloquently intoned—especially that the modern world could not afford the kind of hyper-destructive war that advanced industrial states were now capable of waging. In this, Wilson's vision was prophetic. In any case, probably no other argument could have successfully converted the American people from their historic hostility to involvement in European squabbles. Americans, it seemed, could be either isolationists or crusaders, but nothing in between.

Wilson's appeal worked—perhaps too well. Holding aloft the torch of idealism, the president fired up the public mind to a fever pitch. "Force, force to the utmost, force without stint or limit," he cried, while the country responded less elegantly with, "Hang the kaiser!" Lost on the gale was Wilson's earlier plea for "peace without victory."

Fourteen Points (1918) *Woodrow Wilson's proposal to ensure peace after World War I, calling for an end to secret treaties, widespread arms reduction, national self-determination, and a new league of nations.*

Committee on Public Information (1917) *A government office during World War I known popularly as the Creel Committee for its chairman George Creel, dedicated to winning everyday Americans' support for the war effort. It regularly distributed prowar propaganda and sent out an army of "four-minute men" to rally crowds and deliver "patriotic pep."*

Wilson's Fourteen Potent Points

Wilson quickly came to be recognized as the moral leader of the Allied cause. He scaled a summit of inspiring oratory on January 8, 1918, when he delivered his famed **Fourteen Points** Address to an enthusiastic Congress. Wilson's vision inspired all the drooping Allies to make mightier efforts and demoralized the enemy governments by holding out alluring promises to their dissatisfied minorities.

The first five of the Fourteen Points were broad in scope: (1) A proposal to abolish secret treaties pleased liberals of all countries. (2) Freedom of the seas appealed to the Germans, as well as to Americans who distrusted British sea power. (3) A removal of economic barriers among nations had long been the goal of liberal internationalists everywhere. (4) Reduction of armament burdens was gratifying to taxpayers of all countries. (5) An adjustment of colonial claims in the interests of both native peoples and the colonizers was a potentially revolutionary appeal that helped delegitimize old empires and inspire "subject peoples."

Other points among the fourteen proved to be no less seductive. They held out the promise of independence ("self-determination") to oppressed minority groups, such as the Poles, millions of whom lay under the heel of Germany and Austria-Hungary. The capstone point, number fourteen, foreshadowed the League of Nations—an international organization that Wilson dreamed would provide a system of collective security.

Yet Wilson's appealing points, though raising hopes the world over, were not everywhere applauded. Certain leaders of the Allied nations, with an eye to territorial booty, were less than enthusiastic. Hard-nosed Republicans at home grumbled, and some openly mocked the "fourteen commandments" of "God Almighty Wilson."

Library of Congress Prints and Photographs Division [LC-USZC4-4441]

Anti-German Propaganda The government relied extensively on emotional appeals and hate propaganda to rally support for the First World War, which most Americans regarded as a distant "European" affair. This poster used gendered imagery to evoke the brutal German violation of Belgian neutrality in August 1914.

Manipulating Minds and Stifling Dissent

Mobilizing people's minds for war, both in America and abroad, was an urgent task facing the Washington authorities. The **Committee on Public Information**, headed by journalist George Creel, was therefore created to sell America on the war and to sell the world on Wilsonian war aims. Creel's organization, employing 150,000 workers at home and overseas, proved that words were indeed weapons. It sent out an army of 75,000 "four-minute men"—often longer-winded than that—who delivered countless speeches full of "patriotic pep."

Creel's propaganda took varied forms. Posters were splashed on billboards in the "Battle of the Fences," as artists "rallied to the colors." Millions of pamphlets containing the most pungent Wilsonisms were showered like confetti upon the world. Hang-the-kaiser movies, carrying such titles as *The Kaiser, The Beast of Berlin* and *To Hell with the Kaiser*, portrayed the helmeted "Hun" at his bloodiest. Arm-waving conductors by the thousands led huge audiences in songs that poured scorn on the enemy and glorified the "boys" in uniform.

The entire nation, catching the frenzied spirit of a religious revival, burst into song. Most memorable of many anthems was George M. Cohan's spine-tingling "Over There":

Over there, over there
Send the word, send the word over there,
That the Yanks are coming, the Yanks are coming
The drums rum-tumming ev'rywhere.

Creel typified American war mobilization, which relied more on aroused passion and voluntary compliance than on formal laws. But he oversold the ideals of Wilson and led the world to expect too much. When the president proved to be a mortal and not a god, the resulting disillusionment at home and abroad was disastrous.

Patriotic fervor also had a darker side. German Americans numbered over 8 million, counting those with at least one parent foreign-born, out of a total population of 100 million. Most proved to be loyal to the United States. But as emotion mounted, hysterical hatred of Germans and things Germanic swept the nation. Orchestras found it unsafe to present German-composed music, like that of Wagner and Beethoven. German books were removed from library shelves, and German classes were canceled in high schools and colleges. Sauerkraut became "liberty cabbage" and hamburger "liberty steak." Even beer became suspect, as patriotic Americans fretted over the loyalty of breweries with names like Schlitz or Pabst.

Brey, Laura/Library of Congress Prints and Photographs Division [LC-USZC4-9659]

Patriotic Persuasion Worried about the public's enthusiasm for the war, the government employed all the arts of psychology and propaganda to sustain the martial spirit. The prewar song "I Didn't Raise My Boy to Be a Soldier" was changed to "I Didn't Raise My Boy to Be a Slacker," which in turn inspired the cruel parody "I Didn't Raise My Boy to Be a Sausage."

Both the **Espionage Act** of 1917 and the Sedition Act of 1918 reflected current fears about Germans and antiwar Americans. Especially visible among the nineteen hundred prosecutions undertaken under these laws were antiwar Socialists and members of the radical union Industrial Workers of the World (IWW). Kingpin Socialist Eugene V. Debs was tried under the Espionage Act in 1918 and sentenced to ten years in a federal penitentiary. IWW leader William D. ("Big Bill") Haywood and ninety-nine associates were similarly convicted. Virtually any criticism of the government could be censored and punished. Some critics claimed the new laws were bending, if not breaking, the First Amendment. But in ***Schenck* v. *United States*** (1919), the Supreme Court affirmed their legality, arguing that freedom of speech could be revoked when such speech presented a "clear and present danger" to the nation.

These prosecutions form an ugly chapter in the history of American civil liberty. With the dawn of peace, presidential pardons were rather freely granted, including President Harding's to Eugene Debs in 1921. Yet a few victims lingered behind bars into the 1930s.

Espionage Act (1917) *A law prohibiting interference with the draft and other acts of national "disloyalty." Together with the Sedition Act of 1918, which added penalties for abusing the government in writing, it created a climate that was unfriendly to civil liberties.*

***Schenck* v. *United States* (1919)** *A Supreme Court decision that upheld the Espionage and Sedition Acts, reasoning that freedom of speech could be curtailed when it posed a "clear and present danger" to the nation.*

Forging a War Economy

Victory was no foregone conclusion, especially because the Republic was caught flatfootedly unready for its leap into global war. Wilson had only belatedly backed some mild preparedness measures beginning in 1915. It would take a herculean effort to mobilize America's daunting but disorganized resources and throw them into the field quickly enough to bolster the Allied war effort.

Towering obstacles confronted economic mobilizers. Sheer ignorance was among the biggest roadblocks. No one knew precisely how much steel or explosive powder the country was capable of producing. Traditional fears of big government hamstrung efforts to orchestrate the economy from Washington. The largely voluntary character of economic war organization testified to ocean-insulated America's safe distance from the fighting—as well as to the still-modest scale of government powers in the progressive-era Republic.

Late in the war, Wilson finally succeeded in imposing some order on this economic confusion. In March 1918 he appointed Wall Street's Bernard Baruch to head the **War Industries Board**. Although the board had only feeble formal powers, it set a precedent for the federal government to take a central role in economic planning in moments of crisis.

War Industries Board (1917) *Federal agency, headed by Bernard Baruch, that coordinated industrial production during World War I, setting production quotas, allocating raw materials, and pushing companies to increase efficiency and eliminate waste. Under the economic mobilization of the War Industries Board, industrial production in the United States increased 20 percent during the war.*

As the larder of democracy, America had to feed itself and its allies. Herbert C. Hoover, the Quaker-humanitarian head of the Food Administration, shared his fellow war administrators' preference for relying on voluntary compliance rather than compulsory edicts. Instead of rationing food supplies, he waged a whirlwind propaganda campaign through posters, billboards, newspapers, pulpits, and movies. To save food for export, Hoover proclaimed wheatless Wednesdays and meatless Tuesdays—all on a voluntary basis. Even children, when eating apples, were urged to be "patriotic to the core." The country soon broke out in a rash of vegetable "victory gardens." Thanks to the fervent patriotic wartime spirit, Hoover's voluntary approach worked, greatly increasing farm production and food exports to the Allies.

Congress severely restricted the use of foodstuffs for manufacturing alcoholic beverages. The wartime drive against German-descended brewers aided in the passage of the Eighteenth Amendment in 1919, which prohibited not only beer but all alcoholic drinks.

As prohibition indicated, despite the Wilson administration's preference for voluntary means of mobilizing the economy, over the course of the war the federal government expanded in size and power. The War Industries Board eventually issued production quotas, allocated raw materials, and set prices for government purchases. Following indescribably tangled traffic snarls in late 1917, Washington took over the railroads. Time itself came under Uncle Sam's control when the entire country was ordered to observe daylight saving time to extend the workday and save on fuel.

Industrial Workers of the World (1905) *Also known as the "Wobblies," a radical organization that sought to build "one big union" and advocated industrial sabotage to advance that goal. At its peak in 1923, it claimed 100,000 members and was supported by 300,000. The IWW particularly appealed to migratory workers in agriculture and lumbering and to miners, all of whom suffered from horrific working conditions.*

Workers in Wartime

Spurred by the slogan "Labor Will Win the War," American workers sweated their way to victory. In 1918 the War Department threatened to draft any unemployed male, but for the most part the government tried to treat labor fairly. Samuel Gompers and his American Federation of Labor (AF of L) loyally supported the war and were rewarded for it. At war's end, the AF of L had more than doubled its membership, to over 3 million. In the most heavily unionized industries, wages had risen by more than 20 percent over prewar levels.

Yet labor still harbored grievances. Six thousand strikes, several bloody, broke out in the war years. The radical antiwar **Industrial Workers of the World**, known as the "Wobblies," engineered some damaging industrial sabotage, and not without reason. Transient laborers in such industries as fruit and lumber, the Wobblies were victims of some of the shabbiest working conditions in the country.

Great Migration *The movement of 6 million African Americans from the rural South to the urban North and West in two major waves. The first, from World War I until the onset of the Great Depression, brought more than 1.5 million migrants to northern cities. From 1940 to 1970, another 5 million left the South, pushed off the land by the mechanization of cotton farming and lured north and west by hopes for greater economic opportunity and more equitable political participation. After 1970, increasing numbers of African Americans trekked back to the South in what was called the New Great Migration, as new jobs became more plentiful in the South than in the older industrial cities of the North and racial relations improved in the South.*

In 1919, the greatest strike in American history rocked the steel industry. More than a quarter of a million workers walked off the job in a bid to force their employers to recognize their right to bargain collectively. The steel companies refused to negotiate and brought in thirty thousand African American strikebreakers to keep the mills running. After bitter confrontations that left more than a dozen workers dead, the steel strike collapsed, a grievous setback that crippled the union movement for more than a decade.

Nineteenth Amendment (1920) *Gave women the right to vote, more than seventy years after the first organized calls for woman's suffrage in Seneca Falls, New York.*

The black workers who entered the steel mills in 1919 were but a fraction of the tens of thousands of southern blacks drawn to the North by the magnet of war-industry employment. These migrants made up the small-scale beginnings of the **Great Migration**, a northward trek that would eventually grow to massive proportions. Their sudden appearance in previously all-white areas sometimes sparked interracial violence. An explosive riot in East St. Louis, Illinois, in July 1917 left nine whites and at least forty blacks dead. An equally gruesome riot ripped through Chicago in July 1919, fanned by tensions between white working-class neighborhoods and African Americans toiling as strikebreakers in meatpacking plants. Fifteen whites and twenty-three blacks were killed during nearly two weeks of terror.

Suffering Until Suffrage

Women also heeded the call of patriotism and opportunity. Thousands of female workers flooded into factories and fields, taking up jobs vacated by men who left the assembly line for the front line. But the war split the women's movement deeply. Many progressive feminists were pacifists, inclined to oppose both the participation of America in the war and women in the war effort. This group found a voice in the National Woman's party, led by Quaker activist Alice Paul, which demonstrated against "Kaiser Wilson" with marches and hunger strikes.

But the larger part of the suffrage movement, represented by the National American Woman Suffrage Association, supported Wilson's war. Leaders echoed Wilson's justification for fighting by arguing that women must take part in the war effort to earn a role in shaping the peace. The fight for democracy abroad was women's best chance for winning true democracy at home.

War mobilization gave new momentum to the suffrage fight. Impressed by women's war work, President Wilson endorsed woman suffrage as "a vitally necessary war measure." In 1917 New York voted for suffrage at the state level; Michigan, Oklahoma, and South Dakota followed. The next year, governments in Great Britain, Austria-Hungary, and Germany extended the suffrage to women. Not long after, the United States followed suit. In 1920, more than seventy years after the first calls for suffrage at Seneca Falls, the **Nineteenth Amendment** was ratified, giving all American women the right to vote. (See the Appendix.)

Despite political victory, women's wartime economic gains proved fleeting. When peace arrived, most women workers soon gave up their war jobs. Meanwhile, Congress reaffirmed its support for women in their traditional role as mothers when it passed the **Sheppard-Towner Maternity Act** of 1921, providing federally financed instruction in maternal and infant health care. In doing so, Congress also expanded the responsibility of the federal government for family welfare. Partial though the feminist victories were, the developments of the World War I era foreshadowed a future when women's wage-labor and political power would reshape the American way of life.

Contending Voices

Battle of the Ballot

In an open address to Congress in 1917, suffragist Carrie Chapman Catt (1859–1947) capitalized on the idealism of the day and invoked the founding principles of American democracy in arguing the case for women's right to vote:

"How can our nation escape the logic it has never failed to follow, when its last unenfranchised class calls for the vote? Behold our Uncle Sam floating the banner with one hand, 'Taxation without representation is tyranny,' and with the other seizing the billions of dollars paid in taxes by women to whom he refuses 'representation.' . . . Is there a single man who can justify such inequality of treatment, such outrageous discrimination? Not one."

Female anti-suffrage activists, for their part, often depicted their opposition to the ballot as a means to protect women's unique role in promoting reform free of corrupt politics, as Mrs. Barclay Hazard (1861–1938) explained in a 1907 speech:

"[We] must accept partisanship, political trickery, and office-seeking as necessary evils inseparable from modern conditions, and the question arises what can be done to palliate the situation. To our minds, the solution has been found by the entrance of women into public life. Standing in an absolutely independent political position, freed from all partisan affiliations, untrammeled by any political obligations, the intelligent, self-sacrificing women of today are . . . a third party whose disinterestedness none can doubt."

How did progressive-era notions inform the debate over suffrage?

Making Plowboys into Doughboys

Most citizens, at the outset, did not dream of sending a mighty force to France, assuming American naval power and material support would suffice. But in April and May of 1917, the Europeans confessed that they were scraping the bottom not only of their money

Sheppard-Towner Maternity Act (1921) *Designed to appeal to new women voters, provided federally financed instruction in maternal and infant health care and expanded the role of government in family welfare.*

National Archives

David J. & Janice L. Frent Collection/Historical/Corbis

In the Trenches and to the Polls Wars often bring opportunities and innovations as well as danger and destruction. As U.S. Army nurses went into harm's way at the fighting front in France, the century-long struggle for women's suffrage intensified on the home front, culminating in the Nineteenth Amendment in 1920.

chests but, more ominously, of their manpower barrels. A huge American army would have to be raised, trained, and transported, or the whole western front would collapse. And America's small existing army of 100,000 regulars ranked only fifteenth among the armies of the world.

Conscription was the only answer to the need for raising an immense army with all possible speed. Wilson disliked a draft, but he eventually accepted and eloquently supported conscription as a disagreeable and temporary necessity. Six weeks after declaring war, Congress grudgingly passed conscription to supply manpower for the American Expeditionary Forces (AEF) in Europe.

The draft machinery, on the whole, worked effectively. Within a few frantic months the army grew to over 4 million men. For the first time, women were admitted to the armed forces: some 11,000 to the navy and 269 to the marines. African Americans also served in the AEF, though in strictly segregated units and usually under white officers.

Recruits were supposed to receive six months of training in America and two more months overseas. But so great was the urgency that many doughboys were swept swiftly into battle scarcely knowing how to handle a rifle, much less a bayonet.

Ignoring grisly tales of the agonies of trench warfare, many young American men saw an opportunity for adventure and seized it. Author John Dos Passos (1896–1970) recollected how he felt going off to war in 1917:

"We had spent our boyhood in the afterglow of the peaceful nineteenth century. . . . What was war like? We wanted to see with our own eyes. We flocked into the volunteer services. I respected the conscientious objectors, and occasionally felt I should take that course myself, but hell, I wanted to see the show."

America Helps Hammer the Hun

Russia's collapse underscored the need for haste. After the communist Bolsheviks withdrew their beaten country from the "capitalist" war early in 1918, Germany moved hundreds of thousands of its battle-tested soldiers from the eastern front facing Russia to the western front in France, where, for the first time in the war, they were developing a dangerous superiority in manpower—and the Yanks were yet to arrive.

France gradually began to bustle with American doughboys (see Map 29.3). The first trainees to reach the

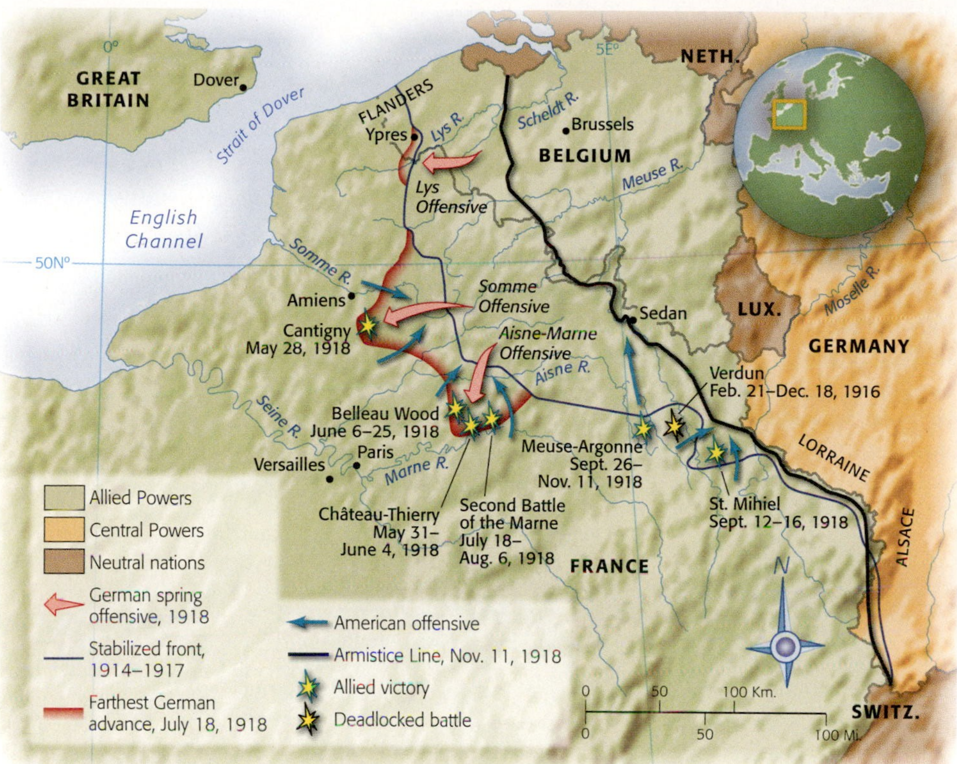

Map 29.3 Major U.S. Operations in France, 1918 One doughboy recorded in his diary his baptism of fire at St. Mihiel: "Hiked through dark woods. No lights allowed, guided by holding on the pack of the man ahead. Stumbled through underbrush for about half mile into an open field where we waited in soaking rain until about 10:00 P.M. We then started on our hike to the St. Mihiel front, arriving on the crest of a hill at 1:00 A.M. I saw a sight which I shall never forget. It was the zero hour and in one instant the entire front as far as the eye could reach in either direction was a sheet of flame, while the heavy artillery made the earth quake."

front were used as replacements in the Allied armies. The newcomers soon made friends with the French girls—or tried to. One of the most sung-about women in history was the fabled "Mademoiselle from Armentières." A printable stanza ran

> *She was true to me, she was true to you,*
> *She was true to the whole damned army, too.*

Not surprisingly, American soldiers suffered from high rates of venereal disease.

The dreaded German drive on the western front exploded in the spring of 1918. Spearheaded by about half a million troops, the enemy rolled forward with terrifying momentum. So dire was the peril that the Allied nations for the first time united under a supreme commander, the quiet French Marshal Ferdinand Foch, whose axiom was "To make war is to attack."

At last the ill-trained "Yanks" were coming—and not a moment too soon. Late in May 1918, the German juggernaut, smashing to within forty miles of Paris, threatened to knock out France. Newly arrived American troops, numbering fewer than thirty thousand, were thrown into the breach at the **Battle of Château-Thierry**, right in the teeth of the German advance. This was a historic moment—the first significant engagement of American troops in a European war. Battle-fatigued French soldiers gaped as the roads filled with inexhaustible truckloads of American doughboys. With their arrival, it was clear that a new American giant had arisen in the West to replace the dying Russian titan in the East.

Château-Thierry, Battle of (1918) *The first significant engagement of American troops in World War I—and, indeed, in any European war. To weary French soldiers, the American doughboys were an image of fresh and gleaming youth.*

America had now put decisive military weight on the scales. By July 1918 the awesome German drive had spent its force, and the AEF joined a Foch counteroffensive in the Second Battle of the Marne. This engagement marked the beginning of a German

Examining the Evidence

"Mademoiselle From Armentières"

Some familiar songs, such as Julia Ward Howe's stirring Civil War–era melody "Battle Hymn of the Republic," were penned by known composers and have well-established scores and lyrics. But many ballads have no specific author. Songwriters may fit new verses to known tunes, but the songs essentially grow out of the soil of popular culture and take on a life of their own. "Yankee Doodle Dandy," for example, originated during the seventeenth-century English Civil War, was adapted by the American revolutionaries more than a century later, and was parodied by Southerners during the American Civil War:

Yankee Doodle had a mind
To whip the Southern "traitors,"
Because they didn't choose to live
On codfish and potaters.

"Stagger Lee," or "Stagolee," a blues ballad supposedly based on a murder in Memphis in the 1930s, has been played in countless renditions, with its homicidal subject variously portrayed as a ruthless badman or a civil rights hero.

This process of accretion and adaptation can furnish valuable clues to historians about changing sentiments and sensibilities, just as the ballads themselves give expression to feelings not always evident in the official record. Folklorist Alan Lomax spent a lifetime tracking down American ballads, documenting layers of life and experience not usually excavated by traditional scholars. In the case of the First World War's most notorious song, "Mademoiselle from Armentières" (or "Hinky Dinky, Parley-Voo?"), Lomax compiled from various sources more than six hundred soldier-authored stanzas, some of which are reproduced here (others he delicately described as "not mailable").

Mademoiselle from Armentières,
She hadn't been kissed in forty years.
She might have been young for all we knew,
When Napoleon flopped at Waterloo. . . .
You'll never get your croix de Guerre,
If you never wash your underwear. . . .

The French, they are a funny race,
They fight with their feet and save their face.

The cootie [louse] is the national bug of France.
The cootie's found all over France,
No matter where you hang your pants. . . .

Oh, the seventy-seventh went over the top,
A sous lieutenant, a Jew, and a Wop. . . .

The officers get all the steak,
And all we get is the belly-ache.

The general got a Croix de Guerre,
The son-of-a-gun was never there. . . .

There's many and many a married man,
Wants to go back to France again.

'Twas a hell of a war as we recall,
But still 'twas better than none at all.

1. What fresh—and irreverent—perspectives do these stanzas reveal about the soldier's-eye view of military life?
2. What view of France and the French people is implied in the lyrics? How do the ordinary American soldiers view their own experience of being in France?
3. What does the implied sexual content of the song and the "Mademoiselle" who supposedly inspired it reveal about this war as a "gendered" activity?

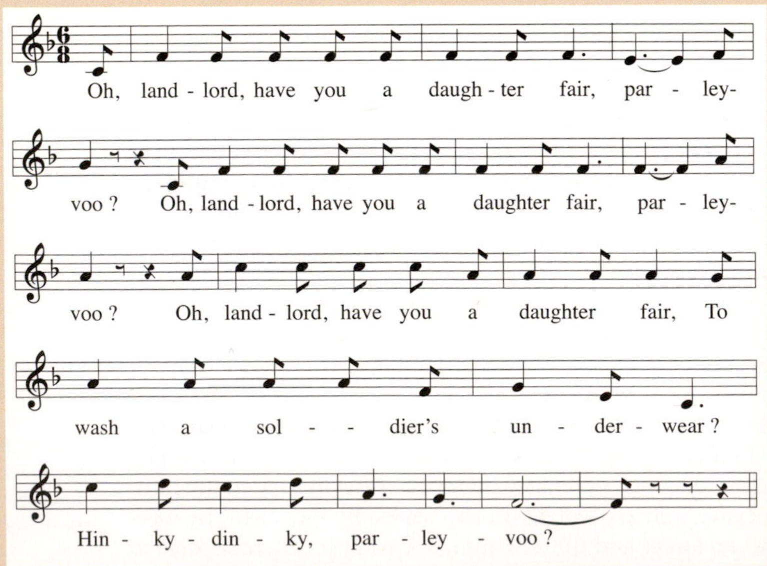
Oh, land - lord, have you a daugh - ter fair, par - ley-
voo ? Oh, land - lord, have you a daughter fair, par - ley-
voo ? Oh, land - lord, have you a daughter fair, To
wash a sol - - dier's un - der - wear ?
Hin - ky - din - ky, par - ley - voo ?

From John A. Lomax and Alan Lomax, *American Ballads and Folksongs*, pp. 558–560. Reprinted by permission of Odyssey Productions, Inc.)

withdrawal that was never effectively reversed. In September 1918 nine American divisions (about 243,000 men) joined four French divisions to push the Germans from the St. Mihiel salient, a German dagger in France's flank.

The Americans meanwhile demanded and got a separate army under their own command. General John J. Pershing was assigned a front stretching northwestward from the Swiss border to the French lines. As part of the last mighty Allied assault, Pershing's army undertook the **Meuse-Argonne offensive**, from September 26 to November 11, 1918. This battle, the most gargantuan thus far in American history, lasted forty-seven days and engaged 1.2 million American troops. With especially heavy fighting in the rugged Argonne Forest, the killed and wounded mounted to 120,000.

Meuse-Argonne offensive (1918) *Effort led by General John J. ("Black Jack") Pershing to cut the German railroad lines supplying the western front. One of the few major battles that Americans participated in during the entire war, it was still under way when the war ended.*

Victory was in sight—and fortunately so. The slowly advancing American armies in France were eating up their supplies so rapidly that they were in grave danger of running short. But the battered Germans were staggering under the sledgehammer blows of the Allies and suffering from critical food shortages caused by the British blockade. Propaganda leaflets containing seductive Wilsonian promises rained upon their crumbling lines from balloons, shells, and rockets.

Berlin was now ready to hoist the white flag. In October 1918 the Germans first sought a peace based on the Fourteen Points. But Wilson made it clear that the kaiser must be thrown overboard before an armistice could be negotiated. The war-weary Germans took the hint and forced the kaiser to flee to Holland.

The exhausted Germans laid down their arms at eleven o'clock on the eleventh day of the eleventh month of 1918, and an eerie, numbing silence fell over the western front. War-taut America burst into a delirium of around-the-clock rejoicing, the streets jammed with laughing, whooping, milling, dancing masses as the "war to end wars" had ended. But the costs exceeded comprehension: nearly 9 million soldiers had died and more than 20 million had suffered grievous wounds. To make matters even worse, some 30 million people perished in a worldwide influenza pandemic in 1918-1919. Over 550,000 Americans—more than ten times the number of U.S. combat casualties—died from flu.

The United States' main contribution to the ultimate victory had been foodstuffs, munitions, credits, oil, and manpower—but not battlefield victories. The AEF fought only two major battles, St. Mihiel and the Meuse-Argonne. It was the *prospect* of endless U.S. troop reserves, rather than America's actual military performance, that eventually demoralized the Germans.

General Pershing's army itself, meanwhile, purchased more of its supplies in Europe than it shipped from the United States, including most of its artillery and nearly all of its aircraft. America was no arsenal of democracy in this war; that role awaited it in the next global conflict, two decades later.

Wilson Steps Down from Olympus

Woodrow Wilson had helped to win the war. What part would he now play in shaping the peace? Expectations ran extravagantly high. As the fighting in Europe crashed to a close, the American president towered at the summit of his popularity and power. No other man had ever occupied so dizzy a pinnacle as moral leader of the world. Wilson also had behind him the prestige of victory and the economic resources of the mightiest nation on earth. But at this fateful moment, his sureness of touch deserted him, and he began to make a series of tragic fumbles.

Hoping to strengthen his hand at the Paris peace table, Wilson personally appealed for a Democratic victory in the congressional elections of November 1918. But the maneuver backfired when voters instead returned a narrow Republican majority to Congress. Having staked his reputation on the outcome, Wilson went to Paris as a diminished leader. Unlike all the parliamentary statesmen at the table, he did not command a legislative majority at home.

Wilson's decision to go in person to Paris to help make the peace infuriated Republicans, who saw it as flamboyant grandstanding. He further ruffled Republican feathers when he neglected to include a single Republican senator in his official peace delegation. The logical choice was the new chairman of the Senate Committee on Foreign

The English science fiction writer H. G. Wells (1866–1946), soon a strong proponent of the League of Nations, spoke for many Europeans when he praised Woodrow Wilson in 1917:

"In all the world there is no outstanding figure to which the world will listen, there is no man audible in all the world, in Japan as well as Germany and Rome as well as Boston—except the President of the United States."

Relations, slender and aristocratically bewhiskered Henry Cabot Lodge of Massachusetts. But Wilson loathed him, and the feeling was hotly reciprocated. An accomplished author with a Harvard Ph.D., Lodge had been known as "the scholar in politics" until Wilson came on the scene. The two men were at daggers drawn, personally and politically.

An Idealist amid the Imperialists

Idealist Woodrow Wilson received tumultuous welcomes from the masses of France, Britain, and Italy, even as their wary statesmen tried to keep the new messiah at arm's length from worshipful crowds. When it came to negotiating the shape of the postwar world at the Paris Conference of great and small nations begun on January 18, 1919, the Allies formed an inner circle known as the Big Four, with Wilson, representing the richest and freshest great power, more or less in charge. He was joined by genial Premier Vittorio Orlando of Italy, Prime Minister David Lloyd George of Britain, and cynical, hard-bitten Premier Georges Clemenceau of France, known as "the Tiger."

Wilson first bent his energies to preventing any vengeful parceling out of the former colonies of the vanquished powers. He tried to force through a compromise between naked imperialism and idealism. The victors would not take possession of conquered territories, like Syria and Iraq, but would receive them as trustees of the League of Nations. In practice this half-loaf solution was little more than the old colonialism, thinly disguised. But in decades to come anticolonial independence movements would wield the Wilsonian ideal of self-determination against their imperial occupiers.

League of Nations (1919) *A world organization of national governments proposed by President Woodrow Wilson and established by the Treaty of Versailles in 1919. It worked to facilitate peaceful international cooperation. Despite emotional appeals by Wilson, isolationists' objections to the League created the major obstacle to American signing of the Treaty of Versailles.*

Meanwhile, Wilson had been serving as midwife for a world parliament known as the **League of Nations**, which he envisioned as containing an assembly with seats for all nations and a council to be controlled by the great powers. To his great satisfaction, in February 1919, his fellow treatymakers agreed to make the League Covenant, Wilson's brainchild, an integral part of the final peace treaty. But tough bargains and grinding compromises loomed ahead in Paris.

The hardheaded Clemenceau pressed French demands for the German-inhabited Rhineland and the Saar Valley, a rich coal area. Faced with fierce Wilsonian opposition to this violation of self-determination, France settled for a compromise whereby the Saar basin would remain under the League of Nations for fifteen years, and then a popular vote would determine its fate. (The Saar population voted overwhelmingly to rejoin Germany in 1935.) Wilson's next battle was with Italy over Fiume, a valuable seaport inhabited by both Italians and Yugoslavs. When Italy demanded Fiume, Wilson insisted that the seaport go to Yugoslavia and appealed over the heads of Italy's leaders to the country's masses. The maneuver fell flat. The Italian delegates went home in a huff, while the Italian masses turned savagely against Wilson.

Another crucial struggle was with Japan over China's Shandong (Shantung) Peninsula and the German islands in the Pacific, which the Japanese had seized during the war. Japan received the strategic Pacific islands under a League of Nations mandate,* But Wilson staunchly opposed Japanese control of Shandong as a violation of self-determination for its 30 million Chinese residents. When the Japanese threatened to walk out, however, Wilson reluctantly accepted a compromise whereby Japan kept Germany's economic holdings in Shandong and pledged to return the peninsula to China at a later date. The Chinese were outraged by this imperialistic solution, while Clemenceau jeered that Wilson "talked like Jesus Christ and acted like Lloyd George."

---

*In due time the Japanese illegally fortified these islands—the Marshalls, Marianas, and Carolines—and used them as bases against the United States in World War II.

National Archives

Wilson in Dover, England, 1919 Hailed by many Europeans in early 1919 as the savior of the Western world, Wilson was a fallen idol only a few months later, when his own countrymen repudiated the peace treaty he had helped to craft.

A completed **Treaty of Versailles** was handed to the Germans in June 1919—almost literally on the point of a bayonet. Excluded from the settlement negotiations in Paris, Germany had capitulated in the hope that it would be granted a peace based on the Fourteen Points. A careful analysis of the treaty shows that only four of the original Wilsonian points were fully honored. Vengeance, not reconciliation, was the treaty's dominant tone. Loud and bitter cries of betrayal burst from German throats—charges that Adolf Hitler would soon reiterate during his meteoric rise to power in Germany.

Wilson was guilty of no conscious betrayal. But the Allied powers were torn by conflicting aims, many of them sanctioned by secret treaties. There had to be compromise at Paris, or there would be no agreement. Faced with hard realities, Wilson was forced to abandon some of his less-cherished Fourteen Points in order to salvage the more precious League of Nations. All the same, the loudly condemned treaty actually had much to commend it. Not least among its merits was its liberation of many oppressed peoples, such as the Poles, from the yoke of imperial dynasties.

Treaty of Versailles (1919) *Treaty signed after six months of tough negotiations, establishing terms of settlement of the First World War. Article 231, "the war guilt clause," blamed the war on Germany, forcing German disarmament and saddling Germany with heavy reparations payments. Germans detested the treaty as too harsh, the French feared it was too weak, and the U.S. Senate rejected it, largely because it obliged the United States to join the League of Nations.*

Wilson's Battle for Ratification

Returning to America, Wilson sailed straight into a political typhoon. Isolationists raised a whirlwind of protest against the treaty, especially against Wilson's commitment to ushering the United States into his newfangled League of Nations, which they regarded as either a useless "sewing circle" or an overpotent "superstate." The opposition's hard core

irreconcilables *Hardcore group of militant isolationists, led by Senators William Borah of Idaho and Hiram Johnson of California, who opposed Wilson's dream of international cooperation in the League of Nations after World War I. Played an important part in preventing American participation in the organization.*

was composed of a dozen or so militants, led by Idaho Senator William Borah and California Senator Hiram Johnson, known as **irreconcilables**. Invoking the revered advice of Washington and Jefferson, they wanted no part of any "entangling alliance."

Nor were isolationists Wilson's only problem. Critics showered the Treaty of Versailles with abuse from all sides. Rabid Hun-haters regarded the pact as not harsh enough. Principled liberals thought it too punitive. German Americans, Italian Americans, and others whom Wilson had termed "hyphenated Americans" were aroused because the peace settlement was not sufficiently favorable to their native lands. Irish Americans in particular feared that the League would empower Britain in the face of any movement for Irish independence.

Despite mounting discontent, a strong majority of the people still seemed favorable to the treaty, with the "Wilson League" firmly riveted as Part I. At this time—early July 1919—Senator Lodge had no real hope of defeating the Treaty of Versailles. His strategy was merely to amend it in such a way as to "Americanize," "Republicanize," or "senatorialize" it.

Lodge effectively used delay to muddle and divide public opinion. He read the entire 264-page treaty aloud in the Senate Foreign Relations Committee and held protracted hearings in which people of various nationalities aired their grievances. Wilson fretted increasingly as the hot summer of 1919 wore on. The pact was bogged down in the Senate, while the nation was drifting into confusion and apathy. He therefore decided to take his case to the country in a spectacular speechmaking tour. Wilson undertook his strenuous barnstorming campaign despite protests from physicians and friends. Never robust, Wilson's frail body had begun to sag under the strain of his first wife's death in 1914, partisan strife, a global war, and a stressful peace conference. But he declared that he was willing to die, like the soldiers he had sent into battle, for the sake of the new world order.

The presidential tour, begun in September 1919, started off shakily in the Midwest, but the reception improved in the Rocky Mountain region and the Pacific Coast. The high point—and the breaking point—of the return trip came in Pueblo, Colorado, on September 25, 1919. With tears coursing down his cheeks, Wilson pleaded for the League of Nations as the only real hope of preventing future wars. That night he collapsed from physical and nervous exhaustion. A "funeral train" whisked him back to Washington, where several days later a stroke paralyzed one side of his body. During the next few weeks he lay in a darkened room in the White House. For more than seven months he did not meet his cabinet.

Senator Lodge was now at the helm. After failing to amend the treaty outright, he finally came up with fourteen formal reservations to it—a sardonic slap at Wilson's Fourteen Points. These safeguards reserved the rights of the United States under the Monroe Doctrine and otherwise sought to protect American sovereignty. Wilson, hating Lodge, saw red at the mere suggestion of the Lodge reservations.

Too feeble to lead, Wilson remained strong enough to obstruct. When the day finally came for the Senate vote, he sent word to all true Democrats to vote *against* the treaty with the odious Lodge reservations attached. On November 19, 1919, loyal Democrats in the Senate did Wilson's bidding, helping to reject the treaty, by a vote of 55 to 39. So strong was public indignation at the vote that the Senate was forced to act a second time. In March 1920 the treaty was brought up again, with the Lodge reservations tacked on. There was only one possible path to success—passing the pact with the reservations included. But the sickly Wilson again sent word to all loyal Democrats to vote down the treaty with the obnoxious reservations. He thus signed the death warrant of the treaty as far as America was concerned. On March 19, 1920, the treaty netted a simple majority but failed to get the necessary two-thirds majority by a count of 49 yeas to 35 nays.

Who defeated the treaty? The Lodge-Wilson personal feud, traditionalism, isolationism, disillusionment, and partisanship all contributed to the confused picture. But Wilson himself must bear a substantial share of the responsibility. He asked for all or nothing—and got nothing.

The "Solemn Referendum" of 1920

Wilson proposed to settle the treaty issue in the forthcoming presidential campaign by appealing to the people for a "solemn referendum." This was sheer folly, for a true mandate on the League in the noisy arena of politics was clearly impossible.

Jubilant Republicans gathered in Chicago in June 1920 with wayward bull moosers back in the corral (after Theodore Roosevelt's death in 1919) and the senatorial Old Guard back in the saddle. A group of Senate bosses meeting in the historic "smoke-filled" Room 404 of the Hotel Blackstone, informally decided on affable and malleable Senator Warren G. Harding of Ohio as the party's presidential nominee. To run with the "folksy," back-slapping former newspaper editor, the party nominated for vice president frugal, grim-faced Governor Calvin ("Silent Cal") Coolidge of Massachusetts. Meeting in San Francisco, Democrats nominated earnest Governor James M. Cox of Ohio, who strongly supported the League. His running mate was Assistant Navy Secretary Franklin D. Roosevelt, a young, handsome, vibrant New Yorker.

Democratic attempts to make the campaign a referendum on the League were thwarted by Senator Harding, who offered muddled and contradictory statements on the issue from his front porch. With newly enfranchised women swelling the vote totals, Harding was swept into power with a prodigious plurality of over 7 million votes—16,143,407 to 9,130,328 for Cox, the largest victory margin to that date in a presidential election. The electoral count was 404 to 127. Eugene V. Debs, federal prisoner number 9653 in the Atlanta Penitentiary, rolled up the largest vote ever for the left-wing Socialist party—919,799.

Public desire for a change found vent in a resounding repudiation of "high and mighty" Wilsonianism. Tired of star-reaching idealism, and soothed by Harding's promise of a return to "normalcy," voters were willing to accept a second-rate president—and they got a third-rate one.

Republican isolationists successfully turned Harding's victory into a death sentence for the League. Politicians increasingly shunned the League as they would a leper. When the legendary Wilson died in 1924, admirers knelt in the snow outside his Washington home. His "great vision" of a league for peace had perished long before.

The Betrayal of Great Expectations

America's spurning of the League was tragically short-sighted. The Republic had helped to win a costly war, but it foolishly kicked the fruits of victory under the table. Whether a strong international organization would have averted World War II in 1939 will always be a matter of dispute. But there can be no doubt that the orphaned League of Nations was undercut at the start by the refusal of the mightiest power on the globe to join it.

The ultimate collapse of the Treaty of Versailles must be laid, at least in some degree, at America's doorstep. This complicated pact, tied in with the four other peace treaties through the League Covenant, was a top-heavy structure designed to rest on a four-legged table. When the fourth leg, the United States, was never put into place the rickety contraption teetered for over a decade and then crashed in ruins—a debacle that played into the hands of the German demagogue Adolf Hitler.

The United States hurt its own cause when it buried its head in the sand. Granted that the conduct of its Allies had been disillusioning, carrying through the Wilsonian program would have served its own interests. By embracing the role of global leader, the United States could have used its enormous strength to shape the world's future. Instead it permitted the warring nations of World War I blithely to drift toward the abyss of a second and even more bloody international disaster.

Varying Viewpoints

Woodrow Wilson: Realist or Idealist?

As the first president to take the United States into a foreign war, Woodrow Wilson was obliged to make a systematic case to the American people to justify his unprecedented European intervention. His ideas have largely defined the character of American foreign policy ever since—for better or worse.

"Wilsonianism" comprised three closely related principles: (1) the era of American isolation from world affairs had irretrievably ended; (2) the United States must infuse its own founding political and economic ideas—including democracy, the rule of law, free trade, and national self-determination (or anticolonialism)—into the international order; and (3) American influence could eventually steer the world away from rivalry and warfare and toward a cooperative and peaceful international system, maintained by the League of Nations or, later, the United Nations.

Whether that Wilsonian vision constituted hard-nosed realism or starry-eyed idealism has excited scholarly debate for nearly a century. "Realists," such as George F. Kennan and Henry Kissinger, insist that Wilson was anything but a realist. They criticize the president as a naïve, impractical dreamer who failed to understand that the international order was, and always will be, an anarchic, unruly arena, outside the rule of law, where only military force can effectively protect the nation's security. In a sharp critique in his 1950 study, *American Diplomacy*, Kennan condemned Wilson's vision as "moralism-legalism." In this view Wilson dangerously threatened to sacrifice American self-interests on the altar of his admirable but ultimately unworkable ideas.

Wilson's defenders, including his biographers Arthur S. Link and Thomas J. Knock, argue that Wilson's idealism was in fact a kind of higher realism, recognizing as it did that armed conflict on the scale of World War I could never again be tolerated and that some framework of peaceful international relations simply had to be found. The development of nuclear weapons in a later generation gave this argument more force. This "liberal" defense of Wilsonianism derives from the centuries-old liberal faith that, given sufficient intelligence and willpower, the world can be made a better place. Realists reject this notion of moral and political progress as hopelessly innocent, especially as applied to international affairs.

Some leftist scholars, such as William Appleman Williams, have argued that Wilson was in fact a realist of another kind: a subtle and wily imperialist whose stirring rhetoric cloaked a grasping ambition to make the United States the world's dominant economic power. Sometimes called "the imperialism of free trade," this strategy allegedly sought not to decolonialize the world and open up international commerce for the good of peoples elsewhere, but to create a system in which American economic might would irresistibly prevail. Wilson's defenders would claim that in a Wilsonian world, *all* parties would be better off because of free trade and international competition. Still other scholars, especially John Milton Cooper, Jr., have emphasized the absence of economic factors in shaping Wilson's diplomacy. Isolationism, so this argument goes, held such sway over American thinking precisely because the United States had such a puny financial stake abroad—no hard American economic interests were mortally threatened in 1917, nor for a long time thereafter. In these circumstances Wilson—and the Wilsonians who came after him, such as Franklin D. Roosevelt—had no choice but to appeal to abstract ideals and high principles. The "idealistic" Wilsonian strain in American diplomacy, in this view, may have been an unavoidable heritage of America's historically isolated situation. If so, it was Wilson's genius to make practical use of those ideas in his bid for popular support of his diplomacy.

A new generation of scholars has begun to explore the influence of Wilsonian ideals on social movements outside the United States and Europe. Erez Manela has argued that emerging anticolonial and nationalist movements appropriated Wilsonian ideals and adapted them to their own political ends, challenging forms of colonialism that Wilson himself failed to criticize. In this view the legacy of Wilsonian foreign policy may have been felt most strongly outside the United States.

CHAPTER SUMMARY ★ ★ ★ ★ ★ ★ ★ ★ ★ ★ ★ ★ ★ ★

As soon as he assumed the presidency, the eloquent, idealistic, but often ideologically self-righteous Woodrow Wilson successfully carried out a sweeping progressive program of economic reform of the tariff, money and banking, and the trusts—what Wilson called the "triple wall of privilege." He also achieved substantial social reforms that benefited women and the working classes, but his lack of sympathy for blacks actually furthered segregation.

Wilson's attempt to implement similar progressive moral goals in foreign policy was less successful, as he stumbled into military involvements in the Caribbean and revolutionary Mexico. The outbreak of World War I in Europe brought growing risks of American involvement, especially because of the threat to neutral shipping from German submarine warfare. Led by President Wilson, most Americans earnestly sought to stay clear of the war, though all but a minority sympathized more with the Allies than the Germans.

Wilson temporarily avoided war by extracting the precarious *Sussex* pledge from Germany. His progressive campaign of 1916, appealing to workers and former bull moose supporters, narrowly won him reelection over Charles Evans Hughes and the Republicans. While Wilson never promised to stay out of war, many voters were also attracted by his emphasis on peace.

Germany's declaration of unlimited submarine warfare in January 1917, as well as the Zimmermann note proposing a German alliance with Mexico, finally caused the United States to declare war. Wilson aroused the country to patriotic heights by declaring the war an idealistic crusade for democracy and a just peace, based on his ideologically liberal Fourteen Points.

Vigorous wartime propaganda stirred voluntary commitment to the war effort, but at the cost of stifling dissent and curtailing civil liberties. American voluntary mobilization worked wonders in organizing industry, producing food, and financing the war. Labor, including women, made substantial wartime gains, though numerous strikes and the radical Industrial Workers of the World caused disruptions. Some progressive women opposed the war, but the majority of women's wartime efforts helped spur passage of the Nineteenth (Suffrage) Amendment. The beginnings of the Great Migration of blacks from the South to northern cities, sometimes as strikebreakers, led to racial tensions and riots.

Despite the emphasis on voluntarism, the federal government turned to the coercive military draft to produce the vast American Expeditionary Force in a brief time. America's soldiers took nearly a year to arrive in Europe, and they fought in only two major battles at the end of the war. America's main contribution to the Allied victory was to provide new enthusiasm and morale, along with the threat of endless supplies of men and *matériel* to follow. Wilson's immense prestige created high expectations for an idealistic peace based on his Fourteen Points. But his own political blunders and the clever, stubborn opposition of European statesmen forced him to compromise his lofty aims and made the Versailles Treaty considerably harsher than he intended.

Opposition to Wilson and the League of Nations arose not only from traditional isolationists but from militant anti-Germans, liberals, and diverse ethnic groups. As Henry Cabot Lodge stalled the treaty in the U.S. Senate, Wilson tried to rouse the country on behalf of his cherished League. A stroke ended Wilson's pro-League speaking tour, and his stubborn refusal to compromise with Lodge and the Republicans finally killed the treaty and the League. Wilson sought a "solemn referendum" on the League in the election of 1920, but the public delivered a harsh repudiation of Wilsonianism. Republican isolationists turned Harding's victory into a death sentence for the League. America thus turned its back on international affairs and harmed its own best interests in shaping a global order.

KEY TERMS

- Underwood Tariff (497)
- Federal Reserve Act (497)
- Federal Trade Commission Act (497)
- Clayton Anti-Trust Act (497)
- holding companies (497)
- Workingmen's Compensation Act (498)
- Adamson Act (498)
- Jones Act (498)
- Tampico Incident (500)
- Central Powers (500)
- Allies (500)
- U-boats (500)
- *Lusitania* (501)
- Zimmermann note (503)
- Fourteen Points (504)
- Committee on Public Information (504)
- Espionage Act (505)
- *Schenck v. United States* (505)
- War Industries Board (506)
- Industrial Workers of the World (506)
- Great Migration (506)
- Nineteenth Amendment (506)
- Sheppard-Towner Maternity Act (507)
- Château-Thierry, Battle of (509)
- Meuse-Argonne offensive (511)
- League of Nations (512)
- Treaty of Versailles (513)
- irreconcilables (514)

PEOPLE TO KNOW

- Louis D. Brandeis
- Francisco ("Pancho") Villa
- Arthur Zimmermann
- George Creel
- Eugene V. Debs
- William D. ("Big Bill") Haywood
- Herbert C. Hoover
- Alice Paul
- Henry Cabot Lodge

MindTap is a fully online, highly personalized learning experience built upon Cengage Learning content. MindTap combines student learning tools—readings, multimedia, activities, and assessments—into a singular Learning Path that guides students through the course.

Chapter 30

American Life in the "Roaring Twenties"

1920–1929

America's present need is not heroics but healing; not nostrums but normalcy; not revolution but restoration; . . . not surgery but serenity.

Warren G. Harding, 1920

Chapter Outline

- The Red Scare and the Ku Klux Klan
- Immigration Restriction, 1921–1924
- Prohibition and Gangsterism
- Cultural Conflict and the Scopes Trial
- The Mass-Consumption Economy and the Automobile Age
- Radio, Film, and Music in the Jazz Age
- Changes in Sexuality and Race
- The Economic Boom
- *Makers of America: The Poles*
- *Examining the Evidence:* The Jazz Singer, *1927*

Bloodied by the war and disillusioned by the peace, Americans turned inward in the 1920s. Shunning diplomatic commitments to foreign countries, they also denounced "radical" foreign ideas, condemned "un-American" lifestyles, and clanged shut the immigration gates against foreign peoples. They partly sealed off the domestic economy from the rest of the world and plunged headlong into a dizzying decade of homegrown prosperity.

The boom of the golden twenties showered genuine benefits on Americans, as incomes and living standards rose for many. But there seemed to be something incredible about it all, even as people sang:

My sister she works in the laundry,
My father sells bootlegger gin,
My mother she takes in the washing,
My God, how the money rolls in!

New technologies, new consumer products, and new forms of leisure and entertainment made the twenties roar. Yet just beneath the surface lurked widespread anxieties about the future and fears that America was losing sight of its traditional ways.

FOCUS QUESTIONS

1. Why did the United States turn so sharply inward and embrace social conservatism in the wake of World War I?
2. What were the major cultural conflicts that occurred over immigration, cultural pluralism, prohibition, and evolution in the 1920s? Why did these issues create such strong polarization among Americans?
3. What were the major features of the new "mass consumer economy," and what effects did it have on the way Americans lived?
4. How did the "new media" of radio, film, and recorded music help transform sexuality and mass popular culture?
5. How were the new ideas of the times reflected in the American literary renaissance of the 1920s? How was the Harlem Renaissance of black writers similar to and different from artistic movements in the white literary world?

CHRONOLOGY

1903	▪ Wright brothers fly first airplane ▪ First story-sequence motion picture
1908	▪ Henry Ford introduces Model T
1914	▪ W.C. Handy's "St. Louis Blues" debuts
1917	▪ Bolshevik Revolution in Russia
1919	▪ Eighteenth Amendment (prohibition) ▪ Volstead Act ▪ Seattle general strike ▪ Anderson publishes *Winesburg, Ohio*
1919–1920	▪ "Red scare"
1920	▪ Radio broadcasting begins ▪ Fitzgerald publishes *This Side of Paradise* ▪ Lewis publishes *Main Street*
1921	▪ Sacco-Vanzetti trial ▪ Emergency Quota Act ▪ Bureau of the Budget created
1922	▪ Lewis publishes *Babbitt* ▪ Eliot publishes *The Waste Land*
1923	▪ Equal Rights Amendment (ERA) proposed
1924	▪ Immigration Act of 1924
1925	▪ Scopes trial ▪ Florida real estate boom ▪ Fitzgerald publishes *The Great Gatsby* ▪ Dreiser publishes *An American Tragedy*
1926	▪ Hughes publishes *The Weary Blues* ▪ Hemingway publishes *The Sun Also Rises*
1927	▪ Lindbergh flies solo across Atlantic ▪ First talking motion picture, *The Jazz Singer* ▪ Sacco and Vanzetti executed
1928	▪ Eugene O'Neill's *Strange Interlude* debuts on Broadway
1929	▪ Faulkner publishes *The Sound and the Fury* ▪ Hemingway publishes *A Farewell to Arms*
1932	▪ Al Capone imprisoned

Seeing Red

Hysterical fears of red Russia continued to color American thinking for several years after Communists came to power in the **Bolshevik Revolution** of 1917, which spawned a tiny Communist party in America. Tensions were heightened by an epidemic of strikes that convulsed the Republic at war's end, many of them the result of high prices and frustrated union-organizing drives. Upstanding Americans jumped to the conclusion that labor troubles were fomented by bomb-and-whisker Bolsheviks. A general strike in Seattle in 1919, though modest in its demands and orderly in its methods, prompted a call from the mayor for federal troops to head off "the anarchy of Russia." Fire-and-brimstone evangelist Billy Sunday said he would like to "fill the jails so full of [Bolsheviks] that their feet would stick out the window."

Bolshevik Revolution (1917) *The second stage of the Russian Revolution in November 1917 when Vladimir Lenin and his Bolshevik party seized power and established a communist state. The first stage had occurred the previous February when more moderate revolutionaries overthrew the Russian czar.*

The big **red scare** of 1919–1920 resulted in a nationwide crusade against left-wingers whose Americanism was suspect. Attorney General A. Mitchell Palmer earned the title of the "Fighting Quaker" for his excess zeal in rounding up about six thousand suspects. When a bomb shattered both the nerves and the Washington home of Palmer in June 1919, the "Fighting Quaker" was dubbed the "Quaking Fighter." Late in December 1919, a shipload of 249 alleged alien radicals was deported on the *Buford* ("the Soviet Ark") to the "workers' paradise" of Russia. Hysteria was revived in September 1920 when a still-unexplained bomb blast on Wall Street killed thirty-eight people and wounded more than a hundred others.

red scare (1919–1920) *A period of intense anticommunism. The "Palmer raids" of Attorney General A. Mitchell Palmer resulted in about six thousand deportations of people suspected of "subversive" activities.*

Various states joined the pack in the outcry against radicals. In 1919–1920 a number of legislatures passed **criminal syndicalism laws** that outlawed the mere *advocacy* of violence to secure social change. Critics protested that mere words were not criminal deeds, that there was a great gulf between throwing fits and throwing bombs, and that "free screech" was for the nasty as well as the nice. Violence was done to traditional American concepts of free speech as IWW members and other radicals were vigorously prosecuted.

criminal syndicalism laws (1919–1920) *Laws passed by many states during the red scare outlawing the mere advocacy of violence to secure social change. Stump speakers for the Industrial Workers of the World were special targets.*

The hysteria went so far that in 1920 five members of the New York legislature, all lawfully elected, were denied their seats simply because they were Socialists.

The red scare was a godsend to conservative businesspeople, who used it to break the backs of the fledgling unions. Labor's call for the "closed," or all-union, shop was denounced as "Sovietism in disguise." Employers, in turn, hailed their own antiunion campaign for the "open" shop as the **American plan**.

American plan *A business-oriented approach to worker relations popular among firms in the 1920s to defeat unionization. Managers sought to strengthen their communication with workers and to offer benefits like pensions and insurance. They insisted on an "open shop" in contrast to the mandatory union membership through the "closed shop" that many labor activists had demanded in the strike wave after World War I.*

Anti-redism and antiforeignism were reflected in a notorious case regarded by liberals as a "judicial lynching." Nicola Sacco, a shoe-factory worker, and Bartolomeo Vanzetti, a fish peddler, were convicted in 1921 of the murder of a Massachusetts paymaster and his guard. The jury and judge were prejudiced in some degree against the defendants because they were Italians, atheists, anarchists, and draft dodgers.

Liberals and radicals the world over rallied to the defense of the two aliens doomed to die. The case dragged on for six years until 1927, when the condemned men were electrocuted. Communists and other radicals were thus presented with two martyrs in the "class struggle," while many American liberals hung their heads.

Hooded Hoodlums of the KKK

A new Ku Klux Klan, spawned by the postwar reaction, mushroomed fearsomely in the early 1920s. Despite the familiar sheets and hoods, it more closely resembled the antiforeign nativist movements of the 1850s than the antiblack nightriders of the 1860s. The new KKK was antiforeign, anti-Catholic, antiblack, anti-Jewish, antipacifist, anti-Communist, anti-internationalist, anti-evolutionist, anti-adultery, and anti–birth control. It was also pro–Anglo Saxon, pro–"native" American, and pro-Protestant. In short, the besheeted Klan betokened an extremist, ultraconservative uprising against many of the forces of diversity and modernity that were transforming American culture.

As reconstituted, the Klan spread with astonishing rapidity, especially among some white Protestants in the Midwest and South. At its peak in the mid-1920s, the Klan claimed about 5 million dues-paying members and wielded potent political influence. The "Knights of the Invisible Empire" included among their officials Imperial Wizards, Grand Goblins, and King Kleagles. The Klan's most impressive displays were "konclaves" and huge flag-waving parades. Their chief warning was the blazing cross, and their weapon the bloodied lash, supplemented by tar and feathers.

This reign of hooded horror, so repulsive to the best American ideals, collapsed rather suddenly in the late 1920s. The Klan's bubble burst as decent people at last recoiled from its terrorism, while scandalous embezzling by Klan officials launched a congressional investigation that exposed the movement as a vicious racket. The KKK was an alarming manifestation of the intolerance and prejudice plaguing people anxious about the dizzying pace of social change in the 1920s. Despite the Klan's decline, civil rights activists fought in vain for legislation making lynching a federal crime, as lawmakers feared alienating white southern voters.

Hiram Wesley Evans (1881–1966), imperial wizard of the Ku Klux Klan, in 1926 poignantly described the cultural grievances that fueled the Klan and lay behind much of the Fundamentalist revolt against "Modernism":

"Nordic Americans for the last generation have found themselves increasingly uncomfortable and finally deeply distressed. . . . One by one all our traditional moral standards went by the boards, or were so disregarded that they ceased to be binding. The sacredness of our Sabbath, of our homes, of chastity, and finally even of our right to teach our own children in our own schools fundamental facts and truths were torn away from us. Those who maintained the old standards did so only in the face of constant ridicule. . . . We found our great cities and the control of much of our industry and commerce taken over by strangers. . . . We are a movement of the plain people, very weak in the matter of culture, intellectual support, and trained leadership. . . . This is undoubtedly a weakness. It lays us open to the charge of being 'hicks' and 'rubes' and 'drivers of second-hand Fords.'"

Stemming the Foreign Flood

Isolationist America of the 1920s, ingrown and provincial, had little use for the immigrants who began to flood into the country again as peace settled on the war-torn world. Some 800,000 stepped ashore in 1920–1921, about two-thirds of

National Archives

Klanswomen on Parade, 1928 Founded in the Reconstruction Era, the Ku Klux Klan enjoyed a remarkable resurgence in the 1920s. Here, women members, unmasked and unapologetic, march down Pennsylvania Avenue under the very shadow of the Capitol Dome.

them from southern and eastern Europe. The "one-hundred-percent Americans," recoiling at the sight of this resumed "New Immigration," once again cried that the famed poem at the base of the Statue of Liberty was all too literally true: they claimed that a sickly Europe was indeed vomiting on America "the wretched refuse of its teeming shore."

Congress temporarily plugged the breach with the Emergency Quota Act of 1921. This stopgap legislation was soon replaced by the **Immigration Act of 1924**. Quotas for foreigners were drastically cut to 2 percent of persons of each nationality living in the United States in 1890, when comparatively few southern Europeans had arrived.* The purpose was clearly to freeze America's existing ethnic composition, which was largely northern European. A flagrantly discriminatory section of the Immigration Act of 1924 slammed the door absolutely against Japanese immigrants. Only Canadians and Latin Americans were exempt from the quota system.

Immigration Act of 1924 *Established quotas for immigration to the United States. Also known as the "National Origins Act." Immigration from southern and eastern Europe was sharply curtailed, while immigrants from Asia were shut out altogether.*

The quota system effected a pivotal departure in American policy, as the country sacrificed something of its tradition of freedom and opportunity, as well as future ethnic diversity. The Immigration Act of 1924 marked the end of an era—a period of virtually unrestricted immigration that in the previous century had brought some 35 million newcomers to the United States, mostly from Europe (see Figure 30.1). The immigrant tide now dwindled to a mere trickle, but it left on American shores by the 1920s a patchwork of ethnic communities separated from the larger society and from each other by language, religion, and customs. Many Italians, Jews, Poles, and others lived in isolated enclaves

*Five years later the Immigration Act of 1929, using 1920 as the quota base, virtually cut immigration in half by limiting the total to 152,574 a year. In 1965 Congress abolished the national-origins quota system.

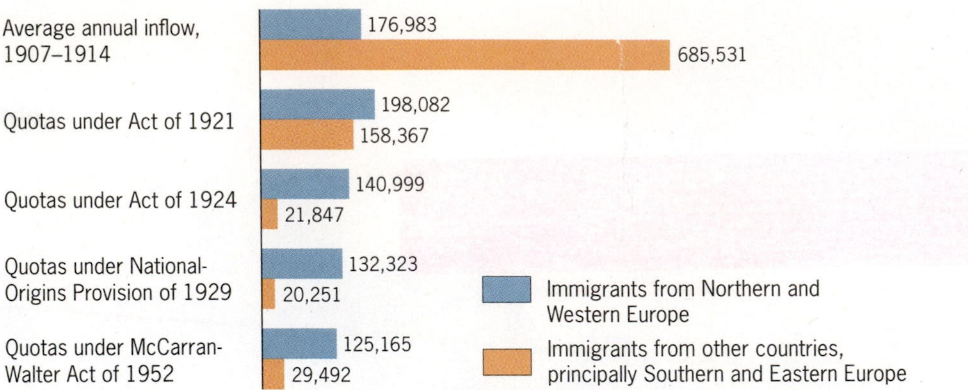

Figure 30.1 Annual Immigration and the Quota Laws

with their own houses of worship, newspapers, and theaters (see "Makers of America: The Poles," p. 523). Efforts to organize labor unions repeatedly foundered on the rocks of ethnic rivalries, which were often played upon by cynical employers. Ethnic variety thus undermined class and political solidarity in America.

Reformers opposed immigration restriction. A chorus of "cultural pluralists" had long criticized the idea that an American "melting pot" would eliminate ethnic differences. Two intellectuals, the philosopher Horace Kallen and critic Randolph Bourne, championed alternative conceptions of the immigrant role in American society. Kallen defended immigrants' right to practice their ancestral customs and preserve their cultural uniqueness. In Kallen's vision, America's ethnic groups should be like the instruments in a symphony orchestra, with each harmonizing with the others while retaining its own identity.

If Kallen stressed the preservation of identity, Bourne advocated greater cross-fertilization among immigrants. Cosmopolitan interchange, Bourne believed, was destined to make America "not a nationality but a trans-nationality, a weaving back and forth . . . of many threads of all sizes and colors." In this view the United States should serve as the vanguard of a more internationalized and multicultural age.

Other intellectuals, including progressives such as John Dewey, Jane Addams, and Louis Brandeis, joined Kallen and Bourne in their defense of ethnic diversity. Vastly outnumbered in the debate over immigration in the 1920s, these early proponents of "cultural pluralism" planted the seeds for the blooming of "multiculturalism" in the last quarter of the twentieth century.

The Prohibition Experiment

One of the last peculiar spasms of the progressive reform movement was prohibition, loudly supported by crusading churches and by many women. The arid new order was authorized in 1919 by the **Eighteenth Amendment** (see the Appendix), as implemented by the **Volstead Act** passed by Congress later that year. Together these laws made the world "safe for hypocrisy."

Eighteenth Amendment (1919) *Prohibited the manufacture, sale, and transportation of alcoholic beverages, ushering in the era known as prohibition.*

Volstead Act (1919) *A federal act enforcing the Eighteenth Amendment, which prohibited the manufacture, sale, and transportation of alcoholic beverages.*

The legal abolition of alcohol was especially popular in the South and the West. Southern whites were eager to keep stimulants out of the hands of blacks, lest they burst out of "their place." In the West, prohibition represented an attack on all the vices associated with the ubiquitous western saloon: public drunkenness, prostitution, and crime. But despite the overwhelming ratification of the "dry" amendment, strong opposition persisted in the larger eastern cities. For many "wet" foreign-born people, sociability was built around drinking in beer gardens and corner taverns.

Prohibitionists were naïve in the extreme. They overlooked the tenacious American tradition of weak control by the central government, especially over private lives. They forgot that the federal authorities had never satisfactorily enforced a law if the majority of

The Poles

The Poles were among the largest immigrant groups to respond to industrializing America's call for badly needed labor after the Civil War. Between 1870 and World War I, some 2 million Polish-speaking peasants boarded steamships bound for the United States. By the 1920s, when antiforeign feeling led to restrictive legislation that choked the immigrant stream to a trickle, Polish immigrants and their American-born children began to develop new identities as Polish Americans.

The first Poles to arrive in the New World had landed in Jamestown in 1608 and helped to develop that colony's timber industry. Over the ensuing two and a half centuries, scattered religious dissenters and revolutionary nationalists also made their way from Poland to America. During the Revolution about one hundred Poles, including two officers recruited by Benjamin Franklin, served in the Continental Army.

But the Polish hopefuls who poured into the United States in the late nineteenth century came primarily to stave off starvation and to earn money to buy land. Known in their homeland as *za chlebem* ("for bread") emigrants, they belonged to the mass of central and eastern European peasants who had been forced off their farms by growing competition from large-scale, mechanized agriculture. An exceptionally high birthrate among the Catholic Poles compounded this economic pressure, creating an army of the land-poor and landless. With wages in the United States more than eight times higher than in Poland, the American magnet was irresistible.

Many Polish immigrants were also lured by glowing letters from friends and relatives already living in the United States. The first wave of Polish immigrants had established a thriving network of self-help and fraternal associations, organized around Polish Catholic parishes. Often, Polish American entrepreneurs helped their European compatriots make travel arrangements or find jobs in the United States. One of the most successful of these, the energetic Chicago grocer Anton Schermann, is credited with "bringing over" a hundred thousand Poles and causing the Windy City to earn the nickname "the American Warsaw."

Most of the Poles arriving in the United States in the late nineteenth century headed for booming industrial cities such as Buffalo, Pittsburgh, Detroit, Milwaukee, and Chicago. In 1907 four-fifths of the men toiled as unskilled laborers in coal mines, meatpacking factories, textile and steel mills, oil refineries, and garment-making shops. Although married women usually stayed home and contributed to the family's earnings by taking in laundry and boarders, children and single girls often joined their fathers and brothers on the job.

When an independent Poland was created after World War I, few Poles chose to return to their Old World homeland. Instead, like other immigrant groups in the 1920s, they redoubled their efforts to integrate into American society. Polish institutions such as churches and fraternal organizations, which had served to perpetuate a distinctive Polish culture in the New World, now facilitated the transformation of Poles into Polish Americans. When Poland was absorbed into the Communist bloc after World War II, Polish Americans clung still more tightly to their American identity, pushing for landmarks such as Chicago's Pulaski Road to memorialize their culture in the New World.

Library of Congress

A Polish Child Laboring Among Men In his notes on this 1910 image of workers at an Illinois Glass Company factory in Alton, Illinois, the renowned photographer Lewis Hine recorded: "Even the tiny chap on left end of photo was working. He is a Polish boy who cannot understand English." Poles' traditionally high birthrates in Europe were replicated in the United States during the great wave of Polish immigration in the late nineteenth and early twentieth centuries. Large families put further pressure on children to contribute economically. (For more on Hine's work chronicling child labor, see "Examining the Evidence: The Photography of Lewis W. Hine," p. 399.)

the people—or a strong minority—were hostile to it. Prohibition simply did not prohibit. The old-time "men-only" corner saloons were replaced by thousands of "speakeasies," each with its tiny grilled window through which the thirsty spoke softly before the barred door was opened. Because of the difficulty of transporting and concealing bottles, hard liquor of high alcoholic content gained in popularity. Illegal rumrunners operating from the West Indies or Canada had their inning. "Home brew" and "bathtub gin" became popular, as law-evading adults engaged in "alky cooking" with toy stills.

Yet the "noble experiment" was not entirely a failure. Bank savings increased, and absenteeism in industry decreased, presumably because of the newly sober ways of formerly soused barflies. On the whole, less alcohol was consumed than in the days before prohibition, though strong drink continued to be available. As a legendary tippler remarked, prohibition was "a darn sight better than no liquor at all."

Prohibition also spawned shocking crimes. The lush profits of illegal alcohol led to bribery of the police. Violent wars broke out in the big cities between rival gangs—often rooted in immigrant neighborhoods—who sought to corner the rich market in booze. Rival triggermen used their sawed-off shotguns and chattering "typewriters" (machine guns) to "erase" bootlegging competitors who were trying to "muscle in" on their "racket." In the gang wars of the 1920s in Chicago, about five hundred mobsters were murdered.

Chicago was by far the most spectacular example of lawlessness. In 1925 "Scarface" Al Capone, a grasping and murderous booze distributor, began six years of gang warfare that netted him millions of blood-spattered dollars. He zoomed through the streets in an armor-plated car with bulletproof windows. Capone could not be convicted of the cold-blooded massacre, on St. Valentine's Day in 1929, of seven rival gang members, but he was finally sent to jail in 1932 for income tax evasion.

Gangsters rapidly moved into other profitable and illicit activities: prostitution, gambling, and narcotics. Honest merchants were forced to pay "protection money" to prevent thugs from destroying their property or beating up their employees. **Racketeers** even invaded the ranks of labor unions as organizers and promoters. Organized crime had come to be one of the nation's most gigantic businesses. By 1930 the annual "take" of the underworld was estimated to be from $12 billion to $18 billion—several times the income of the Washington government.

Racketeers *People who obtain money illegally by fraud, bootlegging, gambling, or threats of violence. Racketeers invaded the ranks of labor during the 1920s, a decade when gambling and gangsterism were prevalent in American life.*

Monkey Business in Tennessee

Education in the 1920s continued to make giant boot-strides. More and more states were requiring young people to remain in school until age sixteen or eighteen, or until graduation from high school. The proportion of seventeen-year-olds who finished high school almost doubled in the 1920s, to more than one in four.

The most revolutionary contribution to educational theory during these yeasty years was made by mild-mannered Professor John Dewey, who served on the faculty of Columbia University from 1904 to 1930. By common consent one of America's few front-rank philosophers, he set forth the principles of "learning by doing" that formed the foundation of so-called progressive education, with its greater "permissiveness." Dewey believed that the workbench was as essential as the blackboard and that "education for life" should be a primary goal of the teacher.

Science also scored wondrous advances in these years. A massive public health program, launched by the Rockefeller Foundation in the South in 1909, had virtually wiped out the ancient affliction of hookworm by the 1920s. Better nutrition and health care helped to increase the life expectancy of a newborn infant from fifty years in 1901 to fifty-nine years in 1929.

Yet both science and progressive education in the 1920s were subjected to unfriendly fire from Fundamentalists. These devoted religionists charged that the teaching of Darwinian evolution was destroying faith in God and the Bible while contributing to the moral breakdown of youth in the jazz age. Numerous attempts were made to secure

The bombastic Fundamentalist evangelist W. A. (Billy) Sunday (1862–1935) declared in 1925:

"If a minister believes and teaches evolution, he is a stinking skunk, a hypocrite, and a liar."

The Battle over Evolution Opponents of Darwin's theories set up shop at the opening of the famed "Scopes Trial" in Dayton, Tennessee, in 1925. The trial was an early battle in an American "culture war" that was still being waged nearly a century later.

laws prohibiting the teaching of evolution, "the bestial hypothesis," in the public schools, and three southern states adopted such shackling measures. The trio of states included Tennessee, in the heart of the so-called **Bible Belt** South, where evangelical religion was especially robust.

Bible Belt *The region of the American South, extending roughly from North Carolina west to Oklahoma and Texas, where Protestant Fundamentalism and belief in literal interpretation of the Bible were traditionally strongest.*

The stage was set for the memorable "Monkey Trial" in the hamlet of Dayton, Tennessee, in 1925. A likable high school biology teacher, John T. Scopes, was indicted for teaching evolution. Batteries of newspaper reporters, armed with notebooks and cameras, descended upon the quiet town to witness the spectacle. Scopes was defended by nationally known attorneys, while former presidential candidate William Jennings Bryan, an ardent Presbyterian Fundamentalist, joined the prosecution. Taking the stand as an expert on the Bible, Bryan was made to appear foolish by the famed criminal lawyer Clarence Darrow. Five days after the trial was over, Bryan died of a stroke, no doubt brought on by the wilting heat and witness-stand strain.

This historic clash between theology and biology proved inconclusive. Scopes, the forgotten man of the drama, was found guilty and fined $100. But the supreme court of Tennessee, while upholding the law, set aside the fine on a technicality. The Fundamentalists at best won only a hollow victory, for the absurdities of the trial cast ridicule on their cause. Yet even though increasing numbers of Christians were coming to reconcile the revelations of religion with the findings of modern science, **Fundamentalism**, with its emphasis on literal reading of the Bible, remained a vibrant force in American spiritual life. It was especially strong in the Baptist Church and in the rapidly growing Churches of Christ, organized in 1906.

Fundamentalism *A Protestant Christian movement emphasizing the literal truth of the Bible and opposing religious modernism, which sought to reconcile religion and science. It was especially strong in the Baptist Church and the Church of Christ, first organized in 1906.*

The Mass-Consumption Economy

Prosperity—real, sustained, and widely shared—put much of the roar into the twenties. The economy kicked off its war harness in 1919, faltered a few steps in the recession of 1920–1921, and then sprinted forward for nearly seven years. Both the recent war and

Treasury Secretary Andrew Mellon's tax policies favored the rapid expansion of capital investment. Ingenious machines, powered by cheap energy from newly tapped oil fields, dramatically increased the productivity of the laborer. Assembly-line production was so advanced at Henry Ford's famed Rouge River plant near Detroit that a finished automobile emerged every ten seconds.

Great new industries suddenly sprouted forth. Supplying electrical power for the humming new machines became a giant business in the 1920s. Above all, the automobile, once the horseless chariot of the rich, now became the carriage of the common citizen. By 1930 Americans owned almost 30 million cars.

The nation's deepening love affair with the automobile headlined a momentous shift in the character of the economy. American manufacturers seemed to have mastered the problems of production; their worries now focused on consumption. Could they find the mass markets for the goods they had contrived to spew forth in such profusion?

Responding to this need, a new arm of American commerce came into being: advertising. By persuasion and ploy, allure and sexual suggestion, advertisers sought to make Americans chronically discontented with their paltry possessions and want more, more, more. A founder of this new Madison Avenue "profession" was Bruce Barton, who published a best seller, *The Man Nobody Knows* (1925), portraying Jesus Christ as the greatest adman of all time. Christ was also an executive who "picked up twelve men from the bottom ranks of business and forged them into an organization that conquered the world."

Sports became big business in the consumer economy of the 1920s. Ballyhooed by the "image makers," home-run heroes such as George H. ("Babe") Ruth were far better known than most statesmen. In 1921 a Jersey City crowd paid more than a million dollars to watch heavyweight champion Jack Dempsey knock out challenger George Carpentier—the first in a series of million-dollar gates in the golden 1920s.

Buying on credit was another innovative feature of the postwar economy. "Possess today and pay tomorrow" was the message directed at buyers. Once-frugal descendants of Puritans went ever deeper into debt to own all kinds of newfangled marvels—refrigerators, vacuum cleaners, and especially cars and radios—*now*. Prosperity thus accumulated an overhanging cloud of debt, and the economy became increasingly vulnerable to disruptions of the credit structure.

Putting America on Rubber Tires

A new industrial revolution slipped into high gear in America in the 1920s. Machinery was the new messiah—and the automobile was its principal prophet. The manufacture of millions of private vehicles heralded an amazing new industrial system based on assembly-line methods and mass-production techniques.

Europeans invented the gasoline engine, but Americans quickly adapted it. By the 1890s a few daring American inventors and promoters, including Henry Ford and Ransom E. Olds (Oldsmobile), were developing the infant automotive industry. By 1910 sixty-nine car companies rolled out a total annual production of 181,000 units. Soon an enormous industry sprang into being, as Detroit became the motorcar capital of America. The mechanized colossus owed much to the stopwatch efficiency techniques of Frederick W. Taylor, a prominent engineer and inventor who became known as the "Father of **Scientific Management**."

Scientific Management *A system of industrial management created and promoted in the early twentieth century by Frederick W. Taylor, emphasizing stopwatch efficiency to improve factory performance. The system gained immense popularity across the United States and Europe.*

The mechanical genius who put America on rubber tires was the lean and silent Henry Ford. This ill-educated, multimillionaire mechanic was socially and culturally narrow. "History is bunk," he once testified. But he dedicated himself with one-track devotion to the gospel of standardization. After two early failures, he grasped and applied fully the techniques of standardization and moving assembly-line production—**Fordism**. He is supposed to have remarked that the purchaser could have his Model T car in any color he desired—just as long as it was black.

Fordism *A system of assembly-line manufacturing and mass production named after Henry Ford, founder of the Ford Motor Company and developer of the Model T car.*

The flood of Fords was phenomenal. In 1914 the "Automobile Wizard" turned out his 500,000th Model T. By 1929, when the great bull market collapsed, Ford had produced nearly 20 million vehicles, and a total of 26 million were registered in the United States. This figure, averaging 1 for every 4.9 Americans, represented far more automobiles than existed in all the rest of the world.

The impact of the self-propelled carriage on various aspects of American life was tremendous. A gigantic new industry emerged, employing directly or indirectly about 6 million people by 1930. Thousands of new jobs, moreover, were created in supporting industries such as rubber, glass, and fabrics, to say nothing of highway construction and thousands of service stations and garages. America's standard of living, responding to this infectious vitality, rose to an enviable level.

Zooming motorcars were agents of social change. At first a luxury, they rapidly became a necessity. Essentially devices for transportation, they soon developed into a badge of freedom and equality—a necessary prop for self-respect. Women were further freed from their dependence on men. Buses made possible the consolidation of schools and to some extent of churches.

Virtuous home life partially broke down as joyriders of all ages forsook the parlor for the highway. What might young people get up to in the privacy of a closed-top Model T? An Indiana juvenile judge voiced parents' worst fears when he condemned the automobile as "a house of prostitution on wheels." Yet no sane American would plead for a return of the old horse and buggy, complete with fly-breeding manure. Life might be cut short on the highways, and smog might poison the air, but the automobile brought more convenience, pleasure, and excitement into more people's lives than almost any other single invention.

★ Humans Develop Wings

Gasoline engines also provided the power that enabled humans to fulfill the age-old dream of sprouting wings. After near-successful experiments by others with heavier-than-air craft, the Wright brothers, Orville and Wilbur, performed "the miracle at Kitty Hawk," North Carolina. On a historic day—December 17, 1903—Orville Wright took aloft a feebly engined plane that stayed airborne for 12 seconds and 120 feet. Thus the air age was launched by two obscure bicycle repairmen.

Airplanes, once "flying coffins" for stuntmen, were first used with marked success for a serious purpose during the Great War of 1914–1918. Shortly thereafter private companies began to operate passenger lines with airmail contracts, which were in effect a subsidy from Washington. The first transcontinental airmail route was established from New York to San Francisco in 1920.

In 1927 modest and skillful Charles A. Lindbergh electrified the world with the first solo west-to-east conquest of the Atlantic. Seeking a prize of $25,000, the lanky flier courageously piloted his single-engine plane, the *Spirit of St. Louis*, from New York to Paris in a grueling thirty-three hours and thirty-nine minutes.

Lindbergh's exploit swept Americans off their feet. Fed up with the cynicism and debunking of the jazz age, they found in this wholesome and handsome youth a genuine hero. "Lucky Lindy" received an uproarious welcome in the canyons of lower Broadway, as eighteen hundred tons of ticker tape and other confetti showered upon him. Lindbergh's achievement did much to dramatize and popularize flying while giving a strong boost to the infant aviation industry.

The impact of the airplane was tremendous. The floundering railroads received another sharp setback through the loss of passengers and mail. A lethal new weapon was given to the gods of war with the coming of city-busting aerial bombs. The Atlantic Ocean was shriveling to about the size of the Aegean Sea in the days of Socrates, while isolation behind ocean moats was becoming a bygone dream.

★ The Radio and Film Revolutions

The speed of the airplane was far eclipsed by the speed of radio waves. Guglielmo Marconi, an Italian, invented wireless telegraphy in the 1890s, and his brainchild was used for long-range communication during World War I. Next came the voice-carrying radio, a triumph of many minds. In November 1920 Pittsburgh station KDKA made history with a live broadcast of the news of the Harding landslide. Radio knitted the nation together and, unlike the automobile, lured the American family back home. By the late 1920s, national commercial networks gained control of the new industry and drowned out much local programming. Various regions heard voices with standardized accents, and countless millions tuned in to perennial comedy favorites such as "Amos 'n' Andy." Advertising "commercials" made radio another vehicle for American free enterprise, and brand-named programs such as the "A&P Gypsies" and the "Eveready Hour" helped make radio-touted labels household words and purchases.

The flickering movie, the inventive fruit of Thomas Edison and others, first attracted attention in the naughty peep-show arcades in the 1890s. The first story-sequence movie, a breathless melodrama called *The Great Train Robbery*, was featured in the five-cent theaters, popularly called "nickelodeons." Spectacular among the first full-length classics was D. W. Griffith's *The Birth of a Nation* (1915), which glorified the Ku Klux Klan of Reconstruction days and defamed both blacks and Northern carpetbaggers. White southerners reputedly fired guns at the screen during the attempted "rape" scene. African Americans were outraged at the film and angrily organized protest marches, petition campaigns, and public hearings.

A fascinating industry was thus launched. Hollywood, California, quickly became the movie capital of the world, for it enjoyed a maximum of sunshine and other advantages. Early movies featured nudity and heavy-lidded female vampires ("vamps"), and an offended public forced the screen magnates to set up their own rigorous code of censorship. The motion picture really arrived during World War I, when it was used as an engine of anti-German propaganda.

A new era began in 1927 with the first "talkie"—*The Jazz Singer*, starring white performer Al Jolson in blackface. About the same time, color films began to be produced. Movies eclipsed all other new forms of amusement in the phenomenal growth of their popularity. Movie "stars" of the first pulchritude commanded much larger salaries than the president of the United States, in some cases as much as $100,000 for a single picture.

Critics bemoaned the vulgarization of popular taste wrought by the technologies of radio and movies. But the effects of the new mass media were not all negative. The insularity of ethnic communities eroded as the immigrants' children, especially, forsook the neighborhood vaudeville theater for the downtown movie palace or turned away from Grandma's Yiddish storytelling to tune in "Amos 'n' Andy." If some of the rich diversity of immigrants' cultures was lost, the standardization of tastes and language hastened entry into the American mainstream—and set the stage for the emergence of a working-class political coalition that, for a time, would overcome the divisive ethnic differences of the past.

The Dynamic Decade

Far-reaching changes in lifestyles and values paralleled the dramatic upsurge of the economy. The census of 1920 revealed that for the first time most Americans no longer lived in the countryside but in urban areas. Women continued to find new opportunities for employment in the cities, though they tended to cluster in a few low-paying jobs (such as retail clerking and office typing) that became classified as "women's work." An organized birth control movement, led by the fiery feminist Margaret Sanger, openly championed the use of contraceptives. Alice Paul's National Woman's party began in 1923 to campaign for an Equal Rights Amendment to the Constitution. To some defenders of traditional ways, it seemed that the world had suddenly gone mad.

Even the churches were affected. Fundamentalists lost ground to Modernists, who liked to think that God was a "good guy." To compete with automobiles and golf, some churches turned to providing entertainment of their own, including wholesome moving pictures for young people.

Even before the war, one observer thought the chimes had struck "sex o'clock in America," and the 1920s witnessed what many old-timers thought was a veritable erotic eruption. Advertisers exploited sexual allure to sell everything from soap to car tires.

Examining the Evidence

The Jazz Singer, 1927

The Jazz Singer was the first feature-length "talkie," a motion picture in which the characters actually speak, and its arrival spelled the end for "silent" films in which the audience read subtitles with live or recorded music as background. Although moviegoers flocked to *The Jazz Singer* to hear recorded sound, when they got there they found a movie concerned with themes of great interest to the urban, first- or second-generation immigrant audiences who were Hollywood's major patrons. *The Jazz Singer* told the story of a poor, assimilating Jewish immigrant torn between following his father's wish that he train as an Orthodox cantor and his own ambition to make a success for himself as a jazz singer, performing in the popular blackface style. The movie's star, Al Jolson, was himself an immigrant Jew who had made his name as a blackface performer. White actors had gradually taken over the southern black minstrel show during the nineteenth century. By the early twentieth century, Jewish entertainers had entirely monopolized these roles. Jolson, like other Jewish blackface performers, used his ability to impersonate a black person to force his acceptance into mainstream white American society. This use of blackface seems ironic because black Americans in the 1920s were struggling with their own real-life battles against Jim Crow–era segregation, a blatant form of exclusion from American society.

1. Besides the novelty of being a "talkie," what may have made *The Jazz Singer* a box office hit in 1927?
2. How might different types of viewers in the audience have responded to the story?
3. Was the "blackface" tradition of performance by white actors an entirely racist one? Or is there a way in which it acknowledges the great importance of blacks within the wider American culture?

Sunset: Boulevard/Corbis

Contending Voices

All that Jazz

Not all Americans welcomed the rising popularity of jazz music. For some stuffy traditionalists, including clergyman and writer Henry van Dyke (1852–1933), jazz symbolized the excessive liberation and dangerous exuberance of modern society.

"As I understand it, [jazz] is not music at all. It is merely an irritation of the nerves of hearing, a sensual teasing of the strings of physical passion. . . . '[J]azz' is an unmitigated cacophony, a combination of disagreeable sounds in complicated discords, a willful ugliness and a deliberate vulgarity."

But for a musical innovator like Duke Ellington (1899–1974), jazz's connection to the modern temper was the key to its authenticity and importance.

"I am trying to play the natural feelings of a people. . . . Beethoven, Wagner, and Bach are geniuses; no one can rob their work of the merit that is due it, but these men have not portrayed the people who are about us today, and the interpretation of these people is our future music."

How do music and other artistic genres reflect "the people who are about us today"?

Once-modest maidens now proclaimed their new freedom as "flappers" in bobbed tresses and dresses. Young women appeared with hemlines elevated, stockings rolled, breasts taped flat, cheeks rouged, and lips a "crimson gash" that held a dangling cigarette. Thus did the "flapper" symbolize a yearned-for and devil-may-care independence (some said wild abandon) in some American women.

Justification for this new sexual frankness could be found in the recently translated writings of Dr. Sigmund Freud. This Viennese physician appeared to argue that sexual repression was responsible for a variety of nervous and emotional ills. Thus not pleasure alone but health demanded sexual gratification and liberation.

Many taboos flew out the window as sex-conscious Americans let themselves go. As unknowing Freudians, teenagers pioneered the sexual frontiers. Glued together in rhythmic embrace, they danced to jazz music squeaking from phonographs. The youthful "neckers" and "petters" also poached upon the forbidden territory of each others' bodies in darkened movie houses or in automobiles.

If the flapper was the goddess of the era, jazz was its sacred music. With its virtuoso wanderings and tricky syncopation, jazz moved up from New Orleans along with migrating blacks during World War I. Tunes such as W. C. Handy's "St. Louis Blues" became instant classics, as the wailing saxophone became the trumpet of the new era. Black performers such as Handy, "Jelly Roll" Morton, Louis Armstrong, and Joseph "King" Oliver gave birth to jazz, but the entertainment industry soon spawned all-white bands—notably Paul Whiteman's. Caucasian impresarios cornered the profits, though not the creative soul, of America's most native music.

A new racial pride also blossomed in the northern black communities that burgeoned during and after the war. Harlem in New York City, counting some 150,000 African American residents in the 1920s, was one of the largest black communities in the world. Harlem sustained a vibrant, creative culture that nourished poets such as Langston Hughes, whose first volume of verse, *The Weary Blues*, appeared in 1926.

Harlem in the 1920s also spawned a charismatic leader, Marcus Garvey. The Jamaican-born Garvey founded the **United Negro Improvement Association (UNIA)** to promote the resettlement of American blacks in Africa. His Black Star Line Steamship Company and other enterprises eventually failed financially, and Garvey himself was convicted of alleged mail fraud in 1927 and deported by a nervous U.S. government. But the race pride that Garvey inspired among his 4 million UNIA followers helped these newcomers to northern cities gain self-confidence and self-reliance. And his example proved important to the later founding of the Nation of Islam (Black Muslim) movement.

United Negro Improvement Association (UNIA) *A black nationalist organization founded in 1914 by the Jamaican-born Marcus Garvey in order to promote resettlement of African Americans to their "African homeland" and to stimulate a vigorous separate black economy within the United States.*

Literary Liberation

Likewise in literature, an older era seemed to have ground to a halt with the recent war. By the dawn of the 1920s, most of the custodians of an aging genteel culture had died—Henry James in 1916, Henry Adams in 1918, and William Dean Howells ("the Dean of American literature") in 1920. A few novelists who had been popular in the previous decades continued to thrive, notably the well-to-do, cosmopolitan New Yorker Edith Wharton and the Virginia-born Willa Cather, esteemed for her stark but sympathetic portrayals of pioneering on the prairies.

But in the decade after the war, a new generation of writers burst on the scene. Many of them hailed from ethnic and regional backgrounds different from that of the Protestant New Englanders who traditionally had dominated American cultural life. The newcomers exhibited the energy of youth, the ambition of excluded outsiders, and, in many cases the smoldering resentment of ideals betrayed. Animated by the spark of the international modernist movement, they bestowed on American literature a new vitality, imaginativeness, and artistic quality.

Frank Driggs Collection/Hulton Archive/Getty Images

King Oliver's Creole Jazz Band, Early 1920s Joseph "King" Oliver arrived in Chicago from New Orleans in 1918. His band became the first important black jazz ensemble and made Chicago's Royal Garden Café a magnet for jazz lovers. Left to right: Honoré Dutrey, trombone; Baby Dodds, drums; King Oliver, cornet; Lil Hardin, piano; Bill Johnson, banjo; and Johnny Dodds, clarinet. Kneeling in the foreground is the young Louis Armstrong, playing a trombone.

Central to **modernism** was its questioning of social conventions and traditional authorities. No one personified this iconoclasm better than H. L. Mencken, the "Bad Boy of Baltimore." As the era's most influential critic, Mencken promoted modernist causes in politics and literature. With his acidic wit, Mencken assailed marriage, patriotism, democracy, prohibition, Rotarians, and the middle-class American "booboisie." The provincial South he contemptuously dismissed as "the Sahara of the Bozart" (a bastardization of *beaux arts*, French for fine arts), and he scathingly attacked do-gooders as "Puritans." Puritanism, he jibed, was "the haunting fear that someone, somewhere, might be happy."

modernism *An artistic and cultural movement that revolted against comfortable Victorian standards and accepted chance, change, contingency, uncertainty, and fragmentation. Originating among avant-garde artists and intellectuals around the turn of the twentieth century, modernism blossomed into a full-fledged cultural movement in art, music, literature, and architecture.*

The war had jolted many young writers out of their complacency about traditional values and literary standards. With their pens they probed for new codes of morals and understanding, as well as fresh forms of expression. F. Scott Fitzgerald, a handsome, Minnesota-born Princetonian then only twenty-four years old, became an overnight celebrity when he published *This Side of Paradise* in 1920. The book became a kind of Bible for the young. It was eagerly devoured by aspiring flappers and their ardent wooers, many of whom affected an air of bewildered abandon toward life. Catching the spirit of the hour (often about 4 A.M.), Fitzgerald found "all gods dead, all wars fought, all faiths in man shaken." He followed this melancholy success with *The Great Gatsby* (1925), a brilliant commentary on the illusory American ideal of the self-made man. Theodore Dreiser's masterpiece of 1925, *An American Tragedy*, similarly explored the pitfalls of social striving, as it dealt with the murder of a pregnant working girl by her socially ambitious young lover.

Ernest Hemingway, who had seen action on the Italian front in 1917, was among the writers most affected by the war. He responded to pernicious propaganda and the overblown appeal of patriotism by devising his own lean, word-sparing but word-perfect style. In *The Sun Also Rises* (1926) Hemingway told of disillusioned, spiritually numb American expatriates in Europe. In *A Farewell to Arms* (1929) he crafted one of the finest novels in any language about the war experience. Hemingway's literary successes and flamboyant personal life made him one of the most famous writers in the world. He won the Nobel Prize in literature in 1954—and blew out his brains with a shotgun blast in 1961.

Hemingway, Fitzgerald, and many other writers and painters found shelter and inspiration in the Paris salon of brainy and eccentric Gertrude Stein, an expatriate American. A literary innovator in her own right, Stein wrote experimental poetry and prose, including *Three Lives* (1909), *Tender Buttons* (1914), and most famously, *The Autobiography of Alice B. Toklas* (1933), named for her lifelong partner.

Stein joined fellow American poets Ezra Pound and T.S. Eliot in the vanguard of modernist literary innovation. These "high modernists" experimented with the breakdown

F. Scott Fitzgerald and His Wife, Zelda They are shown here in the happy, early days of their stormy marriage.

of traditional literary forms and wrote in a self-consciously internationalist mode. Pound, a brilliantly erratic Idahoan who deserted America for Europe, rejected what he called "an old bitch civilization, gone in the teeth," and proclaimed his doctrine: "Make It New." Pound strongly influenced the Missouri born and Harvard-educated T. S. Eliot. After taking up permanent residence in England, Eliot produced *The Waste Land* (1922), one of the most influential poems of the century.

Not all literary efforts of the era proved so radical. Robert Frost, a San Francisco-born poet, wrote hauntingly about the nature and folkways of his adopted New England. Other writers turned to a caustic probing of American small-town life. Sherwood Anderson dissected various fictional personalities in *Winesburg, Ohio* (1919), finding them all in some way warped by their cramped psychological surroundings. Sinclair Lewis, a hotheaded, heavy-drinking writer from Sauk Centre, Minnesota, sprang into prominence in 1920 with *Main Street*, the story of one woman's unsuccessful revolt against provincialism. In *Babbitt* (1922) Lewis affectionately pilloried George F. Babbitt, a prosperous, vulgar, slavishly conformist real estate broker. The word *Babbittry* was quickly coined to describe his all-too-familiar lifestyle.

William Faulkner, a dark-eyed, pensive Mississippian, offered a fictional chronicle of an imaginary, history-rich Deep South county he named "Yoknapatawpha." In powerful books such as *The Sound and the Fury* (1929) and *As I Lay Dying* (1930), Faulkner peeled back layers of time and consciousness from the constricted souls of his ingrown southern characters. His extended meditations on "the rag-tag and bob-ends of old tales and talkings" culminated in what some readers consider his greatest work, *Absalom, Absalom* (1936).

On the stage, Eugene O'Neill, a restless Princeton dropout, emerged as America's first world-class playwright. O'Neill laid bare Freudian notions of sex and the subconscious in plays like *Strange Interlude* (1928). A prodigious playwright, he authored more than a dozen productions in the 1920s and garnered the Nobel Prize in literature in 1936.

O'Neill arose from New York's Greenwich Village, which before and after the war was a seething cauldron of writers, painters, musicians, actors, and other would-be artists. After the war a black cultural renaissance also took root uptown in Harlem, led by such gifted writers as Claude McKay, Langston Hughes, and Zora Neale Hurston, and by jazz artists such as Louis Armstrong and Eubie Blake. In an outpouring of creative expression called the **Harlem Renaissance**, they proudly exulted in their black culture and argued for a "New Negro" who was a full citizen and a social equal to whites.

Harlem Renaissance *A creative outpouring among African American writers, jazz musicians, and social thinkers, centered around Harlem in the 1920s, that celebrated black culture and advocated for a "New Negro" in American social, political, and intellectual life.*

Wall Street's Big Bull Market

Signals abounded that the economic joyride might end in a crash. This something-for-nothing craze was well illustrated by real estate speculation, especially the fantastic Florida boom that culminated in 1925. Numerous underwater lots were sold to eager purchasers for preposterous sums. The whole wildcat scheme collapsed when the peninsula was devastated by a hurricane.

The stock exchange provided even greater sensations. Speculation ran wild. An orgy of boom-or-bust trading pushed the bull market to dizzying peaks, as Wall Street gamblers gored one another and fleeced greedy lambs. The stock market became a veritable gambling den.

As the 1920s lurched forward, everybody seemed to be buying stocks "on margin"—that is, with a small down payment. Barbers, stenographers, and elevator boys cashed in on "hot tips" picked up while on duty. One valet was reported to have parlayed his wages into a quarter of a million dollars. Rags-to-riches Americans eagerly worshiped at the altar of the ticker-tape machine. So powerful was the intoxicant of quick profits that few heeded the warnings raised in certain quarters that this kind of tinsel prosperity could not last forever.

Little was done by Washington to curb money-mad speculators. In the wartime days of Wilson, the national debt had rocketed from the 1914 figure of $1,188,235,400 to the 1921 peak of $23,976,250,608. Conservative principles of money management pointed to a diversion of surplus funds to reduce this financial burden. But to Secretary of the Treasury Andrew Mellon and his fellow millionaires, the burdensome taxes inherited from the war were especially distasteful. Their theory was that such high levies forced the rich to invest in tax-exempt securities rather than in factories that dispensed prosperous payrolls. The Mellonites also argued, with considerable persuasiveness, that high taxes not only discouraged business but also brought a smaller net return to the Treasury than moderate taxes.

Seeking to succor the "poor" rich people, Mellon helped engineer a series of tax reductions from 1921 to 1926. Congress followed his lead by repealing the excess-profits tax, abolishing the gift tax, and reducing excise taxes, the surtax, the income tax, and estate taxes. In 1921 a wealthy person with an income of $1 million had paid $663,000 in income taxes; in 1926 the same person paid about $200,000. Mellon's spare-the-rich policies thus shifted much of the tax burden from the wealthy to middle-income groups.

Langston Hughes (1902–1967) celebrated Harlem's role in energizing a generation of artists and writers in his poem "Esthete in Harlem" (1930):

"Strange,
That in this nigger place
I should meet life face to face;
When, for years, I had been seeking
Life in places gentler-speaking,
Until I came to this vile street
And found Life stepping on my feet!"*

*"Aesthete in Harlem," from *The Collected Poems of Langston Hughes* by Langston Hughes, edited by Arnold Rampersad with David Roessel, Associate Editor, copyright ©1994 by the Estate of Langston Hughes.

Mellon, lionized by conservatives as "the greatest secretary of the Treasury since Hamilton," remains a controversial figure. True, he reduced the national debt by $10 billion—from about $26 billion to $16 billion. But foes of the emaciated multimillionaire charged that he should have bitten an even larger chunk out of the debt, especially while the country was pulsating with prosperity. He was also accused of indirectly encouraging the bull market. If he had absorbed more of the national income in taxes, there would have been less money left for frenzied speculation. His refusal to do so typified the single-mindedly probusiness regime that dominated the political scene throughout the postwar decade.

CHAPTER SUMMARY ★ ★ ★ ★ ★ ★ ★ ★ ★ ★ ★ ★ ★

After the crusading idealism of World War I, America sharply turned inward, as many citizens became hostile to anything foreign or different. Radicals and immigrants were targeted in the red scare and the Sacco-Vanzetti case, while the resurgent Ku Klux Klan reflected many Protestant Americans' fears of change. New restrictions on immigration reflected prejudice against "non-Anglo-Saxon" groups. Sharp cultural and religious conflicts also occurred over the prohibition experiment and evolution.

A new mass-consumption economy fueled the spectacular prosperity of the 1920s. The automobile industry, led by Henry Ford, transformed the economy and altered American lifestyles. Charles Lindbergh's flight symbolized the persistence of individual heroism in an age of cynicism and mass standardization.

The pervasive media of radio and film dramatically altered popular culture and values. Jazz music, the Harlem Renaissance, and Marcus Garvey's movement all reflected African Americans' new cultural energy. Birth control and Freudian psychology overturned traditional sexual standards, especially for women. Young literary rebels, many originally from the Midwest, scorned genteel New England and small-town culture and searched for new values, sometimes as expatriates in Europe. An international modernist movement in the arts and culture self-consciously broke from the past by criticizing traditional authorities and social conventions. The stock-market boom symbolized the free-wheeling spirit of the decade.

KEY TERMS

Bolshevik Revolution (519)
red scare (519)
criminal syndicalism laws (519)
American plan (520)
Immigration Act of 1924 (521)
Eighteenth Amendment (522)
Volstead Act (522)
Racketeers (524)
Bible Belt (525)
Fundamentalism (525)
Scientific Management (526)
Fordism (526)
United Negro Improvement Association (UNIA) (530)
modernism (531)
Harlem Renaissance (532)

PEOPLE TO KNOW

A. Mitchell Palmer
Frederick W. Taylor
Nicola Sacco
Bartolomeo Vanzetti
Horace Kallen
Randolph Bourne
Al Capone
John T. Scopes
Henry Ford
Charles A. Lindbergh
Margaret Sanger
Sigmund Freud
H. L. Mencken
F. Scott Fitzgerald
Ernest Hemingway
T. S. Eliot
William Faulkner
Langston Hughes

MindTap is a fully online, highly personalized learning experience built upon Cengage Learning content. MindTap combines student learning tools—readings, multimedia, activities, and assessments—into a singular Learning Path that guides students through the course.

Chapter 31

The Politics of Boom and Bust

1920–1932

We in America today are nearer to the final triumph over poverty than ever before in the history of any land. We have not yet reached the goal—but . . . we shall soon, with the help of God, be in sight of the day when poverty will be banished from this nation.

Herbert Hoover, 1928

Chapter Outline

- Conservative Republicans Take Power
- Disarmament and Isolation
- The Harding Scandals
- Calvin Coolidge and the Election of 1924
- Foreign Policy and the International Debt Tangle
- Herbert Hoover's Competing Ideologies
- The Great Crash, 1929
- Hoover and the Great Depression
- *Examining the Evidence: Lampooning Hoover, 1932*

Three Republican presidents—Warren G. Harding, Calvin Coolidge, and Herbert Hoover—steered the nation on the roller-coaster ride of the 1920s, a thrilling ascent from the depths of post–World War I recession to breathtaking heights of prosperity, followed by a terrifying crash into the Great Depression. In a retreat from progressive reform, Republicans sought to serve the public good less by direct government action and more through cooperation with big business. Some corrupt officials served themselves as well, exploiting public resources for personal profit. Meanwhile, the United States retreated from its brief international fling during World War I and resumed with a vengeance its traditional foreign policy of military unpreparedness and political isolationism.

FOCUS QUESTIONS

1. How did the political conservatism and economic prosperity of the 1920s lead to policies that attempted to advance the interests of business and isolate America from the world?
2. What was consistent and what was different in the leadership and policies of the three Republican presidents of the 1920s—Harding, Coolidge, and Hoover?
3. How did the United States eventually address the international economic tangle of loans, war debts, and reparations? Why was there so much resentment of America's actions in Europe?
4. What were the immediate and more fundamental causes of the stock market crash and the broader Great Depression?
5. In what ways was Hoover's response to the Great Depression a reflection of the older ideology of individualism and *laissez-faire*, and in what ways did his actions reflect a newer view of government responsibility for the nation's collective economic well-being?

CHRONOLOGY

1919	▪ American Legion founded
1920	▪ Esch-Cummins Transportation Act
1921	▪ Veterans Bureau created ▪ Capper-Volstead Act
1922	▪ Five-Power Naval Treaty signed ▪ Four-Power and Nine-Power Treaties on the Far East ▪ Fordney-McCumber Tariff Law
1923	▪ *Adkins v. Children's Hospital* ▪ Teapot Dome scandal ▪ Harding dies; Coolidge assumes presidency
1924	▪ Adjusted Compensation Act for veterans ▪ Dawes Plan for international finance ▪ U.S. troops leave Dominican Republic ▪ Coolidge wins three-way presidential election
1926	▪ U.S. troops occupy Nicaragua
1928	▪ Kellogg-Briand Pact ▪ Hoover defeats Smith for presidency
1929	▪ Agricultural Marketing Act sets up Federal Farm Board ▪ Stock-market crash
1930	▪ Hawley-Smoot Tariff
1931	▪ Japanese invade Manchuria
1932	▪ Reconstruction Finance Corporation (RFC) established ▪ Norris–La Guardia Anti-Injunction Act ▪ "Bonus Army" dispersed from Washington, D.C.

The Republican "Old Guard" Returns

Warren G. Harding, inaugurated in 1921, *looked* presidential. With erect figure, broad shoulders, bushy eyebrows, and graying hair, he was one of the best-liked men of his generation. An easygoing, warm-handed backslapper, he exuded graciousness and love of people. Yet the charming, smiling exterior concealed a weak, inept interior. With a mediocre mind, Harding quickly found himself beyond his depth in the presidency. "God! What a job!" was his anguished cry on one occasion.

Harding, like Grant, was unable to detect moral halitosis in his associates, and he was soon surrounded by his poker-playing, shirt-sleeved cronies of the "Ohio gang." Harding hated to hurt his friends' feelings by saying no, and designing political leeches capitalized on this weakness. He "was not a bad man," said one Washington observer. "He was just a slob."

Admitting his own scanty mental furnishings, Harding appointed to his cabinet some strong and capable Republicans: imperious and brilliant Charles Evans Hughes as secretary of state; lean and elderly Andrew W. Mellon as secretary of the treasury; and chubby-faced Herbert Hoover, famed wartime feeder of the Belgians, as secretary of commerce. But Harding also brought into his cabinet such corrupt characters as Secretary of the Interior Albert B. Fall, a scheming anticonservationist, and Attorney General Harry M. Daugherty, a member of the "Ohio gang" and a big-time crook.

Well intentioned but weak-willed, Harding was a perfect "front" for enterprising industrialists. A McKinley-style old order settled back into place at war's end, crushing the reform seedlings that had sprouted in the progressive era. This new Old Guard hoped to improve on the old business doctrine of laissez-faire. Their plea was not simply for government to keep its hands off business but for government to help guide business along the path to profits. They subtly and effectively achieved their ends by putting the courts and the administrative bureaus into the safekeeping of fellow stand-patters for the duration of the decade.

Adkins v. Children's Hospital (1923) *A landmark Supreme Court decision reversing the ruling in* Muller v. Oregon, *which had declared women to be deserving of special protection in the workplace.*

The Supreme Court was a striking example of this trend. In his short presidency, Harding appointed four justices who were or became deep-dyed reactionaries. In the first years of the 1920s, the Supreme Court axed progressive legislation. It killed a federal child-labor law, stripped away many of labor's hard-won gains, and rigidly restricted governmental intervention in the economy. In the landmark case of ***Adkins* v. *Children's Hospital*** (1923), the Court reversed its own reasoning in *Muller* v. *Oregon* (see p. 481) and invalidated a minimum-wage law for women. Its strained ruling was that, because females now had the vote (Nineteenth Amendment), they were the legal equals of men and could no longer be protected by special legislation. The contradictory premises of the *Muller* and *Adkins* cases framed a debate over gender differences that would continue for the rest of the century: were women sufficiently different from men that they merited special legal and social treatment, or were they effectively equal in the eyes of the law and therefore undeserving of special protection and preferences?

Justice Oliver Wendell Holmes (1841–1935), wryly dissenting in the Adkins *case, said:*

"It would need more than the Nineteenth Amendment to convince me that there are no differences between men and women, or that legislation cannot take those differences into account."

Under Harding, corporations could once more relax and expand. Antitrust laws were often ignored, circumvented, or feebly enforced by friendly prosecutors in the attorney general's office. The Interstate Commerce Commission, to single out one agency, came to be dominated by members sympathetic to the railroad managers.

Big industrialists, striving to lessen competition, now had a free hand to set up trade associations. Cement manufacturers, for example, would use these agencies to agree upon standardization of product, publicity campaigns, and a united front in dealing with the railroads and labor. Although many of these associations ran counter to the spirit of existing antitrust legislation, their formation was encouraged by Secretary of Commerce Herbert Hoover. His sense of engineering efficiency led him to condemn the waste resulting from cutthroat competition and to encourage business self-regulation.

The Aftermath of War

Wartime government controls on the economy were swiftly dismantled. The War Industries Board disappeared with almost indecent haste. With its passing, progressive hopes for more government regulation of big business evaporated.

Washington likewise returned the railroads to private management in 1920. The Esch-Cummins Transportation Act of 1920 encouraged private consolidation of the railroads and pledged the federal Interstate Commerce Commission to guarantee their profitability.

Labor, suddenly deprived of its wartime crutch of friendly government support, limped along badly in the postwar decade. A bloody strike in the steel industry was ruthlessly broken in 1919, partly by exploiting ethnic and racial divisions among the steelworkers and by branding the strikers as dangerous "reds." The Railway Labor Board, a successor body to the wartime labor boards, ordered a wage cut of 12 percent in 1922, provoking a two-month strike. It ended when Attorney General Daugherty, who fully shared Harding's big-business bias, clamped on the strikers one of the most sweeping injunctions in American history. Unions wilted in this hostile political environment, and membership shriveled by nearly 30 percent between 1920 and 1930.

Needy veterans were among the few nonbusiness groups to reap lasting gains from the war. In 1921 Congress created the Veterans Bureau to operate hospitals and provide vocational rehabilitation for the disabled. The American Legion, founded in Paris in 1919 by Colonel Theodore Roosevelt, Jr., became known for its militant conservative patriotism and aggressive lobbying for veterans' benefits. The Legion demanded "adjusted compensation" to make up for the wages veterans had "lost" while in uniform. Harding vetoed one such bill in 1922, but in 1924 Congress passed the Adjusted Compensation Act over President Calvin Coolidge's veto. This Act gave every former soldier a paid-up insurance policy due in twenty years—adding about $3.5 billion to the total cost of the war.

America Seeks Benefits Without Burdens

Isolation was enthroned in Washington. The Harding administration, with the Senate "irreconcilables" holding a hatchet over its head, continued to regard the League of Nations as a thing unclean.

But disarmament was one international issue on which Harding set isolationism aside and seized the initiative. He was prodded by businesspeople unwilling to dig deeper into their pockets for money to finance the ambitious naval-building program started during the war. A deadly contest was shaping up with Britain and Japan, which watched with alarm as the oceans filled with American vessels. Public agitation in America, fed by worries about British and Japanese cooperation in the Pacific, brought about the headline-making Washington "Disarmament" Conference in 1921–1922. The double agenda included naval disarmament and the situation in East Asia.

At the outset, Secretary of State Charles Evans Hughes dramatically proposed a ten-year "holiday" on construction of battleships and even the scrapping of some of the huge dreadnoughts already built or being built. Hughes proposed that the scaled-down navies of America and Britain should enjoy parity in battleships and aircraft carriers, with Japan on the small end of a 5-5-3 ratio.

The conference's Five-Power Naval Treaty of 1922 embodied Hughes's ideas on ship ratios, but only after face-saving compensation for the insecure Japanese. The British and Americans both conceded that they would refrain from fortifying their East Asian possessions, including the Philippines. The Japanese were not subjected to such restraints in their possessions. In addition, a Four-Power Treaty bound Britain, Japan, France, and the United States to preserve the status quo in the Pacific—another concession to the Japanese. Finally, the Washington Conference gave chaotic China—"the Sick Man of East Asia"—a shot in the arm with the **Nine-Power Treaty** of 1922, whose signatories agreed to nail wide open the Open Door in China.

Nine-Power Treaty (1922) *Agreement coming out of the Washington "Disarmament" Conference of 1921–1922 that pledged Britain, France, Italy, Japan, the United States, China, the Netherlands, Portugal, and Belgium to abide by the Open Door policy in China. The Five-Power Naval Treaty on ship ratios and the Four-Power Treaty to preserve the status quo in the Pacific also came out of the conference.*

The Hardingites boasted of this globe-shaking achievement in disarmament, but their satisfaction was somewhat illusory. No restrictions had been placed on small warships, and the other powers churned ahead with the construction of cruisers, destroyers, and submarines, while penny-pinching Uncle Sam lagged dangerously behind. Ominously, the American people seemed content to rely for their security on words and wishful thinking rather than on weapons and hardheaded realism.

A similar sentimentalism welled up later in the decade, when Americans clamored for the "outlawry of war." Calvin Coolidge's secretary of state, Frank B. Kellogg, signed with the French foreign minister in 1928 the **Kellogg-Briand Pact**, which was ultimately ratified by sixty-two nations. Lacking both muscles and teeth, this parchment peace was a diplomatic derelict—and virtually useless in a showdown. Yet it accurately—and dangerously—reflected the American mind in the 1920s, which was all too ready to be lulled into a false sense of security. This mood took even deeper hold in the ostrich-like neutralism of the 1930s.

Kellogg-Briand Pact (1928) *A sentimental triumph of the 1920s peace movement, this 1928 pact linked sixty-two nations in the supposed "outlawry of war."*

Hiking the Tariff Higher

A comparable lack of realism afflicted foreign economic policy in the 1920s. Businesspeople, shortsightedly obsessed with the dazzling prospects in the prosperous home market, sought to keep that market to themselves by flinging up insurmountable tariff walls around the United States. In 1922 Congress passed the **Fordney-McCumber Tariff Law**, which boosted schedules from the average of 27 percent under Wilson's Underwood Tariff of 1913 to an average of 38.5 percent.

Fordney-McCumber Tariff Law (1922) *A comprehensive bill passed to protect domestic production from foreign competitors. As a direct result, many European nations were spurred to increase their own trade barriers.*

The high-tariff course thus charted by the Republican regimes set off an ominous chain reaction. European producers felt the squeeze, for the American tariff walls prolonged the postwar chaos. An impoverished Europe needed to sell manufactured goods to the United States, particularly if it hoped to achieve economic recovery and to pay its huge war debt to Washington. America needed to give foreign nations a chance to make a profit from it so that they could buy U.S. manufactured articles and repay debts. International trade, Americans were slow to learn, is a two-way street.

Erecting tariff walls was a game that two could play. The American example spurred European nations, throughout the feverish 1920s, to pile up higher barriers themselves. The whole vicious circle further deepened the international economic distress, providing one more rung on the ladder by which Adolf Hitler scrambled to power.

The Stench of Scandal

The loose morality and get-rich-quickism of the Harding era manifested themselves spectacularly in a series of scandals. Early in 1923 the head of the Veterans Bureau, Colonel Charles R. Forbes, was caught with his hand in the till. An appointee of the gullible Harding, he and his accomplices looted the government to the tune of about $200 million, chiefly in connection with the building of veterans' hospitals. Forbes was convicted and sentenced to two years in a federal penitentiary.

The Granger Collection, NYC

The Harding Scandals This 1924 cartoon satirizing the misdemeanors of the Harding administration shows the sale of the Capitol, the White House, and even the Washington Monument.

Most shocking of all was the **Teapot Dome scandal**, an affair that involved priceless naval oil reserves at Teapot Dome (Wyoming) and Elk Hills (California). In 1921 the slippery secretary of the interior, Albert B. Fall, induced his careless colleague, the secretary of the navy, to transfer these valuable properties to the Interior Department. Harding indiscreetly signed the secret order. Fall then quietly leased the lands to oilmen Harry F. Sinclair and Edward L. Doheny, but not until they had paid him some $400,000 in bribes ("loans").

Teapot Dome scandal (1921) *A tawdry affair involving the illegal lease of priceless naval oil reserves in Teapot Dome, Wyoming, and Elk Hills, California. The scandal, which implicated President Harding's secretary of the interior, was one of several that gave his administration a reputation for corruption.*

Teapot Dome, no tempest in a teapot, finally came to a whistling boil. Details of the crooked transaction leaked out in March 1923. Fall, Sinclair, and Doheny were indicted in 1924. Fall was found guilty of taking a bribe and sentenced to one year in jail. The two bribe givers were acquitted, though Sinclair served time in jail for "shadowing" jurors and for refusing to testify before a Senate committee.

Still more scandals erupted. Persistent reports about the underhanded doings of Attorney General Daugherty brought a Senate investigation in 1924 of the illegal sale of pardons and liquor permits. Forced to resign, the accused official was tried in 1927 but released after a jury twice failed to agree. During the trial, Daugherty hid behind the trousers of Harding by implying that persistent probing might uncover crookedness in the White House.

Harding was mercifully spared the full revelation of these iniquities. Just as news of the scandals was beginning to break, he died in San Francisco on August 2, 1923, of pneumonia and thrombosis. Mourning millions, not yet fully aware of the graft in Washington, expressed genuine sorrow.

The brutal fact is that Harding simply was not a strong enough man for the presidency—as he himself privately admitted. Such was his weakness that he tolerated people and conditions that subjected the Republic to its worst disgrace since the days of President Grant.

"Silent Cal" Coolidge

News of Harding's death was sped to Vice President Coolidge, then visiting at his father's New England farmhouse. By the light of two kerosene lamps the elder Coolidge, a justice of the peace, used the old family Bible to administer the presidential oath to his son.

This homespun setting was symbolic of Coolidge. Quite unlike Harding, the stern-faced Vermonter, with his thin nose and tightly set lips, embodied the New England virtues of honesty, morality, industry, and frugality. His dour visage prompted the acerbic observation that he had been "weaned on a pickle."

Coolidge seemed to be a crystallization of the commonplace. Painfully shy, he was blessed with only mediocre powers of leadership. He would occasionally display a dry wit in private; but his speeches, delivered in a nasal New England twang, were invariably boring.

A staunch apostle of the status quo, he became the "high priest of the great god Business." He believed that "the man who builds a factory builds a temple" and that "the man who works there worships there." The hands-off temperament of "Cautious Cal" perfectly suited the times, and Coolidge "luck" held during his five and a half prosperity-blessed years.

Ever a profile in caution, Coolidge slowly gave the Harding regime a badly needed moral fumigation. Teapot Dome had scalded the Republican party badly, but so transparently honest was the vinegary Vermonter that the scandalous oil did not rub off on him.

Frustrated Farmers

Sun-bronzed farmers were caught squarely in a boom-or-bust cycle in the postwar decade. While the fighting had raged, they had raked in money, hand over gnarled fist. But peace brought an end to high farm prices and to massive purchases by other nations, as foreign production reentered the stream of world commerce.

Machines also threatened to plow the farmer under an avalanche of his own overabundant crops. Aided by the efficiency of the new gasoline-engine tractor, agricultural production expanded and piled up more price-dampening surpluses. A withering depression swept through agricultural districts in the 1920s, when one farm in four was sold for debt or taxes.

Schemes abounded for bringing relief to the hard-pressed farmers. A bipartisan "farm bloc" from the agricultural states coalesced in Congress in 1921 and succeeded in driving through some helpful laws. Noteworthy was the Capper-Volstead Act, which exempted farmers' marketing cooperatives from antitrust prosecution. The farm bloc's favorite proposal was the **McNary-Haugen Bill**, pushed energetically from 1924 to 1928. It sought to keep agricultural prices high by authorizing the government to buy up surpluses and sell them abroad. Congress twice passed the bill, but frugal Coolidge twice vetoed it. Farm prices stayed low, and the farmers' political temperatures stayed high, reaching fever pitch in the election of 1924.

McNary-Haugen Bill (1924–1928)
A farm-relief bill that was championed throughout the 1920s and aimed to keep agricultural prices high by authorizing the government to buy up surpluses and sell them abroad. Congress twice passed the bill, but President Calvin Coolidge vetoed it in 1927 and 1928.

A Three-Way Race for the White House in 1924

Self-satisfied Republicans, chanting "Keep Cool and Keep Coolidge," nominated "Silent Cal" for the presidency at their convention in Cleveland in the simmering summer of 1924. Squabbling Democrats had more difficulty choosing a candidate when they met in New York's sweltering Madison Square Garden. Reflecting many of the cultural tensions of the decade, the party was hopelessly split between "wets" and "drys," urbanites and farmers, Fundamentalists and Modernists, northern liberals and southern stand-patters, immigrants and old-stock Americans. Deadlocked for an unprecedented 102 ballots, the convention at last turned wearily, sweatily, and unenthusiastically to John W. Davis. A wealthy Wall Street lawyer, the polished nominee was no less conservative than cautious Calvin Coolidge.

The field was now wide open for a liberal candidate, and white-pompadoured Senator Robert ("Fighting Bob") La Follette of Wisconsin sprang forward to lead a new Progressive party. He gained the support of both the American Federation of Labor and the Socialist party, but his major constituency was the price-pinched farmers. La Follette's new Progressive party, only a shadow of the robust progressive coalition of prewar days, called for government ownership of railroads and relief for farmers, lashed out at monopoly and antilabor injunctions, and urged a constitutional amendment to limit the Supreme Court's power to invalidate laws passed by Congress.

La Follette turned in a respectable showing, polling nearly 5 million votes. But "Cautious Cal" and the oil-smeared Republicans slipped easily back into office, overwhelming Davis, 15,718,211 votes to 8,385,283. The electoral count stood at 382 for Coolidge, 136 for Davis, and 13 for La Follette, all from his home state of Wisconsin (see Map 31.1).

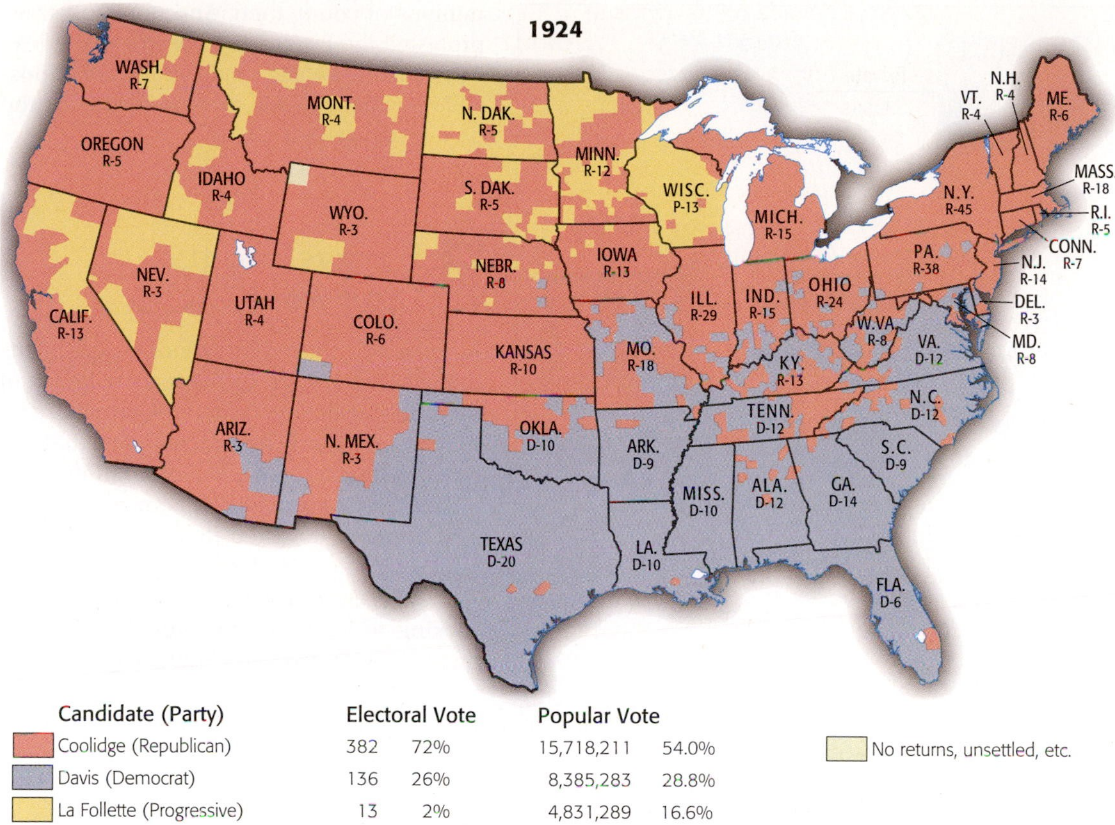

Map 31.1 Presidential Election of 1924 (showing popular vote by county) Note the concentration of La Follette's votes in the old Populist strongholds of the Midwest and the mountain states. His ticket did especially well in the grain-growing districts battered by the postwar slump in agricultural prices.

Foreign-Policy Flounderings

Isolation continued to reign in the Coolidge era. Despite presidential proddings, the Senate proved unwilling to allow America to adhere to the World Court—the judicial arm of the still-suspect League of Nations. Coolidge only halfheartedly—and unsuccessfully—pursued further naval disarmament after the loudly trumpeted agreements worked out at the Washington Conference in 1922.

A glaring exception to the United States' inward-looking indifference to the outside world in the 1920s was the armed interventionism in the Caribbean and Central America. American troops were withdrawn (after an eight-year stay) from the Dominican Republic in 1924, but they remained in Haiti from 1914 to 1934. President Coolidge in 1925 briefly removed American bayonets from troubled Nicaragua, where they had glinted intermittently since 1909, but in 1926 he sent them back, five thousand strong, and they stayed until 1933. When U.S. oil companies clamored for intervention in Mexico in 1926 to protect their interests there, Coolidge kept cool and defused the crisis with some skillful diplomatic negotiating. But his mailed-fist tactics elsewhere bred sore resentments south of the Rio Grande, where angry critics loudly assailed "*yanqui* imperialism."

Overshadowing all other foreign-policy problems in the 1920s was the knotty issue of international debts, a complicated tangle of private loans, Allied war debts, and German reparations (see Figure 31.1). The key knot in the debt tangle was the $10 billion that the U.S. Treasury had loaned to the Allies during and immediately after the war. Uncle Sam held their IOUs—and he wanted to be paid. The Allies, in turn, protested that this was unfair because they had held up a wall of flesh and bone against the common foe until America the Unready had finally entered the fray. America, they argued, should write off its loans as war costs, just as the Allies had been tragically forced to write off the lives of

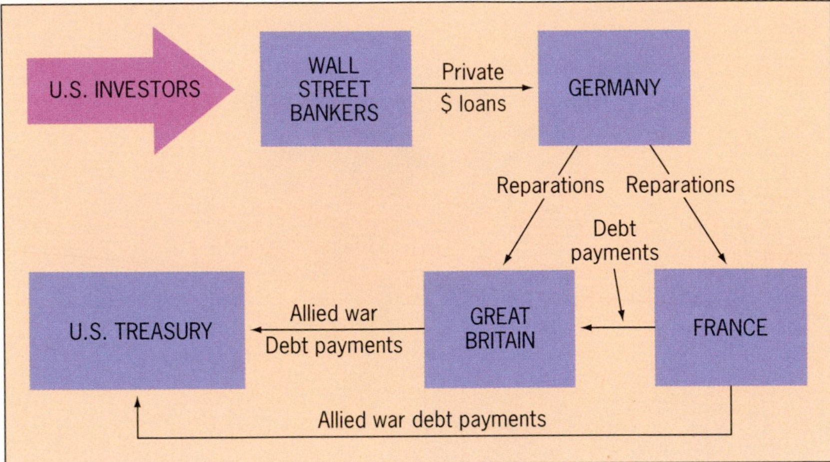

Figure 31.1 Aspects of the Financial Merry-Go-Round, 1921–1933
Great Britain, with a debt of over $4 billion to the U.S. Treasury, had a huge stake in proposals for inter-Allied debt cancellation, but France's stake was even larger. Less prosperous than Britain in the 1920s, and more battered by the war, which had been fought on its soil, France owed nearly $3.5 billion to the United States and additional billions to Britain.

millions of young men. And the final straw, protested the Europeans, was that America's postwar tariff walls made it almost impossible for them to sell the goods to earn the dollars to pay their debts.

Unraveling the Debt Knot

America's tightfisted insistence on getting its money back helped to harden the hearts of the Allies against conquered Germany. The French and the British demanded that the Germans make enormous reparations payments, totaling some $32 billion, as compensation for war-inflicted damages. The Allies hoped to settle their debts to America with the money received from Germany. The French, seeking to extort lagging reparations payments, sent troops into Germany's industrialized Ruhr Valley in 1923. Berlin responded by permitting its currency to inflate astronomically. At one point in October 1923, a loaf of bread cost 480 million marks, or about $120 million in preinflation money. German society teetered on the brink of mad anarchy, and the whole international house of financial cards threatened to flutter down in colossal chaos.

Sensible statesmen now urged that the war debts and reparations alike be drastically scaled down or canceled outright. But to Americans such proposals smacked of "welshing" on a debt. Scroogelike Calvin Coolidge turned aside suggestions of debt cancellation with a typically terse question: "They hired the money, didn't they?"

Dawes Plan (1924) *An arrangement negotiated in 1924 to reschedule German reparations payments. It stabilized the German currency and opened the way for further American private loans to Germany.*

Reality finally dawned in the **Dawes Plan** of 1924. Negotiated largely by Charles Dawes, about to be Coolidge's running mate, it rescheduled German reparations payments and opened the way for further American private loans to Germany. The whole financial cycle now became still more complicated as U.S. bankers loaned money to Germany, Germany paid reparations to France and Britain, and the former Allies paid war debts to the United States. Clearly the source of this monetary merry-go-round was the flowing well of American credit. When that well dried up after the great crash in 1929, the tangled jungle of international finance quickly turned into a desert.

The United States never did get its money, but it harvested a bumper crop of ill will. Throughout Europe Uncle Sam was caricatured as Uncle Shylock, greedily whetting his knife for the last pound of Allied flesh. The bad taste left in American mouths by the whole sorry episode contributed powerfully to the storm-cellar neutrality legislation passed by Congress in the 1930s.

The Triumph of Herbert Hoover in 1928

Poker-faced Calvin Coolidge, the tight-lipped "Sphinx of the Potomac," bowed out of the 1928 presidential race when he announced, "I do not choose to run." His logical successor was super-Secretary (of Commerce) Herbert Hoover. He was nominated on a platform that clucked contentedly over both prosperity and prohibition.

Still-squabbling Democrats nominated Alfred E. Smith, the wisecracking, glad-handing governor of New York and one of the most colorful personalities in American politics. "Al (cohol)" Smith was soakingly "wet" on prohibition, abrasively urban, and Roman Catholic in an overwhelmingly Protestant—and unfortunately prejudiced—land. Many dry, rural, and Fundamentalist Democrats gagged on his candidacy, and they saddled the wet Smith with a dry running mate and a dry platform.

Radio figured prominently in this campaign for the first time, and it helped Hoover more than Smith. The New Yorker had more personal sparkle, but he could not project it through the radio. Iowa-born Hoover, with his double-breasted dignity, came out of the microphone better than he went in.

Chubby-faced, ruddy-complexioned Herbert Hoover, with his painfully high starched collar, was a living example of the American success story and an intriguing mixture of two centuries. As a poor orphan boy who had worked his way through Stanford University, he had absorbed the nineteenth-century copybook maxims of industry, thrift, and self-reliance. As a fabulously successful mining engineer and businessman, he had honed to a high degree the efficiency doctrines of the progressive era.

A small-town boy from Iowa and Oregon, Hoover had traveled and worked abroad extensively. His experiences there had further strengthened his faith in American individualism, free enterprise, and small government. With his unshaken dignity and Quaker restraint, Hoover was a far cry from the typical backslapping politician. Personally colorless in public, he had been accustomed during much of his life to giving orders to subordinates and did not adapt readily to the necessary give-and-take of political accommodation.

As befitted America's newly mechanized civilization, Hoover was the ideal businessperson's candidate. A self-made millionaire, he recoiled from anything suggesting socialism, paternalism, or "planned economy." Yet as secretary of commerce, he had exhibited some progressive instincts. He endorsed labor unions and supported federal regulation of the new radio broadcasting industry. He even flirted for a time with the idea of government-owned radio, similar to the British Broadcasting Corporation (BBC).

Despite the best efforts of Hoover and Smith, below-the-belt tactics were employed to a disgusting degree by lower-level campaigners. Religious bigotry raised its hideous head over Smith's Catholicism. An irresponsible whispering campaign claimed that "A vote for Al Smith is a vote for the Pope" and that the White House, under Smith, would become a branch of the Vatican.

Hoover triumphed in a landslide. He bagged 21,391,993 popular votes to 15,016,169 for his embittered opponent, while rolling up an electoral count of 444 to 87. A huge Republican majority was returned to the House of Representatives. Tens of thousands of dry southern Democrats—"Hoovercrats"—rebelled against Al Smith. Hoover carried all the Border States and five states of the former Confederacy, the first Republican candidate in fifty-two years to carry multiple states that had seceded.

Contending Voices

Depression and Protection

Republican co-sponsor Willis Hawley (1864–1941) touted the Hawley-Smoot Tariff in the House, emphasizing his party's long-standing commitment to protectionism. (Indeed, the idea for this bill originated in 1928, prior to the onset of the depression.)

"[I]f this bill is enacted into law . . . we will have a new era of prosperity such as followed the enactment of every Republican tariff bill, in which all of the people of the United States in every occupation, every industry, and every employment will share as they have always shared."

A petition signed by 1,028 economists and published in the New York Times, *meanwhile, argued strenuously against the bill.*

"The proponents of higher tariffs claim that an increase in rates will give work to the idle. This is not true. We cannot increase employment by restricting trade. . . . Finally, we would urge our government to consider the bitterness which a policy of higher tariffs would inevitably inject into our international relations. . . . A tariff war does not furnish good soil for the growth of world peace."

What might account for the crisis-era enactment of a policy conceived under radically different economic conditions?

President Hoover's First Moves

Prosperity in the late 1920s smiled broadly as the Hoover years began. Soaring stocks on the bull market continued to defy the laws of financial gravitation. But two immense groups of citizens were not getting their share of the riches flowing from the national cornucopia: the unorganized wage earners and especially the disorganized farmers.

Hoover's administration, in line with its philosophy of promoting self-help, responded to the outcry of the farmers with the **Agricultural Marketing Act**. Passed by Congress in

Agricultural Marketing Act (1929) *This act established the Federal Farm Board, a lending bureau for hard-pressed farmers. The act also aimed to help farmers help themselves through new producers' cooperatives. As the depression worsened in 1930, the Board tried to bolster falling prices by buying up surpluses, but it was unable to cope with the flood of farm produce to market.*

June 1929, it was designed to help the farmers help themselves, largely through producers' cooperatives.

Hawley-Smoot Tariff (1930) *The highest protective tariff in the peacetime history of the United States, passed as a result of good old-fashioned horse trading. To the outside world, it smacked of ugly economic warfare.*

Farmers also clutched at the tariff as a possible straw to keep their heads above the water of financial ruin. But the **Hawley-Smoot Tariff** of 1930, which started out in the House as a fairly reasonable measure designed to assist farmers, acquired more than a thousand amendments in the Senate and turned into the highest protective tariff in the nation's peacetime history. The average duty was raised from 38.5 percent to nearly 60 percent. To angered foreigners, the Hawley-Smoot Tariff seemed like a declaration of economic warfare on the entire outside world. It widened the yawning trade gaps and plunged both America and other nations deeper into the terrible depression that had already begun. The Hawley-Smoot Tariff increased international financial chaos and forced the United States further into the bog of economic isolationism, playing directly into the hands of the hate-filled German demagogue Adolf Hitler.

The Great Crash Ends the Golden Twenties

When Herbert Hoover confidently took the presidential oath on March 4, 1929, America's productive colossus—stimulated by the automobile, radio, movie, and other new industries—was roaring along at a breathtaking speed that suggested a permanent plateau of prosperity. Prices on the stock exchange continued to spiral upward and create a fool's paradise of paper profits. A few prophets of disaster sounded warnings, but they were drowned out by the mad chatter of the ticker-tape machine.

Black Tuesday (1929) *The dark, panicky day of October 29, 1929, when over 16,410,000 shares of stock were sold on Wall Street. It was a trigger that helped bring on the Great Depression.*

A catastrophic crash came on **Black Tuesday**, October 29, 1929, when 16,410,030 shares of stock were sold in a save-who-may scramble. Wall Street became a wailing wall as gloom and doom replaced boom and suicides increased alarmingly. Losses, even in blue-chip securities, were unbelievable. By the end of 1929—two months after the initial crash—stockholders had lost $40 billion in paper values, or more than the total cost of World War I to the United States (see Figure 31.2).

The stock-market collapse heralded a business depression, at home and abroad, that was the most prolonged and prostrating in American or world experience. No other industrialized nation suffered so severe a setback. By the end of 1930, more than 4 million workers in the United States were jobless; two years later the figure had about tripled. Hungry and despairing workers pounded pavements in search of nonexistent jobs. Where employees were not discharged, wages and salaries were often slashed. A current jingle ran:

Mellon pulled the whistle,
Hoover rang the bell
Wall Street gave the signal
And the country went to hell.

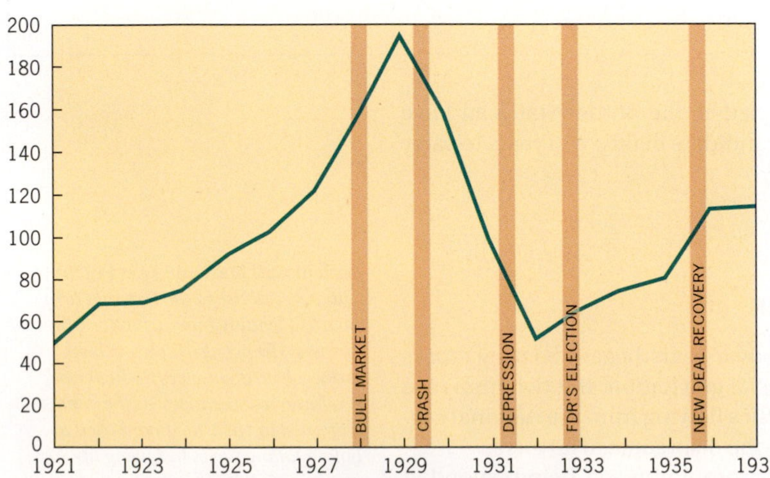

Figure 31.2 Index of Common Stock Prices (1926 = 100)

The misery and gloom were incalculable, as forests of dead chimneys stood stark against the sky. Over five thousand banks collapsed in the first three years of the depression, carrying down with them the life savings of tens of thousands of ordinary citizens. Countless thousands of honest, hard-working people lost their homes and farms to the forecloser's hammer. Breadlines formed, soup kitchens dispensed food, and apple sellers stood shivering on street corners trying to peddle their wares for five cents.

Families felt the stress, as jobless fathers nursed their guilt and shame at not being able to provide for their households. Breadless breadwinners often blamed themselves for their plight, despite abundant evidence that the economic system, not individual initiative, had broken down. Mothers meanwhile nursed fewer babies as hard times reached even into the nation's bedrooms, precipitating a decade-long dearth of births. As cash registers gathered cobwebs, the song "My God, How the Money Rolls In" was replaced with "Brother, Can You Spare a Dime?"

The Depression spectacle of want in the shadow of surplus moved an observer to write in Current History *(1932):*

"We still pray to be given each day our daily bread. Yet there is too much bread, too much wheat and corn, meat and oil and almost every commodity required by man for his subsistence and material happiness. We are not able to purchase the abundance that modern methods of agriculture, mining and manufacture make available in such bountiful quantities. Why is mankind being asked to go hungry and cold and poverty stricken in the midst of plenty?"

Hooked on the Horn of Plenty

What caused the Great Depression? One basic explanation is overproduction by both farm and factory. Ironically, the depression of the 1930s was one of abundance, not want. It was the "great glut" or the "plague of plenty."

The nation's ability to produce goods had clearly outrun its capacity to consume or pay for them. Too much money was going into the hands of a few wealthy people, who invested it in factories and other agencies of production. Not enough was going into salaries and wages, where revitalizing purchasing power could be more quickly felt. Overexpansion of credit on so-called easy terms also caused many consumers to dive in beyond their depth.

This already bleak picture was further darkened by economic anemia abroad. Britain and the Continent had never fully recovered from the upheaval of World War I. A drying up of international trade, moreover, had been hastened by the shortsighted Hawley-Smoot Tariff of 1930.

By 1930 the depression had become a national calamity. Through no fault of their own, a host of industrious citizens had lost everything. They wanted to work—but there was no work. The insidious effect of all this dazed despair on the nation's spirit was incalculable and long lasting. Hitherto the people had grappled with the physical obstacles of

Bettmann/Corbis

"Hooverville" in Seattle, 1934 In the early years of the depression, desperate, homeless people constructed shacks with scavenged materials. These shantytowns sprang up in cities across the country.

Herbert Hoover (1874–1964) spoke approvingly in a campaign speech in 1928 of "the American system of Rugged Individualism." In 1930 he referred to Cleveland's 1887 veto of a bill to appropriate seed grain for the drought-stricken farmers of Texas:

"I do not believe that the power and duty of the General Government ought to be extended to the relief of individual suffering. . . . The lesson should be constantly enforced that though the people support the Government the Government should not support the people."

nature. But the depression was a baffling wraith they could not grasp. Initiative and self-respect were stifled. In extreme cases "ragged individualists" slept under "Hoover blankets" (old newspapers), fought over the contents of garbage cans, or cooked their findings in old oil drums in tin-and-paper shantytowns cynically named **Hoovervilles**. The very foundations of America's social and political structure trembled.

Hoover's exalted reputation as a wonder-worker and efficiency engineer crashed about as dismally as the stock market. The perplexed president was impaled on the horns of a cruel dilemma. As a deservedly famed humanitarian, he was profoundly distressed by the widespread misery about him. Yet as a "rugged individualist," deeply rooted in an earlier era of free enterprise, he shrank from the heresy of government handouts. Convinced that industry, thrift, and self-reliance were the virtues that had made America great, President Hoover feared that a government doling out doles would weaken, perhaps destroy, the national fiber.

Hoovervilles *Grim shantytowns where impoverished victims of the Great Depression slept under newspapers and in makeshift tents. Their visibility (and sarcastic name) tarnished the reputation of the Hoover administration.*

As the depression nightmare steadily worsened, Hoover was finally forced to turn reluctantly from his doctrine of log-cabin individualism and accept the proposition that the welfare of the people in a nationwide catastrophe is a direct concern of the national government. The president at last worked out a compromise between the old hands-off philosophy and the "soul-destroying" direct dole then being used in Britain. He would assist the hard-pressed railroads, banks, and rural credit corporations, in the hope that, if financial health were restored at the top of the economic pyramid, unemployment would be relieved at the bottom on a trickle-down basis.

Reconstruction Finance Corporation (RFC) (1932) *A government lending agency established under the Hoover administration in order to assist insurance companies, banks, agricultural organizations, railroads, and local governments. It was a precursor to later agencies that grew out of the New Deal and symbolized a recognition by the Republicans that some federal action was required to address the Great Depression.*

Early in 1932 Congress, responding to Hoover's belated appeal, established the **Reconstruction Finance Corporation (RFC)**. With an initial working capital of half a billion dollars, this agency became a government lending bank that provided indirect relief to insurance companies, banks, agricultural organizations, railroads, and even hard-pressed state and local governments. But to preserve individualism and character, there would be no loans to individuals from this "billion-dollar soup kitchen."

"Pump-priming" loans by the RFC were of widespread benefit, but the organization was established many months too late for maximum usefulness. RFC projects were largely self-liquidating, and the government as a banker actually profited to the tune of many millions of dollars. Giant corporations so obviously benefited from this assistance that the RFC was dubbed—rather unfairly—"the millionaires' dole."

Norris–La Guardia Anti-Injunction Act (1932) *This law banned "yellow-dog," or antiunion, work contracts and forbade federal courts from issuing injunctions to quash strikes and boycotts. It was an early piece of labor-friendly federal legislation.*

Hoover's administration also provided some indirect benefits for labor. After stormy debate, Congress passed the **Norris–La Guardia Anti-Injunction Act** in 1932, and Hoover signed it. The measure outlawed "yellow dog" (antiunion) contracts and forbade the federal courts from issuing injunctions to restrain strikes, boycotts, and peaceful picketing.

The truth is that Herbert Hoover, despite criticism of his "heartlessness," did inaugurate a significant new policy. In previous panics the masses had been forced to "sweat it out." Slow though Hoover was to abandon this nineteenth-century bias, by the end of his term he had started down the road toward government assistance for needy citizens—a road that Franklin Roosevelt would travel much further.

Many veterans of World War I were numbered among the hard-hit victims of the depression. A drive developed for the premature payment of the deferred bonus voted by Congress in 1924 and payable in 1945. Thousands of impoverished veterans, both of war and of unemployment, prepared to move on Washington, there to demand of Congress the immediate payment of their *entire* bonuses. The "Bonus Expeditionary Force" of about twenty thousand men converged on the capital in the summer of 1932. These supplicants promptly set up unsanitary public camps on vacant lots—a gigantic "Hooverville."

Bonus Army (1932) *Officially known as the Bonus Expeditionary Force (BEF), this rag-tag group of twenty thousand veterans marched on Washington to demand immediate payment of bonuses earned during World War I. General Douglas MacArthur dispersed the veterans with tear gas and bayonets.*

Following riots that cost two lives, Hoover ordered the army to evacuate the remaining members of the **Bonus Army**. The eviction was carried out by General Douglas MacArthur

Examining the Evidence

Lampooning Hoover, 1932

The pages of *The American Pageant* are filled with political cartoons that provide pungent commentary on historical events. With one image rather than many words, a cartoonist can convey a point of view much the way an editorial writer does. This cartoon appeared in the *Washington Daily News* on July 25, 1932, three and a half months before Republican president Hoover lost the presidential election to his Democratic challenger, Franklin D. Roosevelt. The cartoonist foretells Hoover's defeat in November and departure from the White House the following March (not January, as at present) and expresses his support for the Home Loan Bank Bill. With this proposal, Hoover sought to come to the aid of home mortgage lenders in order to forestall them from foreclosing on homeowners. The cartoonist jokes that Hoover supported this bill because he identified with homeowners about to lose their homes, but he also cleverly insinuates that Hoover's banking reform was motivated by electoral opportunism. Surely Hoover sought to win public support in return for his new banking program as he battled for reelection, but the Home Loan Bank Bill also reflected Hoover's growing recognition that the federal government had to take direct action to remedy flaws that had precipitated the crisis of the Great Depression. As Hoover later recorded in his memoirs, "All this seems dull economics, but the poignant American drama revolving around the loss of the old homestead had a million repetitions straight from life, not because of the designing villain but because of a fault in our financial system."

1. How does the cartoonist use caricature to make his point?
2. What accounts for the political cartoon's special power?
3. Are there limitations to this genre? Find another cartoon in this book, and subject it to similar analysis.

FDR Library

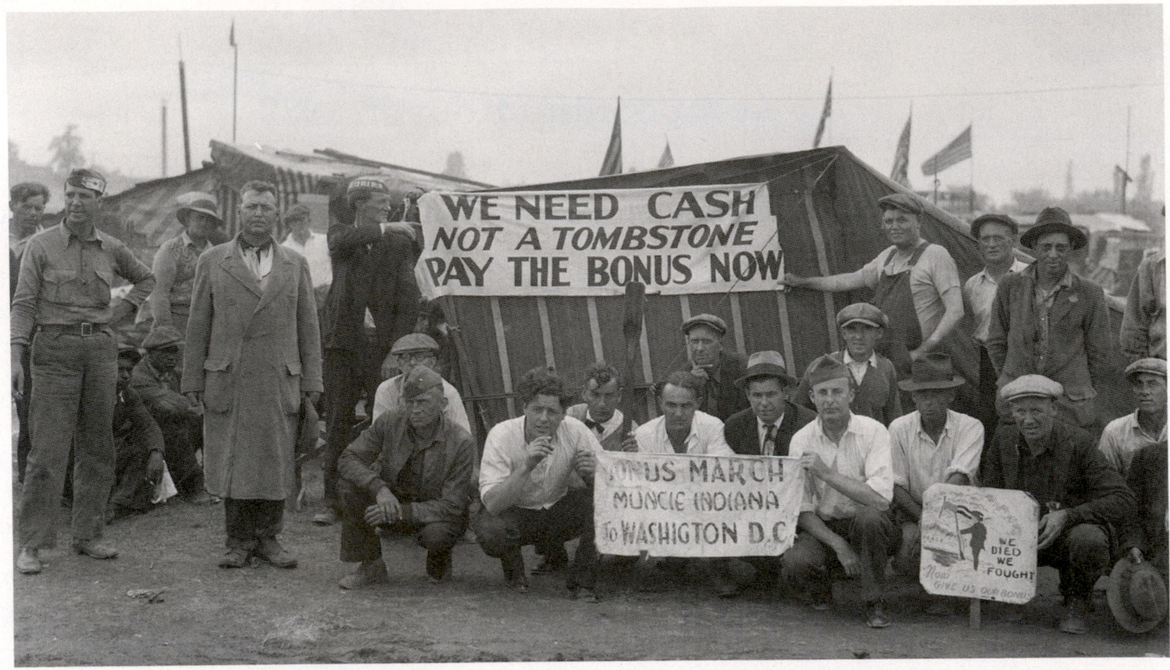

The Bonus Army in Washington, D.C., 1932 World War I veterans from Muncie, Indiana were among many contingents to set up camp in the capital during the summer of 1932, determined to remain there until they received full payment of their promised bonuses.

with bayonets and tear gas in the inglorious "Battle of Anacostia Flats." The veterans' shantytown was put to the torch, a few of the former soldiers were injured, and an eleven-month-old "bonus baby" allegedly died from exposure to tear gas.

This brutal episode brought down additional abuse on the once-popular Hoover, who by now was the most loudly booed man in the country. Cynics sneered that the "Great Engineer" had in a few months "ditched, drained, and damned the country." The existing panic was unfairly branded "the Hoover depression." In truth, Hoover had been oversold as a wizard, and the public grumbled when his magician's wand failed to produce rabbits. The time was ripening for the Democratic party—and Franklin D. Roosevelt—to cash in on Hoover's calamities.

Japanese Aggression

The Great Depression, which brewed enough distress at home, added immensely to difficulties abroad. Militaristic Japan stole the East Asian spotlight. In September 1931 the Japanese imperialists, noting that the Western world was badly mired in depression, plunged into Manchuria. Alleging provocation, they rapidly overran the coveted Chinese province and proceeded to bolt shut the Open Door in the conquered area.

Americans were stunned by this act of naked aggression. Many, though by no means a majority, urged strong measures, ranging from boycotts to a blockade backed by the League of Nations. But the League was handicapped in taking two-fisted action by the nonmembership of the United States. Washington and Secretary of State Henry L. Stimson, in the end, decided to fire only paper bullets at the Japanese aggressors. The so-called Stimson Doctrine, proclaimed in 1932, declared that the United States would not recognize any territorial acquisitions achieved by force. This verbal slap on the wrist did not at all deter the march of the Japanese militarists. But there was no real sentiment for stronger measures among the depression-ridden American people, who remained strongly isolationist during the 1930s.

CHAPTER SUMMARY ★★★★★★★★★★★★★★

The Republican governments of the 1920s carried out active, probusiness policies while undermining much of the progressive legacy by neglect or lack of enforcement. The Washington Naval Conference indicated America's strong desire in the 1920s to withdraw from international involvements. Sky-high tariffs protected America's booming industry but caused severe economic troubles elsewhere in the world and deepened the woes of farmers, who did not share in the nation's prosperity.

As the Harding scandals broke, Harding died and the puritanical Calvin Coolidge took office, thus avoiding political repercussions for the Republicans. Bitterly feuding Democrats—divided by region, religion, and culture—and La Follette Progressives fell easy victims to Republican-managed prosperity in the election of 1924.

American demands for strict repayment of war debts created international economic difficulties and resentment of the United States. The Dawes Plan provided temporary relief, but the Hawley-Smoot Tariff proved another devastating blow to international trade. Herbert Hoover, a renowned businessman and humanitarian, won a landslide victory over Catholic Al Smith in 1928.

The stock-market crash of 1929 brought a sudden end to prosperity and plunged America into a horrible depression. Herbert Hoover's reputation collapsed as he failed to relieve national suffering, although he did make unprecedented but limited efforts to revive the economy through federal assistance. The global depression and American isolationism encouraged Japanese aggression in Chinese Manchuria, which neither the United States nor the feeble League of Nations could thwart.

KEY TERMS

Adkins v. *Children's Hospital* (536)
Nine-Power Treaty (538)
Kellogg-Briand Pact (538)
Fordney-McCumber Tariff Law (538)
Teapot Dome scandal (539)
McNary-Haugen Bill (540)
Dawes Plan (542)
Agricultural Marketing Act (543)
Hawley-Smoot Tariff (544)
Black Tuesday (544)
Hoovervilles (546)
Reconstruction Finance Corporation (RFC) (546)
Norris–La Guardia Anti-Injunction Act (546)
Bonus Army (546)

PEOPLE TO KNOW

Warren G. Harding
Albert B. Fall
Calvin Coolidge
John W. Davis
Robert M. ("Fighting Bob") La Follette
Alfred E. Smith

Chapter 32

The Great Depression and the New Deal

1933–1939

The country needs and . . . demands bold, persistent experimentation. It is common sense to take a method and try it. If it fails, admit it frankly and try another. But above all, try something.

FRANKLIN D. ROOSEVELT, CAMPAIGN SPEECH, 1932

Chapter Outline

- Franklin D. Roosevelt as President
- The Hundred Days Congress, 1933
- The National Recovery Administration, 1933–1935
- The Agricultural Adjustment Administration, 1933–1936
- The Tennessee Valley Authority
- The Social Security Act, 1935
- Gains for Organized Labor
- The Election of 1936 and the "Roosevelt Coalition"
- The Supreme Court Fight, 1937
- The New Deal Assessed
- *Varying Viewpoints: How Radical Was the New Deal?*

Voters were in an ugly mood as the presidential campaign of 1932 neared. Countless factory chimneys remained ominously cold, while more than 11 million unemployed workers and their families sank ever deeper into the pit of poverty.

Hoover, sick at heart, was renominated by the Republican convention in Chicago without great enthusiasm. The rising star in the Democratic firmament was Governor Franklin Delano Roosevelt of New York, a fifth cousin of Theodore Roosevelt. Like the Rough Rider, Franklin Roosevelt had been born to a wealthy New York family, had graduated from Harvard, had been elected as a kid-gloved politician to the New York legislature, had served as governor of the Empire State, had been nominated for the vice presidency (though not elected), and had served capably as assistant secretary of the navy. Although both men were master politicians, adept with the colorful phrase, TR was pugnacious and confrontational, whereas FDR was suave and conciliatory—qualities that appealed strongly to a people traumatized by one of the greatest crises in American history.

FOCUS QUESTIONS

1. What personal qualities did Franklin Roosevelt bring to the presidency, and how did these shape both public attitudes and the New Deal policies designed to combat the Great Depression?
2. What were the primary New Deal efforts to achieve relief, recovery, and reform? Which were most successful and enduring, and which largely failed?
3. How did the early New Deal affect business, agriculture, and labor? Why did it meet such strong opposition from some quarters, including the Supreme Court?
4. How did Roosevelt politically mobilize the "New Deal coalition" of Southerners, Catholics, Jews, African Americans, and women to achieve his goals and lay the foundations for two generations of Democratic party dominance?
5. What did the New Deal truly accomplish? Is the idea of a large federal government role in the economy best understood as a response to an emergency, or a necessary feature of modern industrial life?

CHRONOLOGY

1932	▪ Roosevelt defeats Hoover for presidency
1933	▪ Bank holiday ▪ Emergency Banking Relief Act ▪ Beer and Wine Revenue Act ▪ Hundred Days Congress enacts HOLC, AAA, NRA, PWA, and TVA ▪ Federal Securities Act ▪ Glass-Steagall Banking Reform Act ▪ CWA established ▪ Twentieth Amendment (changed calendar of congressional sessions and date of presidential inauguration) ▪ Twenty-first Amendment (prohibition repealed)
1934	▪ Gold Reserve Act ▪ Securities and Exchange Commission authorized ▪ Indian Reorganization Act ▪ FHA established ▪ Frazier-Lemke Farm Bankruptcy Act
1935	▪ WPA established ▪ Wagner Act ▪ Resettlement Administration ▪ Social Security Act ▪ Public Utility Holding Company Act ▪ *Schechter* "sick chicken" case ▪ CIO organized
1936	▪ Soil Conservation and Domestic Allotment Act ▪ Roosevelt defeats Landon for presidency
1937	▪ USHA established ▪ Roosevelt announces "court-packing" plan
1938	▪ Second AAA ▪ Fair Labor Standards Act
1939	▪ Hatch Act ▪ Reorganization Act

FDR: Politician in a Wheelchair

Infantile paralysis, while putting steel braces on Franklin Roosevelt's legs, put additional steel into his soul. Until 1921, when the dread disease struck, young Roosevelt—tall, athletic, and handsome—impressed observers as charming and witty yet at times as a superficial and arrogant "lightweight." But suffering humbled him to the level of common clay. In courageously fighting his way back from complete helplessness to a hobbling mobility, he schooled himself in patience, tolerance, compassion, and strength of will. He once remarked that, after trying for two years to wiggle one big toe, all else seemed easy.

Another of Roosevelt's great personal and political assets was his wife, Eleanor Roosevelt. The niece of Theodore Roosevelt, she was Franklin Roosevelt's distant cousin as well as his spouse. Tall, ungainly, and toothy, she overcame the misery of an unhappy childhood and emerged as a champion of the dispossessed—and ultimately as the "conscience of the New Deal." Through her lobbying of her husband, her speeches, and her syndicated newspaper column, Eleanor powerfully influenced the policies of the national government. Always she battled for the impoverished and the oppressed. At one meeting in Birmingham, Alabama, she confounded local authorities and flouted the segregation statutes by deliberately straddling the aisle that separated the black and white seating sections.

Eleanor Roosevelt marched to her own drummer. As a young woman she had worked in a New York settlement house, and later on she joined the Women's Trade Union League and the League of Women Voters. When she and Franklin moved into the White House, she brought an unprecedented number of women activists with her to Washington. This network of reformers helped make her the most active First Lady in history. Sadly, her personal relationship with her husband was often rocky due to his occasional infidelity. Condemned by conservatives and

In his successful campaign for the governorship of New York in 1928, Franklin Roosevelt (1882–1945) had played down alleged Democratic "socialism":

"We often hear it said that government operation of anything under the sun is socialistic. If that is so, our postal service is socialistic, so is the parcel post which has largely taken the place of the old express companies; so are the public highways which took the place of the toll roads."

AP Images

Eleanor Roosevelt (1884–1962) America's most active First Lady, she commanded enormous popularity and influence during FDR's presidency. Here she emerges, miner's cap in hand, from an Ohio coal mine.

loved by liberals, Eleanor was one of the most controversial—and consequential—public figures of the twentieth century.

Franklin Roosevelt's political appeal was amazing. His commanding presence and his golden speaking voice, despite a sophisticated accent, combined to make him the premier American orator of his generation. He could turn on charm in private conversations as one would turn on a faucet. As a popular depression governor of New York, he had sponsored heavy state spending to relieve human suffering. Though favoring frugality, he believed that money, rather than humanity, was expendable. Roosevelt revealed a deep concern for the plight of the "forgotten man"—a phrase he used in a 1932 speech—although he was assailed by the rich as a "traitor to his class."

Exuberant Democrats met in Chicago in June 1932 and speedily nominated Roosevelt, who flew daringly through stormy weather to Chicago where he smashed precedent to accept the nomination in person. He electrified the delegates and the public with these words: "I pledge you, I pledge myself to a new deal for the American people."

Roosevelt Routs Hoover in 1932

In the campaign that followed, Roosevelt consistently preached a New Deal for the "forgotten man," but he was annoyingly vague and somewhat contradictory. Many of his speeches were ghost-written by the "Brains Trust" (popularly the **Brain Trust**), a small group of reform-minded intellectuals. They were predominantly young college professors who, as a kind of kitchen cabinet, later authored much of the **New Deal** legislation. Roosevelt rashly promised a balanced budget and denounced deficits. All of this was to make ironic reading in later months.

Brain Trust *Specialists in law, economics, and welfare, many of them young university professors, who advised President Franklin D. Roosevelt and helped develop the policies of the New Deal.*

New Deal *The economic and political policies of Franklin Roosevelt's administration in the 1930s, which aimed to solve the problems of the Great Depression by providing relief for the unemployed and launching efforts to stimulate economic recovery. The New Deal built on reforms of the progressive era to expand greatly an American-style welfare state.*

The high spirits of the Democrats found expression in the catchy air, "Happy Days Are Here Again." This theme song fit FDR's indestructible smile, his jauntily angled cigarette holder, his breezy optimism, and his promises to do something, even at the risk of bold experimentation. Meanwhile, grim-faced Herbert Hoover predicted on the campaign trail that if the Hawley-Smoot Tariff were repealed, the grass would grow "in the streets of a hundred cities." Such down-at-the-mouth gloom contrasted sharply with Roosevelt's tooth-flashing optimism and sparkling promises.

Hoover had been swept into office on the rising tide of prosperity; he was swept out by the receding tide of depression. The flood of votes totaled 22,809,638 for Roosevelt and 15,758,901 for Hoover; the electoral count stood at 472 to 59. In all, the loser carried only six rock-ribbed Republican states.

One striking feature of the election was a distinct shift of blacks from their traditional home in the Republican party of Lincoln to the Roosevelt camp. Beginning with the election of 1932, they became, notably in the great urban centers of the North, a vital element in the Democratic party.

Defeated and repudiated, Hoover continued to be president for four long months, until March 4, 1933. But he was helpless to embark on any long-range policies without the cooperation of Roosevelt. In two meetings with Roosevelt, Hoover tried to bind his successor to an anti-inflationary policy that would have made impossible many of the later New Deal experiments. But Roosevelt refused to assume responsibility without authority and airily remarked to the press, "It's not my baby."

With Washington deadlocked, the vast and vaunted American economic machine clanked to a virtual halt. One worker in four tramped the streets, feet weary and hands idle. Banks were locking their doors all over the nation as people nervously stuffed paper money under their mattresses.

FDR and the Three Rs: Relief, Recovery, and Reform

Great crises often call forth gifted leaders, and the hand of destiny tapped Roosevelt on the shoulder. On a dreary inauguration day, March 4, 1933, his vibrant voice provided the American people with inspirational new hope. He denounced the "money changers" who had brought on the calamity, and he declared that the government must wage war on the Great Depression as it would wage war on an armed foe. His clarion note was, "Let me assert my firm belief that the only thing we have to fear is fear itself."

Roosevelt moved decisively. Now that he had full responsibility, he boldly declared a nationwide bank holiday, March 6–10, as a prelude to opening the banks on a sounder basis. He then summoned the overwhelmingly Democratic Congress into special session to cope with the national emergency. For the so-called **Hundred Days** (March 9–June 16, 1933), members hastily ground out an unprecedented basketful of remedial legislation (see Table 32.1).

Hundred Days (1933) *The first hundred days of Franklin D. Roosevelt's administration, stretching from March 9 to June 16, 1933, when an unprecedented number of reform bills were passed by a Democratic Congress to launch the New Deal.*

Table 32.1 Principal New Deal Acts During Hundred Days Congress, 1933 (items in parentheses indicate secondary purposes)

Recovery	Relief	Reform
FDR closes banks, March 6, 1933 Emergency Banking Relief Act, March 9, 1933		
(Beer Act)	(Beer Act)	Beer and Wine Revenue Act, March 22, 1933
(CCC)	Unemployment Relief Act, March 31, 1933, creates Civilian Conservation Corps (CCC)	
FDR orders gold surrender, April 5, 1933 FDR abandons gold standard, April 19, 1933		
(FERA)	Federal Emergency Relief Act, May 12, 1933, creates Federal Emergency Relief Administration (FERA)	
(AAA)	Agricultural Adjustment Act (AAA), May 12, 1933	
(TVA)	(TVA)	Tennessee Valley Authority Act (TVA), May 18, 1933 Federal Securities Act, May 27, 1933
Gold-payment clause repealed, June 5, 1933		
(HOLC)	Home Owners' Refinancing Act, June 13, 1933, creates Home Owners' Loan Corporation (HOLC)	
National Industrial Recovery Act, June 16, 1933, creates National Recovery Administration (NRA), Public Works Administration (PWA)	(NRA, PWA)	(NRA)
(Glass-Steagall Act)	(Glass-Steagall Act)	Glass-Steagall Banking Reform Act, June 16, 1933, creates Federal Deposit Insurance Corporation

For later New Deal measures, see Table 32.2, p. 556

Roosevelt's New Deal program aimed at three *R*'s—relief, recovery, and reform. Short-range goals were relief and immediate recovery, especially in the first two years. Long-range goals were permanent recovery and reform of current abuses, particularly those that had produced the boom-or-bust catastrophe. The three-*R* objectives often overlapped and got in one another's way. But amid all the topsy-turvy haste, the gigantic New Deal program lurched forward.

Firmly ensconced in the driver's seat, President Roosevelt cracked the whip. A green Congress so fully shared the panicky feeling of the country that it was ready to rubber-stamp bills drafted by White House advisers. More than that, Congress gave the president extraordinary blank-check powers: some laws it passed expressly delegated legislative authority to the chief executive.

Roosevelt was delighted to exert executive leadership. He was inclined to do things by intuition—off the cuff. He was like the quarterback, as he put it, whose next play depends on the outcome of the previous play. So desperate was the mood of an action-starved public that any movement, even in the wrong direction, seemed better than no movement at all.

The frantic Hundred Days Congress passed many essentials of the New Deal's "three *R*'s," though important long-range measures were added in later sessions. These reforms owed much to the legacy of the pre–World War I progressive movement. Many of them were long overdue, sidetracked by the war in Europe and the Old Guard reaction of the 1920s. In an explosive burst of pent-up energy, New Dealers raided file cabinets full of old pamphlets on German social insurance, English housing and garden cities, Danish agricultural recovery, and American World War I collectivization. In time, the New Dealers

Bettmann/Corbis

The Champ: FDR Chatting with Reporters Roosevelt mastered the press as few presidents before or since have been able to do. He was also ingenious in finding opportunities to converse with reporters without revealing his physical limitations.

embraced progressive ideas such as unemployment insurance, old-age insurance, minimum-wage regulations, conservation and development of natural resources, and restrictions on child labor. They also invented some new schemes, such as the Tennessee Valley Authority (see pp. 561–562). Soon, depression-weary Europeans came to marvel at the exciting din of reform activity underway in the United States.

Roosevelt Tackles Money and Banking

Banking chaos cried aloud for immediate action. Congress pulled itself together and in an incredible eight hours had the Emergency Banking Relief Act of 1933 ready for Roosevelt's busy pen. The new law invested the president with power to regulate banking transactions and foreign exchange and to reopen solvent banks.

Roosevelt, the master showman, next turned to the radio to deliver the first of thirty famous "fireside chats." As some 35 million people hung on his soothing words, he gave assurances that it was now safer to keep money in a reopened bank than "under the mattress." Confidence returned with a gush, and the banks unlocked their doors.

The Hundred Days Congress also buttressed public reliance on the banking system by enacting the memorable **Glass-Steagall Banking Reform Act**. This measure provided for the Federal Deposit Insurance Corporation, which insured individual deposits up to $5,000 (later raised).

Glass-Steagall Banking Reform Act (1933) *A law creating the Federal Deposit Insurance Corporation, which insured individual bank deposits and ended a century-long tradition of unstable banking that had reached a crisis in the Great Depression.*

Roosevelt moved swiftly elsewhere on the financial front, seeking to protect the melting gold reserve and to prevent panicky hoarding. He ordered all private holdings of gold to be surrendered to the Treasury in exchange for paper currency and then took the nation off the gold standard.

The goal of Roosevelt's "managed currency" was inflation, which he believed would relieve debtors' burdens and stimulate new production. Roosevelt's principal instrument for achieving inflation was gold buying. He instructed the Treasury Department to purchase gold, ratcheting its price up from $21 an ounce in 1933 to $35 an ounce in 1934, a price that held for nearly four decades. This policy did increase the amount of dollars in circulation, as holders of gold cashed it in at the newly elevated prices, although "sound-money" critics gagged on the "baloney dollar." The gold-buying scheme came to an end in February 1934, when FDR returned the nation to a limited gold standard of $35 an ounce for purposes of international trade only. The Treasury thereafter stopped minting gold coins for domestic circulation.

Creating Jobs for the Jobless

Overwhelming unemployment clamored for prompt remedial action. One out of every four workers was jobless when FDR took his inaugural oath—the highest level of unemployment in the nation's history. Roosevelt had no hesitancy about using federal money to assist the unemployed and at the same time to "prime the pump" of industrial recovery. (A farmer has to pour a little water into a dry pump—that is, "prime it"—to start the flow.)

The Hundred Days Congress responded to Roosevelt's spurs when it created the **Civilian Conservation Corps (CCC)**. This agency provided employment in fresh-air government camps for about 3 million uniformed young men. Their useful work included reforestation, fire fighting, flood control, and swamp drainage. The recruits were required to help their parents by sending home most of their pay. Both human resources and natural resources were thus conserved.

Civilian Conservation Corps (CCC) (1933) *A government program created by Congress to hire young unemployed men to improve the rural, out-of-doors environment with such work as planting trees, fighting fires, draining swamps, and maintaining national parks. The CCC proved to be an important foundation for the post–World War II environmental movement.*

The first major effort of the new Congress to grapple with the millions of adult unemployed was the Federal Emergency Relief Act. Its chief aim was immediate relief rather than long-range recovery. The resulting Federal Emergency Relief Administration (FERA) was handed over to zealous Harry L. Hopkins, a painfully thin, shabbily dressed, chain-smoking New York social worker who became one of Roosevelt's closest friends and most influential advisers. Hopkins's agency finally granted about $3 billion to the states for direct dole payments or preferably for wages on work projects.

Table 32.2 Later Major New Deal Measures, 1933–1939
(items in parentheses indicate secondary purposes)

Recovery	Relief	Reform
(CWA)	FDR establishes Civil Works Administration (CWA), November 9, 1933	
		Securities and Exchange Commission (SEC) authorized by Congress, June 6, 1934 Indian Reorganization Act, June 18, 1934
(FHA)	National Housing Act, June 28, 1934, authorizes Federal Housing Administration (FHA)	(FHA)
(Frazier-Lemke Act)	Frazier-Lemke Farm Bankruptcy Act, June 28, 1934	
(Resettlement Administration)	FDR creates Resettlement Administration, April 30, 1935	
(WPA)	FDR creates Works Progress Administration (WPA), May 6, 1935, under act of April 8, 1935	
(Wagner Act)	(Wagner Act)	(Wagner) National Labor Relations Act, July 5, 1935 Social Security Act, August 14, 1935 Public Utility Holding Company Act, August 26, 1935
(Soil Conservation Act)	Soil Conservation and Domestic Allotment Act, February 29, 1936	
(USHA)	(USHA)	United States Housing Authority (USHA) established by Congress, September 1, 1937
(Second AAA)	Second Agricultural Adjustment Act, February 16, 1938	
(Fair Labor Standards)	(Fair Labor Standards)	Fair Labor Standards Act (Wages and Hours Bill), June 25, 1938 Reorganization Act, April 3, 1939 Hatch Act, August 2, 1939

Immediate relief was also given to two large and hard pressed special groups by the Hundred Days Congress. One section of the Agricultural Adjustment Act (AAA) made available many millions of dollars to help farmers meet their mortgages. Another law created the Home Owners' Loan Corporation (HOLC). Designed to refinance mortgages on nonfarm homes, it ultimately assisted about a million badly pinched households while simultaneously bailing out mortgage-holding banks.

Harassed by the continuing plague of unemployment, FDR himself established the Civil Works Administration (CWA) under Hopkins's direction late in 1933 (see Table 32.2). Designed to provide temporary jobs during the cruel winter emergency, it employed tens of thousands of jobless people in leaf raking and other make-work tasks. The CWA served a useful purpose, although it was heavily criticized as "boondoggling."

Direct relief from Washington to needy families helped pull the nation through the ghastly winter of 1933–1934. But the disheartening persistence of unemployment and suffering demonstrated that emergency relief measures must be not only continued but supplemented.

In 1935 Father Charles Coughlin (1891–1979) single-handedly defeated President Roosevelt's effort to win Senate ratification of a treaty providing for American membership in the World Court, a judicial body of limited authority established by the League of Nations. What FDR saw as a symbolic embrace of international responsibility Coughlin convinced his radio listeners was a conspiracy of international moneyed interests against American sovereignty:

"Our thanks are due to Almighty God in that America retains her sovereignty. Congratulations to the aroused people of the United States who, by more than 200,000 telegrams containing at least 1,000,000 names, demanded that the principles established by Washington and Jefferson shall keep us clear from foreign entanglements and European hatreds."

A Day for Every Demagogue

One danger signal was the appearance of various demagogues, notably a magnetic "microphone messiah," Father Charles Coughlin, a Catholic priest in Michigan who began broadcasting in 1930 with the slogan "Social Justice." His anti–New Deal harangues to some 40 million radio fans finally became so anti-Semitic, fascistic, and demagogic that he was silenced in 1942 by his ecclesiastical superiors.

Also notorious among the new brood of agitators were those who capitalized on popular discontent to make pie-in-the-sky promises. Most conspicuous of these individuals were Dr. Francis E. Townsend, a retired California physician who promised everyone over sixty $200 a month, and Senator Huey P. ("Kingfish") Long of Louisiana, who was said to have more brass than a government mule. Long used his abundant rabble-rousing talents to publicize his "Share Our Wealth" program, which promised to make "Every Man a King." Every family was to receive $5,000, supposedly at the expense of the prosperous. H. L. Mencken called Long's chief lieutenant, former clergyman Gerald L. K. Smith, "the deadliest and damndest orator ever heard on this or any other earth, the champion boob-bumper of all time." Fear of Long's becoming a fascist dictator ended when he was shot by an assassin in the Louisiana state capitol in 1935.

Father Coughlin and Huey Long frightened many Americans because they raised troubling questions about the link between fascism and economic crisis. Danger seemed to be lurking ominously in many corners of the world. Authoritarian rule was strengthening in Japan, while Adolf Hitler was acquiring absolute authority in Germany. Some even worried that Franklin Roosevelt himself would turn into a dictator.

Partly to quiet the groundswell of unrest that might lead to a political explosion, Congress authorized the Works Progress Administration (WPA) in 1935. The objective was employment on useful projects. Launched under the supervision of the energetic Hopkins, this remarkable agency ultimately spent about $11 billion on thousands of public buildings, bridges, and hard-surfaced roads. One of the best-loved WPA programs was the Federal Art Project, which hired artists to create posters and murals—many still adorning post office walls. Critics sneered that WPA meant "We Provide Alms." But the fact is that over a period of eight years, nearly 9 million people were given jobs, not handouts.

Agencies of the WPA also found part-time occupations for needy high school and college students and for such unemployed white-collar workers as actors, musicians, and writers. John Steinbeck, later a Nobel Prize novelist, counted dogs in his California county. Cynical taxpayers condemned lessons in tap dancing, as well as the painting of scenes on post office walls. But much precious talent was nourished, self-respect was preserved, and more than a million pieces of art were created, many of them publicly displayed.

New Visibility for Women

Just over a decade after the ratification of the Nineteenth Amendment, American women began to carve a larger space for themselves in the nation's political and intellectual life. First Lady Eleanor Roosevelt may have been the most visible woman in the Roosevelt

White House, but she was hardly the only female voice. Secretary of Labor Frances Perkins (1880–1965) became the first woman cabinet member. Mary McLeod Bethune (1875–1955), director of the Office of Minority Affairs in the National Youth Administration, served as the highest ranking African American in the Roosevelt administration.

Women also made important contributions in the social sciences, and especially in the relatively new field of anthropology. The landmark book by Ruth Benedict (1887–1948), *Patterns of Culture*, established the study of cultures as collective personalities. One of Benedict's students, Margaret Mead (1901–1978), drew from her own scholarly studies of adolescence among Pacific island peoples to advance bold new ideas about sexuality, gender roles, and intergenerational relationships.

Pearl S. Buck, raised in China by missionary parents, gained fame as a novelist by introducing American readers to Chinese peasant society. Her best-selling novel, *The Good Earth* (1931), earned her the Nobel Prize for literature in 1938.

Helping Industry and Labor

National Recovery Administration (NRA) (1933) *An early New Deal program designed to assist industry, labor, and the unemployed through centralized planning mechanisms that monitored workers' earnings and working hours to distribute work and established codes for "fair competition" to ensure that similar procedures were followed by all firms in any particular industrial sector.*

A daring attempt to stimulate a nationwide comeback was initiated when the Hundred Days Congress authorized the **National Recovery Administration (NRA)**. This ingenious scheme was by far the most complex and far-reaching effort by the New Dealers to combine immediate relief with long-range recovery and reform. Triple-barreled, the NRA was designed to assist industry, labor, and the unemployed.

Individual industries—over two hundred in all—were to work out codes of "fair competition," under which hours of labor would be reduced so that employment could be spread over more people. A ceiling was placed on the maximum hours of labor; a floor was placed under wages to establish minimum levels.

Labor, under the NRA, was granted additional benefits. Workers were formally guaranteed the right to organize and bargain collectively through representatives *of their own choosing*. The hated "yellow dog," or antiunion, contract was expressly forbidden, and certain safeguarding restrictions were placed on the use of child labor.

Enthusiasm for industrial recovery through the NRA was stirred by patriotic mass meetings and huge parades, which included 200,000 marchers on New York City's Fifth Avenue. A handsome blue eagle was designed as the symbol of the NRA, and Philadelphia's newly formed professional football team was named the Eagles. Such was the enthusiasm for the NRA that for a brief period there was a marked upswing of business activity.

But the high-flying eagle gradually fluttered to earth. The "fair competition" codes required too much sacrifice by labor, industry, and the public for such a scheme to work. Critics began to brand the NRA "Nuts Running America," symbolized by what Henry Ford called "that damn Roosevelt buzzard." Complete collapse was imminent when, in 1935, the Supreme Court shot down the dying eagle in the *Schechter* "sick chicken" decision. The learned justices unanimously held that Congress could not "delegate legislative powers" to the executive. They further declared that congressional control of interstate commerce could not properly apply to a local fowl business, such as that of the Schechter brothers in Brooklyn. Roosevelt was incensed by this "horse and buggy" interpretation of the Constitution, but actually the Court helped him out of a bad jam.

The same act of Congress that hatched the NRA eagle also authorized the Public Works Administration (PWA), likewise intended both for industrial recovery and for unemployment relief. The agency was headed by acid-tongued Secretary of the Interior Harold L. Ickes, a free-swinging former bull mooser. Long-range recovery was the primary purpose of the new agency, and in time over $4 billion was spent on some thirty-four thousand projects, which included public buildings, highways, and parkways.

One spectacular PWA achievement was the Grand Coulee Dam on the Columbia River. In the depths of the depression, the towering dam seemed the height of folly. It made possible the irrigation of millions of acres of new farmland—at a time when the government was desperately trying to reduce farm surpluses. It created vast amounts of electrical power—in a region with little industry and virtually no market for additional power. But with the outbreak of World War II and then postwar prosperity, the dam would come to seem a stroke of genius, transforming the entire region with abundant water and power.

Josef Scaylea/CORBIS

Grand Coulee Dam on the Columbia River, Washington State The Grand Coulee Dam was one of the most ambitious projects of the New Deal's Public Works Administration. It is one of the few man-made constructions visible from outer space, the largest concrete structure in the United States, and the central facility in the Columbia Basin Project, which generates electricity for the Pacific Northwest and provides irrigation for half a million acres of Columbia Valley farmland—services that have transformed the life of the region.

Special stimulants aided the recovery of one segment of business—the liquor industry. The Hundred Days Congress, in one of its earliest acts, legalized and taxed "light" wine and beer (3.2 percent alcohol), providing new employment and federal revenue. Prohibition was officially repealed by the Twenty-first Amendment late in 1933 (see Appendix), and the saloon doors swung open.

Paying Farmers Not to Farm

Ever since the war-boom days of 1918, farmers had suffered from low prices and overproduction, especially of grain. During the depression, conditions became desperate as innumerable mortgages were foreclosed, corn was burned for fuel, and embattled farmers tried to prevent shipment of crops to glutted markets. In Iowa several volatile counties were placed under martial law.

A radical new approach to farm recovery was embraced when the Hundred Days Congress established the **Agricultural Adjustment Administration (AAA)**. Through "artificial scarcity" this agency was to establish "parity prices" for basic commodities. "Parity" was the price set for a product that gave it the same real value, in purchasing power, that it had enjoyed during the prosperous period from 1909 to 1914. The AAA would eliminate price-depressing surpluses by paying growers to reduce their crop acreage.

Agricultural Adjustment Administration (AAA) (1933)
A New Deal program designed to raise agricultural prices by paying farmers not to farm. It was based on the assumption that higher prices would increase farmers' purchasing power and thereby help alleviate the Great Depression.

Unhappily, the AAA got off to a wobbly start. It was begun after much of the cotton crop for 1933 had been planted, and balky mules, trained otherwise, were forced to plow under countless young plants. Several million squealing pigs were purchased and

Novelist John Steinbeck (1902–1968) related in his novel The Grapes of Wrath *(1939) that when the "Okies" and "Arkies" reached California, they found the big growers unwilling to pay more than twenty-five cents an hour for work in the fields. One owner mutters:*

"A Red is any son-of-a-bitch that wants thirty cents an hour when we're paying twenty-five!"

slaughtered. Much of their meat was distributed to persons on relief, but some of it was used for fertilizer. This "sinful" destruction of food, at a time when thousands of citizens were hungry, increased condemnation of the American economic system by many left-leaning voices. When the Supreme Court finally killed the AAA in 1936 by declaring its regulatory tax unconstitutional, foes of the plow-under program rejoiced loudly.

The New Deal quickly recovered from this blow by passing the Soil Conservation and Domestic Allotment Act (1936), which paid subsidies to farmers if they planted soil-conserving crops, like soybeans, or let their land lie fallow. The Second Agricultural Adjustment Act of 1938 permitted parity payments if farmers observed acreage restrictions on commodities like cotton and wheat. Other provisions of the new AAA were designed to give farmers not only a fairer price but a more substantial share of the national income. Both goals were partially achieved.

Dust Bowls and Black Blizzards

Dust Bowl *Grim nickname for the Great Plains region devastated by drought and dust storms during the 1930s. The disaster led to the migration into California of thousands of displaced "Okies" and "Arkies."*

Nature meanwhile had been providing some unplanned scarcity. Late in 1933 a prolonged drought struck the states of the trans-Mississippi Great Plains. Rainless weeks were followed by furious, whining winds, while the sun was darkened by millions of tons of powdery topsoil torn from homesteads that stretched from eastern Colorado to western Missouri—soon to be dubbed the **Dust Bowl** (see Map 32.1). Despondent citizens sat on front porches with protective masks on their faces, watching their farms swirl by.

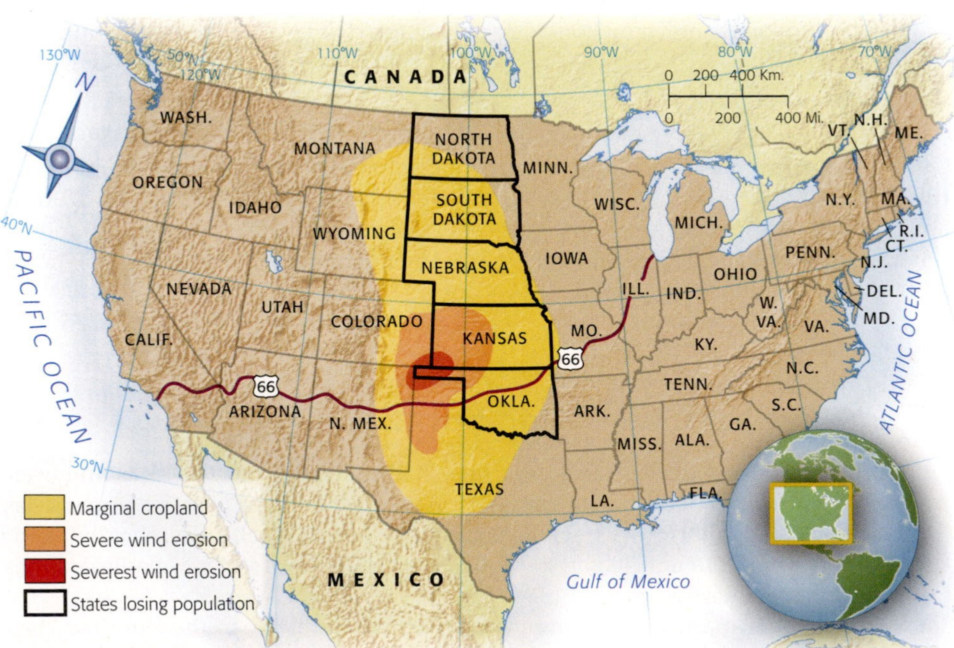

Map 32.1 The Extent of Erosion in the 1930s Note the extensive wind erosion in the western Oklahoma panhandle region, which was dubbed the "Dust Bowl" in the 1930s. Mechanized farmers had "busted" the sod of the southern plains so thoroughly that they literally broke the back of the land. Tons of dust blew out of the Dust Bowl in the 1930s and blotted the sun from the skies as far away as New York. A Kansas newspaperman reported in 1935 that in his dust-darkened town, "Lady Godiva could ride through streets without even the horse seeing her."

Overawed victims of the Dust Bowl disaster predicted the end of the world or the second coming of Christ.

Burned and blown out of the Dust Bowl, tens of thousands of refugees fled their ruined acres. In five years about 350,000 Oklahomans and Arkansans—"Okies" and "Arkies"—trekked to southern California in "junkyards on wheels." Undeterred by signs telling them to "KEEP OUT," many found new homes in the San Joaquin Valley, which shared much in common with the southern plains—arid climate, cotton growing, newfound oil deposits, and abundant land. Yet the transition was cruel. Food, shelter, and clothing were scarce; the winter months, without work and heat, proved nearly unendurable for the migrants. The dismal story of these human tumbleweeds was realistically portrayed in John Steinbeck's best-selling novel *The Grapes of Wrath* (1939), which proved to be the *Uncle Tom's Cabin* of the Dust Bowl.

Zealous New Dealers, sympathetic toward these desperate soil-tillers, made various efforts to relieve their burdens. The Frazier-Lemke Farm Bankruptcy Act, passed in 1934, made possible a suspension of mortgage foreclosures for five years; a revised version was upheld by the Supreme Court. In 1935 the president set up the Resettlement Administration to help farmers move to better land. And more than 200 million young trees were successfully planted on the bare prairies as windbreaks by the young men of the Civilian Conservation Corps.

Native Americans also felt the far-reaching hand of New Deal reform. Commissioner of Indian Affairs John Collier ardently sought to reverse the forced-assimilation policies in place since the Dawes Act of 1887. The Indian Reorganization Act of 1934 (the "Indian New Deal") encouraged tribes to establish local self-government, helped stop the loss of Indian lands, and revived tribes' interest in their identities and cultures. Nearly two hundred tribes established governments under its provisions, though seventy-seven others refused to organize.

★ Reforming Business and Creating Public Power

Reformist New Dealers were determined from the outset to curb the "money changers" who had played fast and loose with gullible investors before the Wall Street crash of 1929. The Hundred Days Congress passed the "Truth in Securities Act" (Federal Securities Act), which required promoters to transmit to the investor sworn information regarding the soundness of their stocks and bonds. In 1934 Congress took further steps to protect the public against fraud, deception, and inside manipulation. It authorized the Securities and Exchange Commission (SEC), which was designed as a watchdog administrative agency. Stock markets henceforth were to operate more as trading marts and less as gambling casinos.

New Dealers likewise directed their fire at public utility holding companies, those supercorporations. When Chicagoan Samuel Insull's multibillion-dollar financial empire crashed in 1932, citizens rebelled against such pyramided layers of big business. The Public Utility Holding Company Act of 1935 delivered a "death sentence" to this type of bloated growth.

Inevitably, the sprawling electric-power industry attracted the fire of New Deal reformers. Within a few decades it had risen from nothingness to a behemoth with an investment of $13 billion. As a public utility, it reached directly and regularly into the pocketbooks of millions of consumers for vitally needed services. Ardent New Dealers accused the electric-power industry of gouging the public with excessive rates, especially because it owed its success to having secured, often for a song, priceless water-power sites from the public domain.

The tempestuous Tennessee River provided New Dealers with a rare opportunity. With its tributaries, the river drained a badly eroded area about the size of England, containing some 2.5 million of the most poverty-stricken people in America. The federal government already owned valuable properties at Muscle Shoals, where it had erected plants for needed nitrates in World War I. By developing the hydroelectric potential of the entire area, Washington could combine the immediate advantage of putting thousands of people to work with a long-term project for reforming the power monopoly.

Tennessee Valley Authority (TVA) (1933) *One of the most revolutionary of the New Deal public works projects, which brought cheap electric power, full employment, low-cost housing, and environmental improvements to Americans in the Tennessee Valley.*

An act that created the **Tennessee Valley Authority (TVA)** was passed in 1933 by the Hundred Days Congress. This far-ranging enterprise was largely a result of the steadfast vision and unflagging zeal of Senator George W. Norris of Nebraska, after whom one of the mighty dams was named. From the standpoint of "planned economy," the TVA was by far the most revolutionary of all New Deal schemes.

New Dealers pointed a prideful finger at the amazing achievements of the TVA, despite critics who called it "creeping socialism." The gigantic project brought to the area not only cheap electric power but full employment, low-cost housing, abundant cheap nitrates, restoration of eroded soil, reforestation, improved navigation, and flood control.

Exulting New Dealers agitated for parallel enterprises in the valleys of the Columbia, Colorado, and Missouri Rivers. Hydroelectric power from federally built dams would drive the growth of the urban West, and the waters the dams diverted would nurture agriculture in the previously bone-dry western deserts. But conservative reaction against the "socialistic" New Deal confined the TVA's brand of federally guided resource management and comprehensive regional development to the Tennessee Valley.

Housing and Social Security

The New Deal had meanwhile framed sturdy new policies for housing construction. To speed recovery and improve homes, Roosevelt set up the Federal Housing Administration (FHA) as early as 1934. The building industry was to be stimulated by small loans to householders. So popular did the FHA prove to be that it was one of the few "alphabetical agencies" to outlast the age of Roosevelt.

Congress bolstered the program in 1937 by authorizing the United States Housing Authority (USHA)—an agency designed to lend money to states or communities for low-cost construction. Although units for about 650,000 low-income people were started, new building fell tragically short of needs. New Deal efforts to expand the project collided with brick-wall opposition from real estate promoters, builders, and landlords ("slumlords"), to say nothing of anti–New Dealers who attacked what they considered down-the-rathole spending. Nonetheless, for the first time in a century the slum areas in America ceased growing and even shrank.

Social Security Act (1935) *A flagship accomplishment of the New Deal, providing for unemployment and old-age insurance financed by a payroll tax on employers and employees. It has long remained a pillar of the "New Deal Order."*

Incomparably more important was the success of New Dealers in the field of unemployment insurance and old-age pensions. Their greatest victory was the **Social Security Act** of 1935—one of the most complicated and far-reaching laws ever to pass Congress. To cushion future depressions, the measure provided for federal-state unemployment insurance. To provide security for old age, specified categories of retired workers were to receive regular payments from Washington, ranging from $10 to $85 a month (raised periodically). These pensions were financed by a payroll tax on both employers and employees. Provision was also made for the blind, the physically handicapped, and dependent children.

Social Security was largely inspired by the example of some of the more highly industrialized nations of Europe. The United States government was now recognizing its responsibility for the economic welfare of its citizens. By 1939 more than 45 million people were eligible for Social Security benefits. In subsequent years further categories of workers were added, including, belatedly, farm and domestic workers. For decades, millions of poor men and women were excluded from Social Security. In contrast to Europe, where welfare programs generally were universal, American workers had to be employed and in certain kinds of jobs to get coverage.

A New Deal for Labor

The NRA blue eagles, with their call for collective bargaining, had been a godsend to organized labor. As New Deal expenditures brought some slackening of unemployment, labor began to feel more secure and hence more self-assertive. A rash of walkouts occurred in the summer of 1934, including a paralyzing general strike in San Francisco. When the Supreme Court axed the blue eagle, a Congress sympathetic to labor unions undertook to fill the vacuum. The fruit of its deliberations was the National Labor Relations Act of 1935, more commonly known as the **Wagner Act** after its congressional sponsor, New York Senator Robert F. Wagner. This trailblazing law created a powerful new National Labor Relations Board and reasserted the right of labor to organize and bargain collectively through representatives of its own choice. Considered the Magna Carta of American labor, the Wagner Act proved to be a major milestone for American workers.

Wagner Act (1935) *Also known as the National Labor Relations Act, protected the right of labor to organize in unions and bargain collectively with employers and established the National Labor Relations Board to monitor unfair labor practices on the part of employers. Its passage marked the culmination of decades of labor protest.*

Under the encouragement of a highly sympathetic National Labor Relations Board, a host of unskilled workers began to organize themselves into effective unions. The leader of this drive was beetle-browed, domineering, and melodramatic John L. Lewis, boss of the United Mine Workers. In 1935 he succeeded in forming the Committee for Industrial Organization (CIO) within the ranks of the skilled-craft American Federation of Labor. But skilled workers, ever since the days of the ill-fated Knights of Labor in the 1880s, had shown only lukewarm sympathy for the cause of unskilled labor, especially blacks. In 1936, following inevitable friction with the CIO, the older federation suspended the upstart unions associated with the newer organization.

Undaunted, the rebellious CIO moved on a concerted scale into the huge automobile industry. Late in 1936 the workers resorted to a revolutionary technique known as the sit-down strike: they refused to leave the factory buildings of General Motors at Flint, Michigan, and thus prevented the importation of strikebreakers. Conservative respecters of private property were scandalized. The CIO finally won a resounding victory when its union, after heated negotiations, was recognized by General Motors as the sole bargaining agency for its employees.

Roosevelt's "Coddling" of Labor

Unskilled workers now pressed their advantage. The United States Steel Corporation, previously an impossible nut for labor to crack, averted a costly strike when it voluntarily granted rights of unionization to its CIO-organized employees. But the "little steel" companies fought back savagely. Citizens were shocked in 1937 by the Memorial Day massacre at the plant of the Republic Steel Company in Chicago, where police gunfire killed or wounded several score picketers.

A better deal for labor continued when Congress, in 1938, passed the memorable **Fair Labor Standards Act** (Wages and Hours Bill). Industries involved in interstate commerce were to set up minimum-wage and maximum-hour levels. The eventual standards were forty cents an hour (later raised) and a forty-hour week. Labor by children under sixteen (under eighteen if the occupation was dangerous) was forbidden. But the exclusion of agricultural, service, and domestic workers meant that blacks, Mexican Americans, and women, who were concentrated in these fields, did not benefit from the act.

Fair Labor Standards Act (1938) *Important New Deal labor legislation that regulated minimum wages and maximum hours for workers involved in interstate commerce. The law also outlawed labor by children under sixteen. The exclusion of agricultural, service, and domestic workers meant that many blacks, Mexican Americans, and women—who were concentrated in these sectors—did not benefit from the act's protection.*

In later New Deal days, labor unionization thrived. "Roosevelt wants you to join a union" was the rallying cry of professional organizers. The president received valuable support at the ballot-box from labor leaders and many appreciative working people. One mill worker remarked that Roosevelt was "the only man we ever had in the White House who would know that my boss is an s.o.b."

The CIO surged forward, breaking completely with the AF of L in 1938. On that occasion the *Committee* for Industrial Organization was formally reconstituted as the **Congress of Industrial Organizations** (the new **CIO**), under the visionary though high-handed presidency of John L. Lewis. By 1940 the CIO could claim about 4 million members in its constituent unions, including some 200,000 blacks.

Congress of Industrial Organizations (CIO) *A New Deal–era labor organization that broke away from the American Federation of Labor (AFL) in order to organize unskilled industrial workers regardless of their particular economic sector or craft. The CIO gave a great boost to labor organizing in the midst of the Great Depression and during World War II. In 1955, the CIO merged with the AFL.*

Landon Challenges "the Champ" in 1936

As the presidential campaign of 1936 neared, the New Dealers were on top of the world. They had achieved considerable progress, and millions of "reliefers" were grateful to their bountiful government. The exultant Democrats renominated Roosevelt on a platform squarely endorsing the New Deal.

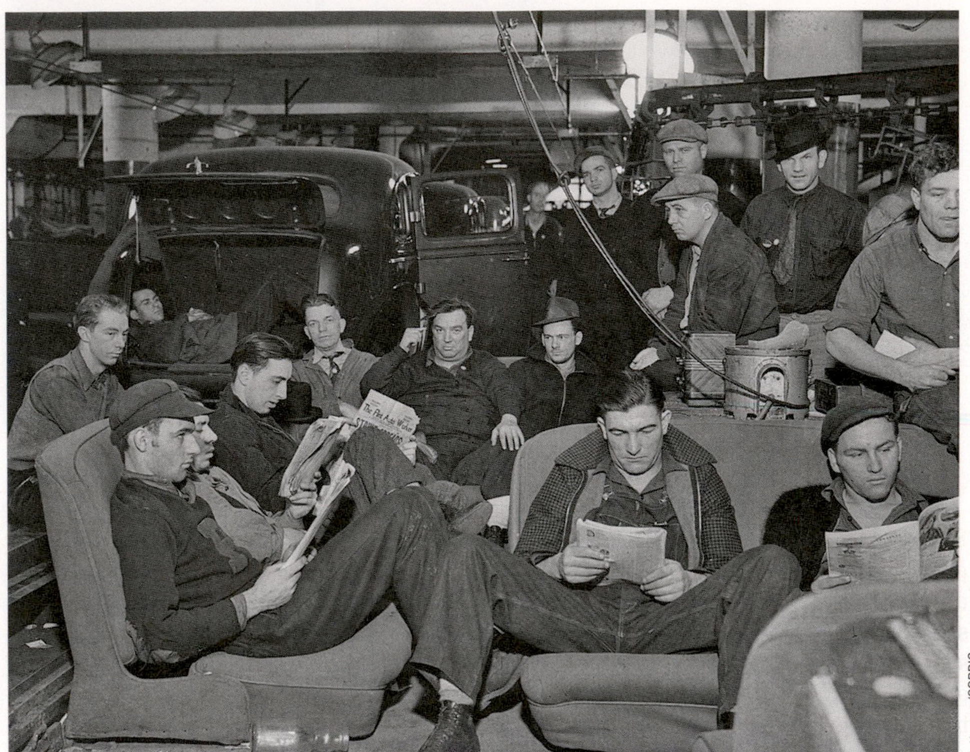

Bettmann/CORBIS

General Motors Sit-Down Strikers, Flint, Michigan, 1937 Strikers like these sometimes kept their spirits up with the song "Sit Down":

When the boss won't talk
Don't take a walk;
Sit down, sit down.

The Republicans were hard pressed to find someone to feed to "the Champ." They finally settled on the colorless but homespun and honest governor of Kansas, Alfred M. Landon. Landon himself was a moderate who accepted some New Deal reforms, although not the popular Social Security Act. But the Republican platform vigorously condemned the New Deal for its radicalism, experimentation, confusion, and "frightful waste." Backing Landon, ex-president Hoover called for a "holy crusade for liberty," echoing the cry of the American Liberty League, a group of wealthy conservatives organized to fight "socialistic" New Deal schemes.

Roosevelt gave as good as he got. Angry enough to stretch sheet iron, Roosevelt took to the stump and denounced the "economic royalists" who sought to "hide behind the flag and the Constitution." "I welcome their hatred," he proclaimed.

A landslide overwhelmed Landon as the demoralized Republicans carried only two states, Maine and Vermont. The popular vote was 27,752,869 to 16,674,665; the electoral count was 523 to 8—the most lopsided in 116 years. A good-humored newspaper columnist quipped, "If Landon had given one more speech, Roosevelt would have carried Canada, too." Democratic majorities were again returned to Congress. Jubilant Democrats could now claim more than two-thirds of the seats in the House and a like proportion in the Senate.

The battle of 1936, perhaps the most bitter since Bryan's defeat in 1896, partially bore out Republican charges of class warfare. Even more than in 1932, the needy economic groups were lined up against the so-called greedy economic groups. CIO units contributed generously to FDR's campaign chest. Many left-wingers turned to Roosevelt, as the customary third-party protest vote sharply declined. Blacks, several million of whom had also appreciated relief checks, had by now largely shaken off their traditional allegiance to the Republican party. To them, Lincoln was "finally dead."

FDR won primarily because he appealed to the "forgotten man," whom he never forgot. Roosevelt in fact had forged a powerful and enduring coalition of southerners, blacks, urbanites, and the poor. He proved especially effective in marshaling the support of the multitudes of "New Immigrants"—mostly Catholics and Jews who had swarmed into the great cities since the turn of the century. These once-scorned newcomers, with their now-numerous sons and daughters, had at last come politically of age. In the 1920s, one out of every twenty-five federal judgeships went to a Catholic; Roosevelt appointed Catholics to one out of every four.

Nine Old Men on the Bench

Bowing his head to the sleety blasts, Roosevelt took the presidential oath on January 20, 1937, instead of the traditional March 4. The Twentieth Amendment to the Constitution had been ratified in 1933. (See the Appendix.) It swept away the postelection lame duck session of Congress and shortened by six weeks the awkward period before inauguration.

Flushed with victory, Roosevelt interpreted his reelection as a mandate to continue New Deal reforms. But in his eyes the cloistered old men on the supreme bench, like fossilized stumbling blocks, stood stubbornly in the pathway of progress. In nine major cases involving the New Deal, the Roosevelt administration had been thwarted seven times. The Supreme Court was ultraconservative, and six of the nine oldsters in black were over seventy. As luck would have it, not a single member had been appointed by FDR in his first term.

Roosevelt, his "Dutch up," viewed with mounting impatience what he regarded as the obstructive conservatism of the Court. To overcome such obstructionism, Roosevelt finally hit upon a Court scheme that he regarded as "the answer to a maiden's prayer." In fact, it proved to be one of the most costly political misjudgements of his career. Roosevelt's brainstorm, which surprised and shocked the country, asked Congress for legislation to permit him to add a new justice to the Supreme Court for every member over seventy who would not retire. The maximum membership could then be fifteen.

Contending Voices

The New Deal at High Tide

Three days before the 1936 election, President Franklin Roosevelt (1882–1945) took the moral high ground in his fiery speech at New York's Madison Square Garden:

"I should like to have it said of my first Administration that in it the forces of selfishness and of lust for power met their match. I should like to have it said of my second Administration that in it these forces met their master."

One day prior to that, his predecessor Herbert Hoover (1874–1964) voiced the sentiments of many conservatives when he depicted the New Deal as a dangerous power grab:

"Through four years of experience this New Deal attack upon free institutions has emerged as the transcendent issue in America. All the men who are seeking for mastery in the world today are using the same weapons. They sing the same songs. They all promise the joys of Elysium without effort. But their philosophy is founded on the coercion and compulsory organization of men."

What ideologies about the nature of government lay behind Roosevelt's and Hoover's very different opinions of the New Deal? In what ways have their respective views persisted in American political life?

Congress and the nation were promptly convulsed over Roosevelt's **Court-packing plan** to expand the Supreme Court. Franklin "Double-crossing" Roosevelt was savagely condemned for attempting to break down the delicate checks and balances among the three branches of the government.

Court-packing plan (1937) *Franklin Roosevelt's politically motivated and ill-fated scheme to add a new justice to the Supreme Court for every member over seventy who would not retire. His objective was to overcome the Court's objections to New Deal reforms.*

The Court had meanwhile seen the ax hanging over its head. Whatever his motives, Justice Owen J. Roberts, formerly regarded as a conservative, began to vote on the side of his liberal colleagues. "A switch in time saves nine" was the classic witticism inspired by this change. By a five-to-four decision, the Court, in March 1937, upheld the principle of a state minimum wage for women, thereby reversing its stand on a different case a year earlier. In succeeding decisions a Court more sympathetic to the New Deal upheld the National Labor Relations Act (Wagner Act) and the Social Security Act.

With these changes under way, Congress refused to endorse the court-packing scheme, and Roosevelt suffered his first major legislative defeat at the hands of his own party. Yet in losing this battle, Roosevelt incidentally won his campaign. The Court, as he had hoped, became markedly more friendly to New Deal reforms. Furthermore, a succession of deaths and resignations enabled him to make nine appointments to the tribunal.

Yet in a sense FDR lost both the Court battle and the war. He so aroused conservatives of both parties in Congress that few New Deal reforms were passed after 1937, the year of the fight to "pack" the Supreme Court. With this catastrophic miscalculation, he squandered much of the political goodwill that had carried him to such a resounding victory in the 1936 election.

The Twilight of the New Deal

Roosevelt's first term, from 1933 to 1937, did not banish the depression from the land. Unemployment stubbornly persisted in 1936 at about 15 percent, down from the grim 25 percent of 1933 but still miserably high. Despite the inventiveness of New Deal programs and the billions of dollars in "pump priming," recovery had been dishearteningly modest, though the country seemed to be inching its way back to economic health.

Then, in 1937, the economy took another sharp downturn, a surprisingly severe depression-within-the-depression that the president's critics quickly dubbed the "Roosevelt recession." In fact, government policies had caused the nosedive, as new Social Security taxes began to bite into payrolls and as the administration cut back on spending out of continuing reverence for the orthodox economic doctrine of the balanced budget.

Only at this late date did Roosevelt at last frankly and deliberately embrace the recommendations of the British economist John Maynard Keynes. The New Deal had run deficits for several years, but all of them had been rather small and none was intended. Now, in April 1937, FDR announced a bold program to stimulate the economy by planned deficit spending. Although the deficits were still undersized for the herculean task of conquering the depression, this abrupt policy reversal marked a turning point in the government's relation to the economy. **Keynesianism**—the use of government spending and fiscal policy to "prime the pump" of the economy and encourage consumer spending—became the new economic orthodoxy and remained so for decades.

Keynesianism *An economic theory based on the work of British economist John Maynard Keynes, holding that central banks should adjust interest rates and governments should use deficit spending and tax policies to increase purchasing power and hence prosperity.*

Roosevelt had meanwhile been pushing the remaining reform measures of the New Deal. But only a few of his proposals made it through an increasingly conservative Congress. The Reorganization Act gave him limited power for administrative reforms, including the key new Executive Office in the White House. The Hatch Act of 1939 barred federal officials from political campaigning or using government funds for political purposes. But such clever ways of getting around it were found that the legislation proved disappointing.

By 1938 the New Deal had clearly lost most of its early momentum. Magician Roosevelt could find few dazzling new reform rabbits to pull out of his tall silk hat. In the congressional elections of 1938 the Republicans, for the first time, cut heavily into the New Deal majorities in Congress, though failing to gain control of either house. The international crisis that came to a boil in 1938–1939 shifted public attention away from domestic reform and no doubt helped save the political hide of the Roosevelt "spendocracy." The New Deal, for all practical purposes, had shot its bolt.

A basic objective of the New Deal was featured in Roosevelt's second inaugural address (1937):

"I see one-third of a nation ill-housed, ill-clad, ill-nourished. . . . The test of our progress is not whether we add more to the abundance of those who have much; it is whether we provide enough for those who have too little."

New Deal or Raw Deal?

Foes of the New Deal condemned its alleged radicalism, incompetence, confusion, and cross-purposes. New Dealers conceded some weaknesses but defended their record as a necessary and effective response to the depression.

To some conservatives, the New Deal was a radical attempt to make America over in a Bolshevik-Marxist image. They condemned "Rooseveltski" for bringing to Washington "crackpot" college professors, leftist "pinkos," and outright Communists. The Hearst newspapers lambasted:

The Red New Deal with a Soviet seal
Endorsed by a Moscow hand,
The strange result of an alien cult
In a liberty-loving land.

Roosevelt was further accused by conservatives of tapping too many bright young leftists for his "Jew Deal," or even of being Jewish himself ("Rosenfeld").

More widespread was the charge that the New Deal brought bureaucracy, waste, and a welfare-state mentality that undermined the old American virtues of individualism, thrift, self-reliance, and limited government. The federal government, with its hundreds of thousands of employees, became incomparably the largest single business in the country, as the states faded further into the background. Promises of budget balancing went out the window as the national debt skyrocketed from $19,487,000,000 in 1932 to $40,440,000,000 by 1939. Critics charged that the lavish benefactions of the "handout state" were turning once self-reliant Americans into relief-seeking loafers, with wishbones larger than their backbones.

Business was bitter. Accusing the New Deal of fomenting class strife, countless businesspeople, especially Republicans, declared that they could pull themselves out of the depression if they could only get an interventionist big government off their backs. Private enterprise, they charged, was being stifled by a "planned economy" and "creeping socialism." Roosevelt's aggressive leadership also came in for denunciation and charges that he was trying to create a "one-man supergovernment."

The most damning indictment of the New Deal was that it failed to cure the depression. Despite some $20 billion poured out in six years of deficit spending and lending, many economists came to believe that better results would have been achieved by much greater deficit spending. The New Deal had merely administered aspirin, sedatives, and Band-Aids, with the result that in 1939 millions of dispirited men and women were still unemployed. Not until World War II increased the national debt from $40 billion in 1939 to $258 billion in 1945 was the unemployment headache solved.

New Dealers staunchly defended their record. Admitting imperfection, they argued that the bureaucratic inefficiency and waste had been trivial in view of the immense sums spent and the obvious need for haste. The New Deal, they insisted, relieved a crisis by demonstrating that the Washington regime was to be used, not feared. The collapse of America's economic system was averted; a fairer distribution of the national income was achieved; and the citizens were enabled to regain and retain their self-respect.

Though hated by business tycoons, FDR should have been their patron saint, so his admirers claimed. He deflected popular resentments against business and may have saved the American system of free enterprise. Roosevelt's quarrel was not with capitalism but with capitalists; he purged American capitalism of some of its worst abuses so that it might be saved from itself. He may even have headed off a more radical swing to the left by a mild dose of what was mistakenly reviled as "socialism." The head of the American Socialist party, when once asked if the New Deal had carried out the Socialist program, reportedly replied that it had indeed—on a stretcher.

Roosevelt, like Jefferson, provided reform without a bloody revolution—at a time in history when some foreign nations were suffering armed uprisings and when many Europeans were predicting either communism or fascism for America. He was upbraided by the left-wing radicals for not going far enough, by the right-wing radicals for going too far. Choosing the middle road, he has been called the greatest American conservative since Hamilton. He was in fact Hamiltonian in his espousal of big government, but Jeffersonian in his concern for the "forgotten man." Demonstrating anew the value of powerful presidential leadership, he exercised that power to relieve the erosion of the nation's greatest physical resource—its people. He helped preserve democracy in America at a time when democracies abroad were disappearing down the sinkhole of dictatorship. And in playing this role, he unwittingly girded the nation for its part in the titanic war that loomed on the horizon—a war in which democracy the world over would be at stake.

Varying Viewpoints

How Radical Was the New Deal?

The Great Depression was both a great calamity and a great opportunity. How effectively Franklin Roosevelt responded to the calamity and what use he made of the opportunity are the two questions that have animated historical debate about the New Deal.

Some historians have denied that there was much of a connection between the depression and the New Deal. Arthur M. Schlesinger, Jr., for example, who believed in "cycles" of reform and reaction in American history, wrote that "there would very likely have been some sort of New Deal in the 1930s even without the Depression." But most of the first generation of historians who wrote about the New Deal (in the 1940s, 1950s, and early 1960s) agreed with Carl Degler's judgment that the New Deal was "a revolutionary response to a revolutionary situation." In this view, though Roosevelt never found a means short of war to bring about economic recovery, he shrewdly utilized the stubborn economic crisis as a means to enact sweeping reforms.

Some leftist scholars writing in the 1960s, however, notably Barton J. Bernstein, charged that the New Deal did not reach far enough. This criticism echoed the socialist complaint in the 1930s that the depression represented the total collapse of American capitalism and that the New Deal muffed the chance truly to remake American society. Roosevelt had the chance, these historians argue, to redistribute wealth, improve race relations, and bring the giant corporations to heel. Instead, said these critics, the New Deal simply represented a conservative holding action to shore up a sagging and corrupt capitalist order.

Those charges against the New Deal stimulated another generation of scholars in the 1970s, 1980s, and 1990s to look closely at the concrete institutional, attitudinal, and economic circumstances in which the New Deal unfolded. Historians such as James Patterson, Alan Brinkley, Kenneth Jackson, Harvard Sitkoff, and Lizabeth Cohen—sometimes loosely referred to as the "constraints school"—concluded that the New Deal offered just about as much reform as circumstances allowed and as the majority of Americans wanted. The findings of these historians are impressive: the system of checks and balances limited presidential power; the disproportionate influence of southern Democrats in Congress stalled attempts to move toward racial justice; the federal system, in fact, inhibited all efforts to initiate change from Washington.

Most important, a majority of the American people at the time wanted to reform capitalism, not overthrow it. Industrial workers, for example, were not hapless pawns upon whom the New Deal was foisted, frustrating their yearning for more radical change. Instead, as David Kennedy has argued, they sought security and self-determination in ways quite compatible with the New Deal's programs for unemployment insurance, old-age pensions, and guarantees of labor's right to organize.

More recently, scholars such as Alice Kessler-Harris, Linda Gordon, and Susan Mettler have argued that the New Deal had a more radical effect on men than women. Social Security, for example, was designed to assist male breadwinners, who were then expected to share their benefits with their dependent wives and children. Ira Katznelson, meanwhile, has re-centered scholarly attention on the key role of southern Democrats in Congress in constricting the New Deal along racial lines.

Perhaps William Leuchtenburg summed it up best when he described the New Deal as a "half-way revolution," neither radical nor conservative but accurately reflecting the American people's needs and desires in the 1930s—and for a long time thereafter. The great "New Deal coalition" that dominated American politics for nearly four decades after Roosevelt's election in 1932 represented a broad consensus in American society about the opportunities and legitimate limits of government efforts to shape the social and economic order.

CHAPTER SUMMARY ★ ★ ★ ★ ★ ★ ★ ★ ★ ★ ★ ★ ★ ★

Franklin Roosevelt, a confident aristocrat with a common touch, swept into office with an urgent mandate to cope with the depression emergency. His bank holiday and frantic Hundred Days legislation lifted America's spirits and created a host of new agencies to provide relief to the unemployed, economic recovery, and hoped-for permanent reform of a largely unregulated capitalist system.

Roosevelt's early programs put millions of the unemployed back on the job through federal action, but failed to achieve the full economic recovery he sought. As popular demagogues such as Senator Huey Long and Father Charles Coughlin gained followings among the suffering population, Roosevelt developed further ambitious programs to reform American industry, labor, and agriculture. The Supreme Court declared unconstitutional the most sweeping effort, the National Recovery Administration, and farmers continued to suffer from the Dust Bowl. But the TVA, Social Security, and the Wagner Act brought far-reaching social changes that especially benefited the economically disadvantaged.

Conservatives furiously denounced the New Deal, but Roosevelt formed a powerful coalition of urbanites, labor, "new immigrants," blacks, and southerners that swept him to victory in 1936. FDR and especially his vigorously reformist wife Eleanor brought new visibility to women in his administration and the country.

Roosevelt's overreaching court-packing plan failed, but the Supreme Court finally began approving New Deal legislation. The later New Deal encountered mounting conservative opposition and the stubborn persistence of unemployment. Although the New Deal was highly controversial, it steered a middle course between unregulated capitalism and socialism that prevented America from turning toward dictatorship or extreme right-wing or left-wing solutions.

KEY TERMS

- Brain Trust (552)
- New Deal (552)
- Hundred Days (553)
- Glass-Steagall Banking Reform Act (555)
- Civilian Conservation Corps (CCC) (555)
- National Recovery Administration (NRA) (558)
- Agricultural Adjustment Administration (AAA) (559)
- Dust Bowl (560)
- Tennessee Valley Authority (TVA) (562)
- Social Security Act (562)
- Wagner Act (563)
- Fair Labor Standards Act (563)
- Congress of Industrial Organizations (CIO) (563)
- Court-packing plan (565)
- Keynesianism (566)

PEOPLE TO KNOW

- Franklin Delano Roosevelt
- Eleanor Roosevelt
- Harry L. Hopkins
- Father Charles Coughlin
- Francis E. Townsend
- Huey P. ("Kingfish") Long
- Frances Perkins
- Mary McLeod Bethune
- Robert F. Wagner

MindTap is a fully online, highly personalized learning experience built upon Cengage Learning content. MindTap combines student learning tools—readings, multimedia, activities, and assessments—into a singular Learning Path that guides students through the course.

Chapter

33

Franklin D. Roosevelt and the Shadow of War

1933–1941

The epidemic of world lawlessness is spreading. When an epidemic of physical disease starts to spread, the community approves and joins in a quarantine of the patients in order to protect the health of the community against the spread of the disease. . . . There must be positive endeavors to preserve peace.

Franklin D. Roosevelt, Chicago "Quarantine Speech," 1937

Chapter Outline

- Roosevelt's Early Foreign Policies
- The Rise of Fascism and American Isolationism
- War in Europe and the Debate over American Neutrality
- Roosevelt's Third-Term Victory and Lend-Lease Aid to Britain
- Refugees from Hitler's Holocaust
- The Japanese Attack on Pearl Harbor, December 7, 1941
- *Examining the Evidence: Public Opinion Polling in the 1930s*

Americans in the 1930s tried to turn their backs on the world's problems. Their president at first seemed to share these views. The only battle Roosevelt sought was against the Depression. America had its own burdens to shoulder, and the costs of foreign involvement, whether in blood or treasure, simply seemed too great.

But as the clouds of war gathered over Europe, Roosevelt eventually concluded that the United States could no longer remain aloof. Events gradually brought the American people around to his thinking: No nation was safe in an era of international anarchy, and the world could not remain half-enchained and half-free.

FOCUS QUESTIONS

1. What were the goals and results of Franklin Roosevelt's early foreign policy?
2. How and why did isolationism come to dominate American public opinion and foreign policy in the 1930s?
3. How did the United States gradually awaken to the threat of totalitarian aggression in the late 1930s while still attempting to avoid foreign entanglements?
4. Why did FDR's increasingly bold moves to aid Britain in the fight against Hitler stir such a fierce national debate over the risk of being drawn into war and the best way to preserve America's security?
5. What issues and developments in Japanese-American relations led up to the surprise Japanese attack on Pearl Harbor?

CHRONOLOGY

1933	▪ FDR torpedoes London Economic Conference ▪ United States recognizes Soviet Union ▪ FDR declares Good Neighbor policy toward Latin America ▪ Hitler becomes German chancellor ▪ Germany quits League of Nations
1934	▪ Tydings-McDuffie Act provides for Philippine independence on July 4, 1946 ▪ U.S. Marines vacate Haiti
1935	▪ Mussolini invades Ethiopia ▪ U.S. Neutrality Act of 1935 ▪ Japan quits League of Nations
1936	▪ U.S. Neutrality Act of 1936 ▪ Mussolini and Hitler form Rome-Berlin Axis ▪ Stalin begins Great Purge ▪ German troops invade Rhineland
1936–1939	▪ Spanish Civil War
1937	▪ U.S. Neutrality Act of 1937 ▪ *Panay* incident ▪ Japan invades China
1938	▪ Hitler seizes Austria ▪ Munich Conference ▪ *Kristallnacht* in Germany
1939	▪ Hitler seizes all of Czechoslovakia ▪ Nazi-Soviet pact ▪ World War II begins in Europe with Hitler's invasion of Poland ▪ U.S. Neutrality Act of 1939
1940	▪ Hitler invades Denmark, Norway, Netherlands, and Belgium ▪ Fall of France ▪ United States institutes first peacetime draft ▪ Battle of Britain ▪ Bases-for-destroyers deal with Britain ▪ FDR defeats Willkie for presidency
1941	▪ Lend-Lease Act ▪ Hitler attacks Soviet Union ▪ Atlantic Charter ▪ Japan attacks Pearl Harbor

Roosevelt's Early Foreign Policies

The sixty-six nation **London Economic Conference** in the summer of 1933 revealed how thoroughly Roosevelt's early foreign policy was subordinated to his strategy for domestic economic recovery. The delegates hoped to organize a coordinated international attack on the global depression by stabilizing national currencies and exchange rates. But Roosevelt, unwilling to subordinate his gold-juggling and other inflationary policies to an international agreement that might tie his hands, torpedoed the conference with a bombshell message that scolded the delegates for even trying to stabilize currencies and withdrew America from the negotiations.

London Economic Conference (1933) *A sixty-six-nation economic conference organized to stabilize international currency rates. Franklin Roosevelt's decision to revoke American participation contributed to a deepening world economic crisis.*

Whether the conference could have arrested the worldwide economic slide is debatable, but Roosevelt's every-man-for-himself attitude plunged the planet even deeper into economic crisis. The collapse of the London Conference also strengthened the global trend toward extreme nationalism—a trend that played directly into the hands of power-mad dictators who were determined to shatter the peace of the world.

Roosevelt matched isolationism from Europe with withdrawal from Asia. With the descent into hard times, American taxpayers were eager to throw overboard their expensive tropical liability in the Philippine Islands. Congress passed the Tydings-McDuffie Act in 1934, which provided for the future independence of the Philippines in 1946. In truth, the American people were not so much giving freedom to the Philippines as they were freeing themselves *from* the Philippines by imposing economic terms so ungenerous as to threaten the islands with economic prostration. American isolationists rejoiced once again, and Japanese militarists calculated that they had little to fear from an inward-looking America.

Closer to home, Roosevelt inaugurated a refreshing new era in relations with Latin America. He proclaimed in his inaugural address, "I would dedicate this nation to the policy of the Good Neighbor." Roosevelt's hope-inspiring **Good Neighbor policy** renounced

Good Neighbor policy *A policy stressing nonintervention in Latin America, a major departure from the Roosevelt Corollary to the Monroe Doctrine. It was begun by Herbert Hoover but is most strongly associated with Franklin D. Roosevelt, who put it into practice in Mexico and elsewhere.*

further armed intervention in Latin America, particularly the vexatious corollary to the Monroe Doctrine devised by his cousin Theodore Roosevelt. It also sought a new attitude of friendliness and consultation with America's southern neighbors rather than aggressive assertion of U.S. economic interests.

Accordingly, the United States withdrew the last marines from Haiti in 1934. That same year, after military strongman Fulgencia Batista came to power, restive Cuba was released from the worst hobbles of the interventionist Platt Amendment, although the United States retained its naval base at Guantanamo (see p. 461). The United States similarly relaxed its grip on Panama in 1936. The acid test of the Good Neighbor policy came when the Mexican government seized Yankee oil properties in 1938. Roosevelt successfully resisted strong business badgering to intervene and eventually threshed out a settlement in 1941. These earnest acts of friendliness paid rich dividends in goodwill among the peoples to the south, and Roosevelt was cheered with tremendous enthusiasm when he traveled to an Inter-American Conference at Buenos Aires, Argentina, in 1936. The Colossus of the North now seemed less a vulture and more an eagle.

Rome-Berlin Axis (1936) *Treaty by which Nazi Germany, under Adolf Hitler, and Fascist Italy, led by Benito Mussolini, allied themselves together. The pact was signed after both countries had intervened on behalf of the fascist leader Francisco Franco during the Spanish Civil War.*

Turning Toward Isolationism

Post-1918 chaos in Europe, followed by the Great Depression, spawned the ominous spread of totalitarianism. The individual was nothing; the state was everything. The communist USSR led the way, with the crafty and ruthless Joseph Stalin finally emerging as dictator. In 1936, Stalin began to purge his communist state of all suspected dissidents, ultimately executing hundreds of thousands and banishing millions to remote Siberian forced-labor camps. Blustery Benito Mussolini, a swaggering Fascist, seized the reins of power in Italy during 1922. And Adolf Hitler, a fanatic with a toothbrush mustache, plotted and harangued his way into control of Germany in 1933 with liberal use of the "big lie."

NSDAP election poster, April 1932. Germany./Photo © Tarker/The Bridgeman Art Library

The Wages of Despair Disillusioned and desperate, millions of Germans in the 1930s looked to Adolf Hitler as their savior from the harsh terms of the Treaty of Versailles, which had concluded World War I. This Nazi poster reads, "Our Last Hope: Hitler."

Hitler was the most dangerous of the dictators because he combined tremendous power with impulsiveness. A frustrated Austrian painter, with hypnotic talents as an orator and leader, Hitler had led the Nazi party to power in Germany by making political capital of the Treaty of Versailles and Germany's depression-spawned unemployment. The desperate German people had fallen in behind the new Pied Piper, for they saw no other hope of escape from the plague of economic chaos and national disgrace. Hitler began clandestinely (and illegally) rearming in 1933, and in 1936 the Nazi Hitler and the Fascist Mussolini allied themselves in the **Rome-Berlin Axis**.

International gangsterism was likewise spreading in East Asia, where imperial Japan was on the make. Like Germany and Italy, Japan was a so-called have-not power. Like them, Japan resented the ungenerous Treaty of Versailles. Like them, Japan demanded additional space for its teeming millions, cooped up in their crowded island nation. Determined to find a place in the Asian sun, Tokyo terminated the Washington Naval Treaty in 1934, and in the following year accelerated its construction of giant battleships. In 1940 Japan joined arms with Germany and Italy in the Tripartite Pact.

Jut-jawed Mussolini, seeking both glory and empire in Africa, brutally attacked Ethiopia in 1935. The members of the League of Nations could have halted Mussolini's war machine with an oil embargo. But fearing global hostilities they failed to act, and the brave but poorly armed Ethiopians were speedily crushed by Mussolini's bombers and tanks.

Isolationism, long festering in America, received a strong boost from these alarms abroad. Though disapproving the dictators, Americans still believed that their encircling seas conferred a kind of mystic immunity. They were continuing to suffer the disillusionment born of their participation in World War I, which they now regarded as a colossal blunder. Americans likewise nursed bitter memories of the ungrateful and defaulting debtors. As early as 1934, a spiteful Congress passed the **Johnson Debt Default Act**, which prevented debt-dodging nations from borrowing further in the United States.

Mired down in the Great Depression, Americans had no real appreciation of the revolutionary forces being harnessed by the dictators. Americans were not so much afraid that totalitarian aggression would cause trouble as they were fearful that they might be drawn into it. Strong nationwide sentiment welled up for a constitutional amendment to forbid a declaration of war by Congress—except in case of invasion—unless there was a favorable popular referendum.

The thirst of Benito Mussolini (1883–1945) for national glory in Ethiopia is indicated by his remark in 1940:

"To make a people great it is necessary to send them to battle even if you have to kick them in the pants."

(The Italians were notoriously unwarlike.)

In 1934 Mussolini proclaimed in a public speech:

"We have buried the putrid corpse of liberty."

As the gloomy 1930s lengthened, an avalanche of lurid articles and books condemning the munitions manufacturers as war-fomenting "merchants of death" poured from American presses. A Senate committee headed by Senator Gerald Nye of North Dakota sensationalized evidence regarding America's entry into World War I, shifting the blame away from German submarines onto American bankers and arms manufacturers. Because the munitions makers had obviously made money out of the war, many a naïve citizen leaped to the illogical conclusion that these soulless scavengers had *caused* the war in order to make money. This kind of reasoning suggested that if the profits could only be removed from the arms traffic—"one hell of a business"—the country could steer clear of any future world conflict.

Johnson Debt Default Act (1934) *A spiteful act, steeping in ugly memories of World War I, that prevented debt-ridden European nations from borrowing further from the United States.*

Responding to overwhelming popular pressure, Congress made haste to legislate the nation out of war. Action was spurred by the danger that Mussolini's Ethiopian assault would plunge the world into a new bloodbath. The **Neutrality Acts of 1935, 1936, and 1937**, taken together, stipulated that *when the president proclaimed* the existence of a foreign war, certain restrictions would automatically go into effect: No American could legally sail on a belligerent ship, sell or transport munitions to a belligerent, or make loans to a belligerent.

Neutrality Acts of 1935, 1936, and 1937 *Short-sighted acts passed to prevent American participation in a European war. Among other restrictions, they prevented Americans from selling munitions to foreign belligerents.*

This storm-cellar neutrality proved to be tragically shortsighted. Through its neutrality laws, America served notice that it would make no distinction between brutal aggressors and innocent victims. By striving to hold the scales even, America actually overbalanced them in favor of the dictators, who had armed themselves to the teeth. By declining to use its vast industrial strength to aid its democratic friends and defeat its totalitarian foes, America helped goad the aggressors along their blood-spattered path of conquest.

The Spanish Civil War of 1936–1939—a proving ground and dress rehearsal in miniature for World War II—was a painful object lesson in the folly of neutrality-by-legislation. Spanish rebels, who rose against the left-leaning republican government in Madrid, were headed by fascistic General Francisco Franco. Generously aided by his fellow conspirators Hitler and Mussolini, he undertook to overthrow the established Loyalist regime, which in turn was assisted on a smaller scale by the Soviet Union. This pipeline from communist Moscow chilled the natural sympathies of many Americans, especially Roman Catholics, for the republican Loyalists. But other Americans burned with passion to defend the struggling republic against Franco's fascist coup. Some three thousand young men and women headed to Spain to fight as volunteers in the **Abraham Lincoln Brigade**.

Abraham Lincoln Brigade *Idealistic American volunteers who served in the Spanish Civil War, defending Spanish republican forces from the fascist General Francisco Franco's nationalist coup. Some three thousand Americans served alongside volunteers from other countries.*

Washington continued official relations with the Loyalist government. But Congress, with the encouragement of Roosevelt and with only one dissenting vote, amended the existing neutrality legislation so as to apply an arms embargo to both Loyalists and rebels.

Uncle Sam thus sat on the sidelines while Franco, abundantly supplied with arms and men by his fellow dictators, strangled the republican government of Spain. The democracies, including the United States, were so determined to stay out of war that they helped to condemn a fellow democracy to death. In so doing they further encouraged the dictators to take the dangerous road that led over the precipice to World War II.

Appeasing Japan and Germany

Sulfurous war clouds had meanwhile been gathering in tension-taut East Asia. In 1937 the Japanese militarists, at the Marco Polo Bridge near Beijing (Peking), touched off the explosion that led to an all-out invasion of China. In a sense this attack was the curtain-raiser of World War II.

Roosevelt shrewdly declined to invoke the recently passed neutrality legislation by refusing to call the China incident an officially declared war. If he had put the existing restrictions into effect, he would have cut off the tiny trickle of munitions on which the Chinese were desperately dependent. The Japanese, of course, could continue to buy mountains of war supplies in the United States.

In Chicago—unofficial isolationist "capital" of America—President Roosevelt delivered his sensational **Quarantine Speech** in the autumn of 1937. Alarmed by the recent aggression of Italy and Japan, he called for "positive endeavors" to "quarantine" the aggressors—presumably by economic embargoes. The speech triggered a cyclone of protest from isolationists and other foes of involvement; they feared that a moral quarantine would lead to a shooting quarantine. Startled by this angry response, Roosevelt retreated and sought less direct means to curb the dictators.

Quarantine Speech (1937) *An important speech delivered by Franklin Roosevelt in which he called for "positive endeavors" to "quarantine" land-hungry dictators, presumably through economic embargoes. The speech flew in the face of isolationist politicians.*

America's isolationist mood intensified in December 1937 when Japanese aviators bombed and sank an American gunboat, the *Panay*, in Chinese waters. After Tokyo apologized and paid an indemnity, Americans breathed a deep sigh of relief that they need not respond to the outrage.

Adolf Hitler meanwhile grew louder and bolder in Europe. In 1935 he had openly flouted the Treaty of Versailles by introducing compulsory military service in Germany. The next year he brazenly marched into the demilitarized German Rhineland, likewise contrary to the detested treaty, while France and Britain looked on in an agony of indecision. Lashing his following to a frenzy, Hitler undertook to persecute and then exterminate the Jewish population in the areas under his control. In the end, he wiped out about 6 million innocent victims, mostly in gas chambers. Calling upon his people to sacrifice butter for guns, he whipped the new German air force and mechanized ground divisions into the most devastating military machine the world had yet seen.

Appeasement (1938) *The policy followed by leaders of Britain and France at the 1938 conference in Munich. Their purpose was to avoid war, but they allowed Germany to take the Sudetenland from Czechoslovakia.*

Hitler-Stalin pact (1939) *Treaty signed on August 23, 1939, in which Germany and the Soviet Union agreed not to fight each other. The fateful agreement paved the way for German aggression against Poland and the Western democracies.*

Neutrality Act of 1939 *Act stipulating that European democracies might buy American munitions, but only if they could pay in cash and transport them in their own ships, a policy known as "cash-and-carry." It represented an effort to avoid war debts and protect American arms-carriers from torpedo attacks.*

Suddenly, in March 1938, Hitler bloodlessly occupied German-speaking Austria, his birthplace. The democratic powers, wringing their hands in despair, prayed that this last grab would satisfy his passion for conquest. But like a drunken reveler calling for madder music and stronger wine, Hitler could not stop. Intoxicated by his recent gains, he began to make bullying demands for the German-inhabited Sudetenland of neighboring Czechoslovakia.

British and French leaders, eager to appease Hitler, frantically arranged a conference with Hitler and Mussolini at Munich, Germany, in September 1938. There they betrayed Czechoslovakia to Germany when they consented to the shearing away of the Sudetenland. Europeans and Americans alike hoped that these concessions would bring "peace in our time." Indeed, Hitler publicly promised that the Sudetenland "is the last territorial claim I have to make in Europe."

Appeasement of the dictators, symbolized by the ugly word *Munich*, turned out to be merely surrender on the installment plan. It was like giving a cannibal a finger in the hope of saving an arm. In March 1939, scarcely six months later, Hitler suddenly erased the rest of Czechoslovakia from the map, contrary to his solemn vows. The democratic world was again stunned.

President Roosevelt was roused at 3 A.M. on September 1, 1939, by a telephone call from Ambassador William Bullitt (1891–1967) in Paris:

"Mr. President, several German divisions are deep in Polish territory. . . . There are reports of bombers over the city of Warsaw."

"Well, Bill," FDR replied, "it has come at last. God help us all."

Hitler's Belligerency and U.S. Neutrality

Joseph Stalin, the sphinx of the Kremlin, was a key to the peace puzzle. When his efforts to secure a mutual defense treaty with Britain and France fell through in the summer of 1939, the Soviet Union astounded the world by signing, on August 23, 1939, a nonaggression treaty with the German dictator. The notorious **Hitler-Stalin pact** meant that, contrary to hopes of wishful thinkers in Western Europe, the two menaces would not bleed each other to death, but rather join hands to share the spoils.

With the signing of the Nazi-Soviet pact, World War II was only hours away. Hitler now demanded from neighboring Poland a return of the areas wrested from Germany after World War I. Failing to secure satisfaction, he sent his mechanized divisions crashing into Poland at dawn on September 1, 1939. Honoring their commitments, Britain and France promptly declared war. But they were powerless to aid Poland, which was quickly divided between Hitler and his partner in crime, Stalin. Long-dreaded World War II was now fully launched, and the long truce of 1919–1939 had come to an end.

Americans were overwhelmingly anti-Nazi and anti-Hitler, but they were desperately determined to stay out of war; they were not going to be "suckers" again. Neutrality promptly became a heated issue in the United States. Britain and France urgently needed American airplanes and other weapons, but the Neutrality Act of 1937 raised a sternly forbidding hand. Roosevelt summoned Congress into special session, and after six weeks of hectic debate it came up with the makeshift **Neutrality Act of 1939**. This law provided that henceforth the European democracies might buy American war materials, but only on a "cash-and-carry" basis. This meant that they would have to pay for munitions in cash and transport them in their own ships. America would thus avoid loans, war debts, and the torpedoing of American arms-carriers.

Despite its defects, this unneutral neutrality law clearly favored the European democracies against the dictators. Because the British and French navies controlled the Atlantic, the European aggressors could not send their ships to buy America's munitions. The United States not only improved its moral position but simultaneously helped its economic position. Overseas demand for war goods brought a sharp upswing from the recession of 1937–1938 and ultimately solved the decade-long unemployment crisis.

Contending Voices

To Intervene or Not to Intervene

Chicago industrialist Sterling Morton (1885–1961), a backer of the isolationist America First Committee, emphasized the American tradition of nonintervention in an August 1940 speech:

"We should follow the advice of [George] Washington: We should maintain friendly relations with all nations, grant special favors to none. We should remember that the Monroe Doctrine was just as emphatic against American interference in Europe as against European interference in the Americas. We should not meddle in the affairs of other nations. . . . We have no mission to impose our ideas of government on others."

That same summer President Franklin Roosevelt (1882–1945) made a compelling case against the isolationists in a speech at the University of Virginia:

"Some indeed still hold to the now somewhat obvious delusion that we of the United States can safely permit the United States to become a lone island, a lone island in a world dominated by the philosophy of force. Such an island may be the dream of those who still talk and vote as isolationists. Such an island represents to me and to the overwhelming majority of Americans today a helpless nightmare of a people without freedom—the nightmare of a people lodged in prison, handcuffed, hungry, and fed through the bars from day to day by the contemptuous, unpitying masters of other continents."

What factors might explain the intense divisions in American opinion about intervening in the war?

The Fall of France

The months following the collapse of Poland, while France and Britain marked time, were known as the "phony war." An ominous silence fell on Europe as Hitler shifted his victorious divisions from Poland for a knockout blow at France. Inaction during this anxious period was relieved by the Soviets, who wantonly attacked neighboring Finland in an effort to secure strategic buffer territory.

An abrupt end to the "phony war" came in April 1940 when Hitler, again without warning, overran his weaker neighbors Denmark and Norway. Hardly pausing for breath, the next month Hitler attacked the Netherlands and Belgium, followed by a paralyzing blow at France. By late June France was forced to surrender, but not until Mussolini had pounced on its rear for a jackal's share of the loot. In a pell-mell but successful evacuation from the French port of Dunkirk, the British managed to salvage the bulk of their shattered army. The crisis providentially brought forth an inspired leader in Prime

Adolf Hitler (1889–1945) promised to win his fellow Germans Lebensraum, *or "living space," and to win it by war if necessary. In his eyes, his nationalist and racist crusade justified every violent means at hand. As he told his commanders:*

"When you start a war, what matters is not who is right, but who wins. Close your hearts to pity. Act with brutality. Eighty million Germans must get what is their due. Their existence must be made secure. The stronger man is in the right."

Minister Winston Churchill, the bulldog-jawed orator who nerved the British to fight off the fearful air bombings of their cities.

France's sudden collapse shocked Americans out of their daydreams. Stouthearted Britons, singing "There'll Always Be an England," were all that stood between Hitler and the death of constitutional government in Europe. If Britain went under, Hitler would have at his disposal the workshops, shipyards, and slave labor of Western Europe. He might even have the powerful British fleet as well. This frightening possibility, which seemed to pose a dire threat to American security, steeled the American people to a tremendous effort.

Roosevelt moved with electrifying energy and dispatch. He called upon an already debt-burdened nation to build huge airfleets and a two-ocean navy, which could also check Japan. Congress, jarred out of its apathy toward preparedness, within a year appropriated the astounding sum of $37 billion, more than the total cost of fighting World War I. Congress also passed a conscription law on September 6, 1940, America's first peacetime draft.

Refugees from the Holocaust

Aroused by Adolf Hitler, the ancient demon of anti-Semitism brutally bared its fangs. In modern Germany primeval violence reappeared with shocking efficiency on the night of November 9, 1938. Instigated by a speech by Nazi propagandist Joseph Goebbels, mobs ransacked more than seven thousand Jewish shops and almost all of Germany's synagogues. At least ninety-one Jews lost their lives and about thirty thousand were sent to concentration camps in the turbulent wake of **Kristallnacht** (the "night of broken glass").

Kristallnacht *German for "night of broken glass," the murderous pogrom that destroyed Jewish businesses and synagogues and sent thousands to concentration camps on the night of November 9, 1938. Thousands more attempted to find refuge in the United States but were ultimately turned away due to restrictive immigration laws.*

Many Jews attempted to escape from Hitler's racist juggernaut. To take one poignant case, in May 1939, 937 passengers, almost all of them Jewish refugees, boarded the ship *St. Louis* in Hamburg and departed for Havana, Cuba. Most, however, were denied entry for lack of valid Cuban visas. The *St. Louis* then sailed to Miami, which proved no more hospitable. President Roosevelt briefly showed some interest in accepting the beleaguered passengers, but restrictive immigration laws, together with opposition from southern Democrats and Secretary of State Cordell Hull, convinced him otherwise. The *St. Louis* eventually deposited its passengers in England, France, Belgium, and the Netherlands, where many of them subsequently perished under the Nazi heel.

After reports of Nazi genocide began to be verified in 1942, Roosevelt created the **War Refugee Board**, which saved thousands of Hungarian Jews from deportation to the notorious death camp at Auschwitz. But all told, only 150,000 Jews—mostly Germans and Austrians—found refuge in the United States. By the end of the war, some 6 million Jews had been murdered in the Holocaust.

War Refugee Board *A U.S. agency formed to help rescue Jews from German-occupied territories and to provide relief to inmates of Nazi concentration camps. The agency performed noble work, but it did not begin operations until very late in the war, after millions had already been murdered.*

Bolstering Britain

Before the fall of France in June 1940, Washington had generally observed a technical neutrality. But now, as Britain alone stood between Hitler and his dream of world domination, the wisdom of neutrality seemed increasingly questionable. Hitler launched air attacks against Britain in August 1940, preparatory to an invasion scheduled for September. For months the Battle of Britain raged in the air over the British Isles. The Royal Air Force's tenacious defense of its native islands eventually led Hitler to postpone his planned invasion indefinitely.

Examining the Evidence

Public Opinion Polling in the 1930s

In 1936 the prominent news publication *Literary Digest* made a monumental gaffe when it relied on public-opinion polling data to forecast a victory for the Republican candidate, Alf Landon, over the incumbent, Franklin D. Roosevelt. As it happened, Roosevelt racked up a monstrous majority, winning the electoral votes of all but two states. The *Digest*'s error had been to compile its polling lists from records of automobile registration and telephone directories—unwittingly skewing its sample toward relatively well-off voters in an era when fewer than half of American families owned either a car or a telephone. The *Digest*'s embarrassing mistake ended an era of informal polling techniques, as new, scientifically sophisticated polling organizations founded by George Gallup and Elmo Roper forged to the fore. From this date forward, polling became a standard tool for marketers and advertisers—as well as for political strategists and historians. Yet controversy has long clouded the relationship between pollsters and politicians, who are often accused of abdicating their roles as leaders and slavishly deferring to public opinion, rather than trying to shape it. Franklin Roosevelt confronted this issue in the 1930s, as polls seemed to confirm the stubborn isolationism of the American people, even as the president grew increasingly convinced that the United States must play a more active international role.

1. What do the poll results suggest about Roosevelt's handling of this issue? What do the results suggest about the reliability of polling data?
2. What are the legitimate political uses of public-opinion polls? How valuable are they to the historian?
3. How might the pollsters' wording of the questions have influenced the results or made them difficult to interpret? Is it possible for polls to avoid terms such as "everything possible" (Question #1) or "becomes necessary" (Question #6) that contain elements of subjective interpretation?

[1.] (U.S. Oct 3 '39) Do you think the United States should do everything possible to help England and France win the war, except go to war ourselves? (AIPO)

Yes 62%	No 38%

[2.] (U.S. Oct 3 '39) If it appears that Germany is defeating England and France, should the United States declare war on Germany and send our army and navy to Europe to fight? (AIPO)

	Yes	No
National total	29%	71%
BY GEOGRAPHICAL SECTION		
New England	33%	67%
Middle Atlantic	27	73
East central	25	75
West central	26	74
South	47	53
West	28	72
(Jan 30 '40) National total	23%	77%

[3.] (U.S. May 29 '40) If the question of the United States going to war against Germany came up for a national vote to go to war (go into the war or stay out of the war)? (AIPO)

	Yes 16%	No 84%
(June 11 '40)	Go in 19%	Stay out 81%

[4.] (U.S. Aug 5 '41) Should the United States go to war now against Japan? (AIPO)

	Yes	No	No opinion
	22%	78% = 100%	11%
(Oct 22 '41)	13	74	13

[5.] (U.S. Sept 17 '41) Should the United States go into the war now and send an army to Europe to fight? (AIPO)

Yes 9%	No 87%	No opinion 4%

[6.] (U.S. Nov 5 '41) If, in trying to defeat Germany, it becomes necessary to send a large American army to Europe, would you favor this step? (AIPO)

Yes 47%	No 46%	No opinion 7%

Source: From Hadley Cantril, ed. *Public Opinion, 1935–1946* (Princeton: Princeton University Press, 1951).

During the precarious months of the Battle of Britain, debate intensified in the United States over what foreign policy to embrace. Radio broadcasts from London brought the drama of German air raids directly into millions of American homes. Sympathy for Britain grew, but it was not yet sufficient to push the United States into war. Roosevelt faced a historic decision: whether to hunker down in a "Fortress America" posture in the Western Hemisphere, or to bolster beleaguered Britain by all means short of war itself.

Both sides had their advocates. Supporters of aid to Britain formed the Committee to Defend America by Aiding the Allies. It proclaimed the slogan that "Britain is Fighting Our Fight," while implying that assisting the democracies could keep the terrible conflict in faraway Europe.

The isolationists, both numerous and sincere, were by no means silent. Determined to avoid American bloodshed at all costs, they organized the America First Committee and proclaimed, "England Will Fight to the Last American." Their basic philosophy was "The Yanks Are Not Coming," and their most effective speechmaker was the famed aviator Colonel Charles A. Lindbergh, who, ironically, had narrowed the Atlantic in 1927.

Britain was in critical need of destroyers, for German submarines were again threatening to starve it out with attacks on shipping. Roosevelt moved boldly when, on September 2, 1940, he agreed to transfer to Great Britain fifty old destroyers left over from World War I. In return, the British promised to hand over to the United States eight valuable defensive bases, stretching from Newfoundland to South America, for ninety-nine years.

Shifting warships from a neutral United States to a belligerent Britain was, beyond question, a flagrant violation of neutral obligations. But public-opinion polls demonstrated that a majority of Americans were determined, even at the risk of armed hostilities, to provide the battered British with "all aid short of war."

Shattering the Two-Term Tradition

In the midst of this crisis came the distracting presidential election of 1940. The two leading Republican aspirants were Senator Robert Taft of Ohio, son of the former president, and the energetic boy wonder Governor Thomas E. Dewey of New York. But in one of the miracles of American political history, the Philadelphia convention was swept off its feet by Wendell L. Willkie, a colorful German-descended son of Hoosier Indiana. This dynamic lawyer and public utilities corporation executive—tousle-headed, broad-faced, and large-framed—was a complete novice in politics. With the convention galleries wildly chanting "We Want Willkie," the delegates finally accepted this magnetic, homespun political upstart as the only candidate who could possibly beat Roosevelt. The outspoken Willkie was opposed not so much to the New Deal as to its extravagances and inefficiencies. Democratic critics branded him "the simple barefoot Wall Street lawyer."

Roosevelt delayed to the last minute the announcement of his decision to challenge the sacred two-term tradition. Despite what he described as his personal yearning for retirement, he avowed that in so grave a crisis he owed his experienced hand to the service of his country and humanity.

Burning with sincerity and energy, Willkie launched a whirlwind, Bryanesque campaign in which he delivered over five hundred speeches. With the country already badly split between interventionists and isolationists, Willkie might have widened the breach dangerously by a violent attack on Roosevelt's aid-to-Britain policies. But the statesmanlike Republican candidate refrained from assailing the president's interventionism and accepted the essential premises of an internationalist foreign policy.

Willkie hit hard against Rooseveltian "dictatorship" and the third term. Roosevelt, busy at his desk with mounting problems, made only a few speeches. But stung by taunts that he was leading the nation by the back door into the European slaughterhouse, he emphatically declared in a Boston speech, "Your boys are not going to be sent into any foreign wars"—a pledge that later came back to plague him.

The time-honored argument that one should not change horses in the middle of a stream was strong, especially in an era of war-pumped prosperity. Roosevelt triumphed, although Willkie ran a strong race. The electoral count was 449 to 82. The popular vote was much closer—27,307,819 to 22,321,018. Democratic majorities in Congress remained about the same.

A Landmark Lend-Lease Law

By late 1940 embattled Britain was nearing the end of its financial tether. But Roosevelt, who had bitter memories of the wrangling over the Allied debts of World War I, was determined, as he put it, to eliminate "the silly, foolish, old dollar sign." He finally hit on the scheme of lending or leasing American arms to the reeling democracies. When the shooting was over, to use his comparison, the guns and tanks could be returned, just as one's next-door neighbor would return a garden hose when a threatening fire was put out. But isolationist Senator Robert Taft retorted that lending arms was like lending chewing gum: "You don't want it back."

The **Lend-Lease Bill**, patriotically numbered 1776, was entitled "An Act Further to Promote the Defense of the United States." The underlying concept was "Send guns, not sons" or "Billions, not bodies." America, so President Roosevelt promised, would be the "arsenal of democracy." It would send a limitless supply of arms to the victims of aggression, who in turn would finish the job and keep the war on their side of the Atlantic. Isolationists assailed the lend-lease scheme as "the blank-check bill." Isolationist Senator Burton Wheeler called it "the new triple-A [Agricultural Adjustment Act] bill"—a measure designed to "plow under every fourth American boy." Nevertheless, lend-lease was finally approved in March 1941 by sweeping majorities in both houses of Congress.

Lend-Lease Bill (1941) *Abandoned pretenses of neutrality by allowing Americans to sell unlimited supplies of arms to any nation defending itself against Axis powers. Based on the motto "Send guns, not sons" and patriotically numbered 1776, the bill was praised as a device for keeping the nation out of World War II.*

Lend-lease was one of the most momentous laws ever to pass Congress; it was a challenge hurled squarely into the teeth of the Axis dictators. America eventually sent about $50 billion worth of arms and equipment to those nations fighting aggressors (see Map 33.1). By its very nature, the Lend-Lease Bill marked the abandonment of any pretense of neutrality. It was no destroyer deal arranged privately by President Roosevelt. The bill was universally debated over drugstore counters and cracker barrels from California to Maine, and the sovereign citizens at last spoke through convincing majorities in Congress. Lend-lease had the somewhat incidental result of gearing U.S. factories for all-out war production. The enormously increased capacity thus achieved helped to save America's own skin when, at long last, the shooting war burst around its head.

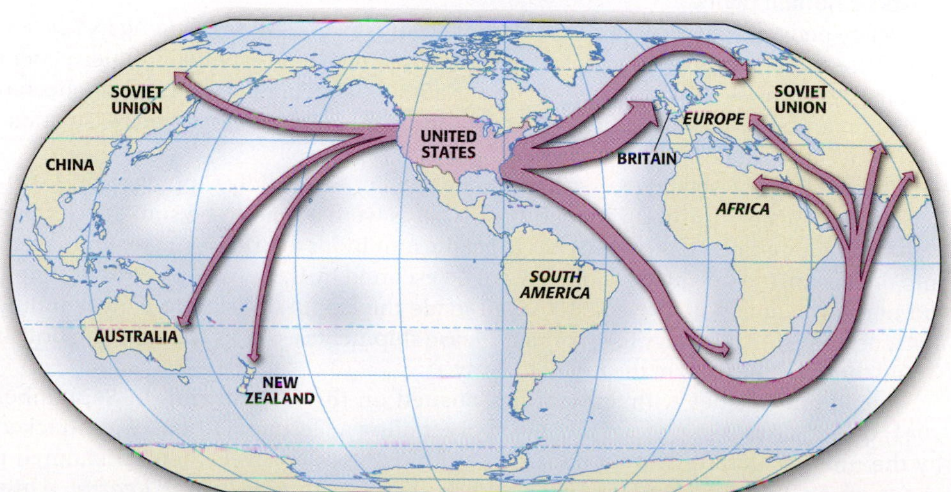

Map 33.1 Main Flow of Lend-Lease Aid (width of arrows indicates relative amount) The proud but desperate British prime minister, Winston Churchill, declared in early 1941: "Give us the tools and we will finish the job." Lend-lease eventually provided the British and other Allies with $50 billion worth of "tools."

Senator (later president) Harry S. Truman (1884–1972) expressed a common reaction to Hitler's invasion of the Soviet Union in 1941:

"If we see that Germany is winning, we ought to help Russia, and if we see Russia is winning, we ought to help Germany, and that way let them kill as many as possible."

Hitler evidently recognized lend-lease as an unofficial declaration of war. Until then Germany had avoided attacking U.S. ships; memories of America's decisive intervention in 1917–1918 were still fresh in German minds. But after the passing of lend-lease there was less point in trying to curry favor with the United States. On May 21, 1941, the *Robin Moor*, an unarmed American merchant ship, was torpedoed and destroyed by a German submarine in the South Atlantic, outside a war zone. The sinkings had started, but on a limited scale.

Charting a New World

Two globe-shaking events marked the course of World War II before the assault on Pearl Harbor in December 1941. One was the fall of France in June 1940; the other was Hitler's invasion of the Soviet Union, almost exactly one year later, in June 1941.

The scheming dictators Hitler and Stalin had been uneasy yoke-fellows under the Nazi-Soviet pact of 1939. As masters of the double cross, neither trusted the other. Believing that his invincible armies would subdue Stalin's "Mongol half-wits" in a few short weeks, Hitler launched a devastating attack on his Soviet neighbor on June 22, 1941.

This assault seemed an incredible stroke of good fortune for the democratic world—if the Soviets did not quickly collapse, as many military experts predicted. Sound American strategy seemed to dictate speedy aid to Moscow while it was still afloat. Roosevelt promised immediate assistance, and a few months later extended $1 billion in lend-lease aid to the USSR—the first installment on an ultimate total of $11 billion.

With the surrender of the Soviet Union still a possibility, Franklin Roosevelt and cherub-faced British Prime Minister Winston Churchill secretly met on a warship off the foggy coast of Newfoundland in August 1941. This was the first of a series of history-making conferences between the two statesmen for the discussion of common problems, including the menace of Japan.

Atlantic Charter (1941) *Covenant signed by Franklin Roosevelt and British prime minister Winston Churchill on a warship off the coast of Newfoundland, outlining the future path toward disarmament, peace, and a permanent system of general security. Its spirit would animate the founding of the United Nations and raise awareness of individual human rights after World War II.*

The most memorable offspring of this get-together was the eight-point **Atlantic Charter**. This covenant, suggestive of Wilson's Fourteen Points, outlined the aspirations of the democracies for a better world at war's end. Arguing for the rights of individuals rather than nations, the Atlantic Charter laid the groundwork for later advocacy on behalf of universal human rights.

Many people were surprised by how specific the document was. Among its key features were self-determination for all peoples, disarmament, and eventually a "permanent system of general security" (a new League of Nations). The Atlantic Charter was cheered by liberals and subject peoples the world over, although roundly condemned by isolationists in the United States.

But the hope of isolating America from the conflict was rapidly slipping away. Lend-lease shipments of arms to Britain on British ships were bound to be sunk by German wolf-pack submarines. If the intent was to get the munitions to Britain, not to dump them into the ocean, the freighters would have to be escorted by U.S. warships. Britain simply did not have enough destroyers. Roosevelt made the fateful decision to convoy in July 1941, ordering the U.S. Navy to escort lend-lease shipments as far as Iceland. The British would then shepherd them the rest of the way.

Inevitable clashes with submarines ensued on the Iceland run. In September 1941, the U.S. destroyer *Greer*, provocatively trailing a German U-boat, was attacked by the undersea craft, without damage to either side. Roosevelt then proclaimed a shoot-on-sight policy. On October 17, 1941, the escorting destroyer *Kearny*, while engaged in a battle with U-boats, lost eleven men when it was crippled but not sent to the bottom. Two weeks later the destroyer *Reuben James* was torpedoed and sunk off southwestern Iceland, with the loss of more than a hundred officers and enlisted men.

Neutrality was still inscribed on the statute books, but not on American hearts. Congress, responding to public pressures and confronted with a shooting war, voted in mid-November 1941 to pull the teeth from the now-useless Neutrality Act of 1939. Merchant ships could henceforth be legally armed. Americans braced themselves for wholesale attacks by Hitler's submarines.

Surprise Assault at Pearl Harbor

The blowup came not in the Atlantic but in the faraway Pacific. This explosion should have surprised no close observer, for Japan, since September 1940, had been a formal military ally of Nazi Germany.

Japan's position in East Asia had grown more perilous by the hour. It was still mired down in the costly and exhausting "China incident," from which it could extract neither honor nor victory. Its war machine was fatally dependent on immense shipments of steel, scrap iron, oil, and aviation gasoline from the United States. Such assistance to the Japanese aggressor was highly unpopular in America. But Roosevelt had resolutely held off an embargo, lest he goad the Tokyo warlords into a descent upon the oil-rich but defense-poor Dutch East Indies (present-day Indonesia).

Washington, late in 1940, finally imposed the first of its embargoes on Japan-bound supplies. This blow was followed in mid-1941 by a freezing of Japanese assets in the United States and a cessation of all shipments of gasoline and other sinews of war. As the oil gauge dropped, the squeeze on Japan grew steadily more nerve-racking. Japanese leaders were faced with two painful alternatives. They could either knuckle under to the Americans or break out of the embargo ring by a desperate attack on the oil supplies and other riches of Southeast Asia.

Final tense negotiations with Japan took place in Washington during November and early December of 1941. The State Department insisted that the Japanese clear out of China, but to sweeten the pill offered to renew limited trade relations. Japanese imperialists, after waging a bitter war against the Chinese for more than four years, were unwilling to lose face by withdrawing at the behest of the United States. Faced with capitulation or continued conquest, they chose the sword.

Officials in Washington, having "cracked" the top-secret code of the Japanese, knew that Tokyo's decision was for war. But the United States, as a democracy committed to public debate and action by Congress, could not shoot first. Roosevelt and other officials, misled by Japanese ship movements in the western Pacific, evidently expected the blow to fall on British Malaya or on the Philippines. No one in high authority in Washington evidently believed that the Japanese were either strong enough or foolhardy enough to strike Hawaii.

But the paralyzing blow struck **Pearl Harbor**, while Tokyo was deliberately prolonging negotiations in Washington. Japanese bombers, winging in from distant aircraft carriers, attacked without warning on the "Black Sunday" morning of December 7, 1941. It was a date, as Roosevelt told Congress, "which will live in infamy." About three thousand casualties were inflicted on American personnel, many aircraft were destroyed, and the battleship fleet was virtually wiped out.

Pearl Harbor (1941) *An American naval base in Hawaii where Japanese warplanes destroyed numerous ships and caused three thousand casualties on December 7, 1941—a day that, in President Roosevelt's words, was to "live in infamy." The attack brought the United States into World War II.*

The next day an angered Congress, with only one dissenting vote, officially recognized that war had been "thrust" upon the United States. When Japan's allies, Germany and Italy, also declared war on December 11, 1941, the challenge was unanimously accepted by Congress the same day. The unofficial war was now official.

Japan's hara-kiri gamble in Hawaii paid off only in the short run. True, the Pacific fleet was largely destroyed or immobilized, but the sneak attack aroused and united America as almost nothing else could have done. To the very day of the blowup, a strong majority of Americans still wanted to keep out of war. But the bombs that pulverized Pearl Harbor blasted the isolationists into silence. The only thing left to do, growled isolationist Senator Wheeler, was "to lick hell out of them."

But Pearl Harbor was not the full answer to the question as to why the United States went to war. This treacherous attack was but the last explosion in a long chain reaction.

U.S. Army

The Battleship *West Virginia* The shocking Japanese attack on Pearl Harbor on December 7, 1941, propelled the United States into World War II. One of the first ships to be hit, the USS *West Virginia* quickly sank at its mooring, taking at least seventy sailors down with it. By September 1944 the *West Virginia* had been repaired and was back in service.

Following the fall of France, Americans were confronted with a devil's dilemma. They desired above all to stay out of the conflict, yet they did not want Britain to be knocked out of the war. They also wished to halt Japan, which menaced American trade, security, and international peace. To keep Britain from collapsing, the Roosevelt administration felt compelled to extend the unneutral aid that invited attacks from German submarines. To keep Japan from expanding, Washington undertook to cut off vital Japanese supplies with embargoes that invited possible retaliation. Rather than let democracy die and dictatorship rule supreme, most citizens were evidently determined to support a policy that might lead to war. It did.

CHAPTER SUMMARY ★ ★ ★ ★ ★ ★ ★ ★ ★ ★ ★ ★ ★ ★

Roosevelt's early foreign policies, such as wrecking the London economic conference and establishing the Good Neighbor policy in Latin America, were governed by his determination to make domestic recovery the national priority and to turn the United States away from commitments elsewhere in the world. America virtually withdrew from all European affairs and promised independence to the Philippines in an attempt to avoid future involvement in East Asia.

Depression-spawned chaos and war in Europe and Asia strengthened the isolationist impulse, as Congress passed a series of Neutrality Acts designed to prevent America from being drawn into foreign wars. The United States adhered to this policy for a time, despite the spreading aggression of Italy, Germany, and Japan. But after the outbreak of World War II in Europe, Roosevelt cautiously began to provide some aid to the Allies.

After the fall of France in June 1940, Roosevelt provided greater assistance to desperate Britain in the destroyers-for-bases deal, and Congress passed the lend-lease program. Still-powerful isolationists protested these measures, but dark-horse Republican nominee Wendell Willkie refrained from attacking Roosevelt's foreign policy in the 1940 campaign.

Roosevelt won an unprecedented third term, but by a closer margin than his previous victories.

The fall of France in June 1940 and Hitler's invasion of the Soviet Union in June 1941 made apparent the threat to the survival of Western democracies. To help prevent a German victory over the USSR, Roosevelt extended lend-lease aid to Stalin. In August 1941 Roosevelt and Winston Churchill issued the Atlantic Charter upholding shared democratic principles and outlining plans for future peace and security. By the summer of 1941, the United States was fighting an undeclared naval war with Nazi Germany in the North Atlantic.

Meanwhile, American economic embargoes against Japan made Japanese militarists desperate. With the United States insisting on Japanese withdrawal from China as a condition of resuming trade, the Japanese leaders decided that only a war with the United States would achieve their goals. The surprise attack on Pearl Harbor in December 1941 united the American people and plunged the United States into World War II.

KEY TERMS

London Economic Conference (571)
Good Neighbor policy (571)
Rome-Berlin Axis (572)
Johnson Debt Default Act (573)
Neutrality Acts of 1935, 1936, and 1937 (573)
Abraham Lincoln Brigade (573)
Quarantine Speech (574)
Appeasement (574)
Hitler-Stalin pact (574)
Neutrality Act of 1939 (574)
Kristallnacht (576)
War Refugee Board (576)
Lend-Lease Bill (579)
Atlantic Charter (580)
Pearl Harbor (581)

PEOPLE TO KNOW

Benito Mussolini
Adolf Hitler
Francisco Franco
Wendell L. Willkie

Chapter 34

America in World War II
1941–1945

Never before have we had so little time in which to do so much.

Franklin D. Roosevelt, 1942

Chapter Outline

- The Grand American Strategy for War
- Mobilizing for War
- Women in Wartime
- Changes for African Americans, Native Americans, and Mexican Americans
- The Social and Economic Impact of War
- Turning the Japanese Tide in the Pacific
- Campaigns in North Africa (1942) and Italy (1943)
- D-Day and the German Surrender
- The Atomic Bomb Ends the War with Japan
- *Makers of America: The Japanese*
- *Examining the Evidence: Franklin Roosevelt at Tehran, 1943*
- *Thinking Globally: America and the World in Depression and War: A Study in Contrasts*
- *Varying Viewpoints: The Atomic Bombs: Were They Justified?*

The United States was plunged into the inferno of World War II with the most stupefying and humiliating military defeat in its history. In the dismal months that ensued, the democratic world teetered on the edge of disaster.

Japan's fanatics forgot that whoever stabs a king must stab to kill. A wounded but still potent American giant pulled itself out of the mud of Pearl Harbor, grimly determined to avenge the bloody treachery. "Get Japan first" was the cry that rose from millions of infuriated Americans, especially on the Pacific Coast. These outraged souls regarded America's share in the global conflict as a private war of vengeance in the Pacific, with the European front a kind of holding operation.

But Washington, in the so-called **ABC-1 agreement** with the British, had earlier and wisely adopted the grand strategy of "getting Germany first." If America diverted its main strength to the Pacific, Hitler might crush both the Soviet Union and Britain and then emerge unconquerable in Fortress Europe. But if Germany was knocked out first, the combined Allied forces could be concentrated on Japan, and its daring game of conquest would be up. Meanwhile, just enough American strength would be sent to the Pacific to prevent Japan from digging in too deeply.

FOCUS QUESTIONS

1. How did the government and the American people mobilize to wage a total war against both Germany and Japan?
2. What was the war's impact on American society, including changing gender roles, regional migration, and race relations?
3. How did the strategy of "island hopping" enable the United States to turn the Japanese tide in the Pacific and advance to within striking distance of the Japanese home islands?
4. How did the British-American and Soviet armies together conquer Nazi Germany and force its surrender?
5. How did the United States develop the atomic bomb, and why was the dropping of two bombs on Japan controversial, despite its immediate ending of the war?

CHRONOLOGY

1941	▪ United States declares war on Japan ▪ Germany declares war on United States ▪ Randolph plans black march on Washington ▪ Fair Employment Practices Commission (FEPC) established ▪ Roosevelt delivers "four freedoms" speech
1942	▪ Japanese Americans sent to internment camps ▪ Japan conquers the Philippines ▪ Battle of the Coral Sea ▪ Battle of Midway ▪ United States invades North Africa ▪ Congress of Racial Equality (CORE) founded
1943	▪ Allies hold Casablanca conference ▪ Allies invade Italy ▪ Smith-Connally Anti-Strike Act ▪ "Zoot-suit" riots in Los Angeles ▪ Race riot in Detroit ▪ Japanese driven from Guadalcanal ▪ Tehran conference
1944	▪ *Korematsu* v. *U. S.* ▪ D-Day invasion of France ▪ Battle of Marianas ▪ Roosevelt defeats Dewey for presidency
1944–1945	▪ Battle of the Bulge
1945	▪ Roosevelt dies; Truman assumes presidency ▪ Germany surrenders ▪ Battles of Iwo Jima and Okinawa ▪ Potsdam conference ▪ Atomic bombs dropped on Hiroshima and Nagasaki ▪ Japan surrenders

The get-Germany-first strategy was the solid foundation on which all American military strategy was built. But it encountered much ignorant criticism from two-fisted Americans who thirsted for revenge against Japan. Aggrieved protests were also registered by short-handed American commanders in the Pacific and by Chinese and Australian allies. But President Roosevelt, a competent strategist in his own right, wisely resisted these pressures.

ABC-1 agreement (1941) *An agreement between Britain and the United States developed at a conference in Washington, D.C., between January 29 and March 27, 1941, that should the United States enter World War II, the two nations and their allies would coordinate their military planning, making a priority of protecting the British Commonwealth. That would mean "getting Germany first" in the Atlantic and the European theater and fighting more defensively on other military fronts.*

The Allies Trade Space for Time

Given time, the Allies seemed bound to triumph. But would they be given time? True, they had on their side the great mass of the world's population, but the wolf is never intimidated by the number of the sheep.

Time, in a sense, was the most needed munition. Expense was no limitation. The overpowering problem confronting America was to retool itself for all-out war production, while praying that the dictators would not meanwhile crush their adversaries who remained in the field—notably Britain and the Soviet Union. Haste was all the more imperative because the highly skilled German scientists might turn up with unbeatable secret weapons, including rocket bombs and perhaps even atomic arms.

America's task was far more complex and backbreaking than during World War I. It had to feed, clothe, and arm itself, as well as transport its forces to regions as far separated as Britain and Burma. More than that, it had to send a vast amount of food and munitions to its hard-pressed allies, who stretched all the way from the USSR to Australia. Could the American people, reputedly "gone soft," measure up to this herculean task? Was democracy "rotten" and "decadent," as the dictators sneeringly proclaimed?

The Shock of War

National unity was no worry, thanks to the electrifying blow by the Japanese at Pearl Harbor. American Communists had denounced the Anglo-French "imperialist" war before Hitler attacked Stalin in 1941, but they now clamored for an unmitigated assault

Monica Sone (b. 1919), a college-age Japanese American woman in Seattle, recorded the shock she and her brother felt when they learned of Executive Order No. 9066, which authorized the War Department to remove Japanese—aliens and citizens alike—from their homes:

"In anger, Henry and I read and reread the Executive Order. Henry crumbled the newspaper in his hand and threw it against the wall. 'Doesn't my citizenship mean a single blessed thing to anyone? Why doesn't somebody make up my mind for me? First they want me in the army. Now they're going to slap an alien 4-C on me because of my ancestry. . . .' Once more I felt like a despised, pathetic two-headed freak, a Japanese and an American, neither of which seemed to be doing me any good."

on the Axis powers. The handful of strutting pro-Hitlerites in the United States melted away, while millions of Italian Americans and German Americans loyally supported the nation's war program. In contrast to World War I, when the patriotism of millions of immigrants was hotly questioned, World War II actually speeded the assimilation of many ethnic groups into American society. Immigration had been choked off for almost two decades before 1941, and America's ethnic communities were now composed of well-settled members, whose votes were crucial to Franklin Roosevelt's Democratic party. Consequently, there was virtually no governmental witch-hunting of minority groups, as had happened in World War I.

A painful exception was the plight of some 110,000 Japanese Americans, concentrated on the Pacific Coast (see "Makers of America: The Japanese," p. 587). The Washington top command, fearing that they might act as saboteurs for Japan in case of invasion, forcibly herded them together in concentration camps, though about two-thirds of them were American-born U.S. citizens. This brutal precaution, authorized under **Executive Order No. 9066**, was both unnecessary and unfair, as the loyalty and combat record of Japanese Americans proved to be admirable. But a wave of post–Pearl Harbor hysteria, backed by the long historical swell of anti-Japanese prejudice on the West Coast, temporarily robbed many Americans of their good sense—and their sense of justice. The internment camps deprived these uprooted Americans of dignity and basic rights; the internees also lost hundreds of millions of dollars in property and foregone earnings. The wartime Supreme Court in 1944 upheld the constitutionality of the Japanese relocation in *Korematsu v. United States*. But more than four decades later in 1988, the U.S. government officially apologized for its actions and approved the payment of reparations of $20,000 to each camp survivor.

Executive Order No. 9066 *Order signed by President Roosevelt on February 19, 1942, authorizing the secretary of war to designate military zones from which certain categories of people could be excluded. Fueled by historic anti-Japanese sentiment as well as panic following the December 7, 1941, attack on Pearl Harbor, the order led to the forced removal of some 120,000 persons of Japanese ancestry (70,000 of them U.S. citizens) from the Western Military Zone (the coastal sections of Washington, Oregon, and California). Most but not all of those removed were interned in relocation camps in the interior West. The order was rescinded in December 1944, and legislation passed in 1988 offered an official government apology and modest financial compensation to surviving citizen internees.*

The war prompted other changes in the American mood. Many programs of the once-popular New Deal were wiped out by the conservative Congress elected in 1942, and even President Roosevelt declared in 1943 that "Dr. New Deal" was going into retirement to be replaced by "Dr. Win-the-War." The era of New Deal reform was over.

World War II was no idealistic crusade, as World War I had been. The Washington government emphasized action rather than propaganda. According to opinion polls during the war, a majority or near-majority of citizens confessed to having "no clear idea what the war is about." All Americans knew was that they had a dirty job on their hands and that the only way out was forward. They went about their bloody task with astonishing efficiency.

★ Building the War Machine

The war crisis snapped the drooping American economy to attention. Massive military orders—over $100 billion in 1942 alone—almost instantly soaked up the idle industrial capacity of the still-lingering Great Depression. Orchestrated by the **War Production Board (WPB)**, American factories poured forth an avalanche of weaponry: 40 billion bullets, 300,000 aircraft, 76,000 ships, 86,000 tanks, and 2.6 million machine guns. Farmers, too, rolled up their sleeves and increased their output. The armed forces drained the farms of workers, but heavy new investment in agricultural machinery and improved fertilizers more than made up the difference. In 1944 and 1945, blue-jeaned farmers hauled in record-breaking billion-bushel wheat harvests.

War Production Board (WPB) *Established in 1942 by executive order to direct all war production, including procuring and allocating raw materials, to maximize the nation's war machine. The WPB had sweeping powers over the U.S. economy and was abolished in November 1945 soon after Japan's defeat.*

The Japanese

In 1853 the American commodore Matthew Perry sailed four gunboats into Japan's Uraga Bay and demanded that the nation open itself to diplomatic and commercial exchange with the United States. Within two decades of Perry's arrival, Japan's new "Meiji" government had launched the nation on an ambitious program of industrialization and militarization designed to make it the economic and political equal of the Western powers.

As Japan rapidly modernized, its citizens increasingly took ship for America. A steep land tax drove more than 300,000 Japanese farmers off their land. In 1884 the Meiji government permitted Hawaiian planters to recruit contract laborers from among this displaced population. By the 1890s many Japanese were sailing beyond Hawaii to the ports of Long Beach, San Francisco, and Seattle.

Between 1885 and 1924, roughly 200,000 Japanese migrated to Hawaii, and around 180,000 more ventured to the U.S. mainland. They were a select group: because the Meiji government saw overseas Japanese as representatives of their homeland, it strictly regulated emigration. Thus Japanese immigrants to America arrived with more money and better education than their European counterparts.

Women as well as men migrated. The Japanese government, wanting to avoid the problems of an itinerant bachelor society that it observed among the Chinese in the United States, actively promoted women's migration. Although most Japanese immigrants were young men in their twenties and thirties, thousands of women also ventured to Hawaii and the mainland as contract laborers or "picture brides," so called because their courtships had consisted exclusively of exchanges of photographs with their prospective husbands.

In Hawaii most Japanese labored on the vast sugar cane plantations. On the mainland they initially found migratory work on the railroads or in fish, fruit, or vegetable canneries. A separate Japanese economy of restaurants, stores, and boardinghouses soon sprang up in cities to serve the immigrants' needs.

From such humble beginnings, many Japanese—particularly those on the Pacific Coast—quickly moved into farming. In the late nineteenth century, the spread of irrigation shifted California agriculture from grain to fruits and vegetables, and the invention of the refrigerated railcar opened hungry new markets in the East. The Japanese, with centuries of experience in intensive farming, arrived just in time to take advantage of these developments. By 1940 Japanese farmers produced most of the state's strawberries, beans, and tomatoes.

But the very success of the Japanese proved a lightning rod for trouble. On the West Coast, Japanese immigrants had long endured racist barbs and social segregation. Increasingly, white workers and farmers, jealous of Japanese success, pushed for immigration restrictions. Bowing to this pressure, President Theodore Roosevelt in 1908 negotiated the "Gentlemen's Agreement," under which the Japanese government voluntarily agreed to limit emigration. In 1913 the California legislature denied Japanese immigrants already living in the United States the right to own land.

Legally barred from becoming citizens, Japanese immigrants (the "Issei," from the Japanese word for *first*) became more determined than ever that their American-born children (the "Nissei," from the Japanese word for *second*) would reap the full benefits of their birthright. Japanese parents encouraged their children to learn English, to excel in school, and to get a college education. Many Nissei grew up in two worlds, a fact they often recognized by Americanizing their Japanese names. Although education and acculturation did not protect the Nissei from the hysteria of World War II, those assets did give them a springboard to success in the postwar era.

Library of Congress

Japanese American Evacuees, 1942 After the U.S. Army's Western Defense Command ordered the forced evacuation of all Japanese and Japanese Americans living on the Pacific Coast, families had no choice but to pack up whatever they could carry and move to the "relocation centers" hastily erected farther inland.

Office of Price Administration (OPA) (1941–1947) *A critically important wartime agency charged with regulating the consumer economy by rationing scarce supplies, such as automobiles, tires, fuel, nylon, and sugar, and by curbing inflation by setting ceilings on the price of goods. Rents were controlled as well in parts of the country overwhelmed by war workers. The OPA was extended after World War II ended to continue the fight against inflation.*

National War Labor Board (NWLB) *Established by President Franklin D. Roosevelt to act as an arbitration tribunal and mediate disputes between labor and management that might have led to war stoppages and thereby undermined the war effort. The NWLB was also charged with adjusting wages with an eye to controlling inflation.*

Smith-Connally Anti-Strike Act (1943) *Allowed the federal government to seize and operate plants threatened by labor disputes. Passed amidst worries about the effects that labor strikes would have on war production, it also criminalized strike action against government-run companies.*

WACs (Women's Army Corps) *The women's branch of the U.S. Army established during World War II to employ women in noncombatant jobs. Women now participated in the armed services in ways that went beyond their traditional roles as nurses.*

WAVES (Women Accepted for Voluntary Emergency Service) *The women's branch of the U.S. Navy established during World War II to employ women in noncombatant jobs.*

SPARs (U.S. Coast Guard Women's Reserve) *The women's branch of the U.S. Coast Guard established during World War II to employ women in noncombatant* jobs.

***Bracero* program (1942)** *Program established by agreement with the Mexican government to recruit temporary Mexican agricultural workers to the United States to make up for wartime labor shortages in the Far West. The program persisted until 1964, by which time it had sponsored 4.5 million border crossings.*

These wonders of production also brought economic strains. Full employment and scarce consumer goods fueled a sharp inflationary surge in 1942. The **Office of Price Administration (OPA)** eventually brought ascending prices under control with extensive regulations. Rationing held down the consumption of critical goods such as meat and butter, though some "black marketeers" and "meatleggers" cheated the system. The **National War Labor Board (WLB)** imposed ceilings on wage increases.

Labor unions, whose memberships grew from about 10 million to more than 13 million workers during the war, fiercely resented the government-dictated wage ceilings. Despite the no-strike pledges of most major unions, a rash of labor walkouts plagued the war effort. Threats of lost production through strikes became so worrisome that Congress, in June 1943, passed the **Smith-Connally Anti-Strike Act**, which authorized the federal government to seize and operate tied-up industries. Under the act, Washington took over the coal mines and, for a brief period, the railroads. Yet work stoppages accounted for less than 1 percent of the total working hours of the United States' wartime laboring force.

Manpower and Womanpower

The armed services enlisted nearly 15 million men in World War II, and some 216,000 women, who were employed for noncombat duties. Best known of these "women in arms" were the **WACS (Women's Army Corps)**, **WAVES (Women Accepted for Voluntary Emergency Service)** (navy), and **SPARS (U.S. Coast Guard Women's Reserve)**.

Despite exemptions for key categories of industrial and agricultural workers, the draft left the nation's farms and factories so short of personnel that new workers had to be found. An agreement with Mexico in 1942 brought thousands of Mexican agricultural workers, called *braceros*, across the border to harvest the fruit and grain crops of the West. The ***Bracero* program** outlived the war by some twenty years, becoming a fixed feature of the agricultural economy in many western states.

Even more dramatic was the march of women onto the factory floor. More than 6 million women took up jobs outside the home; over half of them had never before worked for wages. Many of them were mothers, and the government was obliged to set up some three thousand day-care centers to care for "Rosie the Riveter's" children while she drilled the fuselage of a heavy bomber or joined the links of a tank track. When the war ended, Rosie and many of her sisters wanted to keep on working and often did. The war thus foreshadowed an eventual revolution in the roles of women in American society.

Yet the war's immediate impact on women's lives has frequently been exaggerated. The great majority of women—especially those with husbands present in the home or with small children to care for—did not work for wages in the wartime economy but continued in their traditional roles. In both Britain and the Soviet Union, a far greater percentage of women, including mothers, were pressed into industrial employment as the gods of war laid a much heavier hand on those societies than they did on the United States.

At war's end, two-thirds of women war workers left the labor force. Many of them were forced out of their jobs by employers or unions, but half of them quit their jobs voluntarily because of family obligations. The immediate postwar period witnessed not a permanent widening of women's employment opportunities but a widespread rush into suburban domesticity and the mothering of the "baby boomers," who were born by the tens of millions in the decade and a half after 1945. America was destined to experience a revolution in women's status later in the postwar period, but that epochal change was only beginning to gather momentum in the war years.

Wartime Migrations

The war also proved to be a demographic cauldron, churning and shifting the American population. Many of the 15 million men and women in uniform, having seen new sights and glimpsed new horizons, chose not to go home again at war's end. War industries sucked people into boomtowns like Los Angeles, Detroit, Seattle, and Baton Rouge. California's population grew by nearly 2 million. The South experienced especially dramatic changes. The states of the old Confederacy received a disproportionate share of defense contracts, including nearly $6 billion of federally financed industrial facilities. Here were the seeds of the postwar blossoming of the "Sunbelt" (see Map 34.1).

Despite this economic stimulus in the South, some 1.6 million blacks left the land of their past enslavement to seek jobs in the war plants of the West and North. Forever after, race relations constituted a national, not a regional, issue. Explosive tensions developed over employment, housing, and segregated facilities. Black leader A. Philip Randolph, head of the Brotherhood of Sleeping Car Porters, threatened a massive "Negro March on Washington" in 1941 to demand equal opportunities for blacks in war jobs and in the armed forces. Roosevelt's response was to issue an executive order forbidding discrimination in defense industries and to establish the **Fair Employment Practices Commission (FEPC)** to monitor compliance with his edict.

Blacks were also drafted into the armed forces, though they were generally assigned to service branches rather than combat units. But in general the war helped to embolden blacks in their long struggle for equality. Membership in the National Association for the Advancement of Colored People (NAACP) shot up almost to the half-million mark, and a new militant organization committed to nonviolent "direct action," the **Congress of Racial Equality (CORE)**, was founded in 1942.

National Archives

Workers in Wartime—and Beyond? More than 6 million women—more than 3 million of them homemakers who had never before worked for wages—entered the work force during World War II. That work was valued and encouraged during the war years.

The northward migration of African Americans accelerated after the war, thanks to the advent of the mechanical cotton picker—an invention whose impact rivaled that of Eli Whitney's cotton gin. Overnight, the Cotton South's historic need for cheap labor disappeared. Their muscle no longer required in Dixie, some 5 million black tenant farmers and sharecroppers headed north in the three decades after the war. Within a single generation, a near-majority of African Americans gave up their historic homeland and their rural way of life. By 1970 half of all blacks lived outside the South. The speed and scale of these changes jolted the migrants and sometimes convulsed the communities that received them.

The war also prompted an exodus of Native Americans from the reservations. Thousands of Indian men and women found war work in the major cities, and thousands more answered Uncle Sam's call to arms. More than 90 percent of Indians resided on reservations in 1940; seven decades later more than half lived in cities. Some twenty-five thousand Native American men served in the armed forces. Comanches in Europe and Navajos in the Pacific made especially valuable contributions as "**code talkers**," who transmitted radio messages in their native languages.

The sudden rubbing against one another of unfamiliar peoples produced some distressingly violent friction. In 1943 young "zoot-suit"-clad Mexicans and Mexican Americans in Los Angeles were viciously attacked by Anglo sailors who cruised the streets in taxicabs, searching for victims. At almost the same time, an even more brutal race riot erupted in Detroit, killing twenty-five blacks and nine whites.

Fair Employment Practices Commission (FEPC) (1941) *Set up to monitor compliance with Franklin D. Rooosevelt's executive order forbidding racial discrimination in all defense plants operating under contract with the federal government. The order came in response to the threat of a massive "Negro March on Washington" to demand equal opportunities in war jobs and in the military.*

Congress of Racial Equality (CORE) (1942) *Nonviolent civil rights organization founded in 1942 and committed to the "Double V"—victory over fascism abroad and racism at home. After World War II, CORE would become a major force in the civil rights movement.*

code talkers *Native American men who served in the military by transmitting radio messages in their native languages, which were undecipherable by German and Japanese spies.*

Holding the Home Front

Despite these ugly episodes, Americans on the home front suffered little from the war compared with the peoples of the other fighting nations. By war's end much of the planet was a smoking ruin. But in America the war invigorated the economy and lifted the

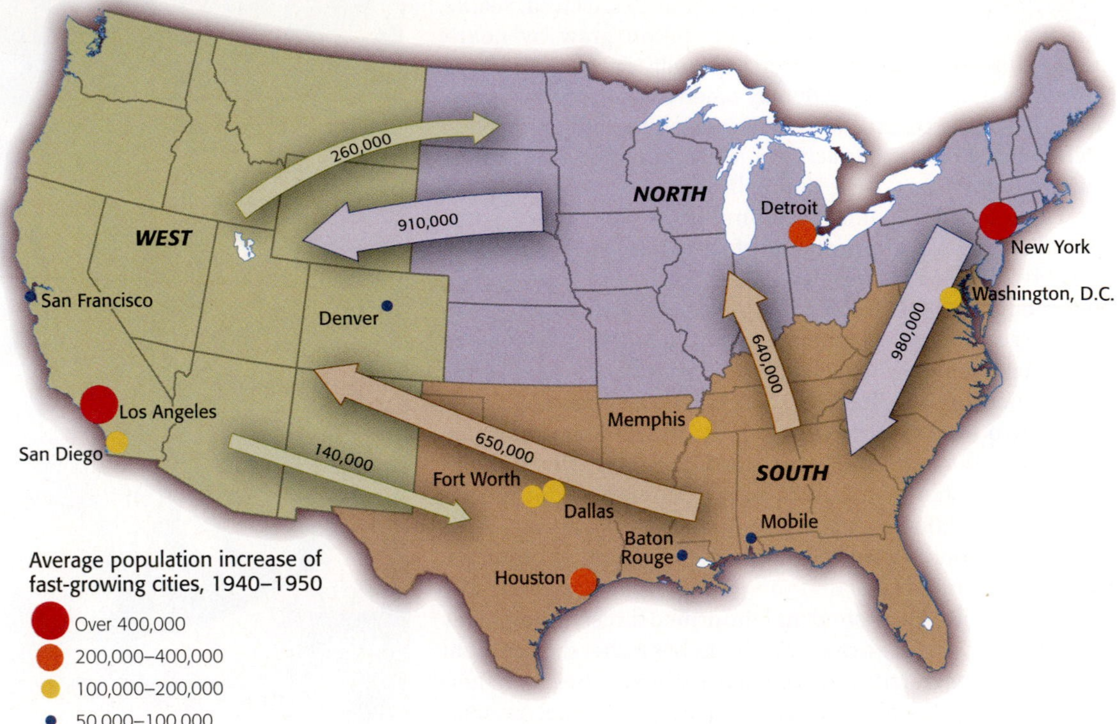

Map 34.1 Internal Migration in the United States during World War II Few events in American history have moved the American people about so massively as World War II. The West and the South boomed, and several war-industry cities grew explosively. A majority of migrants from the South were blacks; 1.6 million African Americans left the region in the 1940s. (Source: United States Department of Labor, Bureau of Labor Statistics.)

country out of a decade-long depression. The gross national product vaulted from less than $100 billion in 1940 to more than $200 billion in 1945. Corporate profits nearly doubled during the war. Despite wage ceilings, overtime pay fattened pay envelopes. On December 7, 1944, the third anniversary of Pearl Harbor, Macy's department store rang up the biggest sales day in its history. Americans had never had it so good—and they wanted it a lot better.

The hand of government touched more American lives more intimately during the war than ever before. The war, perhaps even more than the New Deal, pointed the way to the post-1945 era of big-government interventionism. Millions of men and women worked for Uncle Sam in the armed forces or in defense industries, and their personal needs were cared for by government-sponsored housing projects, day-care facilities, and health plans. The Office of Scientific Research and Development channeled hundreds of millions of dollars into university-based scientific research, establishing the partnership between the government and universities that underwrote America's technological and economic leadership in the postwar era.

The flood of war dollars—not the relatively modest rivulet of New Deal spending—at last swept the plague of unemployment from the land. War, not enlightened social policy, cured the depression. As the postwar economy continued to depend dangerously on military spending for its health, many observers looked back to the years 1941–1945 as the origins of a "warfare-welfare state."

The conflict was phenomenally expensive. The wartime bill amounted to more than $330 billion—ten times the direct cost of World War I and twice as much as *all* previous federal spending since 1776. Despite an expanded income tax and higher tax rates, only about two-fifths of the war costs were paid from current revenues. The remainder was borrowed. The national debt skyrocketed from $49 billion in 1941 to $259 billion in 1945.

The Rising Sun in the Pacific

Early successes of the efficient Japanese militarists were breathtaking: they realized that they would have to win quickly or lose slowly. Simultaneously with the assault on Pearl Harbor, the Japanese launched widespread and uniformly successful attacks on various bastions across the Pacific and East Asia. These included the American outposts of Guam, Wake, and the Philippines, as well as Hong Kong and British Malaya, with its critically important supplies of rubber and tin.

Nor did the Japanese tide stop there. The soldiers of the emperor, plunging into the snake-infested jungles of Burma, cut the famed Burma Road. This was the route over which the United States had been trucking a trickle of munitions to the armies of Chinese generalissimo Jiang Jieshi (Chiang Kai-shek), who was still resisting the Japanese invader in China. Thereafter, intrepid American aviators were forced to fly a handful of war supplies to Jiang "over the hump" of the towering Himalaya Mountains from the India-Burma theater. Meanwhile, the Japanese had lunged southward against the oil-rich Dutch East Indies, which speedily fell to the assailants.

In the Philippines General Douglas MacArthur, the eloquent and egotistical American commander, slowed the invading Japanese army's advance for five months. Twenty thousand American troops and a larger force of Filipinos withdrew to a strong defensive position at Bataan, near Manila, where they held off violent Japanese attacks until April 9, 1942. Before the inevitable American surrender, MacArthur was ordered by Washington to depart secretly for Australia, but he proclaimed as he departed, "I shall return." The battered remnants of his army were treated with vicious cruelty in the infamous eighty-mile Bataan Death March to prisoner-of-war camps. The island fortress of Corregidor, in Manila harbor, held out until May 6, 1942, when it too surrendered and left Japanese forces in complete control of the Philippine archipelago (see Map 34.2).

Contending Voices

War and the Color Line

Activist pressure as well as the need to frame the war as a fight for freedom compelled President Franklin Roosevelt (1882–1945) to support civil rights, as indicated in a 1944 speech endorsing a permanent Fair Employment Practices Commission (FEPC):

"The American people are resolved that when our men and women return home from this war, they shall come back to a place where all persons, regardless of race, color, creed or place of birth, can live in peace, honor and human dignity."

But, with the armed forces still segregated and the home front riven by discrimination, African Americans like this unnamed soldier remained disappointed, even embittered:

"Why is it we Negro soldiers who are as much a part of Uncle Sam's great military machine as any cannot be treated with equality and the respect due us? The same respect which white soldiers expect and demand from us? . . . There is great need for drastic change in this man's Army! How can we be trained to protect America, which is called a *free* nation, when all around us rears the ugly head of segregation?"

How might this contradiction between ideal and reality have mobilized African Americans to take a more politically activist path after World War II?

Japan's High Tide at Midway

The aggressive warriors from Japan, making hay while the Rising Sun shone, pushed relentlessly southward. They invaded the turtle-shaped island of New Guinea, north of Australia, and landed on the Solomon Islands, from which they threatened Australia itself. Their onrush was finally checked by a crucial naval battle in the Coral Sea, in May 1942. An American carrier task force, with Australian support, inflicted heavy losses on the victory-flushed Japanese. For the first time in history, the fighting was all done by carrier-based aircraft.

Japan next undertook to seize Midway Island, more than a thousand miles northwest of Honolulu. From this strategic base, it could launch devastating assaults on Pearl Harbor and perhaps force the weakened American Pacific fleet into destructive combat. The epochal **Battle of Midway** was fought on June 3–6, 1942. Admiral Chester W. Nimitz, a high-grade naval strategist, directed a smaller but skillfully maneuvered carrier force against the powerful invading fleet. The fighting was all done by aircraft, and the Japanese broke off action after losing four vitally important carriers.

Battle of Midway (1942) *A pivotal naval battle fought near the island of Midway on June 3–6, 1942. The victory halted Japanese advances in the Pacific.*

Map 34.2 United States Thrusts in the Pacific, 1942–1945 American strategists had to choose among four proposed plans for waging the war against Japan:

1. Defeating the Japanese in China by funneling supplies over the Himalayan "hump" from India.
2. Carrying the war into Southeast Asia (a proposal much favored by the British, who could thus regain Singapore).
3. Heavy bombing of Japan from Chinese air bases.
4. "Island-hopping" from the South Pacific to within striking distance of the Japanese home islands. The fourth strategy, favored by General Douglas MacArthur, was the one finally emphasized.

The Battle of Midway was a pivotal victory. Combined with the Battle of the Coral Sea, the U.S. success at Midway halted Japan's juggernaut. But the thrust of the Japanese into the eastern Pacific did net them America's fog-girt islands of Kiska and Attu in the Aleutian archipelago, off Alaska. This easy conquest aroused fear of an invasion of the United States from the northwest. Much American strength was consequently diverted to the defense of Alaska.

Yet the Japanese imperialists, overextended in 1942, suffered from "victory disease." Their appetites were bigger than their stomachs. If they had only dug in and consolidated their gains, they would have been much more difficult to dislodge once the tide turned.

American Leapfrogging Toward Tokyo

Following the heartening victory at Midway, the United States for the first time was able to seize the initiative in the Pacific. In August 1942 American ground forces gained a toehold on Guadalcanal Island, in the Solomons, in an effort to protect the lifeline from America to Australia through the Southwest Pacific. After several desperate sea battles for naval control of the area, the Japanese troops evacuated Guadalcanal in February 1943.

American and Australian forces, under General MacArthur, meanwhile had been hanging on courageously to the southeastern tip of New Guinea, the last buffer protecting Australia. Aided by American naval forces, MacArthur eventually fought his way westward through the tropical jungle hells and completed the conquest of New Guinea by August 1944.

The U.S. Navy, with marines and army divisions doing the meat-grinder fighting, had meanwhile been "leapfrogging" the Japanese-held islands in the Pacific. Old-fashioned strategy dictated that the American forces, as they drove toward Tokyo, should reduce the fortified Japanese outposts on their flank. The new American strategy of island-hopping called for bypassing some of the most heavily fortified Japanese posts, capturing nearby islands, setting up airfields on them, and then neutralizing the enemy bases through heavy bombing. Deprived of essential supplies from the homeland, Japan's outposts would slowly wither on the vine—as they did.

With Admiral Nimitz skillfully coordinating the efforts of naval, air, and ground units, the American attacks achieved brilliant success. In May and August 1943, Attu and Kiska in the Aleutians were easily retaken. In November 1943 "bloody Tarawa" and Makin in the Gilbert Islands fell after suicidal resistance. Key outposts in the Marshall Islands succumbed after savage fighting in January and February 1944. The conquest of Guam and other islands in the Marianas in July and August 1944 provided airfields for America's new B-29 super-bombers to carry out round-trip bombing raids on Japan's home islands. With these unsinkable aircraft carriers now available, virtual around-the-clock bombing of Japan began in November 1944.

The Allied Halting of Hitler

Early setbacks for America in the Pacific were paralleled in the Atlantic. Hitler had entered the war with a formidable fleet of ultramodern submarines, which ultimately operated in "wolf packs" with frightful effect. During ten months of 1942 more than five hundred merchant ships were lost. Not until the spring of 1943 did the Allies clearly gain the upper hand against the U-boat. Their antisubmarine tactics were substantially aided by British code breakers, who had cracked the Germans' "Enigma" codes and could therefore pinpoint the locations of the U-boats lurking in the North Atlantic.

The turning point of the land-air war against Hitler came late in 1942. The British launched a thousand-plane raid on Cologne in May, and in August they were joined by the American air force in cascading bombs on German cities. In North Africa, the Germans under Marshal Erwin Rommel—the "Desert Fox"—had driven eastward across the hot sands into Egypt, perilously close to the Suez Canal. A breakthrough would have spelled disaster for the Allies. But late in October 1942, British general Bernard Montgomery delivered a withering attack at El Alamein, west of Cairo. With the aid of several hundred hastily shipped American Sherman tanks, he speedily drove the enemy back to Tunisia, more than a thousand miles away.

On the Soviet front, the unexpected successes of the red army gave a new lift to the Allied cause. In September 1942 the Russians stalled the German steamroller at rubble-strewn Stalingrad, graveyard of Hitler's hopes. In November 1942 the resilient Russians unleashed a crushing counteroffensive, which was never seriously reversed. A year later, Stalin had regained about two-thirds of the blood-soaked Soviet motherland wrested from him by the German invader.

A Second Front from North Africa to Rome

Soviet losses were already staggering in 1942; millions of soldiers and civilians lay dead, and Hitler's armies had laid waste a vast territory equivalent in the United States to the area from Chicago to the Atlantic seaboard. Small wonder that Kremlin leaders clamored for a second front to divert the German strength westward.

Many Americans, including FDR, were eager to begin an invasion of France in 1942 or 1943. They feared that the Soviets might make a separate peace with Germany, as they had in 1918, and leave the Western Allies to face Hitler's fury alone. But British military planners, remembering their appalling losses in France in 1914–1918, preferred to attack Hitler's Fortress Europe through the "soft underbelly" of the Mediterranean. Faced with British boot-dragging, the Americans reluctantly agreed to postpone a massive invasion of Europe.

An assault on French-held North Africa was a compromise second front. The highly secret attack, launched in November 1942, was headed by a gifted and easy-smiling American general, Dwight D. ("Ike") Eisenhower, a master of organization and conciliation. The joint Allied operation, ultimately involving some 400,000 men and about 850 ships, was highly successful. After savage fighting, the remnants of the German-Italian army were finally trapped in Tunisia and surrendered in May 1943.

At Casablanca, in newly occupied French Morocco, President Roosevelt met with Winston Churchill in January 1943 to plan new blows. The Big Two agreed to step up the Pacific war, invade Sicily, increase pressure on Italy, and insist on "unconditional surrender" by the enemy. Designed to hearten the ultra-suspicious Soviets, who professed to fear separate Allied peace negotiations, "unconditional surrender" proved to be one of the most controversial moves of the war. The main criticism was that it steeled the enemy to fight to a last-bunker resistance, while discouraging antiwar groups in Germany from revolting. Although there was some truth in these charges, no one can prove that "unconditional surrender" either shortened or lengthened the war. But this is known: by helping to destroy the German government utterly, the harsh policy forced a thorough postwar reconstruction.

The Allied forces, victorious in Africa, now turned against the not-so-soft underbelly of Europe. Sicily fell in August 1943 after sporadic but sometimes bitter resistance. Shortly before the conquest of the island, Mussolini was deposed, and Italy surrendered unconditionally soon thereafter, in September 1943.

But if Italy dropped out of the war, the Germans did not drop out of Italy. Hitler's well-trained troops stubbornly resisted the Allied invaders now pouring into the toe of the Italian boot. "Sunny Italy" proceeded to belie its name, for in the snow-covered and mud-caked mountains of its elongated peninsula occurred some of the filthiest, bloodiest, and most frustrating fighting of the war.

After a touch-and-go assault on the Anzio beachhead, Rome was finally taken on June 4, 1944. But slow and painful fighting continued in northern Italy, and not until May 2, 1945, only five days before Germany's official surrender, did several hundred thousand Axis troops in Italy lay down their arms. While the Italian second front opened the Mediterranean and diverted some German divisions from the blazing Soviet and French battle lines, it also may have delayed the main Allied invasion of France by many months—allowing more time for the Soviet army to advance into Eastern Europe.

D-Day: June 6, 1944

The Soviets never ceased their clamor for an all-out second front. Plans for a major Allied invasion were finally settled at a conference of Stalin, Churchill, and Roosevelt held in Tehran, the capital of Iran, from November 28 to December 1, 1943. The Soviets agreed to launch attacks on Germany from the east simultaneously with the prospective Allied assault from the west.

Preparations for the cross-channel invasion of France were gigantic. Britain's fast-anchored isle virtually groaned with munitions, supplies, and troops, as nearly 3 million fighting men were readied. Because the United States was to provide most of the Allied warriors, the overall command was entrusted to an American, General Eisenhower.

D-Day (1944) *A massive military operation led by American forces in Normandy beginning on June 6, 1944. The pivotal battle led to the liberation of France and brought on the final phases of World War II in Europe.*

French Normandy, less heavily defended than other parts of the European coast, was pinpointed for the invasion assault. On **D-Day**, June 6, 1944, the enormous operation, which involved some forty-six hundred vessels, unwound. Stiff resistance was encountered from the Germans, who had been misled by a feint into expecting the blow to fall farther north.

The Allied beachhead, at first clung to with fingertips, was gradually enlarged, consolidated, and reinforced. After desperate fighting, the invaders finally broke out of the German iron ring that enclosed the Normandy landing zone. Most spectacular were the lunges across France by American armored divisions, brilliantly commanded by blustery and profane General George S. ("Blood 'n' Guts") Patton. The retreat of the German defenders was hastened when an American-French force landed in August 1944 on the southern

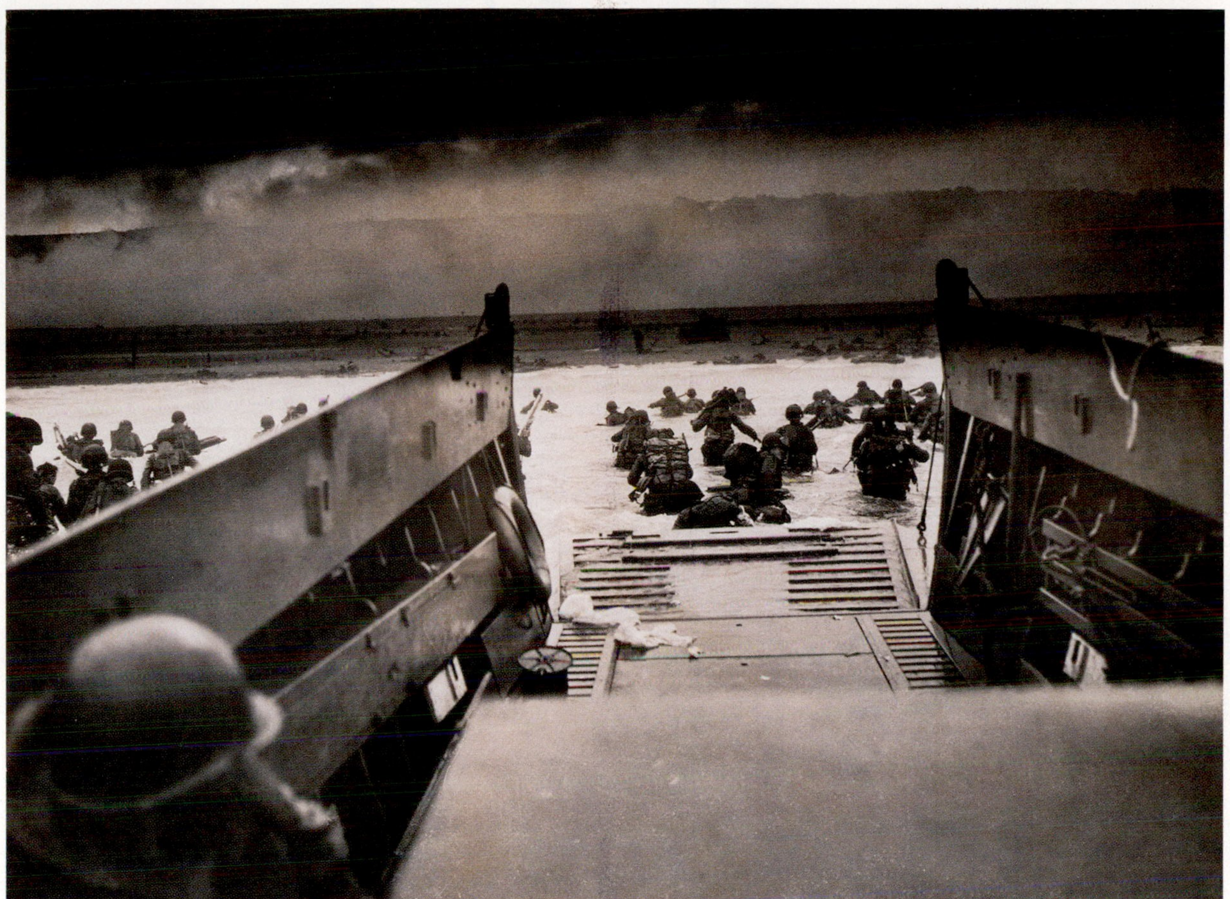

Library of Congress

Allies Landing in Normandy, June 6, 1944 Nine-foot ocean swells on invasion day made loading the assault landing craft, such as the one pictured here, treacherous business. Many men were injured or tossed into the sea as the bathtub-like amphibious vessels bobbed wildly up and down alongside the troop transports. As the vulnerable boats churned toward the beach, some officers led their tense, grim-faced troops in prayer. One major, recalling the remarkable Battle of Agincourt in 1415, quoted from Shakespeare's *Henry V*: "He that outlives this day, and comes safe home / Will stand a tip-toe when this day is named."

coast of France and swept northward. With the assistance of the French "underground," Paris was liberated in August 1944, amid exuberant manifestations of joy and gratitude.

Allied forces rolled irresistibly across France toward Germany. "Lafayette, we are here again," proclaimed American soldiers. The first important German city (Aachen) fell to the Americans in October 1944, and the days of Hitler's "thousand-year Reich" were numbered (see Map 34.3).

FDR: The Fourth-Termite of 1944

The presidential campaign of 1944 came awkwardly as the awful conflict roared to its climax. Meeting in Chicago, victory-starved Republicans nominated short, mustachioed, and dapper Thomas Dewey, the popular governor of New York. A former prosecutor, Dewey was only forty-two years of age, causing one veteran New Dealer to sneer that the candidate had cast his diaper into the ring. To offset Dewey's mild internationalism, the convention nominated for the vice presidency a strong isolationist, Senator John W. Bricker of Ohio.

FDR, aging under the strain, was still the Democrats' "indispensable man." He was nominated by acclamation for a fourth term. The scramble for the vice-presidential plum turned into a free-for-all. Roosevelt's third-term vice president, former agriculture secretary Henry A. Wallace, was a committed liberal who desired renomination. But conservative Democrats who distrusted him as ill-balanced and unpredictable concocted a "ditch Wallace" movement that developed momentum and finally won Roosevelt's blessing.

Map 34.3 World War II in Europe and North Africa, 1939–1945

The vice presidential nomination then went to smiling and self-assured Senator Harry S. Truman of Missouri, who had recently attained national visibility as the efficient chairman of a Senate committee investigating wasteful war expenditures.

A dynamic Dewey took the offensive in the campaign, proclaiming in his beautiful baritone voice that it was "time for a change" after "twelve long years" of New Dealism. In the closing weeks of the campaign, Roosevelt left his desk for the stump. He was eager to show himself, even in chilling rains, to spike well-founded rumors of failing health.

Democrats relied heavily on the new political action committee of the CIO, which provided substantial funds and zealous campaign workers for FDR. Roosevelt, as customary, won a sweeping victory: 432 to 99 in the Electoral College, 25,606,585 to 22,014,745 in the popular totals. Elated, Roosevelt quipped that "the first twelve years are the hardest."

The Last Days of Hitler

By mid-December 1944, the month after Roosevelt's fourth-term victory, Germany seemed to be wobbling on its last legs. The Soviet surge had penetrated eastern Germany. Allied aerial "blockbuster" bombs, making the "rubble bounce" with around-the-clock attacks, were falling like giant explosive hailstones on cities, factories, and transportation arteries. The German western front seemed about to buckle under the sledgehammer blows of the United States and its Allies.

Examining the Evidence

Franklin Roosevelt at Tehran, 1943

In late 1943 the "Big Three" wartime leaders—British prime minister Winston Churchill, American president Franklin Roosevelt, and Soviet leader Marshal Joseph Stalin—gathered together for the first time. They met amid growing Soviet frustration with the British and the Americans for their failure thus far to open a "second front" against Germany in Western Europe, while the Soviets continued to suffer horrendous losses in the savage fighting in Eastern Europe. American military planners were eager to open a second front as soon as possible, but the British, who would necessarily have to supply most of the troops until America was fully mobilized, balked. Tension among the three leaders over the second-front plan—code-named OVERLORD, the operation that resulted in the Anglo-American invasion of Normandy on "D-Day," June 6, 1944—is evident in this report of their discussions in the Iranian city of Tehran on November 28, 1943. The excerpts printed here are actually taken from two separate accounts: one composed by the American diplomat and Roosevelt's official translator Charles Bohlen, the other written by a military officer on behalf of the United States Joint Chiefs of Staff. Both versions were published in *Foreign Relations of the United States*, a compilation of American diplomatic records since 1861. The Soviets and the British also kept their own records of the Tehran meetings, giving historians remarkably rich sources with which to reconstruct the crucial negotiations and decisions that shaped wartime diplomacy.

1. Why might the history of diplomacy be so lavishly documented?
2. At this meeting, what were the principal objectives that each leader pursued? How did each man address his task?
3. In what ways was the future of the war—and the postwar world—here foreshadowed?

FIRST PLENARY MEETING, NOVEMBER 28, 1943, 4 P.M., CONFERENCE ROOM, SOVIET EMBASSY

Bohlen Minutes

SECRET

The President said as the youngest of the three present he ventured to welcome his elders. He said he wished to welcome the new members to the family circle and tell them that meetings of this character were conducted as between friends with complete frankness on all sides with nothing that was said to be made public. . . .

Chief of Staff Minutes

Marshal Stalin asked who will be the commander in this Operation Overlord. (The President and Prime Minister interpolated this was not yet decided.) Marshal Stalin continued, "Then nothing will come out of these operations." . . .

The President said we again come back to the problem of the timing for Overlord. It was believed that it would be good for Overlord to take place about 1 May, or certainly not later than 15 May or 20 May, if possible.

The Prime Minister said that he could not agree to that. . . .

. . . He said he (the Prime Minister) was going to do everything in the power of His Majesty's Government to begin OVERLORD at the earliest possible moment. However, he did not think that the many great possibilities in the Mediterranean should be ruthlessly cast aside as valueless merely on the question of a month's delay in Overlord.

Marshal Stalin said all the Mediterranean operations are diversions, . . .

The President said he found that his staff places emphasis on Overlord. While on the other hand the Prime Minister and his staff also emphasize Overlord, nevertheless the United States does not feel that Overlord should be put off.

The President questioned whether it would not be possible for the *ad hoc* committee to go ahead with their deliberations without any further directive and to produce an answer by tomorrow morning.

Marshal Stalin questioned, "What can such a committee do?" He said, "We Chiefs of State have more power and more authority than a committee. General Brooke cannot force our opinions and there are many questions which can be decided only by us." He said he would like to ask if the British are thinking seriously of Overlord only in order to satisfy the U.S.S.R.

The Prime Minister replied that if the conditions specified at Moscow regarding Overlord should exist, he firmly believed it would be England's duty to hurl every ounce of strength she had across the Channel at the Germans.

The President observed that in an hour a very good dinner would be awaiting all and people would be very hungry. He suggested that the staffs should meet tomorrow morning and discuss the matter. . . .

Source: FDR Library

Hitler then staked everything on one last throw of his reserves. Secretly concentrating a powerful force, he hurled it, on December 16, 1944, against the thinly held American lines in the heavily befogged and snow-shrouded Ardennes Forest. Caught off guard, the outmanned Americans were driven back, creating a deep "bulge" in the Allied line. The ten-day penetration was finally halted after the 101st Airborne Division stood firm at the vital bastion of Bastogne. The commander, Brigadier General A. C. McAuliffe, defiantly answered the German demand for surrender with one word: "Nuts." Reinforcements were rushed up, and the last-gasp Hitlerian offensive was at length bloodily stemmed in the Battle of the Bulge.

In March 1945, forward-driving American troops reached Germany's Rhine River, where, by incredibly good luck, they found one strategic bridge not demolished. Pressing their advantage, General Eisenhower's troops reached the Elbe River in April 1945. There, a short distance south of Berlin, American and Soviet advance guards dramatically clasped hands amid cries of "*Amerikanskie tovarishchi*" (American comrades).

The conquering Americans were horrified to find blood-bespattered concentration camps, where the German Nazis had engaged in scientific mass murder of "undesirables," including an estimated 6 million Jews. The Washington government had long been informed about Hitler's campaign of genocide against the Jews and had been reprehensibly slow to take steps against it. Roosevelt's administration had bolted the door against large numbers of Jewish refugees, and his military commanders declined even to bomb the rail lines that carried the victims to the camps. But until the war's end, the full dimensions of the "Holocaust" were not known. When the details were revealed, the whole world was aghast.

The vengeful Soviets, clawing their way forward from the east, reached Berlin in April 1945. After desperate house-to-house fighting, followed by an orgy of pillage and rape, they captured the bomb-shattered city. Adolf Hitler, after a hasty marriage to his mistress, committed suicide in an underground bunker on April 30, 1945.

Tragedy had meanwhile struck the United States. President Roosevelt, while relaxing at Warm Springs, Georgia, suddenly died from a massive cerebral hemorrhage on April 12, 1945. Knots of confused, leaderless citizens gathered to discuss the future anxiously, as bewildered, unbriefed Vice President Truman took the helm.

On May 7, 1945, what was left of the German government surrendered unconditionally. May 8 was officially proclaimed **V-E (Victory in Europe) Day** and was greeted with frenzied rejoicing in the Allied countries.

V-E (Victory in Europe) Day *The official end to the war in Europe, marked on May 8, 1945, following the unconditional surrender of what remained of the German government.*

Japan Dies Hard

Japan's rickety bamboo empire meanwhile was tottering to its fall. American submarines—"the silent service"—were sending the Japanese merchant marine to the bottom so fast they were running out of prey. All told, these undersea craft destroyed 1,042 ships, or about 50 percent of Japan's entire life-sustaining merchant fleet.

Meanwhile, giant bomber attacks launched from Saipan and other captured Mariana islands were reducing the enemy's fragile cities to cinders. The massive firebomb raid on Tokyo, March 9–10, 1945 destroyed over 250,000 buildings, gutted a quarter of the city, and killed an estimated 83,000 people—a loss comparable to that later inflicted by the atomic bombs.

General MacArthur was also on the move. Completing the conquest of jungle-draped New Guinea, he headed northwest for the Philippines, en route to Japan, with 600 ships and 250,000 men. In a scene well staged for the photographers, he splashed ashore at Leyte Island, on October 20, 1944, with the summons, "People of the Philippines, I have returned . . . Rally to me." The ravaged city of Manila on the main island of Luzon fell in March 1945, but the Philippines were not finally conquered until July, after bitter fighting against holed-in Japanese, who took a toll of over sixty thousand American casualties.

America's steel vise was tightening mercilessly around Japan. The tiny island of Iwo Jima was captured in March 1945, after a desperate twenty-five day assault that cost over four thousand American dead. The island of Okinawa, well defended by Japanese soldiers who fought with incredible courage from their caves, was finally taken in June 1945, at the cost of fifty thousand American casualties and far heavier Japanese losses. The U.S. Navy, which covered the invasion of Okinawa, sustained severe damage. Japanese suicide pilots ("kamikazes"), in an exhibition of mass hara-kiri for their emperor, smashed their bomb-laden planes onto the decks of the invading fleet, sinking over thirty ships and damaging scores more.

The scientific director of the Manhattan Project, J. Robert Oppenheimer (1904–1967), recalled his reaction as he witnessed the detonation of the first atomic bomb at the Trinity test site in Alamogordo, New Mexico, in July 1945. He was not only awed by the extraordinary force of this new weapon. He also feared the power to do harm that it gave to humans:

"I remembered the line from the Hindu scripture, the *Bhagavad-Gita*: 'Now I am become Death, the destroyer of Worlds.'"

The Atomic Bombs

Strategists in Washington were meanwhile planning an all-out invasion of the main islands of Japan—an invasion that presumably would cost hundreds of thousands of American (and even more Japanese) casualties. Tokyo, recognizing imminent defeat, had secretly sent peace feelers to Moscow, which had not yet entered the East Asian war. But bomb-scorched Japan still showed no outward willingness to surrender *unconditionally* to the Allies.

The **Potsdam conference**, held near Berlin in July 1945, sounded the death knell of the Japanese. There President Truman, still new on his job, met in a seventeen-day parley with Joseph Stalin and the British leaders. The conferees issued a stern ultimatum to Japan: surrender or be destroyed. But no encouraging response was forthcoming.

Potsdam conference (1945) *Meeting from July 17 to August 2, 1945 among President Harry S. Truman, Soviet leader Joseph Stalin, and British leaders Winston Churchill and later Clement Attlee (when the Labour party defeated Churchill's Conservative party) near Berlin to deliver an ultimatum to Japan: surrender or be destroyed.*

America had a fantastic ace up its sleeve. Early in 1940, after Hitler's wanton assault on Poland, Roosevelt was persuaded by American and exiled scientists, notably German-born Albert Einstein, to push ahead with preparations for unlocking the secret of an atomic bomb. Congress, at Roosevelt's blank-check request, blindly made available nearly $2 billion.

What was called the **Manhattan Project** pushed feverishly forward, as American know-how and industrial power were combined with the most advanced scientific knowledge. Much technical skill was provided by British and refugee scientists, who had fled to America to escape the torture chambers of the dictators. Finally, in the desert near Alamogordo, New Mexico, on July 16, 1945, the experts detonated the first awesome and devastating atomic device.

Manhattan Project (1942) *Code name for the American commission established in 1942 to develop the atomic bomb. The first experimental bomb was detonated on July 16, 1945, in the desert of New Mexico. Atomic bombs were then dropped on two cities in Japan in hopes of bringing the war to an end: Hiroshima on August 6, 1945, and Nagasaki on August 9, 1945.*

With Japan still refusing to surrender, the Potsdam threat was fulfilled. On August 6, 1945, a lone American bomber dropped one atomic bomb on the city of Hiroshima, Japan. In a blinding flash of death, followed by a funnel-shaped cloud, about 180,000 people were left killed, wounded, or missing. Some 70,000 of them died instantaneously. Sixty thousand more soon perished from burns and radiation disease.

Two days later, on August 8, Stalin entered the war against Japan, exactly on the deadline date previously agreed upon with his allies. Soviet armies speedily overran the depleted Japanese defenses in Manchuria and Korea. Stalin was evidently determined to be in on the kill, lest he lose a voice in the final division of Japan's holdings.

Fanatically resisting Japanese, though facing atomization, still did not surrender. On August 9, American aviators dropped a second atomic bomb on the city of Nagasaki. The explosion took a horrible toll of about eighty thousand people killed or missing (see "Varying Viewpoints," p. 602). The Japanese nation could endure no more. On August 10, 1945, Tokyo sued for peace on one condition: that Hirohito, the bespectacled Son of Heaven, be allowed to remain on his ancestral throne as nominal emperor. Despite their "unconditional surrender" policy, the Allies accepted this condition on August 14, 1945. The official surrender ceremonies took place on the battleship *Missouri* in Tokyo Bay on September 2, 1945. At the same time, Americans at home hysterically celebrated **V-J (Victory in Japan) Day**, after the most horrible war in history had ended in mushrooming atomic clouds.

V-J (Victory in Japan) Day *August 15, 1945, marking the surrender of Japan and the final end to World War II.*

The Allies Triumphant

World War II proved to be terribly costly (see Thinking Globally). American forces suffered some 1 million casualties, more than one-third of which were deaths. Compared with other wars, the proportion killed by wounds and disease was sharply reduced, owing in part to the use of blood plasma and "miracle" drugs, notably penicillin.

Thinking Globally

America and the World in Depression and War: A Study in Contrasts

The Great Depression of the 1930s was a monstrous, planetary-scale economic hurricane that wreaked havoc around the globe. All nations were walloped by its destructive force, but two were especially hard hit: the United States and Germany. In both countries production of goods declined by nearly 50 percent, and unemployment approached 25 percent. Also, in both countries the depression discredited existing political regimes and created opportunities for new leadership to emerge. Fatefully, Germany got Adolf Hitler, while the United States got Franklin D. Roosevelt.

Roosevelt and Hitler were of the same generation, both born in the 1880s. They came to power within weeks of each other—Hitler as Germany's chancellor on January 30, 1933, and Roosevelt as U.S. president on March 4, 1933. Both achieved office through democratic elections, though democracy soon withered under one's hand and flourished under the other's.

Roosevelt's entire presidency unfolded under the looming threat, and eventually the armed challenge, of Hitler's Nazi regime. FDR's record, as well as the very character of American democracy in the mid-twentieth century, can only be properly understood in that larger context.

Consider: In the spring of 1933, Roosevelt was coaxing legislation out of the Hundred Days Congress, forging labor unions and sundry ethnic and racial minorities into a long-lasting Democratic party coalition, and making innovative use of the radio to outflank the hostile media magnates who controlled the nation's newspapers. In those same months, Hitler was dissolving German labor unions and ruthlessly censoring the German press. Soon he declared the Nazis the only legal political party in Germany and proceeded to impose on the German people a reign of terror cruelly enforced by the Gestapo, the Nazis' grimly efficient secret police.

A year later, while Roosevelt worried about a possible political challenge from the swashbuckling Louisiana Senator Huey P. Long, Hitler dispatched with his main Nazi rival, Ernst Rohm, by ordering his execution.

The following year, 1935, Roosevelt shepherded his sweeping reform program through Congress, notably including the Social Security Act, which helped to usher millions of Americans into the mainstream of American life, especially members of the great immigrant communities that had arrived a generation or so earlier. "We are going to make a country," Roosevelt said, "in which no one is left out." That same year Hitler codified the Nazis' viciously anti-Semitic policies in the notorious Nuremberg Laws, stripping German Jews of their citizenship, barring them from the professions and military service, and prohibiting marriage between Jews and "Aryans" (defined by the Nazis as a master race of non-Jewish Caucasians, especially those having Nordic features)—all gruesome steps on the road to the genocidal wartime Holocaust, which would eventually murder some 6 million Jews.

Meanwhile, Hitler was relentlessly building his war machine, while FDR's America clung stubbornly to its traditional isolationism. And when the great conflict of World War II finally erupted, Hitler's Germany and Roosevelt's America fought decidedly different wars. Indeed the United States' experience in the war stands in vivid contrast to the experience of *all* other combatants, including not only Germany but also America's allies in the "Grand Alliance."

Hitler's vaunted "thousand-year Reich" lay in smoldering ruins at war's end, his people dazed, demoralized, and starving. The strutting Führer had brewed a catastrophe so vast that its conclusion seemed to sunder the web of time itself. Germans remember the moment of their surrender on May 7, 1945, as the *Stunde null*, or "zero hour," when history's clock came to a fearful halt. Elsewhere, even America's main wartime partners, Great Britain and the Soviet Union, had paid a far greater price in blood and treasure than the United States. Uniquely among all the belligerents in World War II—perhaps uniquely in the history of warfare—the

FDR Library

Franklin Delano Roosevelt, Thirty-second President of the United States

United States had managed to grow its civilian economy even while waging a hugely costly war. In Germany, Britain, and the Soviet Union, the civilian standard of living had gone down by approximately one-third. In the United States, the civilian economy had actually expanded by 15 percent, preparing the way for phenomenal prosperity in the postwar decades.

And though 405,399 brave American service members died in World War II, proportionate to population American losses were about one-third those of Britain and about one-sixtieth those of the Soviet Union, where some 10 million soldiers and a staggering 17 million civilians perished (see Table 34.1). By glaring contrast, in the forty-eight states in 1945, the U.S. civilian death toll due to enemy action was just six persons, all of them the victims of a crude Japanese balloon-borne firebomb that exploded in their faces near the hamlet of Bly, Oregon, on May 5, 1945.

For all the misery that depression and war visited upon the United States, Americans could count their blessings that fortune had spared them the enormous deprivations and horrors that were all too common elsewhere. Yet some observers worried that America was now assuming leadership in a world where the depths of other peoples' wounds and woes could scarcely be imagined.

U.S. Army Center of Military History

German Chancellor Adolf Hitler

Table 34.1 The Comparative Costs of World War II

Country	Military Deaths	Civilian Deaths	Government Expenditures	Damage to Civilian Property
China	2,000,000	7,750,000		
France	250,000	350,000		
Poland	123,000	6,000,000		
USSR	10,000,000	17,000,000	$192 billion	$128 billion
United Kingdom	300,000	60,600	$120 billion	$5 billion
United States	405,399	6*	$317 billion	
Germany (including Austria)	3,500,000	1,600,000	$272 billion	$50–$75 billion
Italy	242,000	60,000	$94 billion	
Japan	2,000,000	650,000		

*In the forty-eight states; additional civilian deaths occurred in Hawaii, Alaska, and the Philippines.

Sources: World War II casualty estimates vary widely. The figures here are largely taken from David M. Kennedy, ed., *The Library of Congress World War II Companion*; I. C. B. Dear, ed., *The Oxford Companion to the Second World War*; Louis L. Snyder, *Historical Guide to World War II*; and John Ellis, *World War II: A Statistical Survey*.

America was fortunate in emerging with its mainland virtually unscathed. Much of the rest of the world was utterly destroyed and destitute. America alone was untouched and healthy—oiled and muscled like a prize bull, standing astride the world's ruined landscape.

This complex conflict was the best-fought war in America's history. Though unprepared for it at the outset, the nation was better prepared than for the others, partly because America had begun to buckle on its armor about a year and a half before the war officially began. In the end the United States showed itself to be resourceful, tough, adaptable—able to accommodate itself to the tactics of an enemy who was relentless and ruthless.

American military leadership proved to be of the highest order. A new crop of war heroes emerged in brilliant generals such as Eisenhower, MacArthur, and George Marshall (chief of staff) and in imaginative admirals like Nimitz. President Roosevelt and Prime Minister Churchill, as kindred spirits, collaborated closely in planning strategy. Industrial leaders were no less skilled, for marvels of production were performed almost daily. Assembly lines proved as important as battle lines, and victory went again to the side with the most smokestacks. The enemy was almost literally smothered by bayonets, bullets, bazookas, and bombs. Hitler and his Axis co-conspirators had chosen to make war with machines, and the ingenious Yankees could ask for nothing better. They demonstrated again, as they had in World War I, that the American way of war was simply more—more men, more weapons, more machines, more technology, and more money than any enemy could hope to match. From 1940 to 1945, the output of American factories was simply phenomenal.

Hermann Goering, a Nazi leader, had sneered, "The Americans can't build planes—only electric iceboxes and razor blades." Democracy had given its answer, as the dictators, despite long preparation, were overthrown and discredited. It is true that an unusual amount of direct control was exercised over the individual by the Washington authorities during the war emergency. But the American people preserved their precious liberties without serious impairment.

Varying Viewpoints

The Atomic Bombs: Were They Justified?

No episode of the World War II era has provoked sharper controversy than the atomic bombings of Japan in August 1945. Lingering moral misgivings about the nuclear incineration of Hiroshima and Nagasaki have long threatened to tarnish America's crown of military victory. Some critics have accused the United States of racist motives because the bombs were dropped on a non-white people. Other commentators believe the bombs—especially the second bomb dropped on Nagasaki—were unnecessary because the Japanese were already on the verge of collapse. Still other scholars, notably Gar Alperovitz, have charged that the atomic bombs were not the last shots of World War II but the first salvos in the emerging Cold War. Alperovitz argues that President Truman dropped the bomb not simply to defeat Japan but because he wanted to intimidate and isolate the Soviet Union.

Each of these accusations has been vigorously rebutted. Richard Rhodes's history of the making of the atomic bomb emphasizes that the Anglo-American atomic project began as a race against the Germans, who were known to be pursuing a nuclear weapons program. From the outset both British and American planners believed this ultimate weapon of destruction would deliver victory into the hands of whoever possessed it. They consequently assumed that it would be used at the earliest possible moment, and German cities could well have been the target if the European war had lasted longer.

It is true that American intelligence sources knew in the early summer of 1945 that some Japanese statesmen were trying to use the Russians' good offices to negotiate a surrender. But as R. J. C. Butow's fine-grained study of Japan's decision to surrender demonstrates, the Japanese clung to several unacceptable conditions, including no military occupation of the home islands and no international trials of alleged war criminals. All this flew squarely in the face of America's demand for nothing less than an *unconditional* surrender. As for the Nagasaki bomb (dropped on August 9), Butow notes that it conclusively dispelled the Japanese government's original assessment that the Hiroshima attack on August 6 was a one-time-only stunt.

Could the use of the atomic bombs have been avoided? Martin J. Sherwin, Barton J. Bernstein, and McGeorge Bundy have shown that few policymakers of the time seriously asked that question. In fact, the "decision" to use the bomb was not made in 1945, but in 1942, when the United States committed itself to a crash program to build—and use—a nuclear weapon as swiftly as possible. Intimidating the Soviets might have been a "bonus" to using the bomb against Japan, but influencing Soviet behavior was never the *primary* reason for the fateful decision.

Doubt and remorse about the atomic conclusion of World War II have plagued the American conscience ever since. Less often remarked on are the deaths of four times more Japanese noncombatants than died at Hiroshima and Nagasaki in the so-called conventional fire-bombing of some five dozen Japanese cities in 1945. Those deaths suggest that the deeper moral questions should perhaps not be addressed to the particular technology of nuclear weaponry, but to the quite deliberate decision, made by several combatants—including the Germans, the British, the Americans, and the Japanese themselves—to designate civilian populations as legitimate military targets.

CHAPTER SUMMARY ★★★★★★★★★★★★★

America was badly wounded but roused to national unity and determination by Pearl Harbor. Roosevelt and Churchill settled on a fundamental strategy of dealing with Hitler first, while doing just enough in the Pacific to block the Japanese advance.

With the ugly exception of the Japanese-American concentration camps, World War II proceeded in the United States without the fanaticism and violations of civil liberties that occurred in World War I. The economy was effectively mobilized, using new sources of labor such as women and Mexican *braceros*. Numerous African Americans and Indians also left their traditional rural homelands and migrated to war-industry jobs in the cities of the North and West. The war brought full employment and prosperity, as well as enduring social changes, as millions of Americans were uprooted and thrown together in the military and in new communities across the country. Unlike European and Asian nations, however, the United States experienced relatively little economic and social devastation from the war. The federal government became vastly more powerful, and touched Americans' lives in numerous new ways.

The tide of Japanese conquest was stemmed at the Battles of Midway and the Coral Sea, and American forces then began a slow strategy of "island hopping" toward Tokyo. Allied troops first invaded North Africa and Italy in 1942–1943, providing a small, compromise "second front" that attempted to appease both the desperate Soviet Union as well as the anxious British. The real second front came in June 1944 with the D-Day invasion of France. The Allies moved rapidly across France, but faced a temporary setback in the Battle of the Bulge in the Low Countries.

Meanwhile, American capture of the Marianas Islands enabled the use of ground bases for extensive bombing of the Japanese home islands. The seriously ill Roosevelt defeated Thomas Dewey and won a fourth term in 1944 just as Allied troops entered Germany. Soon after FDR's death in April 1945 American troops finally met the Russians, bringing an end to Hitler's rule in May 1945. After a last round of brutal warfare on Okinawa and Iwo Jima, the dropping of two atomic bombs ended the war against Japan in August 1945.

KEY TERMS

- ABC-1 agreement (585)
- Executive Order No. 9066 (586)
- War Production Board (WPB) (586)
- Office of Price Administration (OPA) (588)
- National War Labor Board (NWLB) (588)
- Smith-Connally Anti-Strike Act (588)
- WACs (Women's Army Corps) (588)
- WAVES (Women Accepted for Volunteer Emergency Service) (588)
- SPARs (U.S. Coast Guard Women's Reserve) (588)
- *Bracero* program (588)
- Fair Employment Practices Commission (FEPC) (589)
- Congress of Racial Equality (CORE) (589)
- code talkers (589)
- Battle of Midway (591)
- D-Day (594)
- V-E (Victory in Europe) Day (598)
- Potsdam conference (599)
- Manhattan Project (599)
- V-J (Victory in Japan) Day (599)

PEOPLE TO KNOW

- Douglas MacArthur
- Chester Nimitz
- Dwight D. "Ike" Eisenhower
- Harry S. Truman
- Albert Einstein

Part 6

MAKING MODERN AMERICA

1945 To The Present

World War II broke the back of the Great Depression in the United States and also ended the century-and-a-half-old American tradition of isolationism in foreign affairs. Alone among the warring powers, the United States managed to emerge from the great conflict physically unscarred, economically healthy, and militarily muscled up, especially with nuclear weapons. For more than two decades after 1945, Americans enjoyed an exceptional era of broadly shared prosperity at home and dominance abroad, challenged only by the Soviet Union in a protracted confrontation known as the Cold War. But setbacks both domestic and foreign began to bring that era to a close by the 1970s. At home, sustained economic growth in the postwar quarter century nourished a robust sense of national self-confidence and fed a revolution of rising expectations. The lingering ravages of World War II abroad largely insulated American industries from foreign competition, while the Cold War conflict with the Soviet Union spurred huge public investments in infrastructure, scientific research, and human capital. The result was what economists term "The Great Compression"—a generation or more of rising living standards, relative income equality, and a remarkable measure of social peace. Anything and everything seemed possible. Invigorated by the prospect of endlessly spreading affluence, Americans in the postwar years had record numbers of babies, moved by the millions to spanking-new suburbs, generously expanded the welfare state, widened opportunities for women, and even found the will to grapple at long last with the nation's grossest legacy of injustice, its treatment of African Americans. Citizens trusted their government and had faith in the American dream that their children's lives would be richer than their own.

The rising curve of expectations peaked in the 1960s, a stormy decade that saw great gains for civil rights and efforts to abolish poverty through President Lyndon Johnson's "Great Society" initiatives, but also brought turbulent social unrest driven by racial conflict, a rising generation's challenges to cultural mores, and protest against the Vietnam War. As government lost credibility, economic growth flattened in the 1970s, shrinking the horizon of hope in the future that had beckoned over the previous three decades. The seeds of America's economic predicament could be found in the very postwar international order that America had helped to build. Competition from reconstructed European and Japanese economies put new pressure on domestic industries and their unionized workers. Meanwhile, America's vexed Cold War venture in Vietnam unleashed a vicious inflationary cycle that further stressed the American economy. Americans now faced slower and more fitful economic growth, starkly rising income inequality, loss of faith in institutions from government to the media and even churches, intensifying social conflict, and a resurgence of free-market ideas and practices.

Paradoxically, this era of mounting economic inequality also saw widening social inclusion. "Second-wave feminism" enabled women to burst through the barriers that had long excluded them from traditional male domains. The long-reverberating civil rights movement brought greater acceptance in a multicultural America for African Americans and other minorities, including waves of new immigrants and, eventually, gays and lesbians.

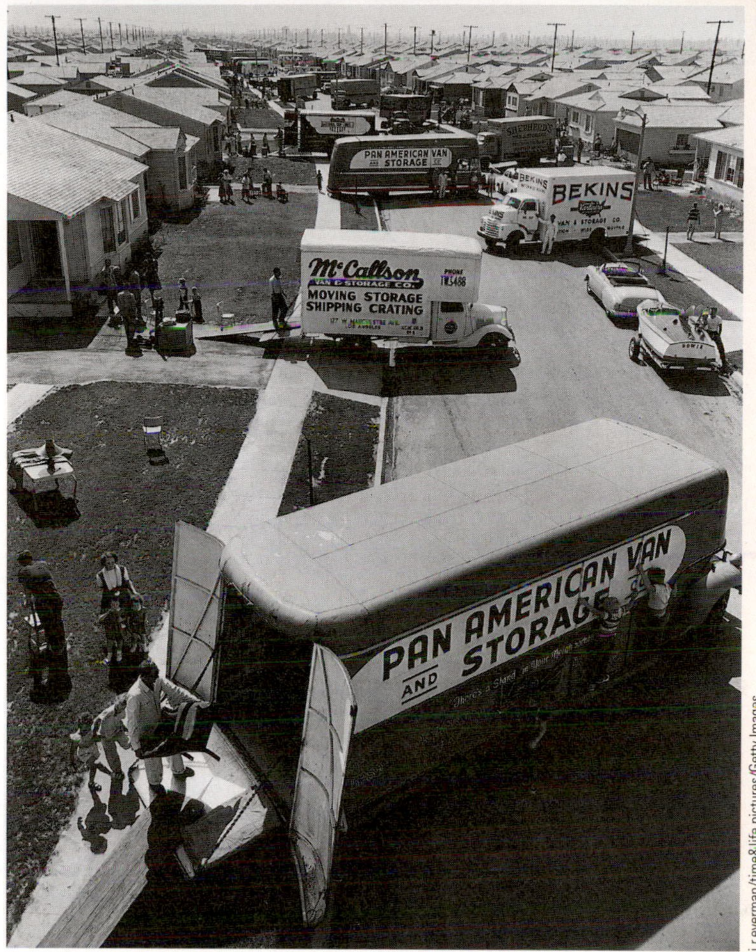

j.r.eyerman/time&life pictures/Getty Images

A Suburban Society In the phenomenally affluent post-WWII years, newly prosperous Americans flocked to new suburban housing developments. By the twentieth century's end, a majority of Americans were suburbanites.

The odd combination of deepening income disparity alongside widening social inclusion profoundly shaped American politics in the post-1970s era. A resurgent conservative movement helped secure Ronald Reagan's election to the presidency in 1980, inaugurating an epoch of cultural, ideological, and political contestation that increasingly divided the country and all but paralyzed the political system. Both Democratic and Republican presidents struggled to achieve lasting accomplishments in the face of a mistrustful public, anemic economy, and a polarized Congress.

For more than forty years after World War II, the fierce competition with the Soviet Union colored almost every aspect of America's foreign relations. When the Cold War ended with the collapse of the Soviet Union in 1991, the United States enjoyed a decade of unchallenged international supremacy. But terrorist attacks on American soil on September 11, 2001 brought the brief moment to a close, leading to wars in Iraq and Afghanistan and a new cycle of domestic conflict over national security, civil liberties, and the role of a superpower in the post-Cold War world.

The attacks of 9/11 brought Americans together for a time in grief and anger. But the "Great Recession" that walloped the American and global economy in 2008 further intensified partisan divisions and threatened to put a permanent end to dreams of ever-expanding personal opportunity and American global hegemony.

What if . . . ?

- **What if the United States had not fought the Vietnam War?**
- **Would the modern American conservative movement have risen to power over a weakened liberalism in the 1980s?**
- **Would American politics have become so sharply polarized in the 1990s and 2000s?**

Chapter 35

The Cold War Begins

1945–1952

America stands at this moment at the summit of the world.

Winston Churchill, 1945

Chapter Outline

- Harry S. Truman as President
- The Yalta Conference, February 1945
- Origins of the Cold War
- The Cold War in East Asia
- The Korean War, 1950–1953
- Anticommunism at Home
- Truman Defeats Dewey, 1948
- Postwar Prosperity
- The Rise of the "Sunbelt" and the Suburbs
- The Postwar Baby Boom
- *Makers of America: The Suburbanites*
- *Varying Viewpoints: Who Was to Blame for the Cold War?*

The American people, 140 million strong, cheered their nation's victories in Europe and Asia at the conclusion of World War II. But before the shouting had even faded, many Americans began to worry about their futures. Four fiery years of global war had not entirely driven from their minds the painful memories of twelve desperate years of the Great Depression. Still more ominously, victory celebrations had barely ended before America's crumbling relations with its wartime ally, the Soviet Union, threatened a new and even more terrible international conflict.

FOCUS QUESTIONS

1. What were the primary causes of the Cold War between the United States and the Soviet Union, and how did the confrontation with communism spread to China and Korea?
2. How did the Cold War affect domestic American society, and what were the results of the widespread fear of both Soviet spying and Communist subversion inside the United States?
3. What were the principal causes of the sustained period of postwar prosperity that began in the late 1940s?
4. How did the postwar "baby boom" and the mass migrations to the suburbs and the Sunbelt alter the character and concerns of American society?
5. How did Harry Truman successfully transform himself from a seemingly unprepared accidental president into a vigorous foreign policy leader and underdog victor in the election of 1948?

CHRONOLOGY

1944	▪ Servicemen's Readjustment Act (GI Bill) ▪ Bretton Woods economic conference
1945	▪ Spock publishes *The Common Sense Book of Baby and Child Care* ▪ Yalta conference ▪ United States ends lend-lease to USSR ▪ United Nations established
1945–1946	▪ Nuremberg war crimes trial in Germany
1946	▪ Employment Act creates Council of Economic Advisers ▪ Iran crisis ▪ Kennan develops containment doctrine
1947	▪ Truman Doctrine ▪ Marshall Plan ▪ Taft-Hartley Act ▪ National Security Act creates Department of Defense, National Security Council (NSC), and Central Intelligence Agency (CIA)
1948	▪ Israel founded; United States recognizes it ▪ Alger Hiss case begins ▪ Truman defeats Dewey for presidency
1948–1949	▪ Berlin blockade
1949	▪ NATO established ▪ Communists defeat Nationalists in China ▪ Soviets explode their first atomic bomb
1950	▪ American economy begins postwar growth ▪ McCarthy red hunt begins ▪ McCarran Internal Security Act passed by Congress over Truman's veto
1950–1953	▪ Korean War
1951	▪ Truman fires MacArthur ▪ Rosenbergs convicted of treason
1952	▪ United States explodes first hydrogen bomb
1957	▪ Postwar peak of U.S. birthrate
1973	▪ U.S. birthrate falls below replacement level

Truman: The "Gutty" Man from Missouri

Presiding over the opening of the postwar period was the "accidental president"—Harry S. Truman. Trim and owlishly bespectacled, with his graying hair and a friendly, toothy grin, Truman was called "the average man's average man." The first president in many years without a college education, he had farmed, served as an artillery officer in France during World War I, and failed as a haberdasher. He then tried his hand at precinct-level Missouri politics, through which he rose from a judgeship to the U.S. Senate. Though a protégé of a notorious political machine in Kansas City, Truman had managed to keep his own hands clean.

The problems of the postwar period were staggering, and the suddenly burdened new president at first approached his tasks with humility. But he gradually evolved from a shrinking pipsqueak into a scrappy little cuss, gaining confidence to the point of cockiness. When the Soviet foreign minister complained, "I've never been talked to like that in my life," Truman shot back, "Carry out your agreements and you won't get talked to like that."

A smallish man thrust suddenly into a giant job, Truman permitted designing old associates of the "Missouri gang" to gather around him and, like Ulysses Grant, was stubbornly loyal to them when they were caught with cream on their whiskers. On occasion he would send critics hot-tempered and profane "s.o.b." letters. Most troubling, in trying to demonstrate to a skeptical public his decisiveness and power of command, he was inclined to go off half cocked or stick mulishly to some wrongheaded notion.

But if Truman was sometimes small in the small things, he was often big in the big things. He had down-home authenticity, few pretensions, rock-solid probity, and a lot of that old-fashioned character trait called moxie. Not one to dodge responsibility, he placed a sign on his White House desk that read, "The buck stops here." Among his favorite sayings was, "If you can't stand the heat, get out of the kitchen."

Yalta: Bargain or Betrayal?

Vast and silent, the Soviet Union continued to be the great enigma. The conference in Tehran in 1943, where Roosevelt had first met Joseph Stalin man to man, had cleared the air somewhat, but much had remained unresolved—especially questions about the postwar fates of Germany, Eastern Europe, and Asia.

Yalta conference (1945) *Meeting of Franklin Roosevelt, Winston Churchill, and Joseph Stalin in February 1945 at an old tsarist resort on the Black Sea, where the Big Three leaders laid the foundations for the postwar division of power in Europe, including a divided Germany and territorial concessions to the Soviet Union.*

The **Yalta conference**, the final fateful conference of the Big Three, took place in February 1945. At this former tsarist resort on the relatively warm shores of the Black Sea, Stalin, Churchill, and the fast-failing Roosevelt reached momentous agreements after pledging their faith with vodka. Stalin agreed that Poland, with revised boundaries, should have a representative government based on free elections—a pledge he soon broke. Bulgaria and Romania were likewise to have free elections—a promise also flouted. The Big Three further announced plans for fashioning a new international peace-keeping organization, the United Nations.

The most controversial decision at Yalta concerned Moscow's entry into the war against Japan. The atomic bomb had not yet been tested, and Washington strategists expected frightful American casualties in the projected assault on Japan. Roosevelt was therefore willing to offer inducements to the Soviets to enter the Asian war and pin down Japanese troops in Manchuria and Korea. Stalin, striking a hard bargain, agreed to attack Japan within three months after the collapse of Germany. In return the Soviets were promised the southern half of Sakhalin Island, Japan's Kurile Islands, and control of key railroads and seaports in China's Manchuria. As it turned out, Moscow's muscle was not necessary to knock out Japan. Critics later charged that Roosevelt had sold Jiang Jieshi (Chiang Kai-shek) down the river and contributed powerfully to his overthrow by the Chinese communists four years later. Roosevelt's defenders countered that Stalin's mighty red army could have secured much more of China if he had wished and that the Yalta conference really set limits to his ambitions. Apologists for Roosevelt also noted that Soviet troops had already occupied much of Eastern Europe, and a war to throw them out was unthinkable.

The fact is that the Big Three at Yalta were not drafting a comprehensive peace settlement; at most they were sketching general intentions and testing one another's reactions. Later critics who howled about the broken promises overlooked that fundamental point. More specific understandings among the wartime allies—especially the two emerging superpowers, the United States and the Soviet Union—awaited the arrival of peace.

The United States and the Soviet Union

History provided little hope that the United States and the Soviet Union would reach cordial understandings about the shape of the postwar world. Mutual suspicions were ancient, abundant, and deep. Communism and capitalism were historically hostile social philosophies. The United States had refused officially to recognize the Bolshevik revolutionary government in Moscow until 1933. Soviet skepticism was nourished by American delays in opening a second front against Germany, by the abrupt termination of vital lend-lease aid in 1945, and by U.S. refusal of Moscow's plea for a $6 billion reconstruction loan—while approving a similar loan of $3.75 billion to Britain in 1946.

Different visions of the postwar world also separated the two superpowers. Stalin aimed above all to guarantee the security of the Soviet Union by establishing friendly governments along its western border, especially in Poland. By maintaining an extensive Soviet sphere of influence in Eastern and Central Europe, the USSR could protect itself and consolidate its revolutionary base as the world's leading communist country.

To many Americans, that "sphere of influence" looked like an ill-gained "empire." Doubting that Soviet goals were purely defensive, they remembered the earlier Bolshevik call for world revolution. Stalin's emphasis on "spheres" also clashed with Franklin Roosevelt's Wilsonian dream of an "open world"—decolonized, demilitarized, and democratized, with a strong international organization to oversee global peace.

Even the ways in which the United States and the Soviet Union resembled each other were troublesome. Both countries had been largely isolated from world affairs

The Communist Menace First appearing in the *New York Daily News* on January 6, 1946, this map reflected the rising anxiety in post–World War II America that the Soviet Union was an aggressively expansionist power, relentlessly gobbling up territory and imposing its will across both Europe and Asia.

before World War II. Both nations also had a history of conducting a kind of "missionary" diplomacy—of trying to export to all the world the political doctrines precipitated out of their respective revolutionary origins.

Unaccustomed to their great-power roles, America and the USSR suddenly found themselves staring eyeball-to-eyeball over the prostrate body of battered Europe. The wartime "Grand Alliance" of the United States, the Soviet Union, and Britain had been a misbegotten child of necessity. When the hated Hitler fell, suspicion and rivalry between communistic, despotic Russia and capitalistic, democratic America were all but inevitable. In a fateful progression of events, marked often by misperceptions as well as by genuine conflicts of interest, the two powers provoked each other into a tense standoff known as the **Cold War**. Enduring four and a half decades, the Cold War not only shaped Soviet-American relations; it overshadowed the entire postwar international order in every corner of the globe.

Cold War (1946–1991) *The forty-five-year-long diplomatic tension between the United States and the Soviet Union that divided much of the world into polarized camps, capitalist against communist. Most of the international conflicts during that period, particularly in the developing world, can be traced to the competition between the United States and the Soviet Union.*

Shaping the Postwar World

Despite these obstacles, the United States did manage at war's end to erect some of the structures that would support Roosevelt's vision of an open world. At the **Bretton Woods Conference** in Bretton Woods, New Hampshire in 1944, the Western Allies established the International Monetary Fund (IMF) to encourage world trade and the World Bank to promote economic growth in war-ravaged and underdeveloped areas. Three years

Bretton Woods Conference (1944) *Meeting of Western allies to establish a postwar international economic order to avoid crises like the one that spawned World War II. Led to the creation of the International Monetary Fund (IMF) and the World Bank, designed to regulate currency levels and provide aid to underdeveloped countries.*

Former British prime minister Winston Churchill (1874–1965), in a highly controversial speech at Fulton, Missouri (March 1946), warned of Soviet expansionism in language that would frame the Cold War in Europe for decades:

"From Stettin in the Baltic to Trieste in the Adriatic an iron curtain has descended across the Continent."

later, the General Agreement on Tariffs and Trade (GATT) reduced trade barriers among member nations, helping spread the economic globalization of the last half of the century. In contrast to its behavior after World War I, the United States took the lead in creating these important international bodies (see "Thinking Globally: The Era of Globalization," pp. 674–675).

Meeting in San Francisco in April 1945, representatives from fifty nations fashioned the United Nations Charter. The **United Nations (U.N.)** was a successor to the old League of Nations, but it differed from its predecessor in significant ways. The League had adopted rules denying veto power to any party in a dispute. The U.N., by contrast, more realistically provided that no member of the Security Council, dominated by the Big Five powers (the United States, Britain, the USSR, France, and China), could have action taken against it without its consent. The League, in short, presumed great-power conflict; the U.N. presumed great-power cooperation. The U.N. also featured the General Assembly, which could be controlled by smaller countries. In contrast to the U.S. rejection of the League in 1919, the Senate overwhelmingly approved the U.N. Charter on July 28, 1945, by a vote of 89 to 2.

United Nations (U.N.) *International body formed in 1945 to bring nations into dialogue in hopes of preventing further world wars. Much like the former League of Nations in ambition, the U.N. was more realistic in recognizing the authority of the Big Five powers in keeping peace in the world. Thus, it guaranteed veto power to all permanent members of its Security Council—Britain, China, France, the Soviet Union, and the United States.*

The United Nations had some gratifying initial successes. It helped preserve peace in Iran, Kashmir, and other trouble spots. It played a large role in creating the new Jewish state of Israel. The U.N. Trusteeship Council guided former colonies to independence. Through such arms as UNESCO (United Nations Educational, Scientific, and Cultural Organization), FAO (Food and Agricultural Organization), and WHO (World Health Organization), the U.N. brought benefits to peoples the world over.

But it proved far less successful in controlling the fearsome new technology of the atom. The suspicious Soviets vetoed an American proposal in 1946 for a U.N. agency to be charged with worldwide authority over atomic energy, weapons, and research. A priceless opportunity to tame the nuclear monster in its infancy was lost.

★ The Problem of Germany

Hitler's ruined Reich posed especially thorny problems for all the wartime Allies. They agreed only that the cancer of Nazism had to be cut out of the German body politic, which involved punishing Nazi leaders for war crimes. The Allies joined in trying twenty-two top culprits at the **Nuremberg war crimes trial** during 1945–1946. Accusations included committing crimes against the laws of war and humanity and plotting aggressions contrary to solemn treaty pledges. Justice, Nuremberg-style, was harsh. Twelve of the accused Nazis swung from the gallows, and seven were sentenced to long jail terms.

Nuremberg war crimes trial (1945–1946) *Highly publicized proceedings against former Nazi leaders for war crimes and crimes against humanity in postwar Germany. The trials led to several executions and long prison sentences.*

Beyond punishing the top Nazis, the Allies could agree on little about postwar Germany. Some American Hitler-haters wanted to completely dismantle all German factories, while the Soviets sought to extract enormous reparations from the Germans. Both these desires clashed headlong with the reality that an industrial, healthy German economy was indispensable to the recovery of Europe. Along with Austria, Germany had been divided at war's end into four military occupation zones, each assigned to one of the Big Four powers (France, Britain, America, and the USSR) (see Map 35.1). Before long, it was apparent that Germany would remain indefinitely divided. West Germany eventually became an independent country, wedded to the West. East Germany and the other Soviet-dominated Eastern European countries, such as Poland and Hungary, became nominally independent "satellite" states, bound to the Soviet Union. Eastern Europe virtually disappeared from Western sight behind the "iron curtain" of secrecy and isolation that Stalin clanged down across Europe from the Baltic to the Adriatic. This division of Europe would endure for more than four decades.

With Germany now split in two, there remained the problem of the rubble heap known as Berlin. Lying deep within the Soviet zone, this beleaguered isle in a red sea had been broken, like Germany as a whole, into sectors occupied by troops of each of the four

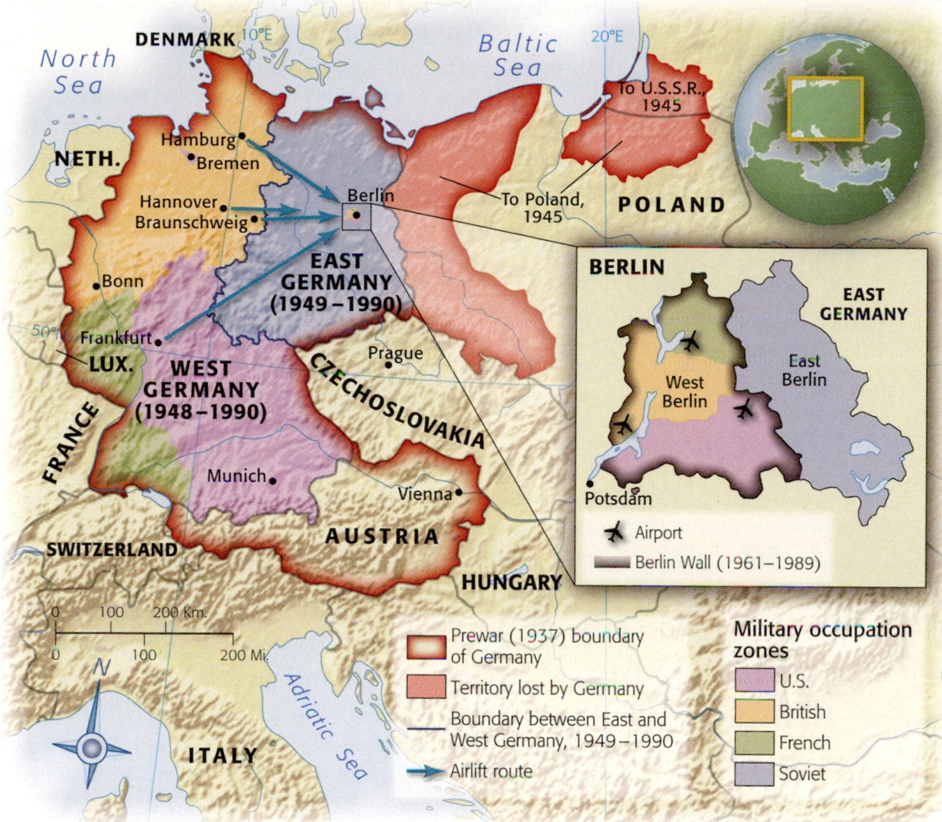

Map 35.1 Postwar Partition of Germany Germany lost much of its territory in the east to Poland and the Soviet Union. The military occupation zones were the bases for the formation of two separate countries in 1949, when the British, French, and American zones became West Germany, and the Soviet zone became East Germany. (The two Germanies were reunited in 1990.) Berlin remained under joint four-power occupation from 1945 to 1990 and became a focus and symbol of Cold War tensions.

victorious powers. In 1948 the Soviets abruptly choked off all rail and highway access to Berlin, evidently reasoning that the Allies would be starved out.

Berlin became a hugely symbolic issue as well as a test of wills for both Moscow and Washington. The Americans organized the gigantic **Berlin airlift** in the midst of hair-trigger tension. For nearly a year American pilots ferried thousands of tons of supplies to the grateful Berliners, their former enemies. The Soviets, their bluff dramatically called, finally lifted their blockade in May 1949. In the same year the governments of the two Germanys, East and West, were formally established. The Cold War had icily congealed.

Berlin airlift (1948–1949) *Year-long mission of flying food and supplies to blockaded West Berliners, whom the Soviet Union cut off from access to the West in the first major crisis of the Cold War.*

The Cold War Deepens

A crafty Stalin also probed the West's resolve at other sensitive points, including oil-rich Iran. In 1946 he broke an agreement to remove his troops from Iran's northernmost province, which the USSR had occupied during World War II. Truman sent off a stinging protest, and the Soviet dictator backed down.

Moscow's hard-line policies in Germany, Eastern Europe, and the Middle East wrought a psychological Pearl Harbor. Any remaining goodwill from the period of comradeship-in-arms evaporated in a cloud of dark distrust. "I'm tired of babying the Soviets," Truman remarked privately in 1946, as attitudes on both sides began to harden frostily.

Truman's piecemeal responses to various Soviet challenges took on intellectual coherence in 1947 with the formulation of the **containment doctrine**. Crafted by

containment doctrine *America's strategy against the Soviet Union based on ideas of George Kennan. The doctrine declared that the Soviet Union and communism were inherently expansionist and had to be stopped from spreading through both military and political pressure. Containment guided American foreign policy throughout most of the Cold War.*

Contending Voices

Debating the Cold War

In February 1946 Kremlin specialist George F. Kennan (1904–2005) sent his landmark "Long Telegram" to the State Department. In the eight-thousand-word message, Kennan assessed the Soviet threat and called for a new kind of response, which would eventually become known as the "containment doctrine."

"In summary, we have here a political force [Stalin's regime] committed fanatically to the belief that with [the] US there can be no permanent *modus vivendi*, that it is desirable and necessary that the internal harmony of our society be disrupted, our traditional way of life be destroyed, the international authority of our state be broken, if Soviet power is to be secure."

Six months later, former Vice President–turned–Secretary of Commerce Henry A. Wallace (1888–1965) wrote to President Truman to urge a more conciliatory policy. Wallace's lonely opposition to America's emerging Cold War policy would propel him into the top spot of a left-wing third-party presidential campaign in 1948.

"How do American actions since V-J Day appear to other nations? I mean by actions the concrete things like $13 billion for the War and Navy Departments, the Bikini tests of the atomic bomb, . . . and the effort to secure air bases spread over half the globe from which the other half of the globe can be bombed. . . . . How would it look to us if Russia had the bomb and we did not, if Russia had 10,000-mile bombers and air bases within a thousand miles of our coast lines and we did not?"

How inevitable was the Cold War between the United States and the Soviet Union and their respective spheres of influence?

a brilliant young diplomat and Soviet specialist, George F. Kennan, this concept held that Russia, whether tsarist or communist, was relentlessly expansionary. But the Kremlin was also cautious, Kennan argued, and the flow of Soviet power into "every nook and cranny available to it" could be stemmed by "firm and vigilant containment."

Truman embraced Kennan's advice when he formally and publicly adopted a "get-tough-with-Russia" policy in 1947. His first dramatic move was triggered by word that heavily burdened Britain could no longer bear the financial and military load of defending Greece against communist pressures. If Greece fell, Turkey would presumably collapse, and the strategic eastern Mediterranean would pass into the Soviet orbit.

In a surprise appearance before Congress on March 12, 1947, the president requested support for what came to be called the **Truman Doctrine**. Specifically, he asked for $400 million to bolster Greece and Turkey, which Congress quickly granted. More generally, he declared that "it must be the policy of the United States to support free peoples who are resisting attempted subjugation by armed minorities or outside pressures"—a sweeping and open-ended commitment of vast and worrisome proportions.

Critics then and later charged that the Truman Doctrine committed the United States to backing any tinhorn despot who claimed to be resisting "Communist aggression," needlessly polarized the world into pro-Soviet and pro-American camps, and unwisely construed the Soviet threat as primarily military in nature. Apologists for Truman have explained that it was Truman's fear of a revived isolationism that led him to exaggerate the Soviet threat and to pitch his message in the charged language of a holy global war against godless communism.

Meanwhile, a threat of a different sort loomed in Western Europe—especially France and, Italy. Still suffering from the hunger and economic chaos spawned by the war, these key nations were in grave danger of being taken over from the inside by Communist parties that could exploit these hardships. President Truman responded with a bold policy, in keeping with America's desire for a liberalized global economy. In an address at Harvard University on June 5, 1947, Secretary of State George C. Marshall invited the Europeans to work out a *joint* plan for their economic recovery. If they did so, then the United States would provide substantial financial assistance. The democratic nations of Europe enthusiastically accepted this life-giving **Marshall Plan** at a Paris conference in July 1947. Marshall offered the same aid to the Soviet Union and its allies, but nobody was surprised when the Soviets denounced the "Martial Plan" as one more capitalist trick.

Congress at first balked at the Marshall Plan's proposal for spending the mammoth sum of $12.5 billion over four years in sixteen countries. But a Soviet-sponsored communist coup in Czechoslovakia finally awakened the legislators to reality, and they voted the initial appropriations in April 1948. Truman's Marshall Plan was a spectacular success. American dollars pumped reviving blood into the economic veins of the anemic Western European nations. Within a few years, an "economic miracle" drenched Europe in prosperity. The Communist parties in Italy and France lost ground, and these two keystone countries were saved from the westward thrust of communism.

A resolute Truman made another fateful decision in 1948. Access to Middle Eastern oil was crucial to the European recovery program and, increasingly, to the health of the U.S. economy, given finite American oil reserves. Yet the Arab oil countries adamantly opposed the creation of the Jewish state of Israel in the British mandate territory of Palestine. Defying Arab wrath and his own State and Defense Departments, Truman officially recognized the state of Israel on the day of its birth, May 14, 1948. Humanitarian sympathy for the Jewish survivors of the Holocaust ranked high among his reasons, as did his wishes to preempt Soviet influence in the Jewish state and to retain the support of American Jewish voters. Truman's policy of strong support for Israel would vastly complicate U.S. relations with the Arab world in the decades ahead.

Truman Doctrine (1947) *President Truman's universal pledge of support for any people fighting any communist or communist-inspired threat. Truman presented the doctrine to Congress in 1947 in support of his request for $400 million to defend Greece and Turkey against Soviet-backed insurgencies.*

Marshall Plan (1948) *Massive transfer of aid money to help rebuild postwar Western Europe, intended to bolster capitalist and democratic governments and prevent domestic communist groups from riding poverty and misery to power. The plan was first announced by Secretary of State George Marshall at Harvard's commencement in June 1947.*

America Begins to Rearm

The Cold War—the struggle to contain Soviet communism—was not war, yet it was not peace. The standoff with the Kremlin banished the dreams of tax-fatigued Americans that tanks could be beaten into automobiles.

The Soviet menace spurred the unification of the armed services as well as the creation of a huge new national security apparatus. Congress in 1947 passed the National Security Act, creating the Department of Defense. The uniformed heads of each service were brought together as the Joint Chiefs of Staff. The National Security Act also established the National Security Council (NSC) to advise the president on security matters and the Central Intelligence Agency (CIA) to coordinate the government's foreign fact gathering. In the same year, Congress resurrected the military draft, providing for the conscription of selected young men from nineteen to twenty-five years of age. The forbidding presence of the Selective Service System shaped millions of young people's educational, marital, and career plans in the following quarter century. The Soviet threat was also forcing the democracies of Western Europe into an unforeseen degree of unity. Proposing a treaty of defensive alliance, five Western European nations invited the United States to join them. American had traditionally avoided entangling alliances, but the emerging coalition could contain the Soviet Union, reintegrate Germany into the European family, and reassure jittery Europeans that a traditionally isolationist Uncle Sam would not abandon them. On April 4, 1949, twelve nations signed the North Atlantic Treaty, which pledged the signatories to regard an attack on one as an attack on all and to respond with "armed force," if necessary. Despite last-ditch howls from immovable isolationists, the U.S. Senate approved the treaty on July 21, 1949, by a vote of 82 to 13.

The NATO pact was epochal. The formation of the **North Atlantic Treaty Organization (NATO)** marked a dramatic departure from American diplomatic convention, a gigantic boost for European unification, and a significant step in the militarization of the Cold War. NATO became the cornerstone of all Cold War American policy toward Europe. With good reason, pundits summed up NATO's threefold purpose: "to keep the Russians out, the Germans down, and the Americans in."

North Atlantic Treaty Organization (NATO) *Military alliance of Western European powers and the United States and Canada established in 1949 to defend against the common threat from the Soviet Union, marking a giant stride forward for European unity and American internationalism.*

Reconstruction and Revolution in Asia

Reconstruction in Japan was simpler than in Germany, primarily because it was largely a one-man show. Under General Douglas MacArthur, the occupying American army went inflexibly ahead with his program for the democratization of Japan, which enjoyed stunning success. The Japanese cooperated to an astonishing degree. They saw that good behavior and the adoption of democracy would speed the end of occupation—and it did. A MacArthur-dictated constitution, adopted in 1946, paved the way for a phenomenal economic recovery that within a few decades made Japan one of the world's mightiest industrial powers.

If Japan proved a postwar success story for American policymakers, the opposite was true in China, where a bitter civil war had raged for years between Nationalists and communists. Washington had halfheartedly supported the Nationalist government of

Generalissimo Jiang Jieshi in his struggle with the communists under Mao Zedong (Mao Tse-tung). But ineptitude and corruption within the generalissimo's regime eroded his people's confidence. The communist armies swept to victory late in 1949. Jiang was forced to flee with the remnants of his force to the island of Taiwan.

The collapse of Nationalist China was a depressing defeat for America and its allies in the Cold War. At one fell swoop nearly one-fourth of the world's population—some 500 million people—was swept into the communist camp. The so-called "fall of China" became a bitterly partisan issue in the United States. Seeking scapegoats, the Republicans charged that President Truman and his bristly mustached secretary of state, Dean Acheson, had "lost China." They insisted that Democratic agencies, wormy with communists, had deliberately withheld aid from Jiang Jieshi and caused his fall.

More bad news came in September 1949 when President Truman shocked the nation by announcing that the Soviets had exploded an atomic bomb—approximately three years earlier than many experts had thought possible. To outpace the Soviets in nuclear weaponry, Truman ordered the development of the "H-bomb" (hydrogen bomb)—a city-smashing thermonuclear weapon that was a thousand times more powerful than the atomic bomb. Physicists Albert Einstein and J. Robert Oppenheimer, former scientific director of the Manhattan Project and current chair of the Atomic Energy Commission, led a group of scientists in opposition to the crash program to design thermonuclear weapons.

But Einstein and Oppenheimer, the nation's two most famous scientists, could not dissuade Truman, anxious over communist threats in East Asia, from proceeding with the H-bomb. The United States exploded its first hydrogen device on a South Pacific atoll in 1952. Not to be outdone, the Soviets exploded their first H-bomb in 1953, and the nuclear arms race entered a perilously competitive cycle, spurred by massive state support for defense-related scientific research in both countries. It was only constrained by the recognition that a truly hot Cold War would leave no world for the communists to communize or the democracies to democratize. Peace through mutual terror brought a shaky stability to the superpower standoff.

The Korean Volcano Erupts

Korea, the Land of the Morning Calm, heralded a new and more ominous phase of the Cold War—a shooting phase—in June 1950. When Japan collapsed in 1945, Soviet troops had accepted the Japanese surrender north of the thirty-eighth parallel on the Korean peninsula, and American troops had done likewise south of that line. Both superpowers professed to want the reunification and independence of Korea, a Japanese colony since 1910. But, as in Germany, each helped to set up rival regimes above and below the parallel.

By 1949, when the Soviets and Americans withdrew, the entire peninsula was a bristling armed camp, with two hostile regimes eyeing each other suspiciously. The explosion came on June 25, 1950, when North Korean army columns with Soviet-made tanks rumbled across the thirty-eighth parallel. Caught flat-footed, the South Koreans were shoved back southward to a dangerously tiny defensive area around Pusan, their weary backs to the sea.

President Truman sprang quickly into the breach. The invasion seemed to provide devastating proof of a fundamental premise in the "containment doctrine" that shaped Washington's foreign policy: even a slight relaxation of America's guard was an invitation to communist aggression somewhere.

National Security Council Memorandum Number 68 (NSC-68) (1950) *National Security Council recommendation to quadruple defense spending and rapidly expand peacetime armed forces to address Cold War tensions. It reflected a new militarization of American foreign policy, but the huge costs of rearmament were not expected to interfere with what seemed like the limitless possibilities of postwar prosperity.*

The Korean invasion prompted a massive expansion of the American military. A few months before, Truman's National Security Council had issued its famous **National Security Council Memorandum Number 68 (NSC-68)**, recommending that the United States quadruple its defense spending. Ignored at first because it seemed politically impossible to implement, NSC-68 got a new lease on life from the Korean crisis. "Korea saved us," Secretary of State Acheson later commented. Truman now ordered a massive military buildup, well beyond what was necessary for Korea. Soon the United States had 3.5 million men under arms and was spending $50 billion per year on the defense budget—some 13 percent of the GNP.

NSC-68 was a key document of the Cold War period, not only because it marked a major step in the militarization of American foreign policy, but also because it vividly reflected the sense of almost limitless possibility that pervaded postwar American society. NSC-68 rested on the assumption that the enormous American economy could bear without strain the huge costs of a gigantic rearmament program.

Truman took full advantage of a temporary Soviet absence from the United Nations Security Council on June 25, 1950, to obtain a unanimous condemnation of North Korea as an aggressor. Two days later, without consulting Congress, Truman ordered American armed forces under General Douglas MacArthur to support South Korea. So began the ill-fated **Korean War**. Officially, the United States was simply participating in a United Nations "police action," but in fact the United States provided 88 percent of the U.N. contingents, and General MacArthur took his orders from Washington, not from the Security Council.

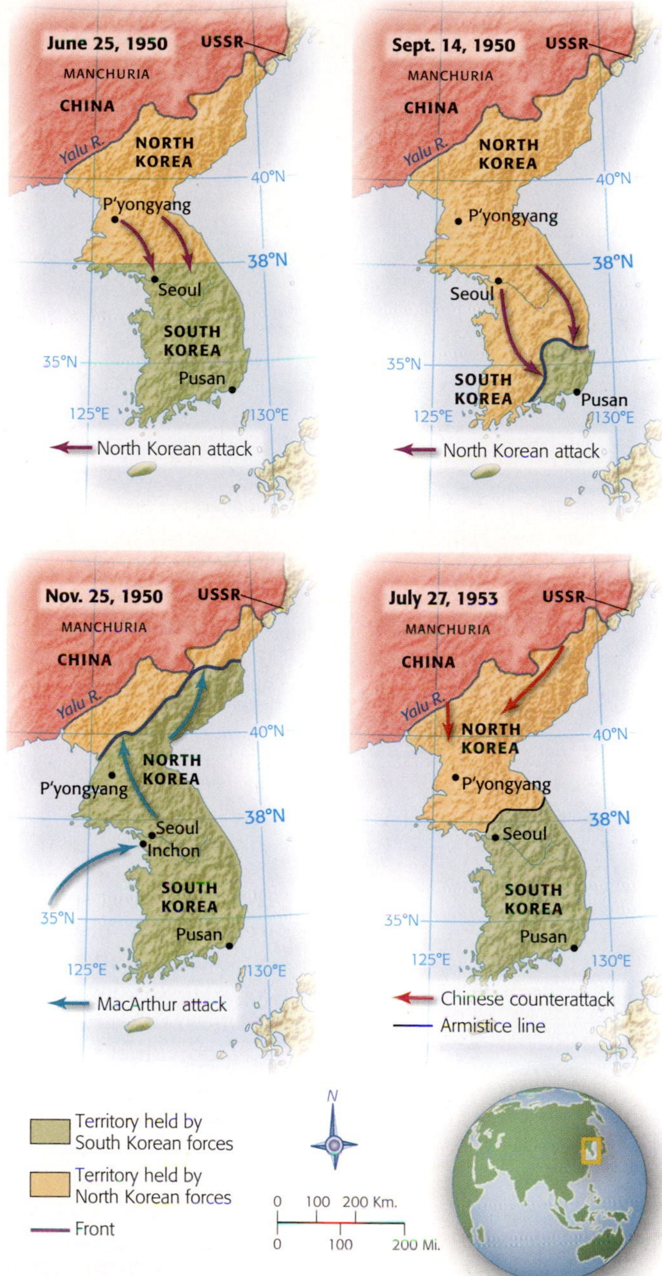

Map 35.2 The Shifting Front in Korea

The Military Seesaw in Korea

Rather than fight his way out of the southern Pusan perimeter, MacArthur launched a daring amphibious landing behind the enemy's lines at Inchon. This bold gamble on September 15, 1950, succeeded brilliantly; within two weeks the North Koreans had scrambled back behind the "sanctuary" of the thirty-eighth parallel. Truman's avowed intention was to restore South Korea to its former borders, but there seemed little point in permitting the North Koreans to regroup north of the parallel and come again. The U.N. General Assembly tacitly authorized a crossing by MacArthur, whom President Truman ordered northward, provided that there was no intervention in force by the Chinese or Soviets (see Map 35.2).

The Americans thus raised the stakes in Korea, and in so doing quickened the fears of another potential player in this dangerous game. The Chinese had publicly warned that they would not sit idly by and watch hostile troops approach the strategic Yalu River boundary between Korea and China. But MacArthur pooh-poohed all predictions of an effective intervention by the Chinese and reportedly boasted that he would "have the boys home by Christmas."

MacArthur erred badly. In November 1950 tens of thousands of Chinese fell upon his rashly overextended lines and hurled the U.N. forces reeling back down the peninsula. The fighting then sank into a frostbitten stalemate on the icy terrain near the thirty-eighth parallel.

Korean War (1950–1953) *First "hot war" of the Cold War. It began when the Soviet-backed North Koreans invaded South Korea and U.N. forces, dominated by the United States, launched a counteroffensive. The war ended in stalemate in 1953.*

An imperious MacArthur, humiliated by this rout, pressed for drastic retaliation. He favored a blockade of the China coast and bombardment of Chinese bases in Manchuria. He even suggested that the United States use nuclear weapons on the advancing Chinese. But Washington policymakers, with anxious eyes on Moscow, refused to enlarge the already costly conflict. The chairman of the Joint Chiefs of Staff declared that a wider clash in Asia would be "the wrong war, at the wrong place, at the wrong time, and with the wrong enemy." Europe, not Asia, was the administration's first concern; and the USSR, not China, loomed as the more sinister foe.

Two-fisted General MacArthur felt that he was being asked to fight with one hand tied behind his back. He sneered at the concept of a "limited war" and insisted that "there is no

Truman Takes the Heat

substitute for victory." Truman bravely resisted calls for nuclear escalation. When MacArthur began to criticize the president's policies publicly, Truman had no choice but to remove the insubordinate general from command on April 11, 1951. By July, truce discussions began near the firing line. Snagged by the issue of prisoner exchange, the talks dragged on for nearly two years while men continued to die.

Meanwhile, MacArthur, a legend in his own mind, returned to an uproarious American welcome, whereas Truman was condemned in many circles as a "pig," an "imbecile," a "Judas," and an appeaser of communism. The domestic response to the Truman-MacArthur conflict offered a hint of the depth of popular passions coursing through the Cold War at home.

The Cold War Home Front

As never before, international events deeply shaped American political and economic developments at home in the years after World War II. The solidifying Cold War with Russia fueled domestic political conflict and drew new boundaries for acceptable political opinion. Meanwhile, the postwar economic order that the United States helped to forge, combined with Cold War spending and investment, laid the foundations for a Long Boom that transformed the country over the next several decades.

A new anti-red chase accelerated within America's borders as U.S.-Soviet relations froze. Many nervous citizens feared that communist spies, paid with Moscow gold, were undermining the government and treacherously misdirecting foreign policy. In 1947 Truman launched a massive "loyalty" program. The attorney general drew up a list of ninety supposedly disloyal organizations. A Loyalty Review Board investigated more than 3 million federal employees, some 3,000 of whom either resigned or were dismissed, none under formal indictment.

Individual states likewise became intensely security-conscious. Loyalty oaths in increasing numbers were demanded of employees, especially teachers. The gnawing question for many earnest Americans was whether the nation could continue to enjoy traditional freedoms—especially freedom of speech and the right of political dissent-in a Cold War climate.

House Un-American Activities Committee (HUAC) *Investigatory body established in 1938 to root out "subversion." Sought to expose communist influence in American government and society, in particular through the case of Alger Hiss.*

In 1949 eleven communists were convicted of advocating the overthrow of the American government under the Smith Act of 1940 and sent to prison. In 1948 Congressman Richard M. Nixon, a member of the **House Un-American Activities Committee (HUAC)** and an ambitious red-catcher, led the chase after Alger Hiss, a prominent ex–New Dealer and a distinguished member of the "eastern establishment." Accused of being a communist agent in the 1930s, Hiss dramatically confronted his chief accuser before HUAC and denied everything. But Hiss was caught in embarrassing falsehoods, convicted of perjury in 1950, and sentenced to five years in prison.

The stunning success of Soviet scientists in developing an atomic bomb was attributed by many to the cleverness of communist spies in stealing American secrets. In 1951 two American citizens, Julius and Ethel Rosenberg, were convicted in a sensational trial of leaking atomic data to Moscow and eventually sent to the electric chair in 1953. Though declassified evidence has subsequently strengthened the case against the Rosenbergs, some citizens at the time believed in their innocence and began to sour on the excesses of the red-hunters.

Was America really riddled with Soviet spies? Soviet agents did infiltrate certain government agencies, and espionage may have helped the Soviets develop an atomic bomb somewhat sooner than they would have otherwise. But for many ordinary Americans, the hunt for communists was not just about fending off the military threat of the Soviet Union. Unsettling dangers lurked closer to home. While men such as Nixon and Senator Joseph

McCarthy led the search for communists in Washington, conservative politicians at the state and local levels discovered that all manner of real or perceived social changes—including declining religious sentiment, increased sexual freedom, and agitation for civil rights—could be tarred with a red brush. Anticommunist crusaders ransacked school libraries for "subversive" books and drove debtors, drinkers, and homosexuals, all alleged to be security risks, from their jobs.

Some Americans, including President Truman, realized that the red hunt was turning into a witch hunt. In 1950 Truman vetoed the McCarran Internal Security Bill, which authorized the president to arrest and detain suspicious persons during an "internal security emergency." But the congressional guardians of the Republic's liberties enacted the bill over Truman's veto.

The demagogic politics of anticommunism found its most dangerous practitioner in Joseph R. McCarthy, an obstreperous Republican senator from Wisconsin. The swaggering senator crashed into the limelight in February 1950 when he accused Secretary of State Dean Acheson of knowingly employing 205 Communist party members—though in the end he failed to identify even one. Some of McCarthy's Republican colleagues realized the partisan usefulness of this kind of attack on the Democratic administration. Ohio Senator John Bricker reportedly said, "Joe, you're a dirty s.o.b. But there are times when you've got to have an s.o.b. around, and this is one of them."

McCarthy's rhetoric grew ever bolder and his accusations wilder over the next several years. Incredibly, he even denounced General George Marshall, former army chief of staff and ex-secretary of state, as "part of a conspiracy so immense and an infamy so black as to dwarf any previous venture in the history of man."

McCarthy—and what became known as **McCarthyism**—flourished in the seething Cold War atmosphere of suspicion and fear. McCarthy was the most ruthless of the red-hunters, and did the most damage to American traditions of fair play and free speech. The careers of countless officials, writers, and actors were ruined after "Low-Blow Joe" had "named" them as communists or communist sympathizers.

McCarthyism *A brand of vitriolic, fear-mongering anticommunism associated with the career of Senator Joseph McCarthy. In the early 1950s, Senator McCarthy used his position in Congress to baselessly accuse high-ranking government officials and other Americans of conspiracy with communism. The term named after him refers to the dangerous forces of unfairness and fear wrought by anticommunist paranoia.*

At the peak of his powers McCarthy effectively controlled personnel policy at the State Department, causing severe damage to the effectiveness and morale of the professional foreign service. In particular, McCarthyite purges deprived the government of a number of Asian specialists who might have counseled a wiser course in Vietnam in the fateful decade that followed.

McCarthy finally bent the bow too far when he attacked the U.S. Army. Up to 20 million Americans watched the televised **Army-McCarthy hearings** in fascination as a boorish, surly McCarthy publicly cut his own throat by parading his essential meanness and irresponsibility. A few months later the Senate formally condemned him, and he died three years later of chronic alcoholism. But "McCarthyism" has passed into the English language as a label for dangerous forces of unfairness and fear.

Army-McCarthy hearings (1954) *Congressional hearings called by Senator Joseph McCarthy to accuse members of the army of communist ties. In this widely televised spectacle, McCarthy finally went too far for public approval. The hearings exposed the senator's extremism and led to his eventual disgrace.*

Beyond fights over security and civil liberties, the Cold War shaped American culture in complex and profound ways. Many Americans interpreted the conflict between the West and the communist East in religious terms. They received support from theologians like the influential liberal Protestant clergyman Reinhold Niebuhr (1892–1971). A vocal enemy of fascism, communism, *and* pacifism in the 1940s and 1950s, Niebuhr divided the world into two polarized camps, the "children of light" and the "children of darkness." For Niebuhr, Christian justice required a "realist" response, including force if necessary, to "children of darkness" like Hitler and Stalin. But Niebuhr's realism also emphasized the dangers of fallibility and the limits of power, in contrast to the crusading spirit of conservative Christian anticommunists. The postwar decades saw an emphasis on religious belief as a distinguishing feature of the "American Way" against atheistic communism. Congress's insertion of the words "under God" into the Pledge of Allegiance in 1954 epitomized this Cold War impulse.

The Cold War influenced domestic politics and society in still other ways. Forceful advocates for racial justice and civil rights in unions, universities, and churches were often slandered as communists and fellow travelers. But at the same time competition with the Soviets for international support placed pressure on the United States to live up to its own stated democratic ideals. An example of the new international politics of civil rights came in 1948, when President Truman issued his landmark **Executive Order 9981** desegregating the armed forces.

Executive Order 9981 (1948) *Order issued by President Truman to desegregate the armed forces. The president's action resulted from a combination of pressure from civil rights advocates, election-year political calculations, and the new geopolitical context of the Cold War.*

Postwar Economic Anxieties

The communist menace was not the only specter haunting Americans after World War II. The decade of the 1930s had left deep scars. Joblessness and insecurity had pushed up the suicide rate and dampened the marriage rate. Babies went unborn as pinched budgets and sagging self-esteem wrought a sexual depression in American bedrooms. The war had banished the blight of depression, but grim-faced observers warned that peace would bring the return of hard times.

The faltering economy in the initial postwar years threatened to confirm the worst predictions of the doomsayers who foresaw another Great Depression. Real gross national product (GNP) slumped sickeningly in 1946 and 1947 from its wartime peak. With the removal of wartime price controls, prices giddily levitated by 33 percent in 1946–1947. An epidemic of strikes swept the country. During 1946 alone some 4.6 million laborers laid down their tools, fearful that soon they would barely be able to afford the autos and other consumer goods their war-commandeered factories would soon manufacture.

The growing muscle of organized labor deeply annoyed many conservatives. They had their revenge against labor's New Deal gains in 1947, when a Republican-controlled Congress (the first in fourteen years) passed the **Taft-Hartley Act** over President Truman's vigorous veto. Labor leaders condemned the Taft-Hartley Act as a "slave-labor law." It outlawed the "closed" (all-union) shop, made unions liable for damages resulting from jurisdictional disputes, and required union leaders to take a noncommunist oath.

Taft-Hartley Act (1947) *Republican-promoted, antiunion legislation passed over President Truman's vigorous veto that weakened many of labor's New Deal gains by banning the closed shop and other strategies that helped unions organize. It also required union leaders to take a noncommunist oath, which purged the union movement of many of its most committed and active organizers.*

Taft-Hartley was one of several obstacles that slowed the growth of organized labor in the years after World War II. The unions' efforts to spread the triumph of their New Deal success in the North to historically antiunion regions of the South and West proved frustrating. The CIO's **Operation Dixie**, aimed at unionizing southern textile workers and steelworkers in 1948, failed miserably, partly due to white workers' fears of racial mixing. Organized labor continued to play a significant role in shaping the American social and economic order for several decades after World War II, but private-sector union membership peaked in the 1950s and then began a long, slow decline.

Operation Dixie (1948) *Failed effort by the CIO after World War II to unionize southern workers, especially in textile factories.*

The Democratic administration meanwhile took steps of its own to forestall an economic downturn. It sold war factories and other government installations to private businesses at fire-sale prices. It secured passage of the **Employment Act of 1946**, which created a three-member Council of Economic Advisers to advise the president on government policy and to "promote maximum employment, production, and purchasing power."

Employment Act of 1946 *Legislation declaring that the government's economic policy should aim to promote maximum employment, production, and purchasing power, as well as to keep inflation low. This general commitment was much shorter on specific targets and rules than its liberal creators had wished. The act created the Council of Economic Advisers to provide the president with data and recommendations to make economic policy.*

Most dramatic was the passage of the Servicemen's Readjustment Act of 1944—better known as the GI Bill of Rights, or the **GI Bill**. Enacted partly out of fear that the employment markets would never be able to absorb 15 million returning veterans at war's end, the GI Bill made generous provisions for sending the former soldiers to school. In the postwar decade, some 8 million veterans advanced their educations at Uncle Sam's expense. The majority attended technical and vocational schools, but colleges and universities were crowded to the blackboards as more than 2 million ex-GIs stormed the halls of higher learning. The total eventually spent for education was some $14.5 billion in taxpayer dollars. The act also enabled the Veterans Administration (VA) to guarantee about $16 billion in loans for veterans to buy homes, farms, and small businesses. By raising educational levels and stimulating the construction industry, the GI Bill powerfully nurtured the robust and long-lived economic expansion that eventually took hold in the late 1940s and that profoundly shaped the postwar era.

GI Bill (1944) *Known officially as the Servicemen's Readjustment Act and more informally as the GI Bill of Rights, this law helped returning World War II soldiers reintegrate into civilian life by securing loans to buy homes and farms and set up small businesses. It also made tuition and stipends available for them to attend college, as well as job training programs. The act was intended to cushion the blow of 15 million returning servicemen on the employment market and to nurture the postwar economy.*

Democratic Divisions in 1948

Attacking high prices and "High-Tax Harry" Truman, the Republicans had won control of Congress in the congressional elections of 1946. Their prospects had seldom looked rosier as they gathered in Philadelphia to choose their 1948 presidential candidate. They noisily renominated New York governor Thomas E. Dewey, still as debonair as if he had stepped out of a bandbox.

Also gathering in Philadelphia, Democratic politicos looked without enthusiasm on their hand-me-down president and sang "I'm Just Mild About Harry." But a "dump

Bettmann/CORBIS

Going to College on the GI Bill Financed by the federal government, thousands of World War II veterans crowded into college classrooms in the late 1940s. Universities struggled to house these older students, many of whom already had families. Pennsylvania State College resorted to setting up hundreds of trailers.

Truman" movement collapsed when war hero Dwight D. Eisenhower refused to be drafted. The peppery president, unwanted but undaunted, was then chosen in the face of vehement opposition by southern delegates, alienated by his strong stand in favor of civil rights for blacks, especially his desegreation of the military.

Truman's nomination split the party wide open. Embittered southern Democrats from thirteen states, like their fire-eating forebears of 1860, met in their own convention in Birmingham, Alabama, with Confederate flags brashly in evidence. Amid scenes of heated defiance, these "Dixiecrats" nominated Governor J. Strom Thurmond of South Carolina on a States' Rights party ticket.

To add to the confusion within Democratic ranks, former vice president Henry A. Wallace threw his hat into the ring. Having parted company with the administration over its get-tough-with-Russia policy, he was nominated by the new Progressive party—a bizarre collection of disgruntled former New Dealers, starry-eyed pacifists, well-meaning liberals, and communist-fronters.

Wallace, a vigorous if misguided liberal, assailed Uncle Sam's "dollar imperialism" from the stump. This so-called Pied Piper of the Politburo took a Soviet-friendly line that earned him drenchings with rotten eggs in hostile cities. But to his supporters, Wallace raised the only hopeful voice in the deepening gloom of the Cold War.

With the Democrats ruptured three ways and the Republican congressional victory of 1946 just past, Dewey's victory seemed assured. Cold, smug, and overconfident, Dewey confined himself to dispensing soothing-syrup trivialities like "Our future lies before us."

The seemingly doomed Truman, with little money and few active supporters, had to rely on his "gut-fighter" instincts and folksy personality. Traveling the country by train to deliver some three hundred "give 'em hell" speeches, he lashed out at the Taft-Hartley "slave labor" law and the "do-nothing" Republican Congress while whipping up

In his inaugural address, January 1949, President Harry S. Truman (1884–1972) said:

"Communism is based on the belief that man is so weak and inadequate that he is unable to govern himself, and therefore requires the rule of strong masters. . . . Democracy is based on the conviction that man has the moral and intellectual capacity, as well as the inalienable right, to govern himself with reason and justice."

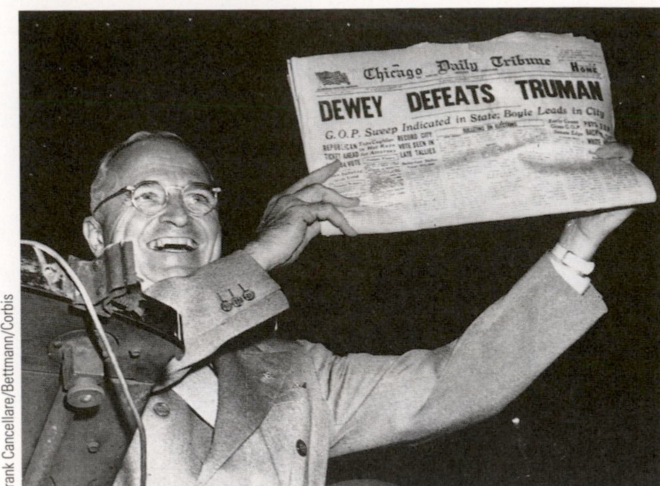

Frank Cancellare/Bettmann/Corbis

That Ain't the Way I Heard It! Truman wins.

support for his program of civil rights, improved labor benefits, and health insurance. "Pour it on 'em, Harry!" cried increasingly large and enthusiastic crowds as the pugnacious president rained a barrage of verbal uppercuts on his opponent.

On election night the *Chicago Tribune* ran off an early edition with the headline "DEWEY DEFEATS TRUMAN." But in the morning it turned out that "President" Dewey had embarrassingly snatched defeat from the jaws of victory. Truman had swept to a stunning triumph, to the complete bewilderment of politicians, pollsters, prophets, and pundits. Even though Thurmond took away 39 electoral votes in the South, Truman won 303 electoral votes, primarily from the South, Midwest, and West, besting Dewey's largely Eastern-based total of 189. To make the victory sweeter, the Democrats regained control of Congress as well, thanks especially to support from Republican-wary farmers, workers, and African Americans.

Smiling and self-assured, Truman sounded a clarion note in the fourth point of his inaugural address, known thereafter as "Point Four." The plan was to lend U.S. money and technical aid to underdeveloped lands to help them help themselves. This farseeing program was officially launched in 1950, and it brought badly needed assistance to impoverished countries, notably in Latin America, Africa, the Middle East, and Asia.

Fair Deal *President Truman's extensive social program introduced in his 1949 message to Congress. Republicans and southern Democrats kept much of his vision from being enacted, except for raising the minimum wage, providing for more public housing, and extending old-age insurance to many more beneficiaries under the Social Security Act.*

At home Truman outlined a sweeping **Fair Deal** program in his 1949 message to Congress. The program called for improved housing, full employment, a higher minimum wage, better farm price supports, new TVAs, and an extension of Social Security. But most of the Fair Deal fell victim to congressional opposition from Republicans and southern Democrats. The only major successes came in raising the minimum wage, providing for public housing in the Housing Act of 1949, and extending old-age insurance to many more beneficiaries in the Social Security Act of 1950. Short-term legislative obstacles to reform, however, paled against the seismic shifts in the domestic economy that brought substantial improvements to many Americans' lives.

The Long Economic Boom, 1950–1970

Gross national product began to climb haltingly in 1948. Then, beginning about 1950, the American economy surged onto a dazzling plateau of sustained growth that was to last virtually uninterrupted for two decades. America's economic performance became the envy of the world. National income nearly doubled in the 1950s and almost doubled again in the 1960s, shooting through the trillion-dollar mark in 1973. Americans, some 6 percent of the world's people, were enjoying about 40 percent of the planet's wealth.

Nothing loomed larger in the history of the post–World War II era than this fantastic eruption of affluence. It did not enrich all Americans, and it did not touch all people evenly, but it transformed the lives of a majority of citizens and molded the agenda of politics and society for at least two generations. Prosperity underwrote social mobility, paved the way for the civil rights movement, funded vast new welfare programs like Medicare, and gave Americans the confidence to exercise unprecedented international leadership in the Cold War era.

As the gusher of prosperity poured forth its riches, Americans drank deeply from the gilded goblet. Millions of depression-pinched souls sought to make up for the sufferings of the 1930s. They determined to "get theirs" while the getting was good. A people who had once considered a chicken in every pot the standard of comfort and security now hungered for two cars in every garage, swimming pools in their backyards, vacation homes, and gas-guzzling recreational vehicles. The size of the "middle class," defined as households earning between $3,000 and $10,000 a year, doubled from pre–Great Depression days and included 60 percent of the American people by the mid-1950s. By the end of that decade, the vast majority of American families owned their own cars and washing machines, and nearly 90 percent owned a television set. In another revolution of sweeping consequences, almost 60 percent of American families owned their own homes by 1960, compared with less than 40 percent in the 1920s.

Of all the beneficiaries of postwar prosperity, none reaped greater rewards than women. More than ever, urban offices and shops provided a bonanza of employment for female workers, as the service sector of the economy dramatically outgrew the old industrial and manufacturing sectors. Women accounted for a quarter of the American work force at the end of World War II and for nearly half the labor pool five decades later. Yet even as women continued their march into the workplace in the 1940s and 1950s, popular culture glorified the traditional feminine roles of homemaker and mother. The clash between the demands of suburban housewifery and the realities of employment eventually sparked a feminist revolt in the 1960s.

What propelled this unprecedented economic explosion? The Second World War itself provided a powerful stimulus. While other countries had been ravaged by years of fighting, the United States had used the war crisis to fire up its smokeless factories and rebuild its depression-plagued economy. America had almost effortlessly come to dominate the ruined global landscape of the postwar period.

Ominously, much of the glittering prosperity of the 1950s and 1960s rested on the underpinnings of colossal military budgets, leading some critics to speak of a "permanent war economy." The economic upturn of 1950 was fueled by massive appropriations for the Korean War, and defense spending accounted for some 10 percent of the GNP throughout the ensuing decade. Pentagon dollars primed the pumps of high-technology industries such as aerospace, plastics, and electronics and also financed much of the scientific research and development ("R and D") that spurred the economy.

Cheap energy also fed the economic boom. Americans doubled their consumption of inexpensive and seemingly inexhaustible oil from the Middle East and elsewhere in the quarter century after the war. Anticipating a limitless future of low-cost fuels, they flung out endless ribbons of highways, installed air conditioning in their homes, and engineered a sixfold increase in the country's electricity-generating capacity between 1945 and 1970.

With the forces of nature increasingly harnessed in their hands, workers chalked up spectacular gains in productivity. In the two decades after the outbreak of the Korean War in 1950, productivity increased at an average rate of more than 3 percent per year. Gains in productivity were also enhanced by the rising educational level of the work force. By 1970 nearly 90 percent of the school-age population were enrolled in educational institutions. Better educated and better equipped, American workers in 1970 could produce nearly twice as much in an hour's labor as they had in 1950. Productivity was the key to prosperity. Rising productivity in the 1950s and 1960s virtually doubled the average American's standard of living in the postwar quarter century.

Also contributing to the vigor of the postwar economy was the accelerating shift of the workforce out of agriculture into industry. Agriculture achieved spectacular gains in productivity, thanks largely to mechanization and rich new fertilizers. Giant agribusinesses replaced the family farm, and farmers whose forebears had busted sod with horses now plowed their fields in air-conditioned cabs. Still some 15 percent of the labor force at the end of World War II, farmers made up a slim 2 percent of working Americans by the turn of the twenty-first century—yet they fed much of the world.

The Smiling Sunbelt

The convulsive economic changes of the post-1945 period shook and shifted the American people, amplifying the population redistribution set in motion by World War II. As immigrants and westward-trekking pioneers, Americans had always been a people on the move, but they were astonishingly footloose in the postwar years. For some three decades after 1945, an average of 30 million persons changed residences every year. Families especially felt the strain, as distance divided parents from children, and brothers and sisters from one another. One sign of this sort of stress was the phenomenal popularity of advice books on child rearing, especially Dr. Benjamin Spock's *The Common Sense Book of Baby and Child Care*. First published in 1945, the book instructed millions of parents during the

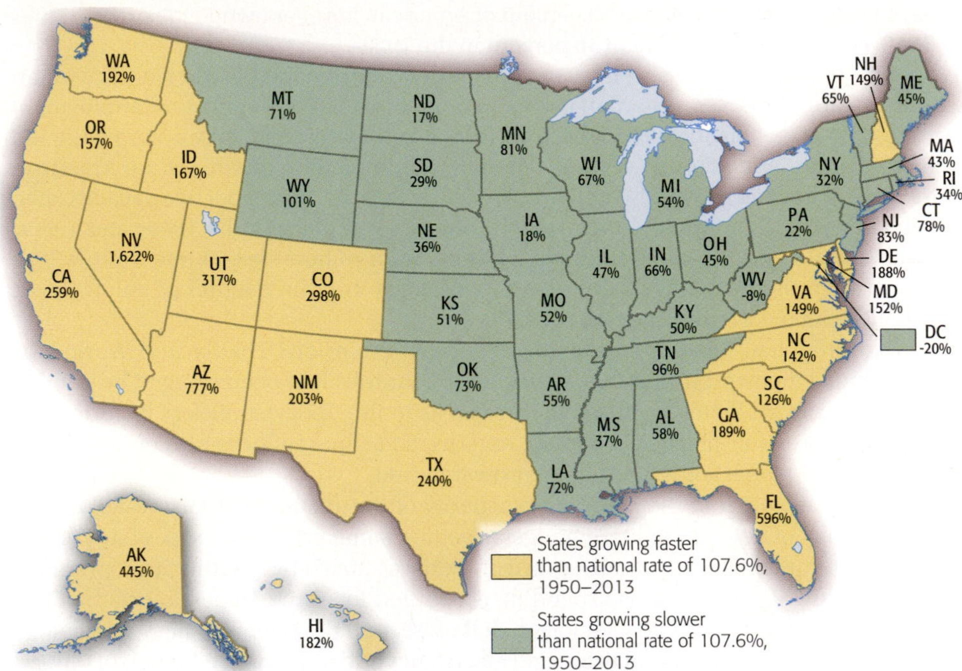

Map 35.3 Distribution of Population Increase, 1950–2013 States with figures higher than 106.7 percent were growing faster than the national average between 1950 and 2013. Note that much of the growth was in the "Sunbelt," a loose geographical concept, as some Deep South states had very little population growth, whereas the mountain and Pacific states were booming.

ensuing decades in the kind of homely wisdom that was once transmitted naturally from grandparent to parent, and from parent to child.

Sunbelt *The fifteen-state crescent through the American South and Southwest that experienced terrific population and productivity expansion during World War II and particularly in the decades after the war, eclipsing the old industrial Northeast (the "Frostbelt").*

Especially striking was the growth of the **Sunbelt**—a fifteen-state area stretching in a smiling crescent from Virginia through Florida and Texas to Arizona and California. This region increased its population at a rate nearly double that of the old industrial zones of the Northeast (the "Frostbelt"). In the 1950s California alone accounted for one-fifth of the entire nation's population growth and by 1963 had outdistanced New York as the most populous state—a position it still holds in the early years of the twenty-first century, with more than 38 million people, or more than one out of every eight Americans.

A Niagara of federal dollars accounted for much of the Sunbelt's prosperity, though, ironically, southern and western politicians led the cry against government spending. By the early twenty-first century, states in the South and West were annually receiving some $444 billion more in federal funds than those in the Northeast and Midwest. Northeasterners and their allies from the hard-hit region of the Ohio Valley tried to rally political support with the sarcastic slogan "The North shall rise again."

These dramatic shifts of population and wealth further broke the historic grip of the North on the nation's political life. Every elected occupant of the White House from 1964 to 2008 hailed from the Sunbelt, and the region's congressional representation rose as its population grew.

The Rush to the Suburbs

In all regions, America's modern migrants—if they were white—fled from the cities to the burgeoning new suburbs (see "Makers of America: The Suburbanites," p. 623). While other industrial countries struggled to rebuild their war-ravaged cities, government policies in the United States encouraged movement away from urban centers. Federal

The Suburbanites

Few images evoke more vividly the prosperity of the postwar era than aerial photographs of sprawling suburbs. Neat rows of look-alike tract houses, each with driveway and lawn and here and there a backyard swimming pool, came to symbolize the capacity of the economy to deliver the "American dream" to millions of families.

Suburbanization was hardly new. Well-off city dwellers had beaten paths to leafy outlying neighborhoods since the nineteenth century. But after 1945 the steady flow became a stampede. The baby boom, new highways, government guarantees for mortgage lending, and favorable tax policies all made suburbia blossom.

Who were the Americans racing to the new postwar suburbs? War veterans led the way in the immediate postwar years, aided by low-interest Veterans Administration mortgages. People of all kinds followed, heading for neighborhoods that varied from the posh to the plain. Yet the overwhelming majority of suburbanites were white and middle class. In 1967 sociologist Herbert Gans published *The Levittowners*, based on his own move to a Levitt-built community outside Philadelphia. He described suburban families in tract developments as predominantly third- or fourth-generation Americans with some college education and at least two children. Men tended to work in either white-collar jobs or upper-level blue-collar positions. Women usually worked in the home, so much so that suburbia came to symbolize domestic confinement for feminists of the 1960s and 1970s.

The house itself became more important than ever as postwar suburbanites built their leisure lives around television, home improvement projects, and barbecues on the patio. The center of family life shifted to the fenced-in backyard, and institutions that had thrived as social centers in the city—churches, women's clubs, fraternal organizations, taverns—had a tougher time attracting patrons in the privatized world of postwar surburbia.

Life in the suburbs was a boon to the automobile, as parents jumped behind the wheel to shuttle children, groceries, and golf clubs to and fro. Drive-thru restaurants and drive-in movies sprang up, and roadside shopping centers edged out downtowns as places to shop. Meanwhile, the new interstate highway system enabled breadwinners to live farther from their jobs and still commute to work daily.

Many suburbanites continued to depend on cities for jobs, though by the 1980s the suburbs themselves became important sites of employment. Wherever they worked, suburbanites turned their backs on the city and its problems. They fought to maintain their independent municipalities as secluded retreats, with their own taxes, schools, and zoning restrictions designed to keep out public housing and the poor. Even the naming of towns reflected the pastoral ideal. East Paterson, New Jersey, was renamed Elmwood Park in 1973. With a majority of Americans living in suburbs by the 1980s, cities lost their political clout. Bereft of state and federal aid, cities festered with worsening social problems: poverty, drug addiction, and crime.

Middle-class African Americans began to move to the suburbs in substantial numbers by the 1980s, but even that migration failed to alter dramatically the racial divide of metropolitan America. Black suburbanites settled in black middle-class suburbs within white-majority counties. By the beginning of the twenty-first century, suburbia as a whole was more racially diverse than at midcentury. But the old patterns of residential segregation endured, and economic inequality increasingly separated older and poorer "inner-ring" suburbs from new more middle-class ones.

Alfred Eisenstaedt/Time Life Pictures/Getty Images

Drive-in Café in Los Angeles, the Mother and Model of All Suburbias

Housing Authority (FHA) and Veterans Administration (VA) home-loan guarantees made it more economically attractive to own a home in the suburbs than to rent an apartment in the city. Tax deductions for interest payments on home mortgages provided additional financial incentive. And government-built highways that sped commuters from suburban homes to city jobs further facilitated this mass migration. By 1960 one in every four Americans dwelt in suburbia, and a half-century later, more than half the nation's population did.

Levittown *Suburban communities with mass-produced tract houses built in the New York and Philadelphia metropolitan areas in the 1950s by William Levitt and Sons. Typically inhabited by white middle-class people who fled the cities in search of homes to buy for their growing families.*

The construction industry boomed in the 1950s and 1960s to satisfy this demand. Pioneered by innovators such as the Levitt brothers, whose first **Levittown** sprouted on New York's Long Island in the 1940s, builders revolutionized the techniques of mass-produced housing construction. Snooty critics wailed about the aesthetic monotony of the suburban "tract" developments, but eager homebuyers nevertheless moved into them by the millions.

"White flight" to the leafy green suburbs left the inner cities—especially in the Northeast and Midwest—black, brown, and broke. Migrating blacks from the South filled up the urban neighborhoods abandoned by the departing white middle class (see "Makers of America: The Great African American Migration," p. 633). Taxpaying businesses fled with their affluent customers from downtown shops to suburban shopping malls.

Government policies sometimes aggravated this spreading pattern of residential segregation. FHA administrators often refused home mortgage loans to blacks and "other unharmonious racial or nationality groups," thus limiting black mobility out of the inner cities. Even public housing programs frequently built housing for blacks in neighborhoods that were already predominantly black—thus solidifying racial separation. Government-supported residential discrimination not only worsened segregation, but also fed the long-term "wealth gap" between whites and blacks, since most Americans' wealth consists primarily of the value of their home.

The Postwar Baby Boom

baby boom (1946–1964) *Demographic explosion from births to returning soldiers and others who had put off starting families during the war. This large generation of new Americans forced the expansion of many institutions such as schools and universities.*

Alongside its economic boom, America experienced an equally dramatic **baby boom**—the huge leap in the birthrate in the decade and a half after 1945. Confident young men and women tied the nuptial knot in record numbers at war's end, and they began immediately to fill the nation's empty cradles. They thus touched off a demographic explosion that added more than 50 million bawling babies to the nation's population by the end of the 1950s. The soaring birthrate finally crested in 1957 and was followed by a deepening birth dearth. By 1973 fertility rates had dropped below the point necessary to maintain existing population figures without further immigration.

This boom-or-bust cycle of births begat a bulging wave along the American population curve. As the oversize postwar generation grew to maturity, it was destined—like the fabled pig passing through the python—to strain and distort many aspects of American life. Elementary-school enrollments, for example, swelled to nearly 34 million pupils in 1970. Then began a steady decline, as the onward-marching age group left in its wake closed schools and unemployed teachers.

The maturing babies of the postwar boom sent economic shock waves undulating through the decades. The baby boomers created lucrative markets for toys and baby food in the 1940s and 1950s and for clothes and recorded rock music in the 1960s. In the 1980s the hordes of baby boomers bumped and jostled one another in the job market, struggling to get a foothold on the crowded ladder of social mobility. As the boomers entered middle age, a "secondary boom" of children peaked in the early 1990s—a faint demographic echo of the postwar population explosion. The impact of the huge postwar generation will continue to ripple through American society well into the twenty-first century, as members pass into retirement and place enormous strains on the Social Security and Medicare systems.

Who Was to Blame for the Cold War?

Whose fault was the Cold War? (And, for that matter, who should get credit for ending it?) For two decades after World War II, American historians generally agreed that the aggressive Soviets were solely responsible. This "orthodox" or "official" appraisal squared with the traditional view of the United States as a virtuous, innocent land with an idealistic foreign policy. This point of view also justified America's Cold War containment policy, which cast the Soviet Union as an aggressor that must be confined by an ever-vigilant United States. America supposedly had only defensive intentions, with no expansionary ambitions of its own.

In the 1960s a vigorous revisionist interpretation flowered, powerfully influenced by disillusion over U.S. involvement in Vietnam. The revisionists stood the orthodox view on its head. The Soviets, they argued, had only defensive intentions at the end of World War II; it was the Americans who behaved provocatively by brandishing their new atomic weaponry. Some of these critics pointed an accusing finger at President Truman, alleging that he abandoned Roosevelt's conciliatory approach to the Soviets and adopted a bullying attitude, emboldened by the American atomic monopoly.

More radical revisionists such as Gabriel and Joyce Kolko even claimed to have found the roots of Truman's alleged belligerence in long-standing American policies of economic imperialism—policies that eventually resulted in the tragedy of Vietnam. In this view the Vietnam War followed logically from America's insatiable "need" for overseas markets and raw materials. Vietnam itself may have been economically unimportant, but revisionists believed that losing in Vietnam would have undermined American hegemony and eventually unraveled the American economy.

In the 1970s a "postrevisionist" interpretation emerged that is widely agreed upon today. Historians such as John Lewis Gaddis and Melvyn Leffler pooh-pooh the economic determinism of the revisionists, while frankly acknowledging that the United States did have vital security interests at stake in the post–World War II era. The postrevisionists analyze the ways in which inherited ideas (such as isolationism) and the contentious nature of post–World War II domestic politics, as well as miscalculations by American leaders, led a nation in search of security into seeking not simply a sufficiency but a "preponderance" of power. The American *overreaction* to its security needs, these scholars suggest, exacerbated U.S.-Soviet relations and precipitated the four-decade-long nuclear arms race that formed the centerpiece of the Cold War.

In the case of Vietnam, the postrevisionist historians focus not on economic necessity but on a failure of political intelligence, induced by the stressful conditions of the Cold War, that made the dubious domino theory—the belief that failure in Vietnam would cause other nations to tumble like dominoes into the Soviet camp—seem plausible. Misunderstanding Vietnamese intentions, exaggerating Soviet ambitions, and fearing to appear "soft on communism" in the eyes of their domestic political rivals, American leaders plunged into Vietnam, sadly misguided by their own Cold War obsessions.

Most postrevisionists, however, still lay the lion's share of the blame for the Cold War on the Soviet Union. By the same token, they credit the Soviets with ending the Cold War—a view hotly disputed by Ronald Reagan's champions, who claim it was his anti-Soviet policies in the 1980s that brought the Russians to their knees (see p. 690). The great unknown, of course, is the precise nature of Soviet thinking in the Cold War years. Were Soviet aims predominantly defensive, or did the Kremlin incessantly plot world conquest? Was there an opportunity for reconciliation with the West following Stalin's death in 1953? Should Mikhail Gorbachev or Ronald Reagan be remembered as the leader who ended the Cold War? With the opening of Soviet archives, scholars are eagerly pursuing answers to such questions.

CHAPTER SUMMARY ★ ★ ★ ★ ★ ★ ★ ★ ★ ★ ★ ★ ★

With the death of Franklin Roosevelt as World War II came to a close, Harry S. Truman was suddenly launched into the presidency. Regarded at first as a weak and fumbling figure, Truman evolved into a courageous statesman who boldly addressed unprecedented international and domestic challenges. The Yalta agreement near the end of World War II left major issues undecided and created growing controversy over postwar relations with the Soviet Union. The two new ideologically incompatible superpowers soon found themselves at odds over Eastern Europe, Germany, and the Middle East. A battered Europe, especially in Italy and France, threatened to succumb to powerful internal Communist parties.

The Truman Doctrine announced military aid to threatened noncommunist nations and an ideological crusade against international communism. The Marshall Plan provided economic assistance to starving and communist-threatened Europe, which soon joined the United States in the permanent NATO military alliance. But the triumph of communism in China created bitter divisions within the United States. Communist North Korea's unprovoked attack on pro-Western South Korea in 1950 led to the seesaw Korean War and to a massive American military buildup. General Douglas MacArthur's insubordination and threats to expand the war to China led Truman to fire him.

The Cold War and revelations of Soviet spying aroused deep fears of communist subversion at home, which spread into a general assault on the socially "deviant." Issues of the Cold War and civil rights fractured the Democratic party three ways in 1948, but a gutsy Truman campaign overcame the divisions to win a triumphant underdog victory over Dewey, Thurmond, and Wallace.

The Cold War and revelations of Soviet spying aroused deep fears of communist subversion at home, which spread into a general assault on alleged communist sympathizers as well as the socially marginal. Demagogic Wisconsin Senator Joseph McCarthy gained immense power with his irresponsible attacks, but finally collapsed after attacking the U.S. Army.

In the immediate postwar years there were widespread fears of a return to depression. But fueled by cheap energy, increased worker productivity, and government programs such as the GI Bill of Rights, the economy began a spectacular expansion that lasted from 1950 to 1970. This burst of affluence transformed American industry and society. More women joined the work force even as popular culture glorified the roles of mother and homemaker.

Footloose Americans migrated to the Sunbelts of the South and West and to the growing suburbs, leaving the northeastern cities with poorer populations. Families grew rapidly, as the "baby boom" created a population bulge that would last for decades.

KEY TERMS

Yalta conference (608)
Cold War (609)
Bretton Woods Conference (609)
United Nations (U.N.) (610)
Nuremberg war crimes trial (610)
Berlin airlift (611)
containment doctrine (611)
Truman Doctrine (613)
Marshall Plan (613)
North Atlantic Treaty Organization (NATO) (613)
National Security Council Memorandum Number 68 (NSC-68) (614)
Korean War (615)
House Un-American Activities Committee (HUAC) (616)
McCarthyism (617)
Army-McCarthy hearings (617)
Executive Order 9981 (617)
Taft-Hartley Act (618)
Operation Dixie (618)
Employment Act of 1946 (618)
GI Bill (618)
Fair Deal (620)
Sunbelt (622)
Levittown (624)
baby boom (624)

PEOPLE TO KNOW

Joseph Stalin
Jiang Jieshi
George F. Kennan
George C. Marshall
Joseph McCarthy
Reinhold Niebuhr
Benjamin Spock

MindTap is a fully online, highly personalized learning experience built upon Cengage Learning content. MindTap combines student learning tools—readings, multimedia, activities, and assessments—into a singular Learning Path that guides students through the course.

Chapter 36

American Zenith

1952–1963

Our soil is fertile, our agriculture productive. The air rings with the song of our industry—rolling mills and blast furnaces, dynamos, dams and assembly lines—the chorus of America the bountiful. . . . We live in a land of plenty, but rarely has this earth known such peril as today.

Dwight D. Eisenhower, January 21, 1957

Chapter Outline

- Affluence and Consumer Culture
- Eisenhower Republicanism
- Martin Luther King, Jr., and the Early Civil Rights Movement
- Eisenhower's Domestic and Foreign Policies
- The Fluctuating Cold War
- John F. Kennedy Defeats Richard Nixon, 1960
- Postwar Literature and Culture
- The Kennedy Promise
- Ventures in Vietnam and Cuba
- Civil Rights Rising
- *Makers of America: The Great African American Migration*
- *Examining the Evidence: The Shopping Mall as New Town Square, 1960*

Unmatched in power or plenty, the United States bestrode the world like a colossus as the 1950s began to unfold. Broadly shared prosperity fueled confidence in the country's capacity to tackle major problems at home and abroad. But problems abounded nonetheless. Americans at midcentury were dug into the frontlines of the global Cold War while bitterly divided at home over the explosive issues of communist subversion and civil rights.

FOCUS QUESTIONS

1. What changes in the American economy and work force fueled the rise of a mass, popular consumer culture in the 1950s?
2. What were the origins of the modern American civil rights movement, and what challenges did it face amidst the generally conservative political and social environment of the 1950s? What enabled the movement to gain political momentum in the early 1960s?
3. What were the fundamental principles of "Eisenhower Republicanism" at home and abroad? How did Eisenhower manage to address numerous Cold War crises while avoiding war?
4. How did the American cultural "renaissance" of the 1950s and early 1960s reflect American affluence and prestige? Which writers and artists were more critical of America and the "American dream"?
5. Why did John F. Kennedy's "New Frontier" raise such high expectations, and to what extent were those expectations met?

CHRONOLOGY

1952	▪ Eisenhower defeats Stevenson for presidency ▪ Ellison publishes *Invisible Man*
1953	▪ CIA-engineered coup installs shah of Iran ▪ Joseph Stalin dies
1954	▪ French defeated at Dien Bien Phu in Vietnam ▪ *Brown v. Board of Education.* ▪ Nasser becomes president of Egypt ▪ CIA-sponsored coup in Guatemala
1955	▪ Montgomery bus boycott by blacks begins; emergence of Martin Luther King, Jr. ▪ Geneva summit meeting on Vietnam ▪ AF of L merges with CIO ▪ Tennessee Williams's *Cat on a Hot Tin Roof* first performed
1956	▪ Soviets crush Hungarian revolt ▪ Suez crisis ▪ Eisenhower defeats Stevenson for presidency ▪ Ginsberg publishes *Howl and Other Poems*
1957	▪ Little Rock school desegregation crisis ▪ Civil Rights Act passed ▪ Southern Christian Leadership Conference (SCLC) formed ▪ Soviet Union launches *Sputnik* satellites ▪ European Economic Community (EEC, Common Market) created
1958	▪ NDEA authorizes loans and grants for science and language education ▪ Galbraith publishes *The Affluent Society*
1958–1959	▪ Berlin crisis
1959	▪ Castro seizes power in Cuba ▪ Landrum-Griffin Act ▪ Alaska and Hawaii attain statehood
1960	▪ Sit-in movement for civil rights begins ▪ U-2 incident sabotages Paris summit ▪ OPEC formed ▪ Kennedy defeats Nixon for presidency ▪ Updike publishes *Rabbit, Run*
1961	▪ Heller publishes *Catch-22* ▪ Berlin Wall built ▪ Alliance for Progress ▪ Bay of Pigs invasion ▪ Kennedy sends "military advisers" to South Vietnam
1962	▪ Pressure from Kennedy results in rollback of steel prices ▪ Trade Expansion Act ▪ Cuban missile crisis
1963	▪ Plath publishes *The Bell Jar* ▪ Anti-Diem coup in South Vietnam ▪ Civil rights march in Washington, D.C. ▪ Kennedy assassinated; Johnson assumes presidency

Affluence and Its Anxieties

The continuing post–World War II economic boom wrought wondrous changes in American society in the 1950s. Prosperity triggered a fabulous surge in home construction: One of every four homes standing in America in 1960 had been built in the 1950s, and 83 percent of those new homes were in the suburbs.

In a period marked by massive military spending and public investment in research, science and technology drove economic growth more than ever. The invention of the transistor in 1948 sparked a revolution in electronics, and especially in computers. The first electronic computers in the 1940s were massive machines with fickle cathode ray tubes, but transistors and, later, printed circuits on silicon wafers made possible dramatic miniaturization and phenomenal computational speed. Computer giant International Business Machines (IBM) became the prototype of the "high-tech" corporation in the dawning "information age." Aerospace industries also grew fantastically in the 1950s, thanks both to the government's building of the Strategic Air Command and to a robustly expanding passenger airline business—as well as to connections between military and civilian aircraft production. Seattle-based Boeing Company brought out the first large passenger jet, the "707," in 1957, whose design owed much to the previous development of SAC's long-range strategic bomber.

The nature of the work force was also changing. A quiet revolution was marked in 1956 when "white-collar" workers for the first time outnumbered "blue-collar" workers, signaling the passage from an industrial to a postindustrial or service-based economy.

Keeping pace with that fundamental transformation, organized labor withered as a percentage of the labor force, after peaking at about 35 percent in 1954.

The surge in white-collar employment opened special opportunities for women. When many women left the work force at the end of World War II, postwar popular culture developed a "cult of domesticity" celebrating the conventional female roles of wife and mother. When popular television programs like "Ozzie and Harriet" and "Leave It to Beaver" depicted idyllic suburban families with a working husband, two children, and a housebound wife they did so without irony; much of middle-class America really did live that way. But as the 1950s progressed, another quiet revolution was gaining momentum that was destined to transform women's roles and even the character of the American family.

Of some 40 million new jobs created in the three decades after 1950, more than 30 million were in clerical and service work. Women filled the huge majority of these new positions. These exploding employment opportunities for women unleashed a groundswell of social and psychological change that mounted to tidal-wave proportions in the decades that followed. In the new urban age, women's dual role as *both* workers and homemakers raised urgent questions about family life and about traditional definitions of gender differences.

Feminist Betty Friedan gave focus and fuel to women's feelings in 1963 when she published ***The Feminine Mystique***, a runaway best-seller and a classic of the modern feminist movement. Friedan spoke in rousing accents to millions of able, educated women who applauded her indictment of the stifling boredom of suburban housewifery.

***The Feminine Mystique* (1963)** *Best-selling book by feminist thinker Betty Friedan. This work challenged women to move beyond the drudgery of suburban housewifery and helped launch what would become second-wave feminism.*

Consumer Culture in the Fifties

The 1950s witnessed a huge expansion of the middle class and the blossoming of a consumer culture that defined a distinctive lifestyle. Diner's Club introduced the plastic credit card in 1949, just one year after the first "fast-food" McDonald's hamburger stand opened in San Bernardino, California. In 1955 Disneyland opened its doors in Anaheim, California. Easy credit, high-volume "fast-food" production, and new forms of leisure marked an emerging culture of consumption that soon moved beyond America's borders.

Crucial to the development of consumerism was the rapid rise of the new technology of television. Only 6 TV stations were broadcasting in 1946; a decade later 442 stations were operating. TV sets were rich people's novelties in the 1940s, but 7 million sets were sold in 1951. By 1960 virtually every American home had one, in a stunning display of the speed with which new technologies can pervade and transform modern societies. By the mid-1950s advertisers annually spent $10 billion to hawk their wares on television, while critics fumed that the wildly popular new mass medium was degrading the public's aesthetic, moral, political, and educational standards.

Even religion capitalized on the powerful new electronic pulpit. Celebrity preachers and priests like the Baptist Billy Graham, the Pentecostal Oral Roberts, and the Roman Catholic Fulton J. Sheen took to the airwaves to spread the Christian gospel. Television also catalyzed the commercialization of professional sports, as viewing audiences that once numbered in the stadium-capacity thousands could now be counted in the couch-potato millions.

Sports also reflected the shift in population toward the West and South. In 1958 baseball's New York Giants moved to San Francisco, and the Brooklyn Dodgers abandoned Flatbush for Los Angeles. Those moves touched off a new westward and southward movement of sports franchises. Shifting population and spreading affluence led eventually to substantial expansion of the major baseball leagues and the principal football and basketball leagues as well.

Popular music was also dramatically transformed in the 1950s. The chief revolutionary was Elvis Presley, a white singer born in 1935 in Tupelo, Mississippi. Fusing black rhythm and blues with white bluegrass and country styles, Elvis created a new musical idiom known forever after as **rock 'n' roll**. Listening and dancing to rock n' roll became a rite of passage for millions of young people around the world, from Japan to working-class Liverpool, England, where Elvis's music inspired teenagers John Lennon and Paul McCartney to form a band that would become the Beatles.

rock 'n' roll *"Crossover" musical style that rose to dominance in the 1950s, merging black rhythm and blues with white bluegrass and country. Featuring a heavy beat and driving rhythm, rock 'n' roll music became a defining feature of the 1950s youth culture.*

Charles Trainor/Time & Life Pictures/Getty Images

The King With his fleshy face, pouting lips, and antic, sexually suggestive gyrations, Elvis Presley became the high priest of rock 'n' roll in the 1950s, to the chagrin of parents everywhere. Bloated by fame, fortune, and drugs, he died in 1977 at the age of forty-two.

Traditionalists were repelled by Presley and much else in the affluent fifties. Movie star Marilyn Monroe, with her ingenuous smile and dangerous curves, helped to popularize—and commercialize—new standards of sensuous sexuality. So did *Playboy* magazine, whose first issue Monroe graced in 1953. As the decade closed, Americans were well on their way to becoming free-spending consumers of mass-produced, standardized products advertised on the electronic medium of television and often sold for their alleged sexual allure.

Many critics lamented the implications of this new consumerist lifestyle. Harvard sociologist David Riesman portrayed the postwar generation as a pack of conformists in *The Lonely Crowd* (1950), as did William H. Whyte, Jr., in *The Organization Man*. Harvard economist John Kenneth Galbraith bemoaned the spectacle of private opulence amidst public squalor in a series of books beginning with *The Affluent Society* (1958). But Galbraith's call to invest in the public good fell on mostly deaf ears in the giddily affluent 1950s.

The Advent of Eisenhower

Democratic prospects in the presidential election of 1952 were blighted by the military deadlock in Korea, Truman's clash with MacArthur, and war-bred inflation. Dispirited Democrats nominated Adlai E. Stevenson, the eloquent governor of Illinois. Republicans enthusiastically chose war hero General Dwight D. Eisenhower. Ike's running mate was California Senator Richard M. Nixon, who had gained notoriety as a relentless red-hunter.

Eisenhower was already the most popular American of his time, as "I Like Ike" buttons everywhere testified. Striking a grandfatherly, nonpartisan pose, Eisenhower left the rough campaigning to Nixon, who relished bare-knuckle political combat. The vice-presidential candidate lambasted his opponents with charges that they had cultivated corruption, caved in on Korea, and coddled communists. He particularly blasted the cerebral Stevenson as "Adlai the appeaser," with a "Ph.D. from [Secretary of State] Dean Acheson's College of Cowardly Communist Containment."

Nixon himself faltered late in the campaign amid accusations that he had accepted illegal donations. Responding with a self-pitying live address on television, Nixon denied the charges and solemnly declared that the only campaign gift he had ever received was the family cocker spaniel, Checkers. The shameless and mawkish **Checkers Speech** saved Nixon's spot on the ticket and spotlighted a fundamental change in American politics. Television allowed candidates to bypass traditional political party machinery and speak directly to voters.

Checkers Speech (1952) *Nationally televised address by vice-presidential candidate Richard Nixon during which he defended himself against allegations of corruption. Using the new mass medium of television shortly before the 1952 election, Nixon saved his place on the ticket by saying the only campaign gift he had received was a cocker spaniel named Checkers.*

The outcome of the presidential election of 1952 was never really in doubt. Given an extra prod by Eisenhower's last-minute pledge to go personally to Korea to end the war, the voters overwhelmingly declared for Ike. He garnered 33,936,234 votes to Stevenson's 27,314,992, ringing up 442 electoral votes to 89 for his opponent. Ike also managed to pull enough Republican legislators into office to gain GOP control of the new Congress by a hairbreadth.

True to his campaign pledge, president-elect Eisenhower flew to Korea in December 1952. Seven months later an armistice was finally signed. The brutal and futile fighting had lasted three years. More than thirty thousand Americans lay dead, joined by perhaps more than a million Chinese, North Koreans, and South Koreans. Tens of billions of American dollars had been poured down the Asian sinkhole. Yet this terrible toll in blood and treasure bought only a return to the conditions of 1950; Korea remained divided at the thirty-eighth parallel, while the broader Cold War remained frigidly frozen. Both in the military and civilian realms, Eisenhower had long cultivated a leadership style that self-consciously projected an image of sincerity, fairness, and optimism. Ike thus seemed ideally suited to soothe the anxieties of troubled Americans who yearned for a period of calm. Ably playing this reassuring role, he presided over a decade of shaky peace and shining prosperity. Yet critics charged that he unwisely hoarded the "asset" of his immense popularity, rather than spend it for a good cause (especially civil rights), and that he displayed opportunism by initially failing to stand up to McCarthyist demagoguery.

A black woman described the day-in, day-out humiliations of life in a Jim Crow South:

"You could not go to a white restaurant; you sat in a special place at the movie house; and Lord knows, you sat in the back of the bus. It didn't make any difference if you were rich or poor, if you were black you were nothing. You might have a hundred dollars in your pocket, but if you went to the store you would wait at the side until all the clerks got through with all the white folks, no matter if they didn't have change for a dollar. Then the clerk would finally look at you and say, 'Oh, did you want something? I didn't see you there.' "

Desegregating American Society

America counted some 15 million black citizens in 1950, two-thirds of whom still made their homes in the South. There they lived bound by the iron set of antiquated rules known as "Jim Crow" laws. Every day of their lives, southern blacks dealt with a bizarre array of separate arrangements that kept them socially insulated from whites, economically inferior, and politically powerless. Blacks in the South not only attended segregated schools but were compelled to use separate public toilets, drinking fountains, restaurants, and waiting rooms. Trains and buses had "whites only" and "colored only" seating. Only about 20 percent of eligible southern blacks were registered to vote, fewer than 5 percent in some Deep South states like Mississippi and Alabama.

Where the law proved insufficient to enforce this regime, vigilante violence did the job. Six black war veterans, claiming the rights for which they had fought overseas, were murdered in the summer of 1946. A Mississippi mob lynched black fourteen-year-old Emmett Till for allegedly leering at a white woman. It is small wonder that a black clergyman declared that "everywhere I go in the South the Negro is forced to choose between his hide and his soul."

Segregation tarnished America's international image, much as McCarthyism did. After the war, African American entertainers like Paul Robeson and Josephine Baker toured widely in Europe and Latin America, informing audiences about the horrors of Jim Crow and raising doubts about America's reputation as the beacon of freedom against Soviet communism. In response, the State Department confiscated Robeson's passport but had to find other ways to silence Baker, who had assumed French citizenship. Intellectuals poured on criticism as well. Swedish scholar Gunnar Myrdal published his landmark book, *An American Dilemma*, exposing the scandalous contradiction between the liberty-loving "American Creed" and the nation's shameful treatment of black citizens.

International pressure combined with grassroots and legal activism to propel some racial progress in the North after World War II. In a growing number of northern cities and states, African Americans battled for—and won—equal access to public accommodations like restaurants, hotels, theaters, and beaches (see "Makers of America: The Great African American Migration," p. 633). Jackie Robinson cracked baseball's color barrier when the Brooklyn Dodgers signed him in 1946. The repeal of the Chinese Exclusion Act in 1943 and the repeal of many state-level anti-miscegenation laws signaled the decline of legal discrimination against not only African Americans but other racial and ethnic minorities as well.

New York Times Co./Archive Photos/Getty Images

The Face of Segregation These women in the segregated South of the 1950s were compelled to enter the movie theater through the "Colored Entrance." Once inside, they were restricted to a separate seating section, usually in the rear of the theater.

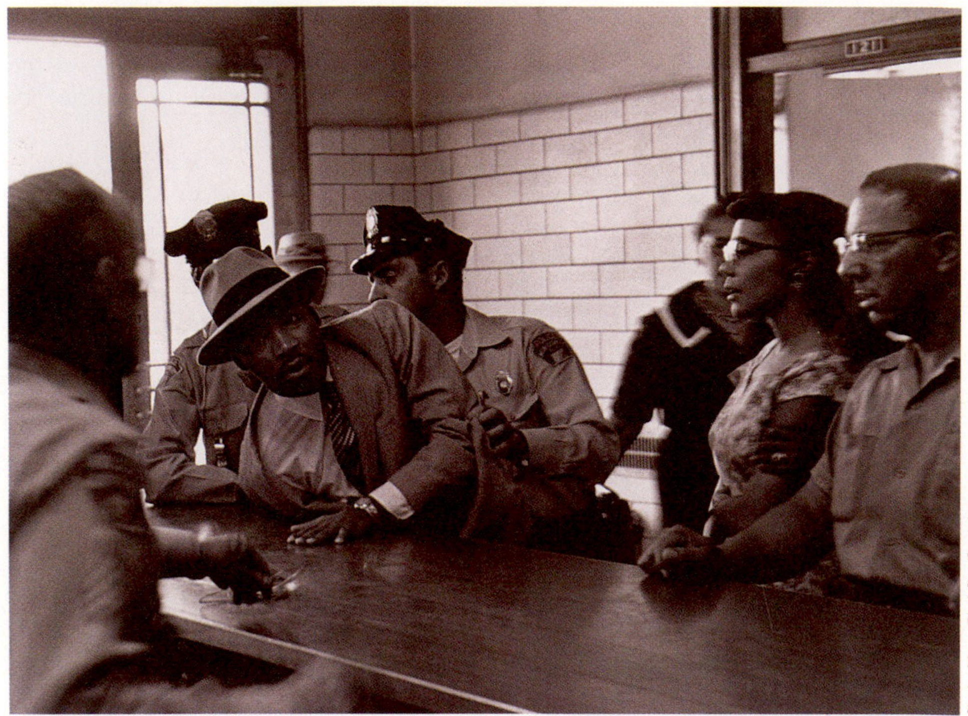

Charles Moore/Black Star/Stockphoto.com

Martin Luther King, Jr., and His Wife, Coretta, Arrested King and his wife were arrested for the first time in Montgomery, Alabama, in 1955 while organizing a bus boycott.

The South saw little of that progress in the early postwar years—but increasingly, African Americans refused to suffer in silence. On a chilly day in December 1955, Rosa Parks, a college-educated black seamstress, made history in Montgomery, Alabama. She boarded a bus, took a seat in the "whites only" section, and refused to give it up. Her arrest for violating the city's Jim Crow statutes sparked a yearlong black boycott of the city buses and served notice throughout the South that blacks would no longer submit meekly to the absurdities and indignities of segregation.

The **Montgomery bus boycott** also catapulted to prominence a young pastor at Montgomery's Dexter Avenue Baptist Church, the Reverend Martin Luther King, Jr. Only twenty-seven years old, the well-educated King became a champion of the downtrodden and disfranchised. His oratorical skill, strategic savvy, mastery of biblical and constitutional conceptions of justice, and devotion to the nonviolent principles of India's Mohandas Gandhi all thrust him to the forefront of the black revolution that soon pulsed across the South and the rest of the nation.

Montgomery bus boycott (1955)
Protest by black Alabamians against segregated seating on city buses, sparked by Rosa Parks's defiant refusal to move to the back of the bus. The bus boycott lasted from December 1, 1955, until December 26, 1956, and became one of the foundational moments of the civil rights movement. It led to the rise of Martin Luther King, Jr., and ultimately to a Supreme Court decision opposing segregated busing.

Seeds of the Civil Rights Revolution

In 1946 President Harry Truman commissioned a report on blacks entitled "To Secure These Rights." Following the report's recommendations, Truman in 1948 ended segregation in federal civil service and the armed forces. Yet Congress stubbornly resisted passing civil rights legislation, and Truman's successor, Dwight Eisenhower, showed no real interest in the racial issue.

In the 1950s it was the Supreme Court that assumed civil rights leadership. Chief Justice Earl Warren, a former Republican governor of California, shocked traditionalists with his active judicial intervention in previously taboo social issues. Publicly snubbed and privately scorned by Ike, Warren courageously led the Court to address urgent issues that Congress and the president preferred to avoid.

The Great African American Migration

Among the groups most affected by the great social upheavals of World War II were African Americans. Predominantly a rural, southern people before 1940, African Americans were propelled by the war into the cities of the North and West, and by 1970 a majority lived outside the states of the Old Confederacy. The results of that massive demographic shift were momentous, for African Americans and for all of American society.

So many black southerners took to the roads during World War II that local officials lost track of the numbers. Black workers on the move crowded into boardinghouses, camped out in cars, and clustered in the juke joints of roadside America en route to their new lives.

Southern cotton fields and tobacco plantations had yielded but slender sustenance to African American farmers, most of whom struggled to make ends meet as tenants and sharecroppers. The Great Depression dealt yet another blow, for when New Deal farm programs paid growers to leave their land fallow, many landlords simply pocketed the money and evicted their tenants—white as well as black. As the Depression deepened, dispossessed former sharecroppers toiled as seasonal farmworkers or languished without jobs.

The spanking new munitions plants and bustling shipyards of the South offered little solace to African Americans. In 1940 and 1941 the labor-hungry war machine soaked up unemployed white workers but commonly denied jobs to blacks. Fed up with such injustices, many African Americans headed for shipyards, factories, and foundries on the Pacific Coast or north of the Mason-Dixon line, where their willing hands found work awaiting them.

Angered by continuing racism, black leaders cajoled President Roosevelt into issuing Executive Order 8802 in June 1941 declaring that "there shall be no discrimination in the employment of workers in defense industries or government because of race, creed, color, or national origin." Roosevelt's action was a tenuous, hesitant step, yet it was the first time since Reconstruction that the federal government had committed itself to ensuring justice for African Americans.

By war's end the great wartime exodus had scattered hundreds of thousands of African Americans to new regions and ways of life. In western and northern cities, blacks now competed for housing and jobs, and they also voted—many of them for the first time in their lives.

As early as 1945, NAACP leader Walter White concluded that the war "immeasurably magnified the Negro's awareness of the disparity between the American profession and practice of democracy." The wartime migration thus set the stage for the success of the civil rights movement. With their new political base outside the Old South, and with new support from the Democratic party, African Americans eventually forced an end to the hated segregationist practices that kept them from enjoying their full rights as citizens.

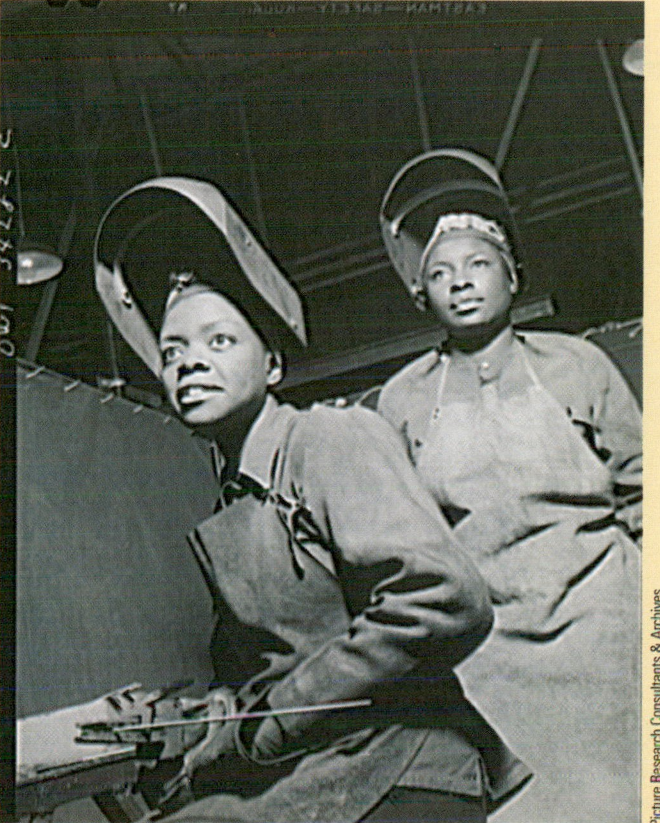

Picture Research Consultants & Archives

The Home Front Though often confronted by prejudice and discrimination, many African American migrants from the rural South found their first industrial jobs in wartime defense plants during World War II.

***Brown* v. *Board of Education of Topeka, Kansas* (1954)** *Landmark Supreme Court decision that overturned* Plessy *v.* Ferguson *(1896) and abolished racial segregation in public schools. The Court reasoned that "separate" was inherently "unequal," rejecting the foundation of the Jim Crow system of racial segregation in the South. This decision was the first major step toward the legal end of racial discrimination and a major accomplishment for the civil rights movement.*

The unanimous decision of the Warren Court in ***Brown* v. *Board of Education of Topeka, Kansas*** in May 1954 was epochal. In a forceful opinion, the learned justices ruled that segregation in the public schools was "inherently unequal" and thus unconstitutional. The uncompromising decision reversed the Court's earlier declaration of 1896 in *Plessy* v. *Ferguson* (see p. 374) that "separate but equal" facilities were allowable under the Constitution. That doctrine was now dead. Desegregation, the justices insisted, must go ahead with "all deliberate speed."

The Border States generally made reasonable efforts to comply with this ruling, but in the Deep South diehards organized "massive resistance" against desegregation. More than a hundred southern congressmen and senators pledged their unyielding resistance to desegregation, and several states diverted funds to hastily created "private" schools where the integration order was more difficult to apply. Throughout the South, white citizens' councils, sometimes by the light of burning crosses, thwarted attempts to make integration a reality. Ten years after the Court's momentous ruling, fewer than 2 percent of the eligible blacks in the Deep South were sitting in classrooms with whites.

President Eisenhower remained reluctant to promote integration. He shied away from employing his vast popularity and the prestige of his office to educate white Americans about the need for racial justice. He complained that the Supreme Court's decision in *Brown* v. *Board of Education* had upset "the customs and convictions of at least two generations of Americans," and he steadfastly refused to issue a public statement endorsing the Court's conclusions.

But in September 1957 Ike was forced to act. Arkansas Governor Orval Faubus mobilized the National Guard to prevent nine black students from enrolling in Little Rock's Central High School. Confronted with a direct challenge to federal authority, Eisenhower sent troops to escort the children to their classes. In the same year Congress passed the first Civil Rights Act since Reconstruction, a mild measure that set up a Civil Rights Commission to investigate violations of civil rights. Blacks meanwhile continued to take the civil rights movement into their own hands. Martin Luther King, Jr., formed the Southern Christian Leadership Conference (SCLC) in 1957. The churches were the largest and best-organized black institutions that had been allowed to flourish in a segregated society, and the SCLC aimed to mobilize their vast power on behalf of black rights.

More spontaneous was the "sit-in" movement launched on February 1, 1960, by four black college freshmen in Greensboro, North Carolina. Without a detailed plan or institutional support, they demanded service at a whites-only Woolworth's lunch counter. The following day, eighty-five students joined in; by the end of the week, a thousand. The sit-in movement rolled swiftly across the South, swelling into a wave of wade-ins, lie-ins, and pray-ins to compel equal treatment in restaurants, transportation, employment, housing, and voter registration. In April 1960 southern black students formed the **Student Non-Violent Coordinating Committee (SNCC**, pronounced "snick"**)** to give more focus and force to these efforts. Young and impassioned, SNCC members would eventually lose patience with the tactics of the SCLC and the deliberate legalisms of the NAACP.

Student Non-Violent Coordinating Committee (SNCC) *Youth organization founded by southern black students in 1960 to promote civil rights. Drawing on its members' youthful energies, SNCC in its early years coordinated demonstrations, sit-ins, and voter registration drives.*

★ Eisenhower Republicanism at Home

Eisenhower had entered the White House in 1953 pledging his administration to a philosophy of "dynamic conservatism." While accepting basic New Deal reforms like Social Security and unemployment insurance, he was also determined to balance the federal budget and guard the Republic from what he called "creeping socialism." Eisenhower won southern support by endorsing the transfer of control over offshore oil fields from the federal government to the states. Ike also tried to curb the TVA by encouraging a private power company to build a generating plant to compete with the massive public utility.

Eisenhower responded to both domestic pressure and the Mexican government's worries that border crossings undercut the *Bracero* program of legally imported farmworkers (see p. 588). In a massive roundup dubbed **Operation Wetback** in reference to the migrants' watery route across the Rio Grande, as many as 1 million Mexicans were apprehended and returned to Mexico in 1954.

Operation Wetback (1954) *A government program to round up and deport as many as 1 million illegal Mexican migrant workers in the United States. The program was promoted in part by the Mexican government and reflected burgeoning concerns about non-European immigration to America.*

Meanwhile, in another of the rude and arbitrary reversals that have long afflicted the government's relations with Native Americans, Eisenhower sought to cancel the tribal preservation policies of the "Indian New Deal," in place since 1934 (see p. 561). He proposed to "terminate" the tribes as legal entities and to return to the assimilationist goals of the Dawes Severalty Act of 1887 (see p. 432). Most Indians resisted termination, and the policy was abandoned in 1961.

Eisenhower also backed a public works project that dwarfed anything the New Dealers had dreamed of. The **Federal Highway Act of 1956** authorized a $27 billion plan to build forty-two thousand miles of sleek, fast motorways. The president believed that such roads were essential to national defense, allowing U.S. troops to mobilize anywhere in the country in the event of a Soviet invasion. Beyond being a defense strategy, the construction of these modern, multilane roads created countless construction jobs, speeded the suburbanization of America, and exacerbated problems of air quality and energy consumption. It had disastrous consequences in many cities, as once-vibrant downtowns withered while shopping malls flourished in the far-flung suburbs.

Federal Highway Act of 1956 *Federal legislation signed by Dwight D. Eisenhower to construct thousands of miles of modern highways in the name of national defense. Officially called the National Interstate and Defense Highways Act, this bill dramatically increased the move to the suburbs, as white middle-class people could more easily commute to urban jobs.*

A "New Look" in Foreign Policy

The 1952 Republican platform called for a "new look" in foreign policy. It condemned the mere "containment" of communism as "negative, futile, and immoral." Incoming secretary of state John Foster Dulles promised not merely to stem the red tide but to "roll back" its gains and "liberate captive peoples." At the same time, the new administration promised to balance the budget by cutting military spending.

How were these two contradictory goals to be reached? Dulles answered with a **policy of boldness** in early 1954. Eisenhower would relegate the army and navy to the back seat and build up the Strategic Air Command's fleet of superbombers equipped with city-flattening nuclear bombs. These fearsome weapons would inflict "massive retaliation" on the Soviets or the Chinese in the event of hostilities. At the same time, Eisenhower sought a thaw in the Cold War through negotiations with the new Soviet leaders who came to power after Joseph Stalin's death in 1953.

policy of boldness (1954) *Foreign-policy objective of Dwight Eisenhower's secretary of state John Foster Dulles, who believed in changing the containment strategy to one that more directly engaged the Soviet Union and attempted to roll back communist influence around the world. This policy led to a buildup of America's nuclear arsenal to threaten "massive retaliation" against communist enemies, expanding the Cold War's arms race.*

In the end, the touted "new look" proved illusory. The new Soviet premier, burly Nikita Khrushchev, rudely rejected Ike's call in 1955 for "open skies" mutual inspection over both the Soviet Union and the United States. In 1956 the Hungarians rose up against their Soviet masters and felt badly betrayed when the United States turned a deaf ear to their desperate appeals for aid. The brutally crushed **Hungarian uprising** revealed the sober truth that America's mighty nuclear sledgehammer was too heavy a weapon to be used in such a relatively minor crisis. The strategic limitations of the "massive retaliation" doctrine were thus starkly exposed.

Hungarian uprising (1956) *Series of demonstrations in Hungary against the Soviet Union. Soviet Premier Nikita Khrushchev violently suppressed this pro-Western uprising, highlighting the limitations of America's power in Eastern Europe.*

Southeast Asia provided further illustration of those limitations. In Vietnam and elsewhere, nationalist movements had sought for years to throw off the yoke of French colonial rule. The legendary Vietnamese leader, goateed Ho Chi Minh, had tried to appeal personally to Woodrow Wilson as early as 1919 to support self-determination for the peoples of Southeast Asia.

But Cold War events dampened the dreams of anticolonial Asian peoples. Their leaders—including Ho Chi Minh—became increasingly communist while the United States became increasingly anticommunist. By 1954 American taxpayers were financing nearly 80 percent of the costs of a bottomless French colonial war in Indochina. Despite this massive aid, French forces continued to crumble under pressure from Ho Chi Minh's nationalist guerilla forces, called the Viet Minh. In March 1954 a key French garrison was trapped hopelessly in the fortress of Dien Bien Phu. The new "policy of boldness" was now put to the test. Secretary Dulles, Vice President Nixon, and the chairman of the Joint Chiefs of Staff favored American intervention to bail out the beleaguered French. But Eisenhower held back.

The **Battle of Dien Bien Phu** proved a victory for the nationalists, and a multination conference at Geneva roughly halved Vietnam at the seventeenth parallel (see Map 36.2). The victorious Ho Chi Minh in the north consented to this arrangement on the assurance that Vietnam-wide elections would be held within two years. In the south a pro-Western

Battle of Dien Bien Phu (1954) *Military engagement in French colonial Vietnam in which French forces were defeated by Vietnamese nationalists loyal to Ho Chi Minh. With this loss, the French ended their colonial involvement in Indochina, paving the way for America's entry.*

government under Ngo Dinh Diem was soon entrenched in Saigon. After Diem's regime and its American backers refused to hold the promised elections, communist guerillas heated up their campaign against Diem. The Americans had evidently backed a losing horse but could see no easy way to call off their bet.

Cold War Crises in the Middle East

Fears of Soviet penetration into the oil-rich Middle East further heightened Cold War tensions. The government of Iran, supposedly influenced by the Kremlin, began to resist the power of the gigantic Western companies that controlled Iranian petroleum. In response, the American Central Intelligence Agency (CIA) engineered a coup in 1953 that installed the youthful shah of Iran, Mohammad Reza Pahlavi, as dictator. Though successful in the short run in securing Iranian oil for the West, the American intervention left a bitter legacy of resentment among many Iranians. More than two decades later, they took their revenge on the shah and his American allies (see pp. 681–682).

Suez crisis (1956) *International crisis launched when Egyptian president Gamal Abdel Nasser nationalized the Suez Canal, which had been owned mostly by French and British stockholders. The crisis led to a British and French attack on Egypt, which failed without aid from the United States. The Suez crisis marked an important turning point in the post-colonial Middle East and highlighted the rising importance of oil in world affairs.*

The **Suez crisis** proved far messier than the swift strike in Iran. President Gamal Abdel Nasser of Egypt, an ardent Arab nationalist, had tentatively obtained American and British aid to build an immense dam on the Nile. But when Nasser began to flirt openly with the communist camp, Secretary of State Dulles dramatically withdrew the dam offer. Nasser promptly regained face by nationalizing the Suez Canal, owned chiefly by British and French stockholders.

Nasser's action placed a razor's edge at the jugular vein of Western Europe's oil supply. America's jittery British and French allies, deliberately keeping Washington in the dark, joined with Israel in an attack on Egypt late in October 1956. The invaders calculated

Egyptian Independence Leader Gamal Abdel Nasser, 1954 Shown here greeting exuberant supporters alongside the visiting Sudanese prime minister (left), Nasser became the first president under Egypt's new constitution in 1956. He was long a thorn in the flesh of American and European policymakers anxious to protect the precious oil resources of the Middle East. "Nasserism," his version of Pan-Arabism, won a great following in the Arab world during the 1950s and 1960s.

that the United States would supply them with oil while their Middle Eastern supplies were disrupted. But a furious President Eisenhower resolved to let them "boil in their own oil" and refused to release emergency supplies. The oil-less allies resentfully withdrew their troops.

The Suez crisis marked the last time that the United States could brandish its "oil weapon." As recently as 1940, the United States had produced two-thirds of the world's oil, but by 1948 America had become a net oil importer. The economic and strategic importance of the Middle East oil region began to grow dramatically.

The region's sandy sheikdoms increasingly resolved to reap for themselves the lion's share of the enormous oil wealth that Western companies pumped out of the scorching Middle Eastern deserts. In a portentous move, Saudi Arabia, Kuwait, Iraq, and Iran joined with Venezuela in 1960 to form the **Organization of Petroleum Exporting Countries (OPEC)**. In the next two decades, OPEC tightened its stranglehold on the Western economies.

Organization of Petroleum Exporting Countries (OPEC) *Cartel comprising Middle Eastern states and Venezuela first organized in 1960. OPEC aimed to control access to and prices of oil, wresting power from Western oil companies and investors. In the process, it gradually strengthened the hand of non-Western powers on the world stage.*

Round Two for Ike

The election of 1956 was a replay of the 1952 contest, with President Eisenhower pitted once more against Adlai Stevenson. Voters still liked Ike. Eisenhower piled up an enormous majority of 35,590,472 popular votes to Stevenson's 26,022,752; in the Electoral College the vote was an even more unbalanced 457 to 73. But Eisenhower failed to win for his party either house of Congress.

Ike nevertheless bestirred himself when it came to organized labor. Congressional investigations produced scandalous revelations of gangsterism and brass-knuckle tactics in many American unions, especially the Teamsters Union. The AFL-CIO, born of a merger of the two giants in 1955, expelled the Teamsters in 1957 for choosing leaders like mob-connected James R. "Jimmy" Hoffa. Later convicted of jury tampering, Hoffa served part of his sentence before disappearing without a trace—evidently the victim of gangsters he had crossed. To counter such corruption, Eisenhower persuaded Congress to pass the Landrum-Griffin Act in 1959. Designed to bring labor leaders to book for financial shenanigans and bullying tactics, it also expanded some of the anti-labor strictures of the earlier Taft-Hartley Act.

Soviet scientists astounded the world on October 4, 1957, by lofting into orbit around the globe a beep-beeping 184-pound "baby moon" (*Sputnik I*). A month later they launched 1,120-pound *Sputnik II* with a dog aboard. These amazing breakthroughs rattled American self-confidence. They cast doubts on America's vaunted scientific superiority and raised sobering military questions. If the Soviets could fire heavy objects into outer space, they certainly could reach America with intercontinental ballistic missiles (ICBMs).

"Rocket fever" swept the nation. Eisenhower established the National Aeronautics and Space Administration (NASA) and directed billions of dollars to missile development. After humiliating and well-advertised failures—notably the Vanguard missile, which blew up on national television just a few feet above the ground in 1957—in February 1958 the United States managed to put into orbit a grapefruit-sized satellite weighing 2.5 pounds. By the end of the decade, several satellites had been launched, and the United States had successfully tested its own ICBMs. The **Sputnik** scare also led to a critical comparison of the American educational system with that of the Soviet Union. In 1958 Congress passed the National Defense and Education Act (NDEA) to promote research and teaching in science, engineering, and foreign languages.

Sputnik (1957) *Soviet satellite first launched into earth orbit on October 4, 1957. This scientific achievement marked the first time human beings had put a man-made object into orbit and pushed the USSR noticeably ahead of the United States in the space race. A month later, the Soviet Union sent a larger satellite, Sputnik II, into space, prompting the United States to redouble its space exploration efforts and raising American fears of Soviet superiority.*

The Continuing Cold War

The fantastic race to create weapons of nuclear annihilation continued unabated. Worried scientists urged halting nuclear tests before the atmosphere became so polluted as to produce generations of mutants. The Soviets, after completing an intensive series of exceptionally "dirty" tests, proclaimed a suspension in March 1958 and urged the Western world to follow. Beginning in October 1958, Washington did halt both underground and

Contending Voices

The "Kitchen Debate"

To promote cultural exchange between the United States and the Soviet Union, both governments agreed to sponsor exhibits in each other's countries during the summer of 1959. On July 24, Vice President Richard Nixon (1913–1994) led Soviet Premier Nikita Khrushchev (1894–1971) on a tour of the American National Exhibition at Sokolniki Park in Moscow. As they explored the facilities, including a state-of-the-art kitchen in a model suburban home, the two leaders engaged in an impromptu debate that ranged from foreign policy to the relative merits of communism and capitalism to the significance of technological innovation for citizens. Nixon said (pointing to a washing machine):

"This is the newest model. This is the kind which is built in thousands of units for direct installation in the houses. . . . What we want to do is make easier the life of our housewives. . . . To us, diversity, the right to choose, the fact that we have 1,000 builders building 1,000 different houses, is the most important thing. We don't have one decision made at the top by one government official. . . . We have many different manufacturers and many different kinds of washing machines so that the housewives have a choice."

Khrushchev replied:

"Don't you have a machine that puts food into the mouth and pushes it down? Many things you've shown us are interesting but they are not needed in life. They have no useful purpose. They are merely gadgets. . . . You think the Russian people will be dumbfounded to see these things, but the fact is that newly built Russian houses have all this equipment right now. Moreover, all you have to do to get a house is to be born in the Soviet Union. You are entitled to housing. I was born in the Soviet Union. So I have a right to a house. In America, if you don't have a dollar, you have the right to choose between sleeping in a house or on the pavement."

What does the exchange reveal about the premises of the ideological conflict between the United States and the Soviet Union during the Cold War?

atmospheric testing. But attempts to regularize suspensions by proper inspection sank on the reef of mutual mistrust.

The brusque Khrushchev, meanwhile, demanded in late 1958 that the Western powers remove their forces from West Berlin, and sought a face-to-face meeting with Eisenhower. Despite grave doubts about any tangible results, the president invited the Soviet leader to America in 1959. Khrushchev appeared in front of the U.N. General Assembly in New York before holding an encouraging meeting with Eisenhower at Camp David, the presidential retreat in Maryland's Catoctin Mountains.

Optimism evaporated when a follow-up Paris "summit conference," scheduled for May 1960, turned into an embarrassing fiasco. On the eve of the conference, the Soviets shot down an American U-2 spy plane deep in the heart of Russia. After bungling bureaucratic denials in Washington, "honest Ike" took the unprecedented step of assuming personal responsibility. Khrushchev stormed into Paris filing the air with invective, and the conference collapsed before it could get off the ground. The concord of Camp David was replaced with the grapes of wrath.

Meanwhile, the Cold War shook America's relations with its hemispheric neighbors. Latin Americans bitterly resented Uncle Sam's lavishing of billions of dollars on Europe while doling out only millions to its poor relations to the south. They also chafed at Washington's habit of intervening in Latin American affairs—as in a CIA-directed coup that ousted a leftist government in Guatemala in 1954. At the same time Washington continued to support—even decorate—bloody dictators who claimed to be combating communists.

One Latin American dictator, ironfisted Fulgencio Batista of Cuba, had encouraged huge investments of American capital, and Washington in turn had given him some support. But early in 1959 black-bearded Fidel Castro engineered a revolution that ousted Batista. Castro then denounced the Yankee imperialists and began to expropriate valuable American properties while pursuing a land-distribution program. Washington, finally losing patience, released Cuba from "imperialistic slavery" by cutting off the heavy U.S. imports of Cuban sugar. Castro retaliated with further wholesale confiscations of Yankee property and in effect made his left-wing dictatorship an economic and military satellite of Moscow. An exodus of anti-Castro Cubans headed for the United States, especially Florida. Nearly 1 million arrived between 1960 and 2000. Washington broke diplomatic relations with Castro's government early in 1961 and imposed a strict embargo on trade with Cuba.

Kennedy Challenges Nixon for the Presidency

Republicans approached the 1960 presidential campaign with Vice President Richard Nixon as their heir apparent. The "old" Nixon had been a no-holds-barred campaigner, especially in assailing Democrats and left-wingers. The "new" Nixon was represented as a mature, seasoned statesman. He had gained particular notice in a finger-pointing **kitchen debate** with Khrushchev in Moscow in 1959, where Nixon extolled the virtues of American consumerism over Soviet economic planning. The next year he handily won the Republican nomination.

On the Democratic side, John F. Kennedy, a youthful millionaire senator from Massachusetts, scored impressive victories in several primaries, overcoming the reluctance of many party bosses to nominate a Roman Catholic. Kennedy's closest rival, Texas Senator Lyndon B. Johnson, accepted second place on the ticket in a marriage of political convenience.

Senator Kennedy was the first Roman Catholic to be nominated by either party since Al Smith's ill-starred campaign in 1928. Smear artists revived the ancient charges about the Pope's controlling the White House. Kennedy rebutted the attacks and asked if some 40 million Catholic Americans were to be condemned to second-class citizenship from birth.

The Protestant Bible Belt South, ordinarily Democratic, had particular misgivings about the candidate's faith. "I fear Catholicism more than I fear communism," declaimed one Baptist minister in North Carolina. But if many southern Democrats stayed away from the polls because of Kennedy's Catholicism, northern Democrats in unusually large numbers supported Kennedy because of the bitter attacks on their Catholic faith.

Television may well have tipped the scales. The contestants crossed words in millions of living rooms. The debates reinforced the importance of image over substance in the television age. Many viewers found Kennedy's glamour and vitality far more appealing than Nixon's tired and pallid appearance.

1960

Candidate (Party)	Electoral Vote		Popular Vote	
Kennedy (Democrat)	303	56.50%	34,266,731	49.7%
Nixon (Republican)	219	40.75%	34,108,157	49.5%
Byrd (Independent)	15	2.75%	501,643	0.7%

Map 36.1 Presidential Election of 1960 (with electoral vote by state) Kennedy owed his hairbreadth triumph to his victories in twenty-six of the forty largest cities—and to Lyndon Johnson's strenuous campaigning in the South, where Kennedy's Catholic religion may have been a hotter issue than his stand on civil rights.

kitchen debate (1959) *Televised exchange in 1959 between Soviet premier Nikita Khrushchev and American vice president Richard Nixon. Meeting at the American National Exhibition in Moscow, the two leaders sparred over the relative merits of capitalist consumer culture versus Soviet state planning. Nixon won applause for his staunch defense of American capitalism, helping lead him to the Republican nomination for president in 1960.*

Kennedy squeezed through with 303 electoral votes to 219,* but with a breathtakingly close popular margin of only 118,574 votes out of over 68 million cast (see Map 36.1). He was not only the first Roman Catholic but also, at forty-three, the youngest person to date to be elected president. Like Franklin Roosevelt, Kennedy ran well in the large industrial centers, where he had strong support from workers, Catholics, and African Americans. (During the campaign Kennedy had solicitously telephoned the pregnant Coretta King, whose husband, Martin Luther King, Jr., was then imprisoned in Georgia for a sit-in. Nixon declined to comment or communicate with Mrs. King, an early signal of the two parties' diverging racial strategies.)

President Eisenhower continued to enjoy extraordinary popularity to the final curtain. Despite Democratic gibes about "eight years of golfing and goofing," Eisenhower was widely admired and respected for his decency, goodwill, and moderation. The old soldier left office warning of the dangers of a burgeoning "**military-industrial complex**." Under his watch America had not only grown economically, but geographically as well: Alaska and Hawaii attained statehood in 1959.

military-industrialized complex *Term popularized by President Dwight Eisenhower in his 1961 Farewell Address, referring to the political and economic ties between arms manufacturers, elected officials, and the U.S. armed forces that created self-sustaining pressure for high military spending during the Cold War. Eisenhower also warned that this powerful combination left unchecked could "endanger our liberties or democratic process," favoring defense concerns over more peaceful goals that balanced security and liberty.*

A Cultural Renaissance

America's unprecedented global power in the heady post-World War II decades was matched by its new international ascendancy in the arts. Shedding the national inferiority complex that had vexed earlier generations, American creative genius exerted a powerful worldwide influence in painting, architecture, and literature.

New York became the art capital of the world after World War II. The tradition-free American environment seemed especially congenial to the experimental mood of much

*Six Democratic electors in Alabama, all eight unpledged Democratic electors in Mississippi, and one Republican elector in Oklahoma voted for Virginia Senator Harry F. Byrd, who ran as an independent.

Candidate John F. Kennedy (1917–1963), in a speech to a Houston group of Protestant ministers (September 12, 1960), declared:

"I believe in an America where the separation of church and state is absolute—where no Catholic prelate would tell the President, should he be a Catholic, how to act, and no Protestant minister would tell his parishioners for whom to vote . . . and where no man is denied public office because his religion differs from the President who might appoint him or the people who might elect him."

modern art. Jackson Pollock pioneered **abstract expressionism** in the 1940s and 1950s, dripping paint on huge flats stretched across his studio floor. Mark Rothko and his fellow "color field" painters also dispatched with representation, enveloping whole canvases with bold, shimmering swaths of color. "Pop" (short for *popular*) artists like Andy Warhol depicted mundane consumer items like soup cans and soda bottles, while Roy Lichtenstein parodied comic strips.

American architecture also reached new heights in the postwar era. Ultramodern skyscrapers conceived in the modernist or **International Style** arose in the nation's urban centers. High-rises like New York's United Nations headquarters (1952) and Seagram Building (1957) were essentially giant steel boxes wrapped in glass. Meanwhile, old master Frank Lloyd Wright continued to produce strikingly original designs like the round-walled Guggenheim Museum (1959) in New York. Louis Kahn employed plain geometric forms to make beautiful, simple buildings, like the serene Salk Institute (1965) in La Jolla, California. Chinese-born I.M. Pei designed numerous graceful buildings on college campuses as well as the dramatic National Gallery of Art (1978) in Washington.

abstract expressionism *An experimental style of mid-twentieth-century modern art exemplified by Jackson Pollock's spontaneous "action paintings," created by flinging paint on canvases stretched across the studio floor.*

International Style *Archetypal, post-World War II modernist architectural style, best known for its "curtainwall" designs of steel-and-glass corporate high-rises.*

Postwar America reaped its greatest cultural harvest in the field of literature. Searing realism characterized the earliest novels that portrayed soldierly life in World War II, like Norman Mailer's *The Naked and the Dead* (1948) and James Jones's *From Here to Eternity* (1951). But as time passed, realistic war writing fell from favor. Authors tended increasingly to write about the war in fantastic and even psychedelic prose. Joseph Heller's savagely satirical *Catch-22* (1961) dealt with the antics and anguish of American airmen in the wartime Mediterranean. The supercharged imagination of Kurt Vonnegut, Jr., produced works of puzzling complexity in inventive prose, including the darkly comic war tale *Slaughterhouse Five* (1969).

In the 1950s the broader culture as well as America's literary imagination became engaged as never before with psychological and particularly Freudian concepts, and postwar pens documented the internal effects of the nation's newly affluent, exuberantly consumerist society. One group of countercultural "Beat" writers rejected modern American life outright, seeking self-expression in stridently nonconformist lifestyles. Striving for liberation, these social drifters advocated marching to one's own "beat." Once "beaten down" by the relentless pressures of bourgeois existence, these bohemian hedonists also deemed themselves capable of "beatitude" or blessedness.

Among the close cohort of prominent Beat writers were Jack Kerouac (1922-1969), whose wild series of transcontinental road trips became the substance of his landmark novel *On the Road* (1957), a sort of pocket bible for social rebels in the late 1950s. Bearded and bespectacled Allen Ginsberg, the most eloquent spokesman of the **Beat Generation**, produced compelling poetry like "Howl" (1955), which proclaimed, "I saw the best minds of my generation destroyed by madness. . . ." A public reading of Ginsberg's "Howl" in San Francisco launched a literary renaissance in that city centered around Lawrence Ferlinghetti's City Lights Bookstore. To literature, the Beats contributed a new style of free-form narration. Beyond the page their promotion of jazz, Eastern religious mysticism, sexual liberation, and extreme experience was eventually taken up by the 1960s "hippie" counterculture. But long after hippies had passed out of fashion, youngsters in America and elsewhere found inspiration in the writings of Kerouac, Ginsberg, and their fellow Beats.

Beat Generation *A small coterie of mid-twentieth-century bohemian writers and personalities, including Jack Kerouac, Allen Ginsberg, and Lawrence Ferlinghetti, who bemoaned bourgeois conformity and advocated free-form experimentation in life and literature.*

A larger group of mainstream writers tackled the realities and dilemmas of postwar American society head-on. Pennsylvania-born John Updike celebrated the feats and failings of ordinary, small-town America in his four-part "Rabbit" series, beginning with *Rabbit, Run* (1960). Massachusetts-bred John Cheever, the "Chekhov of the exurbs," chronicled suburban manners and morals in novels like *The Wapshot Chronicle* (1957). Poets were often highly critical, even despairing, about the conformist character of mid-century American life. Descended from a long line of patrician New Englanders, Robert Lowell sought to apply the wisdom of the Puritan past to the perplexing present in allegorical poems like *For the Union Dead* (1964). Troubled Sylvia Plath crafted the moving

Examining the Evidence

The Shopping Mall as New Town Square, 1960

In this photograph Democratic presidential candidate John F. Kennedy is campaigning at the Bergen Mall in Paramus, New Jersey. Just one presidential contest earlier, a regional shopping center would have been a rare campaign stop. The Bergen Mall opened in 1957, a time when similar shopping centers were popping up in suburbanizing metropolitan areas all over the United States. Real estate developers watched Americans flee cities for suburbs, and they followed the money, locating shopping centers strategically at new highway intersections or along the busiest thoroughfares. As suburbanites increasingly found branches of their favorite department and chain stores closer to home during the 1950s and 1960s, they found it less and less necessary to go downtown. Shopping centers for their part went out of their way to sell themselves as modern-style downtowns worthy of being the public core of new suburban communities, even though legally they were privately owned space. They provided the full range of shops and services once found in city centers, including restaurants, post offices, Laundromats, banks, and even chapels. Shopping centers offered entertainment, from movie theaters and skating rinks to free open-air concerts, carnivals, and exhibitions. They made auditoriums available for community meetings. And they attracted public events such as Kennedy on the stump.

1. Look closely at this photograph. What kind of audience greeted candidate Kennedy at the Bergen Mall in 1960? How different might the crowd have looked in a more socially diverse urban center such as Manhattan or in nearby Newark, the largest city in New Jersey at the time?
2. What did it mean for sites of consumption, such as privately owned shopping centers, to take on the roles and responsibilities previously associated with urban streets, squares, and parks?
3. How might current struggles of downtown merchants against "big-box" chain stores such as Walmart be compared to this history of continuing changes in American public and consumer spaces?

Picture Research Consultants & Archives/Courtesy of The Newark Public Library verses of *Ariel* (published posthumously in 1966) and a disturbing autobiographical novel, *The Bell Jar* (1963), but her career was cut short when she took her own life in 1963. Playwrights were also acute observers of postwar American social mores. Tennessee Williams wrote a series of searing dramas about psychological misfits struggling to hold themselves together amid the disintegrating forces of modern life. Noteworthy were *A Streetcar Named Desire* (1947) and *Cat on a Hot Tin Roof* (1955), each delivering powerful critiques of the contemporary restrictions placed on women's lives. Arthur Miller brought to the stage searching probes of American values, notably *Death of a Salesman* (1949) and *The Crucible* (1953), which treated the Salem witch trials as a dark parable warning against the dangers of McCarthyism. Lorraine Hansberry offered an affecting portrait of African American struggles in *A Raisin in the Sun* (1959). Edward Albee exposed the rapacious underside of middle-class life in *Who's Afraid of Virginia Woolf?* (1962).

Underrepresented groups gained new prominence in midcentury literary circles. Ralph Ellison depicted the African American's often tortured quest for personal identity in *Invisible Man* (1952), a haunting novel narrated by a nameless black person who finds that none of his supposed supporters can see him as a real man. James Baldwin won plaudits as a novelist and essayist, particularly for his sensitive reflections on the racial question in *The Fire Next Time* (1963). Black nationalist LeRoi Jones, who changed his name to Imamu Amiri Baraka, crafted powerful plays such as *Dutchman* (1964).

The South boasted its own literary revival, led by veteran Mississippi author William Faulkner, a Nobel Prize winner in 1950. The **Southern Renaissance** writers brought a new critical appreciation to the region's burdens of history and racism. Tennesseean Robert Penn Warren immortalized Louisiana politico Huey Long in *All the King's Men* (1946). Southern renaissance writers like Georgian Flannery O'Connor perceptively tracked the changes reshaping the postwar South. Virginian William Styron confronted the harsh history of his home state in a controversial fictional representation of an 1831 slave rebellion, *The Confessions of Nat Turner* (1967).

Southern Renaissance *A literary outpouring among mid-twentieth-century southern writers, begun by William Faulkner and marked by a new critical appreciation of the region's burdens of history, racism, and conservatism.*

Especially bountiful was the harvest of books by Jewish novelists. Bernard Malamud rendered a touching portrait of a family of New York Jewish storekeepers in *The Assistant* (1957). Philip Roth wrote comically about young New Jersey suburbanites in *Goodbye, Columbus* and penned an uproarious account of a sexually obsessed New Yorker in *Portnoy's Complaint* (1969).

Kennedy's "New Frontier" Spirit

Complacent and comfortable as the 1950s closed, Americans elected in 1960 a young, vigorous president who pledged "to get the country moving again." As John F. Kennedy announced in his stirring inaugural address on January 20, 1961, "the torch has been passed to a new generation of Americans." Speaking crisply with staccato finger jabs at the air, Kennedy personified the glamour and vitality of the new generation.

The youngest president ever elected assembled one of the youngest cabinets, including his brother, Robert F. Kennedy, as attorney general. Business whiz Robert S. McNamara left the presidency of the Ford Motor Company to take over the Defense Department. Along with other young advisers (many boasting Harvard degrees), these appointees made up an inner circle notable for its aura of brash confidence and self-conscious sophistication.

New Frontier (1961–1963) *President Kennedy's nickname for his domestic policy agenda. Buoyed by youthful optimism, the program included proposals for the Peace Corps and efforts to improve education and health care.*

Peace Corps *A federal agency created by President Kennedy in 1961 to promote voluntary service by Americans in foreign countries. The Peace Corps provides labor power to help developing countries improve their infrastructure, health care, educational systems, and other aspects of their societies. Part of Kennedy's New Frontier vision, the organization represented an effort by postwar liberals to promote American values and influence through productive exchanges across the world.*

From the outset Kennedy inspired high expectations, especially among the young. His depiction of America's potential for greatness as a "**New Frontier**" quickened patriotic pulses. He brought a warm heart to the Cold War when he proposed the **Peace Corps**, an army of idealistic and mostly youthful volunteers bringing American know-how to underdeveloped countries. He summoned citizens to service with his clarion call to "ask not what your country can do for you but what you can do for your country."

But the soaring rhetoric did not quite match the political situation. Kennedy came into office with fragile Democratic majorities in Congress. Southern Democrats threatened to team up with Republicans and ax New Frontier proposals like medical assistance for the aged and increased federal aid to education. Kennedy forced an expansion of the conservative-dominated House Rules Committee, but despite this victory his key medical and education bills stalled in Congress. In 1963 Congress even voted down an administration-endorsed bill slashing income and corporate tax rates to boost the economy.

Richard Goodwin (b. 1931), a Kennedy aide and Peace Corps staffer, eloquently summed up the buoyantly optimistic mood of the early 1960s:

"For a moment, it seemed as if the entire country, the whole spinning globe, rested, malleable and receptive, in our beneficent hands."

That tax bill hinted at the Kennedy administration's complex relationship with big business. Kennedy intended his tax cutting to mollify businessmen wary of a big-government liberal in the White House. But he could also be a tough negotiator with corporate titans when he wanted to. When steel managers raised prices after a noninflationary wage agreement with labor in 1962, Kennedy called them onto the Oval Office carpet and unleashed his Irish temper. Overawed, they backed down.

Kennedy's New Frontier vision also extended to the "final frontier." Early in his term, the president promoted a multibillion-dollar project dedicated, as he put it, to "landing a man on the Moon and returning him safely to earth." Though he summoned stirring rhetoric about expanding human possibilities, the moon shot was really a calculated plan to restore America's international prestige, severely damaged by the Soviet *Sputnik* successes (see p. 637). $24 billion later, in July 1969, two NASA astronauts triumphantly planted their footprints—and the American flag—on the moon's dusty surface. As people around the globe huddled around televisions to watch the **Apollo** mission live, the world had never seemed so small and interconnected, nor the United States so dominant.

Apollo (1961–1975) *Program of manned space flights run by America's National Aeronautics and Space Administration (NASA). The project's highest achievement was the landing of Apollo 11 on the moon on July 20, 1969.*

Foreign Flare-ups and "Flexible Response"

A few months after settling into the White House, in June 1961, the new president met Soviet Premier Nikita Khrushchev in Vienna. The tough-talking Soviet leader adopted a belligerent attitude, threatening to cut off Western access to Berlin. Though visibly shaken, the president refused to be bullied.

The Soviets backed off from their most bellicose threats, but their "puppet" East German regime suddenly began to construct the **Berlin Wall** in August 1961. A barbed-wire-and concrete barrier, the "Wall of Shame" looked like a gigantic enclosure around a prison. The Wall stood for almost three decades as an ugly scar symbolizing the post-World War II division of Europe into two hostile camps.

Berlin Wall *Fortified and guarded barrier between East and West Berlin erected on orders from Soviet premier Nikita Khrushchev in 1961 to stop the flow of people to the West. Until its destruction in 1989, the wall was a vivid symbol of the divide between the communist and capitalist worlds.*

Kennedy meanwhile turned his attention to Western Europe, now miraculously prospering after the Marshall Plan and the growth of the American-encouraged **European Economic Community (EEC)**, the free-trade area that later evolved into the European Union. Kennedy secured passage of the Trade Expansion Act in 1962, authorizing tariff cuts of up to 50 percent to promote trade with the EEC countries. This act led to the so-called Kennedy Round of tariff negotiations, concluded in 1967. These liberalized trade policies inaugurated a new era of such robustly invigorated international commerce that a new word was coined to describe it: *globalization*.

European Economic Community (EEC) *Free-trade zone in Western Europe created by Treaty of Rome in 1957. Often referred to as the "Common Market," this collection of countries originally included France, West Germany, Italy, Belgium, the Netherlands, and Luxembourg. The body eventually expanded to become the European Union, which by 2005 included twenty-seven member states.*

Special problems for U.S. foreign policy emerged from the worldwide decolonization of European overseas possessions after World War II. Cold War entanglements in these new nations threatened to escalate all too quickly into a nuclear confrontation between the United States and the USSR. Kennedy felt hamstrung by the knowledge that in a crisis he had the Devil's choice between humiliation and nuclear incineration. With Defense Secretary McNamara, he pushed an alternative strategy of "flexible response"—developing an array of military "options" that could be precisely matched to gravity of the crisis at hand. To this end, Kennedy increased spending on conventional military forces and bolstered the Special Forces (Green Berets) specializing in anti-guerilla fighting.

The doctrine of "flexible response" seemed sane enough, but it too contained lethal logic. It potentially lowered the level at which diplomacy would give way to shooting. It also provided a mechanism for a progressive, and possibly endless, stepping-up of the use of force. Vietnam soon presented a grisly proof of these pitfalls.

The corrupt, right-wing Ngo Dinh Diem government in Saigon, despite a deluge of American dollars, had ruled shakily since the partition of Vietnam in 1954 (see p. 635).

Anti-Diem agitators threatened to topple the pro-American government from power. In a fateful decision late in 1961, Kennedy ordered a sharp increase in the number of "military advisers" (U.S. troops) in South Vietnam.

American forces allegedly entered Vietnam to foster political stability—to help protect Diem from the communists long enough to allow him to enact promised social reforms. But the Kennedy administration eventually despaired of the reactionary Diem and in November 1963 encouraged a successful coup against him. Ironically, the United States thus contributed to precisely the process of political disintegration that its original policy had meant to prevent. Kennedy still told the South Vietnamese that it was "their war," but he had made dangerously deep political commitments. By the time of his death, he had ordered more than fifteen thousand American men into the Asian slaughter pen. A graceful pullout was becoming increasingly difficult (see Map 36.2).

Bay of Pigs invasion (1961) *CIA plot in 1961 to overthrow Fidel Castro by training Cuban exiles to invade and supporting them with American airpower. The mission failed and became a public relations disaster early in John F. Kennedy's presidency.*

Cuban missile crisis (1962) *Standoff between John F. Kennedy and Soviet premier Nikita Khrushchev in October 1962 over Soviet plans to install nuclear weapons in Cuba. Although the crisis was ultimately settled in America's favor and represented a foreign-policy triumph for Kennedy, it brought the world's superpowers perilously close to the brink of nuclear confrontation.*

Cuban Confrontations

Although the United States regarded Latin America as its backyard, its southern neighbors feared and resented the powerful Colossus of the North. In 1961 Kennedy extended the hand of friendship with the Alliance for Progress (*Alianza para el Progreso*), hailed as a Marshall Plan for Latin America and intended to quiet communist agitation. But results were disappointing; there was little alliance and even less progress. American handouts had little positive impact on Latin America's immense social problems.

President Kennedy also struck below the border with brass knuckles. He had inherited from the Eisenhower administration a CIA-backed scheme to topple Fidel Castro from power by invading Cuba with anticommunist exiles. On April 17, 1961, some twelve hundred exiles landed at Cuba's Bay of Pigs. When the ill-starred **Bay of Pigs invasion** bogged down, Kennedy stood fast in his decision to keep hands off, and the bullet-riddled band of anti-Castroites surrendered.

Hulton-Deutsch Collection/CORBIS

Failed Bay of Pigs Invasion, 1961 Cuban soldiers demonstrate a beach gun they used against a brigade of ex-Cubans who furtively invaded Cuba as agents of the United States. The debacle was one of several unsuccessful American attempts to overthrow Cuban leader Fidel Castro.

The Bay of Pigs blunder, along with continuing American covert efforts to assassinate Castro and overthrow his government, naturally pushed the Cuban leader even further into the Soviet embrace. Wily Chairman Khrushchev lost little time taking full advantage of his Cuban comrade's location just ninety miles off Florida's coast. In October 1962 aerial photographs by American spy planes revealed that the Soviets were secretly and speedily installing nuclear-tipped missiles in Cuba.

Kennedy and Khrushchev now began a nerve-racking game of "nuclear chicken." The president, on October 22, 1962, ordered a naval "quarantine" of Cuba and demanded immediate removal of the threatening weaponry. He also served notice on Khrushchev that any attack on the United States from Cuba would trigger nuclear retaliation against the Russian heartland. For an anxious week, Americans waited while Soviet ships approached the patrol line established by the U.S. Navy off Cuba. The world teetered breathlessly on the brink of global atomization. In this tense eyeball-to-eyeball confrontation, Khrushchev finally flinched. On October 28 he agreed to a partially face-saving compromise, by which he would pull the missiles out of Cuba. The United States in return quietly agreed not to invade the island and to remove from Turkey some of its own missiles targeted at the Soviet Union.

Fallout from the **Cuban missile crisis** was considerable. A disgraced Khrushchev was ultimately hounded out of the Kremlin and became an "unperson." Kennedy, apparently sobered by the appalling risks he had just run, pushed harder for a nuclear test-ban treaty with the Soviet Union. After prolonged negotiations in Moscow, a pact prohibiting trial nuclear explosions in the atmosphere was signed in late 1963.

Map 36.2 Vietnam and Southeast Asia, 1954–1975 Le Ly Hayslip (b. 1949) was born in a peasant village in South Vietnam, just south of Da Nang. In her memoir, *When Heaven and Earth Changed Places*, she describes the trauma endured by ordinary Vietnamese as a result of America's fight against the Viet Cong: "In 1963—the year the Viet Cong came to my village—American warplanes bombed Man Quang. It was at noon, just when the children were getting out of school. My aunt Thu and her pregnant daughter-in-law were making lunch for her husband and four grandchildren when the air-raid signal blared. They all jumped under the wooden table and sheltered the pregnant woman with their bodies—even the little kids. A bomb fell in Aunt Thu's front yard. . . . Hot shrapnel tore through everyone except the pregnant woman. Aunt Thu and one of her grandchildren were killed. The passing fragment left only a weeping hole where her generous heart had been."

Most significant was Kennedy's speech at American University in Washington, D.C., in June 1963. The president urged Americans to abandon a view of the Soviet Union as a Devil-ridden land filled with fanatics and instead to deal with the world "as it is, not as it might have been had the history of the last eighteen years been different." Kennedy thus tried to lay the foundations for a realistic policy of peaceful coexistence with the Soviet Union. Here were the modest origins of the policy that later came to be known as "détente" (French for "relaxation of tension").

The Struggle for Civil Rights

Freedom Riders *Organized mixed-race groups who rode interstate buses deep into the South to draw attention to and protest racial segregation, beginning in 1961. This effort to challenge racism, which involved the participation of many northern young people as well as southern activists, proved a political and public relations success for the civil rights movement.*

Voter Education Project (1962–1968) *Effort by SNCC and other civil rights groups to register the South's historically disenfranchised black population. The project typified a common strategy of the civil rights movement, which sought to counter racial discrimination by empowering people at grassroots levels to exercise their civic rights through voting.*

Kennedy had campaigned with a strong appeal to black voters, but he proceeded gingerly to redeem his promises on civil rights. Political concerns stayed his hand. Elected by a wafer-thin margin, he needed southern legislators to pass his medical and educational bills, which he believed would eventually benefit black Americans. Bold moves for racial justice would have to wait.

But events soon scrambled these careful calculations. After the wave of sit-ins that surged across the South in 1960, groups of **Freedom Riders** fanned out to end segregation in facilities serving interstate bus passengers. A white mob torched a Freedom Ride bus near Anniston, Alabama in May 1961, and Attorney General Robert Kennedy's personal representative was beaten unconscious in another anti–Freedom Ride riot in Montgomery. When southern officials proved unwilling or unable to stem the violence, Washington dispatched federal marshals to protect the Freedom Riders.

Reluctantly but fatefully, the Kennedy administration had now joined hands with the civil rights movement. For the most part, the relationship between Martin Luther King, Jr., and the Kennedys was a fruitful one. Encouraged by Robert Kennedy, the Student Non-Violent Coordinating Committee and other civil rights groups inaugurated the **Voter Education Project** to register the South's historically disfranchised blacks.

Integrating southern universities was as challenging as registering African Americans to vote. Some desegregated painlessly, but the University of Mississippi ("Ole Miss") became a volcano. A twenty-nine-year-old air force veteran, James Meredith, encountered

Bettmann/Bettmann Premium/CORBIS

Freedom Ride, 1961 Rampaging whites near Anniston, Alabama, burned this bus carrying an interracial group of Freedom Riders on May 14, 1961.

violent opposition when he attempted to register in October 1962. In the end President Kennedy was forced to send in four hundred federal marshals and three thousand troops to enroll Meredith in his first class—in colonial American history.

In the spring of 1963, Martin Luther King, Jr., launched a campaign against discrimination in Birmingham, Alabama, the most segregated big city in America. Previous attempts to crack the city's rigid racial barriers had produced more than fifty cross burnings and eighteen bomb attacks since 1957. King advised his organizers that "some of the people sitting here will not come back alive from this campaign." Events soon confirmed this grim prediction of violence. Watching developments on television screens, a horrified world saw peaceful civil rights marchers repeatedly repelled by police with attack dogs and electric cattle prods. High-pressure fire hoses shot water at demonstrators with enough force to knock bricks loose from buildings or strip bark from trees at a distance of one hundred feet. Little children were bowled down the street like tumbleweeds.

In his civil rights address of June 11, 1963, President John F. Kennedy (1917–1963) said:

"If an American, because his skin is dark, cannot eat lunch in a restaurant open to the public; if he cannot send his children to the best public school available; if he cannot vote for the public officials who represent him; if, in short, he cannot enjoy the full and free life which all of us want, then who among us would be content to have the color of his skin changed and stand in his place?"

Jolted by these vicious confrontations, President Kennedy delivered a memorable televised speech to the nation on June 11, 1963. Calling the situation a "moral crisis," and drawing on the same spiritual traditions as Martin Luther King, Jr., he declared that the principle at stake "is as old as the Scriptures and as clear as the American Constitution." He called for new civil rights legislation to protect black citizens. In August King led 200,000 black and white demonstrators in a peaceful **March on Washington** in support of the proposed legislation. In an electrifying speech from the Lincoln Memorial, King declared, "I have a dream that my four little children will one day live in a nation where they will not be judged by the color of their skin but by the content of their character."

March on Washington (1963) *Massive civil rights demonstration in August 1963 in support of Kennedy-backed legislation to secure legal protections for American blacks. One of the most visually impressive manifestations of the civil rights movement, the march was the occasion of Martin Luther King's famous "I Have a Dream" speech.*

Still the violence continued. On the very night of Kennedy's stirring television address a white gunman shot down Medgar Evers, a black Mississippi civil rights worker. In September 1963 an explosion blasted a Baptist church in Birmingham, killing four black girls who had just finished their Sunday school lesson called "The Love That Forgives."

The Killing of Kennedy

Violence haunted America in the mid-1960s, and it stalked onto center stage on November 22, 1963. While riding in an open limousine in downtown Dallas, Texas, President Kennedy was shot in the brain by a concealed rifleman and died within seconds. Vice President Johnson was promptly sworn in as president on a waiting airplane and flown back to Washington with Kennedy's body.

As a stunned nation grieved, the tragedy grew still more unbelievable. The alleged assassin, a furtive figure named Lee Harvey Oswald, was himself shot to death in front of the television cameras by a self-appointed avenger, Jack Ruby. So bizarre were the events surrounding the two murders that even an elaborate official investigation conducted by Chief Justice Warren could not quiet all doubts and theories about what had really happened.

For several days, the nation was steeped in sorrow. Not until then did many Americans realize how fully their young, vibrant president and his captivating wife had cast a spell over them. Chopped down in his prime after only slightly more than a thousand days in the White House, Kennedy was acclaimed more for the ideals he had enunciated and the spirit he had kindled than for his concrete achievements. In later years revelations about Kennedy's womanizing and allegations about his involvement with organized crime figures tarnished his reputation. But despite those accusations, his apparent vigor, charisma, and idealism made him an inspirational figure for a rising "baby boom" generation. Few could foresee that the decade following his death would explode into extraordinary ferment at home and abroad.

CHAPTER SUMMARY ★★★★★★★★★★★★★

American society grew ever more prosperous in the postwar era, as science, technology, and the Cold War fueled burgeoning new industries such as electronics and aviation. Women joined the movement into the increasingly white-collar work force and chafed at widespread restrictions they faced. A new consumer culture, centered around television, fostered an ethic of leisure and enjoyment, including more open expressions of sexuality in popular entertainment.

Enormously popular as the victorious Supreme Allied Commander in World War II, Dwight Eisenhower was nominated by enthusiastic Republicans and breezed to victory in the election of 1952. "Ike" was ideally suited to soothe an America badly shaken by the Cold War and Korea. Seeking stability in domestic affairs, Eisenhower reacted cautiously to the beginnings of the civil rights movement led by Martin Luther King, Jr., but sent troops to Little Rock to enforce court orders for desegregation. Eisenhower's domestic policies were moderately conservative, leaving most of the New Deal in place while spending vast sums on a new interstate highway system.

Despite John Foster Dulles's tough talk, Eisenhower's foreign policies were also generally cautious. He avoided direct military intervention in Vietnam, although aiding South Vietnamese leader Diem, and pressured Britain, France, and Israel to resolve the Suez crisis. Eisenhower also sought negotiations to thaw the frigid Cold War. Dealing with Nikita Khrushchev proved difficult, however, as *Sputnik*, the Berlin Crisis, the U-2 incident, and Fidel Castro's Cuban revolution all kept Cold War tensions high. In a tight election, Senator John Kennedy defeated Eisenhower's vice president, Richard Nixon. Kennedy called for the country to "get moving again" by more vigorously countering the Soviets.

America's power and affluence contributed to a postwar cultural renaissance. Painting and architecture undertook bold experiments in modernism. In literature, the Beat writers challenged conventional forms as well as conformist lifestyles. African American, southern, and Jewish writers all had a striking impact on American thought and writing.

Kennedy's vigorous New Frontier initiatives stirred a spirit of idealism, but many of his programs became bogged down in Congress. Cold War confrontations over Berlin and Russian missiles in Cuba created threats of nuclear war but were successfully defused. Countering communism's threat through the doctrine of "flexible response" led the administration into dangerous involvement in Vietnam and elsewhere.

Kennedy was slow to endorse the civil rights movement, but eventually King and other activists created a moral groundswell that led Kennedy to endorse racial justice and new civil rights legislation. While Kennedy's sudden death left most of his goals unfulfilled, his charisma and idealism had inspired a generation.

KEY TERMS

The Feminine Mystique (629)
rock 'n' roll (629)
Checkers Speech (630)
Montgomery bus boycott (632)
Brown v. *Board of Education of Topeka, Kansas* (634)
Student Non-Violent Coordinating Committee (SNCC) (634)
Operation Wetback (634)
Federal Highway Act of 1956 (635)
policy of boldness (635)
Hungarian uprising (635)
Battle of Dien Bien Phu (635)
Suez crisis (636)
Organization of Petroleum Exporting Countries (OPEC) (637)
Sputnik (637)
kitchen debate (639)
military-industrial complex (639)
abstract expressionism (640)
International Style (640)
Beat Generation (640)
Southern Renaissance (642)
New Frontier (642)
Peace Corps (642)
Apollo (643)
Berlin Wall (643)
European Economic Community (EEC) (643)
Bay of Pigs invasion (644)
Cuban missile crisis (644)
Freedom Riders (646)
Voter Education Project (646)
March on Washington (647)

PEOPLE TO KNOW

- Dwight D. ("Ike") Eisenhower
- Richard M. Nixon
- Betty Friedan
- Elvis Presley
- Rosa Parks
- Martin Luther King, Jr.
- Earl Warren
- John Foster Dulles
- Nikita Khrushchev
- Ho Chi Minh
- Gamal Abdel Nasser
- Fidel Castro
- John F. Kennedy
- Lyndon B. Johnson
- Jackson Pollock
- Andy Warhol
- Jack Kerouac
- Allen Ginsberg
- Arthur Miller
- Ralph Ellison
- Robert F. Kennedy
- Robert S. McNamara
- Ngo Dinh Diem
- James Meredith

Chapter 37

The Stormy Sixties

1963–1973

There's a battle outside and it is ragin'
It'll soon shake your windows and rattle your walls
For the times they are a-changin'

Bob Dylan, 1963

Chapter Outline

- Lyndon Baines Johnson and the "Great Society"
- From Civil Rights to Black Power
- The Vietnam Disaster
- The Election of Richard Nixon
- The Cultural Upheavals of the 1960s
- Nixon and the Vietnam War
- New Policies toward China and the Soviet Union
- Nixon's Domestic Policies
- Nixon's Re-election and Watergate
- Israelis, Arabs, and Oil
- *Thinking Globally: The Global 1960s*
- *Varying Viewpoints: The Sixties: Constructive or Destructive?*

Iconic historical decades rarely align perfectly with the actual calendar. What many Americans remember as the tumultuous "sixties" did not truly come to pass until after the shocking slaying of President John F. Kennedy, and its several upheavals in culture and politics extended well into the following decade. Between President Kennedy's assassination in 1963 and President Nixon's resignation in 1974, Americans experienced a sexual revolution, a civil rights revolt, the emergence of a "youth culture," a devastating war in Vietnam, a massive enlargement of the federal government, and the beginnings of a feminist uprising. The era's close left Americans exhausted, divided, and disillusioned—but also permanently transformed in myriad ways.

FOCUS QUESTIONS

1. What was Lyndon Johnson's distinctive style in the presidency, and what were the legislative goals of his "Great Society"?
2. How was the idealistic and nonviolent spirit of the civil rights movement transformed in the mid-1960s by white racial "backlash," black power, and urban rioting?
3. How did Lyndon Johnson and his advisers lead the United States deeper into the Vietnam quagmire, and why did that war create such deep divisions in American politics and society?
4. What were the roots of the cultural rebellion of the 1960s, and what were its short-term and long-term consequences?
5. What were Richard Nixon's greatest foreign and domestic policy achievements, and how was his presidency destroyed by the Watergate crimes?

CHRONOLOGY

1963	▪ Kennedy assassinated; Johnson assumes presidency
1964	▪ Twenty-fourth Amendment (abolishing poll tax in federal elections) ratified ▪ "Freedom Summer" voter registration in the South ▪ Gulf of Tonkin Resolution ▪ Johnson defeats Goldwater for presidency ▪ War on Poverty begins ▪ Civil Rights Act
1965	▪ Great Society legislation ▪ Voting Rights Act
1965–1968	▪ Race riots in U.S. cities
1966	▪ France withdraws from NATO
1967	▪ Six-Day War between Israel and Egypt
1968	▪ North Vietnamese army launches Tet offensive in South Vietnam ▪ Worldwide protests ▪ Martin Luther King, Jr., and Robert Kennedy assassinated ▪ Prague Spring crushed by Soviet army ▪ Nixon defeats Humphrey and Wallace for presidency
1969	▪ Astronauts land on moon ▪ Stonewall Inn riot in New York City
1970	▪ Nixon orders invasion of Cambodia ▪ Kent State and Jackson State incidents ▪ Environmental Protection Agency (EPA) created ▪ Clean Air Act
1971	▪ Pentagon Papers published ▪ Twenty-sixth Amendment (lowering voting age to eighteen) passed
1972	▪ Nixon visits China and Soviet Union; Shanghai Communiqué begins "normalization" of U.S.-Chinese relations ▪ ABM and SALT I treaties ratified ▪ Nixon defeats McGovern for presidency
1973	▪ Treaty of Paris enacts cease-fire in Vietnam and U.S. withdrawal ▪ War Powers Act ▪ OPEC oil embargo ▪ Endangered Species Act ▪ Chilean president Salvador Allende killed in CIA-backed coup ▪ *Roe v. Wade*
1974	▪ OPEC ends embargo, increases oil prices

The LBJ Brand on the Presidency

With President Kennedy struck down, the torch passed to craggy-faced Lyndon Baines Johnson, a Texan who towered six feet three inches. The new president hailed from the populist hill country west of Austin, Texas, and had supported New Deal measures as a young Congressman. But Johnson had trimmed his sails to the right in order to win statewide elections in Texas, including an eighty-seven vote victory in the 1948 Senate race that earned him the nickname "Landslide Lyndon."

Entrenched in the Senate, Johnson became the powerful majority leader and a master wheeler-dealer. He could move political mountains or checkmate opponents as the occasion demanded, using what came to be known as the "Johnson treatment"—a flashing display of backslapping, flesh-pressing, and arm-twisting that overbore friend and foe alike. His ego and vanity were legendary.

As president, Johnson quickly shed the conservative coloration of his Senate years to reveal the latent liberal underneath. With Johnson's vigorous prodding, and after a lengthy conservative filibuster, Congress at last passed the landmark **Civil Rights Act of 1964**. The act banned racial discrimination in most private facilities open to the public, including theaters, hospitals, and restaurants. It strengthened the federal government's power to end segregation in schools and other public places. Title VII of the Act barred employers from discriminating based on race or national origin in hiring, and empowered the Equal Employment Opportunity Commission (EEOC, a body Kennedy had created in 1961) to enforce the law.

Civil Rights Act of 1964 *Federal law that banned racial discrimination in public facilities and strengthened the federal government's power to fight segregation in schools. Title VII of the act prohibited employers from discriminating based on race in their hiring practices, and empowered the Equal Employment Opportunity Commission (EEOC) to regulate fair employment.*

When conservatives tried to derail the legislation by adding a prohibition on sexual, as well as racial, discrimination, the tactic backfired. The bill's opponents cynically calculated that liberals would not be able to support a bill that threatened to wipe out laws that singled out women for special protection because of their sex. But the act's Title VII passed with the sexual clause intact. It soon proved to be a powerful instrument of federally enforced gender equality, as well as racial equality. Johnson struck another blow for women and minorities in 1965 when he issued an executive order requiring all federal contractors to take **affirmative action** against discrimination.

affirmative action *Program designed to redress historic racial and gender imbalances in jobs and education. The term grew from an executive order issued by Lyndon B. Johnson in 1965 mandating that projects paid for with federal funds take concerted action against discrimination based on race in their hiring practices. In the late 1960s, President Nixon's Philadelphia Plan changed the meaning of affirmative action to require attention to certain groups, rather than protect individuals against discrimination.*

Johnson rammed Kennedy's stalled tax bill through Congress and added proposals of his own for a billion-dollar "War on Poverty." Initial political impetus for the antipoverty campaign came from Michael Harrington's surprise bestseller *The Other America* (1962), which revealed that in affluent America 20 percent of the population—and over 40 percent of the black population—suffered in poverty. Johnson's War on Poverty became part of a far-reaching reform program that he dubbed the **Great Society**. Epitomizing the confidence of the era, the Great Society project entailed a sweeping array of measures encompassing New-Deal style social programs and major public investment in education and the arts.

Great Society (1964–1968) *President Lyndon Johnson's term for his domestic policy agenda. Billed as a successor to the New Deal, the Great Society aimed to extend the postwar prosperity to all people in American society by promoting civil rights and fighting poverty. Great Society programs included the War on Poverty, which expanded the Social Security system by creating Medicare and Medicaid to provide health care for the aged and the poor. Johnson also signed laws protecting consumers and empowering community organizations to combat poverty at grassroots levels.*

Johnson Battles Goldwater in 1964

Johnson's nomination by the Democrats in 1964 was a foregone conclusion; he was chosen by acclamation in Atlantic City. The Republicans, convening in San Francisco, nominated box-jawed Senator Barry Goldwater of Arizona, a bronzed and bespectacled champion of rock-ribbed conservatism. The American stage was thus set for a historic clash of political principles.

Goldwater's forces had galloped out of the Southwest to ride roughshod over the moderate Republican "eastern establishment." Insisting that the GOP offer "a choice, not an echo," Goldwater attacked the federal income tax, the Social Security system, the Tennessee Valley Authority, civil rights legislation, the nuclear test-ban treaty, and, most loudly, the Great Society. His fiercely dedicated followers proclaimed, "In Your Heart You Know He's Right," which prompted the Democratic response, "In Your Guts You Know He's Nuts." Goldwater warmed right-wing hearts when he proclaimed that "extremism in the defense of liberty is no vice. And . . . moderation in the pursuit of justice is no virtue."

The senator owed his nomination to a burgeoning conservative movement that was gaining strength in the mushrooming middle-class suburbs of the Sunbelt. Led intellectually by vibrant writers like William F. Buckley and others on the *National Review* magazine, enthusiastic conservatives organized groups like Young Americans for Freedom. They were especially well received in the once-solidly Democratic South, where the civil rights movement met strong white opposition. Upon signing the Civil Rights Act of 1964 Lyndon Johnson had reputedly told an aide, "We have lost the South for a generation."

Democrats gleefully exploited the image of Goldwater as a trigger-happy cowboy who would "Barry us" in the rubble of World War III. Johnson cultivated the contrasting image of a resolute statesman by seizing upon the Tonkin Gulf episode early in August 1964. Unbeknownst to the American public or Congress, U.S. Navy ships had been cooperating with South Vietnamese gunboats in provocative raids along the coast of North Vietnam. Two of these American destroyers were allegedly fired upon by the North Vietnamese on August 2 and 4, although exactly what happened still remains unclear.

Johnson nevertheless promptly called the attacks "unprovoked" and ordered a "limited" retaliatory air raid. He loudly proclaimed that he sought "no wider war"—thus implying that the truculent Goldwater did. Johnson also used the incident to spur congressional passage of the all-purpose Tonkin Gulf Resolution. With only two dissenting votes in both chambers, the lawmakers virtually abdicated their war-declaring powers and handed the president a blank check to use further force in Southeast Asia.

The towering Texan rode to a spectacular victory in November 1964. A stampede of 43,129,566 Johnson votes trampled the Republican ticket with its 27,178,188 supporters. The tally in the Electoral College was 486 to 52. Goldwater carried only his native Arizona and five other states—all of them, tellingly, in the racially restless South. Johnson's record-breaking 61 percent of the popular vote swept lopsided Democratic majorities into both houses of Congress.

The Great Society Congress

Johnson's huge victory temporarily smashed the conservative congressional coalition of southern Democrats and northern Republicans. A wide-open legislative road stretched before the Great Society programs, as the president skillfully ringmastered his two-to-one Democratic majorities. Congress poured out a flood of legislation, comparable only to the output of the New Dealers in the Hundred Days Congress of 1933, as Johnson delivered at last on long-deferred Democratic promises of social reform.

Besides a greatly expanded War on Poverty, Johnson also prodded Congress into creating two new cabinet offices: the Department of Transportation and the Department of Housing and Urban Development (HUD), to which he named the nation's first black cabinet secretary, respected economist Robert C. Weaver. Other noteworthy laws established the National Endowments for the Arts and the Humanities, designed to lift the level of American cultural life.

Even more impressive were the Big Four legislative achievements that crowned LBJ's Great Society: aid to education, medical care for the elderly and indigent, immigration reform, and a new voting rights bill.

Johnson's federal program for education neatly avoided the thorny question of church and state by channeling educational aid to students, not schools, thus allowing funds to flow to hard-pressed parochial institutions. With a keen eye for the dramatic, LBJ signed the education bill in the humble one-room Texas schoolhouse he had attended as a boy.

Medicare for the elderly, accompanied by Medicaid for the poor, became a reality in 1965. Like the New Deal's Social Security program, Medicare and Medicaid created "entitlements." That is, they conferred rights on certain categories of Americans in perpetuity, without the need for repeated congressional approval. These programs were part of a spreading "rights revolution" that materially improved the lives of millions of Americans—but also eventually undermined the federal government's financial health.

Immigration reform was the third of Johnson's Big Four feats. The Immigration and Nationality Act of 1965 abolished at last the "national-origins" quota system that had been in place since 1921 (see p. 521). The act also doubled to 290,000 the number of immigrants allowed to enter annually, and provided for the admission of close relatives of U.S. citizens without limits. The "family unification" provision swelled immigration, and to the surprise of the act's sponsors, the sources of immigration shifted heavily from Europe to Latin America and Asia, dramatically changing the racial and ethnic composition of the American population.

Great Society programs came in for rancorous political attack in later years. Conservatives charged the billions spent for "social engineering" had simply been flushed down the waste pipe. Yet the poverty rate declined measurably in the ensuing decade. Medicare dramatically reduced poverty among America's elderly, and antipoverty programs like Project Head Start sharply improved the educational performance of underprivileged youth. Infant mortality rates also fell in minority communities as general health conditions improved.

Battling for Black Rights

With the last of his Big Four reforms, the Voting Rights Act of 1965, Johnson made heartening headway against one of the most persistent American evils, racial discrimination. The Civil Rights Act of 1964 had prohibited racial discrimination in public accommodations and employment and strengthened school desegregation. But the problem of voting rights remained. Throughout the South, only about 5 percent of eligible blacks were registered to vote. Ballot-denying devices like the poll tax, literacy tests, and barefaced intimidation still barred black people from the political process.

Beginning in 1964, opening up the polling booths became the chief goal of the black movement in the South. The Twenty-fourth Amendment, ratified in January 1964, abolished the poll tax in federal elections. (See the Appendix.) Singing "We Shall Overcome," blacks joined hands with white civil rights workers—many of them student volunteers from the North—in a massive voter-registration drive in Mississippi during the **Freedom Summer** of 1964.

Freedom Summer (1964) *A voter registration drive in Mississippi spearheaded by a coalition of civil rights groups. The campaign drew the activism of thousands of black and white civil rights workers, many of whom were students from the North, and was marred by the abduction and murder of three such workers at the hands of white racists.*

Mississippi Freedom Democratic party (1964) *Political party organized by civil rights activists to challenge Mississippi's delegation to the Democratic National Convention, who opposed the civil rights planks in the party's platform. Claiming a mandate to represent the true voice of Mississippi, where almost no black citizens could vote, the MFDP demanded to be seated at the convention but were denied by party bosses. The effort was both a setback to civil rights activism in the South and a motivation to continue to struggle for black voting rights.*

Voting Rights Act of 1965 *Legislation pushed through Congress by President Johnson that prohibited ballot-denying tactics, such as literacy tests and intimidation. The Voting Rights Act was a successor to the Civil Rights Act of 1964 and sought to make racial disenfranchisement explicitly illegal.*

But events soon blighted bright hopes. In late June 1964, one black and two white civil rights workers disappeared in Mississippi. Their badly beaten bodies were later found buried beneath an earthen dam. In August an integrated **Mississippi Freedom Democratic party** delegation was denied its seat at the national Democratic convention.

Early in 1965 Martin Luther King, Jr., resumed the voter-registration campaign in Selma, Alabama. State troopers with tear gas and whips assaulted King's peaceful demonstrators as they marched to Montgomery. A Boston Unitarian minister was killed, and a few days later a white Detroit woman was shotgunned to death by Klansmen on the highway near Selma.

As the nation recoiled in horror before these violent scenes, President Johnson, speaking in soft southern accents, delivered a compelling address on television. What happened in Selma, he insisted, concerned all Americans, "who must overcome the crippling legacy of bigotry and injustice." Then, in a stirring adaptation of the anthem of the civil rights movement, the president concluded: "And we shall overcome." Following words with deeds, Johnson speedily shepherded through Congress the landmark **Voting Rights Act of 1965**, signed into law on August 6. It outlawed literacy tests and sent federal voter registrars into several southern states.

The passage of the Voting Rights Act, exactly one hundred years after the conclusion of the Civil War, climaxed a century of awful abuse and robust resurgence for African Americans in the South. The act did not end discrimination and oppression overnight, but it placed an awesome lever for change in blacks' hands. Black southerners now had power and began to wield it without fear of reprisals. In the following decade, for the first time since emancipation, African Americans began to migrate *into* the South.

★ Black Power

The Voting Rights Act of 1965 marked the last major victory of the southern-focused, integrationist, nonviolent civil rights struggle—what one activist called the "classical phase" of the movement. From then on, racial conflict, especially in the urban North, took on new potency and ideological coloring after Jim Crow's final demise in the South. As if to symbolize this shift, just five days after President Johnson signed the voting law, a bloody riot erupted in Watts, a black ghetto in Los Angeles. The week-long violence left thirty-one blacks and three whites dead, more than a thousand people injured, and hundreds of buildings charred and gutted. The Watts explosion heralded a new phase of the black struggle—increasingly marked by militant confrontation, focusing on northern and western cities, led by radical and sometimes violent spokespersons, and often aiming not at interracial cooperation but at black separatism.

The pious Christian moderation of Martin Luther King, Jr., came under heavy fire from this second wave of younger black leaders. Embodying this new militancy was Malcolm X. Born Malcolm Little, he was at first inspired by the militant black nationalists in the Nation of Islam, founded by Elijah Muhammad. A brilliant and charismatic preacher, Malcolm X trumpeted black separatism and inveighed against the "blue-eyed white devils." Eventually, Malcolm distanced himself from Elijah Muhammad's separatist preachings and moved toward mainstream Islam. In early 1965 he was cut down by Nation of Islam gunmen while speaking to a large crowd in New York City.

Black Panther party *Organization of armed black militants formed in Oakland, California, in 1966 to protect black rights. The Panthers represented a growing dissatisfaction with the nonviolent wing of the civil rights movement and signaled a new direction to that movement after the legislative victories of 1964 and 1965.*

Black Power *Doctrine of militancy and separatism that rose in prominence after 1965. Black Power activists rejected Martin Luther King's pacifism and desire for integration. Rather, they promoted pride in African heritage and an often militant position in defense of their rights.*

The **Black Panther party** meanwhile openly brandished weapons in the streets of Oakland, California. Then in 1966 Trinidad-born Stokely Carmichael, a leader of the Student Non-Violent Coordinating Committee (SNCC), began to preach the doctrine of **Black Power**, which, Carmichael said, "will smash everything Western civilization has created." Some advocates of Black Power insisted that they simply intended the slogan to describe a broad-front effort to exercise the political and economic rights gained by the civil rights movement. But other African Americans, recollecting previous black nationalist movements such as that of Marcus Garvey earlier in the century (see p. 530), breathed a vibrant separatist meaning into the concept of Black Power. They emphasized African American distinctiveness, shed their "white" names for new African identities, and demanded black studies programs in colleges and universities.

Ironically, just as the civil rights movement had achieved its greatest legal and political triumphs, city-shaking riots erupted in the black ghettos of several American cities. A bloody outburst in Newark, New Jersey, in the summer of 1967, took twenty-five lives. Federal troops restored order in Detroit, Michigan, after forty-three people died in the streets. As in Los Angeles, black rioters torched their own neighborhoods, attacking police officers, and even firefighters, who had to battle both flames and mobs chanting, "Burn, baby, burn." These outbursts angered many white Americans, who threatened to retaliate with their own "backlash" against ghetto arsonists and killers. Inner-city anarchy baffled many northerners, who had considered racial problems a purely "southern" question. But black concerns had moved north—as had nearly half the nation's black people. Residential discrimination and deindustrialization all directly affected African Americans, who suffered unemployment at twice the rate of whites. Despair deepened when the magnetic and moderate voice of Martin Luther King, Jr., was forever silenced by a sniper's bullet in Memphis, Tennessee, on April 4, 1968. A martyr for justice, King had bled and died on the peculiarly American thorn of race. The killing of King cruelly robbed the American people of one of the most inspirational leaders in their history—at a time when they could least afford to lose him. This outrage triggered a nationwide outburst of violent riots that cost over forty lives.

Rioters noisily made news, but thousands of other blacks quietly made history. Their voter registration had shot upward, and by the late 1960s several hundred blacks held elected office in the Old South. Cleveland, Ohio, and Gary, Indiana, elected black mayors. By 1972 nearly half of southern black children sat in integrated classrooms. Actually, more schools in the South were integrated than in the North. About a third of black families had risen economically into the ranks of the middle class—though an equal proportion remained below the "poverty line." King left a shining legacy of racial progress, but he was cut down when the job was far from done.

Contending Voices

Differing Visions of Black Freedom

Dr. Martin Luther King, Jr. (1929–1968) and Malcolm X (1925–1965) not only differed in the goals they held out to their fellow African Americans—King urging racial integration and Malcolm X black separatism—but also in the means they advocated to achieve them. In his famous "I Have a Dream" speech during the interracial March on Washington on August 28, 1963, King spoke to a quarter of a million people assembled at the Lincoln Memorial:

"In the process of gaining our rightful place we must not be guilty of wrongful deeds. Let us not seek to satisfy our thirst for freedom by drinking from the cup of bitterness and hatred. . . . We must not allow our creative protest to degenerate into physical violence. Again and again we must rise to the majestic heights of meeting physical force with soul force."

About three months later, Malcolm X rejected King's "peaceful, turn-the-other-cheek revolution":

"Revolution is bloody, revolution is hostile, revolution knows no compromise, revolution overturns and destroys everything that gets in its way. And you, sitting around here like a knot on the wall, saying, 'I'm going to love these folks no matter how much they hate me,' . . . Whoever heard of a revolution where they lock arms . . ., singing 'We shall overcome?' You don't do that in a revolution. You don't do any singing, you're too busy swinging."

Why did King see nonviolence as key to achieving movement goals? What might explain some African Americans' growing receptivity to militant and separatist appeals over the course of the 1960s?

Vietnam Vexations

While violence at home eclipsed Johnson's legislative triumphs, foreign flare-ups were threatening his political life. The United States was sinking deeper into the monsoon mud of Vietnam. After communist guerillas attacked an American air base in February 1965, Johnson ordered retaliatory air strikes and for the first time sent regular American troops. Before 1965 was ended, some 184,000 American soldiers were slogging through the jungles and rice paddies of South Vietnam searching for guerillas.

Johnson had now taken the first fateful steps down a slippery path. He and his advisers believed that a fine-tuned, step-by-step "escalation" of American force would drive the enemy to defeat with a minimum loss of life. But the enemy matched every increase in American firepower with more men and more wiliness in the art of guerrilla warfare.

The South Vietnamese themselves were meanwhile becoming spectators in their own war, as the fighting became increasingly Americanized. Corrupt and collapsible governments succeeded each other in Saigon with bewildering rapidity. Yet American officials continued to talk of defending a faithful democratic ally. Washington "hawks" also defended the action as a test of Uncle Sam's commitment and of the reliability of his numerous treaty pledges to resist communist encroachment. Persuaded by such panicky thinking, Johnson steadily raised the military stakes in Vietnam. By 1968 he had poured more than half a million troops into Southeast Asia, and the annual bill for the war was exceeding $30 billion. Still, the end was nowhere in sight.

America could not defeat the enemy in Vietnam, but it seemed to be defeating itself. World opinion grew increasingly hostile; the blasting of an underdeveloped country by a mighty superpower struck many critics as obscene. Several nations expelled American Peace Corps volunteers. President Charles de Gaulle withdrew France from NATO in 1966 and ordered all American troops out of the country.

Overcommitment in Southeast Asia also tied America's hands elsewhere. Attacked by Soviet-backed Egypt, Jordan, and Syria, a beleaguered Israel stunned the world with a military triumph in June 1967. When the smoke cleared after the **Six-Day War**, Israel expanded to control new territories in the Sinai Peninsula, the Golan Heights, the Gaza Strip, and the West Bank of the Jordan River, including Jerusalem. The Israelis eventually withdrew from the Sinai after signing a peace treaty with Egypt, but they refused to relinquish the other areas without a treaty and began moving Jewish settlers into the heavily Arab district of the West Bank. The Six-Day War markedly intensified the problems of the already volatile Middle East, leading to an intractable standoff between the Israelis and more than a million resentful Palestinians under their control.

Six-Day War (1967) *Military conflict between Israel and its Arab neighbors, including Syria, Egypt, and Jordan. The war ended with an Israeli victory and territorial expansion into the Sinai Peninsula, the Golan Heights, the Gaza Strip, and the West Bank. The 1967 war was a humiliation for several Arab states, and the territorial disputes it created formed the basis for continued conflict in the region.*

Domestic discontent festered as the Vietnamese entanglement dragged on. Antiwar demonstrations had begun on a small scale with campus "teach-ins" in 1965. Gradually these protests mounted to tidal-wave proportions. As the long arm of the military draft dragged more and more young men off to the Southeast Asian slaughter pen, resistance stiffened. Thousands of draft registrants fled to Canada; others publicly burned their draft cards. Hundreds of thousands of chanting marchers filled the streets of New York, San Francisco, and other cities. Many Americans felt pangs of conscience at the ghastly spectacle of their countrymen burning peasant huts and blistering civilians with napalm.

Opposition in Congress to the Vietnam involvement centered in the influential Senate Committee on Foreign Relations, headed by Senator J. William Fulbright of Arkansas. A constant thorn in the side of the president, he staged a series of widely viewed televised hearings in 1966 and 1967, during which prominent personages aired their views, largely antiwar. Gradually the public came to feel that it had been lied to about the causes and "winnability" of the war. A yawning credibility gap opened between the government and the people. New flocks of antiwar "doves" were hatching daily.

By early 1968 the brutal and futile struggle had become the longest and most unpopular foreign war in the nation's history. The government had failed utterly to explain to the people what was supposed to be at stake in Vietnam. American casualties, killed and wounded, already exceeded 100,000. More bombs had been dropped on Vietnam than on all enemy territory in World War II.

The war was also ripping apart the fabric of American society and even threatening to shred the Constitution. In 1967 President Johnson ordered the CIA, in clear violation of its charter as a *foreign* intelligence agency, to spy on domestic antiwar activities. He also encouraged the FBI to turn its counterintelligence program against the peace movement, subverting leading "doves" with false accusations that they were communist sympathizers. These clandestine tactics made the FBI look like a totalitarian state's secret police rather than a guardian of American democracy.

As the war dragged on, evidence mounted that America had been entrapped in an Asian civil war, fighting against highly motivated rebels who were striving to overthrow an oppressive regime. Yet Johnson clung to his basic strategy of ratcheting up the pressure bit by bit. He stubbornly assured doubting Americans that he could see "the light at the end of the tunnel." But to growing numbers of Americans, it seemed that Johnson was bent on "saving" Vietnam by destroying it.

AP Photo

The Mechanized War High technology and modern equipment, such as this helicopter, gave the Americans in Vietnam a huge military advantage. But unaccompanied by a clear political purpose and a national will to win, technological superiority was insufficient to achieve final victory.

Vietnam Topples Johnson

Hawkish illusions that the struggle was about to be won were shattered by a blistering communist offensive launched in late January 1968, during Tet, the Vietnamese New Year. At a time when the Viet Cong were supposedly licking their wounds, they suddenly and simultaneously mounted savage attacks on twenty-seven key South Vietnamese cities, including the capital, Saigon. Although eventually beaten off with heavy losses, they demonstrated anew that victory could not be gained by Johnson's strategy of gradual escalation. With an increasingly insistent voice, American public opinion demanded a speedy end to the war. But American military leaders responded to the Tet attacks with a request for 200,000 more troops. The size of the request staggered many policymakers.

Meanwhile, Senator Eugene J. McCarthy of Minnesota was sharply challenging the president from within his own party for the 1968 Democratic presidential nomination. McCarthy, a sometime poet and devout Catholic, gathered a small army of antiwar college students as campaign workers. Going "clean for Gene," with shaven faces and shortened locks, they helped him gain an impressive 41.4 percent of the Democratic vote in the New Hampshire primary on March 12, 1968. Although still second to Johnson's 49.6 percent, McCarthy's showing was devastating for the president. Johnson's star fell further four days later when Senator Robert F. Kennedy of New York, an outspoken dove on the war, threw his hat into the ring. The charismatic and handsome Kennedy, heir to his murdered brother's mantle of leadership, stirred a passionate response among workers, African Americans, Latinos, and young people.

These startling events abroad and at home were not lost on LBJ. In a bombshell address on March 31, 1968, he announced that he would freeze American troop levels and scale down the bombing. Then, Johnson startled his vast television audience by firmly declaring that he would not be a candidate for the presidency in 1968.

Johnson's "abdication" had the effect of preserving the military status quo. The United States could maintain the maximum *acceptable* level of military activity in Vietnam with one hand, while trying to negotiate a settlement with the other. North Vietnam shortly agreed to negotiations in Paris, but progress was glacially slow, as prolonged bickering developed over the very shape of the conference table.

The Presidential Sweepstakes of 1968

The summer of 1968 was one of the hottest political seasons in the nation's history. Johnson's heir apparent for the Democratic nomination was his loyal vice president, Hubert Humphrey. Senators McCarthy and Kennedy meanwhile dueled in several state primaries, with Kennedy's bandwagon gathering ever-increasing speed. But on June 5, 1968, on the night of his exciting victory in the California primary, Kennedy was shot to death by a young Arab immigrant.

Angry antiwar forces, deprived by an assassin's bullet of one of their candidates, streamed menacingly into Chicago for the Democratic convention in August 1968. Mayor Richard Daley responded by arranging for barbed-wire barricades around the convention hall, as well as thousands of police and National Guard reinforcements. Some militant demonstrators baited the officers in blue by calling them "pigs," shouting obscenities, and hurling cans of excrement at police lines. As people the world over watched on television, the exasperated "peace officers" broke into a "police riot," clubbing and manhandling innocent and guilty alike. Acrid tear gas fumes hung over the city even as Humphrey steamrollered to a first-ballot nomination. The Humphrey forces also blocked the dovish McCarthyites' attempt to secure an antiwar platform plank and hammered into place their own declaration that armed force would be relentlessly applied until the enemy showed more willingness to negotiate.

Scenting victory over the badly divided Democrats, the Republicans convened in plush Miami Beach, Florida, where former vice president Richard Nixon arose from his political grave to win the nomination. As a "hawk" on Vietnam and a right-leaning middle-of-the-roader on domestic policy, Nixon was acceptable to both the Goldwater

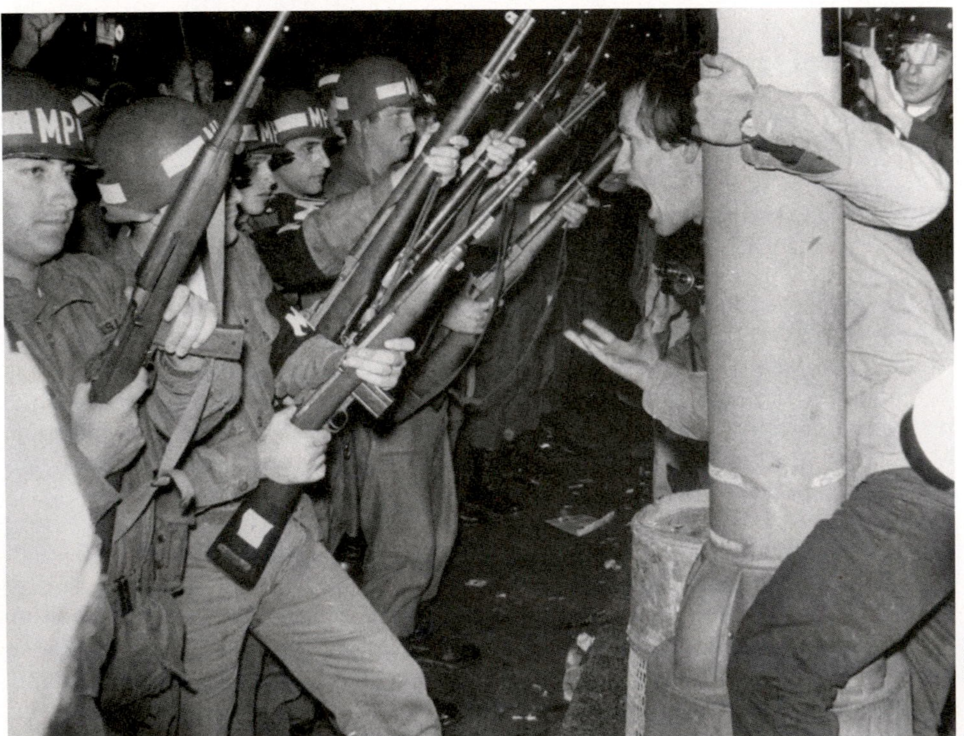

Bettmann/CORBIS

The Siege of Chicago, 1968 Antiwar protesters staged demonstrations in the streets of Chicago during the Democratic National Convention in August 1968. Some 2,500 members of the radical Youth International Party (known as the Yippies) planned a peaceful "festival of light" across the street from the convention hall, but instead found themselves drawn into a melee with the police and National Guardsmen. The confrontation in Chicago badly tarnished Democratic candidate Hubert Humphrey's presidential campaign. His Republican opponent, Richard Nixon, won the presidency with calls for an "honorable peace" in Vietnam and "law and order" at home.

conservatives and party moderates. He appealed to white southern voters and to the "law and order" element when he tapped as his running mate Maryland Governor Spiro T. Agnew, noted for his tough stands against dissidents and black militants. The Republican platform called for victory in Vietnam and a strong anticrime policy.

Adding color and confusion to the campaign was the third-party candidacy of the segregationist former Alabama governor George C. Wallace. Wallace jabbed repeatedly at "pointy-headed bureaucrats" and taunted hecklers as "bums" who needed a bath. He also called for prodding blacks back into their place. Wallace and his running mate, former air force general Curtis LeMay, also proposed smashing the North Vietnamese to smithereens by "bombing them back to the Stone Age."

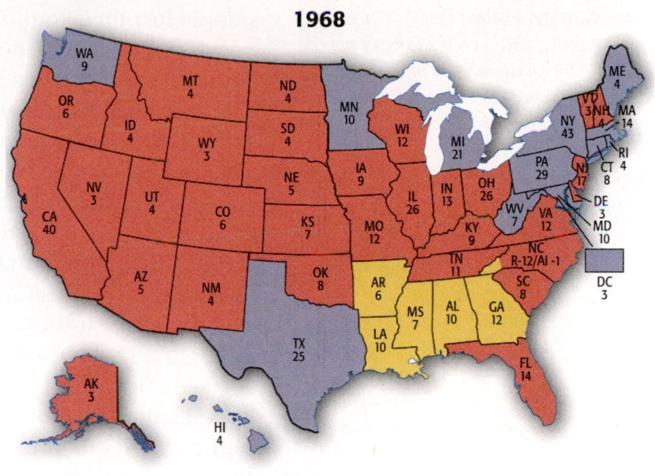

Candidate (Party)	Electoral Vote		Popular Vote	
Nixon (Republican)	301	56.1%	31,785,480	43.4%
Humphrey (Democrat)	191	35.5%	31,275,166	42.7%
Wallace (American Independent)	46	8.4%	9,906,473	13.5%

Map 37.1 Presidential Election of 1968 (with electoral vote by state) George Wallace won in five states and denied a clear majority to either of the two major-party candidates in twenty-five other states. A shift of some fifty thousand votes might have thrown the election into the House of Representatives, giving Wallace the strategic bargaining position that he sought.

Between the positions of the Republicans and the Democrats on Vietnam, there was little choice. Both candidates were committed to keeping on the war until the enemy would settle for an "honorable peace," which seemed to mean an "American victory." The millions of "doves" had no place to roost, and many refused to vote at all. Humphrey, scorched by the LBJ brand, went down to defeat as a loyal prisoner of his chief's policies.

Nixon, who had lost a cliffhanger to Kennedy in 1960, won one in 1968. He garnered 301 electoral votes with 43.4 percent of the popular tally (31,785,480), compared with 191 electoral votes and 42.7 percent of the popular votes (31,275,166) for Humphrey (see Map 37.1). Unlike most new presidents, Nixon faced congressional majorities of the opposing party in both houses. Wallace won an impressive 9,906,473 popular votes and 46 electoral votes, all from five states of the Deep South, four of which the Republican Goldwater had carried in 1964. Wallace remained a formidable force, for he had amassed the largest third-party popular vote in American history to that point and was the last third-party candidate to win any electoral votes. (Ross Perot in 1992 enjoyed a greater popular vote margin but won no states; see p. 704.) Wallace had also resoundingly demonstrated the continuing power of "populist" politics, which appealed to voters' fears and resentments rather than to the better angels of their nature. His candidacy foreshadowed a coarsening of American political life that would take deep root in the ensuing decades.

Talented but tragedy-struck Lyndon Johnson returned to his Texas ranch in January 1969 and died there four years later. His party and his vice president Humphrey had been defeated, yet Johnson's legislative leadership for a time had been remarkable. No president since Lincoln had worked harder or done more for civil rights. None had shown more compassion for the poor, blacks, and the ill educated.

But by 1966 Johnson was already sinking into the Vietnam quicksand. His attempt to provide both guns and butter prevented him from delivering on either in sufficient quantity. The War on Poverty met resistance as stubborn as the Viet Cong and eventually went down to defeat. Johnson crucified himself on the cross of Vietnam. His decision to enlarge the conflict cost him his political future. By not escalating the fighting further he offended the "hawks," by refusing to back off altogether he antagonized the "doves." Like the Calvinists of colonial days, luckless Lyndon Johnson was damned if he did and damned if he did not.

The Cultural Upheaval of the 1960s

The struggles of the 1960s against racism, poverty, and the war in Vietnam had momentous cultural consequences. Everywhere in 1960s America, a newly negative attitude toward all kinds of authority began to take hold. Disillusioned by the discovery that American society was not free of racism, sexism, imperialism, and oppression, many young

Stonewall Rebellion (1969) *Uprising in support of equal rights for gay people sparked by an assault by off-duty police officers at a gay bar in New York. The rebellion led to a rise in activism and militancy within the gay community and furthered the sexual revolution of the late 1960s.*

Students for a Democratic Society (SDS) *A campus-based political organization founded in 1961 by Tom Hayden that became an iconic representation of the New Left. Originally geared toward the intellectual promise of "participatory democracy," SDS emerged at the forefront of the civil rights, antipoverty, and antiwar movements during the 1960s.*

people lost their traditional moral rudders. Neither families nor churches nor schools seemed to be able to define values and shape behavior with the certainty of shared purpose that many people believed had once existed.

The nation's mainstream Protestant denominations, which had dominated American religious life for centuries, lost their grip and many of their churchgoing parishioners. The liberal Protestant churches suffered the most. They increasingly ceded religious authority to conservative evangelicals while surrendering cultural authority to secular professionals and academic social scientists. Religious upheaval even churned the tradition-bound Roman Catholic Church, among the world's oldest and most conservative institutions. The Second Vatican Council, meeting from 1962 to 1965, passed reforms aimed at modernizing church liturgy and practices and encouraging more ecumenical interactions with other faiths. Clerics abandoned their Roman collars and the Latin Mass; folk songs replaced Gregorian chants; and meatless Fridays became ancient history.

Skepticism about authority had deep historical roots in American culture, and it had even bloomed in the supposedly complacent and conformist 1950s. "Beat" poets like Allen Ginsberg and iconoclastic novelists like Jack Kerouac had voiced dark disillusion with the materialistic pursuits of "establishment" arrogance of the Eisenhower era. In movies like *Rebel Without a Cause* (1955), the attractive young actor James Dean expressed the restless frustration of many young people.

University of California at Berkeley, Bancroft Library

The Free Speech Movement, Berkeley, California, 1964 The Free Speech Movement on the campus of the University of California at Berkeley marked the first of the large-scale student mobilizations that rocked campuses across the country throughout the rest of the 1960s. Here a student schooled in passive resistance is dragged by police to a waiting bus.

The disaffection of the young crescendoed in the tumultuous 1960s, as the first baby boomers reached college age. One of the first organized protests against established authority broke out at the University of California at Berkeley in 1964, in the aptly named Free Speech Movement. Students objected to an administrative ban on the use of campus space for political debate, and accused the Cold War "megaversity" of promoting corporate interests rather than humane values.

But in only a few years, the clean-cut Berkeley activists and their sober-minded sit-ins would seem downright quaint. Fired by outrage against the war in Vietnam, some sons and daughters of the middle class became radical political rebels. Others turned to mind-bending drugs, tuned in to "acid rock," and dropped out of "straight" society. Others joined communes or "alternative" institutions. *Patriotism* became a dirty word. Beflowered women and long-haired men with earrings heralded the rise of a self-conscious "counterculture" stridently opposed to traditional American ways.

Social upheaval in the 1960s was hardly confined to the United States as youth-driven political and social conflict roiled nations around the world (see "Thinking Globally: The Global 1960s," p. 661). The newfound power of popular youth culture—especially the urgent rock 'n' roll of the Beatles, Janis Joplin, and Jimi Hendrix—proved global in its reach, helping to stitch together generational styles, norms, and touchstones across borders.

The 1960s also witnessed a "sexual revolution," though its novelty and scale are often exaggerated. Without doubt, the introduction of the birth-control pill in 1960 made unwanted pregnancies much easier to avoid and sexual appetites much easier to satisfy. The Mattachine Society, founded in Los Angeles in 1951, was a pioneering advocate for gay rights. A brutal attack on gay men by off-duty police officers at New York's Stonewall Inn in 1969 proved a turning point, when the victims fought back in what became known as the **Stonewall Rebellion**.

Launched in youthful idealism, many of the cultural "revolutions" of the 1960s sputtered out in violence and cynicism. **Students for a Democratic Society (SDS)**, once at the forefront of antipoverty and antiwar campaigns, had by decade's end spawned an underground terrorist group called the Weather

The Global 1960s

Social upheaval in the 1960s was a global phenomenon. As young people born in the wake of World War II came of age around the world, they everywhere challenged established authority, customs, and institutions. Antiwar protests and demonstrations for social rights shook the political and cultural foundations of peoples on every inhabited continent.

Worldwide turmoil was propelled by worldwide forces. A massive "baby boom" swelled the demographic profile of nations on all continents. Western youth approached adulthood buoyed by postwar prosperity and major public investments in higher education. The leading edge of boomers entered college in the 1960s, just as the international equilibrium was increasingly challenged by Cold War tensions, threats of thermonuclear war, and rapid decolonization in Asia and Africa. Affluent, educated, and idealistic, conscious of their shared generational identity, and impatient with their elders, these young people formed the vanguard of political and social turmoil in one country after another.

Western Europe, long culturally aligned with the United States, paralleled the American experience most closely. Young people in the North Atlantic world adopted what one historian has called an "international language of dissent." Thinkers as disparate as Berlin-born philosopher Herbert Marcuse, American sociologist C. Wright Mills, and Martinique-born psychiatrist Frantz Fanon rejected the stark Cold War dichotomies between capitalist and communist states and inspired Western youth to ferociously condemn repressive and imperialistic tendencies in their own societies. On both sides of the Atlantic, the American war in Vietnam catalyzed protest.

Upheaval was hardly confined to the capitalist West. Peace, economic growth, and expanding education also emboldened a postwar generation in Soviet bloc countries to voice political dissent. A Soviet intelligence officer cabled Soviet premier Leonid Brezhnev in 1968 that "opposition" was one of the "harmful developments among our youth."

The global tumult swept up peoples in the "Third World" as well, even as Western radicals made folk heroes of revolutionaries like Cuba's Che Guevara and Congo's Patrice Lumumba. In China, Mao Zedong launched the "Cultural Revolution" in 1966 to purge all bourgeois vestiges from the emerging Chinese nation. Young and ideologically hypercharged Red Guards made war on the "Four Olds": old customs, old culture, old habits, and old ideas. Millions perished before Mao finally began to rein in the rampaging bullies in 1969.

The year 1968 became synonymous with unrest in many lands. Within the Soviet bloc, Western-inspired Czechoslovakian reformers launched the liberating "Prague Spring." For eight months political freedom blossomed, until ruthlessly cut down by Soviet tanks. In May, leftist French students, backed by massive workers' strikes, nearly toppled the government of President Charles de Gaulle.

By the early seventies, repression and exhaustion began to dissipate the global unrest. But despite backlash and disillusionment, the upheavals of the 1960s left a permanent mark on societies around the world. New "post-materialist" concerns about culture, identity, the environment, and human rights began to enter the political mainstream. A new skepticism about authority and a loosening of cultural mores transformed societies the world over as a lasting consequence of the global 1960s.

Bruno Barbey/Magnum Photos

Paris, 1968 Protests ripped through the world in 1968. In Paris student battles with campus authorities and police triggered a massive nationwide labor strike and nearly brought down the French government.

Underground. Peaceful civil rights demonstrations had given way to blockbusting urban riots. What started as apparently innocent experiments with drugs like marijuana and LSD had fried many youthful brains and spawned a loathsome underworld of drug lords and addicts.

Strait-laced guardians of respectability denounced the self-indulgent romanticism of the "flower children" as the beginning of the end of modern civilization. Sympathetic observers hailed the "greening" of America—the replacement of materialism and imperialism by a new consciousness of human values. But the upheavals of the 1960s could be largely attributed to three *P*'s: the youthful population bulge, protest against racism and the Vietnam War, and the prosperity that seemed a permanent fixture of postwar America The counterculture may not have fully replaced traditional values by the end of the "sixties," but it had weakened their grip, perhaps permanently.

Vietnamization *Military strategy launched by Richard Nixon in 1969. The plan reduced the number of American combat troops in Vietnam and left more of the fighting to the South Vietnamese, who were supplied with American armor, tanks, and weaponry.*

Nixon Doctrine *President Nixon's plan for "peace with honor" in Vietnam. The doctrine stated that the United States would honor its existing defense commitments but, in the future, countries would have to fight their own wars.*

silent majority *Nixon administration's term to describe generally content, law-abiding, middle-class Americans who supported both the Vietnam War and America's institutions. As a political tool, the concept attempted to make a subtle distinction between believers in "traditional" values and the vocal minority of civil rights agitators, student protesters, counterculturalists, and other seeming disruptors of the social fabric.*

Nixon "Vietnamizes" the War

Inaugurated on January 20, 1969, Richard Nixon urged the American people, torn with dissension over Vietnam and race relations, to "stop shouting at one another." The new president seemed an unlikely conciliator of the clashing forces that appeared to be ripping apart American society. Solitary and suspicious by nature, Nixon could be brittle and testy in the face of opposition. He also harbored bitter resentments against the "liberal establishment." But Nixon brought one hugely valuable asset with him to the White House—his expertise in foreign affairs.

The first burning need was to quiet the public uproar over Vietnam. President Nixon's announced policy, called **Vietnamization**, was to withdraw the 540,000 U.S. troops in South Vietnam over an extended period. The South Vietnamese—with American money, weapons, training, and advice—could then gradually take over the burden of fighting their own war. This so-called **Nixon Doctrine** furthermore proclaimed that in the future, America's allies would have to fight their own wars without the support of large bodies of American ground troops.

Nixon sought to win the war by other means without the further spilling of American blood. But even this much involvement was distasteful to the American "doves," many of whom demanded a prompt, complete, and unconditional withdrawal. Antiwar protesters staged a massive national Vietnam moratorium in October 1969, as nearly 100,000 people jammed Boston Common and some 50,000 filed by the White House carrying lighted candles.

A Marine Corps officer expressed the disillusion that beset many American troops in Vietnam:

"For years we disposed of the enemy dead like so much garbage. We stuck cigarettes in the mouths of corpses, put *Playboy* magazines in their hands, cut off their ears to wear around our necks. We incinerated them with napalm, atomized them with B-52 strikes, shoved them out the doors of helicopters above the South China Sea. . . . All we did was count, count bodies. Count dead human beings. . . . That was our fundamental military strategy. Body count. And the count kept going up."

Undaunted, Nixon launched a counteroffensive by appealing to the "**silent majority**" who presumably supported the war and rejected the counterculture. Though ostensibly conciliatory, Nixon's appeal was in fact deeply divisive. His intentions soon became clear when he unleashed tough-talking Vice President Agnew to attack the "nattering nabobs of negativism" who demanded quick withdrawal from Vietnam. Nixon himself in 1970 sneered at the student antiwar demonstrators as "bums."

By January 1970 the Vietnam conflict had become grotesquely unpopular, even among troops in the field. Because draft policies largely exempted college students and those with high skills, the armed forces in Vietnam were mainly composed of the least privileged young Americans. African Americans were disproportionately represented in the army and accounted for a disproportionately high share of combat casualties. Black and white soldiers alike floundered through booby-trapped swamps and steaming jungles, often unable to distinguish friend from foe among the Vietnamese peasants. Morale plummeted, as drug abuse, mutiny, and sabotage dulled the army's fighting edge, and rumors spread that soldiers were murdering ("fragging") their own officers with fragmentation grenades. Domestic disgust with the war further deepened amid revelations that American troops had slaughtered innocent women and children in the village of **My Lai** in 1968.

My Lai *Vietnamese village that was the scene of a military assault on March 16, 1968, in which American soldiers under the command of 2nd Lieutenant William Calley murdered hundreds of unarmed Vietnamese civilians, mostly women and children. The atrocity produced outrage and reduced support for the war in America and around the world when details of the massacre and an attempted cover-up were revealed in November 1969.*

"Cambodianizing" the Vietnam War

For several years the North Vietnamese and Viet Cong had been using Cambodia, bordering South Vietnam on the west, as a springboard for troops, weapons, and supplies. Suddenly, on April 29, 1970, without consulting Congress, Nixon ordered American troops to invade officially neutral Cambodia.

Angry students nationwide responded to this newest escalation of the fighting with rock throwing, window smashing, and arson. At **Kent State University** in Ohio, jumpy members of the National Guard fired into a noisy student crowd, killing four and wounding many more. At historically black Jackson State College in Mississippi, the highway patrol killed two students.

Kent State University *Scene of massacre of four college students by National Guardsmen on May 4, 1970, in Ohio. In response to Nixon's announcement that he had expanded the Vietnam War into Cambodia, college campuses across the country exploded in violence. On May 14 and 15, students at historically black Jackson State College in Mississippi were protesting the war as well as the Kent State shooting when highway patrolmen fired into a student dormitory, killing two students.*

Nixon withdrew the American troops from Cambodia after only two months. But in America the Cambodian invasion amplified the bitterness between "hawks" and "doves." Disillusionment with "whitey's war" increased ominously among African American troops. The Senate (though not the House) overwhelmingly repealed the Gulf of Tonkin blank check that Congress had given Johnson in 1964. American youths were only slightly mollified when the government reduced draft calls, introduced a draft lottery, and lowered the voting age to eighteen through approval of the Twenty-sixth Amendment in 1971 (see Appendix).

New combustibles fueled the fires of antiwar discontent in June 1971, when a former Pentagon official leaked to the *New York Times* the **Pentagon Papers**, a top-secret Pentagon study that documented the blunders and deceptions of the Kennedy and Johnson administrations, especially the provoking of the 1964 North Vietnamese attack in the Gulf of Tonkin.

Pentagon Papers *Secret U.S. government report detailing early planning and policy decisions regarding the Vietnam War under Presidents Kennedy and Johnson. Leaked to the New York Times in 1971, it revealed instances of governmental secrecy, lies, and incompetence in the prosecution of the war.*

John Filo/Getty Images

The War at Home, Spring 1970 President Nixon's order to invade Cambodia sparked angry protests on American campuses. At Kent State University in Ohio, the nation watched in horror as four student demonstrators were shot by jittery National Guardsmen.

Nixon's Détente with Beijing (Peking) and Moscow

Even as the war in Vietnam ground on, Nixon pursued a dramatic Cold War diplomatic initiative in Beijing and Moscow. The two great communist powers, China and the Soviet Union, were clashing bitterly over their rival interpretations of Marxism. Nixon astutely perceived that the Chinese-Soviet tension afforded the United States an opportunity to play off one antagonist against the other, gaining new leverage on the world stage. Nixon's thinking was reinforced by his bespectacled and German-accented national security adviser, Dr. Henry A. Kissinger, who in 1969 had begun negotiating secretly with North Vietnamese officials in Paris while preparing the president's path to Beijing and Moscow.

Nixon, heretofore an uncompromising anticommunist, startled the nation by making an historic journey to China in February 1972. He capped the visit with the Shanghai Communiqué, in which the two nations agreed to "normalize" their relationship. Nixon next traveled to Moscow in May 1972 to play his "China card" in a game of high-stakes diplomacy in the Kremlin. The Soviets, hungry for American foodstuffs and alarmed over the possibility of intensified rivalry with an American-backed China, were ready to deal.

détente *From the French for "reduced tension," the period of Cold War thawing when the United States and the Soviet Union negotiated reduced armament treaties under Presidents Nixon, Ford, and Carter. As a policy prescription, détente marked a departure from the policies of proportional response, mutually assured destruction, and containment that had defined the earlier years of the Cold War.*

Nixon's visits ushered in an era of **détente**, or relaxed tension, with the two communist powers and led to several significant agreements in 1972, including an antiballistic missile (ABM) treaty and a series of arms-reduction agreements known as SALT (Strategic Arms Limitations Talks) aimed at freezing the numbers of long-range nuclear missiles for five years. The ABM and SALT accords constituted long-overdue first steps toward slowing the arms race, though both parties forged ahead with the development of "MIRVs" (multiple independently targeted reentry vehicles) equipped with large numbers of warheads, several to a rocket.

Nixon's détente diplomacy did, to some extent, de-ice the Cold War. Yet Nixon remained staunchly anticommunist when the occasion seemed to demand it. He strongly opposed the election of the outspoken Marxist Salvador Allende as president of Chile in 1970. His administration and the Central Intelligence Agency worked covertly to undermine the legitimately elected leftist president. When the Chilean army overthrew and killed Allende in 1973, many observers smelled a Yankee rat—an impression that deepened when Washington warmly embraced Allende's successor, military dictator General Augusto Pinochet.

Nixon on the Home Front

Nixon had lashed out during the campaign at the "permissiveness" and "judicial activism" of the Supreme Court, presided over by Chief Justice Earl Warren. The Warren Court's controversial decisions on sexual freedom, civil rights, criminal law, the practice of religion, and the structure of political representation had reflected its deep concern for the individual, no matter how lowly.

Miranda warning *A statement of an arrested person's constitutional rights, which police officers must read during an arrest. The warning came out of the Supreme Court's decision in* Miranda v. Arizona *in 1966 that accused people have the right to remain silent, consult an attorney, and enjoy other protections. The Court declared that law enforcement officers must make sure suspects understand their constitutional rights, thus creating a safeguard against forced confessions and self-implication.*

In *Griswold v. Connecticut* (1965), the Court struck down a state law that prohibited the use of contraceptives, even among married couples. The Court proclaimed (critics said "invented") a "right of privacy" that soon provided the basis for decisions protecting women's abortion rights. Controversial decisions in the cases of *Escobedo* (1964) and *Miranda* (1966) gave accused criminals the right to remain silent. The latter case gave rise to the **Miranda warning** that arresting officers must read to suspects. These several court rulings sought to prevent abusive police tactics, but they appeared to conservatives to coddle criminals and subvert law and order.

Conservatives also objected to the Court's views on religion. In two stunning decisions, *Engel* v. *Vitale* (1962) and *School District of Abington Township* v. *Schempp* (1963), the justices argued that the First Amendment's separation of church and state meant that public schools could not require prayer or Bible reading. From 1954 on, the Court came under relentless criticism, the bitterest since New Deal days. Fulfilling campaign promises, President Nixon undertook to change the Court's philosophical complexion.

He sought appointees who would strictly interpret the Constitution, cease "meddling" in social and political questions, and not coddle radicals or criminals. The Senate in 1969 speedily confirmed his nomination of white-maned Warren E. Burger of Minnesota to succeed the retiring Earl Warren as chief justice. Before the end of 1971 the Court counted four conservative Nixon appointments out of nine members.

Yet Nixon was to learn the ironic lesson that many presidents have learned about their Supreme Court appointees: once seated on the high bench, the justices are fully free to think and decide according to their own consciences, not according to the president's expectations. The Burger Court that Nixon shaped proved reluctant to dismantle the "liberal" rulings of the Warren Court; it even produced the most controversial judicial opinion of modern times, the momentous *Roe v. Wade* decision in 1973, which legalized abortion (see p. 679).

Surprisingly Nixon presided over significant expansion of the welfare programs that conservative Republicans routinely denounced. He approved increased funds for entitlements like Food Stamps, Medicaid, and Aid to Families with Dependent Children (AFDC), while adding a generous new program, Supplemental Security Income (SSI), to assist the indigent, blind, and disabled. Nixon also guaranteed automatic Social Security cost-of-living increases to protect the elderly against the ravages of inflation. Ironically, this "indexing" actually helped to fuel the inflationary fires.

Amid much controversy, Nixon in 1969 implemented his so-called **Philadelphia Plan** requiring construction unions to establish "goals and timetables" for the hiring of black apprentices. Soon extended to all federal contracts, the Philadelphia Plan required employers to meet hiring quotas or to establish "set-asides" for minority contractors. Nixon's policy went beyond earlier definitions of "affirmative action" designed to aid *individuals*, and instead conferred privileges on certain *groups*. While opening broad employment and educational opportunities for minorities and women, this approach opened a Pandora's box of protest from critics who assailed this "reverse discrimination" imposed by executive orders and unelected courts, not by democratically elected representatives.

Philadelphia Plan (1969) *Program established by Richard Nixon to require construction trade unions to work toward hiring more black apprentices. The plan altered Lyndon Johnson's concept of "affirmative action" to focus on groups rather than individuals.*

Among Nixon's legacies was the creation in 1970 of the **Environmental Protection Agency (EPA)**, which climaxed two decades of mounting concern for the environment. Scientist and author Rachel Carson gave the environmental movement a huge boost in 1962 when she published *Silent Spring*, an enormously effective piece of latter-day muckraking that exposed the poisonous effects of pesticides. On April 22, 1970, millions of environmentalists around the world celebrated the first **Earth Day** to raise awareness and to encourage their leaders to act. In the wake of what became a yearly event, the U.S. Congress passed the Clean Air Act of 1970 and the Endangered Species Act of 1973. The EPA now stood on the frontline of the battle for ecological sanity and made notable progress in reducing automobile emissions and cleaning up befouled waterways and toxic waste sites.

Environmental Protection Agency (EPA) *A governmental organization signed into law by Richard Nixon in 1970 designed to regulate pollution, emissions, and other factors that negatively influence the natural environment. The creation of the EPA marked a newfound commitment by the federal government to actively combat environmental risks and was a significant triumph for the environmentalist movement.*

Earth Day (1970) *International day of celebration and awareness of global environmental issues launched by conservationists on April 22, 1970.*

The federal government also expanded its regulatory reach on behalf of workers and consumers. Late in 1970 Nixon signed the Occupational Safety and Health Administration (OSHA) into law, creating an agency dedicated to improving working conditions. The Consumer Product Safety Commission (CPSC) followed two years later, holding companies to account for selling dangerous products.

Appointing conservative Supreme Court justices, soft-pedaling civil rights, and opposing school busing to achieve racial balance were all parts of a GOP electoral approach that Nixon advisers called the "**southern strategy**." By deliberately seeking to convert disillusioned white southern Democrats to the Republican cause, Nixon set in motion a sweeping political realignment that eventually transformed the American party system.

southern strategy (1972) *Nixon reelection campaign strategy designed to appeal to conservative whites in the historically Democratic South. The president stressed law and order issues and remained noncommittal on civil rights. This strategy typified the regional split between the two parties as white southerners became increasingly attracted to the Republican party in the aftermath of the civil rights movement.*

★ The Nixon Landslide of 1972

Nearly four years had passed since Nixon had promised, as a presidential candidate, to end the war and "win" the peace. Yet in the spring of 1972 the fighting escalated anew to alarming levels when the North Vietnamese, heavily equipped with foreign tanks, burst through the demilitarized zone (DMZ) separating the two Vietnams. Nixon reacted promptly by launching massive bombing attacks on strategic centers in North Vietnam, including Hanoi, the capital. Either Moscow or Beijing, or both, could have responded explosively, but neither did, thanks to Nixon's shrewd diplomacy.

The continuing Vietnam conflict spurred the rise of South Dakota Senator George McGovern to the 1972 Democratic nomination. McGovern's promise to pull the remaining American troops out of Vietnam in ninety days earned him the backing of the large antiwar element in the Democratic party. But his appeal to racial minorities, feminists, leftists, and youth alienated the traditional working-class backbone of his party. Moreover, the discovery shortly after the convention that McGovern's running mate, Missouri Senator Thomas Eagleton, had undergone psychiatric care—including electroshock therapy—forced Eagleton's ouster from the ticket and virtually doomed the Democrats' hopes of recapturing the White House.

Nixon's campaign emphasized that he had wound down the "Democratic war" in Vietnam from some 540,000 troops to about 30,000. His candidacy received an added boost just twelve days before the election when the high-flying Dr. Kissinger announced that "peace is at hand" in Vietnam and that an agreement would be reached in a few days.

Nixon won the election in a landslide. His lopsided victory encompassed every state except Massachusetts and the nonstate District of Columbia (which was granted electoral votes by the Twenty-third Amendment in 1961 (see Appendix). He piled up 520 electoral votes to 17 and a popular majority of 47,169,911 votes to 29,170,383. McGovern had counted on a large vote from young people, but less than half the eighteen-to-twenty-one age group even bothered to register to vote. Dominated by conflict over both Vietnam and the counterculture, the 1972 presidential election proved to be the last election of the sixties era.

The Secret Bombing of Cambodia and the War Powers Act

The dove of peace, "at hand" in Vietnam just before the balloting, took flight after the election. Nixon launched a furious two-week bombing of North Vietnam that drove the North Vietnamese negotiators to agree to a cease fire in the Treaty of Paris on January 23, 1973, nearly three months after peace was prematurely proclaimed.

Nixon hailed the face-saving cease-fire agreement as "peace with honor," but the boast rang hollow. The United States was to withdraw its remaining 27,000 or so troops and could reclaim some 560 American prisoners of war. The North Vietnamese were allowed to keep some 145,000 troops in South Vietnam, where they still occupied about 30 percent of the country. This shaky "peace" was in reality little more than a thinly disguised American retreat.

The constitutionality of Nixon's continued aerial battering of Cambodia had meanwhile been coming under increasing fire. In July 1973 America was shocked to learn that the U.S. Air Force had already secretly conducted some thirty-five hundred bombing raids against North Vietnamese positions in Cambodia, beginning in March 1969 and continuing for some fourteen months prior to the open American incursion in May 1970. The most disturbing feature of these sky forays was that, while they were going on, American officials, including the president, had sworn that Cambodian neutrality was being respected. Countless Americans began to wonder what kind of representative government they had if they were fighting a war they knew nothing about.

Defiance followed secretiveness. After the Vietnam cease-fire in January 1973, Nixon brazenly continued large-scale bombing of communist forces in order to help the rightist Cambodian government, and he repeatedly vetoed congressional efforts to stop him. The years of bombing inflicted grisly wounds on Cambodia, blasting its people and revolutionizing its politics. The long-suffering Cambodians soon groaned under the sadistic heel of Pol Pot, a murderous tyrant who dispatched as many as 2 million of his people to their graves.

Congressional opposition to the expansion of presidential war-making powers by Johnson and Nixon led to the **War Powers Act** in November 1973. Passed over Nixon's veto, it required the president to report to Congress within forty-eight hours after committing troops to a foreign conflict. Such a limited authorization would have to end within sixty days unless Congress extended it for thirty more days.

The War Powers Act was but one manifestation of what came to be called the "New Isolationism," a mood of caution and restraint in the conduct of the nation's foreign affairs after the bloody and futile misadventure in Vietnam. Meanwhile, the draft ended in January 1973, although it was retained on a standby basis. The armed forces were to be all volunteers.

The Washington Post *(July 19, 1973) carried this news item:*

"American B-52 bombers dropped about 104,000 tons of explosives on Communist sanctuaries in neutralist Cambodia during a series of raids in 1969 and 1970. . . . The secret bombing was acknowledged by the Pentagon the Monday after a former Air Force major . . . described how he falsified reports on Cambodian air operations and destroyed records on the bombing missions actually flown."

The Arab Oil Embargo and the Energy Crisis

War Powers Act (1973) *Law passed by Congress limiting the president's ability to wage war without congressional approval. The act required the president to notify Congress within forty-eight hours of committing troops to a foreign conflict. An important consequence of the Vietnam War, this piece of legislation sought to reduce the president's unilateral authority in military matters.*

The long-rumbling Middle East erupted anew in October 1973, when the rearmed Syrians and Egyptians unleashed surprise attacks on Israel. Kissinger, who had become secretary of state in September, hastily flew to Moscow to restrain the Soviets, who were arming the attackers. Believing that the Kremlin was poised to fly combat troops to the Suez area, Nixon placed America's nuclear forces on alert and ordered a gigantic airlift of nearly $2 billion in war materials to the Israelis. This assistance helped save the day, as the Israelis aggressively turned the tide and threatened Cairo itself until American diplomacy brought about an uneasy cease-fire in what became known as the Yom Kippur War.

America's policy of backing Israel against its oil-rich neighbors exacted a heavy penalty. Late in October 1973, the OPEC nations announced an embargo on oil shipments to the United States and several European allies supporting Israel. What was more, the oil-rich Arab states cut their oil production, further ratcheting pressure on the entire West, whose citizens suffered a long winter of lowered thermostats and speedometers. Lines at gas stations grew longer as tempers grew shorter. The shortage triggered a major economic recession not just in America, but also in France and Britain. In an increasingly globalized, interconnected world, all nations soon felt the crunch of the "energy crisis."

The five months of the Arab "blackmail" embargo in 1974 clearly signaled the end of an era—the era of cheap and abundant energy. American oil production peaked in 1970 and then began a long decline. Blissfully unaware of their dependence on foreign suppliers, Americans, like revelers on a binge, had more than tripled their oil consumption since the end of World War II. The number of automobiles increased 250 percent between 1949 and 1972, and Detroit's engineers gave nary a thought to building more fuel-efficient engines.

By 1974 America was oil-addicted and extremely vulnerable to any interruption in supplies. That stark fact deeply colored the diplomatic and economic history of the next three decades and beyond, as the Middle East loomed ever larger on the map of America's strategic interests. The United States finally began to initiate conservation measures such as a national speed limit of fifty-five miles per hour to conserve fuel. Detroit's automakers began their slow, grudging adjustment to the dawning age of energy dependency. But full reconciliation to that uncomfortable reality was a long time coming.

Varying Viewpoints

The Sixties: Constructive or Destructive?

The 1960s were convulsed by controversy, and they have remained controversial ever since. Conflicts raged in that turbulent decade between social classes, races, sexes, and generations. More than five decades later, conservative Republicans continue to campaign on a repudiation of the government activism that marked the sixties and a reaffirmation of the "traditional values" that sixties culture supposedly trashed. Liberal Democrats, for their part, continued to press for affirmative action for women and minorities, protection for the environment, an expanded welfare state, and sexual tolerance—all legacies of the stormy sixties.

Four issues dominate historical discussion of the 1960s: the civil rights struggle; the Great Society's "War on Poverty"; the Vietnam War and the antiwar movement; and the emergence of the "counterculture."

Although most scholars praise the civil rights achievements of the 1960s, they disagree over how to conceptualize the rise of Black Power and the militants' rejection of nonviolence. The Freedom Riders and Martin Luther King, Jr., find much more approval in most history books than do Malcolm X or the Black Panther party. But such scholars as William L. Van Deburg in *New Day in Babylon* (1992) and Peniel Joseph, *Waiting 'Til the Midnight Hour* (2006), argue that the "flank effect" of radical Black Power radicals like Stokely Carmichael actually enhanced the bargaining position of moderates such as Dr. King. Scholars of what Jacquelyn Hall has term the "long civil rights movement" meanwhile challenge the very notion of a sharp dividing line distinguishing the "classical" phase of the movement from a militant post-1965 phase.

Johnson's War on Poverty has found its liberal defenders in scholars like Allen Matusow (*The Unraveling of America*, 1984) and John Schwarz (*America's Hidden Success*, 1988). Schwarz demonstrates, for example, that Medicare and Social Security reforms virtually eliminated poverty among America's elderly. But conservative writers like Charles Murray (*Losing Ground*, 1984) and Lawrence Meade (*Beyond Entitlements*, 1986) argue that the War on Poverty did not simply fail to eradicate poverty among the so-called underclass; it actually deepened the dependency of the poor on the welfare state and even generated a multigenerational "cycle" of poverty.

The antiwar movement protesting America's policy in Vietnam initiated many young people into politics and "movement culture," with its sense of community and shared purpose. But scholars disagree over the movement's real effectiveness in checking the war. Writers such as John Lewis Gaddis (*Strategies of Containment*, 1982) explain America's eventual withdrawal from Vietnam essentially without reference to the protesters in the streets, while other like Adam Garfinkle (*Telltale Hearts*, 1995) argue that antiwar activism actually prolonged the war. By contrast, Todd Gitlin (*The Sixties: Years of Hope, Days of Rage*, 1987) and Tom Wells (*The War Within*, 1994) insist that mass protest was the force that finally ended the war.

Debate over the counterculture not only pits liberals against conservatives but also pits liberals against radicals. A liberal historian such as William O'Neill (*Coming Apart*, 1971) might sympathize with what he considers some of the worthy values pushed by student activists, but he also claims that much of the sixties "youth culture" degenerated into hedonism, arrogance, and social polarization. In contrast, historians such as Michael Kazin and Maurice Isserman argue that cultural radicalism and political radicalism were two sides of the same coin. Sara Evans shows in *Personal Politics* (1980) that "the personal *was* the political" for many women, and finds the roots of modern feminism in the sexism women activists encountered in the civil rights and antiwar movements.

Some scholars have begun to look at the origins of the conservative movement even during the liberal ascendency of the 1960s. Historians like Lisa McGirr (*Suburban Warriors*, 2001) and Rick Perlstein (*Before the Storm*, 2001) argue that Barry Goldwater's defeat in 1964 actually kick-started the conservatism that led to Ronald Reagan and both George Bushes. Rebecca Klatch shows in *A Generation Divided* (1999) how the New Right fed off the New Left, reshaping American politics in profound ways.

While critics may argue over the "good" versus the "bad" sixties, there is no denying the degree to which that tumultuous decade shaped the world in which we now live.

CHAPTER SUMMARY ★ ★ ★ ★ ★ ★ ★ ★ ★ ★ ★ ★ ★ ★

Johnson succeeded the assassinated Kennedy and overwhelmingly defeated the militantly conservative Goldwater in the 1964 election. Johnson used his strong electoral mandate and huge congressional majorities to push through a mass of liberal Great Society legislation, including Medicare, Medicaid, federal aid to education, and immigration reform.

With Johnson's support, the civil rights movement won great legislative victories with the Civil Rights Act of 1964 and the Voting Rights Act of 1965. But Martin Luther King's nonviolent civil rights movement was increasingly overshadowed by more militant voices, as Northern ghettos erupted in violence amid calls for black power and black nationalism. A growing white backlash reduced sympathies for further integration and civil rights gains.

Faced with the possible collapse of corrupt and unpopular South Vietnamese governments, Johnson escalated military involvement Vietnam. As the number of troops and casualties grew without producing military success, dovish protests against the war gained strength. Political opposition forced Johnson not to seek reelection. Senators Eugene McCarthy and Robert Kennedy led antiwar challenges to Johnson's designated successor, Hubert Humphrey. Humphrey won the nomination, but deep Democratic divisions over the war allowed Nixon to win the White House. The third-party candidacy of George Wallace revealed the growth of an angry "populist" politics. The political upheavals of the 1960s also produced a youthful "counterculture" that revolted against authority and weakened all mainstream American institutions, including government and religion. The counterculture, which began in idealism, eventually faded amidst growing cynicism and economic anxiety in the 1970s.

Nixon's "Vietnamization" policy reduced American ground participation in the war, but his Cambodia invasion sparked massive domestic protest. Nixon's journeys to Communist Moscow and Beijing (Peking) established a new rapprochement with these powers, which Nixon and Kissinger used to advantage in continuing the Vietnam War. In domestic policy, Nixon appointed more conservative justices to the Supreme Court. He expanded social welfare programs and promoted environmental protection and workplace safety. On race relations he pursued a "southern strategy" that successfully moved southern white Democrats into the Republican party.

Nixon won a landslide victory in 1972 over the strongly antiwar Democratic nominee McGovern. After a fierce post-election bombing campaign, a cease fire agreement allowed the remaining U.S. troops to leave Vietnam. But revelations of the secret bombing of Cambodia led to congressional outrage and the War Powers Act. The Middle East war of 1973 and the Arab oil embargo created an energy and economic crisis. Americans gradually awoke to their costly and dangerous dependence on increasingly expensive Middle Eastern oil, and slowly began to take tentative steps toward conservation.

KEY TERMS

Civil Rights Act of 1964 (651)
affirmative action (652)
Great Society (652)
Freedom Summer (653)
Mississippi Freedom Democratic party (654)
Voting Rights Act of 1965 (654)
Black Panther party (654)
Black Power (654)
Six-Day War (656)
Stonewall Rebellion (660)
Students for a Democratic Society (SDS) (660)
Vietnamization (662)
Nixon Doctrine (662)
silent majority (662)
My Lai (663)
Kent State University (663)
Pentagon Papers (663)
détente (664)
Miranda warning (664)
Philadelphia Plan (665)
Environmental Protection Agency (EPA) (665)
Earth Day (665)
southern strategy (665)
War Powers Act (667)

PEOPLE TO KNOW

Malcolm X
Eugene McCarthy
George C. Wallace
Henry A Kissinger
Warren E. Burger
Rachel Carson
George McGovern

Chapter 38

Challenges to the Postwar Order
1973–1980

I must say to you that the state of the Union is not good.

Gerald Ford, 1975

Chapter Outline

- Watergate
- Economic Stagnation
- Nixon's Resignation and the Ford Presidency
- Feminism and Race in the 1970s
- Carter's Troubled Presidency
- The Energy Crisis and Inflation
- The Iranian Hostage Humiliation
- *Examining the Evidence: The "Smoking Gun" Tape, June 23, 1972, 10:04–11:39 A.M.*
- *Thinking Globally: The Era of Globalization*
- *Makers of America: The Vietnamese*
- *Makers of America: The Feminists*

"stagflation" *Term referring to the simultaneous occurrence of low employment growth and high inflation in the national economy. The phenomenon characterized the economic troubles of the 1970s and posed both an intellectual challenge to economists and a policymaking challenge to government officials.*

Americans in the 1970s struggled through a crisis of confidence in their leaders and institutions, as well as wrenching transformations in the nation's economy and politics. The engines of postwar economic growth and broadly shared prosperity sputtered to a near-halt, giving way to a bewildering mixture of stagnation and inflation that was soon dubbed **"stagflation."** Some of the major pillars of the postwar order began to crumble: Keynesian economic policies (see p. 566); an expanding welfare state; shared prosperity; and stable corporations matched by strong labor unions. Simultaneously, conflicts intensified about gender, religion, and America's role in the world. The patterns that emerged out of the crucible of these unsettling years persisted into the new century, including political polarization, a weakened federal government, the invigoration of free-market economic doctrines, rising inequality, and the re-assertion of traditionalist cultural values.

FOCUS QUESTIONS

1. How did the Watergate scandal lead to Nixon's resignation? How successful was Gerald Ford's "unelected presidency" in restoring trust in government after the disillusionment of Watergate and Vietnam?
2. How were the stagnating economy, the energy crisis, and Middle East foreign policy all closely linked in the 1970s? Why did both Republican and Democratic administrations have so little success in addressing these issues?
3. Why did the feminist movement make such dramatic gains in the 1970s, at a time when others like the civil rights movement stalled or prompted political backlash?
4. How did Jimmy Carter's presidential campaign and the turn toward "market economics" both reflect Americans' growing disillusionment with government in the 1970s?
5. How did the Iranian crisis intensify public disaffection with the Carter administration?

CHRONOLOGY

1972	▪ Nixon defeats McGovern for presidency ▪ Equal Rights Amendment passes Congress (not ratified by states) ▪ Title IX of Education Amendments passed
1973	▪ Treaty of Paris enacts cease-fire in Vietnam and U.S. withdrawal ▪ Agnew resigns; Ford appointed vice president ▪ *Frontiero* v. *Richardson* ▪ *Roe* v. *Wade*
1973–1974	▪ Watergate hearings and investigations
1974	▪ Nixon resigns; Ford assumes presidency ▪ *Milliken* v. *Bradley*
1975	▪ Helsinki accords ▪ South Vietnam falls to communists
1976	▪ Carter defeats Ford for presidency
1978	▪ Camp David accords between Egypt and Israel ▪ *United States* v. *Wheeler*
1979	▪ Iranian revolution and oil crisis ▪ SALT II agreements signed (never ratified by Senate) ▪ Soviet Union invades Afghanistan
1979–1981	▪ Iranian hostage crisis
1980	▪ United States boycotts Summer Olympics in Moscow

Watergate and the Unmaking of a President

Watergate *Series of scandals that resulted in President Richard Nixon's resignation in August 1974 amid calls for his impeachment. The episode sprang from a failed burglary attempt at Democratic party headquarters in Washington's Watergate Hotel during the 1972 election.*

Richard Nixon's electoral triumph in 1972 was almost immediately sullied—and eventually undone—by the **Watergate** scandal. On June 17, 1972, five men were arrested inside the Watergate office complex in Washington after attempting to plant electronic "bugs" in the Democratic party's headquarters. They were soon revealed to be working for the Republican Committee to Re-Elect the President—-popularly known as CREEP. The Watergate break-in turned out to be just one in a series of Nixon administration "dirty tricks" that included forging documents to discredit Democrats, using the Internal Revenue Service to harass innocent citizens named on a White House "enemies list," burglarizing the office of the psychiatrist who had treated the leaker of the Pentagon Papers, and perverting the FBI and CIA to cover the tricksters' tracks.

The moral stench hanging over the White House worsened when Vice President Spiro Agnew was forced to resign in October 1973 for taking bribes from Maryland contractors. In the first use of the Twenty-fifth Amendment (see the Appendix), Nixon nominated and Congress confirmed Agnew's successor, a twelve-term congressman from Michigan, Gerald ("Jerry") Ford.

Amid a mood of growing national outrage, a select Senate committee conducted widely televised hearings about the Watergate affair in 1973–1974. Nixon indignantly denied any prior knowledge of the break-in and any involvement in the legal proceedings against the burglars. But when a former White House aide revealed that a secret taping system had recorded Nixon's Oval Office conversations, a Pandora's Box of incriminating evidence lay open.

Nixon at first agreed only to the publication of the "relevant" portions of the tapes, with many sections missing (including Nixon's frequent obscenities, which were excised with the phrase "expletive deleted"). But on July 24, 1974, the president suffered a disastrous setback when the Supreme Court unanimously ruled that "executive privilege" gave him no right to withhold evidence relevant to possible criminal activity. Skating on thin ice over hot water, Nixon reluctantly complied.

New York Newsday

Nixon, the Law-and-Order Man

Examining the Evidence

The "Smoking Gun" Tape, June 23, 1972, 10:04–11:39 A.M.

The technological capability to record Oval Office conversations combined with Richard Nixon's obsession with documenting his presidency to give the public—and the Senate committee investigating his role in the break-in of the Democratic National Committee headquarters in the Watergate Office Tower—rare access to personal conversations between the president and his closest advisers. This tape, which undeniably exposed Nixon's central role in constructing a "cover-up" of the Watergate break-in, was made on Nixon's first day back in Washington after the botched burglary of June 17, 1972. In this conversation with White House Chief of Staff H. R. Haldeman, Nixon devised a plan to block a widening FBI investigation by instructing the director of the CIA to deflect any further FBI snooping on the grounds that it would endanger sensitive CIA operations. Nixon refused to turn over this and other tapes to Senate investigators until so ordered by the Supreme Court on July 24, 1974. Within four days of its release on August 5, Nixon was forced to resign. After eighteen months of protesting his innocence of the crime and his ignorance of any effort to obstruct justice, Nixon was finally undone by the evidence in this incriminating "smoking gun" tape. While tapes documented two straight years of Nixon's Oval Office conversations, other presidents, such as Franklin Roosevelt, John F. Kennedy, and Lyndon Baines Johnson, recorded important meetings and crisis deliberations. Since Watergate, however, it is unlikely that any president has permitted extensive tape recording, depriving historians of a unique insight into the inner workings of the White House.

1. Should taped White House discussions be part of the public record of a presidency? If so, who should have access to the records?
2. What else might historians learn about the president and the administration from a tape such as this one, besides the specific details of the Watergate cover-up?
3. Why did this conversation especially lead to near-unanimous calls for Nixon's impeachment or resignation from Republicans and Democrats alike?

Haldeman: . . . yesterday, they concluded it was not the White House, but are now convinced it is a CIA thing, so the CIA turn off would . . .

President: Well, not sure of their analysis, I'm not going to get that involved. I'm (unintelligible).

Haldeman: No, sir. We don't want you to.

President: You call them in.

President: Good. Good deal! Play it tough. That's the way they play it and that's the way we are going to play it.

Haldeman: O.K. We'll do it.

President: Yeah, when I saw that news summary item, I of course knew it was a bunch of crap, but I thought ah, well it's good to have them off on this wild hair [*sic*] thing because when they start bugging us, which they have, we'll know our little boys will not know how to handle it. I hope they will though. You never know. Maybe, you think about it. Good!

President: When you get in these people when you . . . get these people in, say: "Look, the problem is that this will open the whole, the whole Bay of Pigs thing, and the President just feels that" ah, without going into the details . . . don't, don't lie to them to the extent to say there is no involvement, but just say this is sort of a comedy of errors, bizarre, without getting into it, "the President believes that it is going to open the whole Bay of Pigs thing up again. And, ah because these people are plugging for, for keeps and that they should call the FBI in and say that we wish for the country, don't go any further into this case," period!

Source: Nixon Presidential Materials Project, National Archives and Records Administration

"smoking gun" tape *Recording made in the Oval Office in June 1972 that proved conclusively that Nixon knew about the Watergate break-in and endeavored to cover it up. The tape's release led to a complete breakdown in congressional support for Nixon after the Supreme Court ordered he hand the tape to investigators.*

Three subpoenaed tapes of conversations with his chief aide on June 23, 1972 proved fatal. One of them—the notorious **"smoking gun" tape** (see Examining the Evidence box above)—revealed the president giving orders, six days after the Watergate break-in, to use the CIA to hold back an inquiry by the FBI. Nixon's own tape-recorded words convicted him of having been an active party to the attempted cover-up. The House Judiciary Committee proceeded to draw up articles of impeachment, based on obstruction of justice, abuse of the powers of the presidential office, and contempt of Congress.

The public's wrath proved to be overwhelming. Republican leaders in Congress concluded that the guilty and unpredictable Nixon was a loose cannon on the deck of the ship of state. They frankly informed the president that his impeachment by the full House and removal by the Senate were foregone conclusions and that he would do best to resign.

Left with no better choice, Nixon choked back his tears and announced his resignation in a dramatic television appearance on August 8, 1974. Few presidents had flown so high, and none had sunk so low. In his Farewell Address, Nixon admitted having made some "judgments" that "were wrong." Unconvinced, countless Americans would change the song "Hail to the Chief" to "Jail to the Chief."

The nation had survived a wrenching constitutional crisis, confirming that the impeachment machinery forged by the Founding Fathers could work when public opinion overwhelmingly demanded that it be implemented. The principles that no person is above the law and that presidents must be held to strict accountability for their acts were strengthened. The United States of America, on the eve of its two-hundredth birthday as a republic, had eventually cleaned its own sullied house, giving an impressive demonstration of self-discipline and self-government to the rest of the world. But the toll exacted by Watergate on the public's faith in government proved steep indeed. Americans' disillusionment deepened as the economy fell into a prolonged slump.

Sources of Stagnation

Even as the 1960s lurched to a close, the fantastic quarter-century economic boom of the post-World War II era was already showing signs of petering out. Americans had doubled their average standard of living in the twenty-five years after World War II, But in the years after 1970 the median income of the average family stagnated and failed to decline only because of the addition of working wives' wages to family incomes. The rising baby-boomers now faced the depressing prospect of a living standard lower than that of their parents. As the postwar wave of robust economic growth crested in the early 1970s, the "can-do" American spirit gave way to an unaccustomed sense of limits.

What caused the sudden slump in productivity? Some observers cited the increasing presence in the work force of women and teenagers, who typically had fewer skills than male adult workers and were less likely to take the full-time long-term jobs where skills might be developed. Other commentators blamed declining investment in new machinery, the heavy costs of compliance with government-imposed safety and health regulations, and the general shift of the economy from manufacturing to services, where productivity gains were allegedly more difficult to achieve. Yet in the last analysis much mystery attended the productivity slowdown, and economists continued to wrestle inconclusively with the puzzle.

The Vietnam War also precipitated painful economic distortions. The disastrous conflict in Southeast Asia drained tax dollars from needed improvements in education, deflected scientific skill and manufacturing capacity from the civilian sector, and touched off a sickening spiral of inflation. Sharply rising oil prices in the 1970s also fed inflation, but its deepest roots lay in deficit spending in the 1960s—especially Lyndon Johnson's insistence on simultaneously fighting the war in Vietnam and funding Great Society programs at home, all without a tax increase to finance the added expenditures.

The effects of inflation were deeply felt. Prices increased astonishingly throughout the 1970s. The cost of living tripled in the dozen years after Richard Nixon's inauguration, in the longest and steepest inflationary cycle in American history.

Other weaknesses in the nation's economy were also laid bare by the abrupt reversal of America's financial fortunes in the 1970s. The competitive advantage of many American businesses had been so enormous after World War II that businesses had small incentive to modernize plants and seek more efficient methods of production. The defeated German and Japanese people had meanwhile clawed their way out of the ruins of war and built wholly new factories with the most up-to-date technology and management techniques. The sale of the first Japanese-made Toyota automobile in the United States

Thinking Globally

The Era of Globalization

Early in the twentieth century, Woodrow Wilson envisioned a world order organized around the principles of self-determination and free trade. But his dream perished in the turbulent aftermath of World War I. Two decades later President Franklin Roosevelt, who had served in Wilson's administration, was determined not to squander another opportunity for American international leadership at the conclusion of World War II. He championed a Wilsonian set of principles promoting national self-determination and global free trade—as famously outlined in the "Atlantic Charter" that he and British prime minister Winston Churchill announced in August 1941.

To a remarkable degree, the world order that the United States helped to construct at the end of World War II embodied those very principles. Washington midwifed an array of multilateral institutions to promote international trade and investment, support the rule of law, and nurture democracy. They included the World Bank, to fund postwar reconstruction; the International Monetary Fund (IMF), to stabilize world currencies; and the General Agreement on Tariffs and Trade (GATT), to lower barriers to international commerce. In the ensuing decades, 102 nations, accounting for 80 percent of world trade, signed GATT (succeeded by the World Trade Organization, or WTO, in the 1990s). The United States also took the lead in founding and funding the United Nations (U.N.), which worked to arbitrate international disputes, improve standards of living worldwide, and encourage decolonization, particularly in Asia and Africa.

Outside the Soviet bloc, these institutions nourished a golden era of economic growth that stretched through the 1960s. America boomed. Bolstered by international trade and investment, Europe and Japan also experienced a postwar quarter-century of dazzlingly rapid "catch-up" growth as their economies chased American levels of productivity and living standards.

But globalization bred new dilemmas as well as opportunities. It intensified international competition as well as cooperation. And it ensured that economic shocks could no longer be easily contained within national borders.

First Europe and Japan and then nations in the postcolonial "developing" world like South Korea and eventually China began to challenge American products in world markets—and to threaten American jobs at home. Meanwhile, the end of the Bretton Woods system of fixed exchange rates in 1973 and the growing ease with which capital could cross borders weakened governments' capacity to manage their own national economies. Alongside these international pressures emerged a worldwide political and intellectual shift to the right. In the late 1970s and early 1980s, free-market, anti-regulatory, labor-skeptical governments came to power not only in Ronald Reagan's America but also in countries such as Britain, Australia, and West Germany.

UNITED NATIONS, 1947 by Henry Rowland Eveleigh/Picture Research Consultants and Archives

Great Hopes for World Peace with the United Nations, 1947 The achievements of the new international regime were dramatic. International trade doubled in the 1950s and again in the 1960s. By century's end, the volume of global commerce was ten times larger than in 1950. Increased trade fueled postwar recovery in Europe and Japan and set several underdeveloped countries—notably Taiwan, Singapore, South Korea, India, and China—on the path to modernization and prosperity.

The full effects of an economically liberalized world order were long muffled by the Cold War, since Eastern Europe and the Soviet Union were conspicuous nonparticipants in the emerging global economy. But the dissolution of the Soviet bloc in the early 1990s unleashed the full force of globalization. International trade, investment, and migration exploded. Global trade, already at record levels, nearly quadrupled between 1990 and 2012. The exponential growth of manufacturing in the developing world put still more pressure on workers and wages in the developed world. And as economies have globalized, so has inequality both within and between nations. Environmental degradation and exploitative labor practices have also accompanied worldwide industrial growth.

But such problems should not obscure the profound benefits of the global order forged in the wake of World War II. As goods, workers, and investment capital have flowed across borders, so have advances in medicine, nutrition, and standards of living. Since 1950 the average life expectancy worldwide has increased by twenty years, with the biggest gains in the developing world. Rising prosperity has also strengthened the middle classes in developing countries, with democracy often following in the footsteps of prosperity. The number of electoral democracies increased from 44 in 1950 to 118 in 2012. Recent studies confirm that states with open trade policies are three times more likely to protect civil liberties than those without such policies. On balance, the liberalized world order that the United States took the lead in building after World War II left an impressive legacy of international stability, global growth, and freedom from fear and want for millions of human beings—a lasting testament to Woodrow Wilson's vision and to Franklin Roosevelt's leadership. The challenge remains to bring to this new global order the same aspiration for economic equality that propelled Roosevelt's New Deal many decades ago.

in 1957 proved to be a harbinger of the dawning era of global economic competition (see "Thinking Globally: The Era of Globalization," above). By the 1970s Japanese efforts paid handsome rewards, as they came to dominate industries like steel, automobiles, and consumer electronics—fields in which the United States had once been unchallengeable.

The sickly economic performance of the 1970s hung over the decade like a pall. It frustrated both policymakers and citizens who keenly remembered the growth and optimism of the postwar years. The overachieving generation who had won the war had never met a problem they could not solve. Now a stalemated, unpopular war and a stagnant, unresponsive economy ended the liberal dream, vivid since New Deal days, that an affluent society could spend its way to social justice.

The First Unelected President

Gerald Rudolph Ford, the first man to be made president solely by a vote of Congress, entered the besmirched White House in August 1974 with serious handicaps. He was widely—and unfairly—suspected of being little more than a dim-witted former college football player. President Johnson had sneered that "Jerry" was so lacking in brainpower that he could not walk and chew gum at the same time. Worse, Ford had been selected, not elected, vice president, following Spiro Agnew's resignation in disgrace. The sour odor of illegitimacy hung about this president without precedent.

Then, out of a clear sky, Ford granted a complete pardon to Nixon for any crimes he may have committed as president, discovered or undiscovered. Democrats were outraged, and lingering suspicions about the pardon cast a dark shadow over Ford's prospects of being elected president in his own right in 1976.

Ford at first sought to enhance the so-called détente with the Soviet Union that Nixon had crafted. In July 1975 President Ford joined leaders from thirty-four other nations in Helsinki, Finland, to sign several sets of historic accords. One group of agreements officially wrote an end to World War II by finally legitimizing the Soviet-dictated boundaries of Poland and other Eastern European countries. In return, the Soviets signed a "third basket" of agreements, guaranteeing more liberal exchanges of people and information between East and West and protecting certain basic human rights. The Helsinki accords kindled small dissident movements in Eastern Europe and even in the USSR itself, but the Soviets soon poured ice water on these sputtering flames of freedom.

Western Europeans cheered the Helsinki conference as a milestone of détente. But in the United States critics increasingly charged that détente was proving to be a one-way street. American grain and technology flowed to the USSR, and little of comparable importance flowed back. Moscow also continued its human rights violations, including restrictions on Jewish emigration. Despite these difficulties, Ford at first clung stubbornly to détente. But the American public's fury over Moscow's double-dealing steadily grew. The thaw in the Cold War was threatening to prove chillingly brief.

Defeat in Vietnam

Early in 1975 the North Vietnamese gave full throttle to their long-expected drive southward. President Ford urged Congress to vote still more weapons for Vietnam. But his plea was in vain, and the South Vietnamese quickly and ingloriously collapsed.

The dam burst so rapidly that the remaining Americans had to be frantically evacuated by helicopter, the last of them on April 29, 1975. Also rescued were about 140,000 South Vietnamese, most of them so dangerously identified with the Americans that they feared a bloodbath by the victorious communists. Ford compassionately admitted these people to the United States, where they added further seasoning to the melting pot. Eventually some 500,000 arrived (see "Makers of America: The Vietnamese," p. 677).

The long, frustrating Vietnam War thus ended not with a bang but a whimper. In a technical sense the Americans had not lost the war; their client nation had. The United States had fought the North Vietnamese to a standstill and had then withdrawn its troops in 1973, leaving the South Vietnamese to fight their own war, with generous shipments of costly American weaponry. The estimated cost to America was $118 billion in current outlays, together with some 56,000 dead and 300,000 wounded. The people of the United States had in fact provided just about everything, except the will to win—and that could not be injected by outsiders.

Technicalities aside, America had lost more than a war. It had lost face in the eyes of foreigners, lost its own self-esteem, lost confidence in its political leadership and its military prowess, and lost much of the economic muscle that had made possible its global preemince since World War II. Americans reluctantly came to realize that their power as well as their pride had been deeply wounded in Vietnam and that recovery would be slow and painful.

Feminist Victories and Defeats

As the army limped home from Vietnam, most of the protest movements of the 1960s, including the antiwar movement, had long since splintered and stalled. One major exception to this pattern stood out: the American feminist movement. Although they had their differences, feminists showed vitality and momentum by winning legislative and judicial victories and provoking an intense rethinking of gender roles. (On the roots of this movement, see "Makers of America: The Feminists," p. 678).

Equal Rights Amendment (ERA)
An amendment that declared full constitutional equality for women. Although it passed both houses of Congress in 1972, a concerted grassroots campaign by antifeminists led by Phyllis Schlafly persuaded enough state legislatures to vote against ratification. The amendment failed to become part of the Constitution.

Thousands of women marched in the Women's Stride for Equality on the fiftieth anniversary of woman suffrage in 1970. In 1972 Congress passed Title IX of the Education Amendments, prohibiting sex discrimination in any federally assisted educational program. This act created opportunities for girls' and women's athletics at schools and colleges, giving birth to a new "Title IX generation" that would reach maturity by century's end and help professionalize women's sports as well. The **Equal Rights Amendment (ERA)** to the Constitution won congressional approval in 1972. It declared, "Equality of rights under the law shall not be denied or abridged by the United States or by any State

The Vietnamese

At first glance, the towns of Westminster and Fountain Valley, California seem to resemble other California communities nearby. Tract homes line residential streets; shopping centers flank the busy thoroughfares. But these are no ordinary American suburbs. Instead, they make up "Little Saigons," vibrant outposts of Vietnamese culture in the contemporary United States.

Before South Vietnam fell in 1975, few Vietnamese ventured across the Pacific. Only in 1966 did U.S. immigration authorities even designate "Vietnamese" as a separate category of newcomers, and most early immigrants were the wives and children of U.S. servicemen. But as the communists closed in on Saigon, many Vietnamese, particularly those who had worked closely with American or South Vietnamese authorities, feared for their future. Gathering together as many of their extended-family members as they could assemble, thousands of Vietnamese fled for their lives. In a few hectic days in 1975, some 140,000 Vietnamese escaped before the approaching gunfire, a few dramatically clinging to the bottoms of departing helicopters. Another 60,000 refugees escaped at the same time over land and sea to Hong Kong and Thailand, where they waited nervously for permission to move on.

To accommodate the refugees, the U.S. government set up camps across the United States. Arrivals were crowded into army barracks affording little room and less privacy. These were boot camps not for military service but for assimilation into American society. A rigorous program trained the Vietnamese in English, forbade children from speaking their native language in the classroom, and even immersed them in American slang. Many resented this attempt to mold them, to strip them of their culture.

Vietnamese discontent boiled over when authorities prepared to release the refugees from camps and board them with families around the nation. The resettlement officials had decided to find a sponsor for each Vietnamese family—an American family that would provide food, shelter, and assistance for the refugees until they could fend for themselves. But the Vietnamese people cherish their traditional extended families—grandparents, uncles, aunts, and cousins living communally with parents and children. As soon as refugees could, they relocated from the rural districts where they had been scattered to established Vietnamese enclaves around San Francisco, Los Angeles, and Dallas.

Soon a second throng of Vietnamese immigrants pushed into these Little Saigons. Fleeing from the ravages of poverty and from the oppressive communist government, these stragglers had crammed themselves and their few possessions into little boats, hoping to reach Hong Kong or get picked up by friendly ships. Eventually, many of these "boat people" reached the United States. Usually less educated than the first arrivals and receiving far less resettlement aid from the U.S. government, they were, however, more willing to start at the bottom. Today these two groups total more than half a million people. Differing in experience and expectations, the Vietnamese share a new home in a strange land. Their uprooting is an immense, unreckoned consequence of America's longest war.

Lawrence Migdale/PIX

Preserving the Past A Vietnamese American boy learns classical calligraphy from his grandfather.

The Feminists

A well-to-do housewife and mother of seven, Elizabeth Cady Stanton (1815–1902) was an unlikely revolutionary. Yet this founding mother of American feminism devoted seven decades of her life to the fight for women's rights.

Young Elizabeth Cady drew her inspiration from the fight against slavery. When she and her new husband, abolitionist Henry Stanton, attended the World Anti-Slavery Convention in London, she was insulted that women were forced to sit in a screened-off balcony above the convention floor. Stanton went on to organize the Seneca Falls Convention in 1848. There she presented her Declaration of Sentiments, which proclaimed that "all men *and women* are created equal" and demanded women's rights to own property, enter the professions, and vote.

Early feminists encountered a mountain of hostility to their cause. Stanton failed in her struggle to include women in the Fourteenth Amendment to the U.S. Constitution, which granted equal citizenship to African Americans. She died before her dream of woman suffrage was realized in the Nineteenth Amendment (1920). Yet by imagining women's emancipation as an expansion of America's founding principles of citizenship, Stanton charted a path that other feminists would follow a century later.

Historians use the terms *first wave* and *second wave* to distinguish the women's movement of the nineteenth century from that of the late twentieth century. The woman most often credited with launching the "second wave" is Betty Friedan (1921–2006). Growing up in Peoria, Illinois, Friedan had seen her mother grow bitter over sacrificing a journalism career to raise her family. Friedan's best seller *The Feminine Mystique* (1963) exposed the quiet desperation of millions of housewives trapped in the "comfortable concentration camp" of the suburban home. In 1966 Friedan cofounded the National Organization for Women (NOW), the chief political arm and more moderate wing of second-wave feminism.

Just as first-wave feminism grew out of abolitionism, the second wave drew ideas, leaders, and tactics from the civil rights movement of the 1960s. Civil rights workers and feminists alike focused on equal rights. NOW campaigned vigorously for an Equal Rights Amendment, which fell just three states short of ratification in 1982.

Second-wave feminism also had an avowedly radical wing, supported by younger women eager to challenge almost every traditional male and female gender role and to take the feminist cause to the streets. Among these women was Robin Morgan (b. 1941), a civil rights activist who encountered in the movement the same sexism that plagued society at large. Women in the movement who protested against gender discrimination met ridicule, as in SNCC leader Stokely Carmichael's retort, "The only position for women in SNCC is prone." Morgan went on to found WITCH (Women's International Terrorist Conspiracy from Hell), made famous by its protest at the 1968 Miss America pageant in Atlantic City, New Jersey. There demonstrators threw symbols of women's oppression—bras, girdles, and dishcloths—into trash cans. (Contrary to news stories, they did not burn the bras.)

As the contrast between WITCH and NOW suggests, second-wave feminism was a remarkably diverse movement. Feminists disagreed over many issues—from pornography and marriage to how much to expect from government, capitalism, and men. Some feminists placed a priority on gender equality—for example, full female service in the military. Others defended a feminism of gender difference—such as maternity leave and other special protections for women in the workplace.

Still, beyond these differences feminists had much in common. Most advocated a woman's right to choose abortion and regarded the law as a key weapon against gender discrimination. By the early twenty-first century radical and moderate feminists alike could take pride in a host of achievements that had changed the landscape of gender relations beyond what most people could have imagined at midcentury. Yet, like Elizabeth Cady Stanton, second-wave feminists also shared the burden of understanding that the goals of genuine equality would take more than a lifetime to achieve.

Steve Northup/Time Life Pictures/Getty Images

Marching for Women's Rights, 1977 A multiethnic and multiracial group of women, accompanied by noted "second-wave" feminists Bella Abzug (in hat) and Betty Friedan (far right), helped to carry a torch from Seneca Falls, New York, birthplace of the feminist movement, to Houston, Texas, site of the National Women's Conference.

on account of sex." Twenty-eight of the necessary thirty-eight states quickly ratified the amendment, first proposed by suffragists in 1923. Hopes rose that the ERA might soon become the law of the land.

Even the Supreme Court seemed to be on the movement's side. In *Reed* v. *Reed* and *Frontiero* v. *Richardson* (1973), the Court challenged sex discrimination in legislation and employment. And in the landmark case of ***Roe* v. *Wade*** (1973), the Court struck down laws prohibiting abortion, arguing that a woman's decision to terminate a pregnancy was protected by the constitutional right of privacy.

***Roe* v. *Wade* (1973)** *Landmark Supreme Court decision that forbade states from barring abortion by citing a woman's constitutional right to privacy. Seen as a victory for feminism and civil liberties by some, the decision provoked a strong counterreaction by opponents to abortion, galvanizing the pro-life movement.*

But the feminist movement soon faced a formidable backlash. In 1972 President Nixon vetoed a proposal to set up nationwide public day care, saying it would weaken the American family. The Catholic Church and evangelical denominations organized a powerful grassroots movement to oppose the legalization of abortion.

For many feminists, the most bitter defeat was the death of the ERA. Antifeminists, led by conservative activist Phyllis Schlafly, argued that the ERA would remove traditional protections women enjoyed by forcing the law to see them as men's equals. They further believed the amendment would threaten the basic family structure of American society. Schlafly charged that the ERA's advocates were just "bitter women seeking a constitutional cure for their personal problems." Her STOP ERA movement proved stunningly successful. Grassroots antifeminist activists organized state-level efforts to block ratification. In 1979 Congress extended the deadline for ratification of the amendment. But the battle was lost. The ERA died in 1982, three states short of success.

Politics and policy made up only part of the story of second-wave feminism, however. The women's movement proved to be an undeniably transformative force in the 1970s. Women's labor force participation accelerated, as medicine, law, and higher education opened their doors to female career-seekers. Feminist enterprises proliferated, from battered women's shelters to women's support groups. Newly frank discussions of women's sexuality abounded. Perhaps most profoundly, ongoing transformations of the size and structure of American families—including the growing numbers of divorced, single-parent, and dual-income households—would ensure women's centrality to battles over lifestyle choices and family values for years to come.

The Seventies in Black and White

Although the civil rights movement had fractured, race remained an explosive issue in the 1970s. The Supreme Court in *Milliken* v. *Bradley* blind-sided school integrationists when it ruled that desegregation plans could not require students to move across school-district lines. The decision effectively exempted suburban districts from shouldering any part of the burden of desegregating inner-city schools, thereby reinforcing "white flight" to the suburbs and forcing all the problems of desegregation into the least prosperous districts. Conflicts over desegregation thereafter often pitted the poorest, most disadvantaged elements of the white and black communities against one another.

Affirmative action programs also remained highly controversial. White workers who were denied advancement and white students who were refused college admission cried "reverse discrimination," charging that racial or ethnic background was now outweighing ability and achievement.

In 1978 the Supreme Court, in a five-to-four decision, upheld the claim of one white Californian, Allan Bakke, that his application to medical school had been turned down because of an admission policy that favored minority applicants. In a tortured decision, the Court ordered the University of California at Davis medical school to admit Bakke and declared that preference in admissions could not be based on ethnic or racial identity alone. Yet at the same time, the Court said that racial factors might be taken into account in a school's overall admissions policy for purposes of assembling a diverse student body. In an impassioned dissent, the Court's only black justice, Thurgood Marshall, warned that the denial of racial preferences might sweep away years of civil rights progress. But many conservatives cheered the decision as affirming the principle that justice is colorblind.

Inspired by the civil rights movement, Native Americans in the 1970s gained remarkable power through using the courts and well-planned acts of civil disobedience.

But while blacks had fought against segregation, Indians used the tactics of the civil rights movement to assert their status as separate semi-sovereign peoples. Indian activists captured the nation's attention by seizing the island of Alcatraz in San Francisco Bay in 1970 and the village of Wounded Knee, South Dakota, in 1972. In the case of *United States* v. *Wheeler* (1978), the Supreme Court declared that Indian tribes possessed a "unique and limited" sovereignty, subject to the will of Congress but not to individual states.

The Bicentennial Campaign and the Carter Victory

America's two-hundredth birthday, in 1976, fell during a presidential election year—a fitting coincidence for a proud democracy. President Gerald Ford energetically sought the Republican nomination in his own right and defeated challenger Ronald Reagan, former actor and governor of California. Reagan's pursuit of the GOP nomination was propelled by a swelling conservative movement that came to be known as the **"New Right."**

"New Right" *Term for a loose network of conservative political activists and organizations that emerged in the 1970s and 1980s. More populist in tone than previous generations of conservatives, the New Right emphasized hot-button cultural issues like abortion, busing, and prayer in school. They also espoused a nationalist foreign policy outlook that rejected détente and international treaties.*

The New Right's cadre of activists and political organizers were mainly veterans of Barry Goldwater's failed 1964 presidential campaign. They spent the 1970s building a network of advocacy groups, political action committees, and think tanks. More populist in tone than previous generations of political conservatives, the New Right emphasized hot-button cultural issues—from the ERA and abortion to busing and school curricula—as well as a nationalist foreign-policy outlook. Though Reagan fell short at the Republican convention in 1976, he and the movement behind him grew substantially more powerful over the next four years.

The Democratic standard-bearer in 1976 was fifty-one-year-old James Earl Carter, Jr., a dark-horse candidate who galloped out of obscurity during the long primary-election season. A former Georgia governor who insisted on the humble "Jimmy" as his first name, this born-again Baptist touched many people with his down-home sincerity. Untainted by ties with a corrupt and cynical Washington, Carter ran against the memory of Nixon and Watergate as much as he ran against Ford. His most effective campaign pitch was his promise that "I'll never lie to you."

Carter squeezed out a narrow victory on election day, with 51 percent of the popular vote. The electoral count stood at 297 to 240. The winner swept every state except Virginia in his native South. Especially important were the votes of African Americans, 97 percent of whom cast their ballots for Carter. But in yet another sign of the changing political alignments in the South, Ford actually beat Carter among white southerners, garnering 53 percent of their votes to Carter's 46 percent.

Carter enjoyed hefty Democratic majorities in both houses of Congress. Hopes ran high that the stalemate of the Nixon-Ford years between a Republican White House and a Democratic Capitol Hill would now be ended. At first Carter enjoyed notable political success, as Congress granted his requests to create a new cabinet-level Department of Energy and to cut taxes.

But Carter's honeymoon did not last long. An inexperienced outsider, he had campaigned against the Washington "establishment" and never quite made the transition to being an insider himself. Carter repeatedly rubbed congressional fur the wrong way, and critics charged that he isolated himself in a shallow pool of fellow Georgians, whose ignorance of the ways of Washington compounded the problems of their greenhorn chief.

Carter's Humanitarian Diplomacy

As a committed Christian, President Carter displayed from the outset an overriding concern for "human rights" as the guiding principle of his foreign policy. In the African nations of Rhodesia (later Zimbabwe) and South Africa, Carter and his eloquent United Nations ambassador, Andrew Young, championed the oppressed black majority.

The president's most spectacular foreign-policy achievement came in September 1978 when he invited President Anwar Sadat of Egypt and Prime Minister Menachem Begin of Israel to the woodsy presidential retreat at Camp David, Maryland. Skillfully serving as go-between, Carter persuaded the two visitors to sign a preliminary accord (September 17, 1978) whereby Israel agreed to withdraw from territory conquered in the 1967 war and Egypt promised to respect Israel's borders. Both parties pledged themselves to sign a formal peace treaty within three months.

Carter achieved further diplomatic success by resuming full diplomatic relations with China in 1979. He also concluded two treaties turning over the Panama Canal to the Panamanians. Over the protests from conservatives, including Ronald Reagan, the United States agreed to give up complete control on December 31, 1999.

Despite these dramatic accomplishments, trouble stalked Carter's foreign policy. Overshadowing all international issues was the ominous reheating of the Cold War with the Soviet Union. Détente fell into disrepute as Cuba deployed thousands of troops, assisted by Soviet advisers, in Angola, Ethiopia, and elsewhere in Africa to support revolutionary factions. Arms-control negotiations with Moscow stalled in the face of this Soviet military meddling.

Economic and Energy Woes

Adding to Carter's mushrooming troubles was the failing health of the economy. A stinging recession during Ford's presidency had brought the inflation rate down slightly to just under 6 percent, but from the moment Carter took over, prices resumed their dizzying ascent, driving the inflation rate well above 13 percent by 1980. The soaring bill for imported oil plunged America's balance of payments deeply into the red.

The "oil shocks" of the 1970s taught Americans a painful but necessary lesson: that they could never again seriously consider a policy of economic isolation, as they had tried to do between the two world wars. For most of American history, foreign trade had accounted for no more than 10 percent of gross national product (GNP). But huge foreign-oil bills drove that figure upward in the 1970s. By century's end, some 27 percent of GNP depended on foreign trade. Unable to dominate international trade and finance as they once had, Americans would have to master foreign languages and study foreign cultures if they wanted to prosper in the rapidly globalizing economy.

Yawning deficits in the federal budget, reaching nearly \$60 billion in 1980, further aggravated the U.S. economy's inflationary ailments. The elderly and other Americans living on fixed incomes suffered from the shrinking dollar. People with money to lend pushed interest rates ever higher. The "prime rate" (the rate of interest that banks charged their very best customers) vaulted to an unheard-of 20 percent in early 1980. The high cost of borrowing money shoved small businesses to the wall and strangled the construction industry.

Carter diagnosed America's economic disease as stemming primarily from the nation's costly dependence on foreign oil. Unfortunately, his legislative proposals in April 1977 for energy conservation ignited a blaze of indifference among the American people, who had already forgotten the long gasoline lines of 1973.

Events in Iran jolted Americans out of their complacency about energy supplies in 1979. The imperious Mohammad Reza Pahlavi, installed as shah of Iran with help from America's CIA in 1953, had long ruled his oil-rich land with a will of steel. His repressive regime was finally overthrown in January 1979 in a violent revolution spearheaded by Muslim fundamentalists who denounced the United States as the "Great Satan." The crippling upheavals soon spread to Iran's oil fields. As Iranian oil supplies stopped flowing, Americans once more found themselves waiting impatiently in long lines at gas stations or buying gasoline only on specified days.

President Jimmy Carter (b. 1924) delivered what became known as his "malaise" speech (although he never used the word) on television in 1979. In time cultural conservatives would take up his theme to support their call for a return to "traditional values":

"In a nation that was proud of hard work, strong families, close-knit communities, and our faith in God, too many of us now tend to worship self-indulgence and consumption. Human identity is no longer defined by what one does, but by what one owns. But we've discovered that owning things and consuming things does not satisfy our longing for meaning. We've learned that piling up material goods cannot fill the emptiness of lives which have no confidence or purpose. . . . The symptoms of this crisis of the American spirit are all around us."

Contending Voices

The Political Mobilization of Business

In August 1971, the corporate lawyer Lewis Powell (1907–1998)—soon to be appointed by President Nixon to the Supreme Court—wrote a confidential memo to the director of the U.S. Chamber of Commerce decrying what he described as a broad-based ideological assault on capitalist principles under way in American academia, media, and politics. Powell then presciently proposed that American businesses collectively marshal a long-range countermovement within those same institutions to reclaim public favor and power.

"No thoughtful person can question that the American economic system is under broad attack. . . . [T]he time has come—indeed, it is long overdue—for the wisdom, ingenuity and resources of American business to be marshalled against those who would destroy it. . . . [O]ne should not postpone more direct political action, while awaiting the gradual change in public opinion to be effected through education and information. Business must learn the lesson, long ago learned by labor and other self-interest groups. This is the lesson that political power is necessary; that such power must be assiduously cultivated; and that when necessary, it must be used aggressively and with determination—without embarrassment and without the reluctance which has been so characteristic of American business."

Seven years later, in 1978, United Auto Workers president Douglas Fraser (1916–2008) announced his resignation from a joint forum for business and labor leaders in a scathing open letter. He decried what he saw as a new aggressiveness and political hostility on the part of American business.

"I believe leaders of the business community, with few exceptions, have chosen to wage a one-sided class war today in this country—a war against working people, the unemployed,

As this second oil crisis deepened, President Carter sensed the rising temperature of popular discontent. In July 1979 he retreated to the presidential mountain hideaway of Camp David, where he remained largely out of public view for ten days. Like a royal potentate of old summoning the wise men of the realm for their counsel in a time of crisis, Carter called in more than one hundred leaders from all walks of life to give him their views. Meanwhile, the nation waited anxiously for the results of these extraordinary deliberations.

When Carter finally came down from the mountaintop on July 15, 1979, he stunned a perplexed nation with his **malaise speech**, chiding his fellow citizens for falling into a "moral and spiritual crisis" and for being too concerned with "material goods." A few days later, the president fired four of his cabinet secretaries and circled the wagons of his Georgia advisers more tightly around the White House. Critics began to wonder aloud whether Carter, the professed man of the people, was losing touch with the popular mood of the country.

The Turn Toward the Market

The energy crisis, stagflation, and Carter's political woes helped to nurture a powerful conservative challenge to the very foundations of the postwar American "social contract," which had featured a strong federal government, active economic regulation, expanded social provision, and a large measure of income equality. Now the emphasis shifted to the energy and promise of the free market, and the burdens and dangers of "big government."

An influential group of thinkers known as "neoconservatives," many of them former liberals appalled by what they regarded as the excesses of the 1960s, spearheaded this conservative revival. They championed free-market capitalism liberated from government restraints and sharply questioned the efficacy of the welfare programs spawned by Lyndon Johnson's Great Society. They called for the restoration of traditional values at home and took tough, harshly anti-Soviet positions in foreign policy.

Prominent among pro-market thinkers was the Nobel Prize–winning economist Milton Friedman, a long-standing critic of Keynesian economics and activist government. He achieved a new level of popular influence in 1979 with a best-selling book he co-wrote with his wife Rose called *Free to Choose*. The book and an accompanying public television documentary argued for the superiority of free markets in solving social problems and protecting individual liberty.

Conservative thinking complemented conservative action. Corporate political action committees mushroomed from 89 in 1974 to 1,024 in 1980, while the number of companies with registered lobbyists shot up from 175 in 1971 to nearly 2,500 in 1982. Concerted conservative opposition killed two labor law reform bills during Carter's presidency, as well as a minimum wage hike and the establishment of a Consumer Protection Agency. Critics also pinned the blame for stagflation on onerous government regulations, contributing to a sweeping deregulatory movement in areas as disparate as transportation, communications, and banking.

Significantly, President Carter also supported deregulation and the liberation of market forces. Younger congressional Democrats also began to move away from the New Deal–era positions of their elders. "We're not a bunch of little Hubert Humphreys," one of them declared in 1974, scornfully repudiating his party's 1968 presidential nominee and one of the most prominent liberals of the postwar era. Though spearheaded by a resurgent Republican right, the turn toward the market attracted bipartisan support—in America and elsewhere (see "Thinking Globally: The Era of Globalization" pp. 674–675).

The most politically explosive aspect of the new antigovernment politics centered on taxes. A "tax revolt" in California and other states in 1978 soon snowballed into a revolutionary new tax-cutting agenda for the conservative movement nationwide—one that rewrote the script of American politics in the following decade (see Chapter 39, pp. 689–690).

the poor, the minorities, the very young and the very old, and even many in the middle class of our society. The leaders of industry, commerce and finance in the United States have broken and discarded the fragile, unwritten compact previously existing during a past period of growth and progress."

How accurate were Powell's and Fraser's descriptions of the American scene in the 1970s? What underlying changes in the economy and society supported their assertions?

Foreign Affairs and the Iranian Imbroglio

Hopes for a less dangerous world rose slightly in June 1979, when President Carter met with Soviet leader Leonid Brezhnev in Vienna to sign the long-stalled **SALT II** (Strategic Arms Limitation Talks II) agreements, limiting the levels of lethal strategic weapons in the Soviet and American arsenals. But conservative critics of the president's defense policies, still regarding the Soviet Union as the Wicked Witch of the East, unsheathed their long knives to carve up the SALT treaty when it came to the Senate for debate in the summer of 1979.

Political earthquakes in the petroleum-rich Persian Gulf region finally buried all hopes of ratifying the SALT II treaty. On November 4, 1979, a mob of passionately

Associated Press

An Apostle for Capitalism Milton Friedman receives the cash award that accompanied his Nobel Prize in economics in 1976. Friedman won the Nobel at just the point in the 1970s that the free-market outlook he espoused began to gain new prominence in the broader political culture.

malaise speech *National address by Jimmy Carter in July 1979 in which he chided American materialism and urged a communal spirit in the face of economic hardships. Although Carter intended the speech to improve both public morale and his standing as a leader, it had the opposite effect and was widely perceived as a political disaster for the embattled president.*

SALT II *Strategic Arms Limitation Treaty agreement between Soviet leader Leonid Brezhnev and American president Jimmy Carter. Despite an accord to limit weapons between the two leaders, the agreement was ultimately scuttled in the U.S. Senate following the Soviet invasion of Afghanistan in 1979.*

anti-American Muslim militants stormed the United States embassy in Tehran, Iran and took all of its occupants hostage. The captors then demanded that American authorities ship the exiled shah from the United States back to Iran.

Americans agonized over both the fate of the hostages and the stability of the entire Persian Gulf region, so dangerously close to the Soviet Union. The Soviet army then aroused the West's worst fears on December 27, 1979, when it blitzed into the mountainous nation of Afghanistan, next door to Iran, and appeared to be poised for a thrust at the oil jugular of the gulf.

President Carter reacted vigorously to these alarming events. He slapped an embargo on the export of grain and high-technology machinery to the USSR, called for a boycott of the upcoming Olympic Games in Moscow, and requested that young people (including women) be made to register for a possible military draft. Proclaiming that the United States would "use any means necessary, including force," to protect the Persian Gulf against Soviet incursions, Carter grimly conceded that he had misjudged the Soviets. The SALT II treaty became a dead letter in the Senate. Meanwhile, the Soviet army met unexpectedly stiff resistance in Afghanistan and became bogged down in a nasty, decade-long guerrilla war that came to be called "Russia's Vietnam."

Iranian hostage crisis *The 444 days, from November 1979 to January 1981, in which American embassy workers were held captive by Iranian revolutionaries. The hostage crisis began when revolutionaries stormed the American embassy, demanding that the United States return the shah to Iran for trial. After diplomatic efforts proved unable to gain the hostages' relief, a military rescue attempt by the Carter administration ended in failure and loss of American life. The crisis ended with the hostages' release the day Ronald Reagan became president, January 20, 1981.*

The **Iranian hostage crisis** was Carter's—and America's—bed of nails. The captured Americans languished in cruel captivity, while the nightly news broadcasts showed humiliating scenes of Iranian mobs burning the American flag and spitting on effigies of Uncle Sam.

Carter at first tried to apply economic sanctions and the pressure of world opinion against the Iranians. But the president's frustration grew as the political turmoil in Iran rumbled on endlessly. Carter at last ordered a daring rescue mission. A highly trained commando team penetrated deep into Iran's sandy interior, but when equipment failures prevented some members of the team from reaching their destination, the mission had to be scrapped. As the commandos withdrew in the dark desert night, two of their aircraft collided, killing eight of the would-be rescuers.

The disastrous failure of the rescue raid proved anguishing for Americans. The episode seemed to underscore the nation's helplessness and even incompetence in the face of a mortifying insult to the national honor. The stalemate with Iran dragged on throughout the rest of Carter's term, providing an embarrassing backdrop to the embattled president's struggle for reelection.

As the 1980 presidential race approached, a discontented and divided American public looked to close the book on a frustrating decade. What Americans could not fully know at the time was how much lasting change had already taken place in such a relatively brief period. The long postwar boom and broadly shared prosperity were gone for good, replaced in coming decades by more fitful and less equitable spurts of growth. An ascendant conservative movement criticized government activism and promoted free-market policies. Economic inequality and political polarization grew alike in the decades to come. Yet perhaps paradoxically, the dawning era of dampened economic growth, governmental paralysis, and widening income disparity also witnessed increasing tolerance and inclusion of racial and ethnic minorities, immigrants, gays and lesbians, and women, all of whose horizons broadened dramatically in the decades ahead.

CHAPTER SUMMARY ★ ★ ★ ★ ★ ★ ★ ★ ★ ★ ★ ★ ★ ★

Nixon's landslide 1972 election victory was negated as the widespread Watergate scandal erupted. Nixon fought efforts by prosecutors to obtain relevant evidence, but the revelation of his own involvement in the Watergate crimes and coverup finally compelled him to resign in 1974.

Unelected President Gerald Ford took office amidst an emerging "stagflation" that combined low economic growth with inflation, signaling the end of the long postwar era of prosperity and relative economic equality. Ford attempted to sustain Nixon's détente policy with the Soviet Union, but faced growing criticism that the Soviets had turned the policy entirely to their advantage. The Communist Vietnamese finally overran the South Vietnamese government in 1975, confirming Americans' sense of diminished world power and pride.

The major social movement to survive the sixties was feminism, which achieved widespread breakthroughs in employment, culture, and social organization, though failing to pass the Equal Rights Amendment. Race remained an explosive issue, as divisive issues of busing and affirmative action eroded the good will created by the civil rights movement. A growing New Right movement throughout the 1970s mobilized around cultural issues like abortion and affirmation action as well as a militantly anticommunist foreign policy,

Campaigning against Watergate and a corrupt Washington, outsider Jimmy Carter won a slender victory over Ford in 1976, but proved unable to work with Congress or improve the economy once he took office. His Camp David agreement brought peace between Egypt and Israel, but the Iranian revolution led to a new energy crisis that compounded already severe inflation and recession. Growing criticism of big government and federal regulation of the economy led to a major turn toward free-market solutions.

The Soviet invasion of Afghanistan and the holding of American hostages in Iran added to Carter's woes and a general American sense of frustration and helplessness. Economic weakness and foreign policy failures did not, however, prevent a growing tolerance and inclusion of minorities and immigrants within American society.

KEY TERMS

"stagflation" (670)
Watergate (671)
"smoking gun" tape (672)
Equal Rights Amendment (ERA) (676)
Roe v. Wade (679)
New Right (680)
malaise speech (683)
SALT II (683)
Iranian hostage crisis (684)

PEOPLE TO KNOW

Gerald ("Jerry") Ford
Phyllis Schlafly
James Earl ("Jimmy") Carter, Jr.
Milton Friedman
Robin Morgan
Leonid Brezhnev

Chapter 39

The Resurgence of Conservatism
1980–1992

It will be my intention to curb the size and influence of the federal establishment and to demand recognition of the distinction between the powers granted to the federal government and those reserved to the states or to the people.

Ronald Reagan, Inaugural Address, 1981

Chapter Outline

- Ronald Reagan and the New Right
- "Reaganomics" and Its Consequences
- Reagan Renews the Cold War
- The Iran-Contra Scandal
- Reagan's Economic Legacy
- The Religious Right and Conflict over Abortion
- George H.W. Bush
- The End of the Cold War
- The Persian Gulf War, 1991
- Bush's Battles at Home
- *Varying Viewpoints: Where Did Modern Conservatism Come From?*

"It's morning in America" was the slogan of Republican candidate Ronald Reagan in his 1984 presidential campaign. Certainly the 1980s were a new day for America's conservative right. Census figures confirmed that the average American was older than in the stormy sixties and much more likely to live in the South or West, the traditional bastions of conservatism, where many citizens harbored suspicions of federal power. The conservative cause drew added strength from the emergence of a "New Right" movement that focused on cultural issues like abortion, pornography, homosexuality, feminism, and affirmative action. Increasingly politicized evangelical Christian groups such as the Moral Majority became leading actors in New Right campaigns. Together, the culture-focused New Right and more traditional anti-government conservatives added up to a powerful political combination, devoted to changing the very character of American society.

FOCUS QUESTIONS

1. What social and cultural forces led to the dramatic rise of Ronald Reagan and the "New Right" in the early 1980s?
2. What were the essential elements of the "Reagan revolution" in economic and social policy, and what were Reaganism's short-term and long-term consequences?
3. How and why was the renewed Cold War of the early 1980s followed by the easing of tensions and the Reagan-Gorbachev agreements later in the decade? What caused the collapse of communism first in Eastern Europe and then in Soviet Union in 1989–1991?
4. How did the religious right transform American politics, and how were issues like abortion and affirmative action addressed by the public and the Supreme Court?
5. What were the causes and consequences of the Persian Gulf War? Why did President George H.W. Bush leave Saddam Hussein in power in Iraq?

CHRONOLOGY

1980	▪ Reagan defeats Carter for presidency
1981	▪ Iran releases American hostages ▪ "Reaganomics" spending and tax cuts passed ▪ Solidarity movement in Poland ▪ O'Connor appointed to Supreme Court (first woman justice)
1981–1991	▪ United States aids anti-leftist forces in Central America
1982	▪ Recession hits U.S. economy ▪ Israel invades Lebanon
1983	▪ Reagan announces SDI plan (Star Wars) ▪ U.S. marines killed in Beirut, Lebanon ▪ U.S. invasion of Grenada
1984	▪ Reagan defeats Mondale for presidency ▪ Soviet Union boycotts Summer Olympics in Los Angeles
1985	▪ Gorbachev comes to power in Soviet Union, announces *glasnost* and *perestroika* ▪ First Reagan-Gorbachev summit meeting in Geneva
1986	▪ Reagan administration backs Aquino in Philippines ▪ Iran-Contra affair revealed ▪ Second Reagan-Gorbachev summit meeting in Reykjavik, Iceland
1987	▪ Stock market plunges 508 points ▪ Third Reagan-Gorbachev summit meeting in Washington, D.C.; INF treaty signed
1988	▪ Fourth Reagan-Gorbachev summit meeting in Moscow ▪ Bush defeats Dukakis for presidency
1989	▪ Chinese government suppresses prodemocracy demonstrators in Tiananmen Square ▪ *Webster* v. *Reproductive Health Services* ▪ Eastern European countries oust communist governments ▪ Berlin Wall torn down
1990	▪ Iraq invades Kuwait ▪ East and West Germany unite ▪ Americans with Disabilities Act (ADA)
1991	▪ Persian Gulf War ▪ Thomas appointed to Supreme Court ▪ Gorbachev survives coup attempt and resigns as Soviet president ▪ Soviet Union dissolves
1992	▪ Twenty-seventh Amendment (prohibiting congressional pay raises from taking effect until an election seats a new session of Congress) ratified ▪ *Planned Parenthood* v. *Casey*

The Election of Ronald Reagan, 1980

Ronald Reagan was well suited to lead the gathering conservative crusade. Reared in a generation whose values were formed well before the upheavals of the 1960s, he naturally sided with the New Right on social issues. In economic and social matters alike, he denounced the activist government and failed "social engineering" of the 1960s. Just as his early political hero, Franklin Roosevelt, had championed the "forgotten man" against big business, Reagan championed the "common man" against big government. He condemned federal intervention in local affairs, favoritism for minorities, and the elitism of arrogant bureaucrats. He aimed especially to win over from the Democratic column working-class and lower-middle-class white voters by implying that the Democratic party had become the the party of big government and the exclusive tool of its minority constituents.

An actor-turned-politician, Reagan enjoyed enormous popularity with his crooked grin and aw-shucks manner. The son of an impoverished Irish-American father from a small Illinois town, Reagan got his start in the depressed 1930s as a radio sports announcer in Iowa. He became a B-grade Hollywood star in the 1940s and helped purge communists from the Screen Actors Guild as the organization's president in the 1950s. In 1954 he became a spokesman for General Electric and began preaching a conservative, antigovernment line. Reagan's growing skill at promoting the conservative cause inspired a group

In a speech to the National Association of Evangelicals on March 8, 1983, President Ronald Reagan (1911–2004) defined his stand on school prayer:

"The Declaration of Independence mentions the Supreme Being no less than four times. 'In God We Trust' is engraved on our coinage. The Supreme Court opens its proceedings with a religious invocation. And the Members of Congress open their sessions with a prayer. I just happen to believe the schoolchildren of the United States are entitled to the same privileges as Supreme Court Justices and Congressmen."

of wealthy California businessmen to help him launch his political career as governor of California from 1966 to 1974.

By 1980 the Republican party was ready to challenge the Democrats' hold on the White House. Bedeviled abroad and becalmed at home, Jimmy Carter's administration struck many Americans as bungling and befuddled. Carter's inability to control double-digit inflation was especially damaging.

Disaffection with Carter's apparent ineptitude ran deep even in his own Democratic party, in which an "ABC" (Anybody But Carter) movement gathered steam. The liberal wing of the party found its champion in Senator Edward Kennedy of Massachusetts, the last survivor of the assassin-plagued Kennedy brothers. He and Carter slugged it out in a series of bruising primary elections, while delighted Republicans decorously proceeded to name Reagan their presidential nominee. In the end Kennedy's candidacy fell victim to the country's conservative mood and to lingering suspicions about a 1969 automobile accident on Chappaquiddick Island, Massachusetts, in which a young woman assistant was drowned when Kennedy's car plunged off a bridge. A badly battered Carter, his party divided and in disarray, was left to do battle with Reagan.

The Republican candidate proved to be a formidable campaigner. Using his professional acting skills to great advantage, Reagan attacked the incumbent's fumbling performance in foreign policy and blasted the Democratic party's "big-government philosophy." Galloping inflation, sky-high interest rates, and a faltering economy put Carter on the defensive. He countered ineffectively that Reagan was a trigger-happy cold warrior who might push the country into nuclear war.

Carter's spotty record in office was no defense against Reagan's popular appeal. On election day Reagan rang up a spectacular victory, bagging more than 51 percent of the popular vote while 41 percent went to Carter. Reflecting a small but vocal protest against both candidates, nearly 7 percent of the electorate voted for liberal Republican congressman John Anderson, who ran as an independent. The electoral count stood at 489 for Reagan and 49 for Carter, making Carter the first elected president to be unseated by voters since Herbert Hoover in 1932. Equally startling, the Republicans gained control of the Senate for the first time in twenty-six years. Leading Democratic liberals, including George McGovern, had been targeted for defeat by well-heeled New Right groups. They went down like dead timber in the conservative windstorm that swept the country.

Carter showed dignity in defeat. An unusually intelligent, articulate, and well-meaning president, he had been hampered by his lack of managerial talent and badly buffeted by events beyond his control, such as the soaring price of oil, runaway inflation, and the galling insult of the hostages still held in Iran. Though unsuccessful in the White House, Carter earned much admiration in later years for his humanitarian and human rights activities. He received the Nobel Peace Prize in 2002.

Picture Research Consultants & Archives

President Ronald Reagan Older than any man previously elected to the presidency, Reagan displayed youthful vigor both on the campaign trail and in office.

The Reagan Revolution

Reagan's arrival in Washington was triumphal. The Iranians contributed to the festive mood by releasing the hostages on Reagan's Inauguration Day, January 20, 1981, after 444 days of captivity.

The new president, a hale and hearty sixty-nine-year-old devoted to fiscal fitness, sought nothing less than the dismantling of the welfare state and the reversal of the political evolution of the preceding half century. Years of New Deal–style tax-and-spend programs, Reagan jested, had created a federal government that reminded him of the definition of a baby as a creature who was all appetite at one end, with no sense of responsibility at the other.

On his conservative crusade for smaller government, less bureaucracy, and freer markets, Reagan found common cause with the new leader of America's oldest ally, Great Britain. Conservative Margaret Thatcher became Britain's first female Prime Minister in 1979. With a mandate to improve her nation's economy, which had suffered through the 1970s as the United States had, she embarked on a mission to reduce the power of labor unions and government involvement in business, two of Reagan's chief goals. The philosophic kinship between "Ronnie and Maggie," as the press dubbed the two heads of state, went beyond economics. Emboldened by each other, they strengthened the Anglo-American alliance through muscular foreign policy against a number of foes, especially the Soviet bloc. Their common refrain was that free markets made free peoples and that shrinking government meant keeping their nations safer from communism.

By the early 1980s, this antigovernment message found a receptive audience in the United States. In the two decades since 1960, federal spending had risen from about 18 percent of gross national product to nearly 23 percent. After four decades of advancing New Deal and Great Society programs, a strong countercurrent took hold. Californians staged a "tax revolt" in 1978 (known by its official ballot title of **Proposition 13**) that slashed property taxes and forced painful cuts in government services. The California "tax quake" jolted other state capitals and even rocked the pillars of Congress in Washington, D.C. Ronald Reagan had ridden this political shock wave to presidential victory in 1980 and proceeded to rattle the "welfare state" to its very foundations.

Proposition 13 (1978) *A successful California state ballot initiative that capped the state's real estate tax at 1 percent of assessed value. The proposition radically reduced average property tax levels, decreasing revenue for the state government and signaling the political power of the "tax revolt," increasingly aligned with conservative politics.*

Reagan pursued his smaller-government policies with near-religious zeal and remarkable effectiveness. He proposed a new federal budget that necessitated cuts of some $35 billion, mostly in social programs like food stamps and federally funded job-training centers. Reagan worked naturally in harness with the Republican majority in the Senate, while in the Democratic House he enterprisingly wooed a group of mostly southern conservative Democrats (dubbed **boll weevils**), who abandoned their own party's leadership to follow the president. The new president's political hand was further strengthened after a failed assassination attempt in March 1981 brought an outpouring of sympathy and support.

boll weevils *Term for conservative southern Democrats who voted increasingly for Republican issues during the Carter and Reagan administrations.*

The Battle of the Budget

Swept along on a tide of presidential popularity, Congress swallowed Reagan's budget proposals. The new president's triumph amazed political observers, especially defeated Democrats. He had descended on Washington like an avenging angel of conservatism, kicking up a blinding whirlwind of political change in pursuit of his Reaganomics agenda. His impressive performance demonstrated the power of the presidency with a skill not seen since Lyndon Johnson's day.

Reagan hardly rested to savor the sweetness of his victory. The second part of his economic program called for substantial reductions in marginal tax rates over a period of three years. Many Democrats, the president quipped, had "never met a tax they didn't hike." Thanks largely to Reagan's skill as a television performer and the continued defection of the "boll weevils" from the Democratic camp, the president again had his way. In late 1981 Congress approved a set of far-reaching tax reforms that lowered individual tax rates, reduced federal estate taxes, and created new tax-free savings plans for small investors. Reagan's "supply-side" economic advisers argued that a combination of budgetary discipline and tax reduction would stimulate new investment, boost productivity, foster dramatic economic growth, and eventually even boost tax revenues and reduce the deficit.

At first, **supply-side economics** seemed to be a beautiful theory mugged by a gang of brutal facts, as the economy slid into its deepest recession since the 1930s. Unemployment

supply-side economics *Economic theory that underlay Ronald Reagan's tax and spending cuts. Contrary to Keynesianism, supply-side theory declared that government policy should aim to increase the supply of goods and services, rather than the demand for them. It held that lower taxes and decreased regulation would increase productivity by providing increased incentives to work, thus increasing productivity and the tax base.*

reached nearly 11 percent in 1982, businesses folded, and several bank failures jolted the nation's entire financial system. The automobile industry, once the brightest jewel in America's industrial crown, reported losses in the hundreds of millions of dollars.

Ignoring the yawping pack of Democratic critics, President Reagan and his economic advisers serenely waited for their supply-side economic policies to produce the promised results. The supply-siders seemed to be vindicated when a healthy economic recovery finally got under way in 1983. Yet the economy of the 1980s was not uniformly sound. For the first time in the post-World War II era, income gaps widened between the richest and the poorest Americans. The poor got poorer and the very rich grew fabulously richer, while middle-class incomes largely stagnated. Symbolic of the new income stratification was the emergence of "yuppies," or young urban professionals. Sporting Rolex watches and BMW sports cars, they made a near-religion out of conspicuous consumption. Though numbering only about 1.5 million people, yuppies showcased the values of materialism and the pursuit of wealth that came to symbolize the high-rolling 1980s.

Some economists located the sources of the economic upturn neither in the president's budget cuts and tax reforms nor in the go-get-'em avarice of the yuppies. It was massive military expenditures, they argued, that constituted the real foundations of 1980s prosperity. Reagan cascaded nearly 2 trillion dollars onto the Pentagon in the 1980s, asserting the need to close the "window of vulnerability" in the armaments race with the Soviet Union. Ironically, this conservative president thereby plunged the government into a red-ink bath of deficit spending that made the New Deal look downright stingy. Federal budget deficits topped $100 billion in 1982, and the government's books were nearly $200 billion out of balance in every subsequent year of the 1980s.

Reagan Renews the Cold War

Hard as nails toward the Soviet Union in his campaign speeches, Reagan saw no reason to soften up after he checked in at the White House. He claimed that the Soviets were "prepared to commit any crime, to lie, to cheat" in pursuit of their goals of world conquest. He denounced the Soviet Union as "the focus of evil in the modern world."

Reagan believed in negotiating with the Soviets—but only from a position of overwhelming strength. Accordingly, his strategy for dealing with Moscow was simple: by enormously expanding U.S. military capabilities, he could threaten the Soviet leaders with a fantastically expensive new round of the arms race. Desperate to avoid economic ruin, Kremlin leaders would come to the bargaining table and sing Reagan's tune.

This strategy resembled a riverboat gambler's ploy. It wagered the enormous sum of Reagan's defense budgets on the hope that the other side would not call Washington's bluff and initiate a new cycle of arms competition. Reagan played his trump card in this risky game in March 1983 when he announced his intention to pursue a high-technology missile defense system called the **Strategic Defense Initiative (SDI)**, popularly known as Star Wars. The plan called for orbiting battle stations in space that could fire laser beams or other forms of concentrated energy to vaporize intercontinental missiles on liftoff. Most scientists considered this an impossible goal, but the deeper logic of SDI lay in its fit with Reagan's overall Soviet strategy. By pitching the arms contest onto a stratospheric plane of technology and astronomical expense, it would help force the Kremlin's hand.

Strategic Defense Initiative (SDI) *Reagan administration plan announced in 1983 to create a missile defense system over American territory to block a nuclear attack. Derided as "Star Wars" by critics, the plan typified Reagan's commitment to vigorous defense spending even as he sought to limit the size of government in domestic matters.*

Relations with the Soviets further nose-dived in late 1981 when the government of Poland, needled by a popular union movement called "Solidarity," clamped martial law on the troubled country. Reagan saw the heavy fist of the Kremlin inside this Polish iron glove, and he imposed economic sanctions on Poland and the USSR alike.

Dealing with the Soviet Union was additionally complicated by the inertia and ill health of the aging oligarchs in the Kremlin, three of whom died between late 1982 and early 1985. Relations grew even more tense when the Soviets, in September 1983, blasted from the skies a Korean airliner that had inexplicably violated Soviet airspace. Hundreds of civilians, including many Americans, plummeted to their deaths. By the end of 1983, all arms-control negotiations with the Soviets were broken off. The Cold War chill deepened further in 1984, when USSR and Soviet-bloc athletes boycotted the Olympic Games in Los Angeles.

Map 39.3 The End of the Cold War Changed the Map of Europe

The Persian Gulf War

Sadly, the end of the Cold War did not mean the end of all wars. President Bush flexed the United States' still-intimidating military muscles in tiny Panama in December 1989, when he sent airborne troops to capture dictator Manuel Noriega.

Still more ominous events in the summer of 1990 severely tested Bush's dream of a democratic and peaceful new world order. On August 2 Saddam Hussein, the brutal and ambitious ruler of Iraq, sent his armies to overrun Kuwait, a tiny, oil-rich sheikdom on Iraq's southern frontier. Saddam design was to seize Kuwait's oil, gain control of the world's economic jugular in the Persian Gulf, and perhaps totally extinguish the Arabs' enemy, Israel.

On August 2, 1990, Saddam's army roared into Kuwait. The speed and audacity of the invasion were stunning, but the world responded just as swiftly. The United Nations Security Council unanimously condemned the invasion on August 3 and demanded the immediate and unconditional withdrawal of Iraq's troops. In November the Security Council delivered an ultimatum to Saddam to leave Kuwait by January 15, 1991, or U.N. forces would "use all necessary means" to expel his troops.

In a logistical operation of astonishing complexity, the United States spearheaded a massive international military deployment on the sandy Arabian Peninsula. As the January 15 deadline approached, some 539,000 U.S. soldiers, sailors, and pilots swarmed into the Persian Gulf region. They were joined by nearly 270,000 troops from twenty-eight other countries in the coalition opposed to Iraq. When all diplomatic efforts to resolve the crisis failed, the U.S. Congress voted on January 12, 1991, to approve the use of force.

The United States and its U.N. allies unleashed a thirty-seven-day air attack that pummeled targets in occupied Kuwait and in Iraq itself. On February 23, 1991, the dreaded and long-awaited land war began. Dubbed **Operation Desert Storm**, it lasted only four days—the "hundred-hour war." With lightning speed the U.N. forces penetrated deep into

Operation Desert Storm (1991) *U.S.-led multicountry military engagement in January and February of 1991 that drove Saddam Hussein's Iraqi army out of neighboring Kuwait. In addition to presaging the longer and more protracted Iraq War of the 2000s, the 1991 war helped undo what some called the "Vietnam Syndrome," a feeling of military uncertainty that plagued many Americans.*

Iraq, outflanking the occupying army in Kuwait. Allied casualties were amazingly light, whereas much of Iraq's remaining fighting force was quickly destroyed or captured. On February 27 Saddam accepted a cease-fire, and Kuwait was liberated.

Most Americans cheered the war's rapid and enormously successful conclusion. Many people echoed President Bush's sentiments when he declared, "By God, we've kicked the Vietnam Syndrome once and for all!" But when the smoke cleared, Saddam Hussein had survived to menace the world another day. America and its allies had agreed to the liberation of Kuwait, but Bush, fearing that a full assault on Baghdad would cost many lives and much public support, stopped well short of overthrowing the tyrant Saddam. The perpetually troubled Middle East knew scarcely less trouble after Desert Storm had ceased to thunder, and the United States, for better or worse, found itself more deeply ensnared in the region's web of mortal hatreds and intractable conflicts.

Bush on the Home Front

Americans with Disabilities Act (ADA) (1990) *Landmark law signed by President George H.W. Bush that prohibited discrimination against people with physical or mental handicaps. It represented a legislative triumph for champions of equal protections to all.*

George H.W. Bush partly redeemed his pledge to work for a "kinder, gentler America" when he signed the **Americans with Disabilities Act (ADA)** in 1990, a landmark law prohibiting discrimination against the 43 million U.S. citizens with physical or mental disabilities. The president also signed a major water projects bill in 1992 that put the interests of the environment on a par with those of agriculture, especially in California's heavily irrigated Central Valley.

The new president continued to aggravate the explosive "social issues" that had so divided Americans throughout the 1980s, especially the nettlesome questions of affirmative action and abortion. Bush challenged the legality of college scholarships targeted for racial minorities, and repeatedly threatened to veto civil rights legislation that would make it easier for employees to prove discrimination in hiring and promotion. Most provocatively, in 1991 Bush nominated for the Supreme Court the conservative African American jurist Clarence Thomas, a stern critic of affirmative-action policies. Thomas's nomination was loudly opposed by labor, civil rights, and women's organizations. Reflecting irreconcilable divisions over affirmative action and abortion, the Senate Judiciary Committee concluded its hearings with a divided seven-to-seven vote and forwarded the matter to the full Senate without a recommendation. Then, just days before the Senate was scheduled to vote in early October 1991, a press leak revealed that Anita Hill, a University of Oklahoma law professor, had accused Thomas of sexual harassment. The Senate Judiciary Committee was forced to reopen its hearings.

For days a prurient American public sat glued to their television sets as Hill graphically detailed her charges of sexual improprieties and Thomas angrily responded. In the end, by a fifty-two to forty-eight vote, the Senate confirmed Thomas as the second African American ever to sit on the supreme bench (Thurgood Marshall was the first). While many hailed Hill as a heroine for focusing the nation's attention on issues of sexual harassment, Thomas maintained that her widely publicized, unproved allegations amounted to "a high-tech lynching for uppity blacks who in any way deign to think for themselves, to do for themselves." Many women, enraged by the all-male judiciary committee's behavior in the Thomas hearings, grew increasingly critical of the president's uncompromising stand on abortion. A "gender gap" opened between the two political parties, as pro-choice women grew increasingly cool toward the strong anti-abortion stand of the Republicans.

Still more damaging to President Bush's political health, the economy sputtered and stalled almost from the outset of his administration. By 1992 the unemployment rate exceeded 7 percent, while the federal budget deficit continued to mushroom cancerously, topping $250 billion in each of Bush's years as president. In a desperate attempt to stop the hemorrhage of red ink, Bush agreed in 1990 to a budget that included $133 billion in new taxes.

Bush's 1990 tax and budget package added up to a political catastrophe. In his 1988 presidential campaign, Bush had belligerently declared, "Read my lips—no new taxes." Now he had flagrantly broken that campaign promise. The budget deal deeply divided his own party. An ascendant congressional wing of hard-line conservatives, led by Georgia congressman Newt Gingrich, voted against their own president's hard-fought agreement. After Bush's debacle, a blanket opposition to tax increases of any kind became an entrenched part of mainstream Republican orthodoxy, setting the stage for irreconcilable political conflicts ahead.

Where Did Modern Conservatism Come From?

Ronald Reagan's elections surprised many historians. Reflecting a liberal political outlook that is common among academic scholars, they were long accustomed to understanding American history as an inexorable, almost evolutionary, unfolding of liberal principles, including the quests for economic equality, social justice, and active government. Even the "New Left" revisionists of the 1960s who decried liberalism's deficiencies assumed that the deep currents of American history flowed leftward. Whether liberal or revisionist, most scholars writing in the first three post–World War II decades dismissed conservatism as an obsolete political creed and psychoanalyzed its adherents as fringe wackos—paranoid McCarthyites or racist demagogues who, in the words of liberal critic Lionel Trilling, trafficked only in "irritable mental gestures which seem to resemble ideas." Such an outlook is conspicuous in books such as Daniel Bell's *The Radical Right* (1963), and Richard Hofstadter's *The Paranoid Style in American Politics* (1965).

Yet what flowed out of the turbulent decade of the 1960s was not a strengthened liberalism but a revived conservatism. Ronald Reagan's huge political success, followed by continued conservative strength through the 1990s and 2000s, compelled a thorough reexamination of the tradition of American conservatism and the sources of its modern resurgence.

Historians such as Leo Ribuffo and Alan Brinkley have argued that characters from earlier eras once dismissed as irrational crackpots—including religious Fundamentalists and depression-era figures like Huey Long and Father Charles Coughlin—articulated values deeply rooted and widely shared in American culture. They offered a vision of free individuals, minimal government, and autonomous local communities that harked back to the "civic republicanism" in the era of young nationhood.

But modern conservatism, however deep its roots, is also a product of the recent past. Many students of the postwar right emphasize the theme of "backlash." They explain conservatism's rise as a populist reaction among working-class whites to the racial, cultural, and economic disruptions of the 1960s. Thomas and Mary Edsall's *Chain Reaction* (1991) and Ron Formisano's *Boston Against Busing* (1991) emphasize class tensions and economic insecurity as causes of battles over taxes and busing.

Other historians have challenged the "backlash" proponents' depiction of conservative politics in reactionary terms. Kim Phillips-Fein (*Invisible Hands*, 2006) outlined the role of conservative businessmen in promoting premarket ideology, while Rick Perlstein (*Before the Storm*, 2001) and Jonathan Schoenwald (*A Time for Choosing*, 2001) unearthed the deliberate conservative movement-making of the 1960s. Other scholars like Lisa McGirr, Thomas Sugrue, and Lizabeth Cohen have shown how the New Deal and Cold War ironically served to foster a suburban politics hostile to taxes and government redistributism.

Even as they trace the roots of the conservative revival to the early postwar years, scholars have come to see the 1970s as a "*Pivotal Decade*" (the title of Judith Stein's 2010 book). The work of Bruce Schulman, Jefferson Cowie, and Laura Colman shows how 1970s activists took advantage of disillusionment with government to mobilize new constituencies on behalf of conservatism. Their agenda combined antigovernment, free-market economic policies with an emphasis on hot-button "social issues" related to gender, reproductive policy, and cultural production. Scholars like Donald Critchlow and Darren Dochuk have shown that this latter cultural element of conservative mobilization had origins dating to the midcentury.

The flowering of scholarship on American conservatism has demonstrated, above all, that the forces that propelled Reagan to power in 1980 were neither aberrant not fleeting. Rather, they reflected outlooks deeply rooted in American culture and drew strength from core developments in the American state and economy in the twentieth century. American historians, like American citizens, are unlikely to ignore the conservative tradition again.

CHAPTER SUMMARY ★ ★ ★ ★ ★ ★ ★ ★ ★ ★ ★ ★ ★

Reagan led Republicans to sweeping victories in 1980 and 1984 over divided and demoralized Democrats. Riding a conservative national tide, Reagan pushed both his "supply-side" economic program of reduced social welfare programs, lower taxes, and massive military expenditures. These policies brought economic recovery and lower inflation, as well as high interest rates and dramatically bigger federal budget deficits.

Reagan revived the Cold War confrontation with the Soviet Union, and engaged the United States in assertive military support for anti-leftist forces in Latin America and elsewhere. The ratcheting up of military spending, along with the attempted reforms led by Mikhail Gorbachev, contributed to a series of successful arms limitation talks that reduced Cold War tensions in the mid-1980s. The Iran-Contra affair tarnished Reagan's international legacy, but his economic policies guaranteed success for his goal of curbing further growth in the welfare state.

Religious conservatives of the New Right assumed growing influence on American politics, borrowing many tactics from the sixties New Left. The Supreme Court under Reagan and his successor, George H.W. Bush, became increasingly conservative, as the Court partially overturned previous rulings on issues of abortion and affirmative action.

In foreign affairs, Bush promoted a "new world order" after the collapse of communism in Eastern Europe and the Soviet Union in 1989–1991. But Saddam Hussein's invasion of Kuwait brought war to the Middle East. With America as the only remaining superpower, Bush led an international coalition to victory in the Persian Gulf War, but the Middle East remained a dangerous tinderbox despite new efforts to resolve the Israel-Arab conflict. Bush supported the Americans with Disabilities Act, but also pushed conservative social issues and nominated the controversial Clarence Thomas to the Supreme Court. Economic recession and Bush's tax increase created a growing conservative opposition within the Republican party, led by Congressman Newt Gingrich.

KEY TERMS

- Proposition 13 (689)
- boll weevils (689)
- supply-side economics (689)
- Strategic Defense Initiative (SDI) (690)
- Sandinistas (692)
- contras (692)
- glasnost (693)
- perestroika (693)
- Intermediate-Range Nuclear Forces (INF) Treaty (693)
- Iran-Contra affair (694)
- Moral Majority (695)
- Black Monday (696)
- Operation Desert Storm (699)
- Americans with Disabilities Act (ADA) (700)

PEOPLE TO KNOW

- Ronald Reagan
- Margaret Thatcher
- Mikhail Gorbachev
- Saddam Hussein
- Jerry Falwell
- Sandra Day O'Connor
- George H.W. Bush
- Boris Yeltsin
- Manuel Noriega
- Clarence Thomas

Chapter

40

America Confronts the Post–Cold War Era

1992–2000

As the Cold War gives way to the global village, our leadership is needed more than ever, because problems that start beyond our borders can quickly become problems within them.

William J. Clinton, 1995

Chapter Outline

- Bill Clinton in the White House
- Congressional Republicans Battle Clinton
- Clinton and the Prosperous '90s Economy
- Racial Gains and Tensions
- Globalization and U.S. Foreign Policy
- Clinton's Impeachment and Acquittal
- The Controversial 2000 Election
- Postmodern American Culture
- *Makers of America: The Latinos*

The collapse of the Soviet Union and the democratization of its client regimes in Eastern Europe ended the four-decade-old Cold War and left the United States the world's sole remaining superpower. Americans welcomed these changes but seemed unsure how to exercise their unprecedented economic and military might in this new international scenario. The culture wars that had started in the 1960s fed ferociously partisan political squabbles that distracted the nation from the urgent task of clearly defining its role in the age of globalization.

Amidst this deepening partisan polarization, a sustained ten-year economic expansion powerfully shaped American society and politics in the 1990s. The second half of the decade was a particularly giddy boom era, as an exuberant financial sector and ascendant information technology firms helped to propel the economy to near-full employment—and the federal budget to record surpluses. But the good times were not to last.

FOCUS QUESTIONS

1. How did President Bill Clinton attempt to navigate between traditional liberal Democratic values and his claim to be a centrist "new Democrat"?
2. What caused the growing polarization between the conservative Republican movement and the Clinton administration?
3. Why did issues of race and women's rights remain controversial in the 1990s, even as many blacks and women made substantial social and economic gains?
4. How did President Clinton survive the Lewinsky scandal and subsequent impeachment?
5. How did multiculturalism, postmodernism, and new media change and splinter American culture?

CHRONOLOGY

1992	▪ Clinton defeats Bush and Perot for presidency
1993	▪ NAFTA signed
1994	▪ Republicans win majorities in both houses of Congress
1996	▪ Welfare Reform Bill becomes law ▪ Clinton defeats Dole for presidency
1998	▪ Clinton-Lewinsky scandal ▪ Al Qaeda bombing of the U.S. embassies in Kenya and Tanzania ▪ House of Representatives impeaches Clinton
1999	▪ Senate acquits Clinton on impeachment charges ▪ Kosovo crisis; NATO warfare with Serbia ▪ Protest in Seattle against World Trade Organization
2000	▪ United States normalizes trade relations with China ▪ George W. Bush wins presidency in Electoral College; Albert Gore takes popular vote

Bill Clinton: The First Baby-Boomer President

As the last decade of the twentieth century opened, a slumbering economy, a widening gender gap, and a rising anti-incumbent spirit spelled opportunity for Democrats, frozen out of the White House for all but four years since 1968. In a bruising round of primary elections, Governor William Jefferson ("Bill") Clinton of Arkansas weathered blistering accusations of womanizing and draft evasion to emerge as his party's standard-bearer, with another southern white male moderate, Tennessee Senator Albert Gore, as his vice presidential running mate.

Democratic Leadership Council (DLC) *Nonprofit organization of centrist Democrats founded in the mid-1980s. The group attempted to push the Democratic party toward pro-growth, strong defense, and anti-crime policies. Among its most influential early members was Bill Clinton, whom it held up as an example of "third way" politics.*

Clinton claimed to be a "New Democrat," chastened by his party's long exile in the political wilderness. With other centrist Democrats, he had formed the **Democratic Leadership Council (DLC)** to point the party away from its traditional anti-business, dovish, champion-of-the-underdog orientation and toward pro-growth, strong defense, and anticrime policies. The DLC's ascendance as a business-friendly faction within the country's center-left party underscored the degree to which market-oriented thinking and policies had come to dominate American politics in the last decades of the twentieth century.

Trying to wring one more win out of the social issues that had underwritten two Reagan and one Bush presidential victories, the 1992 Republican convention emphasized "family values" as it nominated President George H.W. Bush and Vice President J. Danforth Quayle for a second term. But Bush's listless campaign could not keep pace with the super-energetic and phenomenally articulate Clinton. Bush claimed credit for ending the Cold War and trumpeted his leadership in the Persian Gulf War. But pocketbook problems as the economy dipped into recession swayed more voters than pride in past foreign policy.

At Clinton's campaign headquarters, a simple sign reminded staffers of his principal campaign theme: "It's the economy, stupid." Reflecting pervasive economic unease and the virulence of the throw-the-bums-out national mood, nearly 20 percent of voters cast their ballots for independent presidential candidate H. Ross Perot, a bantamweight, jug-eared Texas billionaire who harped incessantly on federal deficit problems and boasted of the fact that he had never held any public office.

With a record turnout of 100 million voters on election day, the final tally gave Clinton 44,909,889 popular votes and 370 votes in the Electoral College. He was the first baby boomer to ascend to the White House, a distinction reflecting the electoral profile of the population. Bush polled 39,104,545 popular votes and 168 electoral votes. Perot won no electoral votes but did gather 19,742,267 popular votes—the strongest showing for an independent or third-party candidate since Theodore Roosevelt ran on the Bull Moose ticket in 1912. Democrats also racked up clear majorities in both houses of Congress. The new Congress included thirty-nine African Americans, forty-eight women, and record numbers of Hispanics, Asian Americans, and Indians.

AFP/Getty Images

The Clintons Campaign, 1992 Bill and Hillary Clinton wave to a crowd of forty thousand in St. Louis on the last stop of the Clinton-Gore campaign's cross-country bus tour. The Arkansas governor was a famously tireless and effective campaigner, and he and his wife, an attorney and political force in her own right, would prove to be a powerful team in national politics for decades to come.

A False Start for Reform

Badly overestimating his electoral mandate for liberal reform, the young president made a series of costly blunders upon entering the White House. He stirred a hornet's nest of controversy by advocating an end to the ban on gays and lesbians in the armed forces. Confronted with fierce opposition, the president finally settled for a **"Don't Ask, Don't Tell"** policy that quietly accepted gay and lesbian soldiers and sailors without officially acknowledging their presence in the military. (Congress finally repealed the discriminatory policy in 2010.)

"Don't Ask, Don't Tell" *From 1993 to 2010, the policy affecting homosexuals in the military. It emerged as a compromise between the standing prohibition against homosexuals in the armed forces and President Clinton's push to allow all citizens to serve regardless of sexual orientation. Military authorities were forbidden to ask about a service member's orientation, and gay service personnel could be discharged if they publicly revealed their homosexuality. At President Obama's urging, Congress repealed DADT in 2010, permitting gays to serve openly in uniform.*

Even more damaging to Clinton's political standing was the fiasco of his attempt to reform the nation's health care system. In a dramatic but risky move, the president appointed his wife, Hillary Rodham Clinton, as the director of a task force charged with redesigning the medical-service industry. Their stupefyingly complicated plan was dead on arrival when presented to Congress in October 1993. The First Lady was doused with a torrent of abuse for her role in producing this legislative turkey, but she eventually rehabilitated herself sufficiently to win election as U.S. senator from New York in 2000—the first First Lady ever to hold elective office.

President Clinton had better luck with a deficit-reduction bill that passed Congress in 1993, which combined with an increasingly buoyant economy help shrink federal deficits. By 1998 Clinton's policies seemed to have caged the ravenous deficit monster, as Congress argued over the unfamiliar question of how to spend projected federal budget *surpluses*.

Clinton succeeded in getting through Congress a far-reaching anti-crime bill that provided for 100,000 new police officers, construction of more prisons, and a ban on some assault weapons (the ban expired in 2004). Several states also stiffened law enforcement practices, until America's incarceration rate became the highest in the world. The country's violent crime rate began to decline substantially after 1995—a striking nationwide trend that continued into the new century.

AP Images/David Glass

Bombing of Federal Building in Oklahoma City, 1995 A truck bomb killed 168 people in this federal office building in the worst act of terrorism in the United States until September 11, 2001. Convicted on eleven counts for the attack, antigovernment militant Timothy McVeigh became the first person executed by the federal government in nearly forty years in 2001.

Oklahoma City bombing (1995) *Truck-bomb explosion that killed 168 people in a federal office building on April 19, 1995. The attack was perpetrated by right-wing and antigovernment militant Timothy McVeigh, who was later executed by the U.S. government for the crime.*

Contract with America (1994) *Multipoint program offered by Republican candidates and sitting politicians in the 1994 midterm election. The platform proposed smaller government, congressional ethics reform, term limits, greater emphasis on personal responsibility, and a general repudiation of the Democratic party. This articulation of dissent was a significant blow to the Clinton administration and led to the Republican party's takeover of both houses of Congress for the first time in half a century.*

Despite such legislative achievements, a sour antigovernment mood persisted. A huge explosion destroyed a federal office building in Oklahoma City in 1995, taking 168 lives, in retribution for a 1993 standoff in Waco, Texas, between federal agents and the Fundamentalist sect known as the Branch Davidians. That showdown had ended in the destruction of the sect's compound and the deaths of many Branch Davidians, including women and children. Events like the **Oklahoma City bombing** brought to light a secretive underground of paramilitary private "militias" composed of alienated citizens armed to the teeth and ultra-suspicious of all government.

Even many law-abiding citizens shared to some degree in the antigovernment attitudes that drove the militia members to murderous extremes. Thanks largely to the disillusioning agony of the Vietnam War and the naked cynicism of Richard Nixon in the Watergate scandal, the confidence in government that came naturally to the generation that had licked the Great Depression and won the Second World War was in short supply by century's end. Reflecting that pervasive disenchantment with politics and politicians, several states passed term-limit laws for elected officials, although the Supreme Court ruled in 1995 that the restrictions did not apply to federal officeholders.

★ The Politics of Distrust

Clinton's failed initiatives and widespread antigovernment sentiment afforded conservative Republicans a golden opportunity in 1994, and they seized it aggressively. Led by outspoken Georgia representative Newt Gingrich, Republicans offered voters a **Contract with America** that promised an all-out assault on budget deficits and radical reductions in welfare programs. Their campaign succeeded fabulously, as a conservative tornado roared across the land in the 1994 congressional elections. Republicans picked up eleven governorships, eight Senate seats, and fifty-three seats in the House (where Gingrich became Speaker), giving them control of both chambers of Congress for the first time in forty years. The 1994 midterms wiped out the remaining conservative congressional Democrats, concentrated in the South. Their replacement by newly empowered southern Republicans accelerated the ideological and geographical sorting of the two parties, which in turn only intensified the political combat in Washington.

In 1996 the new Congress achieved a major conservative victory when it compelled a reluctant Clinton to sign the **Welfare Reform Bill**, which made deep cuts in welfare grants and required able-bodied welfare recipients to find employment. Though liberal Democrats howled with pain at this law, Clinton's acceptance of welfare reform was part of his shrewd political strategy of accommodating the electorate's conservative mood by moving to the right.

Even as he signed the welfare-reform bill, Clinton denounced provisions that tightly restricted welfare benefits for both legal and illegal immigrants. These measures, like the Illegal Immigration Act of 1996 and a proposal to declare English the country's "official language," reflected a rising tide of anti-immigrant sentiment as the numbers of newcomers climbed to all-time highs, especially in the Southwest. Though anti-immigrant sentiment galvanized many voters, it also risked alienating the country's rapidly growing Latino population (see "Makers of America: The Latinos," p. 709).

Welfare reform marked a landmark legislative victory for the so-called "Republican Revolution" in Congress, but Republicans then proceeded to overplay their mandate for conservative retrenchment. Many Americans gradually came to feel that the Gingrich Republicans were bending the bow too far, especially when Speaker Gingrich advocated provocative ideas like sending the children of welfare families to orphanages. In a tense confrontation in 1995 between the Democratic president and the Republican Congress over proposed cuts to Medicare and education, the federal government was forced to shut down for nearly a month until a budget package was agreed upon. The shutdown bred a backlash against the GOP that helped President Clinton rebound from his political near-death experience.

Contending Voices

Welfare Reform Divides the Democrats

The 1996 Welfare Reform Bill, formally named the Personal Responsibility and Work Opportunity Act, badly split the president's fellow Democrats. Bill Clinton's (b. 1946) decision to sign it—after having vetoed two previous versions passed by the Republican-controlled Congress—occurred on the eve of a looming reelection campaign. His signing reflected his determination to be a "New Democrat" open both to market-based reform and scaled-back welfare programs.

Fellow New Democrats like Connecticut senator Joseph Lieberman (b. 1942) supported this approach. As Lieberman explained in an op-ed endorsing the Senate version of the bill:

"Welfare makes it feasible for a man to father a child without worrying about being a parent. It makes it possible for a young woman (too often a teen-age girl) to have a child, move away from home, get an apartment and survive—without working. . . .

The Senate bill provides hope for poor Americans, and for taxpayers who want a Government that spends their money wisely and better reflects American values of work, family, and responsibility. . . . Most important, it would put an end to the policy of something for nothing, of penalizing work and marriage, and isolating the poor from the economic and cultural mainstream."

But leading liberal activists, among them the Clinton ally and Children's Defense Fund president Marian Wright Edelman (b. 1939), lambasted Clinton:

(continued)

Clinton Comes Back

As the 1996 election approached, the Republicans chose Kansas Senator Robert Dole as their presidential candidate. A decorated World War II veteran, Dole had a dry wit and deadpan manner that did not translate well on the campaign trail. In a bland contest, both parties fought for moderate "swing voters." One such swing constituency—middle class female suburbanites—introduced the term *soccer moms* into the national lexicon. Targeting soccer moms made excellent political sense because for the first time a majority of Americans now lived in the suburbs.

Welfare Reform Bill (1996)
Legislation that made deep cuts in welfare grants and required able-bodied welfare recipients to find employment. Part of Bill Clinton's campaign platform in 1992, the reforms were widely seen by liberals as an abandonment of key New Deal/Great Society provisions to care for the impoverished.

(continued)

"President Clinton's signature on pending 'welfare reform' legislation makes a mockery of his pledge not to hurt children. It will leave a moral blot on his presidency and on our nation that will never be forgotten.

This legislation is the biggest betrayal of children and the poor since the Children's Defense Fund began. It takes no political courage to stand up to two-month-old babies or to play election year games of political chicken at preschoolers' expense."

What explains the emergence of a pro-welfare-reform wing within the Democratic party during the prosperous 1990s? How did both sides invoke traditional American values in making their cases?

Buoyed by a healthy economy and by his artful trimming to the conservative wind, Clinton breezed to an easy victory, with 47,401,898 popular votes to Dole's 39,198,482. Dole's victory in eight southern states, however, underscored how the once safely-Democratic "solid South" had by century's end become Republican territory. The Reform party's egomaniacal leader, Ross Perot, ran a distant third, picking up less than half the votes he had garnered in 1992. Clinton won 379 electoral votes, Dole only 159. But Republicans retained control of Congress.

As Clinton began his second term—the first Democratic president since Franklin Delano Roosevelt to be reelected—the heady promises of far-reaching reform with which he had entered the White House four years earlier were no longer heard. Still facing Republican majorities in both houses of Congress, Clinton proposed only modest legislative goals, even though soaring tax revenues generated by the prosperous economy produced in 1998 a balanced federal budget for the first time in three decades.

Racial Progress and Perils

In his second term, Clinton cleverly managed to put Republicans on the defensive by claiming the political middle ground on contentious issues. He now warmly embraced the landmark Welfare Reform Bill of 1996 that he had initially been slow to endorse. Juggling the political hot potato of affirmative action, Clinton pledged to "mend it, not end it." When voters in California in 1996 approved Proposition 209, prohibiting affirmative-action preferences in government and higher education, the number of minority students in the state's public universities temporarily plummeted. A federal appeals court decision, *Hopwood v. Texas*, had a similar effect in Texas. Clinton criticized these broad assaults on affirmative action but stopped short of trying to reverse them, aware that public support for affirmative action, especially among white Americans, had diminished since the 1970s.

Beyond affirmative action, the racial divisions that still loomed large in American culture and politics became searingly apparent in Los Angeles in 1992. Like New York a century earlier, the southern California metropolis had become a magnet for minorities, especially immigrants from Asia and Latin America. When a mostly white Los Angeles jury exonerated white police officers who had been videotaped ferociously beating a black suspect, the minority neighborhoods in South Central Los Angeles erupted in rage. Arson and looting laid waste to entire city blocks, and scores of people were killed. In a sobering demonstration of the complexity of modern American racial rivalries, many black rioters vented their anger at the white police by attacking Asian shopkeepers.

The Los Angeles riots vividly testified to black skepticism about the American justice system. Just three years later, again in Los Angeles, the televised spectacle of former football star O.J. Simpson's trial for allegedly murdering his white former wife fed white disillusionment with the state of race relations. After months of testimony that seemed to point to Simpson's guilt, the jury acquitted him, presumably because certain Los Angeles police officers involved in the case had been shown to harbor racist sentiments. The reaction to the Simpson verdict revealed the yawning chasm that separated white and black America, as most whites believed Simpson guilty, while a major of African-Americans felt the not-guilty verdict was justified.

In 1990 the African American intellectual Shelby Steele (b. 1946) declared in his provocative book, The Content of Our Character,

"What is needed now is a new spirit of pragmatism in racial matters where blacks are seen simply as American citizens who deserve complete fairness and in some cases developmental assistance, but in no case special entitlements based on color. We need deracinated social policies that attack poverty rather than black poverty and that instill those values that make for self-reliance."

The Latinos

Today Mexican food is handed through fast-food drive-up windows in all fifty states and Spanish-language broadcasts fill the airwaves. Latinos send representatives to Congress and mayors to city hall, record hit songs, paint murals, and teach history. Latinos, among the fastest-growing segments of the U.S. population, include Puerto Ricans, frequent voyagers between their native island and northeastern cities; Cubans, many of them refugees from the communist dictatorship of Fidel Castro, concentrated in Miami and southern Florida; and Central Americans, fleeing the ravages of civil war in Nicaragua and El Salvador.

But the most populous group of Latinos derives from Mexico. The first significant numbers of Mexicans began heading for *El Norte* ("the North") around 1910, when the upheavals of the Mexican Revolution stirred and shuffled the Mexican population into more or less constant flux. Their northward passage was briefly interrupted during the Great Depression, when thousands of Mexican nationals were deported. But immigration resumed during World War II, and since then a steady flow of legal immigrants has passed through border checkpoints, joined by countless millions of their undocumented countrymen and countrywomen stealing across the frontier on moonless nights.

Many of these Mexicans came to work in the fields, following the ripening crops northward to Canada through the summer and autumn months. Others found work in the cities of the Southwest—El Paso, Los Angeles, Houston, and San Bernardino. Houses may have been shabby in the barrios, but these Mexican neighborhoods provided a sense of togetherness, a place to raise a family, and the chance to join a mutual aid society. Such societies, or *mutualistas*, sponsored baseball leagues, helped the sick and disabled, and defended their members against discrimination.

Mexican immigrants lived so close to the border that their native country acted like a powerful magnet, drawing them back time and time again. Mexicans frequently returned to see relatives, and relatively few became U.S. citizens. In addition, the Mexican government sometimes discouraged Mexicans from becoming citizens of their adopted country. In the 1910s and 1920s the Mexican consulate in Los Angeles launched a Mexicanization program among the immigrants. The consulate sponsored parades on *Cinco de Mayo* ("Fifth of May"), celebrating Mexico's defeat of a French army in 1862, and opened Spanish-language schools for children.

Since World War II, American-born generations have carried on the fight for political representation, economic opportunity, and cultural preservation. After years of struggle, the United Farm Workers Organizing Committee (UFWOC), headed by Cesar Chavez, succeeded in improving working conditions for mostly Chicano farm laborers. Flexing their political muscles, Latinos have since the 1980s helped elect their co-ethnics as mayors of Miami, Denver, San Antonio, and Los Angeles.

Fresh arrivals from Mexico and other Latin American nations daily swell Latino communities across America. By 2012, Latinos made up 17 percent of the total U.S. population, with an even greater proportion in California (38 percent), Arizona (30 percent), New Mexico (47 percent), and Texas (38 percent). As the United States moves through the twenty-first century, it is taking on a pronounced Spanish accent.

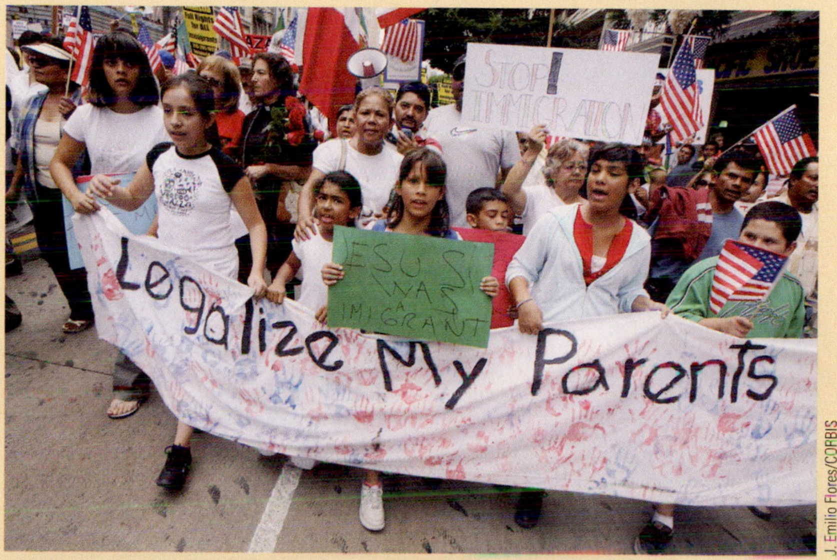

J. Emilio Flores/CORBIS

Demonstrating for Immigrant Rights, Los Angeles, 2007 Latinos march in downtown Los Angeles in support of legalizing undocumented parents who have children born in the United States. U.S. law gives the right of citizenship to anyone born on American soil ("jus soli"), but not necessarily to the parents of that child.

America's increasingly segmented residential landscapes reflected the stubborn racial divide. At the end of the twentieth century, minorities made up majorities within many American cities, while whites dominated the suburbs. In 2002, 52 percent of all blacks lived in central cities compared with only 21 percent of whites. Some of these urban white residents were well-to-do gentrifiers, whose restoration of decaying neighborhoods sent real estate values soaring and many minority residents packing to deepening concentrations of inner-city poverty.

Many successful black beneficiaries of the civil rights revolution of the 1950s and 1960s followed whites to the prosperous middle-class suburbs, while less affluent minorities began populating the first ring of post-World War II suburbs, now often badly deteriorated. Some cities like New York and San Francisco boomed with finance and technology economies, while others like Detroit and Cleveland struggle to replace once-prosperous industries.

African American gains in the wake of the civil rights victories of the 1950s and 1960s could be measured in other ways than shifting residential addresses. The number of black elected officials rose above the nine thousand mark in 2000, including more than three dozen members of Congress and the mayors of several large cities. By the turn of the new century, blacks had also dramatically advanced in higher education, although the political assault against affirmative action in California and elsewhere compounded obstacles to advancement for many young African Americans.

Racial divisions in the 1990s also manifested themselves politically in massive partisan disparities among black and white voters. African Americans proved themselves among Bill Clinton's most fiercely loyal supporters, giving him 83 percent of their vote in 1992 and 84 percent in 1996. As a politician, Clinton had an easy and authentic personal connection with the African American community. But far more significant was the electoral sorting of the two major parties, with racial minorities becoming ever larger and more consequential components of the Democratic base.

Globalization and Its Discontents

Clinton's major political advantage in his second term was the roaring economy, which by 2000 had sustained the longest period of growth in American history. The Federal Reserve's low-interest, easy-money policies and the explosive growth of new Internet ("dot-com") businesses helped fuel the boom. Unemployment crept down to 4 percent, sending employers scrambling madly for workers, while inflationary pressure remained remarkably low.

In this heady atmosphere, Clinton and congressional Republicans found common ground in pursuing fateful new efforts at financial deregulation. These included loosening federal regulation of "derivatives" trading as well as repealing the depression-era Glass-Steagall Act that had barred commercial banks from dealing in securities. Later, amidst the financial tumult of the 2000s, the deregulatory wave of the go-go nineties came in for heavy retrospective criticism.

North American Free Trade Agreement (NAFTA) (1993) *Free-trade zone encompassing Mexico, Canada, and the United States. A symbol of the increased reality of a globalized marketplace, the treaty passed despite opposition from protectionists and labor leaders.*

World Trade Organization (WTO) (1995) *An international body to promote and supervise liberal trade among nations. The successor to the General Agreement on Tariffs and Trade, it marked a key world trade policy achievement of the Clinton administration.*

Clinton encountered more controversy over trade policy. He had shown political courage by supporting the **North American Free Trade Agreement (NAFTA)** in 1993, creating a free-trade zone encompassing Mexico, Canada, and the United States. Clinton took another step in 1994 toward a global free-trade system when he vigorously promoted the creation of the **World Trade Organization (WTO)**. But simmering discontent over trade policy boiled over when Clinton hosted the meeting of the WTO in Seattle. The city's streets filled with protesters railing against what they viewed as the human and environmental costs of economic globalization.

Speaking in Hanoi, Vietnam, in November 2000, Bill Clinton declared:

"Globalization is not something we can hold off or turn off. It is the economic equivalent of a force of nature—like wind or water."

Despite such protests, Clinton vigorously pursued trade-expansion initiatives through his presidency. As the emerging powerhouse of China loomed ever larger, Clinton soft-pedaled his earlier criticism of Beijing's human rights record and began seeking improved trade relations.

His controversial China trade bill, passed by Congress in 2000, marked one more stride in the forward march of globalization.

Communications technology helped to accelerate the pace of globalization. The old industrial age was rapidly giving way to a new "information age" in which storing, organizing, and processing data were the most important industries of all. As the pace of the information age accelerated, the world shrank. Businesspeople could now instantaneously girdle the planet with transactions of prodigious scope and serpentine complexity.

But the very speed and efficiency of the new communications tools threatened to wipe out entire occupational categories, and even entire ways of life. Workers whose business was to mediate between product and client, like travel agents and bank tellers, were in danger of becoming casualties of the computer. White-collar jobs in financial services and engineering could now be "out-sourced" to countries such as Ireland and India. The related forces of the computer revolution and economic globalization defined the central opportunities and challenges for American workers as the new millennium dawned.

Protesting NAFTA, 1993 These members of the Teamsters Union feared that the adoption of the North American Free Trade Agreement would mean the replacement of high-paying American jobs with low-wage, nonunion Mexican labor. More than a decade later, the treaty still rankled. Policymakers disagreed about whether NAFTA had been damaging to American workers. In the 2008 election, the Republicans endorsed it, while the Democrats attacked it.

NAFTA/Office of the United States Trade Representative/Picture Research Consultants & Archives

The Feminist Revolution

All Americans were caught up in the great economic changes of the late twentieth century, but no group was more profoundly affected than women. When that century opened, women made up about 20 percent of all workers. Over the next five decades they increased their presence in the labor force at a fairly steady rate, except for a temporary spurt during World War II. Then, beginning in the 1950s, women's entry into the workplace accelerated dramatically. By the 1990s nearly half of all workers were women, and the majority of working-age women held jobs outside the home.

Most astonishing was the upsurge in employment of mothers. In 1950, nearly 90 percent of mothers with children under the age of six did not work for pay. But half a century later, a majority of women with children as young as one year old were wage earners. Because most men did not take on tasks such as cooking, childcare, and housework, working women were expected to bring home the bacon and cook it, too.

The greater burdens of parenthood on women helped explain the persistence of occupational segregation and pay disparities through the 1990s. Women were far more likely than men to interrupt their careers to bear and raise children. Partly as a result, women continued to receive lower wages than men doing the same full-time work, and they tended to concentrate in lower paying occupations—the so-called the "pink-collar ghetto." And although they made up more than half the population, women in 2010 accounted for just 33 percent of lawyers and judges (up from 5 percent in 1970) and 32 percent of physicians (up from 10 percent in 1970).

Recognizing the new realities of the modern American household, Congress passed and President Clinton signed the Family and Medical Leave Act of 1993, which mandated job protection for working fathers as well as mothers who needed time off from work for family-related reasons. Over the course of the decade, some employers began providing paternity leave as well, but such leave was overwhelmingly unpaid. The concept of gender equality in family leave policies was more aspirational than real in most workplaces.

Picture Research Consultants & Archives

Reuters/CORBIS

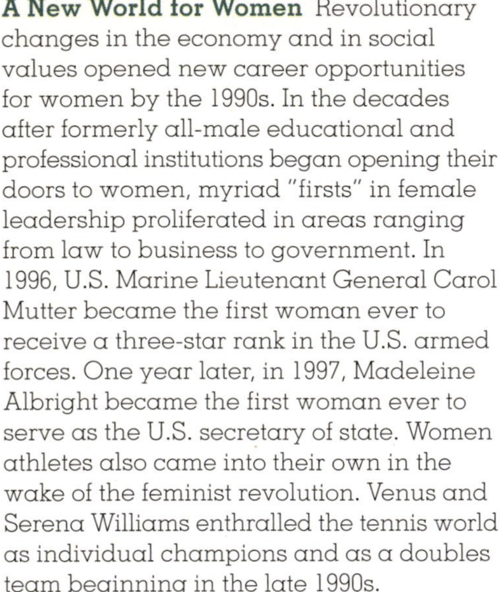

A New World for Women Revolutionary changes in the economy and in social values opened new career opportunities for women by the 1990s. In the decades after formerly all-male educational and professional institutions began opening their doors to women, myriad "firsts" in female leadership proliferated in areas ranging from law to business to government. In 1996, U.S. Marine Lieutenant General Carol Mutter became the first woman ever to receive a three-star rank in the U.S. armed forces. One year later, in 1997, Madeleine Albright became the first woman ever to serve as the U.S. secretary of state. Women athletes also came into their own in the wake of the feminist revolution. Venus and Serena Williams enthralled the tennis world as individual champions and as a doubles team beginning in the late 1990s.

© Wally McNamee/Sygma/CORBIS

Women's full-scale entrance into the work force inevitably affected family practices and structures, provoking passionate political conflicts over "family values." Indeed, the traditional nuclear family, once prized as the foundation of society and the nursery of the Republic, suffered heavy blows in the late twentieth century. By the 1990s one out of every two marriages ended in divorce. Births to unmarried women, once rare, became common. In the 1990s one out of four white babies, one out of three Latino babies, and two out of three African American babies were born to single mothers.

But if the *traditional* family was increasingly rare, the family itself remained a bedrock of American society at the close of the twentieth century. Children in households led by a single parent, stepparent, or grandparent, as well as children with gay or lesbian parents, encountered a degree of acceptance that would have been unimaginable a generation earlier. The family was not evaporating, but evolving into multiple, apparently viable forms.

Searching for a Post-Cold War Foreign Policy

The end of the Cold War dismantled the framework within which the United States had conducted foreign policy for nearly half a century. Throughout his presidency, Bill Clinton groped for a new formula to replace anticommunism as the basic premise of American diplomacy.

Absorbed by domestic issues, Clinton at first seemed uncertain and even amateurish in his conduct of foreign policy. He followed his predecessor's lead in dispatching American peacekeeping troops to Somalia, but quietly withdrew them after Somali rebels killed more than a dozen Americans in late 1993. Burned in Somalia, Washington stood on the sidelines in 1994 when catastrophic ethnic violence in the central African country of Rwanda resulted in the deaths of half a million people.

The Rwandan genocide painfully underscored a question dogging the sole remaining superpower in the post-Cold War era: What obligations did America have to intervene in military and humanitarian crises abroad? Events in the tormented Balkans in southeastern Europe provoked similar uncertainty. As vicious ethnic conflict raged through Bosnia, Washington dithered until finally committing American troops to a NATO peacekeeping contingent in 1995.

Yet NATO's presence in Bosnia failed to pacify the Balkans. When Serbian president Slobodan Milosević in 1999 unleashed a new round of "ethnic cleansing" in the region, this time against ethnic Albanians in the province of Kosovo, U.S.-led NATO forces launched an air war against Serbia. The bombing campaign eventually forced Milosević to accept a NATO peacekeeping force in Kosovo.

The Middle East remained a major focus of American diplomacy right up to the end of Clinton's tenure—and beyond. At a historic White House meeting in 1993, Israeli premier Yitzhak Rabin and Palestinian Liberation Organization (PLO) leader Yasir Arafat agreed in principle on Israeli withdrawal from the West Bank and Gaza Strip and self-rule for the Palestinians living there. But hopes flickered low two years later when Rabin fell to an assassin's bullet. Clinton and his second-term secretary of state, Madeleine Albright, spent the rest of the 1990s struggling in vain to broker the permanent settlement that continued to elude Israelis and Palestinians.

The Middle East served as the regional source for another thorny problem in the 1990s: the growth of radical, anti-American Islamic terrorism, organized most effectively in the transnational network known as Al Qaeda ("the base" in Arabic). The terrorist organization killed more than 230 people in simultaneous bombings of the American embassies in Kenya and Tanzania in 1998. Operatives bombed the USS *Cole* in Yemen two years later. Denouncing America's growing military presence in the Middle East, Al Qaeda leader Osama bin Laden declared war against all Americans and their Allies in a *fatwa* issued in 1998.

In his final years as president, Clinton stepped up his efforts to leave a legacy as an international peacemaker. He sought to reduce or end festering conflicts between Catholics and Protestants in Northern Ireland, between North and South Korea, and between India and Pakistan in South Asia. But despite these gestures, the guiding principles of American foreign policy in the post–Cold War era remained ill-defined and elusive.

Scandal and Impeachment

Scandal had dogged Bill Clinton from the beginning of his presidency. Critics brought charges of everything from philandering to illegal financial transactions. Allegations of corruption stemming from a real estate deal called **Whitewater** while he was governor of Arkansas triggered an investigation by a special prosecutor, but no indictment ever materialized. A mobilized conservative movement, with its own humming media infrastructure in print and talk radio, amplified each new whiff of scandal throughout the Clinton years.

Whitewater *A series of scandals during the Clinton administration that stemmed from a failed real estate investment from which the Clintons were alleged to have illicitly profited. The accusations prompted the appointment of a special federal prosecutor, though no indictments.*

All previous scandals were overshadowed by the revelation in January 1998 that Clinton had engaged in a sexual affair with a young White House intern, Monica Lewinsky, and then blatantly lied about it when he testified under oath in another woman's civil suit accusing him of sexual harassment. Caught in his bold lie, the president made a humiliating confession, but his political opponents smelled blood in the water. In September 1998, the special prosecutor investigating Whitewater, who had broad powers to investigate *any* evidence of presidential malfeasance, presented a stinging report, including lurid sexual details, to the Republican-controlled House of Representatives. That report charged Clinton with eleven possible grounds for impeachment, all related to lying about the **Lewinsky affair**.

Lewinsky affair (1998–1999) *Political sex scandal that resulted in Bill Clinton's impeachment and trial by Congress. In 1998, Clinton gave sworn testimony in a sexual harassment case that he had never engaged in sexual activity with a White House intern named Monica Lewinsky. When prosecutors discovered evidence that the president had lied under oath about the affair, to which Clinton admitted, Republicans in Congress began impeachment proceedings. Although Clinton was ultimately not convicted by the Senate, the scandal put a lasting blemish on his presidential legacy.*

The House quickly cranked up the rusty machinery of impeachment. As an acrid partisan atmosphere enveloped the capital, House Republicans in December 1998 eventually passed two articles of impeachment against the president: perjury before a grand jury and obstruction of justice. Crying foul, the Democratic minority charged that, however deplorable Clinton's personal misconduct, sexual transgressions did not rise to the level of "high crimes and misdemeanors" prescribed in the Constitution (see Art. II, Sec. IV in the Appendix). The House Republican managers (prosecutors) of impeachment replied that perjury and obstruction were grave public issues and that nothing less than "the rule of law" was at stake.

As cries of "honor the Constitution" and "sexual McCarthyism" filled the air, the nation debated whether the president's peccadilloes amounted to high crimes or low follies. Most Americans apparently leaned toward the latter view. In the 1998 midterm elections, voters reduced the House Republicans' majority, causing fiery House Speaker Newt Gingrich to resign his post. Although Americans held a low opinion of Clinton's slipshod personal morals, most liked the president's political and economic policies and wanted him to stay in office.

In early 1999, for the first time in 130 years, the nation witnessed an impeachment proceeding in the U.S. Senate. Dusting off ancient precedents from Andrew Johnson's trial, the one hundred senators solemnly heard arguments and evidence in the case. With the facts widely known and the two parties' political positions firmly locked in, the trial's outcome was a foregone conclusion. On the key obstruction of justice charge, five northeastern Republicans joined all forty-five Democratic senators in voting not guilty. The fifty Republican votes for conviction fell far short of the constitutionally required two-thirds majority. The vote on the perjury charge was forty-five guilty, fifty-five not guilty.

Clinton's Legacy and the 2000 Election

Beyond the obvious stain of impeachment, Clinton's legacy was mixed. His sound economic policies encouraged growth and trade in a rapidly globalizing, post–Cold War world. Yet as a New Democrat and avowed centrist, Clinton did more to consolidate than to reverse the Reagan-Bush revolution against New Deal liberalism that had for half a century provided the compass for the Democratic party and the nation. Further, by setting such a low standard in his personal conduct, he replenished the sad reservoir of public cynicism about politics that Vietnam and Watergate had created a generation before.

Nonetheless, as the end of the Clinton term and the beginning of the new millennium approached, the Democrats stayed on their political course and nominated loyal vice president Albert Gore for president. Gore faced the tricky challenge of linking himself to Clinton-era peace and prosperity while at the same time distancing himself from his boss's personal foibles. He chose as his running mate Connecticut Senator Joseph Lieberman, an outspoken Clinton critic and the first Jew nominated to a major national ticket. Their Republican challenger, George W. Bush, won the nomination on the strength of his father's name and his years as governor of Texas. Bush surrounded himself with Washington insiders, including vice-presidential nominee Richard Cheney, and, in a clear jab at Clinton, promised to "restore dignity to the White House."

Rosy estimates that the federal budget would produce a surplus of some $2 trillion in the coming decade set the stage for the presidential contest. Echoing the Republican creed of smaller government, Bush argued for returning the budget surplus to "the people" through massive tax cuts and for promoting private sector programs, such as school vouchers and a reliance on "faith-based" institutions to help the poor. Gore proposed smaller tax cuts, targeted at middle-income and lower-income people, and strengthening Social Security. In an era of peace, foreign policy figured hardly at all in the campaign.

Pollsters predicted a close election, but none foresaw the epochal cliffhanger that the election became. On election day, the country split nearly evenly between the two candidates, and it was soon clear that Florida's electoral votes would determine the winner. Television news programs announced that Bush had won the Sunshine State, and Al Gore called the Texas governor to concede defeat. Yet just an hour later Gore's camp decided that Florida was too close to call and the vice president—in perhaps the most awkward phone call in modern politics—retracted his concession.

What ensued was a five-week political standoff over how to count the votes in Florida. Democrats argued that some ballots were confusing or misread by machines, and asked for recounts in several counties. Republicans claimed that such a recount would amount to "changing the rules in the middle of the game" and thus thwart the rule of law. After weeks of legal bickering, the Supreme Court finally intervened. By a five-to-four vote along partisan lines, the Court reasoned that, because neither Florida's legislature nor its courts had established a uniform standard for evaluating disputed ballots, the hand counts amounted to an unconstitutional breach of the Fourteenth Amendment's equal protection clause.

That ruling gave Bush the White House but cast a dark shadow of illegitimacy over his presidency. Bush officially won Florida by 537 votes out of 6 million cast, and he squeaked by in the Electoral College, 271 to 266 (see Map 40.1). The national popular vote went decisively to Gore, 50,999,897 to 50,456,002. For the first time since 1888, a candidate had won the White House with fewer popular votes than his opponent. Calls to abolish the Electoral College, however, were few and muted (see Art. V of the Constitution).

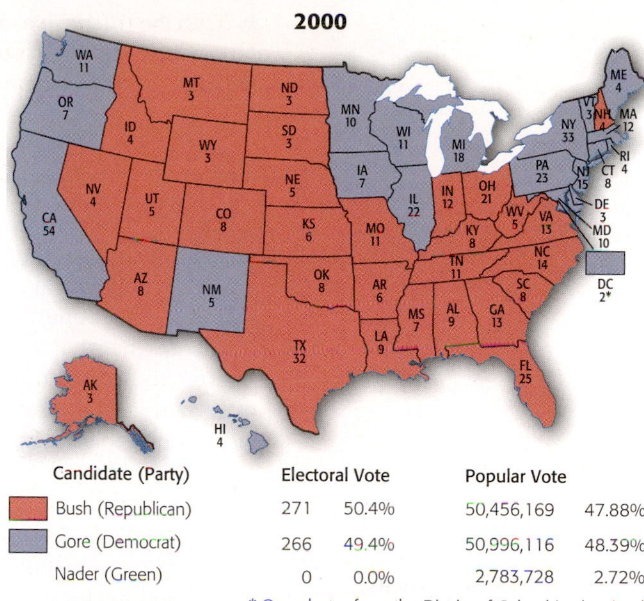

Map 40.1 Presidential Election of 2000 (with electoral vote by state) Although Democrat Albert Gore won the popular election for president by half a million votes, George W. Bush's contested 537-vote advantage in Florida gave him a slight lead in the Electoral College. The 2.7 million popular votes won by Green party candidate and consumer activist Ralph Nader almost surely deprived Gore of victory, casting Nader in the role of spoiler. Bush's failure to win the popular vote inspired critics to protest at his inauguration with placards reading "Hail to the Thief."

African Americans voted for Gore over Bush by a ratio of ten to one, signaling the deepening racial polarization of party politics at the turn of the new century. Many black Floridians also complained that election officials had unfairly disqualified their votes or even turned them away from the polls, as in the "Jim Crow" era.

E Pluribus Plures

America's culture proved no less fractious than the nation's politics as the century drew to a close. What united many key late-century developments in American intellectual life and artistic production became—ironically enough—diversity itself.

Controversial issues of color and culture also pervaded the realm of ideas in the late twentieth century. Echoing early-twentieth-century "cultural pluralists" like Horace Kallen and Randolph Bourne, many intellectuals after 1970 embraced the creed of "multiculturalism." The new mantra celebrated diversity for its own sake and stressed the need to preserve and promote, rather than squash, a variety of distinct ethnic and racial cultures in the United States.

The nation's classrooms became battlegrounds for the debate over America's commitment to pluralism. Multiculturalists attacked the traditional curriculum as "Eurocentric" and advocated greater focus on the achievements of African Americans, Asian Americans, Latinos, and Native Americans. In response, critics charged that too much stress on ethnic difference would come at the expense of national cohesion and an appreciation of common American values.

The Census Bureau further enlivened the debate when in 2000 it allowed respondents to identify themselves with more than one of the six standard categories (black, white, Latino, American Indian, Asian, and Native Hawaiian or Pacific Islander). Signifying a mounting revolution in attitudes toward race, nearly 7 million Americans chose to describe themselves as biracial or multiracial. By the early twenty-first century many Americans, including public figures like golfer Tiger Woods, actress Rosario Dawson, and Barack Obama, were proclaiming their mixed heritage with pride.

The Postmodern Mind

A growing comfort with multiplicity not only characterized Americans' attitudes toward race, ethnicity, and identity in the later twentieth century. This same outlook energized much of the cultural and intellectual output of the era. Commentators often described contemporary Americans as living in a "postmodern" age, though few could agree on precisely what that term meant. But whatever else it denoted, *postmodernism* generally referred to a condition of fragmented perspectives, multiple truths, and constructed identities. The postmodern mind rejected rational, totalizing descriptions of the self or the world, and replaced modernism's faith in certainty, objectivity, and unity with an eclectic celebration of diverse and overlapping outlooks.

Postmodern architecture made the most visible imprint on the American cultural landscape. Rejecting austere modernist functionalism and minimalism, postmodernists like Robert Venturi and Michael Graves revived decorative details and celebrated a playful mix of architectural elements. The flight from stark modernism took especially fanciful forms in Frank Gehry's use of luminous, undulating sheets of metallic skin in the widely hailed Guggenheim Museum (1997) in Bilbao, Spain, and the Walt Disney Concert Hall (2003) in Los Angeles.

Visual artists also felt the eclectic urge. Cindy Sherman, Jenny Holzer, and Kara Walker combined old and new media to confront, confound, and even offend the viewer. Jeff Koons and Shepard Fairey used industrial materials and pop culture to blur the hidebound distinction between highbrow and lowbrow cultures. These pastiches of disparate fragments came to symbolize postmodern art.

Atlantide Phototravel/CORBIS

Architect Frank Gehry's Walt Disney Concert Hall, Los Angeles, California, Completed in 2003

Postmodern literature, like art, had deep roots in the second half of the twentieth century, as writers like Kurt Vonnegut and Thomas Pynchon pioneered the use of nonlinear narratives and other experimental forms. A new generation of writers working in the 1990s, including Jeffrey Eugenides and Michael Chabon, adapted these techniques for contemporary audiences. David Foster Wallace playfully lampooned North America's dystopian future in *Infinite Jest* (1996), complete with calendar years named after corporate sponsors.

Other major works of contemporary fiction complemented postmodernism's ethos of pluralism and cultural diversity. Toni Morrison wove a bewitching portrait of maternal affection amidst the horrors of slavery in *Beloved* (1987), and in 1993 became the first African American woman to win the Nobel Prize for literature. E. Annie Proulx's moving tale of homoerotic love between two cowboys in "Brokeback Mountain" (1997) reached a mass audience in 2005 in an award-winning motion picture.

Immigration also yielded a rich cultural harvest. Asian American authors flourished, among them playwright David Hwang, novelist Amy Tan, and novelist Jhumpa Lahiri, whose *Interpreter of Maladies* (1999) explored the sometimes painful relationship between immigrant Indian parents and their American-born children. Latino writers made their mark as well. Junot Diaz's Pulitzer Prize-winning *The Brief Wondrous Life of Oscar Wao* (2007) brilliantly bridged the worlds of the Dominican Republic and New Jersey in a dazzling concoction of street-smart Spanglish. On the stage, the AIDS epidemic inspired Tony Kushner's sensationally inventive *Angels in America* (1991) as well as Jonathan Larson's musical *Rent* (1996).

In her touching novel The Joy Luck Club, *Amy Tan explored the complex dilemmas of growing up as a Chinese American:*

"'A girl is like a young tree,' [my mother] said, 'You must stand tall and listen to your mother standing next to you. That is only way to grow strong and straight. But if you bend to listen to other people you will grow crooked and weak. . . .' Over the years I learned to choose from the best opinions. Chinese people had Chinese opinions. American people had American opinions. And in almost every case, the American version was much better. It was only later that I discovered there was a serious flaw with the American version. There were too many choices, so it was easy to get confused and pick the wrong thing."

Niche Nation

When it came to popular arts—music, film, television—the postmodern cast of much late- and turn-of-the-century work was even more pronounced, and for good reason. Basic changes in communications technology and media markets simultaneously enabled artists to mix disparate elements in new ways while rendering commercial popular culture itself ever more microtargeted and niche-oriented. As crowning exemplars of the mix-and-mash approach to cultural production, hip-hop artists from Public Enemy to Jay-Z "sampled" beats from other sound recordings to create something simultaneously familiar and new.

From the rise of cable television, which smashed the dominance of the Big Three broadcast networks, to the coming of the Internet, with its endless capacity to forge specialized networks of the likeminded, late-twentieth-century communications technology fragmented the consuming public in such a way as to give new voices the potential to find sustaining audiences. An independent film movement transformed the world of American cinema in the late 1980s and 1990s, as iconoclasts like Quentin Tarantino, the Coen brothers, and Kathryn Bigelow found commercially viable strategies for pursuing unconventional cinematic visions. Tarantino's *Pulp Fiction* (1994) and David Lynch's *Mulholland Drive* (2001), notable for their nonlinear storylines, cinematic allusions, and dark comedic stylings, were prime examples of postmodern film. Beginning in the late 1990s, cable television entered a golden era, as high-quality dramas such as *The Sopranos* (1999–2007) and *The Wire* (2002–2008) enjoyed commercial and critical success.

In the niche logic of popular art in the postmodern age, audience fragmentation enabled more and fresher voices to be heard. But it also ensured that, compared to previous eras, fewer national experiences and cultural events were collectively shared by large numbers of citizens. In this way, popular culture matched ongoing developments in the society at large, as turn-of-the-century America became an ever more pluralist, hybridized, and boisterously diverse nation.

CHAPTER SUMMARY

The dynamic young "baby-boomer" Bill Clinton defeated President George H.W. Bush in 1992, and promoted an ambitious reform agenda within the context of his centrist New Democrat ideology, which broke the traditional Democratic affinity for labor and government social programs. Clinton's efforts to reform health care and promote gun control met strong resistance, but his economic policies helped to spark a decade-long expansion. Presenting an aggressively conservative agenda, Republicans gained control of Congress in 1994 for the first time in forty years. But overreaching by the Newt Gingrich-led Republicans enabled Clinton to revive and win a second term by defeating Kansas Senator Robert Dole in 1996.

In his second term, Clinton downplayed reform and successfully claimed the political middle ground. Racial issues, including affirmative action and criminal justice, caused continuing controversies as well as periodic outbursts of violence. While some African Americans made great social and economic gains, residential segregation sustained the strong link between poverty and race.

The booming economy encouraged bipartisan deregulation efforts, and enhanced Clinton's efforts to develop even more free trade agreements in line with the successful North American Free Trade Agreement (NAFTA). Women became nearly half of the work force, but continued to suffer low pay and less opportunities, partly because of family responsibilities. Family life adapted in striking ways to social economic change, even as the "traditional" family came under severe pressure.

Clinton recovered from early foreign policy stumbles in Africa with a successful intervention in the former Yugoslavia. But efforts at Middle East peace stalled. Clinton's affair with Monica Lewinsky led to his highly partisan impeachment in 1998 and acquittal in 1999. Clinton's vice president, Albert Gore, won a majority of the popular vote in the close election of 2000, but lost to Texas governor George W. Bush in the Electoral College by four votes after a Supreme Court ruling.

American culture grew more diverse and sometimes conflict-ridden in the late twentieth century. Multiculturalism, postmodernism, and the fragmentation of once-national media opened doors to fresh voices and minority perspectives, though the sense of shared cultural experience and ideas diminished.

KEY TERMS

- Democratic Leadership Council (DLC) (704)
- Don't Ask, Don't Tell (705)
- Oklahoma City bombing (706)
- Contract with America (706)
- Welfare Reform Bill (707)
- North American Free Trade Agreement (NAFTA) (710)
- World Trade Organization (WTO) (710)
- Whitewater (713)
- Lewinsky affair (714)

PEOPLE TO KNOW

- William Jefferson ("Bill") Clinton
- H. Ross Perot
- Hillary Rodham Clinton
- Newt Gingrich
- Robert Dole
- Monica Lewinsky

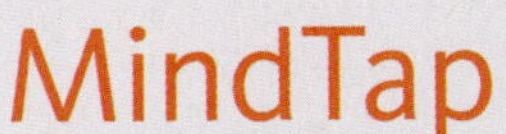

Chapter 41

The American People Face a New Century

2001–2015

We remain a young nation. But in the words of Scripture, the time has come to set aside childish things.

BARACK OBAMA, INAUGURAL, 2009

Chapter Outline

- George W. Bush and September 11, 2001
- The Iraq War
- George W. Bush's Troubled Second Term
- Barack Obama and the "Great Recession"
- Obama's Foreign and Domestic Policies
- The Politics of Inequality
- Obama's Reelection and Second-Term Stalemate
- Immigration and Civil Rights
- The American Prospect

weapons of mass destruction (WMD) *Refers to weapons—nuclear, biological, and chemical—that can kill large numbers of people and do great damage to the built and natural environment. The term was used to refer to nuclear weapons during the Cold War. The Bush administration's claim that Saddam Hussein had developed WMD provided the rationale for the United States' invasion of Iraq in 2003. These weapons were never found after the invasion.*

In 2000 George W. Bush won a bitterly contested presidential election that left the nation more rancorously divided than ever, until the spectacular terrorist attacks on September 11, 2001, called forth, at least temporarily, a resurgent sense of national unity. Bush responded to the 9/11 attacks by invading the terrorist haven of Afghanistan. And then, controversially claiming that Iraq possessed **weapons of mass destruction (WMD)** and had ties to terrorists, Bush proceeded to invade Iraq as well. After the failure to find WMD and with over four thousand American battle deaths in the prolonged Iraq War, a war-weary country, nostalgic for the prosperity and peace of the 1990s, made history by electing the first African American president, Barack Obama, in 2008.

President Obama inherited a crushing economic crisis, soon dubbed "The Great Recession." Its scale was exceeded in modern times only by the Great Depression of the 1930s. Like Franklin Roosevelt in the depression era, Obama seized the occasion to pursue major reforms in health care and financial regulation. But unlike FDR, Obama triggered a powerful Republican backlash that erased the Democratic majority in the House of Representatives in the congressional elections of 2010. Obama's reelection two years later neither restored Democratic control to the House nor tempered the rancor of political divisions in the country, which threatened to turn the federal government into a useless laughing-stock. A standoff between the House and the president over the nation's debt ceiling led to an unprecedented downgrade in the government's credit rating in 2011, and a second standoff over funding the Patient Protection and Affordable Care Act shut down the government entirely for more than two weeks in 2013.

The paradox of rising economic inequality amidst expanding social inclusiveness continued to shape the new century as it had the closing decades of the previous one. A painfully slow economic recovery and stubbornly high unemployment in the years following the 2008 financial crisis highlighted growing gaps in income and wealth, even as the country remained intractably divided over appropriate remedies. At the same time, American society grew more diverse in the twenty-first century, as evidenced by the biracial president and the multiracial political coalition that twice elected him. No less dramatic was the extraordinarily rapid expansion of popular acceptance of gay and lesbian Americans.

CHRONOLOGY

2000	■ George W. Bush wins presidency in Electoral College; Albert Gore takes popular vote
2001	■ Bush's $1.3 trillion tax cut passes Congress ■ Congress passes No Child Left Behind Act ■ Terrorists attack New York City and Washington, D.C., on September 11 ■ U.S. invades Afghanistan ■ Congress passes USA Patriot Act
2002	■ Bush labels Iraq, Iran, and North Korea "axis of evil" ■ Congress authorizes use of force against Iraq ■ U.N. Security Council demands that Iraq comply with weapons inspections ■ Republicans regain Senate
2003	■ U.S. invades Iraq ■ Second Bush tax cut ■ Saddam Hussein captured in Iraq ■ Supreme Court narrowly approves affirmative action
2004	■ Gay marriage controversy erupts ■ Iraqi interim government installed ■ Bush defeats Kerry for presidency
2005	■ Iraq elects permanent government but quickly descends into sectarian conflict
2006	■ Saddam Hussein executed ■ Democrats retake control of Congress
2007	■ U.S. troop surge in Iraq
2008	■ Barack Obama elected 44th president of the United States
2009	■ American Recovery and Reinvestment Act passed
2010	■ Patient Protection and Affordable Care Act passed ■ Wall Street Reform and Consumer Protection Act passed ■ "Don't Ask, Don't Tell" policy repealed ■ Supreme Court decision in *Citizens United* v. *Federal Election Commission* ■ Republicans retake control of the House
2011	■ U.S. withdraws from Iraq ■ U.S. begins troop withdrawal from Afghanistan ■ U.S. forces kill Osama Bin Laden ■ First debt-ceiling crisis between President Obama and the GOP-led House
2012	■ Supreme Court upholds the Affordable Care Act ■ Obama defeats Romney to win reelection
2013	■ Supreme Court repeals Section 4 of the Voting Rights Act ■ Supreme Court rules the Defense of Marriage Act unconstitutional ■ Second debt-ceiling crisis between President Obama and GOP-led House ■ Budget dispute causes a 16-day federal government shutdown
2014	■ U.S. begins air attacks against Islamic State in Iraq and Syria ■ Republicans gain control of Senate in mid-term confessional elections
2015	■ U.S. and Cuba resume diplomatic relations ■ Congress authorizes Obama to negotiate Pacific Partnership free trade agreement ■ *King* v. *Burwell* upholds Affordable Care Act ■ *Obergefell* v. *Hodges* declares same-sex marriage a constitutional right

FOCUS QUESTIONS

1. What was the impact of the September 11 terrorist attacks on the United States? What were the accomplishments and failures of the post–9/11 wars in Afghanistan and Iraq?
2. How did George W. Bush's troubled second term and the "Great Recession" of 2008 contribute to the election of the upstart Barack Obama?
3. What were Obama's strongest efforts to respond to the "Great Recession," and how did his assertive policies provoke the angry Tea Party backlash?
4. What caused the dramatic rise in economic inequality in early twenty-first century America, and how did the widening income gap contribute to growing political and social polarization?
5. How did controversial issues of immigration, civil rights, and civil liberties contribute to political "gridlock" in Washington, and why were political leaders unable to find suitable room for compromise?

Bush Begins

As the son of the forty-first president, George W. Bush became the first presidential offspring since John Quincy Adams to reach the White House. Affecting the chummy manner of a self-made good ol' boy—though he held degrees from Yale and Harvard—Bush promised to bring to Washington the conciliatory skills he had honed as the Republican governor of Texas.

But as president, Bush soon proved to be more of a divider than a uniter, less a "compassionate conservative" than a crusading ideologue. Religious traditionalists cheered, but liberals jeered, when he withdrew American support from international health programs that sanctioned abortion and sharply limited government-sponsored research on embryonic stem cells. Bush pleased corporate chieftains but angered environmentalists by repudiating a major international effort to slow global warming, the **Kyoto Treaty** limiting greenhouse gas emissions.

Kyoto Treaty *International treaty to limit greenhouse gas emissions. It was negotiated and opened for signatories in 1997 and took effect in 2005. Although it was signed by 169 (of 192) countries, the Bush administration rejected the plan as too costly in 2001.*

The centerpiece of Bush's fiscal policy was a whopping $1.3 trillion tax cut, passed by Congress in 2001, followed by a second cut in 2003. Together with a softening economy, these measures turned the federal budget surpluses of the late 1990s into yawning deficits that reached nearly $460 billion by 2008.

Terrorism Comes to America

On September 11, 2001, the long era of America's impregnable national security violently ended. On a balmy late-summer morning, suicidal terrorists slammed two hijacked airliners, loaded with passengers and jet fuel, into the twin towers of New York City's World Trade Center. They flew a third plane into the military nerve-center of the Pentagon, near Washington, D.C., killing 189 people. Heroic passengers forced a fourth hijacked aircraft to crash in rural Pennsylvania, killing all 44 aboard but depriving the terrorists of a fourth weapon of mass destruction.

As the two giant New York skyscrapers thunderously collapsed, some three thousand innocent victims perished, including hundreds of New York's police and fire department rescue workers. A stunned nation blossomed with flags, as grieving and outraged Americans struggled to express their sorrow and solidarity in the face of catastrophic terrorism of **9/11**.

9/11 (2001) *Common shorthand for the terrorist attacks that occurred on September 11, 2001, in which nineteen militant Islamist men hijacked and crashed four commercial aircraft. Two planes hit the twin towers of the World Trade Center in New York City, causing them to collapse. One plane crashed into the Pentagon in Washington, D.C., and the fourth, overtaken by passengers, crashed into a field in rural Pennsylvania. Nearly three thousand people were killed in the worst case of domestic terrorism in American history.*

President Bush responded with a sober but stirring address to Congress nine days later. His solemn demeanor and the gravity of the situation helped to dissipate the cloud of illegitimacy that had shadowed his presidency since the disputed election of 2000. While emphasizing his respect for the Islamic religion and Muslim people, Bush identified the principal enemy as Osama bin Laden, head of a shadowy terrorist network **Al Qaeda**. Since 1998 bin Laden had taken refuge in landlocked Afghanistan, ruled by an Islamic fundamentalist party, the Taliban. Bin Laden drew on popular Muslim opposition to Washington's policies in the Middle East, including its military presence there and its unwavering support of Israel. He also benefited from broader, worldwide resentment of America's enormous economic, military, and cultural power. Ironically, America's most conspicuous strengths had made it a conspicuous target.

Al Qaeda *Arabic for "The Base," an international alliance of anti-Western Islamic Fundamentalist terrorist organizations founded in the late 1980s by veterans of the Afghan struggle against the Soviet Union. The group was headed by Osama bin Laden and has taken responsibility for numerous terrorist attacks, especially after the late 1990s. Al Qaeda organized the attacks of September 11, 2001, in the United States from its headquarters in Taliban-controlled Afghanistan. Since the U.S.-led invasion of Afghanistan in 2001 and the launch of the "global war on terror," the group has been weakened but still poses significant threats around the world.*

When the Taliban refused to hand over bin Laden, Bush ordered a massive military campaign against Afghanistan. Within three months, American and Afghan rebel forces had overthrown the Taliban but failed to find bin Laden, and Americans continued to live in fear of future attacks. Confronted with this unconventional, diffuse menace, antiterrorism experts called for new tactics of "asymmetrical warfare," employing not just traditional military muscle but also counterinsurgency tactics like innovative intelligence gathering and the training of local police forces.

The terrorists' blows diabolically coincided with the onset of a recession. The already gathering economic downdraft worsened as edgy Americans shunned air travel and the tourist industry withered. In the anxious atmosphere Congress in 2001 rammed through the **USA Patriot Act**, which permitted extensive telephone and e-mail surveillance and authorized the detention and deportation of immigrants suspected of terrorism. Just over

USA Patriot Act (2001) *Legislation passed shortly after the terrorist attacks of September 11, 2001 that granted broad surveillance and detention authority to the government.*

David Turnley/CORBIS

The Toll of Terror Grief overcame this exhausted firefighter during the search for survivors in the wreckage of New York City's World Trade Center.

a year later, Congress created a new cabinet-level **Department of Homeland Security** to protect the nation's borders and ferret out potential attackers. The Justice Department meanwhile rounded up hundreds of immigrants and held them without *habeas corpus* (formal charges in an open court). As hundreds of Taliban fighters captured in Afghanistan languished in legal limbo and demoralizing isolation in the **Guantanamo Detention Camp** on the American military base at Guantanamo, Cuba, public-opinion polls showed Americans sharply divided on whether the terrorist threat fully warranted such drastic encroachments on America's venerable tradition of protecting civil liberties.

Catastrophic terrorism posed an unprecedented challenge to the United States. The events of that murderous September morning brought a long chapter in American history to a dramatic climax. All but unique among modern peoples, American for nearly two centuries had been spared from foreign attack on their homeland. That unusual degree of virtually cost-free national security had undergirded the values of openness and individual freedom that defined the distinctive character of American society. Now American security and American liberty alike were dangerously imperiled.

Bush Takes the Offensive against Iraq

On only its second day in office, the Bush administration warned that it would not tolerate Iraq's continued defiance of United Nations weapons inspections, mandated after Iraq's defeat in the 1991 Persian Gulf War. Iraqi dictator Saddam Hussein, after playing hide and seek with the inspectors for years, expelled them from his country in 1998. President Clinton then declared, with congressional approval, that Saddam's removal ("regime change") was an official goal of U.S. policy. But no sustained military action against Iraq had followed. Now, in the context of the new terrorist threat, the Bush administration focused on Iraq with a vengeance.

Department of Homeland Security *Cabinet-level agency created in 2003 to unify and coordinate public safety and antiterrorism operations within the federal government.*

Guantanamo Detention Camp *Controversial prison facility constructed after the U.S.-led invasion of Afghanistan in 2001. Located on territory occupied by the U.S. military, but not technically part of the United States, the facility serves as an extra-legal holding area for suspected terrorists.*

In January 2002, mere months after the September 11 attacks, Bush claimed that Iraq, along with Iran and North Korea, constituted an "axis of evil" that gravely menaced American security. Iraqi tyrant Saddam Hussein, defeated but not destroyed by Bush's father in 1991, became the principal object of the new president's wrath. Unlike the elder Bush, who had carefully assembled a broad international coalition to fight the Persian Gulf War, his son was brashly determined to break with longstanding American traditions and wage a preemptive war against Iraq—and to go it alone if necessary. The younger Bush thus stood revealed as a daring risk-taker willing to embrace bold, dramatic policies, foreign as well as fiscal.

Itching for a fight, and egged on by hawkish Vice President Richard Cheney and other "neoconservative" advisers, Bush accused the Iraqi regime of developing weapons of mass destruction ("WMD") and supporting terrorist organizations like Al Qaeda. Most controversially, Bush also suggested that a liberated, democratic Iraq might provide a beacon of hope to the Islamic world and thereby begin to improve the political equation in the volatile Middle East. To skeptical observers, including America's European allies, Bush's ambition to create a democracy in long-suffering Iraq, burdened with centuries of internecine conflict, seemed naïvely utopian. Secretary of State Colin Powell warned about the long-term consequences of invading and occupying an unstable, religiously and culturally divided nation of 25 million people. "You break it, you own it," he told the president.

Congress nevertheless passed a resolution in October 2002 authorizing the president to employ armed force to defend against Iraqi threats to America's national security. But with United Nations inspectors unable to find weapons of mass destruction in Iraq, the U.N. Security Council declined to authorize the use of force against Saddam Hussein.

In this tense and confusing atmosphere, Bush, with Britain his only major ally, launched the long-anticipated invasion of Iraq on March 19, 2003. Saddam Hussein's vaunted military machine collapsed almost immediately. In less than a month Baghdad had fallen and Saddam had been driven from power. From the deck of a U.S. aircraft carrier off the California coast, speaking beneath a banner declaring "Mission Accomplished," Bush triumphantly announced on May 1, 2003, that "major combat operations in Iraq have ended."

In his 2002 state of the union address, President Bush declared:

"Iraq continues to flaunt its hostility toward America and to support terror. The Iraqi Regime has plotted to develop anthrax, and nerve gas, and nuclear weapons for over a decade. . . . This is a regime that has agreed to international inspections, then kicked out the inspectors. This is a regime that has something to hide from the civilized world.

States like these, and their terrorist allies, constitute an axis of evil, arming to threaten the peace of the world. By seeking weapons of mass destruction, these regimes pose a grave and growing danger. They could provide these arms to terrorists, giving them the means to match their hatred. They could attack our allies or attempt to blackmail the United States. In any of these cases, the price of indifference would be catastrophic."

Owning Iraq

President Bush's words quickly came back to haunt him and America's forces in Iraq. Neoconservative pundits in Washington had predicted that American soldiers would be greeted as liberators and that Saddam's ouster would lead to flowering democracy across the Middle East. In reality, post-Saddam Iraq quickly devolved into a seething cauldron of violence.

The country's largest religious groups, Sunni and Shia Muslims, clashed violently, especially in the capital city of Baghdad. Both groups attacked American forces, especially after their decision to disband the Iraqi army. A locally grown insurgency quickly spread, and occupying Iraq became ever more perilous for American troops. Hatred for Americans only worsened with revelations in April 2004 that Iraqi prisoners in Baghdad's **Abu Ghraib prison** had been tortured and humiliated by their American captors. Amid this chaos, jihadist terrorists from around the region flooded into Iraq, often fueling the intra-Iraqi conflicts to further their own radical Islamic vision. Although Al Qaeda had had no link to Iraq under Saddam, as Bush had falsely alleged, the organization certainly moved in afterward. These three sources—Shia/Sunni violence, counter-occupation insurgency, and jihadist terrorism—fed a spiraling maelstrom of bloodshed. By the end of 2006, more Americans had died in Iraq than in the attacks of September 11.

Abu Ghraib prison *A detention facility near Baghdad, Iraq. Under Saddam Hussein, the prison was the site of infamous torturing and execution of political dissidents. In 2004, during the U.S. occupation of Iraq, the prison became the focal point of a prisoner-abuse and torture scandal after photographs surfaced of American soldiers mistreating, torturing, and degrading Iraqi war prisoners and suspected terrorists. The scandal was one of several dark spots on the public image of the Iraq War and led to increased criticism of Secretary of Defense Donald Rumsfeld.*

In the summer of 2004, the American military ceded political power and limited sovereignty to an interim Iraqi government. A series of national elections led to a constitution, parliamentary representatives, and eventually a president. But the minority Sunnis, who had held power under Saddam Hussein, feared reprisals under a majority Shia government. Many Sunnis turned to bombings and political assassinations.

Reelecting George W. Bush

Americans had rarely been as divided as they were in the first years of the twenty-first century. Civil libertarians worried that the government was trampling personal freedoms in the name of fighting terrorism. Revelations in 2002 about flagrant corporate fraud fed rampant popular disillusion with the business community. Cultural tensions brewed over the rights of gay and lesbian Americans when leaders in San Francisco and Massachusetts permitted same-sex couples to marry in 2004. Affirmative action continued to spark sharp debate, as the Supreme Court permitted some preferential treatment in admitting minority undergraduate and law students to the University of Michigan in 2003.

No Child Left Behind Act (2001) *An education bill created and signed by the George W. Bush administration. Designed to increase accountability standards for primary and secondary schools, the law authorized several federal programs to monitor those standards and increased choices for parents in selecting schools for their children. The program was highly controversial, in large part because it linked results on standardized tests to federal funding for schools and school districts.*

Amid these divisions, George W. Bush positioned himself to run for reelection. He proclaimed that his tax cuts had spurred economic growth. Targeting what he called "the soft bigotry of low expectations," he championed the **No Child Left Behind Act** of 2001, which mandated sanctions against schools that failed to meet federal performance standards. He played to cultural conservatives by opposing stem cell research and called for a constitutional amendment to ban gay marriage. But most of all, he promoted himself as a stalwart leader in wartime, warning the country not to "change horses midstream."

After an intense round of primary elections, the embattled Democrats chose lanky and long-jawed Massachusetts Senator John Kerry to represent their ticket. A more old-fashioned liberal than Clinton, Kerry pushed progressive visions of government and counted on his Vietnam War record to counter charges that he would be weak in the face of terrorism. In spite of increased public misgivings about the war in Iraq, Bush nailed down a decisive victory in November 2004. He received the first popular vote majority in more than a decade, 60,639,281 to 57,355,978, and won the Electoral College, 286 to 252. This time his victory was clear, constitutional, and uncontested.

Bush's Bruising Second Term

Reelection, George W. Bush announced, gave him "political capital," which he intended to spend on an aggressive domestic agenda. The appointment of two new conservative Supreme Court justices (John G. Roberts and Samuel A. Alito, Jr.) upon the retirement of Sandra Day O'Connor and the death of Chief Justice William Rehnquist seemed to bode well for his ambitions. But Bush soon overplayed his hand. Attacking the core of New Deal liberalism, Bush proposed a radical program to privatize much of Social Security, providing incentives for younger Americans to fund their own retirements through personal accounts. A massive outcry led by the American Association of Retired Persons (AARP) and other liberal groups reminded Americans how much they loved Social Security, warts and all. Bush's proposal faded away within six months of his reelection. The same fate befell a proposed constitutional amendment to ban same-sex marriage, which had been a major issue in the 2004 campaign.

The president also took (faulty) aim at the contentious issue of immigration reform. Bush worked with a bipartisan group of legislators on a proposed law to establish a guest-worker program for undocumented workers and to create a path to citizenship, albeit after paying a fine. But nativist forces condemned the plan as "amnesty," businesses protested the burden of verifying the right to work, and immigrant rights advocates charged that the program would create "second class citizens." In the end the compromise bill pleased no one and died an ignominious political death.

Hurricane Katrina (2005) *The costliest and one of the deadliest hurricanes in the history of the United States, which killed over a thousand Americans. The storm ravaged the Gulf Coast, especially the city of New Orleans, in late August 2005. In New Orleans, high winds and rain caused the city's levees to break, leading to catastrophic flooding, particularly in the city's most impoverished wards. A tardy and feeble response by local and federal authorities exacerbated the damage and led to widespread criticism of the Federal Emergency Management Agency (FEMA).*

Perhaps the most tragic and avoidable of Bush's missteps came in the botched response to the deadly **Hurricane Katrina**, which devastated New Orleans and much of the Gulf Coast in late August 2005, flooding 80 percent of the historic city and causing over 1,300 deaths and $150 billion in damages. The Federal Emergency Management Agency (FEMA) proved pathetically inept in New Orleans, and Bush came in for still more criticism. A consensus began to build that Bush was a genial personality but an impetuous, unreflective, and frequently feckless leader, a president in over his head.

As charges of dictatorial power-grabbing and incompetence mounted during Bush's second term, Republicans fell victim in midterm elections of 2006 to the same anti-incumbency sentiment they had ridden to power twelve years before. Democrats regained control of both houses of Congress, and California Democrat Nancy Pelosi became the first woman to serve as Speaker of the House.

The biggest factor in the Democratic sweep was the perceived mishandling of the war in Iraq. By late 2005 polls revealed that a majority of Americans considered the war a mistake. Secretary of Defense Donald Rumsfeld, who had badly mismanaged events on the ground, resigned after the Republicans "thumping" in the 2006 midterm elections. In 2007 Bush launched a "surge" of twenty thousand additional American troops that brought a modest measure of stability to Iraq, but public opinion solidified even more strongly against the war.

The Presidential Election of 2008

With neither the sitting president nor vice president running, the 2008 election was truly "open" for the first time in eighty years. The Democratic race soon tightened into a fiercely fought contest between forty-six-year-old Illinois Senator Barack Obama and the pre-campaign favorite, former First Lady and New York Senator Hillary Rodham Clinton. Obama narrowly prevailed, surviving Clinton's attacks on his inexperience. Son of a black Kenyan father and a white mother from Kansas, Obama had a cosmopolitan background well suited to the age of globalization. He strengthened his national security credentials by picking Delaware Senator Joseph Biden as his running mate.

In keeping with the country's anti-Bush mood, Republicans nominated long-time Arizona Senator John McCain, a Vietnam War hero with a record of bipartisan reform. To galvanize the conservative base of his party, McCain chose telegenic Alaska Governor Sarah Palin as his running mate. But Palin's inexperience and weak grasp of issues made her at least as much a liability as an asset to the Republican ticket.

Armed with an unprecedented war chest of nearly $700 million, Obama seized the advantage in both the "air war" (television) and the "ground war" (door-to-door campaigning by his legions of volunteers). His poise and gravitas in televised debates favorably impressed many voters, and his campaign slogan "Yes we can" excited widespread hope and enthusiasm. Then, just six weeks before election day, a sudden economic maelstrom gave his campaign a buoyant boost.

The American housing price bubble, fed by the Federal Reserve System's easy-money policies and banks' lax lending practices, burst at last. By 2008 the collapse in real estate values was generating a tsunami of mortgage defaults. Bankers and other lenders watched in horror as countless homeowners defaulted and mortgage-backed securities sank precipitously. Aggressive "**deleveraging**" set in worldwide, as financial institutions from Tokyo to New York sold assets at ever-declining prices. Credit markets soon froze everywhere, and stocks fell into a deep swoon. The gravest financial hurricane since the Great Depression of the 1930s was gathering ever-increasing force.

deleveraging *The inverse of "leveraging," whereby businesses increase their financial power by borrowing money (debt) in addition to their own assets (equity). In times of uncertainty or credit tightening, the same businesses seek to improve their debt-to-equity ratios by shedding debt through the sale of assets purchased with borrowed money.*

John Zich/zrImages/CORBIS

The New First Family President-elect Barack Obama, wife Michelle, and daughters Sasha and Malia, on election night 2008 in Chicago's Grant Park.

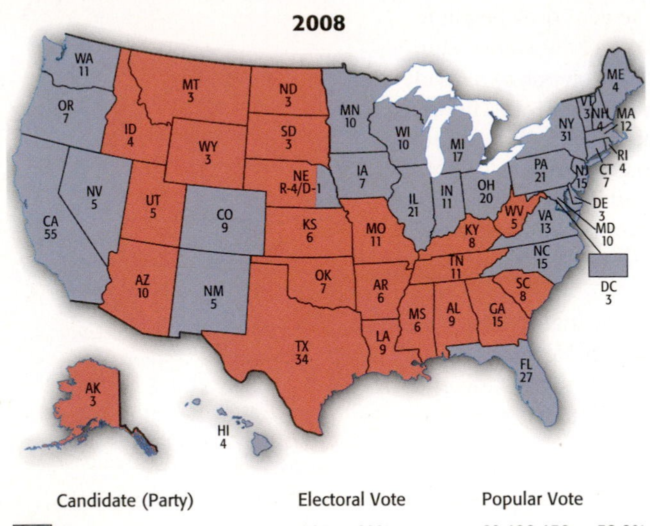

Candidate (Party)	Electoral Vote		Popular Vote	
Obama (Democrat)	365	68%	69,498,459	52.9%
McCain (Republican)	173	32%	59,948,283	45.6%

Map 41.1 Presidential Election of 2008 A record voter turnout, swelled by millions of young new voters, African Americans, and Latinos, gave Senator Barack Obama an Electoral College landslide and the Democratic party solid control of both houses of Congress. Obama redrew the electoral map by taking nine states won by George W. Bush in 2004.

In contrast to the infamous 1929 crash, it took days, not years, for a terrified Bush Administration to intervene on a gigantic scale. The federal government nationalized the country's two biggest mortgage companies, the Federal National Mortgage Association ("Fannie Mae") and the Federal Home Mortgage Corporation ("Freddie Mac"), and effectively took over the world's biggest insurance company, the American International Group (AIG). Treasury Secretary Henry Paulson next persuaded Congress to create the Troubled Assets Relief Program (TARP), authorizing a whopping $700 billion to buy "toxic" assets and inject cash directly into the nation's biggest banks and corporations.

Candidate Obama seized the political opportunity presented by the mounting economic crisis and declared that electing McCain would amount to a "third Bush term." Obama called for reviving the faltering economy with bold public investments and infrastructure repair, which McCain derided as "socialism."

Unsettled by the galloping economic calamity, voters delivered a historic victory to Barack Obama. He garnered 53 percent of the popular vote, prevailing even in such traditional Republican strongholds such as Virginia, Nevada, and Colorado, and won the Electoral College 365 to 173 (see Map 41.1). Democrats also enlarged their majorities in the House and the Senate. Obama's victory reflected important, long-term demographic developments reshaping American politics. He drew support from youth, educated professionals, and racial and ethnic minorities. Thanks to the increased preponderance of such voters in the population, what had once been a marginal coalition behind George McGovern's candidacy in 1968 had become a formidable political force by 2008.

Obama's election opened a new chapter in the long-vexed history of American race relations. It also confronted the nation's first African American president with the daunting challenge of governing a country even as it sank into the deepest economic stress since the 1930s. "Black Man Given Nation's Worst Job" jibed the satirical magazine, *The Onion*.

Obama in the White House

Inspired by Barack Obama's vision of "hope," a vast and exuberant crowd gathered in Washington, D.C., to celebrate his inauguration. Youthful energy was in the air, though in his inaugural address Obama struck a sober note by calling on Americans to "put away childish things" and embrace "a new era of responsibility."

Obama's solemn tone was fitting. Even as he spoke, home construction was grinding to a halt, mortgage foreclosures were soaring, and countless businesses were shutting their doors. Most alarmingly, the economy was shedding a sickening 700,000 jobs a month. The unemployment climbed above 10 percent—the highest level since the early 1980s and perhaps heralding a return to the catastrophic joblessness of the Great Depression of the 1930s.

American Recovery and Reinvestment Act (2009) *Among the earliest initiatives of the Obama administration to combat the Great Recession. It was based on the economic theories of John Maynard Keynes that called for increased government spending to offset decreased private spending in times of economic downturn. The act was controversial from the outset, passing with no Republican votes in the House and only three in the Senate, and helping to foster the "Tea Party" movement to curb government deficits, even while critics on the left argued that the act's $787 billion appropriation was not enough to turn the economy around.*

Obama strongly counterpunched against the deepening crisis. In his first hundred days he pushed through a series of major initiatives that included a new round of help for troubled banks, tax and mortgage relief, and a huge "stimulus" bill—the **American Recovery and Reinvestment Act**—that contained nearly a trillion dollars of tax cuts as well as new spending for jobs, infrastructure projects, and relief to state and local governments. The government also shored up bankrupt automakers General Motors and Chrysler as well as threatened banks and insurance companies. The nonpartisan Congressional Budget Office later estimated that those measures saved up to 3 million jobs, helping substantially to arrest the economy's freefall.

By the summer of 2009, the worst of the panic was over, and the economy began to expand once more. Economists tempered their comparisons with the Great Depression and gave the turmoil the less frightening label "Great Recession." But the economy had been badly wounded and continued to suffer. Hopes for a rapid recovery proved false, and the first steps toward growth were feeble and faltering. The unemployment rate stayed stuck above 9 percent. As millions of Americans lost jobs and homes, and many more succumbed to anxiety and fear, the effects of the Great Recession wormed their way deeply into the American psyche and would not be quickly dislodged. Psychology and economics intersected, as newly anxious consumers cut back on spending, further burdening an already sluggish recovery.

Even while pursuing economic recovery, President Obama sought to achieve the long-sought goal of health-care reform. When attempts to enlist Republican support bogged down, he had to rely on Democrats alone to pass a landmark health bill, the **Patient Protection and Affordable Care Act** in March 2010. The new health-care law (popularly known as "Obamacare") mandated all Americans to purchase health insurance starting in 2014, provided subsidies for those below certain income thresholds, and funded a major expansion of public Medicaid insurance for the poorest Americans

Scarcely pausing, Obama soon followed his health-care success with the 2010 **Wall Street Reform and Consumer Protection Act**. The act aimed to curb the risky, high-flying practices that had contributed to the debacle of 2008 with new controls on banks, investment houses, and stock markets, and with new truth-in-lending rules to protect consumers.

Patient Protection and Affordable Care Act (2010) *Also known as "Obamacare," the act extended health-care insurance to some 30 million Americans, marking a major step toward achieving the century-old goal of providing universal health-care coverage.*

Wall Street Reform and Consumer Protection Act (2010) *Also known as the Dodd-Frank Act, after its Democratic sponsors, Connecticut senator Christopher Dodd and Massachusetts representative Barney Frank. In an effort to avoid another financial crisis like the Great Recession, the act updated many federal regulations affecting the financial and banking systems and created some new agencies, such as the Bureau of Consumer Financial Protection.*

Back to Backlash

Yet, in a polarized political environment, Obama had unusual difficulty reaping the political rewards of these legislative achievements. Critics on the left condemned him as too timid in merely halting, not reversing, the economy's decline. Critics on the right excoriated him as a big-government spendthrift who fostered ballooning federal budget deficits (though Bush-era tax cuts and declining tax revenues from the recession contributed to the deficits).

The conjunction of expanding federal programs and mounting deficits tapped into a deep vein of American wariness of "big government." Starting with vehement attacks on the health-care bill in the summer of 2009, angry protesters accused the Obama administration of promoting "socialism" and "unconstitutional" controls over individual lives. Calling themselves the "**Tea Party**" after the American Revolutionary Patriots, these aggrieved citizens combined a knack for street-theater demonstrations with nonstop Internet and media fulminations against the president and his party.

Heartened by the Tea Party's mobilization, Republicans determined to fight the administration tooth and nail. The president did succeed in appointing two new Supreme Court justices, Sonia Sotomayor (the Court's first Hispanic) on 2009 and Elena Kagan in 2010, bringing the number of female justices to three. But other efforts fell victim to the fervent minority's opposition, as gridlock held Washington in an iron grip.

As the Great Recession continued to weigh on the land, Republicans gained six Senate seats and a whopping sixty-three House seats in the midterm elections of 2010. President Obama glumly acknowledged his party's "shellacking," but did achieve several notable goals in the "lame duck" congressional session in December 2010, including a repeal of the military's "Don't Ask, Don't Tell" policy toward gays.

But legislative productivity came to an end in the new Congress, as partisans closed their ranks ever tighter. The once-routine matter of raising the federal debt ceiling turned into a fiercely partisan game of fiscal "chicken" in the summer of 2011. As the deadline for raising the ceiling loomed, the stock market swooned and the credit rating of the United States was downgraded for the first time in history. Only a last-minute deal between Obama and House Speaker John Boehner averted the exhaustion of America's borrowing authority. Republicans looked to the upcoming 2012 election with increasing hope for victory, while the spectacle of protracted partisan bickering deeply disillusioned many Americans of both parties.

Tea Party *A grassroots conservative political movement mobilized in opposition to Barack Obama's fiscal, economic, and health care policies. Named after the Boston Tea Party of the Revolutionary era, Tea Party protestors first demonstrated in early 2009, and they grew steadily in visibility and power as a pressuring force within the Republican Party through the 2010 midterm elections and beyond.*

New Directions in Foreign Policy

Along with economic problems, Obama inherited America's wars in Iraq and Afghanistan, as well as a raft of other foreign policy headaches. Seeking to chart a more tempered and pragmatic course after the neoconservative ventures of the Bush years, Obama assembled a veteran foreign policy team headed by former First Lady Hillary Rodham Clinton as secretary of state.

The president sought to wind down the Iraq War while leaving behind a reasonably stable country. Shortly after taking office, Obama announced that American combat operations in Iraq would end in summer 2010 and that all American combat troops would be withdrawn by 2011. Despite continuing violence and the agonizingly slow birth of a viable Iraqi government, the deadline for ending American-led operations was met and all combat forces removed from the country in December 2010. All told, nearly five thousand Americans—and vastly greater numbers of Iraqis—had perished in the years of the invasion and occupation.

Afghanistan was a pricklier nettle to grasp. Obama had declared the Afghan war necessary to defeat Al Qaeda and prevent future terrorism. But Afghan *jihadi* (militant Islamic) fighters grew stronger against an Afghan government plagued by incompetence and corruption. More ominously, the Taliban and Al Qaeda found refuge across the border in unstable but nuclear-armed Pakistan, creating the danger of an expanded conflict there as well.

Pressed by some to bolster the American commitment, and by others to seek a way out of the increasingly costly conflict, Obama chose to do both. In December 2009 he declared that American troops would begin to withdraw by 2011—but that in order to achieve that goal an additional thirty thousand U.S. soldiers would be sent to combat the insurgency. Despite this deployment, little progress was made in securing the country from terrorists, even as casualties mounted. Meanwhile, American forces achieved a dramatic success in neighboring Pakistan in May 2011 when they concluded a ten-year manhunt by killing 9/11 mastermind Osama bin Laden.

Falling short of his goals in Afghanistan, Obama made good on his pledge to begin withdrawing troops in 2011. But even as American ground combat operations in Afghanistan ended in 2014, the Obama administration increasingly relied on a controversial policy of aerial attacks by unmanned remotely piloted aircraft, popularly called "drones." The intensity of U.S. drone attacks sparked national and international outcries about this revolutionary new kind of warfare.

Obama also came under increasing pressure to honor his promise to roll back Bush-era antiterrorism policies. His administration did ban water-boarding and other practices widely considered torture. But the president's efforts to shut down the controversial military detention center in Guantanamo Bay, Cuba, were thwarted by Congress.

The Politics of Inequality

Occupy Wall Street *Name of the original protest that launched the populist, anti-Wall Street "Occupy" movement in late 2010 and early 2011. Youthful radicals pitched tents and occupied Zuccotti Park in New York's financial district beginning in September 2010 to protest inequality and corporate political power. This demonstration inspired similar occupations in many other cities.*

Chronically high unemployment and stubbornly anemic economic growth after the 2008 financial meltdown helped sharpen a national debate over class, inequality, and the role of government in the economy. The financial sector provided a particularly rich target for many Americans' ire. Financiers' soaring incomes helped to drive the surge in the richest Americans' income share. The fall of 2011 saw the emergence of an eclectic protest movement that colorfully dramatized the issue of rising inequality. "**Occupy Wall Street**" began as a small demonstration by youthful radicals who pitched their tents in New York's financial district. Similar encampments soon sprang up in other cities and popularized the slogan "We are the 99 Percent"—a reference to the concentration of wealth and income among the highest earning 1 percent of Americans. Though the protesters gradually decamped, President Obama acknowledged their cause in January 2012 by describing the challenge to restore broadly shared prosperity as "the defining issue of our time."

Growing inequality had deep roots and assumed dramatic proportions as the new century opened. In American society, during the last two decades of the twentieth century the rich had grown fabulously richer, middle-class incomes had stagnated, and the poor were left to make do with an ever-shrinking share of the economic pie. Between 1968 and 2012, the share of the nation's income that flowed to the top 20 percent of household swelled from 40 percent to 51 percent. And the top 1 percent so frequently targeted by the Occupy movement saw their share of national income rise from 8.4 percent in 1968 to a whopping 19.3 percent in 2012.

Widening inequality could be measured in other ways as well. In 1965, chief executives typically earned 20 times as much as the average worker in their corporations. In 2012 they earned 273 times as much. Some 46.5 million people remained mired in poverty in 2012, or 15 percent of all Americans—up from 11.3 percent in 1973.

These figures offered a depressing indictment of the inequities afflicting an affluent and allegedly egalitarian republic. A similar trend toward inequality was evident in many industrial societies, but it was most pronounced in the United States. In the new century, Americans were no longer the world's wealthiest people, as they had been in the quarter-century after World War II.

What caused the widening income gap? Some critics pointed to the tax and fiscal policies of the Reagan and both Bush (father and son) presidencies, which favored the wealthy. But deeper running historical currents probably played a more powerful role, as suggested by similar trends lines in other industrialized societies. Among the most conspicuous causes were intensifying global competition; the shrinkage in high-paying manufacturing jobs for semiskilled and unskilled workers; the greater economic rewards commanded by educated workers in high-tech industries; the rise of the financial sector as a percentage of national GDP; the decline of unions; the growth of part-time and temporary work; the rising tide of relatively low-skill immigrants; and the increasing tendency of educated men and women to marry one another and both work, creating households with very high incomes.

Educational opportunities also had a way of perpetuating inequality, starting with the underfunding of many schools in poor urban areas and the soaring cost of higher education. A 2004 study revealed that at the 146 most selective colleges, two-thirds of the students came from families with incomes in the top 25 percent, compared to 6 percent of the students from the bottom income quartile.

The very nature of the contemporary economy seemed to pose daunting obstacles to creating more equitably shared prosperity. When the twentieth century opened, United States Steel Corporation was the flagship business of America's industrial revolution. A generation later, General Motors became the characteristic American corporation, signaling the historic shift to a mass consumer economy. Following World War II, the rise of International Business Machines (IBM) symbolized the transformation to the fast-paced "information age." But in a sobering illustration of the dynamics of the new economy, the most iconic American company of the contemporary age—Apple—only employed 43,000 Americans in 2012. When General Motors occupied a similar status in the American economy half a century earlier, it employed over 600,000 Americans.

Contending Voices

Populist Politics in a Polarized Age

Two grassroots movements with starkly differing political agendas but a similarly populist character emerged in the wake of the ongoing economic turmoil that broke out in 2008. Conservative Tea Party activists in 2009 and 2010 erupted in full-throated wrath against Barack Obama's policies—as well as against the moderate congressional Republicans they accused of being enablers. In September 2011, a small protest in New York City's Zuccotti Park grew into a short-lived but broad movement known as Occupy Wall Street, which condemned the capitalist system in general and economic inequality in particular.

Nancy Ripley (ca. 1935–2011), a Florida Tea Party participant, explained her motivation in 2010:

"People dissent when they feel they're not being heard. . . . We are outraged over the disregard for [the] Constitution, the way it is being diminished to provide more government programs that promote dependence and thwart motivation."

Bennett Weiss (born ca. 1948), interviewed in Zuccotti Park in 2011, described the chief goal of the Occupy activists:

"Economic justice, that's why we're here. . . . [W]e have to level the economic playing field so that we don't have an extreme concentration of wealth. It's pretty damn simple."

What might account for the emergence of such ideologically disparate movements in the context of a shared economic crisis? Why were some Americans motivated to target "big government" even while others called on government to step up and address economic inequality?

Jan Isachsen/Art Directors/Alamy Limited

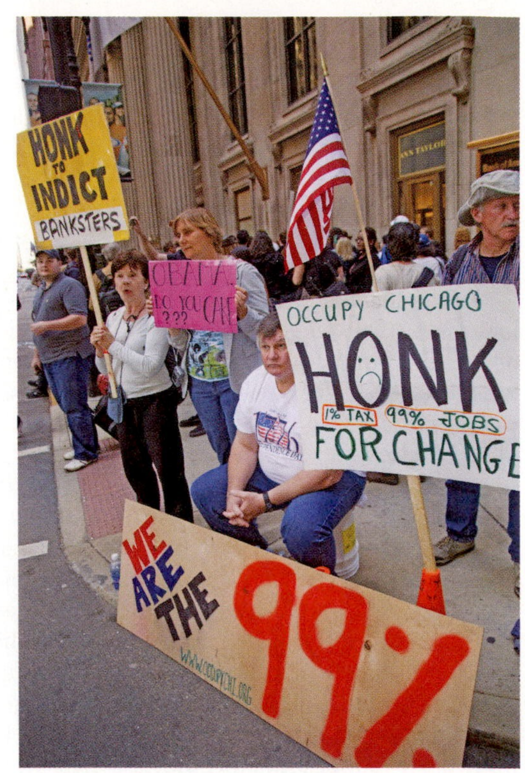

Jim West/Alamy

An Age of Discontent Dramatic protests from both the right and left sprang up during Barack Obama's first term as president. Tea Party rallies, such as this one in Washington, D.C. (left), expressed conservative resistance to the president's promise of "change." On the political left, meanwhile, the Occupy Wall Street protests in New York City against economic inequality spread like wildfire across the country, sparking satellite Occupy demonstrations like this one in Chicago (right).

Battling for the White House in 2012

To a striking degree, inequality—both economic and political—remained a central theme of the heated 2012 presidential race. Barack Obama sought reelection on the basis of his stewardship of the economy in crisis times, his signature health-care law (narrowly upheld in a Supreme Court decision that summer), and his winding down of two unpopular wars.

After a long, feisty primary season, the Republican party nominated former Massachusetts governor Mitt Romney and ultraconservative Wisconsin congressman Paul Ryan as their presidential and vice-presidential nominees. Romney, the first Mormon presidential candidate of a major party in American history, had a record as a moderate governor of liberal Massachusetts, but he secured the GOP's presidential nomination in 2012 by hewing to a much more conservative line, promising to repeal both the Affordable Care Act and the Wall Street Reform Act, cut domestic spending, and slash taxes.

The role of money in politics became a divisive issue in the race, thanks to a highly controversial 2010 Supreme Court decision, *Citizens United* v. *Federal Election Commission*. In a five-to-four ruling, the Court held that the First Amendment prohibited the government from limiting political expenditures made by corporations, unions, and advocacy groups. The decision helped to spur the proliferation of so-called "super-PACS," which, by avoiding any direct contributions to candidates and parties, could pour unlimited sums into the political arena. With the floodgates of political spending open as never before, the presidential race of 2012 proved to be the most expensive in American history, with both campaigns and their allies spending a combined total of over $2 billion.

On election day, Obama won a decisive victory over Romney, with 65,915,796 popular and 332 electoral votes to Romney's 60,933,500 and 206 votes. Obama prevailed in all of the states he had won in 2008 with the exception of Indiana and North Carolina. Democrats managed to retain control of the Senate but the House remained in GOP hands.

Second-Term Stalemate

Obama had expressed hope that a victory over Mitt Romney might "break the fever" of intractable opposition afflicting congressional Republicans. But with the partisan balance of power largely unchanged by the election and deep-seated ideological disagreements still defining the partisan divide, such a hope proved wishful thinking.

The first year of the president's second term was defined by legislative gridlock and a new period of white-knuckle budget brinksmanship with the John Boehner–led House. Spurred on by a still-potent Tea Party faction, House Republicans threatened once again to refuse to lift the debt ceiling without policy concessions from Obama. The stalemate led to a sixteen-day government closure in October 2013 before the GOP backed down and allowed for a vote temporarily raising the debt ceiling and funding the government.

These seemingly endless rounds of politically induced budget crises and governance-through-showdown raised alarming questions about the very capacity of the American political system to function in times of divided government and ideologically sorted parties. But they also rendered all the more unlikely any grand compromise to restore the country's long-term fiscal balance in the face of a rapidly aging population. Over 13 percent of Americans were over sixty-five in 2012, and projections were that one of every five people would be in the "sunset years" by 2050.

This greying of America brought fiscal strains, especially on the Social Security and Medicare systems. As the huge wave of post–World War II baby boomers entered retirement age, those programs' long-term "unfunded liability"—the difference between what the government had promised to pay to the elderly and the taxes it expected to take in over the next seventy-five years—reached $9.6 trillion. But the electoral power of older Americans, the Republicans' no-new-taxes orthodoxy, and the intractability of partisan warfare in government made addressing this imbalance ever more challenging.

Citizenship and Civil Rights

The vexed issue of immigration reform, especially with respect to the nation's 11 million "illegals," also continued to elude resolution during Obama's presidency. Obama and congressional Democrats in 2010 had pushed the DREAM Act (Development, Relief, and Education for Alien Minors Act), which would have created a path to citizenship for undocumented youths who either graduated from college or served in the U.S. armed forces, but

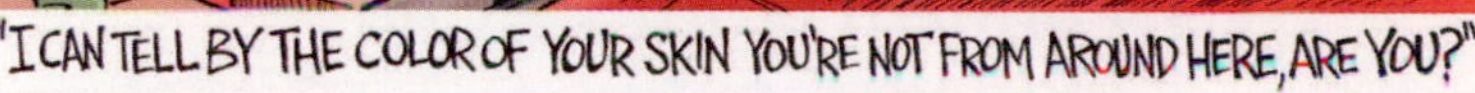

© 2010 Joe Heller PoliticalCartoons.com

Picture Research Consultants & Archives/Iowa Presidential Watch PAC

Immigration Confrontation When Arizona governor Jan Brewer signed a tough new bill in 2010 authorizing local police to crack down on illegal immigrants, the national debate over immigration policy grew still more bitterly divisive. Champions of the bill hailed Arizona for taking a stand in the void left by federal inaction. Critics denounced it as an invitation to the harassment of all Latinos—indeed, all people of color—regardless of their citizenship status.

it fell to a Republican filibuster in the Senate. Obama tried to make more comprehensive immigration reform a centerpiece of his second term. But though a bill offering undocumented immigrants a route to citizenship passed the Senate in the summer of 2013, the House refused to bring it to a vote.

House Republicans' opposition to the bill reflected deep anxieties felt by many Americans over the presence of millions of undocumented immigrants seeking jobs and benefiting from public services. The economic crisis had only exacerbated such anxiety. In 2010, legislators in Arizona, provoked by continuing immigrant flows over the state's long desert border with Mexico, passed a harsh anti-immigrant law requiring local police to detain people if there was "reasonable suspicion" that they were illegal. Critics complained that the law amounted to unfair "racial profiling" and that the state was unconstitutionally usurping federal responsibility for controlling immigration.

The Supreme Court waded further into politically charged waters in two landmark decisions in 2013. In *Shelby County* v. *Holder*, a narrow conservative majority declared unconstitutional Section 4 of the 1965 Voting Rights Act, which set a formula for determining which states—namely, those with a history of racial discrimination—were required to seek federal clearance for any changes to voting laws. The 2012 elections had occasioned controversy over state-level anti-voter-fraud laws featuring strict voter identification requirements and limited registration periods, which critics charged unfairly penalized minority, poor, and young voters. The Supreme Court's *Shelby* decision intensified the debate over voting rights in the twenty-first century.

Later the same year, a narrow *liberal* majority on the Court declared unconstitutional the 1996 Defense of Marriage Act, which had denied federal benefits to same-sex couples in states where gay marriage was legal. Though not explicitly declaring a blanket right to same-sex marriage in all states, the strongly worded decision provided a galvanizing spur to the legalization of gay marriage in more and more states.

Obama faced criticism in his second term for explosive revelations that his administration had approved sweeping National Security Administration (NSA) spying operations covering both domestic and international telephone and Internet communications. The revelations sparked anew impassioned debates over the tradeoff between security and civil liberties. They also served as a vivid reminder to Americans of the transformative impact of the Internet on their daily lives—and of the potential threats to privacy that the Internet enabled.

First created by the government for Cold War intelligence sharing, the Internet had spread like wildfire through American homes, schools, and offices starting in the mid-1990s. The percentage of households with Internet access skyrocketed from 18 percent in 1997 to about 75 percent in 2012. In rapidly increasing numbers, Americans turned to the Internet to communicate, shop, work, pay bills, and electronically bond with family, friends, and lovers. Fulfilling the promises of its early boosters, the Internet seemed to have a democratizing effect, spreading power and information among more and more people while upending the worlds of traditional media, business, and politics. But the growing centrality of the electronic online world to Americans' everyday lives also served to increase their vulnerability to potentially unwanted intrusions—from businesses, governments, and criminals alike.

In Obergefell *v.* Hodges, *a five-to-four Supreme Court majority declared gay marriage a fundamental right under the Fourteenth Amendment. (See Appendix p. A-16.) As Justice Anthony Kennedy (b. 1936) wrote in the majority decision:*

"No union is more profound than marriage, for it embodies the highest ideals of love, fidelity, devotion, sacrifice, and family. In forming a marital union, two people become something greater than once they were. As some of the petitioners in these cases demonstrate, marriage embodies a love that may endure even past death. It would misunderstand these men and women to say they disrespect the idea of marriage. Their plea is that they do respect it, respect it so deeply that they seek to find its fulfillment for themselves. Their hope is not to be condemned to live in loneliness, excluded from one of civilization's oldest institutions. They ask for equal dignity in the eyes of the law. The Constitution grants them that right."

Political Gridlock and Judicial Change

In the 2014 mid-term elections, Republicans cashed in on President Obama's declining job approval ratings, which sank to nearly 40 percent in some polls. Public frustration with an economic recovery that lit up the stock market but failed to boost most household incomes fed discontent with the president's party, as did the stubborn unpopularity in some quarters of the Affordable Care Act, the signature achievement of Obama's first term. A rash of troubles abroad also plagued the president and his party alike. The unexpected emergence of the Islamic State of Iraq and Syria (ISIS), a ferocious jihadist movement, alarming in its brutality and in its territorial advance, cast doubts on the president's foreign policy skills, and further discredited his party's candidates.

As a result, in the 2014 midterm elections Republicans expanded their majority in the House and gained control of the Senate for the first time since 2006. Many observers attributed those results not to blossoming affection for Republicans, but to deep disillusionment with the Democratic administration.

With the Republicans in complete control of Congress, there seemed little chance of easing the stalemate with President Obama on the issues of immigration, gun control, and environmental policy. Republicans also remained sharply critical of Obama's Middle East policies, including his attempted agreement on nuclear weapons development with Iran, as well as his limited aerial responses aimed at weakening the Islamic State. Obama also sparked controversy when he met with Cuban President Raul Castro in April 2015 and announced that the two nations would work to restore normal diplomatic relations.

Obama did garner strong Republican support in 2015 for successful passage of the Trans-Pacific Partnership, a major free trade agreement among twelve Asia-Pacific nations, including the United States and China. Many Democrats voted against the deal, fearing a loss of U.S. jobs and the weakening of environmental protections.

With the president and Congress still largely at loggerheads, it was the Supreme Court that in 2015 decisively addressed two fiercely contested political issues. In *King* v. *Burwell*, the Court rejected a last-gasp legal challenge to federal subsidies for health insurance under the Affordable Care Act. Republicans still vowed to repeal and replace "Obamacare," but they would need to elect another president to do so. In *Obergefell* v. *Hodges*, the Court's majority declared that same-sex marriage was a fundamental right under the Constitution's Fourteenth Amendment, making it legal in all fifty states. The decision was a testimony to the power of the American commitment to the idea of equal rights for all, as well as to the lightning-speed transformation in public attitudes toward gay sexuality, marriage, and family, especially among younger citizens.

As a legion of candidates began to line up for the 2016 presidential elections, the two major parties were still sharply divided on issues of economics, immigration, and foreign policy. Whether new leadership or some fresh turn of events might make room for common ground to move the nation forward remained to be seen.

The American Prospect

Well beyond its two-hundredth birthday as the twenty-first century's second decade unspooled, the United States was both an old and a new nation. It boasted one of the longest uninterrupted traditions of democratic government of any country on earth. Indeed, it had pioneered the techniques of mass democracy and was, in that sense, the oldest modern polity. As one of the earliest countries to industrialize, America had also dwelt in the modern economic era longer than most nations. But the Republic was in many ways still youthful as well. Innovation, entrepreneurship, and risk-taking—all characteristics of youth—were honored national values.

America's twenty-first century had begun much like the twentieth, as society continued to be rejuvenated by fresh waves of immigrants, full of energy and ambition. The U.S. economy, despite the impact of the "Great Recession," remained an important engine of world economic growth. American inventions—especially computer and communications technologies—continued to transform the face of global society. Consumers from Berlin to Beijing seemed to worship the icons of American culture—downing soft drinks and donning blue jeans, watching Hollywood films and television series, listening to rock or country music, even adopting indigenous American sports like baseball and basketball. In the realm of consumerism, American products appeared to have Coca-Colonized the globe.

The history of American society also seemed to have increased global significance as the third millennium of the Christian era opened. Americans were a pluralistic people who had struggled for centuries to offer opportunity, tolerance, and justice to many different religious, ethnic, and racial groups. Their historical trials and triumphs could offer valuable lessons to the rapidly internationalizing planetary society that was emerging at the dawn of the twenty-first century.

Much history remained to be made as the country entered its third century of nationhood. The great social experiment of American democracy was far from completed as the United States faced its future. Astonishing breakthroughs in science and technology, especially in genetics, bioengineering, and communications, presented Americans with stunning opportunities as well as wrenching ethical choices. Global climate change made the responsible stewardship of a fragile planet more urgent than ever. Inequality and prejudice continued to challenge Americans to close the gap between their most hallowed values and the stark realities of society in the twenty-first-century United States. The terrorist attacks of September 11, 2001 violently heralded a new era of fear and anxiety. And the severe economic crisis that convulsed the nation and the world in 2008 demonstrated that free-market capitalism could still produce abundant misery as well as material abundance.

But men and women make history only within the framework bequeathed to them by earlier generations. For better or worse, they march forward along time's path bearing the burdens of the past. Knowing when they have come to a truly new turn in the road, when they can lay part of their burden down and when they cannot, or should not—all this constitutes the sort of wisdom that only historical understanding can engender. As Americans confront the unending challenges of the twenty-first-century world, they would do well to remember Woodrow Wilson's admonition of 1893, long before he became president. "Democratic Institutions are never done; they are like living tissue, always a-making. It is a strenuous thing, this of living the life of a free people."

CHAPTER SUMMARY ★★★★★★★★★★★★★★

George W. Bush took office after the close, bitter election of 2000, and began governing as a highly activist and often divisive conservative leader. His heavy defense expenditures and sharp tax cuts created huge federal budget deficits.

The September 11, 2001 terrorist attacks shocked and unified the nation, while propelling it out of its long centuries of relative safety from foreign attack on domestic soil. Bush responded by launching a "war on terror" that included a swift ouster of the Taliban in Afghanistan. He also launched a highly controversial war against Iraqi dictator Saddam Hussein, claiming that Iraq possessed weapons of mass destruction that threatened the United States. While Saddam was quickly overthrown, Iraq soon fell into chaos, featuring bloody factional religious conflicts and militant attacks on occupying American troops.

Bush won reelection in 2004 as a strong leader, but he suffered numerous failures and decreasing popularity in his second term. The administration's disastrous response to Hurricane Katrina and the continuing conflict in Iraq led to Democratic gains in 2006 midterm elections. In the 2008 campaign Democrats nominated youthful Senator Barack Obama, who defeated Republican Senator John McCain; Obama became the first black president in American history.

Obama's victory came partly because of a major financial crisis and economic collapse that began in fall 2008. The "Great Recession" cost millions of Americans their jobs and homes, and led to a stagnant economic environment that lingered for years. Obama responded vigorously to the crisis with a huge "stimulus" spending bill as well as reforms of health care and the financial system. But Obama's surge of federal activism prompted a fierce backlash by ultraconservative "Tea Party" citizens who attacked "big government" and the Democrats who supported it. Democrats suffered setbacks in the midterm elections of 2010.

Obama successfully wound down the Iraq War and brought American troops home, though the country remained unstable. Afghanistan proved more difficult to pacify, and even when ground troops left they were increasingly replaced by aerial "drone warfare" against terrorists. Al Qaeda leader Osama bin Laden was killed in neighboring Pakistan.

America's attention turned to issues of growing economic inequality in the early twenty-first century. A radical "Occupy Wall Street" movement attacked the wealthiest "1 percent." The movement faded, but the weak economic environment fostered growing debates about poverty and wealth, and especially the power of the immensely rich and growing financial sector.

Barack Obama won reelection against Republican Mitt Romney, a former Massachusetts governor and the first Mormon presidential candidate in American history. Obama attempted to expand his activist reforms in his second term, but conservative Republicans in control of the House blocked his efforts. The standoff between the president and Congress over the budget ceiling and other issues forced the government into "gridlock." Immigration reform remained a hotly contested issue in the country, but all attempts to find compromise legal solutions failed. Republicans made further gains in the midterm elections of 2014, and the partisan conflict between the president and Congress deepened. In 2015 the Supreme Court declared gay marriage a right under the Fourteenth Amendment.

American democracy remains a dynamic force in a new global and technological age. Issues of economic inequality, environmental degradation, and ethnic conflict demand urgent attention and engagement by American citizens. American culture and democracy can provide powerful resources for addressing the challenges of the nation's third century.

KEY TERMS

weapons of mass destruction (WMD) (719)
Kyoto Treaty (721)
9/11 (721)
Al Qaeda (721)
USA Patriot Act (721)
Department of Homeland Security (722)
Guantanamo Detention Camp (722)
Abu Ghraib prison (723)
No Child Left Behind Act (724)
Hurricane Katrina (724)
deleveraging (725)
American Recovery and Reinvestment Act (726)
Patient Protection and Affordable Care Act (727)
Wall Street Reform and Consumer Protection Act (727)
Tea Party (727)
Occupy Wall Street (729)

PEOPLE TO KNOW

John McCain
Sarah Palin
George W. Bush
Richard Cheney
Nancy Pelosi
Barack Obama
Joseph R. ("Joe") Biden

Documents

Declaration of Independence

In Congress, July 4, 1776

The Unanimous Declaration of the Thirteen United States of America

[Bracketed material in color has been inserted by the authors. For adoption background see pp. 105–106.]

When, in the course of human events, it becomes necessary for one people to dissolve the political bonds which have connected them with another, and to assume, among the powers of the earth, the separate and equal station to which the laws of nature and of nature's God entitle them, a decent respect to the opinions of mankind requires that they should declare the causes which impel them to the separation.

We hold these truths to be self-evident: That all men are created equal; that they are endowed by their Creator with certain unalienable rights; that among these are life, liberty, and the pursuit of happiness; that, to secure these rights, governments are instituted among men, deriving their just powers from the consent of the governed; that whenever any form of government becomes destructive of these ends, it is the right of the people to alter or to abolish it, and to institute new government, laying its foundation on such principles, and organizing its powers in such form, as to them shall seem most likely to effect their safety and happiness. Prudence, indeed, will dictate that governments long established should not be changed for light and transient causes; and accordingly all experience hath shown that mankind are more disposed to suffer, while evils are sufferable, than to right themselves by abolishing the forms to which they are accustomed. But when a long train of abuses and usurpations, pursuing invariably the same object, evinces a design to reduce them under absolute despotism, it is their right, it is their duty, to throw off such government, and to provide new guards for their future security. Such has been the patient sufferance of these colonies; and such is now the necessity which constrains them to alter their former systems of government. The history of the present King of Great Britain is a history of repeated injuries and usurpations, all having in direct object the establishment of an absolute tyranny over these states. To prove this, let facts be submitted to a candid world.

He has refused his assent to laws, the most wholesome and necessary for the public good. [See royal veto, p. 89.]

He has forbidden his governors to pass laws of immediate and pressing importance, unless suspended in their operation till his assent should be obtained; and, when so suspended, he has utterly neglected to attend to them.

He has refused to pass other laws for the accommodation of large districts of people [by establishing new countries], unless those people would relinquish the right of representation in the legislature, a right inestimable to them, and formidable to tyrants only.

He has called together legislative bodies at places unusual, uncomfortable, and distant from the depository of their public records, for the sole purpose of fatiguing them into compliance with his measures [e.g., removal of Massachusetts Assembly to Salem, 1774].

He has dissolved representative houses repeatedly, for opposing, with manly firmness, his invasions on the rights of the people [e.g., Virginia Assembly, 1765].

He has refused for a long time, after such dissolutions, to cause others to be elected; whereby the legislative powers, incapable of annihilation, have returned to the people at large for their exercise; the state remaining, in the mean time, exposed to all the dangers of invasions from without and convulsions within.

He has endeavored to prevent the population [populating] of these states; for that purpose obstructing the laws for naturalization of foreigners; refusing to pass others to encourage their migration hither, and raising the conditions of new appropriations of lands [e.g., Proclamation of 1763, p. 84].

He has obstructed the administration of justice, by refusing his assent to laws for establishing judiciary powers.

He has made judges dependent on his will alone, for the tenure of their offices, and the amount and payment of their salaries. [See Townshend Acts, p. 92.]

He has erected a multitude of new offices, and sent hither swarms of officers to harass our people and eat out their substance. [See enforcement of Navigation Laws, pp. 89, 90.]

He has kept among us, in times of peace, standing armies, without the consent of our legislatures. [See pp. 90, 92.]

He has affected to render the military independent of, and superior to, the civil power.

He has combined with others to subject us to a jurisdiction foreign to our constitution, and unacknowledged by our laws, giving his assent to their acts of pretended legislation:

For quartering large bodies of armed troops among us [see Boston Massacre, pp. 92–93];

For protecting them, by a mock trial, from punishment for any murders which they should commit on the inhabitants of these states [see 1774 "Intolerable Acts," p. 95];

For cutting off our trade with all parts of the world [see Boston Port Act, p. 95];

For imposing taxes on us without our consent [see Stamp Act, pp. 90–91];

For depriving us, in many cases, of the benefits of trial by jury;

For transporting us beyond seas, to be tried for pretended offenses;

For abolishing the free system of English laws in a neighboring province [Quebec], establishing therein an arbitrary government, and enlarging its boundaries, so as to render it at once an example and fit instrument for introducing the same absolute rule into these colonies [Quebec Act, pp. 95–96];

For taking away our charters, abolishing our most valuable laws, and altering fundamentally the forms of our governments [e.g., in Massachusetts, p. 95];

For suspending our own legislatures, and declaring themselves invested with power to legislate for us in all cases whatsoever. [See Stamp Act repeal, pp. 91–92.]

He has abdicated government here, by declaring us out of his protection and waging war against us. [See George III's proclamation of colonies in rebellion, p. 103.]

He has plundered our seas, ravaged our coasts, burned our towns, and destroyed the lives of our people [e.g., the burning of Falmouth (Portland), p. 103].

He is at this time transporting large armies of foreign mercenaries [Hessians, p. 103] to complete the works of death, desolation, and tyranny already begun with circumstances of cruelty and perfidy scarcely paralleled in the most barbarous ages, and totally unworthy the head of a civilized nation.

He has constrained our fellow-citizens, taken captive on the high seas [by impressment], to bear arms against their country, to become the executioners of their friends and brethren, or to fall themselves by their hands.

He has excited domestic insurrection among us [i.e., among slaves], and has endeavored to bring on the inhabitants of our frontiers the merciless Indian savages, whose known rule of warfare is an undistinguished destruction of all ages, sexes, and conditions.

In every stage of these oppressions we have petitioned for redress in the most humble terms; our repeated petitions have been answered only by repeated injury [e.g., p. 103]. A prince, whose character is thus marked by every act which may define a tyrant, is unfit to be the ruler of a free people.

Nor have we been wanting in our attentions to our British brethren. We have warned them, from time to time, of attempts by their legislature to extend an unwarrantable jurisdiction over us. We have reminded them of the circumstances of our emigration and settlement here. We have appealed to their native justice and magnanimity; and we have conjured them, by the ties of our common kindred, to disavow these usurpations, which would inevitably interrupt our connections and correspondence. They, too, have been deaf to the voice of justice and of consanguinity [blood relationship]. We must, therefore, acquiesce in the necessity which denounces [announces] our separation, and hold them, as we hold the rest of mankind, enemies in war, in peace friends.

We, therefore, the representatives of the United States of America, in General Congress assembled, appealing to the Supreme Judge of the world for the rectitude of our intentions, do, in the name and by the authority of the good people of these colonies, solemnly publish and declare, That these United Colonies are, and of right ought to be, FREE AND INDEPENDENT STATES; that they are absolved from all allegiance to the British crown, and that all political connection between them and the state of Great Britain is, and ought to be, totally dissolved; and that, as free and independent states, they have full power to levy war, conclude peace, contract alliances, establish commerce, and do all other acts and things which independent states may of right do. And for the support of this declaration, with a firm reliance on the protection of Divine Providence, we mutually pledge to each other our lives, our fortunes, and our sacred honor.

[Signed by]

John Hancock [President]
[and fifty-five others]

Constitution of the United States of America

[Boldface headings and bracketed explanatory matter and marginal comments (both in color) have been inserted for the reader's convenience. Passages that are no longer operative are printed in italic type.]

Article I. PREAMBLE

Section I. We the people of the United States, in order to form a more perfect union, establish justice, insure domestic tranquility, provide for the common defense, promote the general welfare, and secure the blessings of liberty to ourselves and our posterity, do ordain and establish this Constitution for the United States of America.

Section II. *Legislative Department*

Congress

Legislative power vested in a two-house Congress. All legislative powers herein granted shall be vested in a Congress of the United States, which shall consist of a Senate and a House of Representatives.

House of Representatives

1. The people elect representatives biennially. The House of Representatives shall be composed of members chosen every second year by the people of the several States, and the electors [voters] in each State shall have the qualifications requisite for electors of the most numerous branch of the State Legislature.

2. Who may be representatives. No person shall be a Representative who shall not have attained the age of twenty-five years, and been seven years a citizen of the United States, and who shall not, when elected, be an inhabitant of that State in which he shall be chosen.

See 1787 compromises, pp. 129–131.

3. Representation in the House based on population; census. Representatives and direct taxes[1] shall be apportioned among the several States which may be included within this Union, according to their respective numbers, *which shall be determined by adding to the whole number of free persons, including those bound to service for a term of years* [apprentices and indentured servants], *and excluding Indians not taxed, three-fifths of all other persons* [slaves].[2] The actual enumeration [census] shall be made within three years after the first meeting of the Congress of the United States, and within every subsequent term of ten years, in such manner as they shall by law direct. The number of Representatives shall not exceed one for every thirty thousand, but each State shall have at least one Representative; *and until such enumeration shall be made, the State of New Hampshire shall be entitled to choose three, Massachusetts eight, Rhode Island and Providence Plantations one, Connecticut five, New York six, New Jersey four, Pennsylvania eight, Delaware one, Maryland six, Virginia ten, North Carolina five, South Carolina five, and Georgia three.*

See 1787 compromises, pp. 129–131.

---

[1]Modified in 1913 by the Sixteenth Amendment re income taxes (see p. 497).

[2]The word *slave* appears nowhere in the original, unamended Constitution. The three-fifths rule ceased to be in force when the Thirteenth Amendment was adopted in 1865 (see p. 332 and amendments below).

4. Vacancies in the House are filled by election. When vacancies happen in the representation from any State, the Executive authority [governor] therefore shall issue writs of election [call a special election] to fill such vacancies.

See Johnson trial, pp. 360–361; Nixon trial preliminaries, pp. 671–673; and discussion of Clinton's impeachment, pp. 713–714.

5. The House selects its Speaker; has sole power to vote impeachment charges (i.e., indictments). The House of Representatives shall choose their Speaker and other officers; and shall have the sole power of impeachment.

Section III. Senate

1. Senators represent the states. The Senate of the United States shall be composed of two Senators from each State, *chosen by the legislature thereof,*[1] for six Years; and each Senator shall have one vote.

2. One-third of senators chosen every two years; vacancies. *Immediately after they shall be assembled in consequence of the first election, they shall be divided as equally as may be into three classes. The seats of the Senators of the first class shall be vacated at the expiration of the second year, of the second class at the expiration of the fourth year, and of the third class at the expiration of the sixth year,* so that one-third may be chosen every second year; *and if vacancies happen by resignation or otherwise, during the recess of the legislature of any State, the Executive* [governor] *thereof may make temporary appointments until the next meeting of the legislature, which shall then fill such vacancies.*[2]

3. Who may be senators. No person shall be a Senator who shall not have attained to the age of thirty years, and been nine years a citizen of the United States, and who shall not, when elected, be an inhabitant of that State for which he shall be chosen.

4. The vice president presides over the Senate. The Vice President of the United States shall be President of the Senate, but shall have no vote, unless they be equally divided [tied].

5. The Senate chooses its other officers. The Senate shall choose their other officers, and also a President *pro tempore*, in the absence of the Vice President, or when he shall exercise the office of the President of the United States.

See Johnson trial, pp. 360–361; and discussion of Clinton's impeachment, pp. 713–714.

6. The Senate has sole power to try impeachments. The Senate shall have the sole power to try all impeachments. When sitting for that purpose, they shall be on oath or affirmation. When the President of the United States is tried, the Chief Justice shall preside[3]: and no person shall be convicted without the concurrence of two-thirds of the members present.

7. Penalties for impeachment conviction. Judgment in cases of impeachment shall not extend further than to removal from office, and disqualification to hold and enjoy any office of honor, trust or profit under the United States: but the party convicted shall nevertheless be liable and subject to indictment, trial, judgment and punishment, according to law.

Section IV. Election and Meetings of Congress

1. Regulation of elections. The times, places and manner of holding elections for Senators and Representatives shall be prescribed in each State by the legislature thereof; but the Congress may at any time by law make or alter such regulations, except as to the places of choosing Senators.

2. Congress must meet once a year. The Congress shall assemble at least once in every year, and such meeting *shall be on the first Monday in December, unless they shall by law appoint a different day.*[4]

---

[1]Repealed in favor of popular election in 1913 by the Seventeenth Amendment.

[2]Changed in 1913 by the Seventeenth Amendment.

[3]The vice president, as next in line, would be an interested party.

[4]Changed in 1933 to January 3 by the Twentieth Amendment (see p. 565 and below).

Section V. Organization and Rules of the Houses

1. Each house may reject members; quorums. Each house shall be the judge of the elections, returns and qualifications of its own members, and a majority of each shall constitute a quorum to do business; but a smaller number may adjourn from day to day, and may be authorized to compel the attendance of absent members, in such manner, and under such penalties, as each house may provide.

See "Bully" Brooks case, pp. 300–301.

2. Each house makes its own rules. Each house may determine the rules of its proceedings, punish its members for disorderly behavior, and with the concurrence of two-thirds, expel a member.

3. Each house must keep and publish a record of its proceedings. Each house shall keep a journal of its proceedings, and from time to time publish the same, excepting such parts as may in their judgment require secrecy; and the yeas and nays of the members of either house on any question shall, at the desire of one-fifth of those present, be entered on the journal.

4. Both houses must agree on adjournment. Neither house, during the session of Congress, shall, without the consent of the other, adjourn for more than three days, nor to any other place than that in which the two houses shall be sitting.

Section VI. Privileges of and Prohibitions upon Congressmen

1. Congressional salaries; immunities. The Senators and Representatives shall receive a compensation for their services, to be ascertained by law and paid out of the treasury of the United States. They shall in all cases except treason, felony and breach of the peace, be privileged from arrest during their attendance at the session of their respective houses, and in going to and returning from the same; and for any speech or debate in either house, they shall not be questioned in any other place [i.e., they shall be immune from libel suits].

2. A congressman may not hold any other federal civil office. No Senator or Representative shall, during the time for which he was elected, be appointed to any civil office under the authority of the United States, which shall have been created, or the emoluments whereof shall have been increased, during such time; and no person holding any office under the United States shall be a member of either house during his continuance in office.

Section VII. Method of Making Laws

See 1787 compromises, p. 130.

1. Money bills must originate in the House. All bills for raising revenue shall originate in the House of Representatives; but the Senate may propose or concur with amendments as on other bills.

Nixon, more than any predecessors, "impounded" billions of dollars voted by Congress for specific purposes because he disapproved of them. The courts generally failed to sustain him, and his impeachment foes regarded wholesale impoundment as a violation of his oath to "faithfully execute" the laws.

2. The president's veto power; Congress may override. Every bill which shall have passed the House of Representatives and the Senate, shall, before it become a law, be presented to the President of the United States; if he approve he shall sign it, but if not he shall return it with his objections to that house in which it shall have originated, who shall enter the objections at large on their journal, and proceed to reconsider it. If after such reconsideration two-thirds of that house shall agree to pass the bill, it shall be sent, together with the objections, to the other house, by which it shall likewise be reconsidered, and, if approved by two-thirds of that house, it shall become a law. But in all such cases the votes of both houses shall be determined by yeas and nays, and the names of the persons voting for and against the bill shall be entered on the journal of each house respectively. If any bill shall not be returned by the President within ten days (Sundays excepted) after it shall have been presented to him, the same shall be a law, in like manner as if he had signed it, unless the Congress by their adjournment prevent its return, in which case it shall not be a law [this is the so-called pocket veto].

3. All measures requiring the agreement of both houses go to president for approval. Every order, resolution, or vote to which the concurrence of the Senate and House of Representatives may be necessary (except on a question of adjournment) shall be presented to the President of the United States; and before the same shall take effect, shall be approved by him, or being disapproved by him, shall be repassed by two-thirds of the Senate and House of Representatives, according to the rules and limitations prescribed in the case of a bill.

Section VIII. Powers Granted to Congress

Congress has certain enumerated powers:

1. It may lay and collect taxes. The Congress shall have power to lay and collect taxes, duties, imposts, and excises, to pay the debts and provide for the common defense and general welfare of the United States; but all duties, imposts and excises shall be uniform throughout the United States;

2. It may borrow money. To borrow money on the credit of the United States;

3. It may regulate foreign and interstate trade. To regulate commerce with foreign nations, and among the several States, and with the Indian tribes;

For 1798 naturalization, see p. 152.

4. It may pass naturalization and bankruptcy laws. To establish an uniform rule of naturalization, and uniform laws on the subject of bankruptcies throughout the United States;

5. It may coin money. To coin money, regulate the value thereof, and of foreign coin, and fix the standard of weights and measures;

6. It may punish counterfeiters. To provide for the punishment of counterfeiting the securities and current coin of the United States;

7. It may establish a postal service. To establish post offices and post roads;

8. It may issue patents and copyrights. To promote the progress of science and useful arts by securing for limited times to authors and inventors the exclusive right to their respective writings and discoveries;

9. It may establish inferior courts. To constitute tribunals inferior to the Supreme Court;

See Judiciary Act of 1789, p. 142.

10. It may punish crimes committed on the high seas. To define and punish piracies and felonies committed on the high seas [i.e., outside the three-mile limit] and offenses against the law of nations [international law];

11. It may declare war; authorize privateers. To declare war,[1] grant letters of marque and reprisal,[2] and make rules concerning captures on land and water;

12. It may maintain an army. To raise and support armies, but no appropriation of money to that use shall be for a longer term than two years;[3]

13. It may maintain a navy. To provide and maintain a navy;

14. It may regulate the army and navy. To make rules for the government and regulation of the land and naval forces;

See Whiskey Rebellion, pp. 144–145.

15. It may call out the state militia. To provide for calling forth the militia to execute the laws of the Union, suppress insurrections, and repel invasions;

16. It shares with the states control of militia. To provide for organizing, arming, and disciplining the militia, and for governing such part of them as may be employed in the service of the United States, reserving to the States respectively the appointment of the officers, and the authority of training the militia according to the discipline prescribed by Congress;

17. It makes laws for the District of Columbia and other federal areas. To exercise exclusive legislation in all cases whatsoever, over such district (not exceeding ten miles square) as may, by cession of particular States, and the acceptance of

[1]Note that presidents, though they can provoke war (see the case of Polk, p. 276) or wage it after it is declared, cannot declare it.

[2]Papers issued private citizens in wartime authorizing them to capture enemy ships.

[3]A reflection of fear of standing armies earlier expressed in the Declaration of Independence.

Congress, become the seat of government of the United States,[1] and to exercise like authority over all places purchased by the consent of the legislature of the State, in which the same shall be, for the erection of forts, magazines, arsenals, dock-yards, and other needful buildings;—and

Congress has certain implied powers:

This is the famous "elastic clause"; see p. 144.

18. It may make laws necessary for carrying out the enumerated powers. To make all laws which shall be necessary and proper for carrying into execution the foregoing powers, and all other powers vested by this Constitution in the government of the United States, or in any departure or officer thereof.

Section IX. Powers Denied to the Federal Government

See 1787 slave compromise, p. 130.

1. Congressional control of slave trade postponed until 1808. *The migration or importation of such persons as any of the States now existing shall think proper to admit shall not be prohibited by the Congress prior to the year 1808; but a tax or duty may be imposed on such importation, not exceeding $10 for each person.*

See Lincoln's unlawful suspension, p. 319.

2. The writ of habeas corpus[2] may be suspended only in cases of rebellion or invasion. The privilege of the writ of habeas corpus shall not be suspended, unless when in cases of rebellion or invasion the public safety may require it.

3. Attainders[3] and ex post facto laws[4] forbidden. No bill of attainder or ex post facto law shall be passed.

4. Direct taxes must be apportioned according to population. No capitation [head or poll tax] or other direct, tax shall be laid, unless in proportion to the census or enumeration herein before directed to be taken.[5]

5. Export taxes forbidden. No tax or duty shall be laid on articles exported from any State.

6. Congress must not discriminate among states in regulating commerce. No preference shall be given by any regulation of commerce or revenue to the ports of one State over those of another; nor shall vessels bound to, or from, one State, be obliged to enter, clear, or pay duties in another.

See Lincoln's unlawful infraction, p. 319.

7. Public money may not be spent without congressional appropriation; accounting. No money shall be drawn from the treasury, but in consequence of appropriations made by law; and a regular statement and account of the receipts and expenditures of all public money shall be published from time to time.

8. Titles of nobility prohibited; foreign gifts. No title of nobility shall be granted by the United States; and no person holding office of profit or trust under them, shall, without the consent of Congress, accept of any present, emolument, office, or title, of any kind whatever, from any king, prince, or foreign state.

Section X. Powers Denied to the States

Absolute prohibitions on the states:

On contracts, see Fletcher v. Peck, *p. 183.*

1. The states are forbidden to do certain things. No State shall enter into any treaty, alliance, or confederation; grant letters of marque and reprisal [i.e., authorize

[1]The District of Columbia, ten miles square, was established in 1791 with a cession from Virginia (see p. 143).

[2]A writ of habeas corpus is a document that enables a person under arrest to obtain an immediate examination in court to ascertain whether he or she is being legally held.

[3]A bill of attainder is a special legislative act condemning and punishing an individual without a judicial trial.

[4]An ex post facto law is one that fixes punishments for acts committed before the law was passed.

[5]Modified in 1913 by the Sixteenth Amendment (see p. 497 and amendments below).

privateers]; coin money; emit bills of credit [issue paper money]; make anything but gold and silver coin a [legal] tender in payment of debts; pass any bill of attainder,[1] ex post facto,[1] or law impairing the obligation of contracts, or grant any title of nobility.

Conditional prohibitions on the states:

Cf. Confederation chaos, p. 125.

2. The states may not levy duties without the consent of Congress. No State shall, without the consent of Congress, lay any imposts or duties on imports or exports, except what may be absolutely necessary for executing its inspection laws: and the net produce of all duties and imposts, laid by any State on imports or exports, shall be for the use of the treasury of the United States; and all such laws shall be subject to the revision and control of the Congress.

3. Certain other federal powers are forbidden the states except with the consent of Congress. No State shall, without the consent of Congress, lay any duty of tonnage [i.e., duty on ship tonnage], keep [nonmilitia] troops or ships of war in time of peace, enter into any agreement or compact with another State, or with a foreign power, or engage in war, unless actually invaded, or in such imminent danger as will not admit of delay.

Article II. Executive Department

Section I. President and Vice President

1. The president is the chief executive; term of office. The executive power shall be vested in a President of the United States of America. He shall hold his office during the term of four years,[2] and, together with the Vice President, chosen for the same term, be elected as follows:

See 1787 compromise, p. 130.

See 1876 Oregon case, p. 373.

2. The president is chosen by electors. Each State shall appoint, in such manner as the legislature thereof may direct, a number of electors, equal to the whole number of Senators and Representatives to which the State may be entitled in the Congress; but no Senator or Representative, or person holding an office of trust or profit under the United States, shall be appointed an elector.

See Burr-Jefferson disputed election of 1800, pp. 157–158.

See Jefferson as vice president in 1796, p. 150.

A majority of the electoral votes needed to elect a president. *The electors shall meet in their respective States, and vote by ballot for two persons, of whom one at least shall not be an inhabitant of the same State with themselves. And they shall make a list of all the persons voted for, and of the number of votes for each; which list they shall sign and certify, and transmit sealed to the seat of government of the United States, directed to the President of the Senate. The President of the Senate shall, in the presence of the Senate and House of Representatives, open all the certificates, and the votes shall be counted. The person having the greatest number of votes shall be the President, if such number be a majority of the whole number of electors appointed; and if there be more than one who have such majority, and have an equal number of votes, then the House of Representatives shall immediately choose by ballot one of them for President; and if no person have a majority, then from the five highest on the list the said house shall in like manner choose the President. But in choosing the President the votes shall be taken by States, the representation from each State having one vote; a quorum for this purpose shall consist of a member or members from two-thirds of the States, and a majority of all the States shall be necessary to a choice. In every case, after the choice of the President, the person having the greatest number of votes of the electors shall be the Vice President. But if there should remain two or more who have equal votes, the Senate shall choose from them by ballot the Vice President.*[3]

[1]For definitions see footnotes 3 and 4 on preceding page.

[2]No reference to reelection; for anti–third term Twenty-second Amendment, see below.

[3]Repealed in 1804 by the Twelfth Amendment (for text see below).

3. Congress decides time of meeting of Electoral College. The Congress may determine the time of choosing the electors and the day on which they shall give their votes; which day shall be the same throughout the United States.

To provide for foreign-born people, like Alexander Hamilton, born in the British West Indies.

4. Who may be president. No person except a natural-born citizen, *or a citizen of the United States at the time of the adoption of this Constitution,* shall be eligible to the office of President; neither shall any person be eligible to that office who shall not have attained to the age of thirty-five years, and been fourteen years a resident within the United States [i.e., a legal resident].

Modified by Twentieth and Twenty-fifth Amendments below.

5. Replacements for president. In case of the removal of the President from office or of his death, resignation, or inability to discharge the powers and duties of said office, the same shall devolve on the Vice President, and the Congress may by law provide for the case of removal, death, resignation, or inability, both of the President and Vice President, declaring what officer shall then act as President, and such officer shall act accordingly, until the disability be removed, or a President shall be elected.

6. The president's salary. The President shall, at stated times, receive for his services a compensation, which shall neither be increased or diminished during the period for which he shall have been elected, and he shall not receive within that period any other emolument from the United States, or any of them.

7. The president's oath of office. Before he enter on the execution of his office, he shall take the following oath or affirmation:—"I do solemnly swear (or affirm) that I will faithfully execute the office of the President of the United States, and will to the best of my ability preserve, protect and defend the Constitution of the United States."

Section II. Powers of the President

See cabinet evolution, p. 141.

1. The president has important military and civil powers. The President shall be commander in chief of the army and navy of the United States, and of the militia of the several States, when called into the actual service of the United States; he may require the opinion, in writing, of the principal officer in each of the executive departments, upon any subject relating to the duties of their respective offices, and he shall have power to grant reprieves and pardons for offenses against the United States, except in cases of impeachment.[1]

For president's removal power, see p. 360.

2. The president may negotiate treaties and nominate federal officials. He shall have power, by and with the advice and consent of the Senate, to make treaties, provided two-thirds of the Senators present concur; and he shall nominate, and by and with the advice and consent of the Senate, shall appoint ambassadors, other public ministers and consuls, judges of the Supreme Court, and all other officers of the United States, whose appointments are not herein otherwise provided for, and which shall be established by law: but the Congress may by law vest the appointment of such inferior officers, as they think proper, in the President alone, in the courts of law, or in the heads of departments.

3. The president may fill vacancies during Senate recess. The President shall have power to fill up all vacancies that may happen during the recess of the Senate, by granting commissions which shall expire at the end of their next session.

Section III. Other Powers and Duties of the President

For president's personal appearances, see p. 497.

Messages; extra sessions; receiving ambassadors; execution of the laws. He shall from time to time give to the Congress information of the state of the Union, and recommend to their consideration such measures as he shall judge necessary and expedient; he may, on extraordinary occasions, convene both houses, or either of

---

[1]To prevent the president's pardoning himself or his close associates, as was feared in the case of Richard Nixon. See pp. 671–673.

them, and in case of disagreement between them, with respect to the time of adjournment, he may adjourn them to such time as he shall think proper; he shall receive ambassadors and other public ministers; he shall take care that the laws be faithfully executed, and shall commission all the officers of the United States.

Section IV. Impeachment

See discussion of Presidents Johnson, pp. 360–361; Nixon, pp. 671–673; and Clinton, pp. 713–714.

Civil officers may be removed by impeachment. The President, Vice President and all civil officers[1] of the United States shall be removed from office on impeachment for, and on conviction of, treason, bribery, and other high crimes and misdemeanors.

Article III. Judicial Department

Section I. The Federal Courts

See Judiciary Act of 1789, p. 142.

The judicial power belongs to the federal courts. The judicial power of the United States shall be vested in one Supreme Court, and in such inferior courts as the Congress may from time to time ordain and establish. The judges, both of the Supreme and inferior courts, shall hold their offices during good behavior, and shall, at stated times, receive for their services a compensation which shall not be diminished[2] during their continuance in office.

Section II. Jurisdiction of Federal Courts

1. Kinds of cases that may be heard. The judicial power shall extend to all cases, in law and equity, arising under this Constitution, the laws of the United States, and treaties made, or which shall be made, under their authority;—to all cases affecting ambassadors, other public ministers and consuls;—to all cases of admiralty and maritime jurisdiction;—to controversies to which the United States shall be a party;—to controversies between two or more States;*—between a State and citizens of another State*[3];—between citizens of different States;—between citizens of the same State claiming lands under grants of different States, and between a State, or the citizens thereof, and foreign states, citizens or subjects.

2. Jurisdiction of the Supreme Court. In all cases affecting ambassadors, other public ministers and consuls, and those in which a State shall be a party, the Supreme Court shall have original jurisdiction.[4] In all the other cases before mentioned, the Supreme Court shall have appellate jurisdiction,[5] both as to law and fact, with such exceptions, and under such regulations, as the Congress shall make.

3. Trial for federal crime is by jury. The trial of all crimes, except in cases of impeachment, shall be by jury; and such trial shall be held in the State where the said crimes shall have been committed; but when not committed within any State, the trial shall be at such place or places as the Congress may by law have directed.

---

[1]i.e., all federal executive and judicial officers, but not members of Congress or military personnel.

[2]In 1978, in a case involving federal judges, the Supreme Court ruled that diminution of salaries by inflation was irrelevant.

[3]The Eleventh Amendment (see below) restricts this to suits by a state against citizens of another state.

[4]i.e., such cases must originate in the Supreme Court.

[5]i.e., it hears other cases only when they are appealed to it from a lower federal court or a state court.

Section III. Treason

See Burr trial, p. 164.

1. Treason defined. Treason against the United States shall consist only in levying war against them, or in adhering to their enemies, giving them aid and comfort. No person shall be convicted of treason unless on the testimony of two witnesses to the same overt act, or on confession in open court.

2. Congress fixes punishment for treason. The Congress shall have power to declare the punishment of treason, but no attainder of treason shall work corruption of blood, or forfeiture except during the life of the person attained.[1]

Article IV. Relations of the States to One Another

Section I. Credit to Acts, Records, and Court Proceedings

Each state must respect the public acts of the others. Full faith and credit shall be given in each State to the public acts, records, and judicial proceedings of every other State.[2] And the Congress may by general laws prescribe the manner in which such acts, records, and proceedings shall be proved [attested], and the effect thereof.

Section II. Duties of States to States

1. Citizenship in one state is valid in all. The citizens of each State shall be entitled to all privileges and immunities of citizens in the several States.

This stipulation is sometimes openly flouted. In 1978 Governor Jerry Brown of California, acting on humanitarian grounds, refused to surrender to South Dakota an American Indian, Dennis Banks, who was charged with murder in an armed uprising.

2. Fugitives from justice must be surrendered by the state to which they have fled. A person charged in any State with treason, felony, or other crime, who shall flee from justice, and be found in another State, shall on demand of the executive authority [governor] of the State from which he fled, be delivered up, to be removed to the State having jurisdiction of the crime.

Basis of fugitive-slave laws; see pp. 287–289.

3. Slaves and apprentices must be returned. *No person held to service or labor in one State, under the laws thereof, escaping into another, shall, in consequence of any law or regulation therein, be discharged from such service or labor, but shall be delivered up on claim of the party to whom such service or labor may be due.*[3]

Section III. New States and Territories

e.g., Maine (1820); see p. 181.

1. Congress may admit new states. New States may be admitted by the Congress into this Union; but no new State shall be formed or erected within the jurisdiction of any other State; nor any State be formed by the junction of two or more States, or parts of States, without the consent of the legislatures of the States concerned as well as of the Congress.[4]

2. Congress regulates federal territory and property. The Congress shall have power to dispose of and make all needful rules and regulations respecting the territory or other property belonging to the United States; and nothing in this Constitution shall be so construed as to prejudice any claims of the United States, or of any particular State.

Section IV. Protection to the States

See Cleveland and the Pullman strike, pp. 444–445.

United States guarantees to states representative government and protection against invasion and rebellion. The United States shall guarantee

---

[1]i.e., punishment only for the offender; none for his or her heirs.

[2]e.g., a marriage in one is valid in all.

[3]Invalidated in 1865 by the Thirteenth Amendment (for text see below).

[4]Loyal West Virginia was formed by Lincoln in 1862 from seceded Virginia. This act was of dubious constitutionality and was justified in part by the wartime powers of the president. See pp. 314–315.

to every State in this Union a republican form of government, and shall protect each of them against invasion; and on application of the legislature, or of the executive [governor] (when the legislature cannot be convened), against domestic violence.

Article V. *The Process of Amendment*

The Constitution may be amended in four ways. The Congress, whenever two-thirds of both houses shall deem it necessary, shall propose amendments to this Constitution, or, on the application of the legislature of two-thirds of the several States, shall call a convention for proposing amendments, which, in either case, shall be valid to all intents and purposes, as part of this Constitution, when ratified by the legislatures of three-fourths of the several States, or by conventions in three-fourths thereof, as the one or the other mode of ratification may be proposed by the Congress; provided *that no amendments which may be made prior to the year one thousand eight hundred and eight shall in any manner affect the first and fourth clauses in the ninth section of the first article;*[1] and that no State, without its consent, shall be deprived of its equal suffrage in the Senate.

Article VI. *General Provisions*

This pledge honored by Hamilton, pp. 142–143.

1. The debts of the Confederation are taken over. All debts contracted and engagements entered into, before the adoption of this Constitution, shall be as valid against the United States under this Constitution, as under the Confederation.

2. The Constitution, federal laws, and treaties are the supreme law of the land. This Constitution, and the laws of the United States which shall be made in pursuance thereof; and all treaties made, or which shall be made, under the authority of the United States, shall be the supreme law of the land; and the judges in every State shall be bound thereby, anything in the Constitution or laws of any State to the contrary notwithstanding.

3. Federal and state officers bound by oath to support the Constitution. The Senators and Representatives before mentioned, and the members of the several State legislatures, and all executive and judicial officers, both of the United States and of the several States, shall be bound by oath or affirmation to support this Constitution; but no religious test shall ever be required as a qualification to any office or public trust under the United States.

Article VII. *Ratification of the Constitution*

See 1787 irregularity, pp. 131–133.

The Constitution effective when ratified by conventions in nine states. The ratification of the conventions of nine States shall be sufficient for the establishment of this Constitution between the States so ratifying the same.

Done in Convention by the unanimous consent of the States present, the seventeenth day of September in the year of our Lord one thousand seven hundred and eighty-seven and of the Independence of the United States of America the twelfth. In witness whereof we have hereunto subscribed our names.

[Signed by]

G° Washington
Presidt and Deputy from Virginia
[and thirty-eight others]

---

[1]This clause, regarding slave trade and direct taxes, became inoperative in 1808.

AMENDMENTS TO THE CONSTITUTION

Amendment I. Religious and Political Freedom

For background of Bill of Rights, see pp. 141–142.

Congress must not interfere with freedom of religion, speech or press, assembly, and petition. Congress shall make no law respecting an establishment of religion,[1] or prohibiting the free exercise thereof; or abridging the freedom of speech, or of the press; or the right of the people peaceably to assemble, and to petition the government for a redress of grievances.

Amendment II. Right to Bear Arms

The people may bear arms. A well-regulated militia being necessary to the security of a free State, the right of the people to keep and bear arms [i.e., for military purposes] shall not be infringed.[2]

Amendment III. Quartering of Troops

See Declaration of Independence and British quartering above.

Soldiers may not be arbitrarily quartered on the people. No soldier shall, in time of peace, be quartered in any house without the consent of the owner, nor in time of war, but in a manner to be prescribed by law.

Amendment IV. Searches and Seizures

A reflection of colonial grievances against the crown.

Unreasonable searches are forbidden. The right of the people to be secure in their persons, houses, papers, and effects, against unreasonable searches and seizures, shall not be violated, and no [search] warrants shall issue but upon probable cause, supported by oath or affirmation, and particularly describing the place to be searched, and the persons or things to be seized.

Amendment V. Right to Life, Liberty, and Property

When witnesses refuse to answer questions in court, they routinely "take the Fifth Amendment."

The individual is guaranteed certain rights when on trial and the right to life, liberty, and property. No person shall be held to answer for a capital, or otherwise infamous crime, unless on a presentment [formal charge] or indictment of a grand jury, except in cases arising in the naval forces, or in the militia, when in actual service in time of war or public danger; nor shall any person be subject for the same offense to be twice put in jeopardy of life or limb; nor shall be compelled in any criminal case to be a witness against himself, nor be deprived of life, liberty, or property, without due process of law; nor shall private property be taken for public use [i.e., by eminent domain] without just compensation.

Amendment VI. Protection in Criminal Trials

See Declaration of Independence above.

An accused person has important rights. In all criminal prosecutions, the accused shall enjoy the right to a speedy and public trial, by an impartial jury of the State and district wherein the crime shall have been committed, which district shall

---

[1]In 1787 "an establishment of religion" referred to an "established church," or one supported by all taxpayers, whether members or not. But the courts have often acted under this article to keep religion, including prayers, out of the public schools.

[2]The courts long held that the right to bear arms was a limited right linked to the maintenance of militias. But in the case of *District of Columbia v. Heller* in 2008, the Supreme Court defined the right to bear arms as an individual right, not contingent on "participation in some corporate body." Yet the Court still left the door open to some kinds of gun-control legislation.

have been previously ascertained by law, and to be informed of the nature and cause of the accusation; to be confronted with the witnesses against him; to have compulsory process [subpoena] for obtaining witnesses in his favor, and to have the assistance of counsel for his defense.

Amendment VII. Suits at Common Law

The rules of common law are recognized. In suits at common law, where the value in controversy shall exceed twenty dollars, the right of trial by jury shall be preserved, and no fact tried by a jury shall be otherwise re-examined in any court of the United States, than according to the rules of the common law.

Amendment VIII. Bail and Punishments

Excessive fines and unusual punishments are forbidden. Excessive bail shall not be required, nor excessive fines imposed, nor cruel and unusual punishment inflicted.

Amendment IX. Concerning Rights Not Enumerated

The Ninth and Tenth Amendments were bulwarks of southern states' rights before the Civil War.

The people retain rights not here enumerated. The enumeration in the Constitution, of certain rights, shall not be construed to deny or disparage others retained by the people.

Amendment X. Powers Reserved to the States and to the People

A concession to states' rights, *p. 143.*

Powers not delegated to the federal government are reserved to the states and the people. The powers not delegated to the United States by the Constitution, nor prohibited by it to the States, are reserved to the States respectively, or to the people.

Amendment XI. Suits Against a State

The federal courts have no authority in suits by citizens against a state. The judicial power of the United States shall not be construed to extend to any suit in law or equity, commenced or prosecuted against one of the United States by citizens of another State, or by citizens or subjects of any foreign state. [Adopted 1798.]

Amendment XII. Election of President and Vice President

Forestalls repetition of 1800 electoral dispute, *pp. 157–158.*

See 1876 disputed election. pp. 371–372.

See 1824 election, pp. 190–192.

1. Changes in manner of electing president and vice president; procedure when no presidential candidate receives electoral majority. The electors shall meet in their respective States, and vote by ballot for President and Vice President, one of whom, at least, shall not be an inhabitant of the same state with themselves; they shall name in their ballots the person voted for as President, and in distinct ballots the person voted for as Vice President, and they shall make distinct lists of all persons voted for as President, and of all persons voted for as Vice President, and of the number of votes for each, which lists they shall sign and certify, and transmit sealed to the seat of government of the United States, directed to the President of the Senate;—the President of the Senate shall, in the presence of the Senate and House of Representatives, open all the certificates and the votes shall be counted;—the person having the greatest number of votes for President shall be the President, if such number be a majority of the whole number of electors appointed; and if no person have such majority, then from the persons having the highest numbers not exceeding three on the list of those voted for as President, the House of

Representatives shall choose immediately, by ballot, the President. But in choosing the President, the votes shall be taken by States, the representation from each State having one vote; a quorum for this purpose shall consist of a member or members from two-thirds of the States, and a majority of all the States shall be necessary to a choice. And if the House of Representatives shall not choose a President whenever the right of choice shall devolve upon them, before *the fourth day of March*[1] next following, then the Vice President shall act as President, as in the case of the death or other constitutional disability of the President.

2. Procedure when no vice presidential candidate receives electoral majority. The person having the greatest number of votes as Vice President, shall be the Vice President, if such number be a majority of the whole number of electors appointed; and if no person have a majority, then from the two highest numbers on the list the Senate shall choose the Vice President; a quorum for the purpose shall consist of two-thirds of the whole number of Senators, and a majority of the whole number shall be necessary to a choice. But no person constitutionally ineligible to the office of President shall be eligible to that of Vice President of the United States. [Adopted 1804.]

Amendment XIII. Slavery Prohibited

For background, see pp. 332–333.

Slavery forbidden. 1. Neither slavery[2] nor involuntary servitude, except as a punishment for crime whereof the party shall have been duly convicted, shall exist within the United States, or any place subject to their jurisdiction.

2. Congress shall have power to enforce this article by appropriate legislation. [Adopted 1865.]

Amendment XIV. Civil Rights for Ex-slaves,[3] etc.

For background, see pp. 354–355.

For corporations as "persons," see p. 395.

1. Ex-slaves made citizens; U.S. citizenship primary. All persons born or naturalized in the United States, and subject to the jurisdiction thereof, are citizens of the United States and of the State wherein they reside. No State shall make or enforce any law which shall abridge the privileges or immunities of citizens of the United States; nor shall any State deprive any person of life, liberty, or property, without due process of law; nor deny to any person within its jurisdiction the equal protection of the laws.

Abolishes three-fifths rule for slaves, Art. I., Sec. II, para. 3.

2. When a state denies citizens the vote, its representation shall be reduced. Representatives shall be apportioned among the several States according to their respective numbers, counting the whole number of persons in each State, excluding Indians not taxed. But when the right to vote at any election for the choice of Electors for President and Vice President of the United States, Representatives in Congress, the executive and judicial officers of a State, or the members of the legislature thereof, is denied to any of the male inhabitants of such State, being twenty-one years of age and citizens of the United States, or in any way abridged, except for participation in rebellion, or other crime, the basis of representation therein shall be reduced in the proportion which the number of such make citizens shall bear to the whole number of male citizens twenty-one years of age in such State.[4]

Leading ex-Confederates denied office. See p. 355.

3. Certain persons who have been in rebellion are ineligible for federal and state office. No person shall be a Senator or Representative in Congress, or Elector of President and Vice President, or hold any office, civil or military, under the

[1]Changed to January 20 by the Twentieth Amendment (for text see below).

[2]The only explicit mention of slavery in the Constitution.

[3]Occasionally an offender is prosecuted under the Thirteenth Amendment for keeping an employee or other person under conditions approximating slavery.

[4]The provisions concerning "male" inhabitants were modified by the Nineteenth Amendment, which enfranchised women. The legal voting age was changed from twenty-one to eighteen by the Twenty-sixth Amendment.

United States, or under any State, who, having previously taken an oath, as a member of Congress, or as an officer of the United States, or as a member of any State legislature, or as an executive or judicial officer of any State, to support the Constitution of the United States, shall have engaged in insurrection or rebellion against the same, or given aid or comfort to the enemies thereof. But Congress may, by a vote of two-thirds of each house, remove such disability.

The ex-Confederates were thus forced to repudiate their debts and pay pensions to their own veterans, plus taxes for the pensions of Union veterans, their conquerors.

4. Debts incurred in aid of rebellion are void. The validity of the public debt of the United States, authorizing by law, including debts incurred for payment of pensions and bounties for services in suppressing insurrection or rebellion, shall not be questioned. But neither the United States nor any State shall assume or pay any debt or obligation incurred in aid of insurrection or rebellion against the United States, or any claim for the loss or emancipation of any slave; but all such debts, obligations, and claims shall be held illegal and void.

5. Enforcement. The Congress shall have power to enforce, by appropriate legislation, the provisions of this article. [Adopted 1868.]

Amendment XV. *Suffrage for Blacks*

For background, see pp. 355–357.

Black males are made voters. 1. The right of the citizens of the United States to vote shall not be denied or abridged by the United States or by any State on account of race, color, or previous condition of servitude.

2. The Congress shall have power to enforce this article by appropriate legislation. [Adopted 1870.]

Amendment XVI. *Income Taxes*

For background, see p. 497.

Congress has power to lay and collect income taxes. The Congress shall have power to lay and collect taxes on incomes, from whatever source derived, without apportionment among the several States, and without regard to any census or enumeration. [Adopted 1913.]

Amendment XVII. *Direct Election of Senators*

Senators shall be elected by popular vote. 1. The Senate of the United States shall be composed of two Senators from each State, elected by the people thereof, for six years; and each Senator shall have one vote. The electors in each State shall have the qualifications requisite for electors of [voters for] the most numerous branch of the State legislatures.

2. When vacancies happen in the representation of any State in the Senate, the executive authority of such State shall issue writs of election to fill such vacancies: Provided, that the Legislature of any State may empower the executive thereof to make temporary appointments until the people fill the vacancies by election as the Legislature may direct.

3. This amendment shall not be so construed as to affect the election or term of any Senator chosen before it becomes valid as part of the Constitution. [Adopted 1913.]

Amendment XVIII. *National Prohibition*

For background, see pp. 522–524.

The sale or manufacture of intoxicating liquors is forbidden. 1. *After one year from the ratification of this article the manufacture, sale, or transportation of intoxicating liquors within, the importation thereof into, or the exportation thereof from the United States and all territory subject to the jurisdiction thereof, for beverage purposes, is hereby prohibited.*

2. *The Congress and the several States shall have concurrent power to enforce this article by appropriate legislation.*

3. *This article shall be inoperative unless it shall have been ratified as an amendment to the Constitution by the legislatures of the several States, as provided by the Constitution, within seven years from the date of the submission thereof to the States by the Congress.* [Adopted 1919; repealed 1933 by Twenty-first Amendment.]

Amendment XIX. Woman Suffrage

For background, see p. 507.

Women guaranteed the right to vote. 1. The right of citizens of the United States to vote shall not be denied or abridged by the United States or by any State on account of sex.

2. Congress shall have power to enforce this article by appropriate legislation. [Adopted 1920.]

Amendment XX. Presidential and Congressional Terms

Shortens lame duck periods by modifying Art. I, Sec. IV, para. 2.

1. Presidential, vice presidential, and congressional terms of office begin in January. The terms of the President and Vice President shall end at noon on the 20th day of January, and the terms of Senators and Representatives at noon on the 3d day of January, of the years in which such terms would have ended if this article had not been ratified; and the terms of their successors shall then begin.

2. New meeting date for Congress. The Congress shall assemble at least once in every year, and such meeting shall begin at noon on the 3d day of January, unless they shall by law appoint a different day.

3. Emergency presidential and vice presidential succession. If, at the time fixed for the beginning of the term of the President, the President-elect shall have died, the Vice President–elect shall become President. If a President shall not have been chosen before the time fixed for the beginning of his term, or if the President-elect shall have failed to qualify, then the Vice President–elect shall act as President until a President shall have qualified; and the Congress may by law provide for the case wherein neither a President-elect nor a Vice President–elect shall have qualified, declaring who shall then act as President, or the manner in which one who is to act shall be selected, and such persons shall act accordingly until a President or Vice President shall have qualified.

4. The Congress may by law provide for the case of the death of any of the persons from whom the House of Representatives may choose a President whenever the right of choice shall have devolved upon them, and for the case of the death of any of the persons from whom the Senate may choose a Vice President whenever the right of choice shall have devolved upon them.

5. Sections 1 and 2 shall take effect on the 15th day of October following the ratification of this article.

6. This article shall be inoperative unless it shall have been ratified as an amendment to the Constitution by the Legislatures of three-fourths of the several States within seven years from the date of its submission. [Adopted 1933.]

Amendment XXI. Prohibition Repealed

For background, see p. 559.

1. Eighteenth Amendment repealed. The eighteenth article of amendment to the Constitution of the United States is hereby repealed.

2. Local laws honored. The transportation or importation into any State, Territory, or Possession of the United States for delivery or use therein of intoxicating liquors, in violation of the laws thereof, is hereby prohibited.

3. This article shall be inoperative unless it shall have been ratified as an amendment to the Constitution by conventions in the several States, as provided in the Constitution, within seven years from the date of the submission thereof to the States by the Congress. [Adopted 1933.]

Amendment XXII. Anti–Third Term Amendment

Sometimes referred to as the anti–Franklin Roosevelt amendment.

1. Presidential term is limited. No person shall be elected to the office of President more than twice, and no person who has held the office of President, or acted as President, for more than two years of a term to which some other person was elected President shall be elected to the office of President more than once. But this article shall not apply to any person holding the office of President when this article was proposed by the Congress [i.e., Truman], and shall not prevent any person who may be holding the office of President, during the term within which this article becomes operative [i.e., Truman] from holding the office of President or acting as President during the remainder of such term.

2. This article shall be inoperative unless it shall have been ratified as an amendment to the Constitution by the legislatures of three-fourths of the several States within seven years from the date of its submission to the States by the Congress. [Adopted 1951.]

Amendment XXIII. District of Columbia Vote

Designed to give the District of Columbia three electoral votes and to quiet the century-old cry of "No taxation without representation." Yet the District of Columbia still has only one nonvoting member of Congress.

1. Presidential electors for the District of Columbia. The District, constituting the seat of government of the United States, shall appoint in such manner as the Congress shall direct:

A number of electors of President and Vice President equal to the whole number of Senators and Representatives in Congress to which the District would be entitled if it were a State, but in no event more than the least populous State; they shall be in addition to those appointed by the States, but they shall be considered for the purposes of the election of President and Vice President, to be electors appointed by a State; and they shall meet in the District and perform such duties as provided by the twelfth article of amendment.

2. Enforcement. The Congress shall have the power to enforce this article by appropriate legislation. [Adopted 1961.]

Amendment XXIV. Poll Tax

Designed to end discrimination against poor people, including southern blacks who were often denied the vote through inability to pay poll taxes. See pp. 653–654.

1. Payment of poll tax or other taxes not to be prerequisite for voting in federal elections. The right of citizens of the United States to vote in any primary or other election for President or Vice President, for electors for President or Vice President, or for Senator or Representative in Congress, shall not be denied or abridged by the United States or any State by reason of failure to pay any poll tax or other tax.

2. Enforcement. The Congress shall have the power to enforce this article by appropriate legislation. [Adopted 1964.]

Amendment XXV. Presidential Succession and Disability

1. Vice president to become president. In case of the removal of the President from office or of his death or resignation, the Vice President shall become President.[1]

Gerald Ford was the first "appointed president." See p. 671.

2. Successor to vice president provided. Whenever there is a vacancy in the office of the Vice President, the President shall nominate a Vice President who shall take office upon confirmation by a majority vote of both Houses of Congress.

[1]The original Constitution (Art. II, Sec. I, para. 5) was vague on this point, stipulating that "the powers and duties" of the president, but not necessarily the title, should "devolve" on the vice president. President Tyler, the first "accidental president," assumed not only the powers and duties but the title as well.

3. Vice president to serve for disabled president. Whenever the President transmits to the President pro tempore of the Senate and the Speaker of the House of Representatives his written declaration that he is unable to discharge the powers and duties of his office, and until he transmits to them a written declaration to the contrary, such powers and duties shall be discharged by the Vice President as Acting President.

4. Procedure for disqualifying or requalifying president. Whenever the Vice President and a majority of either the principal officers of the executive departments or of such other body as Congress may by law provide, transmit to the President pro tempore of the Senate and the Speaker of the House of Representatives their written declaration that the President is unable to discharge the powers and duties of his office, the Vice President shall immediately assume the powers and duties of the office as Acting President.

Thereafter, when the President transmits to the President pro tempore of the Senate and the Speaker of the House of Representatives his written declaration that no inability exists, he shall resume the powers and duties of his office unless the Vice President and a majority of either the principal officers of the executive department[s] or of such other body as Congress may by law provide, transmit within four days to the President pro tempore of the Senate and the Speaker of the House of Representatives their written declaration that the President is unable to discharge the powers and duties of his office. Thereupon Congress shall decide the issue, assembling within forty-eight hours for that purpose if not in session. If the Congress, within twenty-one days after receipt of the latter written declaration, or, if Congress is not in session, within twenty-one days after Congress is required to assemble, determines by two-thirds vote of both Houses that the President is unable to discharge the powers and duties of his office, the Vice President shall continue to discharge the same as Acting President; otherwise, the President shall resume the powers and duties of his office. [Adopted 1967.]

Amendment XXVI. Lowering Voting Age

A response to the current revolt of youth. *See p. 663.*

1. Ballot for eighteen-year-olds. The right of citizens of the United States, who are eighteen years of age or older, to vote shall not be denied or abridged by the United States or any state on account of age.

2. Enforcement. The Congress shall have the power to enforce this article by appropriate legislation. [Adopted 1971.]

Amendment XXVII. Restricting Congressional Pay Raises

Reflects anti-incumbent sentiment of early 1990s. First proposed by James Madison in 1789; took 203 years to be ratified.

Congress not allowed to increase its current pay. No law varying the compensation for the services of the Senators and Representatives shall take effect, until an election of Representatives shall have intervened. [Adopted 1992.]

INDEX